D0793413

THE SWORD OF IMAGINATION

Russell Kirk in his library
Photo by Victoria A. Kailas

'The Sword of Imagination

Memoirs of a Half-Century of Literary Conflict

Russell Kirk

WILLIAM B. EERDMANS PUBLISHING COMPANY
GRAND RAPIDS, MICHIGAN

© 1995 Russell Kirk

Published by Wm. B. Eerdmans Publishing Co.
255 Jefferson Ave. S.E., Grand Rapids, Michigan 49503

Printed in the United States of America

00 99 98 97 96 95   7 6 5 4 3 2 1

ISBN 0-8028-3765-4

To Annette Yvonne Cecile Courtemanche Kirk,
my first and only wife
&
to my four daughters,
Monica Rachel, Cecilia Abigail, Felicia Annette, and Andrea Seton

Acknowledgments

For assistance in preparation of the manuscript:
Andrew Shaughnessy
James E. Person, Jr.
Regis Courtemanche
Several Fellows of The Wilbur Foundation

For financial support during the writing of this volume:
Henry Salvatori and the Salvatori Foundation
The Earhart Foundation
The American Council on Economics and Society

For advice on certain specialized topics:
Daniel Scavone

Contents

Contents

Contents

Preface

Emulating Julius Caesar, Henry Esmond, and Henry Adams, I express my memoirs, throughout the following chapters, in the third person — that mode being less embarrassing to authors who set at defiance the ravenous ego. Besides, when the man within (to borrow a conceit from Sir Thomas Browne) regards critically the life of the outer man, it may be possible to attain some degree of objectivity — using that word in its signification of detachment from strong emotion or personal prejudice.

Enthusiasts for modernity, the global village, the end of history, the gross national product, emancipation from moral inhibitions, abstract rights without concomitant duties, and what Samuel Johnson called "the lust for innovation" — why, such folk may be little pleased by my fulminations and vaticinations. But in the phrases of a chief hero of pop culture, Popeye the Sailorman — my contemporary, for I perused his comic strip daily during my boyhood, and recall his first appearance in a strip earlier denominated Olive Oyl — "I am what I am, and that's all I am." It would be *vanitas vanitatum* to draw an analogy between Popeye's battle with Alice the Goon and Kirk's resistance to the intellectual goons of the latter half of the twentieth century.

RUSSELL KIRK
at Piety Hill

CHAPTER ONE

The Dead Alone Give Us Energy

A Boyhood beside the Railroad Yards

Take this book for "a slotted window bellied like the fig's fruit," looking upon a prospect of the twentieth century — a sanguinary vista of a stricken field, for the most part, although here and there may be descried strong towers or safe houses.

In the pages of this book, the being called Russell Kirk discourses with you, friendly reader, and also discourses with himself, at divers stages in his life. If you will, among these pages you may hear the Soul whispering to the Person, as in that coffin text of the Egyptian Middle Kingdom called "Dispute of a Man, Who Considers Suicide, with His Soul."

These memoirs' author, in his small way, endeavored to restore to a bent world some degree of order in mind and order in conscience. In this book are recorded merely such of his adventures, misadventures, and ruminations as may seem still pertinent to the Common Reader's concerns near the end of the twentieth century. Rather than a study in political thought or an exercise in criticism, this is a personal volume.

In twenty-nine earlier volumes, Russell Kirk aspired, rather like Ben Jonson, "to strip the ragged follies of the time/Naked, as at their birth." Now and again he and his allies were beaten down, horse, foot, and dragoons; yet from time to time they took a castle or a town.

In youth he had thought now and again of becoming a soldier, a professor, a lawyer — or, better, a judge. Yet without quite intending it, he became a man of letters. Having drawn the sword of imagination, he ventured, in the words of Pico della Mirandola, to "join battle as to the sound of a trumpet of war," assailing the vegetative and sensual errors of his time.

In the heat of combat, he learned how to love what ought to be loved and how to hate what ought to be hated. Buffeted in the Battle of the Books, he bore on his shield the device of the Permanent Things. As Flannery O'Connor would come to write of his literary crusade, "Old Russell lays about him." There was no discharge in that Fifty Years' War, so hard fought. Possibly his adventures and misadventures, like those of the Knight of the Sorrowful Countenance, may be found amusing. Yet unlike Don Quixote de la Mancha, Kirk generally kept a cheerful countenance, to the vexation of certain reviewers of his books.

Once upon a time he meant to publish his memoirs when he attained the age of forty years; but time runs on, runs on, as Yeats reminds us, so that only in his eighth decade does this battered knight-errant who means to die in the saddle find opportunity to set down diverse recollections and ruminations that conceivably may be of service to the rising generation.

First, observations about his beginnings and his ancestors; for, as Gustave Le Bon puts it, the dead alone give us energy.

Our Time of Troubles — so Arnold Toynbee instructs us — commenced in 1914. Russell Amos Kirk was born on October 19, 1918, when already the old shell of the social and moral order had been cracked, a few weeks before the Armistice with Germany that concluded the War expected to end all wars. The Bolsheviki had held power in Russia for nearly a year; the Habsburg system was collapsing as the baby was born; the crash of empires would resound throughout his life.

Hard by the railway station at Plymouth, Michigan, there still stands a large house, bungalow-style, in which he was born. This is one of the earliest prefabricated dwellings, sold to Russell's grandfather by Sears, Roebuck, and Company, complete with handsome oak woodwork, leaded-glass bookcases and cupboards built in, bricks for the tall chimney and the fireplace, a long living-room bench of a single heavy plank of oak — this last all of his birthplace that would remain to Kirk half a century later — varandah, entrance hall, ten rooms, two bathrooms. Day and night, the steam locomotives puffed and hooted a few rods distant.

Young and poor, his parents gave the baby much love. His strong father, Russell Andrew Kirk, had left school before the sixth grade; he was a railroad engineman, soft-spoken and kindly, who would have preferred to work with horses, being the son of a drayman. His little mother, tender and romantic, a reader of good poetry, had been a waitress at her father's railroad restaurant, which stood between their house and the railway line. Russell Andrew Kirk passed on to his son the virtue of patience; Marjorie Rachel Pierce Kirk endowed the baby with imagination.

A good town to be born into, Plymouth was old as civilization goes in Michigan, founded by New Englanders in the 1820s. Although only twenty miles by rail to the west of Fort Street station in Detroit, Plymouth in 1918 — and indeed until the Second World War — remained a tranquil place with handsome old houses (nearly all of them vanished today), tree-shaded streets, and a square on the New England model. There were perhaps three thousand residents then; a single town marshal, living next door to little Russell's grandfather's house, sufficed for the police power. (Also the marshal made cigars in a shed at the back of his garden.) The town's prosperity was sustained by the big railway yards and rip-track and by the air-rifle factories, yet the place was wholly spared the grimness of Detroit.

In the 1980s the big Sears, Roebuck bungalow, across an alley from the railway station, would become a doghouse — a kennel for pedigreed poodles. In 1918, it was the residence, amidst lawns and gardens, and sheltered by three immense cottonwood trees, of Mr. Frank Pierce, proprietor of F. J. Pierce's Restaurant. The house was situated in the quarter of Plymouth then known as the North End, or Lower Town, the neighborhood of the railroad yards; nowadays it is styled Old Town. Many of the Lower Town's wage-earners were railwaymen, then somewhat vain of their appellation "the aristocracy of labor."

Dr. Peck, of the white goatee, brought little Russell into first consciousness in a ground-floor bedroom later infested by poodles. After his father the baby was named, and also after certain Baptist-preacher Russells, ancestors on the distaff side. As for his second name, it was taken from the prophet of Tekoa, comminator of kings; also in honor of his great-grandfather Amos Johnson, then dead eighteen years.

[3]

What's in a name? Why, this second name was a memento of the baby's Pilgrim and Bible-reading ancestry. The legacy of Massachusetts Bay, diluted somewhat in its translation to backcountry Michigan, would provide for him a domestic literary and moral culture invulnerable to the thunder of the locomotives or to the manners of the speakeasy that already was flourishing on the opposite side of North Mill Street.

For Russell would grow up among his mother's family, the clannish Pierces and Johnsons. The name of Abraham Pierce or Peirce, their first American ancestor, appears on the tax rolls of Plymouth Colony in 1623. Like the Adams family, the Pierce family of Massachusetts and New Hampshire retained no knowledge whatsoever of their English roots, not even of the port whence they had embarked. (Wondrous to relate, a few years ago a curator at Plimoth Plantation, the twentieth-century replica of the original settlement, declared that he had discovered this Abraham Peirce to have been a black man, perhaps from the West Indies — which, had the theory been sustained by sufficient evidence, might have justified the curious mention in a Harvard University publication, during the 1970s, of "two of America's leading black writers, Ralph Ellison and Russell Kirk . . ."). If not black-skinned, still Abraham Peirce may have been black-hearted: for in 1650 he was tried for neglect of public worship and spending the Sabbath slothfully — though acquitted of the charges. It is recorded that he served as a soldier under Miles Standish, and earlier had exchanged with that train-band captain two shares in a red cow for two ewe lambs.

Although not precisely "the short and simple annals of the poor," the history of the Pierce family over three centuries in America had not been one of famous men. The Pierces had produced a proprietor of privateers during the War of 1812, an obscure poet, a Civil War colonel; they had been, nevertheless, people of the sort that Dicey calls the real shapers of public opinion — those persons, their names seldom seen in print, who influence their neighbors. Farmers and carpenters, most of them, gradually they had shifted westward through New England; then into the Finger Lake country of upper New York; presently into southwestern Michigan, near Mendon and Leonidas; after that, one branch of them, up to Mecosta County, Michigan, in the lumbering regions.

During Russell's boyhood, his grandmother, Eva Pierce, would put into his hands a lively history of the descendants of Abraham

Peirce of the Old Colony, in five hundred pages, published in 1870. Its author, Colonel Ebenezer W. Peirce, who had lost his right arm at White Oak Swamp in 1862, was humorous and censorious — hard especially upon the Puritans of Massachusetts for their inhumanity to Indians and Quakers. This unusual genealogical work, crammed with battles and scandals, waked the boy's historical consciousness at a time when he had read little history aside from Hawthorne's *Grandfather's Chair* (an ancestral copy). It opened his young eyes to Burke's "contract of eternal society" that joins generation to generation and man to the divine.

Beginning in Massachusetts Bay Colony with the Pilgrims' dissidence of dissent, the Pierces seem to have drifted — like so many of their kind — first into Congregationalism and then toward the more exotic varieties of religious experience during their sojourn in the Burnt-Over Country of New York and their migration to Michigan. By the time Russell Kirk was born into their clan at Plymouth, Michigan, the Pierces and their connections had ceased to be churchgoers at all, although retaining a vague stubborn apprehension of a world beyond the world, and endowed with unquestioned moral habits. The baby Russell was not baptized; as matters would turn out, he would postpone that sacrament until he attained the age of forty-five years.

By marriage and friendship, the Pierces were allied with the Johnsons, Eva Johnson Pierce's people; they too had made their way to Michigan from the Burnt-Over Country. Frank Pierce had married Eva Johnson up north in Mecosta County; eventually little Russell would be assimilated to the Johnson line of his family, in the cut-over lands some two hundred miles north of his birthplace.

Russell's father's folk, Kirks and Simmonses, farmers and farm laborers in southeastern Michigan, contended unsuccessfully against the tide of industrialism that swept out of Detroit. Gradually their landmarks were effaced. Scots of Edinburgh and Galloway, a century and a half removed, the Kirks retained some national characteristics and even some Scots words and turns of phrase. (Little Russell was a "tyke" to his father.) The Edinburgh Kirks were said to have been leeches; Russell would inherit a lancet in a little case.

Those rural Kirks and Simmonses were attached to old houses, old trees, old country roads; for the old bucolic ways they expressed a piety almost Roman. But theirs was a setting of moribund farms, barns sagging to their ruin, fields grown up to brush — rural America in retreat. The rising generation went into the factories willy-nilly. Three of the Kirk young men, Russell's uncles, died early, of tuberculosis. How his Kirk grandparents subsisted — John and Maude Kirk, the grandfather a witty old Scot with tremendous beetling white eyebrows — the growing boy did not understand. They were the salt of the earth, those Kirks and Simmonses, unmachined.

If the elder Russell Kirk, shuttling freight trains in the yards at Detroit or Toledo or Erie, did not lead a life of quiet desperation, still he found no satisfaction in the industrial discipline. At various times, in youth, he had been apprenticed to a veterinary, a boilermaker, a mortician; but most of his working life was spent in the service of the Pere Marquette Railroad, later absorbed into the Chesapeake and Ohio system. Sober, dutiful, always gentle and decent of speech, he spent his happiest hours, perhaps, lying with his little son in the shade of a great oak above the millpond at the northern extremity of Plymouth.

Russell Andrew Kirk retained from his brief rural schooling an affection for Washington Irving's tale of the Headless Horseman, but he read only newspapers. From him, the younger Russell acquired a suspicion of the gospel of Progress; for the elder Russell, skeptical of popular fad and foible, was fortified by sound prejudice, which Burke calls the wisdom of unlettered men.

While little Russell was a baby, the family of three tenanted what had been the miller's house above the millpond, a very handsome Greek Revival dwelling, with a gaggle of rat-infested woodsheds to its rear, and spreading lawns. It still stands today, well maintained — the last of Plymouth's fine old houses. House and pond, six decades later, would supply the setting for Kirk's mystical tale "An Encounter by Mortstone Pond." Close by lay the Plymouth Village Cemetery, disused and neglected since 1871, with many curious stones, like a backdrop for a performance of *Our Town*. With his grandfather Pierce, the boy Russell often would poke about that graveyard. There entered his head, early, something like T. S. Eliot's awareness that the communication of the dead is tongued with fire.

His was a cheerful infancy, with hearty Thanksgivings and Christmases and July Fourths and Hallowe'ens, celebrated by the extended family at the grandparents' house. The last of those kin has passed into the dark now.

The first bond of society is marriage, Cicero writes; next, children; then, the family. Little Russell was born into a realm of domestic orders happy in marriages, generous toward its children, close-knit in families, and conscious of their continuity. His family's quick and its dead prepared him to encounter the antagonist world.

The Grandfather with the Tear-Gas Fountain Pen

Frank Pierce, the boy's grandfather, restaurateur and later bank manager, did more to form the boy's mind and character than did anyone else except Russell's mother, Marjorie, Frank Pierce's second daughter. A village Hampden, Frank Pierce was the champion of the working-class North End of Plymouth — a village commissioner, president of the school board, advisor to everybody in Lower Town who sought his counsel.

He had been born in a log cabin in southwestern Michigan; had shifted with his parents to Mecosta, up north; had labored on a farm there, in the wake of the Panic of '93, walking several miles to work every morning; had studied music for a term at Valparaiso University; had become a bank cashier; presently had established a big restaurant and lodging house (since burnt) beside the railroad station at Plymouth; had left that, not long after Russell was born, to become manager of the North End branch of the Plymouth United Savings Bank, "strong as the Rock of Gibraltar" according to its outdoor advertising.

His wife, Eva Johnson Pierce, eldest daughter of Amos Johnson, was a strong-willed and indefatigable woman. Daily she baked marvelous numbers of pies at F. J. Pierce's restaurant. Also, schooled at Big Rapids by Woodbridge Ferris (later governor and United States senator), Eva Pierce possessed some intellectual attainments. Often she commended to her growing grandson (for seven years the family's only child) Pope's *Essay on Man;* also Combe's *Dr. Syntax,* with its Rowlandson caricatures. She cherished a gigantic bull bitch named Towser, little Russell's protector and growling playmate.

Frank Pierce was self-educated, for the most part, and well educated. His bookcases in the living room of the Sears, Roebuck house were crammed with sets of Macaulay, Victor Hugo, Dickens, Mark Twain. He was well read in history, and Ridpath's three-volume illustrated *Cyclopedia of World History,* bound in calf, there on the glazen shelves, became Russell's introduction to historical consciousness. Presently his grandfather gave the boy a Christmas copy of Van Loon's *Story of Mankind,* and later H. G. Wells's *Outline of History;* Russell would sense that the latter, though so interesting, was quite wrongheaded.

On Frank Pierce's library table — later to become the station of the ancestral typewriter on which Kirk would write *The Conservative Mind* and other books — lay copies of *The Bookman* and *The Literary Digest.* These and his books were Frank Pierce's real friends. For although he had many local admirers, Mr. Pierce had no intimates of his own generation. It was with his grandson that he talked and walked.

Even when, collarless, Mr. Pierce strolled the street in his shirtsleeves, he carried himself with a certain leisurely quiet self-confidence and dignity. His clothing exuded the odors of potpourri and fragrant soaps kept in his dresser drawers. Theodore Roosevelt was his hero: once, when grandfather and grandson were at the movie house, the picture of Teddy was flashed briefly upon the screen — and Frank Pierce applauded loudly but alone, to his shy grandson's embarrassment.

As Roosevelt's disciple, Pierce now and again set his face against Vested Interests. On the village council, he defeated a proposal to supply water free of charge to the town's principal industry, the Daisy Air Rifle Company. Charlie Bennett, that firm's president, promptly demanded that the bank dismiss Pierce from his post as manager; but the bank's president stood by his public-spirited lieutenant.

Doubtless untypical of small-town bankers, Mr. Pierce (called "Frank" by his wife only) fell into the habit of lending money interest-free — out of his own munificent salary of two hundred dollars per month, that is. For when young married couples or others without tangible assets should be unable to qualify for a bank loan, Frank Pierce might volunteer a substantial sum of cash from his own pocket. He laid up treasure in heaven — not that he ever talked about heaven — rather than here below.

He was a little man, rather rotund — and perfectly fearless. He had need to be, what with bank robberies in the Twenties. In a drawer at the bank he kept a heavy revolver; in the breast-pocket of his coat, a tear-gas fountain pen. His branch bank was assailed by robbers several times, only once successfully. On one occasion, a mad farmer thrust a shotgun in his face; Pierce outwitted him without violence. At another time, confronted by two armed men, Pierce dropped below his counter and pulled the tear-gas lever: the canister turned out to be empty of gas, but the noise of its explosion frightened the robbers (who took it that they were being fired upon) and they fled, to be caught in the street.

Frank Pierce's one defeat occurred near the end of his life. Starting out early one morning to walk from his house the two blocks to the bank, he was asked directions by two persons sitting in a car parked at the curb. In his courteous way, the old gentleman came close up to reply. On being greeted by the muzzle of a submachine gun, he found it necessary to enter the automobile. One of the occupants, a hard-featured, voluble man, manifestly was an accomplished professional criminal; the other, who never spoke, was dressed as a woman, but presumably was a disguised man.

They drove Pierce to the bank, compelled him to unlock the street door, entered, and demanded that he open the safe. He told his captors, calmly enough, that a time-lock secured the safe until the hour of eight, even against himself. "We already know that, Mr. Pierce," the voluble man told him. "We'll wait the half hour."

During the interval, the principal robber regaled Frank Pierce with some account of his life and hard times. The man subscribed to the argument of the sophist Thrasymachus (although without citation of Plato) that laws are devised by the strong to exploit the weak. This philosophical robber had been born to low estate; but, knowing himself by nature one of the strong, he had set out to redress his condition; and by setting the law at defiance, he had succeeded famously. This dialectical apology — not precisely in formal style, of course — the man with the submachine gun offered for disturbing the even tenor of Mr. Pierce's ways.

The hour of eight having arrived, Mr. Pierce was instructed to open the vault. He refused.

"Then we'll have to kill you," his captor informed him. He went on to explain that this would be a hard necessity, unpleasant, what with the respect he felt for his prisoner's nerve. But his professional reputation depended upon enforcement of his commands. "Where would I be if I let people off and didn't get the cash?"

This predatory Thrasymachus meant business. Meticulously faithful to his trust though Frank Pierce always had been, he opened the vault.

Then the two robbers drove off with the cash and Mr. Pierce. The small boy called Russell Kirk, on his way to school, found a crowd assembled before the bank, and his grandfather and the money missing.

The robber pair took Frank Pierce to a barn on a derelict farm, and there bound him. Thrasymachus scribbled a note: "Mr. Banker had to do it or die." This absolution he civilly deposited in one of Mr. Pierce's pockets. He told the banker that he would be shot if he left the barn in less than half an hour; then the pair disappeared. Contriving to extricate himself from his bonds in less than five minutes, Pierce ran out of the barn in pursuit, vainly.

Years later, after Frank Pierce's death, his neighbor George Springer, the town's marshal and undersheriff, participated in a lawmen's tour of the prison in which was confined the celebrated Machine Gun Kelly. Kelly told Springer that "The Plymouth job was one of mine. I liked that banker, Mr. Pierce." Whether or not this was braggadocio, it was no casual masterless man who defeated Frank Pierce.

Never forgiving himself for having opened that safe — though no one blamed him — he died of heart failure in an elevator three years later, well before all banks fell to their ruin at Franklin Roosevelt's Bank Moratorium. His life, in its narrow compass, had been perfect. (His only extensive travel had been an expedition to Watkins Glen, in New York, just before his death, to visit distant relatives.) His kidnapping had been his grandson's first strong acquaintance with the disorder of the age, and his death the boy's introduction to great sorrow.

They two, on their long walks westward up a glacial moraine or eastward through the railroad yards to a forgotten ravine with ruined milldams (now effaced by the construction of huge factories during the Second World War), had conversed unforgettably, a conscience speaking to a conscience. They, old and young, had talked of the notion of Progress, and the iniquities of Richard III, and the desire for immortality, and the significance of dreams, and why the sea is boiling hot, and whether pigs have wings. Yet it was by example rather than through discourses that the old gentleman taught the boy charity and fortitude.

So much for the beginning of his adventures in a disordered world. Before his grandfather's death, Russell already was winning prizes in essay contests. In the fullness of time, he would learn, in the lines of the Water Poet, that

Pens are most dangerous tools, more sharp by odds
Than swords, and cut more keen than whips or rods.

The Quickening Soul

Of early memories, Kirk's most painful was the recollection of his crying for water in a hospital at Ann Arbor. At the age of three, Russell had contracted acute nephritis, fell scourge, and had puffed up to the likeness of a large ball, too hideous for his mother to be permitted to see him in his hospital sickbed. Even water, being saline, was denied to him; in the hospital he was given to drink only a vegetal slime denominated Imperial Drink, not much more welcome than the molten gold said to have been poured down the throat of the vanquished Crassus by his Parthian captors.

With this distasteful remembrance is mingled a glimpse, perhaps illusory, of a silent blind man, his great-uncle Raymond Johnson, standing at the foot of his hospital bed. Certainly Uncle Ray at that time was dying of a brain tumor in an Ann Arbor hospital — although not the same hospital. At the Traverse City asylum for the insane, where Raymond Johnson had been an attendant, he had been beaten on the head by a madman, and he died in Ann Arbor a year later. Made melancholy from an early age by seances in his father's house, Uncle Ray never had married. Young Russell was to inherit his books, good ones all of them, from *Don Quixote* to a history of Switzerland to Beckford's *Vathek*. Uncle Ray entered into the little boy's imagination. There was something spectral about Raymond Johnson, homesteader, soldier, male nurse: perhaps his bedside appearance at the hospital was spectral too.

Refuting gloomy common expectation, the little boy survived his nephritis. Until the age of seven, he would not be strong — kept in this world, indeed, by the devotion of his mother and his grandmother (who churned unsalted butter for him); even to have consumed a banana, after leaving the hospital, might have ended his life.

Much of his time during those tender years was spent in the Land of Counterpane, marshalling imaginary hosts of chivalry on the bed-spread, with images drawn from a rendering — was it Sidney Lanier's or Howard Pyle's? — of the Arthurian legends.

That sort of childhood had benefited, blessing in disguise, such as Robert Louis Stevenson and Theodore Roosevelt, in like fashion cribbed, cabined, confined. Young Russell taking it for granted, naturally enough, that he would be read to lifelong by his mother, in school did not trouble himself to learn how to read competently. At last, when he was not quite seven and a sibling was in prospect, his mother insisted that he acquire the art, for she would not be able to spend so much time with him thereafter. In two weeks, by some means he could not recollect in later years, that affectionate mother contrived to make him literate; and already he had acquired a large vocabulary by attentive listening. His mother presented him with second-hand sets of the select works of Hawthorne, Fenimore Cooper, and Walter Scott; he dashed into them. This precocious introduction to the immense corpus of English literature may have impeded, in later years, any accomplishment in ancient and foreign languages: there was so much to read in English that he could not trouble himself with other literatures. He would acquire some Latin in high school and some Spanish in college; otherwise, once he ventured into the world, he would find himself confined to asking in a variety of tongues the hour of a train's departure.

The child fell victim to every conceivable childhood disease, then unrestrained by ingenious vaccines and antitoxins. Yet he would emerge from these afflictions deep-chested and hearty, able in manhood to stroll forty miles a day, a hill walker and on occasion a mountain climber. From the age of three until that of sixty-three, he never was bedded in a hospital.

During those months before the birth of his sister Carolyn, Marjorie Pierce tried to fix in her boy's memory everything they did together: it was the close of their isolated intimacy, mother and child, first child. Her tenderness was very great. But usually, like his father, the boy kept his emotions to himself, tight locked except in some desperate hour: for the most part, a pity, that pretended apathy. Pray for us sinners, now, and at the hour of our death.

Between the ages of seven and eight, the boy came to suspect that he already knew everything of importance. He was right, at bottom: mind and character often have taken form by that venerable age, the Jesuits not being mistaken when they declared, "Give us the boy until he is seven, and we will answer for his soul."* Afterward comes experience — a hard master, Ben Franklin wrote, though fools will have no other. Afterward comes the accumulating of a mass of facts, which with difficulty may be fitted into some pattern of knowledge. Yet reason and imagination are shaped early, for good or ill: what else one learns is mere buttressing with fragments of worldly wisdom.

The boy's cast of mind was more mystical than metaphysical. Now and again he would stand between two tall mirrors, glimpsing the terror of infinity — diminished image reflecting dwindled image, until the optic nerve could not suffice to detect what presumably continued *ad infinitum*. "We see through a glass, darkly" — or, as a recent translation has it, "Now we are looking into the riddle of a mirror." What was infinity? What was eternity?

Or he would stare puzzled at his mirrored face — with which he was not much pleased — asking himself silently who or what he was. *Cogito ergo sum?* Of course the seven-year-old-boy, deep in *märchen,* never had heard of Descartes; nevertheless he rejected the Cartesian hypothesis. He knew that he possessed an organic thinking contrivance called a brain; yet he knew, or rather was mysteriously aware, that he was more than brain. Confronting the mirror, he received the intuition that he had a soul; no, that he *was* a soul. No one had told him so, yet he knew it.

The doctrine of the soul, which the old Plato proclaimed his principal teaching, is denied by many today — especially by those styling themselves intellectuals — and uneasily neglected by many more. Nineteenth- and twentieth-century dictionaries are vague about that word "soul." The Christian dogmas of the soul and of the resurrection of the flesh, preached early in three continents, created a new order for mankind. Men and women are made for eternity: such was the first premise of that order. How so? Because they are souls.

For expression and action, Aquinas tells us, the soul requires a corporeal envelope. That premise is far more readily apprehended

---

*There exist variations on this phrase; sometimes "and we care not what is done with him later." Character can be thoroughly formed by proper guidance and instruction, that is, during childhood.

today than it was in Saint Paul's age; for physicists instruct us that we of this seemingly too-solid flesh actually are collections of electrical particles, held in an ephemeral suspension and arrangement by some "laws" that we do not understand in the least. We are energy — and energy, which we can neither create nor destroy, incessantly is being transmuted into new forms. No longer need we say, with Tertullian, *credo quia absurdum est.* For the science of quantum mechanics has undone nineteenth-century concepts of matter, and it becomes conceivable that whatever power has assembled the negative and positive charges composing us may reassemble those electrical particles, if it chooses. What survives (if stained) this present existence is the *anima,* the animating soul transcending mind and body.

Naturally seven-year-old Russell knew nothing of atomic theory or of Platonic and Christian insights, faded in modern minds quite as old pictures grow dim with the passing of centuries, and — to carry the analogy farther — are thickly coated over, during the past two centuries, with the varnish of mechanism and materialism. Nevertheless, in erring reason's spite, the precocious boy, possibly through a perception beyond the five senses, found in the riddle of a mirror the answer to his inquiry, "What am I?" He became aware that he was more than a person: the *persona,* after all, means a mask merely. He was a soul; if a soul in a fleshly prison, still a soul.

That conviction sweeps away the "identity crisis" so much written about in recent years. Few philosophical intellects remain that venture to discuss the soul; it is daring enough nowadays to try to analyze "consciousness." But if the reality of the soul is admitted, mere consciousness ceases to be a problem. A soul is conscious of its own existence — unless blinkered by twentieth-century scientism. The axiom is not "I think, therefore I am," but "I am, therefore I think." Or perhaps it should be put, "I really am, therefore I imagine." With recognition of one's soul, identity is established.

This insight gave the boy whatever strength he was to possess in later years. He knew who he was, with his failings and his powers. The insight did not make him religious: a few Sundays he attended a Baptist Sunday school — encouraged by his parents, who never entered any church themselves — but departed unreproved. Skeptical from early years, in his teens he would twit his elders by professing militant atheism; actually he was too skeptical to accept atheism's dogmata.

Confronting a glass darkly at the age of seven, the boy could not surmise whither imagination, reason, experience, and formal learning would lead him in the end. He did nothing more than seize upon the truth, never afterward doubted, that he was a soul — subject to the infirmities of the flesh, and yet rejoicing in the flesh. For the time, that grand perception sufficed.

The House of Ancestral Shadows

Elder kin and ancestors were much with the small boy. While tiny, Russell, with his mother, commenced pilgrimages by train to the village of Mecosta, away up north. There, in a tall clapboard Italianate house of angular charms, lived his widowed great-grandmother, Estella Russell Johnson, with her two spinster daughters, Norma and Frances. Long later the Mecosta property would become Russell's.

Amos Johnson, a massive man with somber, dominating eyes and a red beard, one of Russell's great-grandfathers, had laid out the village of Mecosta and had been elected its first president; later, judge of probate in Mecosta County. Giles Gilbert, Johnson's uncle and mentor, had been a lumber baron of central Michigan; the towns of Stanton and Mecosta were his creations, although after the depletion of Michigan's forests he pursued the retreating trees to Oregon, where he prospered mightily.

Amos and Estella Johnson, with their children, had stuck to Mecosta and their white-pine house on Piety Hill — the western quarter of the village, so styled by the hard-drinking lumberjacks about the saloons down by the east branch of the Little Muskegon River.

Swedenborgian and Spiritualist doctrines, fetched along from upper New York, fascinated the Johnsons and the Pierces and their friends in the boomtown; a Spiritualist church was erected on Piety Hill but soon burnt. Then, in the 1880s and 1890s, the Johnson house became a center for seances.

Stella Johnson, with the manners of a grand lady, would be levitated in her rocking chair to glide in the air about the upper regions of the high-ceilinged front parlor — so family tradition came down to Russell. The heavy mahogany Second Empire round table, also levitated at those seances, still is among Kirk's goods and chattels. As easily as it had come to the young William Butler Yeats, acceptance of the uncanny came to the young Russell Kirk: it was a matter of course in his family. In the fullness of time, the uncanny would enter into Kirk's mystical tales as it entered into Yeats's. In that haunted house at Mecosta, where time had a stop, Russell's boyhood summers would be spent. The seances had ended with Amos Johnson's death, in 1900; but memories and shadows lingered.

With its bay windows, its kitchen redolent of sage and peppermint, its curious corners, its plaster busts of Plato and Homer looking down from advantageous elevations, the house seemed infinitely old to the boy. Possessing faded grandeur — so far as Mecosta County, a poor land, ever had known grandeur — the place was crowded with good old furniture and books.

The family had been ruined, nearly, by the Panic of '93 — losing much land, a lake, and a partnership in the bank. Seven years later, the death of Amos Johnson had left his widow and his daughters to genteel poverty lifelong — though one might not have fancied them straited, what with the table they set for guests and the hundreds of jars of preserves in the deep Michigan cellar. They retained the house, a cornfield, forty acres of swampy cutover land, a cow, and chickens.

At the height of the lumber boom, in the 1880s, there may have been two thousand people in the village and Giles Gilbert's nearby lumber camps. Four decades later, during Russell's boyhood, the place had shrunk to two hundred souls — living souls, that is. It had become one of Michigan's more pleasant ghost towns: no one seemed to stir except on Saturday nights. Mecosta was a village of a broad street one mile in length, clapboard shops with false fronts scattered along it, with many a gap worked by fire. The hamlet would have suited Wyoming or Colorado well enough, being a perfect set for a Western shoot-out; the country round it, however, belonged peculiarly to the lake states. Glaciated and ravaged, Mecosta County was like the empty land that peers out of the pages of the Mabinogion. Thirty-six lakes lay in a six-mile radius, and picturesque swamps to explore by boat.

Curtis Stadtfeld, in his moving book *From the Land and Back*, touches upon Mecosta's eerieness. Grown up some miles to the east, two decades after Russell's boyhood, Stadtfeld describes Mecosta village as an odd little place left over from the logging days, getting a bit of resort business in the summer from people who stayed at the lakes nearby. There is no particular reason for Mecosta to survive. . . . The single street is so wide it makes the town seem abandoned much of the time; stores change hands, businesses come and go, and there seem to be no roots going out from it. When we were boys, we used to call it "Brigadoon" and drive over now and then to see if it was still there. Even after I drive through it now, I am never quite sure. . . . Strange winds blow there, and odd sounds are heard in the night. Perhaps the ghosts of the lumbermen are keeping it alive, knowing they will need it later.

The boy Russell scarcely understood how the sparse surviving population of Mecosta subsisted: perhaps by taking in one another's laundry. His two maiden great-aunts occasionally shucked and husked at the village's elevator, since vanished. The township's farms, of arid sand or heavy clay, belonged principally to the descendants of Mosel peasants, Catholics, a hard-working race. Also there were colored farmers — rare in the North — called the Old Settlers, descendants of free blacks or escaped slaves who had migrated to Ontario; there (some of them) married Scottish girls, and shifted back to Michigan after the Emancipation Proclamation, homesteading land in southern and eastern Mecosta County. The Berry family, eminent among the Old Settlers, lived across Franklin Street from the Johnsons. (A lively account of the Old Settlers may be found in Richard Dorson's book *Negro Folktales in Michigan;* it would be Russell Kirk, in 1955, who would introduce Professor Dorson to this unique community.) Indian blood was noticeable among the Old Settlers, but no pure Indians remained at Mecosta in Russell's boyhood — only tales of the squaws who often had sat in a silent circle in Estella Johnson's kitchen, and sticks of a balsam medicine for splinters in the flesh that the squaws had taught Mrs. Johnson to compound.

That hospitable autocrat Estella Johnson, in her ankle-long black dresses and high-buttoned black shoes, throughout Russell's boyhood presided over Piety Hill, seeming almost never to exert herself. She was an intelligent old lady, reading many good books; Willa Cather was her favorite author. She had been a pioneer at Mecosta — not a pioneer woman but a pioneer lady.

While in the early years, seated upon a plush sofa, she read Emanuel Swedenborg, just outside on the lawn growled the watch-bear, chained to a log. The creature had been caught as a cub — the name Mecosta, incidentally, signifying in Potawatomi "cub bear" — and pressed into service; later, having grown surly and menacing, he was emancipated to lumber off to Hughes' Swamp, sixteen miles long, with its jungle of cedars. Fifty years earlier, making their way through the forest toward Saginaw, Tocqueville and Beaumont had been greeted at a farmyard by just such a watch-bear. "What a devilish country this is," Tocqueville exclaimed, "where they have bears as watchdogs!" A century ago, Mecosta must have remained devilish still. For that matter, a reputed witch survived in the neighborhood until recent decades, drying up rival farmers' cattle by her curses.

Aye, they were eerie enough, Mecosta Village and Morton Township; they would supply themes and backgrounds, long later, for the stories and vignettes in Kirk's volume *The Surly Sullen Bell* and other collections of his tales. The Old Sand Road and Lost Lake, in particular, worked upon the boy's fancy. (In 1952, Adrian Smith, Kirk's partner in a bookshop, would tell him, "Russell, you are the last of the Romantics, and probably the greatest: for nobody else could make tales out of that God-forsaken Mecosta County.")

In Kirk's entrance hall today hang seven heavy-framed big portraits: those of Amos and Estella Johnson, his great-grandparents; of Isaac and Caroline Pierce, another pair; of Frank and Eva Pierce, his mother's parents; and of Raymond Johnson, the only son of Amos and Estella. Those faces, too, set the boy to imagining.

Isaac Pierce was an adventurer who left Caroline in 1850 to seek riches in the Californian gold fields; after years there and in Montana (where he was a cowboy), and after having eaten pounded grasshoppers with the Digger Indians, he returned with only a poke full of gold-dust and some other gold that he had made into trinkets. At Mecosta, he became a builder of pleasantly simple little houses and for a time village president. Caroline, his wife, struggled tirelessly against poverty; Russell would inherit her pocket-book, still with her tiny savings in archaic dollar bills and fractional currency safe inside.

Those big faces on the wall, Johnsons and Pierces, like death-masks in a Roman triclinium, did not dismay the boy: they told him that he participated in a continuity of the dead, the living, and those yet unborn. From those dead on the wall came his energies.

Over everything at Piety Hill brooded an air, by no means oppressive, of vanished lands, frustrated ambitions, forgotten expectations. One learned not to lay up treasures on earth, where moth and rust doth corrupt. The vanity of human wishes was writ large at Mecosta. Still, the old house much abounded in little treasures dear to a boy's heart, family souvenirs: Amos Johnson's nickel-plated pistol, carried in the vanished lumber-camps; enormous earrings of Californian gold; a half-dozen gold watches; antique toys; no end of books. Such bric-a-brac, evocative of ancestors, would supply the subject for Kirk's first nationally published essay, "Mementos," written when he was sixteen.

We all are full of ghosts, says Lafcadio Hearn: "All our emotions and thoughts and wishes, however changing and growing through the varying seasons of life, are only compositions and recompositions of the sensations and ideas and desires of other folk, mostly of dead people. . . ." There are no dead, Saint Augustine tells us. Russell's ancestors had taken that literally.

There survive at Piety Hill the slates employed at the Johnson and Pierce seances, with messages from the beyond still legible upon them. A travelling medium came to Piety Hill in the Eighties; pairs of slates were fastened face to face, and upon the inner faces of those slates appeared sentences — written, some of them, in the colors of the parlor carpet.

Some of those communications were grim enough. Through the medium, the family had sought to learn what had happened to an older brother of Amos Johnson, vanished in the Civil War; and on a slate appeared the words, "I was shot, shot, shot to pieces." But sometimes the wits of the departed seemed to have suffered by translation to another realm, the boy Russell reflected; inexplicable though the slate-writings seemed, they were platitudinous. Here is one that still may be discerned on a surviving slate, addressed to Frank Pierce:

My dear son,
　　Frank, I will come tonight if I can, but the atmosphere is bad.
　　The conditions are not going to be first class. Frank, I wish to say I am proud of my boy. Only learn everything well.

　　　　　　　　　　　　　　　　　Father Isaac W. Pierce.

Visible manifestations were more startling. A man who belonged to this Spiritualist circle would come from Hall's Corners, bearing a fiddle he did not know how to play; but the instrument would be snatched out of his grasp by invisible hands, carried up toward the ceiling; and there the bow would make music on the strings.

Such episodes preternatural had occurred at Piety Hill in former days, whatever the power behind them; and shadows of those episodes lingered long — indeed, until the house was consumed by fire in 1975. The boy's very sensible and book-reading great-grandmother Stella Johnson, who had been considerable of a medium herself long before Russell was born, was in the habit of retiring to her bedroom promptly after dinner, during the boy's frequent visits to Mecosta. Later, though not while she lived, Russell was told that nightly in her room she had conversed with the dead. For decades, neighborhood children ran full tilt at night when they had to pass the Johnson house, they being mindful of its legendary terrors.

One strong seeming manifestation of the uncanny came to the boy himself. When eight or nine years old, he was at Piety Hill for Christmas. The house being crowded, he was bedded on a sofa in the front parlor. Setting his eyeglasses — which then he had not worn long — upon the floor, he crept between the covers. Snow was falling thickly outside the bay window, which his bed faced.

Abruptly he perceived two men standing just outside that big window, in the storm; heads and shoulders were clearly visible. They appeared to be staring into the room. One man, tall and bearded, wore a tall hat; the other, short, wore a round hat.

Who would be snubbing his nose against the pane in such weather, in the dead of night? This must be an optical illusion, possibly to be dissipated by a pair of spectacles. The boy put his glasses back on.

The two men still stared into the room.

Glasses or no glasses, might not this apparition be produced by a snow-laden branch of some tree close to the window, say — or some such natural cause? The hypothesis might be tested by the boy getting out of bed, proceeding up to the bay window, and standing nose to nose with the two men; but he did not relish that prospect. An alternative would have been to run out of the house barefoot, through the snow, to the bay-window front, there to challenge the intruders; but neither did that scheme please the boy.

[20]

Therefore, discretion being the better part of valor, he tucked his head under the covers and fell asleep. Rising early the next morning, he went out to investigate. No footprints appeared in the snow, and there was no tree-branch anywhere near that bay window.

Until he was middle-aged, Kirk would keep that eldritch episode strictly private. Long later, in the course of a desultory conversation, his old Aunt Fay — to whom he had told nothing of his midnight visitants — happened to mention that when she was a little girl, given to playing outside the front parlor's bay window, from time to time she had enjoyed the companionship of two men seen by no one else. Did she converse with them? She couldn't say, precisely; but somehow they had communicated. The men had names: Dr. Cady and Patti. Dr. Cady was tall and bearded, and wore a tall hat; Patti was short and clean-shaven, and wore a turban.

Later still, after Kirk had married, his first daughter, Monica, two years old, was found waving from the second parlor to an invisible being on the lawn, calling out "Hi, Patti! Hi, Patti!" Many children have invisible playmates of fancy; but this coincidence of names was remarkable, and Monica insisted that her Patti was a rather short man. Spectres persisting through three generations at Piety Hill? And perceived only by innocents, but in consistent form? There are "thin places" here below, says an eminent living minister of the Kirk, where something may be glimpsed as through a veil. Certainly Russell's forebears had labored diligently to peer through that veil; conceivably they had succeeded better than they knew.

The old Arthur Koestler, never encountered by Kirk, might have been fascinated by this brief narration; and William Butler Yeats still more. Whatever it was, it occurred; but Kirk never subscribed to any particular theory of occult phenomena. C. G. Jung might have made much of another of Kirk's experiences: a recurrent dream, coming to Russell from childhood until his fifties, and dreamed at Piety Hill only.

In this recurrent dream, Kirk would find himself in the dining room of the old house, looking at a sealed door. (That door did have a real existence, and as a little boy Kirk often tried to open it, in vain; it led, actually, to a disused cellar stair.) In the dream, he did find it possible to open that door at last, and descended the stairs leading to a region of the house previously unvisited by him — though he long had suspected its existence.

He found himself in a windowless subterranean apartment, consisting of several rooms, low-ceilinged, with floors of packed earth. Heavy timbers showed in walls and ceilings. The rooms were furnished, sparsely, with heavy rustic chairs and tables and beds. All this was much older, apparently, than the Italianate house above.

The dream-adventurer penetrated to the furthest room, and there saw in the opposite wall a stone tablet set. Approaching and bending to read the inscription, he became aware suddenly that the tablet was a tombstone. Before he could make out the inscription, he sensed something at his back; and turning with a shriek, he confronted an amorphous white figure rising out of the earth. At that he awoke.

This nocturnal vision of the House of the Dead made its way into his sleeping consciousness a dozen times at least, over the years. One cannot say that it plagued him; for he took a certain dreadful joy in the adventure. Sometimes he wondered whether the subterranean apartment might bear a resemblance to the log house of one or another of his ancestors; down to his father's time, many of them had been born in log cabins. But those dwellings had been demolished, burnt, or greatly modernized; there was no telling.

Let it not be thought that young Russell, at Piety Hill, suffered an existence of terror, a Gorgon round every corner. *Au contraire,* the preternatural seemed to be part and parcel of the nature of things at Mecosta; he was early inoculated against the darkness at the bottom of the stairs. As he would tell his bride, when Piety Hill had become his, "The darkness belongs to us."

Perhaps a relish for the uncanny worked in his genes; he found such mysteries more entertaining than affrighting. In the course of a vagrant life he would collect narratives of the occult — in haunted St. Andrews, in the castles and country houses of Fife, in the Hebrides, in Ireland, even in the *palazzi* of Florence. At Piety Hill, contrary to the usual course of psychic phenomena, the manifestations of strange presences would grow stronger with the passing of the years — until that house's sudden destruction in 1975.

In fine, Russell's was a childhood of wonder and love, mystery and familial memories. He never knew the tyranny of the "age-peer group," having always the counsel and companionship of family — especially of his grandfather.

Nevertheless he played and scuffled with the stalwart boys of Lower Town, dubbing them knights of the Round Table and outfitting them with wooden swords and cardboard armor. In his grandfather's bank he rubber-stamped endorsements on the reverse of checks, and even (shocking to relate about a bank that called itself "Strong as the Rock of Gibraltar") was permitted in the vault to pile up safety-deposit boxes as if they had been building-blocks.

They are gone now, every one of them, every man and woman, those Pierces and Johnsons a generation older than Russell Kirk. How much more he should have said to them, while there was time! But the boy was shy, keeping his own counsel. They forgave much in him. Reticent though he remained, he was grateful, deep within, to the dead ancestors and the living family; he knew he would have been nothing without them. Surely the communication of the dead exceeds the language of the living.

CHAPTER TWO

Liberal Learning,
North and South

When Public Schools Taught Disciplines

For thirteen years, beginning in 1922, the boy was sent to the public schools of Plymouth, where some of the teachers were very good indeed, and nearly all were competent. He learned a great deal of history, geography, and humane letters, although his progress in mathematics and the sciences was undistinguished. At spelldowns, he was the ablest boy, even if excelled always by at least one girl. From kindergarten to graduation day, he took it for granted that schools were orderly, safe, and reasonably pleasant places — an assumption that would be dispelled swiftly in most public schools seven decades later.

For the primary years he attended Starkweather School, a few blocks distant from his house: a brand-new school building then, handsome, situated next door to an old Lutheran church, on a bluff above the valley of the little River Rouge. Well sited and designed! Its library was a charming room, with hardwood bookcases and panelling, all of the books on its shelves good ones; it was kept open during the summer months, too, for pupils with a bookish turn, some of whom belonged to the poorer families of the North End. Russell's grandfather, president of the Plymouth school board, had a large hand in the designing of the school, meant to be the finest building in the Lower Town. Mr. Pierce took the small boy with him to inspect the construction weekly. Starkweather School rose on the site of a forgotten Lutheran graveyard; now and again fragments of tombstones, or of bones, would be found among the stacks of brick and stone — an intimation to the boy of the mutability of the human condition.

Until 1927 or 1928, say, John Dewey's Instrumentalism or Progressivism in pedagogy did not reach so far as the public schools of Plymouth. Long later, Eric Voegelin would inquire of Kirk, "How did you, who went to American schools, manage to learn so much?" And Kirk would reply, "I ran across the drawbridge before the portcullis fell." A difference could be discerned by the time Russell's sister, Carolyn, seven years younger than he, attended the same schools.

What was taught at Plymouth's schools, in the Twenties? Why, the essentials, by teachers who knew their disciplines. It was printed in Russell's sixth-grade reader, "The foundation of the book must be the acknowledged masterpieces of American and British authors." Literature at Starkweather School truly roused the imagination.

The literary culture imparted by the common school — a culture not in the least diluted for boys who, Russell among them, lived on the wrong side of the tracks — would begin to weaken a few years later. Radio, and then television, would enfeeble it; and the false "humanism" of Dewey, with Dewey's contempt for the literature of the past, would riddle the curriculum within the schools. In 1929 and for some years thereafter, nobody would have thought of suggesting that Starkweather School offered an "elitist" program of literary studies. Kirk's schoolmates came from families of limited and uncertain means. One of the bookworms among them was Philip, a potato-faced Irish boy, truant at least a third of the time — running away from school and home in freight cars, carrying with him an armful of good books from the school library, and returning them dutifully, perhaps at the end of a fortnight.

When Russell entered junior high school, in the middle of the town (high school and junior high being in the same building, approached by tree-lined Main Street, with its handsome houses of yesteryear, then admirable, now destroyed, most of them), he was introduced to a curriculum with only one weak link, the course in civics — a Deweyite innovation. Six years of literature — great English literature; three years of history — ancient, modern, American; a year of physics and one of chemistry; also a year of algebra and one of geometry; two years of Latin; a year of speech, once denominated rhetoric; as concessions to Utilitarianism, a term of wood-shop and a term of first aid; four years of physical training; a term of typewriting; a term of business law, well taught by the superintendent of schools: those courses occupied six years of Russell's life. He was very active on the high school debate squad and on the school newspaper.

In this curriculum, which nobody challenged, there occurred no teaching of religion, except as religious beliefs were examined incidentally in the study of history or humane letters; nor were there ever prayers in school. Yet Christian morals were taken for granted. Nearly all the teachers belonged to one denomination or another — Presbyterian, Methodist, Lutheran, and Baptist chiefly; their assumptions about ultimate questions were derived from Christian doctrine; but dogmatic instruction was left entirely to the several Sunday schools of the churches. Russell's parents and grandparents not being churchgoers, Russell took his religion chiefly from Mark Twain's nihilistic romance *The Mysterious Stranger*, of which a beautifully illustrated copy was on the shelves of his grandfather's library. Not until his prolonged sojourn in the desert, as a soldier, would he begin to think seriously about the transcendent — and then after the fashion of the Stoics.

Although uninterested in team sports, Russell was kept in good condition by running a mile to school every morning, running home for lunch and back to school about noon, and snowballing and scuffling in alleys with kindred spirits; also by organizing nocturnal games of prisoners' base, played in the railroad yards. He was not a zealously diligent student, except in subjects he enjoyed; in a graduating class of some one hundred boys and girls, he stood perhaps ninth in grade-point average but was appointed class poet.

By the time he entered junior high school, he could write well, and on serious subjects. How he acquired this skill, which astonished the majestic Miss Edna Allen, chief teacher of English literature, he did not then know; but it was probably because of his critical study, from an early age, of how Hawthorne, Cooper, Scott, Twain, Dickens, and other great novelists went about their business, how they formed their sentences, how they contrived to give flesh to people and verisimilitude to situations that never had existed here below. Also, from the age of nine or ten onward, he engaged in his juvenile analysis of popular historians, particularly H. G. Wells and Hendrik Willem Van Loon.

From grade school upward, he won literary competitions. In 1932 the *Detroit Times* awarded him its gold medal for an essay on the bicentenary of George Washington's birth. In 1936 he won the first prize in the national competition sponsored by *Scholastic,* the American high school weekly, for the best essay. (The judges, whose names he did not recognize then, were eminent in the literary circles of the Thirties: Irita Van Doren, Fred Lewis Pattee, Robert Cortes Holliday, Charles J. Finger.) His subject was "Mementos"; the piece was published nationally in *Scholastic* in April 1936, and reprinted in an anthology, *Saplings,* and later in a composition textbook published by Ginn. Kirk was sixteen years of age when he wrote the essay; this early venture into the republic of letters was to nurture in some quarters, later, the misapprehension that Kirk was a contemporary of George Bernard Shaw who had outlived his adversary.

"Mementos" described the ancestral keepsakes on either side of Kirk's family and their social and historical significance. Re-reading the piece more than fifty-five years later, Kirk was startled to find it mature enough in both thought and style; yet he had sought nobody's advice as to either substance or technique.

"Such legacies from the past are monuments to what was once America," Kirk wrote in his concluding paragraphs.

They reveal iron wills and reckless courage and unsurpassed devotion and grim stubbornness — and patient labor. They are a part of America itself. These mementos are all that many Americans left to narrate the efforts and the passions of those unrecorded in history. There is humor in those letters, tragedy in those uniforms, and perseverance in that furniture.

Despite all the wealth and pride we have gained by the efforts of these men and women, with all the luxury and culture which they toiled to give us, can we hope to be the people they were?

Nearly all those family mementos described by Kirk in this essay vanished in the Kirks' Great Fire of 1975. Much else of the America of 1936 has been obliterated.

The older America, indeed, was dissolving even as Russell wrote his essays: for those were the years of the Great Depression and the Roosevelt Recession. Only fragmentary mementos would remain of the Plymouth and the Wayne County into which Russell had been born. In that era of swift change, Russell Kirk's political convictions began to take shape.

Education in Hard Times

Sometime in 1928, at the age of ten, Russell began to read the *Detroit Times,* the *Detroit News,* and the *Detroit Free Press.* He took a precocious interest in political news but ignored the financial pages — as, indeed, he has endeavored to ignore them ever since. Thus he was vexed when on the front pages of the papers appeared lengthy, boring stories of the suicide of Ivar Kreuger, the Swedish "match king," and the consequences of his death; thus Russell was still more annoyed when the papers devoted their headlines to fluctuations on the New York stock exchange. Yet in the fullness of time he was made aware that such financial transactions did concern the material interests and the social prospects of even a ten-year-old boy in a town twenty miles west of Detroit's city hall (itself one of those mementos since swept away).

The Kirks lived close to the Pere Marquette depot, the spreading railway yards, the round-house, and the rip-track. They possessed no automobile during Russell's school years. (Grocers then delivered telephoned orders, and physicians made house-calls.) Distinctly they were not of the number of FDR's "malefactors of great wealth"; but neither were the Kirks marchers in the dawn toward some terrestrial Zion.

Upon the Kirk household there descended by degrees the Great Depression. On the Pere Marquette Railroad the volume of freight diminished. Under the seniority system of the Railway Brotherhoods, the elder Russell Kirk was "bumped" repeatedly from the more desirable assignments, until presently he was working only half-time as a fireman. Not being able to pay the rent for their house, Marjorie Kirk told the landlord that they must depart to move in with her parents; but the landlord, Henry Dohmstreich, reduced that rent. A few months later the Kirks could not afford even that reduced rent, so old Mr. "Doomstrike" reduced it a second time. Still the Kirk wage-packet (wages then being paid in bills and silver) shrank, so the decision was made to shift to the biggish house of Russell's widowed grandmother, Eva Pierce. Not wishing his rental property to stand empty, Mr. Doomstrike then begged the Kirks to stay on, paying no rent at all until better times; but regretfully the Kirks abandoned him to shift to the towering bungalow next door to the railway station, where Russell had been born.

The circumstances of people with much-reduced incomes between 1929 and 1933 were not so desperate as certain school textbooks would have the public believe. Railwaymen in particular were resourceful in adversity. When the Kirks' friend Eddie Ebert, the yardmaster at Plymouth, was bumped from his post by an older railway employee from Detroit, he took a job as an ordinary section hand, swinging a pick alongside Mexican laborers — and gradually worked his way back up. Having some time to spare, Eddie and the elder Russell Kirk enrolled in a course in bricklaying at a proprietary trade school in the city, paying scarce cash for instruction.

President Hoover's much-ridiculed anecdote about folk who kept themselves off relief by selling apples on street corners did not seem patently absurd to the Kirks — not that they were ardent admirers of Mr. Hoover. One of Russell's uncles, who had been foreman in a foundry, on losing his job took up selling magazine subscriptions — and did rather well thereat. Another uncle, who ran a small dry-cleaning business, kept his doors open, when he could pay his help no longer, by enrolling his employees in a profit-sharing plan — which succeeded.

The hardest knocks of the Depression did not hit Plymouth until President Franklin Roosevelt, soon after taking office, proclaimed his national bank moratorium. That measure dismayed and much inconvenienced the people with some small savings, but it did not ruin many of them. One such family in Plymouth, who raised chickens on a small holding, were reduced for three years to eating little but eggs, chicken in a variety of forms, and their own vegetables; their health did not suffer.

Across North Mill Street from Russell's grandmother's house stood the Hotel Anderine, Italian-operated, where strong drink could be obtained, Volstead Act or no Volstead Act. (The town marshal and undersheriff lived next door.) Some rough customers were to be encountered there — all of them, though, in awe of Mrs. Eva Pierce's huge bull bitch, Towser. In Italy, say, the Hotel Anderine — the class of its customers considered — might have hung the inn sign "Albergo

Karl Marx." But in Plymouth the Anderine displayed the American flag from the hotel's cornice on every possible occasion, and now and again the strains of a patriotic song of the First World War might issue from the barroom.

During those late years of Hoover and early years of Roosevelt, young Russell ceased to be a political ignoramus. When a junior in high school, he read with high interest Trotsky's *History of the Russian Revolution,* with Rostovtzeff's *Social and Economic History of the Roman Empire* as antidote. (These books were studied privately, of course, not in connection with high school classes.) He became alert to tones of political opinion. His principal school chum, Jack Sessions, thought of himself as a socialist. Years later, when director of political education for the International Ladies' Garment Workers Union in Manhattan, Sessions would become a most effective and intelligent opponent of communist influence, abroad and in the United States. With Comrade Trotsky at the back of his mind, Russell kept an ear open for whispering of sedition in Plymouth, but overheard almost nothing of that sort.

By 1932, a great storm cloud of public disapproval menaced President Hoover; and General Douglas MacArthur's dispersal of the Bonus Marchers at Anacostia Flats undid the Hoover administration altogether. Steadily the newspapers fulminated against Mr. Hoover. For Russell Kirk's part, in the principal radical act of his life, he pulled down a big photograph of the President that the superintendent of schools had posted on the bulletin board, tore it in half, and flung it in the trash can. (Kirk refrained from recounting this episode to Mr. Hoover himself, long later, when they two breakfasted together at the Waldorf Towers.) It became clear, in 1932, that Hoover and his cabinet were on the way out.

The elder Russell Kirk once had been apprenticed to a veterinary; but, horses vanishing from the roads, he had been claimed by the Iron Horse. Although a reliable worker, sober and punctual, he intensely disliked the inhumane scale of modern industry and (though a mild-mannered, good-natured man) was hot against speculators in stocks and bonds, and against the New York stock exchange in particular. He knew avarice for the deadly sin of the twentieth century. There was in him, nevertheless, no spark of political radicalism. So far as he thought at all about socialism, he thought it silly. He was a reactionary, rather, in that he would have shifted Wayne

County and the neighboring counties of Michigan back into the rural life of 1890, had he enjoyed magical power.

The swelling spirit of public unrest did not spare him, for all that, by the summer of 1932. With some emphasis, he said to his wife and son, "If something isn't done, there's going to be a revolution."

Although the younger Russell had rent asunder Mr. Hoover's photograph, he was not disposed toward overthrow of the Constitution. "Who's going to fight in this revolution, Daddy?" he inquired skeptically. "Are you?"

"Oh, no," his father replied. "I don't want any revolution. I'm just saying that there are people who'd start a revolution."

He had read hints of insurrection in the Railway Brotherhood's newspaper *Labor,* which arrived weekly in the family mailbox. That paper's editors rejoiced in cartoons representing the villain Capitalist as a highly rotund person perpetually in evening dress, with a silk top-hat, puffing on a cigar fat as himself. The paper's editorials regularly reviled the wicked owners of the nation's railroads, although by that time many lines had passed into receivership, the stockholders having lost their investment and the bondholders having taken over. Young Russell read avidly the joke column in *Labor,* that being rather good, but his father scarcely glanced at the paper. It printed pretty much the same abuse from week to week. Clearly the paper's editors fancied it their moral obligation to denounce capitalism root and branch without cessation, but they did not expect any violent rising against this infamy, really. They knew well enough that railwaymen desired no overturn; their radicalism resembled the compassion of butchers, in the witticism of Samuel Johnson: "When a butcher says his heart bleeds for you, he means nothing by it." In Russia, incidentally, Lenin had found the railway unions an obstacle to the transformation of society: he had crushed them.

But of course it was not *Labor* merely that denounced Mr. Hoover. The daily papers, particularly the Hearst *Detroit Times,* then ardently Democratic, fulminated against the President. William Randolph Hearst was bound and determined to expel Herbert Hoover from the White House. There was appearing in the newspapers of the Hearst chain, read chiefly by blue-collar families, an ominous serial romance entitled *Gabriel over the White House,* presently made into a film, that foretold the coming of an angel-inspired dictator of the United States who would put down crime, disorder, and male-factors of great wealth, not scrupling to overturn civil rights in the performance of his appointed mission.

An iron-jawed elderly spinster teacher of English took Jack Sessions, young Russell Kirk, and some few of their classmates to meetings in Ann Arbor of League Against War and Fascism, and that sort of thing, but the students joined nothing and demonstrated against nothing. In Detroit, riots broke out downtown, and the rioters were dispersed by mounted police. Young Russell, read in Trotsky, called the police Cossacks, but his mother, laughing, said that the horses merely danced toward the mob without stepping on anybody's toes and that he ought to go to watch them someday. His mother was an optimist, a progressive, conscious of being poor; yet no thought of violent social upheaval ever entered her generous and romantic mind. At one time the household funds sank to a twenty-dollar bill, concealed in Marjorie Kirk's copy of Kipling's novel *The Light That Failed*. To Russell A. Kirk, Jr., that sum seemed wealth equalling the treasures of Midas — of whom Junior had read in Hawthorne's pages.

It has been argued that had Mr. Hoover not been swept out of office, and had there come to pass no New Deal, the Constitution of the United States, the American competitive economy, and the whole pattern of American society would have been swept into the dustbin of history by the rising of the infuriated masses against an inhumane domination. Journalists have declared that there existed "a real threat of armed revolution in Flint and Detroit in the 30s."

But who would have worked this "armed revolution"? Not the elder Russell Kirk, with his Marlin carbine for deer-hunting; not Eddie Ebert, the pistol-packing yardmaster; not the Mexican section hands with their picks; not anybody young Russell encountered in the railroad and manufacturing town of Plymouth. There existed then in the United States no organizations of ideological fanatics, except for the scanty band of Communists, who indeed attempted to provoke confrontations between police and strikers or between Bonus Marchers and the military; but the Communists were little more than irritating, their chief function being to serve as an espionage appara-tus for the Soviet Union.

To make a revolution violently in a great modern state, there must exist a large sullen class of the discontented and unfortunate, their circumstances seemingly desperate. These must be led by able unscrupulous men, so many Dantons, and they must count on the neutrality, at the very least, of the military. An elaborate propaganda must have subverted the loyalty of many persons whose stake in the existing society would incline them otherwise to sustain an established order.

But the United States in 1932 had scarcely any proletariat, strictly speaking, and no coherent mischievous class of ideologues to plot and lead a violent transformation of the American republic. If a class struggle should have occurred in the United States, the yardmaster and the engineman would have adhered to things established.

In a materialistic democracy, the promise that any great possible change will be averted, and economic prosperity will be restored by ingenious measures, usually assures a candidate's success in an hour of crisis — supposing the candidate has command of the art of popular rhetoric. The first New Deal neither averted a revolution nor made a revolution.

The preceding observations, of course, were not altogether coherent in young Russell Kirk's mind when Franklin Delano Roosevelt assumed the presidency. During his senior year in high school, Russell did much reading about Thomas Jefferson, coming to fancy himself a Jeffersonian Democrat — which was as radical as ever he would become. Once President Roosevelt was entrenched and issuing commands, Kirk the precocious political theorist rejected the New Deal's centralizing policies; reacting, he joined Irénée du Pont's Liberty League, becoming perhaps the youngest member of that ineffectual opposition, from which he received a membership card but no information.

As graduation day approached, young Russell had no prospects of employment. Miss Edna Allen inquired of him whether he meant to follow his father's occupation of railroadman; he replied that he didn't, but that he had no notion of what might become of him. His Aunt Leah endeavored to find him a job with a small-town weekly newspaper; she failed. He would have been content, he thought, at any occupation that might secure him a subsistence of two bowls of bread and milk daily, with leisure to read good books.

From this austere prospect he was redeemed by Plymouth High School's principal, Claude Dykhouse. Encountering Russell one day in the corridor, the principal inquired, "What are you going to do when you graduate?"

"I don't know, sir."

"Then why don't you apply for a scholarship at Michigan State College? You could take the test at Detroit, for Wayne County students."

Young Russell felt no desire for higher schooling: thirteen years in classrooms seemed to him sufficient. Yet it would have been rude to respond to the kindly Mr. Dykhouse with a flat "No, I won't!" In Wayne County there lived more than two million people: surely an application by an unknown Russell Kirk would be lost in the shuffle or overwhelmed by the application of brighter wits.

Therefore — "Yes, sir; thank you, sir."

To his chagrin, he won a scholarship. The die was cast. Although later in life Russell Kirk would make many strongly negative decisions, he would come to very few positive or affirmative decisions: by nature he was a no-sayer. Off he went to college against his will, having nothing better to do during the Roosevelt Recession in 1936; and most of his decisions during manhood would arise from necessity or peculiar circumstance rather than from free will.

A Penurious Scholar at the Cow College

In September 1936, seventeen years of age, Russell Kirk arrived at Michigan State College of Agriculture and Applied Science (later to become Michigan State University), derided by undergraduates at the University of Michigan, Ann Arbor, as "the cow college." A pleasantly bucolic aroma lingered at MSC, with its college farms, its riding stables for the Reserve Officers' Training Corps, and the stately trees and gardens under the patronage of the departments of landscape architecture, horticulture, and forestry.

Little could be said for MSC's architecture, however, except for three or four smallish neo-romanesque survivals of red sandstone. One of them, the Old Music Building, Kirk would save from demolition during his undergraduate years there — the one achievement for which he would be mentioned in the official history of Michigan State.

MSC had more than five thousand students when Kirk entered, and would have more than six thousand when he was graduated. By comparison with those campuses of 1994 that take pride in enrollments exceeding thirty thousand students (Michigan State by 1994 boasting of more than forty thousand), MSC in 1936 may seem to have been on the humane scale; but it was not. As Lord Percy of Newcastle was to write, "It is not good to be educated in a crowd." Thomas Griffith's book *The Waist-High Culture* (1959) mordantly describes the degradation of the democratic dogma at big state universities in the Thirties and later; and Kirk, in his book *Decadence and Renewal in the Higher Learning* (1978), would lament the condition of Michigan State, immensely more inflated, after the Second World War. Aside from occupational and technical training (some of it well imparted, some of it sham), MSC existed to sponsor a football squad and — in the words of one of Kirk's professors of history — "to put a veneer of culture on a mass of young people who couldn't care less."

Why did students come to this vast campus? Because their parents had sent them thither. What were the parents' hopes and expectations? Job training, of course; and, with a great many, snobbery: that is, the presumed social advantages of possessing some sort of diploma.

Yet it was possible to obtain a tolerable liberal education, strange to relate, at this land-grant college. In Morrill Hall the professors of history and English literature and European languages and philosophy (well, the one professor of philosophy, anyway) and related humane disciplines had their lairs. Latin and Greek were not offered (except in one year, and thereafter abolished), and the natural sciences at MSC were more applied than theoretical; nevertheless, reading and thinking were not discouraged, and most of the students were amicable.

Kirk found himself a member of an informal circle of undergraduates, a half-dozen of them (including the one male Marxist on campus), who met almost daily at lunch for good-natured serious discussions. The level of learning more general at MSC, however, may be suggested by the dialogue of Kirk with a classmate visiting Kirk's room, where he noticed a full bookcase:

"Gee, Russell, you got a lot of books here. I bet you read a hunnert books in your life."

"I suppose so."

"Well, I read a book once, or most of it. It was *We*, by Charles Lindbergh. I didn't like it much."

[36]

From his first month in East Lansing, Kirk fell in with certain professors possessed of learning and common sense. He was most influenced by John Clark, a tall, lanky, humorous, melancholy man who had played football for the University of Missouri long before, and at Michigan State taught literary criticism and the history of criticism. Later, in a curricular reorganization at MSC, Clark's popular course in literary criticism would be abolished, being found superfluous because the journalism department offered a course in book reviewing. John Clark, who had read everything, had actually been published (a rarity at MSC then) in such periodicals as *Commonweal* and *The South Atlantic Quarterly*.

A. J. M. Smith, the Canadian poet, also taught English literature at East Lansing; and Kirk read students' papers for him. There were lively young instructors fresh out of graduate schools, whose companion in coffee shops Kirk became. The department of history, in those years, was surprisingly thorough, if somewhat dull; Kirk majored in history.

East Lansing's cultural center was situated not on the campus but in the little house of William McCann, MSC alumnus and former baseball player, who had become an insurance actuary after majoring in journalism. His wife, Isabel, was the most vivacious of hostesses and the best of cooks. McCann's library, like John Clark's, overflowed his house; and he was ready to talk at length about everything, but especially matters literary. Kirk spent many, many evenings with the McCanns, who were patient with him.

Thus Kirk found plenty of food for thought but not too much for the body. In retrospect, it is difficult to imagine how he contrived to subsist. His alumni scholarship covered only tuition, then ninety dollars a year; he had savings of two hundred dollars, earned by painting walls, mowing lawns, picking cherries, and some typewriting. His parents had no money to give him, but he held a free pass on the Pere Marquette from Plymouth to Lansing, his father being a railwayman, and he took his laundry home weekly for his mother to wash. So he ate but one substantial meal a day, and thought it extravagance to pay thirty-five cents, occasionally, for the enticing "blue plate special" at Hunt's Cafeteria.

To make ends meet, Kirk had to win all possible scholastic competitions to which some small cash prize was attached for the best essays and short stories, for the best orations, declamations, and extemporaneous speaking. When duty whispers low, "Thou must" — why, he won year after year the prize sums, so surviving.

Much as David Hume had taken pleasure in subsisting upon sixpence a day in his lodgings at James's Court (an Edinburgh tenement later frequented by Kirk), so Kirk, wrapping his poverty about him as if it were a cloak, ate peanut butter and crackers in his rooms; he made himself the George Gissing of East Lansing. Practicing *simplicitas* and *frugalitas*, he read extensively in disciplines his college courses never touched upon — African history, Jacobean tragedy, Lord knows what. Somehow he contrived to buy good second-hand books in downtown Lansing or North Lansing, walking the several miles there to save the bus fare of a nickel or a dime, and walking back, heavy-laden and joyous, to his rooming house — quite as Gissing had walked thrice from Portland Road Station, in London, to his rooms at Islington, carrying the quartos of Gibbon's *Decline and Fall*. Notwithstanding Dr. Johnson's observation to the contrary, poverty really does have its pleasures, at least for bibliophiles. And in the collections of the Library of the State of Michigan, since burnt, Kirk discovered splendid scarce — nay, rare — volumes that nobody had withdrawn before he came.

Joining MSC's debating squad, Kirk for the first time travelled beyond the boundaries of Michigan, traversing Indiana, Ohio, West Virginia, and the District of Columbia, debating at famous universities and obscure little rustic colleges. Urban rot had not yet set in during those late Thirties: Kirk was awed by the splendors of Indianapolis, Columbus, and Washington. He spoke far too rapidly on the platform, but he could draw up a good brief.

And during 1936-37 he commenced to write, encouraged by John Clark, for the serious quarterlies. *College English* accepted and published his essay "Tragedy and the Moderns," unaware that it was submitted by an undergraduate, not a professor; *The South Atlantic Quarterly* printed his first political essay, "Jefferson and the Faithless." Also he wrote reviews for the student newspaper. His term papers widened the eyes of his instructors. He was passionately interested then in the Italo-Ethiopian War, as a partisan of Haile Selassie and the Abyssinians: he wrote a long study, never published and now lost, of the Battle of Adowa, in 1896; also a study of Samuel Johnson's knowledge of Abyssinia.

Kirk grew lean during his freshman year — partly from privation, and partly in consequence of having foolishly enrolled in a class in boxing and wrestling intended for physical-education majors. His classmates were giants who might have stormed Valhalla. "The school of hard knocks" was not a metaphor merely.

Other hard knocks provided the principal excitement of that freshman year. For in the spring there occurred at East Lansing an instance of the civil disorders — far short of revolution — that troubled the early years of Franklin Roosevelt's administration.

In 1937 the United Automobile Workers turned to sit-down strikes in Michigan's automobile factories. One of the more dramatic confrontations of that rough period of labor unrest took place in Lansing and East Lansing, and Kirk was a participant.

Professors and students at MSC in those days were conservative, in the sense that Walter Bagehot described the middle classes of France as conservative: altogether satisfied with their own nature and fearful of any change that might endanger their worldly possessions or advantages. They were of no mind to endure the domination of the militant labor unions that had seized control of industrial plants at Flint and Detroit.

During the spring of 1937, at Lansing, Michigan's capital, unlawful picketing had been carried on by union members at the yard of Capitol Wrecking Company. The union had ignored a judge's order to cease and desist; therefore some union officers had been arrested at night, and jailed.

In wrath, and prideful because of their recent successes in the Flint and Detroit sit-down strikes, the UAW members turned out in strength the following morning. As if playing at revolution, they drove their cars downtown and parked them so as to block the principal streets in the vicinity of the Capitol and the business district; they invaded public buildings and radio stations; they tramped into the jail, but did not venture to lay hands on the armed police who barred the way to the cells where the jailed union members were lodged. In short, for most purposes the United Automobile Workers shut down the capital of Michigan.

Toward evening, union muscle-men — denominated goons, a term derived from the Popeye comic strip — sped on their motorcycles out of Lansing to East Lansing, aspiring to close down the places of business in that college suburb. Unhappily for the goons, they arrived at supper time, and when they attempted to shut the restaurants, the more athletic undergraduates seized upon the goons and flung them and their motorcycles into the shallow Red Cedar River.

When dripping zealots carried back to union headquarters the tidings of disaster, the UAW stalwarts came buzzing and fuming down Michigan Avenue, crying for vengeance upon the student body. Hundreds of them advanced on the campus, but they were met by hundreds of students, Kirk among them, some of the boys armed with sticks and lengths of pipe snatched from a construction site. At the prospect of a defeat yet more humiliating, union stewards prevailed upon their rank and file to straggle back to their Lansing fastnesses. Some students pursued them to their redoubts, late in the evening, but were badly thrashed for their pains.

The ROTC cavalry cadets had hoped to charge the UAW mob on horseback, and had so implored Governor Frank Murphy, who at the moment of the riot happened to be riding horseback on the campus in the company of the college president's daughter, Miss Shaw. Would not the Governor let them take the ROTC mounts to put down civil disorder? Governor Murphy may have fancied that he might escape hard decisions that rough day by forsaking his Capitol office to canter by the river with Miss Shaw; but he was compelled, in the interest of his political adherents of the UAW, to restrain the cavalry of MSC.

After this signal reverse, the big unions made no attempt to take arbitrary control of a state capital. In those days, college students were often more Jacobite than Jacobin. In 1932 or 1937, there was not to be found on many American campuses any counterpart of the passionate student ideologues of Germany or of Latin America during those years.

In East Lansing, the radical menace consisted chiefly of the Fagan family, with whom Russell Kirk was well acquainted. Ruth Fagan, intense, unsmiling, black-haired with bangs, was the member of Kirk's freshman class who held the highest intelligence-quotient score; she produced radical orations and declamations in competition with Kirk's conservative addresses. Her father, Peter Fagan, edited a free-throw radical weekly paper that pilloried all dominations and powers of Lansing and East Lansing. Mrs. Fagan was a hard-line Communist who indoctrinated scientifically her several daughters, seemingly identical except for variations in height. The solemn little things followed their mother about as if they had been goslings tagging behind a goose.

Desirous of being regarded as an intellectual, and eager to persuade other intellectuals of their Marxist duty to gnaw at the foundations of bourgeois society, Mrs. Fagan frequently went to hear visiting lecturers on the MSC campus and was very willing to entertain them and many of their auditors in the Fagan house. On one such occasion, a pleasant, mild-mannered, wispy visiting scholar, a philologist, incautiously accepted Mrs. Fagan's invitation. Kirk was one of the students who tagged along, welcomed by Mrs. Fagan. She knew that the quiet Kirk read books and was to be seen occasionally in company with her eldest daughter; therefore he must be an intellectual; therefore he must be a communist, actual or potential.

At the Fagan house, the philologist, a political innocent, continued his interesting discourse on the roots and development of such words as "goose." Mrs. Fagan's burning eyes were fixed earnestly upon him; she was sure that these philological explanations somehow veiled profound social significance, for clearly this visiting lecturer was an intellectual. And were not all intellectuals the foes of capitalism?

Hostess though she was, at length she could restrain herself no longer. "Yes, yes, Professor," she interrupted, all eagerness for revelation. (The amiable philologist had been in the midst of a digression upon Gothic and Old Norse roots.) "Yes, yes, you know so much! But tell us, explain to us — how does this relate to the class struggle?"

After tea had been served ("Shipped to us by our friends in China," Mrs. Fagan announced), the philologist fled in company with Kirk. As Kirk moved toward the door, Mrs. Fagan cried sharply, perceiving volumes under his arm, "Are you taking some of our books with you?" Kirk presented the books for inspection: they were his own, brought with him to the Fagan house. Mrs. Fagan's laugh had a false ring.

Indeed, the Fagans differed with the apologists of capitalism as to several property. In a grocery store once, Kirk noticed Mrs. Fagan, followed by her gaggle of daughters, carrying out the door a large sack of foodstuffs; each daughter, too, was so burdened. They very nearly had departed when the cashier shouted, "Stop! You didn't pay!" Mrs. Fagan's false laugh was heard again: "How silly of me to forget!" There exists more than one mode of expropriation.

Ruth, fanatic as her mother though more amiable, later came and went in mysterious ways. After the War she would frequent a bookshop owned by Kirk; then there came a time when she was seen no more at the Red Cedar Bookshop, and it was rumored that she had gone mad and had been confined by her parents to the attic of their house. Or was she kept incommunicado there, for reasons best known to the Party? However that may have been, a few years afterward she was in Manhattan, where she married old Maxwell Bodenheim, the bohemian author of *Replenishing Jessica* and other novels at which unco' gude folk raised eyebrows. At last Ruth's name appeared in headlines: a restaurant dishwasher whom Ruth had be-friended came upstairs and used a knife to murder Maxwell and Ruth most savagely. She had been a very bright girl, charitable by instinct, warped by ideology.

Such having been his acquaintance with zealous Marxists, Kirk did not live in any dread that the future would belong to them. As one of those whom Gissing called "the unclassed," Kirk in his college years saw something of the extremes of class. Summers, beginning in 1937, he worked for Mr. Henry Ford, who already had changed America more than any ideologue could.

Henry Ford, Antiquary

At Dearborn, a few miles from Kirk's birthplace at Plymouth, stands the most interesting creation of man in the state of Michigan: the Edison Institute, which Henry Ford began to build in 1928, when Russell was ten years old. This Institute is composed of Greenfield Village, a collection of historic or significant buildings and their contents, all enclosed within a high brick wall; and the Henry Ford Museum, a technological collection on a vast scale, lodged in build-ings that in part are reproductions of the eighteenth-century Inde-pendence Hall, Carpenters' Hall, and Old City Hall in Philadelphia.

Although Ford's interest lay in technology rather than humane disciplines, the liberal education of young Russell Kirk was much advanced by his being employed at Greenfield Village as a guide during his summer vacations from college and for some months after being graduated from Duke University. The best-remembered learn-ing, and often the most salutary, lies beyond the classroom.

The Greenfield Village guides were a fairly select group of young men, expected to be intelligent and personable. How did Kirk come to be numbered among them? Through the connections of his Uncle Glenn Jewell, husband of Russell's Aunt Fay, sister to Marjorie Pierce Kirk. Glenn (usually called "Potter" Jewell) had been one of Henry Ford's early assistants in the Ford Engineering Laboratory at Dearborn and personally close to Henry Ford: often he had chauffeured Mr. Ford on the industrialist's personal errands, and he had been the mechanic aboard Edsel Ford's speedboat in the Detroit River. (One of the confidential errands with the elder Ford had been to an elderly seamstress who darned Henry Ford's socks; for Clara, Mrs. Ford, objected that her husband could afford to buy new socks, and would not herself darn the old ones.)

Jewell was offered a post with the new Ford Motor Company in England, which doubtless would have made him rich; but his wants were simple, kith and kin were all in Michigan, and he chose to remain at Plymouth, where he became successively a foundry foreman, a haberdasher, and the proprietor of a dry-cleaning business. Later he and Fay Jewell shifted north to Mecosta, where they would be joined by Russell Kirk in 1953. Potter Jewell always dressed handsomely and in good taste outside working hours; so did Russell's father and Russell's Uncle Clifford and his Uncle Frank, for although they never thought in terms of class, actually they were members of a class of Americans who worked with their hands and never had indulged in higher education but early acquired good manners, good morals, and good taste. (That class is not yet extinct, but it is much diminished in numbers.) Long later, Glenn would pass on his evening dress to Russell — resplendent garments made for Glenn by a Norwegian tailor that have survived the crash of empires and that Kirk still wears to dinners in Washington, New York, or foreign parts — and that he wore evenings aboard ship, for many years, while liners still plied the Atlantic. For that matter, during his high-school and college years Russell commonly wore suits and coats donated by Potter Jewell and other relatives and cut down for young Russell. Waste not, want not: that adage was approved by the Kirks out of necessity and perhaps out of their Scottish inheritance.

A barber once said of Jewell, "Glenn is a man to ride the river with." Courageous, good-natured, cheerful, and ingenious, Uncle Potter loomed large in young Russell's world. And it was Uncle Potter who found his shy nephew a place at Greenfield Village.

[43]

The Village — which has grown considerably in the number of its buildings since first Kirk was employed there, in 1937 — occupies, or is surrounded by, some 269 acres set aside by Henry Ford in the midst of his industrial enterprises and other developments. No one dwells there: the Village is a charming museum, with lawns, trees, and other amenities, of transported or reconstructed buildings of significance, many of them historic and most of them with machines, furnishings, or other contents either original to the structures or of the periods in which the buildings had been erected and used.

For the Village, as for the Museum, Henry Ford's original intention had been to create a permanent large-scale exhibition of American technology, leading up to the industrial accomplishments of Thomas Edison, the Wright brothers, and Ford himself. Edison's laboratories from Menlo Park, New Jersey; the Wright brothers' bicycle-shop and residence; Ford's backyard machine shop from Bagley Avenue, Detroit — such were the buildings Ford began fetching to his Village. But twentieth-century industry could not be properly understood without knowledge of its background in craft shops and little factories of the nineteenth century and the eighteenth century. So shoemakers' premises, a steam-powered grist mill, a glassblower's building, a little silk mill, blacksmith shops, a tintype studio, and other examples of earlier technology were added. Then the houses of people connected with these buildings were acquired and re-erected in the Village. Presently Henry Ford, notorious for his observation (in a different context) that "history is bunk," was saying of his Village, "When we are through, we shall have reproduced American life as lived; and that, I think, is the best way of preserving at least a part of our history and tradition."

It was found desirable to erect public buildings round the Village green: an inn from Clinton, Michigan; a courthouse in which Lincoln had practiced law; schools; a chapel or church; a town hall. The Village acquired its own antique carriages, its own antique railway, its own antique steamboat. Of course an old country store, stuffed with antique stock, was set upon a prominent site.

As old buildings became available, they were acquired for the Village. Some of them were handsome houses where there had lived eminent men whose names one does not connect with technology — Noah Webster, Robert Frost, Stephen Foster, Joseph Pearson. Buildings from the other side of the Atlantic made their appearance as well: principally a Swiss watchmakers' chalet; Sir John Bennett's jewelry store from London (with Gog and Magog striking the hours over the entrance); and a seventeenth-century Cotswold cottage, sheep and all. Houses from old Massachusetts, old Maryland, old Georgia, and old Michigan were brought in; and more craft shops and mills; and buildings associated with Burbank, with Steinmetz, with McGuffey. Mr. Ford's architectural collection became somewhat incongruous, perhaps, but certainly delightful: two-thirds museum, one-third amusement park. Visitors swarmed in to see the craftsmen at work and to ride the carriages, the railroad, the little steamboat.

Alexis de Tocqueville remarked that it is better far for a country to have rich men who may do magnificent things of public benefit than to have merely a multitude of citizens possessing their petty competences — which they spend for their own consumption. So it was with Henry Ford in his creating of Village and Museum; so it was with the Rockefellers' restoration of Williamsburg. Mr. Ford's hobby became the chief object for everybody to see in Michigan.

To apprehend the past, one must see the things, and not merely pictures of them: Henry Ford said that and knew that. His gigantic display of Americana (and pre-Americana) deserves weeks of study. The ordinary visitor attempts to tour Village and Museum in a single day. But Russell Kirk was there in his youth five or six days a week, for a total of nearly sixteen months, between 1937 and 1942. Visually, Henry Ford gave him a better education than did Michigan State.

Kirk's historical consciousness was roused by Newcomen's mighty steam-engines for pumping water out of mines, invented at the very beginning of the Industrial Revolution (the original engines, not mere reproductions); by the furniture and the china in the Museum's section for decorative arts; by the handsome residence of that great Federalist Noah Webster; by the tall windmill from Cape Cod; by the strong-built Swiss watchmaker's chalet, not then open to visitors, where Kirk sometimes ate his lunch out of his bucket.

In the winter months the Village guides led visitors from building to building through the snow, but during the busy season, stationed in the principal buildings, they stayed at one station all day while visitors straggled through the spreading grounds. Kirk's favorite station, especially on a rainy or a snowy day, was the Cotswold Cottage complex, at the far end of the Village, away beyond the covered bridge. In the warm months, Cotswold sheep grazed on the lawns near the cottage; and a Cotswold blacksmith shop, with a live smith at work, stood across the walled yard from the Cottage. Solitary in the cottage, Kirk could fancy himself in the seventeenth century, he on a settle near the hearth — a fragrant fire smouldering as he browsed through the huge original edition of Foxe's *Book of Martyrs*. The cottage, built of limestone slabs, probably would have fallen wholly into ruin had not Ford's men transplanted it from Gloucestershire to Michigan when it was three centuries old. What was its connection with the history of technology? Why, from the Cotswold sheep came the wool that made English cloth famous; and that wool had been carded and spun and woven by the cottagers.

Aye, Kirk the Guide was liberally educated at the Edison Institute, and was paid for being there. He learned about Greek Revival architecture, and furniture styles of the eighteenth century, and economic history, and Noah Webster, and the history of silk culture, and any number of things. He wrote for the Village a manual about the surviving old houses of Plymouth, Michigan — because there stood in the Village a pedimented and pillared house that once had stood on Mill Street, Plymouth, only two blocks from where Kirk had been born. And on one occasion he was Sunday lector in the Village's Martha-Mary Chapel. A little-schooled man, Mr. Henry Ford much improved the knowledge and the imagination of young Russell Kirk.

Kirk never ventured to tell him so, though opportunity occurred. One summer day in 1938, Kirk and two other guides, strolling past the humble little building called 58 Bagley Avenue, where Ford had constructed his first practical automobile, were accosted by a lean old gentleman who had stepped out of a Lincoln. It was Mr. Henry Ford. "Come on in, boys," he said to them, opening the door of his old machine-shop, "and I'll show you where I made it."

They followed somewhat timidly. He pointed out features of his Quadricycle (it being kept within the machine shop), which three-horsepower vehicle he had first driven on June 4, 1896. By 1899 he had become a manufacturer of cars. From other men he had borrowed four concepts: standardized parts; division of labor, or specialization; automatic conveyance (the assembly line); and production efficiency. These ideas Ford had combined to form the American system of mass production. Ford had been no scientific inventor: Kirk was told by his Uncle Glenn that in the Ford Motor Company's original engineering building, research and development had consisted of buying specimens of all the extant European cars, taking them apart, laying out the parts on the laboratory's floor, comparing them — and then reproducing in the new model of the Ford the best features of each European competitor.

But as an efficient industrialist, nobody surpassed Henry Ford. By 1908, he turned out the first inexpensive automobile, the Model T, priced $809; by 1926, he was able to reduce the price to $280. So early as 1914, he had turned out two hundred and fifty thousand automobiles in a single year.

He had become the richest man in the United States through his practical talents, but his political aspirations had been blighted, and he had wiped out, if inadvertently, the countryside where he had been born. Now he was old, and it was said that he regretted having centralized his operations at the Rouge Plant, where grim labor troubles had plagued Ford Motor in recent years. Possibly he regretted other decisions as well.

The boys hung on his words. Mr. Henry Ford looked out a window in the direction of the towering stacks of the Rouge coke-ovens. "It don't seem long since I made it," he said to them or to himself, meditatively. Perhaps he solicited the reassuring approbation of the young; but the three guides made no response, except "Thank you, Mr. Ford."

He nodded, and was driven away in his car, and the three guides went home from work. *Vanitas vanitatum.*

Henry Ford had the instincts of an antiquary, but also the practical talents that had effaced the rural life and the farmlands where he had been born and reared. Behind the serpentine brick walls of the Village, he had preserved the simple house of his birth, the rural school he had attended, and other buildings of his boyhood. In the valleys of the little rivers Rouge and Huron he had bought old mills and restored them; or, if they were hopelessly decayed, he had built new mills on those sites. These mills, dubious undertakings economically, had made parts for the Ford Motor Company and supplied employment to people in little towns that Henry Ford remembered. Any employee at one of these mills was entitled to cultivate for his own use and profit a plot of ground owned by Ford near the mill. (Since his death, Ford Motor has disposed of the little mills.) So far as it lay in his power, Henry Ford endeavored to save from extinction the rural society of his boyhood; but multimillionaire though he was, all his capital seemed trifling beside the forces of indiscriminate growth that he and other American entrepreneurs had set into operation.

Looking out the little window of that machine shop of his, transferred from downtown Detroit to the Village, Henry Ford conceivably may have wondered about the consequences of his success. He had made it possible for almost anybody to whiz about in a motorcar, escaping for a time from private tribulations; possible also to dwell many miles distant from one's place of employment; possible as well for couples to court in a mobile privacy, for malefactors to prowl and escape with ease, for tipsy youths to blot out others' lives and their own on icy roads, for entrepreneurs to pull down every handsome old house that stood on a corner lot so that gasoline stations might rise there. He had not intended some of these consequences, but they soon came to pass.

Mr. Ford altered the world irrevocably. Fifteen years after this brief encounter at the transplanted No. 58 Bagley Avenue, Kirk would write in his book *The Conservative Mind* that the automobile was a mechanical Jacobin, overthrowing dominations and powers, breaking the cake of custom, running over oldfangled manners and morals, making the very air difficult to breathe. Although no social philosopher, Henry Ford surely must have perceived before he died (alone with his wife, in an unlit house, in 1947, after the Second World War) some of the consequences of the changes worked by himself and other great industrialists of the time.

Those complex consequences cannot be analyzed here. Today they are to be seen in the city of Detroit, which the automobile enriched and ruined. When the Fords lived at 58 Bagley Avenue, in 1896, Detroit was rather a pleasant city. When Kirk worked at Greenfield Village, 1938 to 1941, Detroit still was a tolerable city; Kirk nocturnally explored the streets for miles in every direction from Grand Circus Park. Nobody nocturnally explores those streets in 1994.

Because not every passenger train stopped at Plymouth, in his college years Kirk found it necessary often to ride from Lansing to Detroit, spend some exploratory hours in the heart of the city, and then go out to Plymouth at midnight by a primitive train called The Owl, its single coach heated by a potbellied coal stove. Time was when he walked those dark hard streets unarmed; later, he walked armed; later still, he found it prudent not to walk there at all. But that was in the Forties and Fifties; back in 1938, when Mr. Ford had taken him to see the gasoline-powered quadricycle, inner Detroit had been almost innocent.

Gradually the automobile had drained out of the city to the suburbs almost everybody who could afford to leave. The automobile had caused the abolition of public transportation by streetcar and had prevented the building of subways. The automobile factories had attracted to Detroit a labor force of uprooted people — eastern Europeans, men and women from Appalachia, southern blacks, wave upon wave — and the urban "renewal" and highway building of the Sixties would prevent these people from settling down into community.

In *anno Domini* 1994, if one drives along Woodward Avenue, Detroit's principal street, from the Detroit River a dozen miles north to the city limit, one sees mostly ruin and dereliction. A few large public buildings and some massive churches of yesteryear still function. Detroit's population is but half what it once was, the great department stores have been demolished, and civic activities for the most part are confined to a narrow and short strip along the river, on either side of the foot of Woodward Avenue. But nearly everybody in Detroit possesses an automobile of some sort — except, perhaps, the foul-mouthed, belligerent beggars who harass anybody venturing to enter the Public Library, the Art Institute, or the Historical Museum, all three surviving on Woodward Avenue.

The automobile did not wreak all this mischief, but it has contributed heavily to Detroit's wretchedness. Having been no seer, Henry Ford is not to be blamed overmuch for bestowing upon Americans the cheap car, instrument of civic and familial undoing. Had he not produced the Model T, undoubtedly his competitors soon would have devised some cheap equivalent. Some of these thoughts passed through Kirk's head when, from time to time, he saw Mr. Ford in the Village; but he was not so bold as to utter them; and they could have only saddened Henry Ford, who was no Canute to turn back the industrial tide, and who hoped that the rising generation would approve Thomas Alva Edison, the Wright brothers, and himself.

Kirk does remember him with gratitude; for at Greenfield Village and the Museum, Ford builded more wisely than he knew, joining things humane with things triumphantly technological.

The Culture of the South

To Kirk, in 1940, it seemed as if he had spent infinite time taking courses at Michigan State and ushering people — with especial attention to pretty girls — about Greenfield village. But linear time, the progression of events from day to day, is deceptive. According to the Hebrews, what matters is psychic time: the intensity of psychic consciousness, not mere duration. Kirk's college years, though instructive and for the most part pleasant, had been uneventful. American schooling is too prolonged: nearly everybody now spends thirteen years in the classroom, and half the young people go on to college, and a minority to graduate schools; those intending to enter professions may have attained the age of thirty, or of thirty-five even, before fighting clear of the classroom, and have acquired wives or husbands (and possibly have divorced them), and offspring, meanwhile — so many hostages to fortune. What a snail's pace!

M. de Tocqueville observed that democracies keep young folk of aspiring talents in leading-strings through vexatious and time-consuming requirements and formulas of certification — so that when at length a keen spirit is permitted to act, he has grown so weary (and perhaps middle-aged) that he remains no threat to democratic complacency and mediocrity.

Kirk, who by 1940 had read Tocqueville with close attention, had no plan for escaping from mediocrity, much though he longed for independence. Yet within two years, catastrophic events would liberate Kirk from servitude to linear time — from that quiet desperation which, if we are to believe Thoreau, settles upon most men's lives.

Having arrived at the age of twenty-one, Kirk was eager to enter upon man's estate by taking up some decent work. But upon being graduated from the cow college, whither might he turn? The Roosevelt Recession still afflicted the American economy, and in the spring of 1940 war demand for supplying Britain and her allies was only beginning to reinvigorate American productivity. The German *blitzkrieg* burst into the Low Countries about the middle of May, when Kirk and his classmates became alumni of MSC. What places might be found for bachelors of arts in this exploding world? Despite the technological intentions of Justin Morrill, patron saint of the land-grant colleges, Kirk actually had been liberally schooled at MSC; the only "vocational" course in which he had enrolled had been one (well taught, but valueless) in foreign-trade practice. Not certification for employment but the acquisition of some measure of wisdom and intellectual virtue is the end of the liberal-arts discipline. Kirk had known that very well, even in his high-school years. Yet how was he to obtain a subsistence?

Graduate study was a possibility — not a very desirable prospect, just then, for Kirk, but a tolerable one. In those times scholarships and assistantships were far fewer than nowadays. Kirk applied to Pennsylvania State and to Duke; both universities kindly offered him something in the discipline of history. He took an assistantship (for which, as it turned out, he never was required to perform any duties) at Duke; he was well satisfied to be granted a waiving of tuition (then a modest sum) and a stipend of two hundred dollars — for him, wealth beyond the dreams of avarice.

The tall Gothic buildings of Duke emancipated Kirk from his Michigan provinciality. For austere study, he could not have made a better choice. Duke proper was for men only, the girls being at associated Trinity College, some distance away among the loblolly pines; the odorous tobacco town of Durham, which had few attractions, was yet more distant. On the stately stone campus, the only place (aside from fraternities) for socialization was a snack counter with a half-dozen stools. The graduate students had their own dining room, with waiters and plenty of peanut butter, and their own dormitory, two to a room. Perhaps half the students came from the north, but there prevailed a Southern civility.

He being in the South, it behooved Kirk to acclimate himself by studying Southern history and Southern literature. In this, Providence seemed to lend Kirk a hand, for at Duke, in 1940-41, were two leading professors in those fields, both of them much published and nationally known: Charles Sydnor in history, Jay Hubbell (the founder of the quarterly *American Literature*) in the latter discipline; Kirk never had heard of them until he arrived at Duke. Both were Southern gentlemen and scholars of the old breed, courteous and friendly to those deserving of friendship. Kirk, as was his way, saying little in their seminars, Dr. Sydnor and Dr. Hubbell were considerably surprised by the papers he submitted to them; and Sydnor would express his astonishment at the master's thesis Kirk produced.

Without anybody's advice, Kirk had chosen for the subject of his thesis the politics of John Randolph of Roanoke, the most interesting and unusual man ever to be a power in the Congress of the United States. He first had read of Randolph in a textbook at Plymouth High School and had wished to know more of that burning spirit. His private study of Jefferson, in high school and college, had led him to understand the Virginia and the United States of Randolph's day. At Duke some letters of Randolph were in the library, and related materials; more at Chapel Hill and at Raleigh; others in archives at Richmond; the richest store at the Alderman Library, the University of Virginia. Kirk came to know Raleigh and Richmond well in his pursuit of John Randolph's ghost; both cities have lost a great deal since the early Forties.

His railroad pass enabled him to travel; and in those days, with the Roosevelt Recession undiminished, although the trains were maintained in the old style, he had few fellow-travellers; sometimes he was the only diner in the dining car, with its good food and attentive waiters. And afoot he explored a good deal of North Carolina's piedmont. Hillsborough, the little capital of Revolutionary years, pleased him much. A roommate took him during vacation to Charleston, then approached by shell roads along which stood, here and there, little hovels with their doors painted blue to keep off the ha'nts. At Charleston for the first time, he encountered the eighteenth century visually and at once became a Charlestonian by adoption. Long later, when a syndicated newspaper columnist, he would have a hand in preventing terrible damage to old Charleston through the proposed building of new bridges and a highway.

At the end of the academic year, in 1941, Kirk's study of Randolph's thought, his master's thesis, was accepted by the University; a decade later (a war intervening) it would be published by the University of Chicago Press under the title *Randolph of Roanoke: A Study in Conservative Thought*. Over the years it would go into two other editions, enlarged and with appendices of some of Randolph's speeches and letters. Perhaps no other master's thesis in American history, written in the space of eight months, has enjoyed such long life in print, even unto this very day.

The darting eloquence of John Randolph, and his power of pathos, helped to form Kirk's mind and style and to invigorate his political imagination. About the same time, and in part through his reading of Randolph, he began to apprehend a greater thinker and statesman, Edmund Burke. The power of Burke's *Reflections* did for

Kirk what it had done for Randolph and many others (even for Edward Gibbon, diligently read by Kirk on his front porch at Plymouth, in his high-school days): it expounded the politics of prescription and convention.

Kirk had found in the South a conservative society that had been struck a fearful blow eighty years before and still sometimes seemed dazed by that stroke; but he liked its life far better than the life of Detroit. In the South, then and later, he learned that some of the more oppressive "problems" in life never are solved, unless by Time and Providence. He read deeply about the South "befo' de wah" and poked into its ashes. In Richmond and Charleston he found communities that had not surrendered unconditionally to the new order of American life.

But back to Michigan he rode. Later he was told that Dr. Sydnor and Dr. Hubbell had expected him to return to Duke for doctoral studies and would have provided for him. But, a war intervening, Kirk never again saw the faces of those men of learning and manners.

For some months he was employed again at Greenfield Village. On December 7, 1941, he was in his friend Warren Fleischauer's rooms in East Lansing when over the radio came the news of the bombing of the fleet at Pearl Harbor; Kirk dismissed this news as journalistic exaggeration or invention. Within a few months, nevertheless, he and Warren (a votary of Samuel Johnson) would be in uniform.

Greenfield Village then closing its doors for the duration of the war, Kirk was transferred to the payroll department of the new aircraft engine building at the Rouge Plant. Here he was set to work at an electromatic typewriter, recording payroll statistics. For some weeks he labored alone on the night shift, typing away for eight hours, interrupted occasionally by some assembly-line hand with a thick accent who threatened to cancel his savings-bond assignment.

What dreariness! At a Dearborn rooming house, Kirk sank into an apathy. In Plymouth, twenty miles distant, his mother was beginning to die of cancer, she still young and still hopeful for the twentieth century. He was with her weekends, she abed; but he was too callow to sense how to comfort or to talk of the meaning of life and of death. She was all love, and so doubtless forgave him much.

His mother's decline, and the listlessness that afflicts a good many people who turn the great wheel of circulation of modern industry, sat heavy upon him. During those months Kirk read nothing but the letters of Charles Lamb, endeavoring to ignore the future, being weighed down by the bent condition of the world generally as well as by his own troubles.

In company with a friend from Duke, he made a day's expedition to Ontario, with some notion of enlisting in the Essex Scottish regiment. It was well for the two Americans that they did not enlist, for the Essex Scottish would be blotted out in a desperate British commando raid across the Channel. Kirk applied to the United States Army Air Corps, but his eyesight would not pass muster.

When he had been little, indulgent kinfolk had endowed Russell with regiments of lead soldiers. Now Kirk must put on the uniform himself, although he believed that all wars fought by the American people — the Revolution included — might have been averted. He was only marking time at the fire-belching Rouge, where mass production swaggered triumphant. The Rouge had become the biggest unit in what was being called Detroit's "arsenal of democracy." One did not encounter old Henry Ford at the Rouge; at last he was wearing out.

Kirk was twenty-two years of age now — though fancying himself much older — and a master of arts, without the slightest expectation of ever accomplishing anything here below. From these circumstances the United States Army rescued him in the summer of 1942.

With other conscripts, euphemistically styled inductees, a high-school band playing, he was marched down to the Plymouth railway station, across the alley from his own birthplace, and put aboard a train for Camp Custer, Michigan. Private Kirk never saw again some of the people who waved good-bye. In his life, as in that of many other young men, the War would be a great gulf fixed between family and community on the nearer rim and the antagonist world on the further: the Grand Canyon of a Time of Troubles.

CHAPTER THREE

A Stoical Sergeant
in the Waste Land

The Great Salt Lake Desert

At the induction center, a disused loft opposite the Fort Street Station (since demolished) in Detroit, the conscript Kirk, along with hundreds of other conscripts, was made to strip and to undergo various inspections. Presently, naked, he came to the table at which literacy was tested.

"Do you think you could read a part of this newspaper?" inquired a clothed inspector, holding up a copy of that day's *Detroit News*.

"I believe so," Kirk answered.

"All right, you pass: move on."

In the fullness of time, Kirk arrived at the counter where one's sanity and normality were ascertained. "Do you ever go out with girls?" the psychological inspector demanded.

"Occasionally," Kirk ventured.

"All right, you pass: move on."

From this naked theater of the absurd, Kirk and a great many other draftees were transported by rail to Camp Custer (since abolished), in southern Michigan, where they all were outfitted, staggering to barracks under the weight of mattresses and crammed barracks bags. Kirk, having received no instructions, had no notion of what he was supposed to be doing; he merely remained in his theater-of-operations barracks when a bugle summoned others to various roll calls and chores. Presently the bugle sounded "lights out," and Kirk, with his barracksmates, crept obediently into his cot.

Before Kirk could sink into sleep, heavy boots tramped up the stair to the second floor, bam bam bam, and a stentorian voice roared in the darkness, "I'm CORPORAL POND!"

The conscripts trembled under their covers; clearly this was some great power at Camp Custer. The voice of Ozymandias — look on my works, ye mighty, and despair — sounded again:

"I'm Corporal Pond!" (One could glimpse at the door only a very dim figure, squat and stern. A certain slurring of the words suggested that Corporal Pond had been imbibing spirits of a sort not permitted on military posts.) "I'm Corporal Pond! I'm in charge here! These are my barracks, understand that? There are no bedbugs here! And if there are, tell ME! ME, CORPORAL POND!"

The squat omnipotent figure tramped most heavily back down the stair; and at length the humble new private soldiers slumbered.

The next day Kirk attended a lecture by a real live officer, a lieutenant, the theme of which was that the ankle-high boots issued to the recruits might seem odd at first but that he, the lieutenant, had come to find them very comfortable indeed and so intended to wear such boots for the rest of his life. This lecture, and subsequent personal experience, converted Kirk to the lieutenant's case for boots, which he was to find prudent footwear in a desert swarming with rattlesnakes; and indeed Kirk has worn such boots, British ones usually, ever since that thoughtful military admonition at Camp Custer.

Russell Kirk, M.A, was not permitted to linger at Camp Custer. With a hundred other neophytes, he was handed orders to proceed to Fort Douglas, Utah, the very day of the boot lecture, and off they went westward by a crowded train. It was rumored that the lot of them were assigned for duty to the Chemical Warfare Service. Some of the barracks bags bore the mysterious stencilled letters HTS. "That means Human Target Squad," Kirk, tongue in cheek, informed several comrades. Believing him, some of them were near to tears.

The journey across the plains states, once denominated the Great American Desert, went on day and night — Kirk's first westward expedition. "It seems only last week we went aboard this train," one wag murmured. At North Platte, Nebraska, kindly women in the railway station gave the new soldiery lemonade, sandwiches, and pieces of cake. After a long while, the foothills of the Rockies loomed up. And, in the fullness of time, their train came down from the Wasatch upon Salt Lake City, an amazing sight, with streams of fresh water running in its gutters.

At the station, without being granted time to stretch their legs — for this was the summer of 1942, with a war being fought desperately on the far side of either ocean — the recruits were hurried into buses to be trundled up the mountain bench to Fort Douglas — or so they fancied. But no! They were being transported elsewhere. Leaving behind handsome Salt Lake City, the convoy made its way across barrens south of the Great Salt Lake, west southwestward, thirty-five interminable miles, to the plain sunbaked town of Tooele, where an ordnance depot had been established. By this time the conscripts had ascertained that they would end at a mysterious installation called Dugway (some said Dogway) Proving Ground. Was that at Tooele, on the edge of savagery?

Nay, not so. Straight through little Tooele the convoy proceeded, toward the real desert, the Great Salt Lake Desert, through arid uplands inhabited by a few invisible Indians. Now more mountains loomed before the rookie soldiers — sharp barren dead mountains, with no touch of green, rising defiant from the desert floor. Gradually the buses ascended, making their way through gaunt Skull Valley to a low pass where a sentry post of sorts had been established. Three soldiers, clearly of Mexican stock, stared languidly at the passing buses. The trio held rifles, the first weapons seen by the conscripts in the convoy; the merciless sun glinted upon those guns. As the convoy left the sentry post behind, a tall saturnine grumbler-conscript muttered in relief, "I knew that spot couldn't be Dugway. The army wouldn't dump us in a hole like that, where the only ones who can stand it are Mexicans."

He was mistaken: the convoy now was departing from Skull Valley to enter Dugway Valley, which desolation normally had no human population whatsoever. After more miles of this high desert, quite treeless, the buses came to great sand dunes. Perched upon these dunes were a few theater-of-operations barracks. This was Dugway Proving Ground, some ninety miles distant from Salt Lake City and a long way from the nearest rancher — old Dan Orr, of the splendid oldfangled leather riding breeches, the patriarch of Skull Valley. Once upon a time a few naked Gosiutes may have tried to survive in Dugway Valley; if so, those Indians had left no memorials.

Of Kirk's four years in the army, three would be spent here near the heart of the Great Salt Lake Desert — the famous Bonneville salt flats sprawling a few miles to the west of the Dugway camp — surely one of the most desolate and most salubrious spots in all the world. While millions of men were slaughtering one another upon the Ukrainian steppes or in the Papuan jungles, Kirk lay enchanted, like Merlin in the oak, amidst a desert so long dead that it seemed nothing was permitted to die there any longer. Occasionally Kirk might be blistered by mustard gas or temporarily choked by phosgene, a mere small mishap; but such diversions aside, the Great Salt Lake Desert was a wholesome place for body and soul — once the initial shock of its emptiness diminished.

Dugway Proving Ground was then, and is today, the Chemical Warfare Service's vast experiment field. Aside from conventional spraying of mustard or phosgene gases on goats, to see if such toxic agents would vex the creatures, Dugway became the center for testing two huge deadly experiments: the development of the gel bomb, and the beginnings of bacteriological warfare. Kirk being the only enlisted man at Dugway Proving Ground who possessed a master's degree, and being an experienced typist, he found himself assigned to duty as recorder and custodian of classified documents — some of them "top secret" indeed. Had Germany and Japan won the war, Kirk might have been put on trial as a war criminal.

On the salt flats the CWS built accurate replicas of German and Japanese villages, to scale and of suitable materials, the houses completely furnished. Dugway Proving Ground possessed a solitary bomber, dispatched now and again to drop gel incendiary bombs upon those villages, in hope they might burn. They did. After one holocaust, the villages were rebuilt and refurbished, and then again bombed with gel; this went on and on, month after month. Having been thus thoroughly tested, the gel bomb was employed, very near the end of the war in Europe, to wipe out Dresden and its population, the air being sucked out of Silesian lungs while their dwellings were incinerated. This had been a war to vindicate the democratic and humanitarian way of life.

Away to the west, towering two thousand six hundred feet above the dead level of the salt flats, rose up the solitary splendor of Granite

Peak, where antelope lingered. Kirk climbed that mountain once in company with an experienced mountain man, Werner Schnack-enberg, but very nearly came down dead, head over heels, from a slippery shelf of obsidian. During the latter part of Kirk's duty in Dugway, the CWS established at Granite Peak a testing ground for "germ warfare," a perilous undertaking for which perfect isolation was required. Nevertheless, so far as Kirk knew, nobody died at Granite Peak, or from consequences of experimenting there; and in the toxic gas area nearer Dugway camp, only one elderly civilian employee perished — from walking through a cloud of phosgene without wearing his gas mask.

The healthiness of the high desert notwithstanding, soldiers did die at Dugway, though not from gases or microbes. (Some, true, were wretchedly burned by mustard gas, though not fatally.) Desert soli-tude and monotony provoked two or three suicides, even though weekend passes to Salt Lake City offered relief. The ancient, fat contract surgeon died, apparently of the weight of years — he whose hand trembled so alarmingly as he was about to perform injections; he who had instructed the newly arrived conscripts that they need not fear injury to their lungs during sandstorms, because "the harm is done by silica, and there is no silica in our sand here at Dugway." Old Master Sergeant Emory died — the amiable and efficient veteran who had never applied for weekend passes, lest he become drunken and so forfeit his post as top sergeant. But Technician Fourth Grade Kirk (as he soon became) never felt healthier.

So long as the detachment at Dugway remained small in numbers, it kept a certain homeliness, they being kind one to another out of a common pity; but before long, the American lust for aggrandizement operating, a thousand men were crowded into barracks and were kept busy at occupations rather like taking in one another's washing. Also Dugway acquired a company of Italian prisoners of war, and another company of German prisoners. Kirk applied to teach them English, but permission was denied by Dugway's commanding officer.

Large dunes surrounded the camp. When he had leisure, which was much of the time, Kirk sat upon the sand reading. That strange mountain the Camel's Back stared down at him. It was a thing drowned and then washed up from the ocean bed of time, for on its sides showed the successive benchmarks of seas that dried a million years past. If Kirk sank into sleep — an easy thing to do in the sun, for the nearest tree, a scrubby juniper, was miles distant — little lizards slid across his face; he opened his eyes cautiously to see whether the thing might be a rattler, for one species thereof abounded amidst the sagebrush. He stared across the salt and the alkali where not even snakes, lizards, and rabbits lived, into Nevada on the horizon. This was a region almost without a history: some forlorn savages had lurked on its fringes a hundred years gone, Jed Smith had staggered alone across its waterless expanses, and in the Forties a few shepherds with their flocks occasionally made their way around it; that was all, except for some gold mining, long ago abandoned, on the desert's Nevada side. An Air Force base now was situated on the Nevada side of the salt flats, near Wendover. Once, while Dugway men were laying out targets on their territory, bombers from Nevada came over and, whether by mistake or by malice aforethought, dropped bombs on the Dugway targets; the Dugway CWS personnel, in jeeps and command cars, scurried away to safety. Then Dugway's colonel telephoned his counterpart at the air base and threatened to have Dugway's sole bomber retaliate with mustard or phosgene, were such a blunder to occur a second time. At our own Gehenna, we committed our atrocities in the abstract, as if they were childish games. In Germany and Japan it would be otherwise.

Afoot or in jeep or command car, with comrades, Kirk explored the desert wilderness. There occurred expeditions to the High Uintas, America's only mountain range running east and west, away up at the top of Utah; there, one night, a wildcat quite unacquainted with man sat on Kirk in his sleeping bag, perhaps speculating on whether the strange long creature might be edible; one afternoon Sergeant Kirk, quite alone, contrived to lose himself in a ravine choked with fallen timbers, and extricated himself only by careful orientation of his compass.

His longest expedition, tramping and hitchhiking in company with another Dugway soldier, Alfred Cutler (by coincidence also from Plymouth, Michigan), took him all the way to Hanksville and back again by a different route — remote Hanksville, once a Mormon co-hab settlement, at the time of Kirk's visit a hamlet, wondrously isolated, between the towering Capitol Reef and the Green River country. In those days it was a place of arcadian simplicity; soon it would swell to a boomtown with huge highways leading to it, for uranium had been discovered nearby.

At the shrunken village of Torrey, a far cry from Dugway, Kirk and Cutler were given a ride in the back of a pickup truck driven by a Basque shepherd called Banjo, whose speech suffered from some impediment, compensated for by his geniality. His Anglo wife and her sixteen-year-old son were in the cab beside Banjo.

As they pulled away from Torrey into the Capitol Reef National Monument, Kirk looked upon a tremendous expanse of wild country, quite different from the Utah mountains through which the two soldiers had passed earlier. On their right (they looking over the truck's tailboard) loomed up the Capitol Reef; on their left, the inaccessible desolation of the Aquarius Plateau. One mighty butte rose behind another, stretching away in terrible lifelessness to the horizon. They saw tremendous spires and towers, and balancing rocks, and windows in the cliffs of dull reds and greens.

Snow fell lightly as they jogged into the Capitol Wash, a fantastic wild prospect, a canyon fourteen feet wide or narrower, its sheer walls rising as much as eighteen hundred feet above, the rock worn smooth by water and wind. In this canyon the infant Dirty Devil River had its source. Beyond the wash they crossed a series of fords — the violent floods of spring having taken out what bridges had been constructed once upon a time. Scattered clumps of low-growing rabbit grass were the only life to be seen. The road or track now twisted among great blue-gray cones of what appeared to be eroded shale, with jagged sandstone buttes for background.

Through dangerous washes and over loose sand they plunged into Blue Valley, a region of death, where the alkali gleamed white. There once had stood the town of Blue Valley, or Giles; the ruins of the school and the chapel still stood, and some rotten trunks of fruit trees remained near the track. Not a soul lingered here; the valley's heavy blue clay had won the battle over vainglorious mankind.

After more miles through the treeless and grassless Tophet of the Wayne Wonderland, with its red rock formations, their truck puffed up to Caineville — a sufficiently fitting abode, it looked, for the original Cain — where the valley widened somewhat and a few wretched cabins stood. Here Banjo and his wife invited the soldiers into their living room, of which one wall only was papered — with newsprint. Mrs. Banjo, who smoked cigarettes incessantly, had been born here. On the living room floor survived some fragments of linoleum that had been laid twenty years before.

[61]

Kirk and Cutler were presented to their hosts' kin and neighbors, who crowded into the house to meet these strangers in uniform. They were awkward back-country people, warmhearted and desperately poor, some of them odd in appearance and manner after a lifetime of such subsistence. One pretty girl appeared, and several merry little children.

At length the military guests were served dinner, along with the family; they shared five little sausage patties, a large bowl of tough string beans, preserved apricots, and bread without butter; they all drank coffee out of bowls. At this hamlet, life in the high desert must have been much the same in the outlaw years here, a century earlier.

They were within twenty-five miles of Hanksville, at the end of the world. Asserting that no vehicles would be going east on the Hanksville road that evening, Banjo invited the soldiers to lodge with them that night; but Cutler and Kirk, having given their hosts some large chocolate bars in token of gratitude, tramped on down the road. They might have been wiser to linger; for the folk of Caineville must have folk tales to recount of Butch Cassidy, his Wild Bunch, and other horse thieves, cattle rustlers, and train robbers who had ridden as they listed in these wilds in the closing decades of the nineteenth century. Robbers' Roost, the badmen's stronghold atop the San Rafael Swell, was not far distant — though only as the crow flies.

Five miles east of Caineville, the two wanderers built a roaring fire of brush, to warm them in the night while awaiting some ride. Presently there appeared a large truck, laden with food and gasoline for a road-building crew; they climbed in beside the driver.

On through more washes, along the verge of deep arroyos, they won their way to Hanksville, an old settlement ringed about with cliffs of sandstone, the Dirty Devil entering through one gap in those cliffs and pouring out through another gap. Nine families lived in the town — large extended Mormon families. The town had no store, although in the old time it had been a principal supply station for the Robbers' Roost gunmen, doubtless to the profit of both parties — but the Hanksville of the Forties possessed a ramshackle post office, a cafe, a decayed school, and a chapel of freestone. Standing in the dusty Main Street, Kirk wondered what manner of men first had ventured to this spot, desolation on every side; later he learned that the pioneers had been four Mormon men accused of murder in Salt Lake City. A settlement grew on this spot in the 1860s, and in the 1880s, the time of federal prosecutions for polygamy, Mormon plural wives found sanctuary in this picturesque solitude. The soil was very good, with plenty of clover for grazing; in early days after Ebenezer Hanks settled his wives here, there was a stand of tall grass that made possible two large ranches. Beekeeping thrived here when Kirk and Cutler paid their visit. The villagers' houses, board-and-batten or log, were those built by early settlers. Kirk and Cutler lodged in a converted bunkhouse — or perhaps woodshed — for fifty cents each.

A tortuous, difficult, and dangerous trail had led from Hanksville to Robbers' Roost, north of Hanksville and higher up. So late as 1900, the Roost was outlaws' territory. Kirk asked a tall inhabitant of Hanksville in what direction the trail to Robbers' Roost lay. "Out there somewhere, I guess," said the man, his outstretched arm sweeping the horizon. Could it be that Hanksville folk still thought it imprudent to give strangers information about the Wild Bunch?

Next day the two soldiers made their way northward toward the town of Greenriver. They passed an abandoned ranch some thirty miles north of Hanksville and a good ranch on the San Rafael River — otherwise, no sign of habitation along that vast stretch of territory, parallel with the pinnacles of the San Rafael Swell. Thirty hours after leaving Hanksville, the two wanderers were back at Dugway Proving Ground, having completed in a long weekend a tour of seven hundred miles through the wild heart of Utah — a feat their Dugway friends had thought impossible of attainment.

Never again will anyone make quite that trip; for uranium and vanadium ore, very soon after Kirk slept at Hanksville, would entice the highway engineers and the mining engineers to eastern Utah, and they would alter the face of things. Banjo and his wife were buried long ago, no doubt, and the affluent society has pushed their kind to the wall. As for the uranium mined near Hite, on the Colorado River — Hite, population one man at the time of Kirk's expedition — why, that element, which two months earlier had effaced Hiroshima and Nagasaki, would raise up future Titans and Cyclopes.

Other Utah adventures came to pass: a wild jeep ride with tipsy comrades at the top of the Wasatch, in deep snow; pistol shooting at coyotes in the shadow of the Camel's Back; near-drowning by a flash flood in an arroyo near the ghost town of Gold Hill. Good friendships were formed, but only one of them would endure into years of peace.

Kirk fancied himself miserable in the army, although he was efficient enough in his duties; for one thing, he was the only newcomer to Dugway in his lot of recruits who could perform the manual of arms smartly, that martial skill having been forced upon him at Michigan State by the Reserve Officers' Training Corps. When a film about the British victory at El Alamein in Libya was shown at Dugway, the enlisted men of the Proving Ground observed the similarity between the terrain of Libya and that of the Great Salt Lake Desert.

"This is the desert!" the film's narrator commenced.

"Dugway!" groaned the Dugway audience.

"Sand, heat, thirst," the narrator proceeded.

"Dugway!" shouted Kirk and his comrades.

"The Arabs say," the solemn narrator went on, "that after three days here, a man may go mad."

"Dugway!" the old Dugway hands roared.

Yet the men of Dugway — some of them forty-five years of age or older — really were somewhat proud of their desert toughness, and a number of them, among those some of the worst grumblers, re-enlisted after the war ended. Kirk himself, for years after his honorable discharge, dreamed repeatedly that through some miscarriage of justice he had not been discharged at all; in his dream he would leaf frenziedly through bound volumes of army regulations, that he might prove to the commanding officer his right to go home. In retrospect, those army years would seem almost a prolonged lively vacation at public expense.

He wrote essays and short stories at his desk in headquarters, no one interrupting him or looking over his shoulder, because Kirk was in charge of secret and confidential documents. He was exempted from rising at reveille because of a general belief that "Kirk works so hard every night" — writing letters to friends, actually. He enjoyed liberty to edit a little camp newspaper, *The Sand Blast*. (More than forty years later, a military historian attached to Dugway Proving Ground would discover that Sergeant Kirk, editor of *The Sand Blast*, and Dr. Kirk, the man of letters, were one and the same.) All in all, despite its ghastly function, Dugway was a humane camp — even rousing, long later, friendly memories.

Marcus Aurelius and Epictetus on the Sand Dunes

Late in 1942, word came from Plymouth that Marjorie Rachel Kirk had not long to live: the operation for intestinal cancer had failed. Kirk had been writing to his mother almost daily, letters full of the affection that he had been too shy to show when at home. Yet he and she had planned much together that never could come to pass now. In particular, he had meant to take her on a trip to Guatemala once he was out of the army. In reality, he never had been able to take her anywhere except to Greenfield Village for a few hours: there had been no money and no time. For that matter, his father and mother never had visited him at Michigan State College, although it was merely an hour's train ride to Lansing, and they had free passes; doubtless a campus had seemed to them a foreign land.

How good she had been to him, bringing him back from the verge of the grave when he was three years old, reading to him, teaching him to read, making every sacrifice to advance him! She was tiny, gentle, a reader of poetry, amazingly unselfish. When he was a freshman at college, she had asked him, timidly and hopefully, "Do you remember, Junior, the times we spent together during the months before Carolyn was born?" (Carolyn, his sister, was seven years younger.) "How I read to you so much, and we talked and talked, just the two of us, still alone together?"

"No, I don't remember," said the cross-grained boy, mercilessly, he then detesting sentimentality.

"Oh! I hoped so much that you would remember, my darling." She had been much saddened.

What a fool he had been then, and at many other times, with the one he loved most! But now, at Dugway, he wrote to her in remorse, saying, "I did remember, Mama, and I do remember, those months we had together before Carolyn came."

That letter reached her, thank God, and she read it, the day before she died.

The night of her death, two thousand miles distant, Kirk was on sentry duty, patrolling, walking from building to building, in at one door and out the other, hour upon hour. Although it was a still night, every door that Kirk closed behind him somehow opened again when he turned his back; repeatedly he had to about-face and close every door a second time. In the guard house, at dawn, word was given to him that his mother had died about midnight.

It was a faint consolation that a fortnight earlier Kirk had been granted a "compassionate" furlough of a few days and had read to his mother and sat by her bedside; but even then he had been neglectful and had said nothing consoling. Yet when he had risen early on the last morning to take the train back to Utah, he had entered his mother's room desperately. Did he kiss her? He cannot remember. But the poor tormented loving creature in the bed had seen the tears streaming down her only son's face.

"Why are you crying, my darling?"

"Because I don't want to leave you, Mama." At that, he had fled. Dogma tells us that we are made for eternity. The resurrection of the flesh and the life everlasting are sought not so much that one should prolong his own existence but rather that beyond time one might explain and atone. Almost all boys are unfeeling fools, but that is no consolation.

While still young, Kirk had lost the two created beings — his grandfather and now his mother — that he loved passionately. On the surface, the young man was all constraint and reserve; within, desolate. Not until he was forty-five years old, at which time he married, would he confide deeply in anybody. Those two deaths had hardened him; in Scotland, a few years later, students would speak of him as "the Buddha, dispassionate but benign." But in a Time of Troubles a certain apathy may enable a man to endure with a shrug many slings and arrows of outrageous fortune.

At the hour of his mother's death, Kirk knew next to nothing about any religion. Perhaps the vanishing of Marjorie Pierce Kirk began to wake him to some awareness of the eternal and the sacred. It entered his mind that the Great Salt Lake Desert, though blasted beyond belief, might not be God-forsaken.

In college he had read Marcus Aurelius and Epictetus and Seneca privately; he read them again on the sand dunes at Dugway, in solitude. In Marcus's meditations he came upon such passages as this:

Even as the traveller asks his way of him that he meets, inclined in no wise to bear to the right rather than to the left (for he desires only the way leading whither he would go), so should we come unto God as to a guide; even as we turn our eyes without admonishing them to show us some things rather than others, but content to receive the images of such things as they present to us. But as it is, we stand anxiously watching the victim, and with the voice of supplication call upon the augur: "Master, have mercy on me: vouchsafe unto me a way of escape!" Slave, would you then have aught else than what is best? Is there anything better than what is God's good pleasure? Why, as far as in you lies, would you corrupt your Judge, and lead your Counsellor astray?

The conscience of the Stoic emperor seemed to speak to Kirk's conscience. Pity is a vice, Zeno had said; and self-pity especially, Kirk remarked to himself. About this time, in a Salt Lake City bookshop, he came upon a new volume by Albert Jay Nock, *Memoirs of a Superfluous Man,* by which he was much moved. Somewhat presumptuously, Kirk commenced a correspondence with Nock, who then, near the end of his tether, was living at Canaan, Connecticut. Into the limbo of lost things, together with much else in Kirk's life, the letters of this correspondence have vanished. They discussed Marcus Aurelius. Mr. Nock, although once an Episcopalian priest like his father before him, latterly had abandoned any firm faith in Christian doctrine. He had come to think his own survival beyond the jaws of physical death improbable. Yet in the end, would the imitation of Marcus Aurelius, or Epictetus, or Zeno suffice Nock, or anyone else, on what Nock called "the road to the river" . . . of death?

For his part, Kirk had commenced to move, very languidly, beyond Stoicism to something more. It was not toward pantheism that he shifted, for the rattlesnake, the gray sagebrush, and the bitter juniper berry do not inspire in a soldier Wordsworth's love of divine handiwork. Yet some consciousness of a brooding Presence stirred in Kirk something of the desert prophet Amos, whose name Kirk bore as his second name; this was rather like rousing, as G. K. Chesterton says in another context, "a great wild forest passion in a little Cockney heart." The desert knew no benevolence; it was terrible; but awe and veneration being close allied, truly the fear of God is the beginning of wisdom. Something made Kirk inquire within himself by what authority he presumed to doubt — although he had not yet read Newman's observation that it is better to believe all things than to doubt all things. Upon authority all revealed religion rests, and the authority that lies behind Christian doctrine is massive. By what alternative authority did Kirk question it? Why, chiefly upon the promptings of people like H. G. Wells and Leonard Woolf, with whose other opinions Kirk did not agree in the least. Why should he prefer their negations to the affirmations of men whose precepts he took otherwise for gospel: the principles of Johnson and Burke, of Coleridge and Paul Elmer More? If their minds gave credence to revealed religion, must not Kirk, in mere toleration, open his mind to the possibility of religion's truth? So, by slow degrees, mind and heart are moved; and if Kirk in 1943 was scarcely better than a skeptic, still that was a far cry from the positivism of his teens.

In the Great Salt Lake Desert — whether or not the awfulness of the place worked some change in him — he began to perceive that pure reason has its frontiers and that to deny the existence of realms beyond those borders — why, that's puerility. Yet even within the realm of reason, if disbelief in a transcendent order is suspended, evidences of every sort begin to pour in — proofs drawn from the natural sciences, from psychology, from history, from physics — demonstrating that we are part of some grand mysterious scheme, working upon us providentially. This granted, one must turn for elucidation of those mysteries to a different science, theology — but in the year 1943, in the desert, Kirk got no farther. Knowledge of this sort comes through illation, being borne in upon the mind, in hints and fragments, not systematically; and Kirk's illative sense began to stir in the stony shadow of the Camel's Back.

If Kirk came some way toward an apprehension of the divine, there upon the dunes that were the beaches of a forgotten sea, he moved farther toward a proper understanding of his own nature. He had told himself, ever since beginning to think about such matters, that he admired the intellect of the Enlightenment of the seventeenth and eighteenth centuries; now he came to understand that he had drifted the wrong way. Those had been splendid centuries, but he did not in truth sympathize with the chief currents of thought and feeling in those ages; what he respected in the Enlightenment was the men who had stood against the whole tendency of their epoch — such men as Johnson and Burke.

His was no Enlightenment mind, Kirk now became aware: it was a Gothic mind, medieval in its temper and structure. He did not love cold harmony and perfect regularity of organization; what he sought was a complex of variety, mystery, tradition, the venerable, the awful. He despised sophisters and calculators; he was groping for faith, honor, and prescriptive loyalties. He would have given any number of neoclassical pediments for one poor battered gargoyle. The men of the Enlightenment had cold hearts and smug heads; now their successors, as the middle of the twentieth century loomed up, were in the process of imposing upon all the world a dreary conformity, with Efficiency and Progress and Equality for their watchwords — abstractions preferred to all those fascinating and lovable peculiarities of human nature and human society that are the products of prescription and tradition. This desert of salt would be a cheerful place by comparison with the desolation of human hearts, should the remains of Gothic faith and Gothic diversity be crushed out of civilization.

Yet Kirk's was not a religious mind. Religion is the tie that binds men and women together in worship; for that community Kirk felt no longing. In his loneliness he still turned to Marcus Aurelius. The sense of the vanity of human wishes, though with the Emperor always, was borne with a splendid calm:

> To go on being what you have been hitherto, to lead a life still so distracted and polluted, were stupidity and cowardice indeed, worthy of the mangled gladiators who, torn and disfigured, cry out to be remanded till the morrow, to be flung once more to the same fangs and claws. Enter your claim then to these few attributes. And if stand fast in them you can, stand fast — as one translated indeed to Islands of the Blessed. But if you find yourself falling away and beaten in the fight, be a man and get away to some quiet corner, where you can still hold on, or, in the last resort, take leave of life not angrily, but simply, freely, modestly, achieving at least this much in life, brave leaving of it.

The Islands of the Blessed — were there such, hereafter? If the Islands were but a fable, was not Kirk the most miserable of men? Did there really exist a community of souls, joining the dead, the living, and those yet to be born? A community transcending time and space? Christians called such the mystical body of Christ; but Kirk was no Christian at the age of twenty-five, brooding on some windy talus, hawks wheeling above him, vigilant for Dugway's rabbits; and he, knowing nature red in tooth and claw, vigilant for rattlers.

Burning Men in Florida's Swamps

From time to time, Dugway's colonel commanding and Dugway's executive officer permitted Kirk a considerable change of scene — although eventually summoning him back to his secret and confidential documents amidst the sand dunes. Later he reflected on how good the officers were to him — perhaps because he contrived for their desert parties various treasure hunts, complete with puzzling rhymed clues. It was a simple and relatively innocent life at Dugway, with simple and perfectly innocent diversions.

However that may be, for some months in 1944 and 1945 he was dispatched to the Withlacoochee Land Use Area in central Florida, near the village of Bushnell, north of Tampa. In the swamps of the Withlacoochee, where Osceola's Seminoles had won their principal victory over federal troops, the Chemical Warfare Service had arranged to spray mustard gas in the brush and parade soldiers through it, with or without protective clothing, to see if their flesh might be burned, and how badly. The half-dozen hardened CWS enlisted men dispatched from Dugway, under command of a portly major, were not to be so burnt, except perhaps accidentally or incidentally, they not being expendable: they were to supervise and record the operation, which was to continue for months.

To the abandoned Air Corps tent camp where the Dugway men were lodged, among great diseased and decaying oak trees, was dispatched also a CWS decontamination company, fairly well drilled — which the half-dozen Dugway ruffians were not, being swaggering or stoical individualists. Also presently there arrived another company, composed of men who had volunteered to be the human subjects (goats, who did not volunteer, being burnt with mustard gas, too) of this prolonged experiment. Soon Kirk learned that only three categories of men volunteer to be burnt alive: selfless patriots, the mad, and criminals released from bondage on condition of suffering torment for their country's sake. He encountered few selfless patriots in the Withlacoochee.

The Dugway sourdoughs dwelt apart in their own tiny jungle community; when at length compelled to mess with the decontamination company and finding the food unsavory, they cursed first the cook and then the company's captain, as if they had been gourmets at the Ritz; for they had grown into devil-may-care characters, so many two-legged Dugway coyotes. Their major backing them up, they compelled a great reform of the camp's cuisine. Down with Spam! Camp Swampy, in the cartoon-strip "Beetle Bailey," is the spit and image of their encampment near Bushnell.

One took one's chances in the Withlacoochee, quite aside from the mustard gas. Once, nocturnally, at the door of his tent Kirk was bitten by what appeared to be a deadly coral snake — which, however, turned out either not to be of that species or else degenerate from its sire. On another occasion, exploring solitary in the forest behind the camp, Kirk was confronted in a clearing by a perfectly enormous and belligerent sow, with piglets in her care; being unarmed, he stood very still while the sow glared at him for some minutes, ready to charge; then, walking backward very slowly, he withdrew into the brush.

Lunatics in the strange company of men who had volunteered to be burnt for the greater good of the CWS were as perilous as coral snakes or sows gone wild. Old Sergeant Sheridan, a veteran of the cavalry of the old Army of the United States, for a time shared Kirk's tiny tent. The two sergeants were conversing amicably one evening when shots were fired, successively. Peering cannily from behind a tent flap, Kirk perceived one of those witless volunteers stumbling among the trees, firing a German pistol into trunks and empty (fortuitously) tents. Sergeant Kirk snatched up a sheath knife, Sergeant Sheridan a tent pole; and the two waited for him to burst into their sanctuary. But he lurched past their tent, not perceiving their presence, into the forest; they tracked him down later, better armed and with reinforcements.

The most interesting peril was a hurricane, of which they were given warning. As the wind rose late in the evening, Kirk's immediate comrades and the decontamination company and the company of psychotic volunteers fled in trucks into the little town of Bushnell, for greater security. But Kirk and his tentmate that month were too indolent, or else too fond of their private possessions; they went to bed in their cots, letting the wind howl. When they rose at dawn, they discovered that all the tents save theirs had been blown away during the night, or else had been crushed to earth by falling decayed oaks. Not long later appeared their boon comrade Corporal Muska in a jeep with the tidings that the hurricane, circling round, was on its way back to their camp; he carried them off to the town, which lay just outside the hurricane's path.

[71]

In the Withlacoochee, Kirk learned how to terrify recruits by enticing them to cross a ditch on a plank; when they glanced down, they found alligators in the water below. Also he spent a good deal of time in art museums and historic buildings, at St. Augustine, Jacksonville, Gainesville, Orlando, Tampa, St. Petersburg, Sarasota, and Miami.

Florida in those years was relatively unspoilt, its population a fraction of the state's inhabitants half a century later, with much cattle ranching (open range) and curious old towns, both on the coasts and inland. The grand hotels built by Flagler and other railway magnates still were functioning; the natives about Bushnell were friendly; the county judge kept racial relations tolerable. Only roaches troubled Kirk in his wilderness retreat. One might have lingered pleasantly enough in that lotusland for some years, buying second-hand books and privately preparing for the Foreign Service, diplomatic or consular — something, however, that never came to pass. Sooner than they liked, the major and his six or seven Dugway daredevils were summoned back to the Great Salt Lake Desert: the Withlacoochee project was completed, it having been ascertained that if a man were to walk without protective clothing through brush contaminated by mustard gas, his flesh might be badly burned. One might have guessed that result without having tormented the volunteers for months on end; but then, often the CWS seemed to Sergeant Kirk wondrously wasteful of time and materials. He understood that profligacy better when, at the war's end, Major General Alden Waitt, Chief, CWS, was indicted for accepting bribes from contractors and found guilty.

Later, as the Italian and then the German armies were crushed and Hiroshima and Nagasaki were erased, it was found well to prepare some enlisted men as "separation counsellors" to troops being discharged. Kirk contrived to get himself assigned to training for that particular skill: he was sent for a month of instruction to Camp Lee near Petersburg, Virginia, and so came to know Petersburg, Richmond, and other old towns; and, in charge of a busload of soldiers, he saw Williamsburg for the first time. (Some of the old houses, unrestored, then remained in private possession, their owners setting at defiance the Rockefeller restorers; and tourists were a rare species.)

Invariably he fell asleep at the afternoon lectures by army psychologists. About this reported lassitude he was questioned one day by his commanding officer.

CAPTAIN: Sergeant Kirk, it has been reported to me that you were observed sleeping at 1600 hours yesterday. Were you studying hard the previous night?

KIRK: Yes, sir,

CAPTAIN: Did you think the lecture was boring?

KIRK: Not much more than usual, sir.

CAPTAIN (*involuntarily smiling*): Well, be charge of quarters for two hours tonight.

Then and ever after, Kirk was a nocturnal creature, widest awake at three in the morning, sleepiest about half past three in the afternoon. Only in the American army, probably, would officers and noncoms have recognized such constitutional peculiarities and have indulged them. After all, Kirk performed his duties faithfully enough and never caused trouble: so they let him be.

To complete his training as a separation counsellor, Kirk was sent to the military hospital at Brigham City, Utah, where most of the patients were infantrymen who had lost limbs — sometimes three of them, and in a few cases all four — a number of them from German land mines in the Liri Valley. Most of them had been farmers or farmers' sons, of good outdoor stock, possessed of fortitude. Kirk talked with one, deprived of three limbs, who had spent some weeks at Volterra, in Italy; he was surprised and delighted to find someone who knew about the quarries and the black wine of Volterra. This new friend offered to teach Italian to Kirk, but then Kirk was summoned back to Dugway. Ah, the sadness of that hospital! What could Kirk say to those mutilated men? He might have donated an arm or a leg of his own, had it been possible, to one or another of those brave ruins. After hours in the hospital, Kirk scrambled about the snowy foothills of the Wasatch, by way of relief.

Back at Dugway, Kirk was informed that he would not be converted into a separation counsellor after all: he must get back to those classified documents, being regarded as irreplaceable in that capacity. Of chemistry Kirk knew no more than he had learnt as a C student in high school, but the Federal Bureau of Investigation had found him innocent of subversion, so to the classified files he was tethered. He began to wonder whether indispensable personnel ever would be demobilized.

Yet in 1946, at San Pedro, he was presented with his discharge papers. It had been his intention to walk all the way back to Michigan, but the weather was insalubrious. Slowly he made his journey eastward by rail, spending time along the route in Tucson, San Antonio, and New Orleans. During his army years, on furlough or in the course of travel in line of duty, he had come to know fairly well San Francisco, Los Angeles, St. Louis, and other cities. At St. Louis, nearly all of the old French town already had been demolished, the cathedral standing lonely amid land strewn with rubble; much more of that city has vanished since then, St. Louis being an early and principal victim of miscalled "urban renewal." Yet the town fascinated Kirk, then and later; long after, he would make St. Louis the setting for two of his ghostly tales, "The Surly Sullen Bell" and "Lex Talionis."

What would become of him now? At San Pedro, another sergeant who actually *had* been made a separation counsellor sat across a table from Kirk and after routine remarks had muttered, guardedly, "I got to ask you this, Sarge. Would you like to join the Enlisted Reserve?"

Kirk smiled: "No, thanks."

"That's O.K." The separation counsellor relaxed in his chair. "Some G.I.s get abusive when I ask that question. Now did you suffer any injuries in the service that you might need treatment for, or that might be pensionable?"

Kirk had taken some mustard gas in the throat that occasionally caused coughing and dry vocal chords, but he did not mean to be detained in a military hospital, and the government would have enough pensions to pay without compensating Kirk lifelong for minor damage. "No, thanks." They had let him go, a free man again, and he was in St. Louis again, on his way back to Michigan.

The greatest of all wars had passed him by: Kirk scarcely had heard a voice raised in anger. In the army he had acquired a stock of worldly wisdom and had learnt to consort, unharmed, with the brutal, the fraudulent, the mad — even with the murderous, among them Whiskey Murray at Dugway, who had boasted of being an executioner for a racketeering union in New York, shoving dissidents down elevator shafts. A mad world, my masters! Marcus Aurelius and Epictetus and Seneca had sustained Kirk in such company. Yet there had been good companions, too: Robert Shaw, who was to become an optometrist in Pocatello; and Chico Gonzalez, who kept

[74]

the Dugway gate o' nights, telephoning "Sergeant Kirky" at headquarters now and again to inquire whether he should fire at some trespasser. ("Fire in the air first," was the usual response of the Confidential Clerk, solitary in the headquarters building.)

For good or ill, such comradeship was ended now. Like Sindbad transported by the roc, Kirk found himself back at Plymouth and Mecosta, himself little altered outwardly, but his Plymouth household broken up, his father remarried, his sister off to college, his high-school friends scattered, the fields he had used to walk with his grandfather now covered by factories, and his fortune at a stay. Whither should he turn? He still lacked any discernible bent or purpose, having abandoned any thought of the Foreign Service, although while still in the army he had passed the Service's written examinations with a very high score — one hundred per cent, indeed, on the general-information test.

Then, to his surprise, Kirk sitting in an East Lansing hash house, there came up to him a professor of history whose best student Kirk had been, before the war. "Russell! What are you doing these days?"

"Nothing, sir." It was the laconic answer Kirk had given to Principal Dykhouse at Plymouth, a decade before.

With the veterans flooding into colleges, 1946 was a year of insatiable demand for new instructors possessed of masters' degrees, or even bachelors'. The University of Washington, it was said, had begun to recruit from Skid Row degreed lushes to teach freshman English.

"Come to my office," said Professor Kimber.

Before the sun had set the next day, Russell Kirk, M.A, quondam sergeant, had consented to teach the history of civilization, principally to veterans who now professed a thirst for knowledge or at least for certification in some skill or other.

In the Educational Waste Land

During his years at Dugway and in the Withlacoochee, Kirk had continued to write for publication. In 1944, *Michigan History* published his piece "A Michigan Soldier's Diary, 1863," drawn from the journal of his ancestor Nathan Frank Pierce, who had been at Gettysburg, Antietam, the Wilderness, and the siege of Petersburg. In 1945

The South Atlantic Quarterly published his essay "A Conscript on Education"; in 1946 *College English* brought out his "Cooper and the European Puzzle," about James Fenimore Cooper's politics, written while Kirk had been at Duke University. Later that year, the *South Atlantic* published his lament "Conscription ad Infinitum." At the age of twenty-eight, he had to his credit more serious publications than had the great majority of tenured professors at MSC; so for him the nascent national academic policy of "publish or perish" would hold no terrors.

Yet it was only because he had nothing better to do at the moment that Kirk turned his hand to college lecturing, as earlier for the same empty reason he had turned his hand to college studies and then to graduate-school researches. Never, in 1946 or later, would he endeavor to ride up the "tenure track," nor did he seek increments of salary while at Michigan State: a frugal bachelor and a Scot by descent, he had no great need for money; and — in this somewhat un-Scottish — he took no thought for the morrow.

Accustomed to public debating, well stocked with historical anecdotes of a striking or a comical cast, and himself a recently discharged soldier, Kirk did not encounter half so much difficulty with his students as did most instructors. But circumstances at Michigan State in 1946 and after were unfriendly to the higher learning. A hundred students might be crowded into one classroom, a fair number of them resentful of being expected to read even textbooks; outside, in a frenzy of construction of new buildings, the bulldozers roared ceaselessly; the professor who expected his students to write, as Kirk did, was unassisted in his reading of hundreds of students' test papers every fortnight. Michigan State was a gross caricature of the Grove of Academe.

Kirk taught the history of civilization, in the newly founded Basic College. From its beginnings, that Basic College suffered from grave defects of organization and method. Most of its departments attempted to accomplish too much, and so ended by doing very little. The unconfessed aim of the Basic College was to provide remedial education — somehow to compensate for the wretchedly shallow schooling of the typical graduate of the typical high school — and to wake intellectual curiosity in the minds of single men who, in barracks, hadn't turned into plaster saints. Kirk discerned a tendency to substitute facile generalizations for the inculcation of a genuine body of knowledge. What was yet more serious, the Board of Examiners, a body of educationists who made up the comprehensive or term-end examinations almost independently of the departments concerned, were dedicated to "objective" tests — that is, standardized multiple-choice questions put to students in great number in a short space of time and calculated to encourage the conditioned response of the indoctrinated mediocre student rather than the calculated judgment of the serious student.

As it became apparent to students that they were not expected to write, and scarcely to read, but only to attend lectures and put down their check marks to indicate the doctrines preached by their instructors, a subtle feeling spread among them: the conviction that the Basic College was merely a boondoggle or racket, to be endured if one must, to be escaped so soon as one might; thus their performance fell short of their abilities.

Nevertheless, the Basic College — which paid relatively high salaries — attracted to its staff some men of high abilities and principles in every department, and they combined against this degradation of the democratic dogma, hoping that in time they would be able to improve the College's condition. As for Kirk, having neither taste nor talent for faculty politics, he spent his time with his classes and his writing and his studies (*not* "researches," merely searches), in no way interfering with the administrators of the Basic College.

Now and again a decent student reared his head within the Basic College; but in general the staff were disheartened by their pupils in the College's several departments of literature, history of civilization, natural science, physical science, and effective living. How much civilization the students digested may be measured by the response of a typical student to a question put by Kirk on a typical test:

QUESTION: Can you offer some description of ancient Egyptian sculpture?

ANSWER: Egyptian sculpture was mostly horizontal. They all had that oriental look.

A conversation overheard by Kirk on a local bus may suggest the students' attitude toward the program so inanely entitled Effective Living. Two high-school girls, one small, one ample, were conversing in low tones.

SMALL GIRL: You couldn't tell that, not even to your man.

AMPLE GIRL: They do at the College, though; they talk about things like that all the time. They call it Effective Living.

MSC's freshmen and sophomores, wards or victims of the Basic College, called it Effective Loving. But to acquire that art they needn't have paid tuition.

The educational principles enunciated by Russell Kirk, it will be perceived, were not much honored at Michigan State in 1946 or thereafter. Some passages from his essay "A Conscript on Education," published a year before he began teaching at MSC, may be worth reprinting here, they remaining pertinent to America's present educational discontents.

Kirk had begun his article by replying mordantly to an article in the *Atlantic Monthly* by George Boas, then a famous professor of philosophy at Johns Hopkins. Boas had urged that the humanities and the arts should be swept aside in wartime, so that students might "get to business learning trigonometry and physics and chemistry." Moreover, Boas had written, "All the learning in the world is not worth the experience which he will gain from his military career; and if he is killed, at least he will not have asked someone else to die for him."

What Kirk experienced in his military career did not seem to him worth all the learning in the world; so he thumped Boas manfully. The following Kirk paragraph suggests his substance and style when he was twenty-eight years of age:

It might not be surprising to hear the headmaster of a military preparatory school expounding a doctrine which exalts above his victim the legionary who slew Archimedes; but to listen to this cry of "sound, sound the clarion, fill the fife" coming from the ivory tower is another matter. It is an opinion which differs only in degree from an important article of faith in the credo of those states now contesting with us the mastery of the earth, whose intellectual principles we profess to despise. [Kirk had written this essay in 1944.] Before commencing our work of world reformation, it might pay us to consider whether we are going to beat the Nazis and enlighten them, or beat the Nazis and join them. We are fit to weigh this question only if we retain some vestige of the liberal learning so quickly cast aside in one crowded hour of glorious life; and it is to be feared that a smattering of trigonometry and physics and chemistry is not sufficient to make the mind liberal. The physical sciences have their place, a respectable one; but they, primarily, do not win wars; the human spirit still does that; and physical sciences certainly cannot suffice for the men who are to make and maintain a peace, who are to establish liberty and justice, who are to set free the body and the mind.

Kirk went on to certain pitiless observations concerning the higher learning in America that have not lost their relevance with the elapse of half a century.

It is true that the average graduate of our colleges knows neither how to live nor how to think. His four years of membership in the academic body served chiefly to muddle his mind, to blur the sound prejudices in it. . . . A liberally educated man has a great store of general knowledge and common sense; ignorant enthusiasm cannot remake the world. . . .

In this war, fought in the name of liberalism, very few think of liberalism of knowledge. We need an Epictetus to remind us that freedom of the mind is more important than freedom of the body. If our thoughts are not liberal, we shall not know how to rule, once we find ourselves masters of the world's destiny.

This was Kirk's first essay on education. It would be followed by some hundreds of essays, articles, and newspaper columns on that general subject, and by three books of his, down into the Nineties.

Sudden restoration of the higher learning not being within his power, what might Kirk do to brighten the arid corner where he found himself? Why, establish an oasis in this East Lansing desert: found a good second-hand bookshop to which his friends on the staff of the college, and the better sort of undergraduate, might resort. They would brew strong coffee and serve plain doughnuts and sell very good books, old and new, and have good talk.

So in partnership with his friend Adrian Smith, employed in the engineering department of Oldsmobile, Kirk found a basement in East Lansing's business district where they might install their Red Cedar Bookshop — not a good site, because invisible from the street.

They borrowed money to acquire two splendid libraries in Lansing: the enormous collection of the late Justice Howard Weist, of Michigan's Supreme Court; and the less gigantic but wondrously rare collections of the late Clarence Bement, a Lansing pioneer in the automobile industry.

The Weist mansion, crammed with books, architecturally was the finest house in Lansing, a massive Italianate building once meant to be the house of the governors of Michigan. Justice Weist, finding it derelict, had acquired and restored it; but since his death the house had been decaying, as had the fortunes of his widow and his daughter, still resident there. "I suppose we could rent rooms," said the ancient and witty Mrs. Weist, "but who'd wish to live here? It's too dirty." Also it was ghostly. After the death of Mrs. and Miss Weist, the beautiful thick-walled house was thoughtfully pulled down. Shagbark, the Justice's country place near Williamston, found a kindly new owner, and stands still. "Red" Smith and Russell Kirk painfully lugged thousands and thousands of books and bound periodicals out of the two houses. From the Weist library, Kirk retained Fuller's *The Holy State and the Profane State,* Harrington's *Oceana* — both the original editions — and a very few lesser books. Out of eerie happenings in the Weist mansion, years later Kirk would make his ghostly tale "What Shadows We Pursue."

Many of the more costly volumes in these two splendid libraries Smith and Kirk sold through mail-order catalogues, produced on their duplicating machine, to such famous New York dealers as Dauber and Pine, who flew from Manhattan, from time to time, to visit the Red Cedar Bookshop. Kirk's sister Carolyn, then an undergraduate at Michigan State, was installed as clerk of the shop.

It was a bold and pleasant venture, but time-consuming and unprofitable; it lasted for two years, at the end of which time Kirk went abroad. In later years Kirk would urge other men to enter into the second-hand book trade but never would be so foolish, despite temptations, as to return to that business himself.

A consolation for lack of profit in bookselling is the diversity of character among bookshop browsers. Kirk's most curious customer was saddled with the name of Leon Lack, an appellation commendably suitable, for he was lean and lank and very shabby, the archetype of the hollow-cheeked radical, straight out of the pages of Dostoevski. He peered lengthily into books of the Marxist persuasion and at intervals bought one such — though Kirk hated to take his money, the student being so very impoverished. Also he approved of Leon Lack because he was a genuine scholar, a breed extremely rare at Michigan State. Daily Leon travelled by bus, between MSC and the Library of the State of Michigan, near the Capitol; and Kirk too haunted that State Library, which then held many rare volumes — later destroyed in a great fire.

After Kirk had left East Lansing, the time came when Leon Lack, having completed all requirements at MSC, was ready to be graduated. At that juncture, someone informed the press that Lack was a Communist — which was true undoubtedly, Leon having made no secret of where his political affections lay. John Hannah, president of Michigan State, then proclaimed that Lack would not be permitted to graduate: Communists had no place at MSC, the friendly campus. But nowhere in the College's charter or regulations was there any prohibition of Communists as students. Having no funds to contest at law this arbitrary denial of his degree, Leon Lack vanished from the campus without a diploma, after his several years of serious study.

Kirk never saw Lack again, but Kirk's friend Mary Moran did, years later. She was seated near the window of a restaurant in Flint, when there appeared outside the skeletal Leon. Glimpsing her, he entered, sat down, and began to talk nervously, having known her in the Red Cedar Bookshop days. Then he noticed someone out in the street, sprang up in great alarm, ran through the restaurant to the back door, and vanished. Mary never saw him after; nor, so far as Kirk knows, did anybody else. Had he been swallowed up by the Communist apparatus? The book trade attracts oddities, some of them tragic.

Another civilizing enterprise undertaken by Kirk in those East Lansing years was the George Ade Society, named in honor of the Indiana humorist, whose books were collected by Adrian Smith, William McCann, John Clark, Warren Fleischauer, and other friends of Kirk. One of East Lansing's radicals of that period, Elizabeth Pollock, sister-in-law to Jackson Pollock, referred to these Ade cronies as "the Death Group" — with special reference to their denial of the Pelagian doctrine of the natural goodness of man. But they were jolly. It would have been more reasonable to style them the East Lansing Inklings, for among them were several much-published writers — most notably, at the time, A. J. M. Smith, the poet, and Richard

Dorson, the folklore authority, the latter a close friend of Kirk for many years afterward.

The Ade Society people talked about books and general ideas, and occasionally attracted speakers from the outer world, in particular Richard Weaver, the author of *Ideas Have Consequences,* and Ross J. S. Hoffman, the Burke scholar, and Father Leo Ward, the writer on education. Often the Society met in the back room of Archie Tarpoff's fashionable restaurant in downtown Lansing. In their small way, the members of the Ade Society, or Death Group, were the heritors of The Club to which Samuel Johnson and Burke and Goldsmith and other eighteenth-century loquacious worthies had belonged. After Kirk had departed from Michigan State, the Ade Society would sink to extinction, few cultural flowers blooming long in East Lansing.

During his Duke year and his army years, Kirk had travelled too much to rest satisfied with the domestic comforts of East Lansing. Besides, on all young instructors there was inflicted the pressure to obtain the doctorate, should they wish to remain on the staff and, as the years should limp by, to have conferred on them the high dignity called tenure. Kirk felt no strong urge to linger in the Academy: a man who hangs about a college after having been graduated, Edmund Burke wrote in 1760, "is like a man who, having built and rigged and victualled a ship, should lock her up in a dry dock."

Still, what other practical prospect had Kirk? He had thought of the profession of the law, with the ambition of becoming a judge; on aptitude tests, Kirk had ranked very high as a potential lawyer. But to attend any law school, a good deal of money was required, and scholarships then were few. Kirk had no savings nor anyone from whom he might borrow money; with a shrug, he abandoned the fancy. In those years, it never entered his head that he might prosper tolerably well as a man of letters and in that occupation exert far stronger influence than he could have at the bar or on the bench.

American graduate schools, pedantic, bureaucratic, and given to excessive supervision, seemed repellent to Kirk. He came upon a slim book by Sir D'Arcy Thompson, professor of natural science at St. Andrews University, in Scotland. Therein he found a charming essay on St. Andrews itself, university and town. "There be sailor towns and weaver towns," Sir D'Arcy wrote of that ancient place, "and market towns and fighting border towns and more besides; but St. Andrews is none of these. It has been, for better for worse, a town of scholars these five hundred years — yea, and for some centuries besides; once upon a time it was a town for kings and cardinals, and monkish saints and hermits came hither more, much more, than a thousand years ago."

Kirk's Scottish ancestry, his assiduous reading of Walter Scott and Robert Louis Stevenson, and his relish for the books of a living Scottish writer, George Scott-Moncrieff — these influences induced Kirk to write to The Secretary, the University of St. Andrews, inquiring whether he might be admitted as a research student at this oldest university of Scotland. A very brief form was sent to him; he filled it out, and was admitted as a candidate for St. Andrews' highest arts degree, doctor of letters. He was to write a book about Edmund Burke's thought. A grant from the American Council of Learned Societies was obtained for his subsistence; and as a veteran he was entitled to the benefits of the G.I. Bill — payment of his St. Andrews fees as a research student (then about forty-five dollars a year!), some books, and a stipend of seventy-five dollars monthly. This he regarded as being in clover, with the style of Senior Fellow of the American Council of Learned Societies.

For travelling companion he had Miss Rosemary Ray, his sister's closest friend, who then meant to study at Trinity College, Dublin. In September they went aboard an oldfangled half-and-half vessel, sheep and other quadrupeds amidships, that slowly made her heaving way out of Boston harbor, by way of Halifax and St. John's, toward Ireland. Kirk suffered his first seasickness; thereafter for some years he would cross the Atlantic at least twice annually.

Arrived at Dublin, Rosemary determined not to become a research student after all, but instead to return soon to Michigan and marry her favorite boy; so she and Kirk visited Killarney, and presently various towns in England and Scotland, and then Russell was left at St. Andrews to his own devices.

Dr. Samuel Johnson remarked that if a man had no duties to perform, he might spend his life happily travelling in a post chaise with a pretty woman. Taking this advice to heart, for the next decade and longer Kirk would induce American girls, all pretty or more than pretty, to explore Europe with him: Dorothy, Corine, Jane, another Rosemary, Beegie, Ilse, Marian, Annette. Train, bus, lake steamer, and shank's mare, though, had supplanted the post chaise. The psycho-biographer may be incredulous to learn that these peregrinate relationships were chaste — and therefore happy enough. Asking no reward but a cheerful face, Kirk would become the most accomplished *cavalier servente*. The earlier fair companions would remain Kirk's friends for life; the last of them would marry him, and she the fairest of them all.

Kirk reached St. Andrews in September 1948, aged nearly thirty years, owning nothing but the contents of the suitcases he brought with him, his portable typewriter, and a few books he had left at Plymouth or Mecosta. From the cozy railway station he found his way through dark streets to a handsome Victorian house in the terrace called Queen's Gardens, where he was to lodge in the former parlor on the first floor. The town and its people promptly enchanted him; he would be drawn back there, most years, for the rest of his life.

Too long Kirk had sojourned in dry deserts, wet deserts, deserts of mind and conscience; now he was settling in a venerable place where thought and prayer had been nurtured for a thousand years and more, from the age of the Culdees to the age of the fissured atom.

CHAPTER FOUR

Scots Imagery and Scots Character

The Haunted Town of Schoolmen

Spreading fanlike from the cathedral close on Kirk Hill, the three ancient streets of the royal burgh of St. Andrews stretched before Russell Kirk, as for the first time he surveyed the town from the summit of St. Rule's Tower. In the Dark Ages this headland frowning upon the North Sea, brown-gray cliffs eroded by the Lammas tides, was a noble site for a hermitage or a tower. Both arose there.

In the sixth century, some Christian anchorite from far away — Saint Rule, the legend names him — lodged himself in the shallow cave to which one still can scramble. Chapels, churches, a cathedral, and a priory successively were raised in veneration of the relics of Andrew the Apostle, fetched here from Northumbria during the chaos of the eighth century. St. Rule's Tower, a hundred and ten feet high, survives from the first grand church, to keep watch over all.

The ruins of ecclesiastical St. Andrews — mighty gables, long stretches of arcading, immense fortified walls, crypts and tombs, the bishops' castle, scraps of friaries — are beautiful in death. The cathedral, grandest church in Scotland, was quarried by the townsfolk for two centuries after the Reformation; half the tomb effigy of Bishop Wardlaw, benefactor of the infant university, was pulled out of the façade of a fish-and-chips saloon a few years past, when the Italian proprietor installed a larger window.

St. Andrews town is said to endure more ghosts than any other place in Scotland, or perhaps the world. Pickled cardinals, defenestrated priors, monks buried in dunghills, witches burnt or drowned, Protestant martyrs tormented, and other terrors walk the wynds. The bottle dungeon of the bishops' castle, in 1948 to be seen only by the eerie light of a swinging lantern, supplied a whole series of dubious legends with which to regale the credulous. "There's but ane ither gaol like it," said the elderly custodian, in the accents of Fife, "and that's in Rome, Italy," meaning the Mamertine.

The very university library, gifted by James VI, cherished its ghost — the revenant of an eighteenth-century janitor who had hanged himself from the stair rail. The university's senate of that time had condemned the suicide's bones to hang in perpetuity, encased, above the stair. And there they had remained until the sepulchral case was brought down by a German bomb that fell in the close during the Second World War. Two centuries' punishment being deemed sufficient, the janitor's remains were interred at last, and his unquiet spirit has not since troubled Parliament Hall, within the Library.

The German bomb also knocked over the ancient thorn tree beside St. Mary's College, planted by Mary Stuart; but, being propped up, it lingers like an old woman leaning upon a stick. Much else antique has lingered in St. Andrews.

Perhaps no place in Britain clung more affectionately to old ways than did the little gray city of St. Andrews, perched on its sandstone headland. When John Knox and his Reformers dinged down the archbishopric of St. Andrews, the soul would have gone out of the place had not the little university remained and come to flourish again. The game of golf had its beginnings at St. Andrews, with Mary Stuart herself on the links; and golf conferred upon nineteenth- and twentieth-century St. Andrews a degree of prosperity.

Cozy is a word originally Scottish, and St. Andrews in 1948 remained faithful to the idea of coziness. The snug residents' parlor of an inn, the cozy that swaddled the pot on every tea table, the compact farms with their pantiled rows of thick-walled cottages and bothies and byres — these embodiments of tidy comfort extended upward to the Scottish universities. Gown and town were snug and douce.

Summers, during the years Kirk spent there, a horde of Glasgow folk descended upon the West Sands and splashed uncomfortably in

Witch Lake, a cove where a gristlier generation had drowned its condemned. Winters, St. Andreans of the tall old mansions in South Street, or of the fishers' cottages near the harbor, sat home keeping the cat out of the ashes while the sea wind swept along the Scores. The town's pulsating heart remained the two colleges of the university, with the bold fifteenth-century tower of Saint Salvator, the university's church, looming defiant of the tooth of time.

Of the town's ancient mansions, the one that Kirk would come to know well was the Roundel, in medieval times the residence of the cathedral's archdeacons, in Kirk's time the house of the professor of history, John Williams Williams, who called himself the last of the Whigs. Although the Roundel's high panelled rooms were draughty, coziness triumphed, so that Sunday tea at the Roundel was a cultural and gastronomical event. Jack Williams, Mrs. Williams, and four or five students would gather in a hearthstone crescent about the wide fireplace with its Dutch tiles, consuming scones and cakes, engaging in good talk of a literary and historical bent. Jack Williams, though he had read everything, had written nothing. His library of old books, every volume with its glosses from his pen, much overflowed that big hospitable drawing room, into bedrooms and corridors.

On weekdays, now and again, Kirk would sit alone with Professor Williams in that fine room, or perhaps join with him at the Royal and Ancient Club by the links for a whisky-and-soda, and yet again a whisky-and-soda. They two would talk of everything except Kirk's doctoral dissertation; the Professor knew that Kirk was writing about Burke, of whom the Professor approved, and that sufficed. Kirk would bring to this venerable mentor — so tall, so learned, so affable — chapter draft upon chapter draft of the dissertation; these would be laid upon the drawing-room piano, the first page of each chapter soon to be profaned by rings deposited by whisky tumblers, the stack of typescript growing from month to month.

Meanwhile Kirk bought many scarce books, relevant to his thesis, in Edinburgh, Glasgow, Dublin, and London; also at country-house auctions in Fife and Angus. He walked a great many miles in Scotland, and in Burke's Ireland and in Burke's London, and also in France, Switzerland, and Italy. Between such expeditions he wrote diligently. Frequently he returned to the Roundel, another chapter in hand.

On one occasion after the elapse of a year, Jack Williams glanced at the accumulation of his only research student's learning and remarked while presenting Kirk with another whisky, "Russell, I hate typescript. I know from our talks that you are the master of your subject. Why don't you simply take all those pages back to your rooms? When your book is published, I'll read it with pleasure."

So it would come to pass. When *The Conservative Mind* appeared in print, Professor Williams was much pleased, offering merely the criticism that he thought the book overemphasized somewhat Burke's Christian belief. (Like some other Whigs, Jack Williams was invincibly suspicious of parsons.) In any American graduate school, even at the relatively humane Duke University then, Kirk would have been compelled to waste his energies upon a congeries of graduate courses and examinations, but St. Andrews cared only for the end product, upon the excellence of which the professors would insist. Kirk was the only American to be awarded the university's highest arts degree, doctor of letters, then or later.

During Kirk's years at St. Andrews, a Royal Commission was appointed by the Labour government to investigate the condition and prospects of the university. This report criticized many of the university's staff for living a life withdrawn, once outside the lecture room, from both the students and their fellow professors, readers, and lecturers. That was true; but it was a scholastic virtue. The St. Andrews scholars of that generation were truly learned men who read, who thought, who were civilization incarnate; no one ever had told them to be salesmen or Rotarians. Kirk reflected that some of his American professorial colleagues had no books in their homes except free copies of textbooks. His frequent hours with J. W. Williams taught him what it is to be a scholar and a gentleman.

St. Andrews was the oldest university in Scotland, the third oldest in Britain, and the smallest in the British Isles except for Aberdeen. From the Reformation onward, the university had struggled against poverty, isolation, and the repeated threat of dissolution. In the twentieth century a huge benefaction by the American Edward Harkness had relieved the university of its more pressing fiscal problems; but, in contrast with Oxbridge, St. Andrews remained austere. Students' tuition and living costs were only half the usual American equivalent. Samuel Johnson, on his Scottish tour, had remarked that St. Andrews seemed eminently suited for study, from the cheapness of living and the cloistered quiet. It was so still in Kirk's time.

St. Andrews had schooled famous men: George Buchanan, Reformer and humanist; the Admirable Crichton, poet, orator, and swordsman; Andrew Melville, pillar of kirk and state; Montrose and Claverhouse, great Jacobite captains; Napier of Merchiston, the inventor of logarithms; James Gregory, of differential calculus; later worthies. Also St. Andrews had schooled local magnates, men of business, dominies, farmers, and sometimes even farm laborers — yes, away back in the seventeenth century — who had carried the leaven of civilization back to the pinched old towns and hardscrabble farmsteads of Scotland.

A gawky farm boy might tramp down from Angus or Perthshire, in the eighteenth century or the nineteenth, with a sack of oatmeal and a few shillings for his sustenance, replenishing his provender at the holidays, wear his scarlet gown — as the undergraduates do still — for three years, and, with proper diligence, become a master of arts. In this fashion the four Scottish universities raised the population to that high standard of literacy and intelligence (sometimes crabbed and arrogant) that became the wonder of Europe. Even in Kirk's time, when county council scholarships were being passed out, he knew students whose clothing under their gowns was remarkably ragged — and not from affectation.

In the first half of the twentieth century, St. Andrews's reputation had stood highest in the disciplines of classics and philosophy. The most celebrated professor had been Sir D'Arcy Thompson, great of frame and attainments, whose essay on St. Andrews in his *Science and the Classics* had enticed Kirk to Scotland — though Professor Thompson died some months before Kirk's arrival. The town still echoed with tales of his genius and his eccentricities — of how, for instance, when a whale was stranded upon the West Sands, Thompson strode down to the beach, abruptly produced a mighty knife from under his cloak, and carved out a steak which he bore majestically homeward. Zoologist, classicist, man of letters, he is said to have been offered his choice of four different chairs when as a young man he came to teach at St. Andrews.

Competence, and more than competence, was expected of St. Andrews students. John Wright, dean of arts when Kirk arrived, alarmed undergraduates by his severity of mien. One young man fainted outside the dean's fifteenth-century office at the mere prospect of having to confront that black-gowned professor of philosophy; and another, edging within, stammered out his salutation with a transposition slight but disastrous: "Are you dizzy, Bean?" What with levelling pressures in Britain over the past several decades, standards have declined somewhat since those times, though not so strikingly as at other British universities.

In Kirk's years, St. Andrews had a thousand students merely — many of them lodging in private "bunks," sometimes gas-lit, in the quaint houses of the Old Town. (They employed their threadbare red gowns as tablecloths in the bunks and cooked on kerosene heating stoves or in oldfangled fireplace ovens.) They debated formally in the Union, which had been the Admirable Crichton's residence, the Conservatives always winning the political debates by acclamation. Many of the pretty girl students came from fashionable boarding schools of northern England. There was a fair sprinkling of African students — a Sudanese called Mahdi obtained the only first-class honors in philosophy during Kirk's years and later became great in the Sudan — but, curiously, no Indians or Pakistanis or Chinese; the only Oriental face was that of Edwin McClellan, half Ulsterman, half Japanese, Kirk's comrade at St. Andrews, now professor of Japanese literature at Yale. "Pongo" McClellan maintained himself by winning prolonged games of poker from hardbitten British soldiers turned students; he seemed to do little else; yet he would become one of St. Andrews's more distinguished scholarly graduates, after some years at the University of Chicago, where he would be assistant to F. A. Hayek.

Lodged in Victorian rooms in the genteel street of Queen's Gardens, and later in the picturesque old suburb of Argyle outside the medieval West Port, from the autumn of 1948 until the spring of 1952 — except for occasional sessions of teaching at Michigan State — Kirk was writing the chapters of the book that was to become *The Conservative Mind:* writing while everyone else slept, about him heaps of forgotten books that he had contrived to purchase at country-house auctions or in Edinburgh bookshops. Also he wrote ghostly tales for the new *London Mystery Magazine,* so doubling his income. For fiction of the preternatural, he could have found no better food for the imagination than that supplied by St. Andrews's atmosphere. As for more substantial fare, he kept in his rooms a stock of brandy and chocolate biscuits and took frugal meals at tearooms; with Pongo, he learned how to acquire the largest possible portion of chips at fish-and-chips shops for the smallest possible expenditure of threepences.

He turned antiquary, too, acquiring an abundance of curious information about university and town, which he was to incorporate in an illustrated book, *St. Andrews,* that the London firm of Batsford would publish in 1954. The old gray town seemed to work upon him magically: he wrote with a speed and a vigor, his brain full of concepts, that seemed almost to come from a source outside himself.

Spirit and Stone: George Scott-Moncrieff

Up seven flights of stairs in the vast tall tumbledown house of James's Court, off the Lawnmarket of Edinburgh, lived George Scott-Moncrieff, Esquire, man of letters. "Scomo" had a country house and a town house, he would say: a but-and-ben in the misty Isle of Eigg and a floor of the eighteenth-century complex where David Hume and Adam Smith and James Boswell had lived in their time.

Having read Scomo's books about the stones of Scotland — *Edinburgh* first, and then several other delightful volumes, for Scott-Moncrieff kept writing them lifelong — while keeping a bookshop in Michigan, Kirk had written to the author months before taking passage to Britain. It was Scomo, warmhearted Scomo with the wisdom of the heart and the blemish of the cleft palate, who received the young American at James's Court; introduced him to no end of writers and gentlefolk, in clubs and country houses; set him an example of cheerfulness in adversity; became his friend forever. "Yours aye," George would sign his many letters to Kirk. Just so: ever yours. Kirk expects him to be his sponsor in Paradise.

Scomo dwelt in James's Court because he loved the ancient dwellings and closes of Edinburgh, Auld Reekie; and because he never had any money. The massive building had been condemned late in the eighteenth century as unfit for habitation because subsidence of the Mound on which it stood had caused the floors to slope dramatically: when one dined at George's little table, one grew adept at catching the soup bowl before it slid into one's lap. Yet a good many people beside George lived and worked there, among them an engraver and an elderly woman artist, defying condemnation; higher up still in the pile gypsies lodged, trundling their perambulators downstairs past Scomo's door. The rent was very low, and the view of the New Town from George's windows (of which the tall frames were rotten) was very fine.

Scott-Moncrieff was the worst-dressed gentleman in all Scotland, indifferent to circumstance, endowed with the consolations of philosophy. The son of an eccentric parson, he was the nephew of C. K. Scott-Moncrieff, Proust's translator. When first Kirk knew Scomo, he was a widower, with two sons and a daughter in boarding schools: his wife, Ann, who wrote inimitable children's books, had drowned in 1948. What a marvellous father Scomo was, comical and tender! Kirk once literally fell off a chair, convulsed with laughter at George's stories. The children, too, would grow up to be Kirk's friends.

David Hume, at James's Court, had prided himself upon subsisting at a cost of sixpence a day; Scomo lived there two centuries later almost as frugally, boiling his tea amidst his books and papers, and writing better than anybody did in Murger's Latin Quarter. Summers, this True Gentleman (to borrow a title from old Thomas Fuller) and his children inhabited his rented cottage in the Isle of Eigg, among crofters, seabirds, and cliffs; Kirk was to join him there and write about Eigg.

Later he occupied handsome Number One Scotland Street (in the New Town), a flat belonging to his brother-in-law, Captain Neil Usher; Sir Compton Mackenzie was a neighbor there. Several times Kirk was a guest in Scotland Street while Mary O'Hara was visiting the Scott-Moncrieffs: the famous Mary O'Hara of the harp, the beautiful voice, the beautiful face, and the ardent Catholic faith. In her autobiography, *The Scent of the Roses,* she writes much of Scomo. One passage must suffice:

> I have always maintained that he was a man of whom not only I, but countless others could say: 'He was my closest friend.' Not physically handsome, but of a noble and endearing countenance, he had immense charm and one of the things that distinguished him from others was his unabated gaiety. . . . Scomo was good and thus 'diffusive of himself' — his playfulness marked him out indeed as one enjoying the freedom of the children of God which, of course, is a participation in the very freedom of the Almighty Himself.

Besides his books about Scotland, Scott-Moncrieff wrote plays, novels, essays, and poems. His mission it was to enrich the present through knowledge and preservation of the past. As he puts this in *Scotland's Dowry,*

> The world about us is not merely ours. We possess it only because our predecessors appreciated and cherished it. We look at it through eyes that are not simply our own but to some considerable degree have learnt their vision from the eyes of others. The eyes of painters and poets, of craftsmen and farmers, and, more personally, of relations and friends who in our childhood, and since, have illuminated our ambience for us. The world seen, as it were, flat, with no associations, none of the subtle hints of other things, no correspondence with ideas and experiences that link us to the first great history of mankind, would be dull and meaningless, hardly sensuous at all.

George Scott-Moncrieff, like Walter Scott before him (though, strange to say, Scomo had read Sir Walter little), contended against the vandalism of purposeless "Progress." Upon the Mound, hard by James's Court, Walter Scott had exclaimed to Jeffrey, the Whig reformer, "No, no — 'tis no laughing matter; little by little, whatever your wishes may be, you will destroy and undermine, until nothing of what makes Scotland Scotland shall endure." By Scomo's time, Scotland had endured a century and a half of neglect and demolition. Scott-Moncrieff and Kirk together often saw the bulldozer, that efficient by-product of war, busy knocking down a great architectural patrimony.

Kirk learnt from this friend much about old towns and old ways: Scomo was the most patriotic of Scots, authoritative on how to prepare and eat porridge, on rare occasions resplendent in his formal dress of kilt, velvet jacket, and sword. But he held something higher even than his Scottish nationalism: and that was his Catholic faith.

Few know his little book of devotional meditations, *This Day,* in which happiness and resignation walk side by side. Fewer still know his essay "Growing Old," though many might be consoled by it. George's spiritual writings brought to Kirk a fuller awareness of the soul. Were Kirk to win a million dollars in a lottery, he would publish in splendid editions Scomo's books of quiet wisdom, beautifully expressed.

George had a power of depicting character convincingly that was shared by few authors of fiction in his time. His *Burke Street* is a masterpiece of pathos; what moved him to write it was the demolition of most of George Square in Edinburgh. He describes the virtues and failings of the inhabitants of eight houses on doomed Burke Street, as summoned up by the memories of the narrator. His portrait of brittle Peggy Neale-Swinton, of Number One Burke Street, obsessed by the dogmas of a mechanistic psychology, is especially and alarmingly vivid. Scomo, who wrote so perceptively of the soul, was no respecter of the twentieth-century alleged science of the soul: "Psychology, the deification of the ulterior motive, had dissolved our wills and cursed our relationships, making us unable to live with ourselves or with each other." From that he had been redeemed by having his eyes opened to the theological virtues.

The friendship of Scott-Moncrieff and Kirk would endure famously. In late middle age, Scomo would marry an American girl, Eileen, the age of Kirk's wife, Annette; and the two couples would seem to compete in producing offspring. The Scott-Moncrieffs would acquire the old miller's house at Traquair, in Peeblesshire, an idyllic place: a happy conclusion to Scomo's lifetime of brave struggle against adversity. George meant to write a book about John Muir, the great naturalist, and Kirk arranged for him a contract with an American publisher. Into that book Scott-Moncrieff would have poured the best of himself.

But it was not to be. Scomo's heart had been giving him grave trouble, and the end was sufficiently pathetic and ironical. Intending to take a bus back to Traquair, he ran toward the bus station within the hideous new commercial complex of St. James Centre in Edinburgh. That bus station and the architectural barbarity about it were what Scott-Moncrieff detested most in Scotland's capital — otherwise so loved by him. In the station his heart failed him altogether: dying or dead, he fell to the pavement. There he was left lying for a time, passersby taking him to be dead drunk. At length there came along Annie, irascible Annie, a feeble-minded woman lodged at Martin House, a compassionate sanctuary for abused women. Annie had been taught to care for those in trouble; she knelt by the fallen man. Defying people who told her to leave the tramp alone, she said, "Drunk or not, he needs help." Then George was taken to a hospital; but the soul had departed. Kirk never missed any friend more.

Beginning in 1948, Kirk saw Scotland through Scomo's eyes; and through the undismayed eyes of that generous friend, he came to see much else besides.

Drink Your Dram, Lad

Anyone who would write lively history — even the history of ideas — ought to see the things and see the men, or at least see what vestiges of them are yet to be discerned. So from time to time Kirk made his way afoot, often solitary, to most of the counties of Great Britain and to many of Ireland, and through several Continental lands — most pleasurably in Flanders, Alsace, Provence, Tuscany, Umbria, and Switzerland; presently in the Rhineland, Austria, Sicily, and Spain. Walking stick across his knees, he took his coffee at Florian's in Venice, or at the Cafe Greco in Rome; but chiefly he was attracted to silent ancient towns and country lanes. How many Gothic or Romanesque churches did he seek out, how many heaps of ruins did he grope through? One might make a whole book about curious corners visited, chance companions encountered.

He came to know Lowlands and Highlands and Islands of Scotland unusually well. There occurred an especially hearty tramp along the Borders and through Galloway in company with another American research-student, Steve Kohlbry, now proprietor of a steel-fabricating plant in St. Louis; they were nearly precipitated from the wallhead of Threave Castle into the Blackwater of Dee. Still better were two expeditions to the Isle of Eigg, in the Hebrides: the first in company with Pongo McClellan, extending over a month; the second, of a week, in company with Miss Dorothy Leston, a girl from Idaho's mountains, whose friend Kirk had become in his Dugway years.

In Eigg, with its great cliffs, the old crofter life survived, and Kirk exchanged ghostly yarns with Hugh MacKinnon, the last man who knew the ancient legends of the island. Kirk's essay "Eigg, in the Hebrides" was published not long later in *The Yale Review* and presently included in his book *Beyond the Dreams of Avarice*. As Kirk (who was lodged in the haunted manse of the island's missionary from the Kirk of Scotland) wrote at the time of the island life, "The turf smokes, a bit of it flares up and is reduced to ash, the night mists convert all Eigg outdoors into a black cellar; and those fragmentary chronicles drift sleepily into the low-ceilinged room. 'I saw pale kings and princes too, death-pale were they all . . .' By the twenty-first century, like enough, Hugh MacKinnon's traditional tales will have been obliterated so thoroughly as have been the legends of the Picts."

During the decade that followed the Second World War, Britain remained the walker's paradise. No day was too hot for exertion; the rainfall prevented dust on road and paths; and with a little planning, one always could arrive by nightfall at some old inn. (As Samuel Johnson instructs us, there is no prospect so noble that it is not improved by a good inn in the foreground; and more than once Kirk followed some stretch of Johnson's and Boswell's pedestrian progress through Scotland.) The apotheosis of the automobile had not yet come to pass in Britain: students, working people, and many others still were mounted upon bicycles, which meant that sturdy walkers were untroubled by speeding cars and gasoline fumes. It would be otherwise a few years later: C. S. Lewis and his friends would have to abandon their countryside expeditions afoot, harassed off the roads by cars.

The following illustration of the charms and vicissitudes of travel afoot, that old human necessity and diversion now so much reduced by the triumph of technology, occurred early in the spring of 1949, in the central highlands of Scotland.

In company with David Ruddy, a fellow American, Kirk had walked thirty miles through the hills that day, all the way — with side excursions — from Dinnet in Deeside to a dot on the Ordnance Survey map denominated Gartly Station, away north in Strathbogie. C. E. M. Joad gives as an example of an absolute truth, to which any rational man will assent, this statement: "Thirty miles in one day is a long walk." Aye, it is; especially through driving snow, as much of Kirk's and Ruddy's walk had been, for it was early March, and Strathbogie long has been infamous for its late snow.

As the sun sank, the two Americans found themselves taking their bearings among old tombstones, by an isolated country kirk on a knoll. They were making for Gartly Station, at which point their map indicated an inn and a passenger stop. If they could not get lodging at the purported inn, at least they might be able to catch a train to Elgin and spend the night in that town. Having ascertained their way, well after dark they stumbled into the hamlet of Gartly Station, a dull little row of cottages by the railway line. They saw no inn; at every window in the place the war-time blanket draperies were drawn, leaving the street to total darkness. Perplexed, cold, hungry, and tired, they huddled in a doorway. But presently, happening to glance up, they perceived nailed to the door-frame just above their heads a dingy notice: "Gartly Station Hotel. Seven Day License." Opening the little green double doors, they entered.

This was an oldfangled Scottish public house. The representative Scots pub, old style, of the Highlands did not much resemble its English counterpart. A Scots bar is a place where two farmers come to seal a bargain — or so it was in the Forties — with no women admitted; and the amenities were sufficiently austere to satisfy the most dogmatic iconoclast. The Americans plodded directly into the bar of the Gartly Station Hotel, which was a very narrow little room with backless wooden benches on either side and a counter at the far end. A single naked lightbulb burned overhead, revealing four men, mugs in hand, seated on the benches; and behind the bar itself, an ancient female being who resembled Azucena in the opera, tip of nose and tip of chin almost meeting.

Diffidently approaching this proprietress, while the four men stared silent from their hard benches, Kirk said, in what he hoped was a conciliatory tone, "We'd like a room for the night."

"Room?" cried Azucena, in a moan compounded of incredulity and scorn. "Room? Na, na." She turned away. That was that.

Of course the pedestrians should have known, from that fatal term "Seven Day License," that Gartly Station Hotel was no hotel at all. "Seven Day License" meant in Scotland that an inn had obtained permission to sell drink on Sundays — but only to *bona fide* travellers making their godless way from place to place on the Sabbath, who might require strong drink to sustain them in their progress. In return for this indulgence, the inn with a seven-day license was expected to have rooms ready for the accommodation of those "bona fides" (in Scots, "bonnie fydies"). But it being whisky rather than beds that brought in money, the bona fide who sought lodging often found it difficult to extract accommodation from such a proprietress as now stared down the feckless Americans. "Na, na," said Azucena. Footsore and heavy laden, they turned back toward the door. There *might* be a train to Huntly.

Yet before Kirk could touch the doorknob, one of the silent drinkers — a tall, lean man with a hat on his head, reasonably well

[97]

dressed, somewhat arrogant of manner — stayed the travellers with a gesture. "Stay, lads," he said, "and hae a dram."

These four Scots did not appear to be travellers. They were natives of Huntly, it turned out. The tall man who had spoken was Donald. Then there was a short and tubby person called Angus, who sang ceaselessly. His companions were proud of him: "Aye, Angus would hae had a braw voice," said they, "had he had the trainin'." Possibly so. There was also an elderly farm laborer in a thick cap and corduroys. And the fourth stalwart was the most impressive of all: Dugald, a giant by nature and a tailor by trade. Dugald sat immense and brooding by the door, seeming seven feet tall, yet muscular out of proportion.

"Stay, lads, and hae a dram," said the lordly Donald, a second time.

"No, thank you, sir," Kirk replied, "but we've strolled some thirty miles today, and we need to find beds in Huntly while there's time." Kirk laid his fingers on the doorlatch.

But Dugald the tailor had stretched across the door his arm, seemingly greater in girth than Kirk's thigh. Dugald's frown was more forbidding than that of Ozymandias. Dugald spoke, rumblingly: "Hae a dram, lads."

"Of course," Ruddy and Kirk replied. "Thank you very much." They scuttled back to the bar, where Azucena poured out drams of whisky, for which Donald paid. "This is Strathbogie, in the north of Scotland," said Donald to the two Americans. "There's no hospitality like Scots hospitality. And the further north in Scotland ye go, the warmer the hospitality gets!"

Aye, the Americans drank those drams; and yet more drams; and yet others. Under the brooding eye of Azucena, they sat upon those hard benches and fell into conversation with their hosts; and later grew the hour.

"Dinna fash, sir," the Farm Laborer whispered to Kirk, at a moment when Donald's attention had been diverted. "Yon's Donald MacDonald. He'll find beds for ye. 'Tis a joke, ye ken. Ha ha, ha ha! 'Tis a joke. For Donald MacDonald's no common mon, mind. Donald's master o' the Huntly Arms, Family and Commercial, in Huntly toon. An' in the fu'ness o' time, Donald'll tak ye to the Huntly Arms Hotel and gie ye lodgin'. 'Tis a joke, ye ken. Ye needna fash: Donald'll no fail ye. Ha ha, ha ha!"

Donald MacDonald had overheard a portion of this colloquy. "Aye, lads," he put in, "ye'll be wanting to sup. And ye shall sup! Up Angus, up Dugald! We're awa' to Huntly!"

"Ane dram mair," said the laconic Dugald.

"Aye, anither dram!" cried Donald, with the wave of an emperor. So the Scottish Azucena gave each his stirrup cup, and then all six drinkers strode out into the bitter Highland night, crowded into Angus's tiny automobile, and careered off through the blizzard along a hill road to Huntly, five miles distant.

Dugald, who drove, had been drinking ale and whisky without stint but was an admirable driver. The road was sheathed in ice, and the snow seemed to be poured out of vast bins. Dugald scooted round bends as if Cutty Sark and her eldritch sisters had been hard on the taillight. Angus the Singer was sitting on Kirk's lap, chanting his favorite song:

> I'm no awa' to bide awa';
> I'm no awa' to leave ye;
> I'm no awa' to bide awa',
> For I'll gang back an' see ye!

At the end of each chorus, Angus the Singer punctuated his refrain with three great cries of "Boom, boom, boom!" And he emphasized the booms by striking his clenched fist upon the head of Dugald, sitting directly in front of him. A lesser man might have been dazed by the first blow; but Dugald, merely shaking his head as if a fly had teased him, drove on intrepidly through the storm, maximum speed. Those five miles to Huntly elapsed as distance slips away in nightmares; the little car roared down Huntly's High Street; Dugald applied the shrieking brakes at the Queen, the chief public house of that sturdy stone-built town.

It was after hours. In those years, drink might not be sold after half past nine — or, at the latest in some Scots towns, ten of the evening. But Donald was nothing daunted. Bidding all follow, he burst into the back door of the Queen, and the six revelers found themselves in a bare little back room ornamented by potted plants. A few tardy customers were lingering in the Victorian splendors of the public bar, glimpsed by Kirk through a door left ajar. There hurried to them a matron called Jeanie, all smiles and remonstrances: "Na, na, gentlemen, but it's lang past time!"

"No matter, Jeanie, lass," said Donald MacDonald; "we've Overseas Guests wi' us, as ye see. Scotland's hospitality is the warmest hospitality in the world, an' the further north in Scotland ye go, the warmer the hospitality gets. Fetch us drams, Jeanie."

Jeanie fetched us drams, and we drank; she fetched us still more drams, and them too we drank. And now the back door opened again, to admit a man in tweeds somewhat shabby, with a long jaw and nose and mustache. "Major Troop!" Donald exclaimed. "Ye'll tak a dram, Major Troop." Major Troop did, and the Overseas Guests were presented to him. While Angus engaged this gentleman in talk, the Farm Laborer (or perhaps Shepherd) drew the Overseas Guests to a corner of the room. "D'ye ken, sirs, wha's yon?" he asked. He doffed his cap in veneration. "Yon's Major Troop, the laird. Aye, Major Troop's a muckle mon in Strathbogie. I worked for his father before him."

David Ruddy had been mixing the whisky with water for all of the party, and for some time now had been giving himself pure water; but at this moment, perceiving Ruddy's duplicity, Dugald seized bottle and glasses. "Noo *I'll* mix the drinks, lad," said Dugald grimly. "Drink your drams, lads." We drank our drams. "Lad," said Angus to Kirk, "sing us a song."

All the Strathbogie faces were turned toward Kirk. "Sing us a song, lad," Angus repeated, and would not be denied. Kirk hurriedly burst into Stephen Collins Foster:

Way down upon the Suwanee River,
Far, far away . . .

There was civil applause for this wretched effort. "Noo, lad," said Donald to Angus the Singer, "do ye sing us a song, and we'll all dance." Angus began: "I'm no awa' to bide awa'." Dugald, seizing upon Kirk as a bear grips a terrier, whirled the Overseas Guest round and round in a Highland fling. "But I'll gang back an' see ye," sang Donald MacDonald, taking the Major for his partner. "This is Huntly toon; Huntly's awa' in the north o' Scotland; Scots hospitality's the warmest in the world; and the further north ye gang in Scotland, the warmer the hospitality gets!"

Fling succeeded fling, song ran into song, dram into dram, until at length Kirk drew Mr. MacDonald aside, pleading that he and Ruddy had not eaten since early morning, and but little then. "Ye needna fear, lads," said Donald; "for we'll no desert ye. Come, Angus, we're awa' to the Huntly Arms. We're no awa' to bide awa', Jeanie. Up, Major Troop; we're all awa' to the Huntly Arms, Family and Commercial. Gi'e us a last dram, a' roun', Jeanie!"

"And it's high time, gentlemen," replied Jeanie, "for the constable's thunderin' at the street door." Out they all went into the wynd, and got once more into Angus's car, and some into the Major's car, and sped through nocturnal Huntly to the Huntly Arms, an old-fashioned inn with a close, or courtyard.

The pend, or gateway, to that close was blocked by the automobile of some unfortunate wretch who was drinking after hours in the public bar of the Huntly Arms. Donald MacDonald cried aloud unto his God and his manservants, and two or three underlings ran into the bar to drag out the miscreant, thrusting him roughly into his misbegotten car, Donald cursing him the while and forbidding him ever to darken again the door of the Huntly Arms. The offending car removed, MacDonald and his boon companions drove into the close and poured out of their cars — into the kitchen, where Donald MacDonald sent a pink-cheeked serving maid scuttling to provide for the wants of Overseas Guests. "Supper for the twa!" was Donald's cry. "And beds for the twa! And noo, lads, while ye wait for supper and beds, we'll into the bar for a dram or twa."

The public bar of the Huntly Arms, somewhat more commodious than that of the Gartly Station Hotel, still was crowded with patrons, though lawful closing time was long past. There are two diversions in Scots pubs: dominoes and darts. A knot of old men huddled round the domino table in one corner; but most of the patrons, though somewhat befuddled, were intent upon a match of darts. Ruddy and Kirk were seated upon a bench, and provided with drams, and the darts whizzed alarmingly close to their noses on the way to the target.

Now they were joined by newcomers, also habitual roisterers with Donald MacDonald, it appeared: the manager of the Scottish Co-operative shop at Elgin, and the Co-operative's van driver. The Manager, a lugubrious person who would take only sherry, set himself to badger Major Troop. He was naming no names, but he understood that many heirs to decadent old families were cowardly in war. Major Troop, though ignoring these studied insults, offered some strictures upon the Labour party. Meanwhile, the van driver poured out to Kirk the interminable tale of his private woes.

"Wha' time hae ye the noo, sir?" he inquired. Having been told that it was nigh to midnight, the Driver sighed heavily. The Manager had come to his door just after high tea, he said, and had cried, "Come, Jock, we're awa' on official business." And the Driver had told his wife he would be home quite early. But it had not been official business; nay, it had been mere pub crawling, compulsory for the Driver, on Co-operative petrol. So it had gone for him, night after night, the imperious Manager intimidating him: "Come awa, Jock: I'm the master, ye're the mon."

The Driver declared that he would emigrate to Australia if he could, "But they want skilled men there, not men like me. My wife, sir, says she'll flit frae me if this pub crawlin' doesna cease."

A woman's face appeared in the doorway at the back of the bar — or, rather, upon a stair that led down to that doorway. "That lady," said Major Troop, "is Donald's wife, Mrs. MacDonald, a long-suffering woman."

Mrs. MacDonald intimated that supper was ready for the latecomers. Ruddy and Kirk made their way up the back stairs to the residents' parlor, where a table was laid for them; and as they passed her, Mrs. MacDonald murmured grimly, "There'll be no beds for ye here, gentlemen. Ye'd best look elsewhere this night." Possibly so, but Kirk and Ruddy suspected that Mrs. MacDonald did not fancy her husband's companions, old or new.

They ate ham and eggs in the residents' parlor, crowded with commercial travelers who sat writing out their orders, reading the evening papers, or staring speechless at the two Overseas Guests. Having gobbled down their food, those Guests made their way quietly back downstairs, hoping to depart by a side door to seek other lodging. But Donald, espying them, haled his two Americans back into the public bar, where things continued merry as ever that Saturday night — and gave them drams.

Of a sudden there came a pounding at the street door. With startling presence of mind, Major Troop hurried Kirk and Ruddy into the bar parlor, separated by a door from the public bar and reserved for more sedate guests. Closing the door carefully, he set a chair against it, and proceeded to make polite conversation in low tones. Presently he learned that Ruddy and Kirk were from St. Andrews University.

"What a pity," Major Troop said, "that we had not met under other circumstances. Had I known you were university men, I might have shown you Huntly Castle and any number of historical curiosities. Really, you can't stay another day or two? This is a very ancient town, and the fishing is good. A pity." He drank his dram sadly. "A pity, I mean, that you have so little time to spend here."

"Why are we sitting here?" Ruddy inquired. "Who is in the bar just now?"

"The police constable," Major Troop said, with some solemnity.

"Is he investigating this drinking after hours?" Kirk inquired.

"No, no," said Major Troop, "that sort of thing is customary in Huntly. Ostensibly, the constable is here to inquire after a man who died in the bar yesterday."

"By violence?"

"No, of natural causes: of drink, to be precise. But the constable is not really interested in that unfortunate death. His true purpose here is to discover whether I am in this public house just now. For you see, I am to be a character witness at a trial on Monday. Could the constable swear that he had found me drinking after hours in the Huntly Arms, he might be able to bring my character into question; he might imply that nightly I drink in public houses after closing hours. I am a witness for the defendant, you must understand, in an important criminal case. So, if you please, do not open the door, nor approach it, nor speak above a whisper." (His own response had been whispered.) "I shall be much obliged to you, gentlemen."

Major Troop stared intently at the door leading into the bar. This seeming a propitious moment for taking French leave, Kirk and Ruddy crept out of the further door — which, they found, opened upon a chill corridor. There abruptly they again encountered Mrs. MacDonald. "I tell ye again, gentlemen," said that worthy woman, "ye'd best seek lodgin' elsewhere. Ye'll find anither hotel up the brae." And the Guests she thrust, packs and all, out of a species of postern door, into the snow. "Oot ye go!"

In a wind fiercer even than before, driving before it snow wetter and more dense than ever, they blundered under a railway viaduct and upward toward the dark brae. Brae? It was a blasted and empty heath. Retracing their steps, Kirk and Ruddy got back into the town, tried another street, and presently found themselves at the gates of an Edwardian villa of ashlar, standing upon a hillock in its own grounds. A sign nailed to one gatepost proclaimed this to be the Royal British Hotel, Luncheons, Teas, Dinners, Weekly Terms. It was utterly dark. Ascending to the porch, the Overseas Guests deliberated as to whether they might dare the wrath of the slumbering proprietor by knocking.

Just then a little car puffed in at the gate, followed by a van; the vehicles fought their way through the drifts up the sweeping drive; they halted at the porch, and out poured a Comus's rout of Strathbogie men: Donald, the Major, Dugald, Angus, the Shepherd, the Manager, the Driver. "Lads, whatever were ye thinkin' of?" demanded Donald MacDonald. "Why did ye tak a powder?"

The Guests protested humbly that they had feared they were inconveniencing him at the Huntly Arms. "No matter, lads," said the magnanimous MacDonald. "We'll rouse Vera here and hae a dram or twa. Go roun' to the back, Major Troop, and try that door; and I'll pound at this one." They thumped and kicked and halloed. Presently a heavy curtain at a bay window was drawn back, and a youngish and well-got-up woman in a kimono appeared against the light. "You can't come in, gentlemen," Vera said through the window. "It's after hours."

"But dinna ye see, Vera, ye've here twa Overseas Guests, and ye're obliged by law to let them in? D'ye want a gude gangin' law plea, Vera?" So Donald roared back to Vera.

"I'll let them in, Donald," called Vera, relenting, "but not you." She went to unbar the door.

"Vera's a gude girl," the Manager whispered to Kirk; "aye, but Donald's corruptin' her."

Once the door was open, the whole crew jostled in, ignoring Vera's entreaties. "Noo, Vera," said Donald, "fetch us all drams and sandwiches." Despairing, Vera retired to the kitchen obediently; the crowd surged into the great parlor and ranged about a huge rosewood table. "Sing us a song!" they cried as one man to Angus. He obliged: "I'm no awa' to bide awa' . . ."

Bearing a platter of ham sandwiches and drams, Vera reappeared. "If you've any pity in your hearts, gentlemen," she said, "you'll not sing so loud, for I've an old, old couple in the room just above, and they sleep badly."

"Weel, bring them doun to drink a dram, Vera!" Donald shouted. "Bring them doun! I'm the mon to pay for the drams." He had been doing just that all evening. Drams then cost two shillings and six-pence.

Vera began to enter into the fun of the thing, and presently everyone joined hands and went dancing round and round the table, to the music of a rosewood grand piano — played by the Manager, perhaps, though by this time details were growing indistinct. Major Troop embraced the dancing Vera too ardently. "*Dear* Major Troop!" she remonstrated, prudently disengaging herself.

As opportunity offered in the course of this revel, Kirk and Ruddy ate the sandwiches, and Kirk drank the drams. Fortune having conspired against him, Kirk now found himself drinking three drams at every round. For Ruddy had got into the way of thrusting his dram in front of Kirk, treacherously; while the Manager, who under a doctor's orders drank sherry only, also passed on his dram to Kirk. "Lad, ye haena drunk your dram!" the colossal Dugald would growl. And the whole company then would stare reproachfully at that Overseas Guest: "Lad, ye haena drunk your dram!" Perforce, he downed more drams.

As they all whirled once more round the table, like the damned crew in the Auld Kirk o' Alloway, an official knock sounded at the back door. Vera and Donald hastily made for that region, and the rest of the crowd fell silent. The Driver reconnoitred. "Aye, the constable," he reported, *sotto voce*.

"Gentlemen, he must not find me here," whispered Major Troop. "My friend's future depends upon my testimony and my good character at Monday's trial. Goodnight, goodnight." He pressed the university men's hands. "We must meet again, under other circumstances, and enjoy a dram or two together. Yes, under other circumstances . . ." Closing the front door behind him, he was gone into the blast.

Now Vera and Donald returned, with the Constable in tow. By a happy coincidence, the Constable had gone off duty, and so could join the company in a dram. "But where has Major Troop got to?" asked he, on entering. The laird's precautions nevertheless had availed him this — that the Constable could not swear he actually had seen Major Troop drinking in a public house after closing hours.

All took a dram with the Constable, then presently fell again to singing — the Constable's deep voice joining in — and Angus was leading the dance round the table. It was long past the witching hour. Donald and the Manager fell into a disputation concerning the merits of the welfare state. Mr. MacDonald was all for giving up Cabinet and Parliament in disgust and turning over the administration of Britain to the Americans, who should rule the British Isles as they did Alaska and Hawaii, making them the subordinate Territory of Britain. He suggested that Russell Kirk become governor or viceroy of this new domination. The Manager, as one might expect of an Aneurin Bevan man, dissented strongly from this proposal and this nomination.

Taking Vera aside at last, Kirk and Ruddy entreated her mercy: that day they had walked thirty miles, much of that distance against the snowfall — or rather, the previous day. Turning businesslike, Vera led them down a corridor to a large and lofty bedchamber, bidding them good night. In the parlor the wassail continued, its noises drifting joyously to the Overseas Guests. That bedroom was so cold a place as ever Kirk had known; without the drams, he might have felt uncomfortable. The Overseas Guests, having flung themselves into bed, soon drifted off to unconsciousness. Kirk at the last heard Donald's refrain from the parlor: "and the further north ye gang in Scotland, the warmer the hospitality gets." Someone, perhaps the Constable, continued to play the piano.

In the morning the Guests found that the room was cold because all the windows had stood open, and snow sloped at an angle of forty-five degrees from sills to floor. Having huddled on their clothes, they went down to breakfast. The neat maid who served them said that Vera had gone shopping. With expedition Ruddy and Kirk got their packs upon their backs and walked briskly but quietly down the High Street of Huntly. In a few minutes they came to the Huntly Arms, Family and Commercial. Although no one seemed to be stirring there, they tiptoed past. Safely got by, they lengthened their strides, so that within a quarter of an hour they were well upon a hill road. But they did not tramp north: the hospitality of Huntly had been quite warm enough.

Some years later, Kirk's eye fell upon an advertisement in *Country Life*. Near Huntly, a large property was being sold to pay death duties: the estate of the late Major Troop, with the big house, several farms, woodlands, fishing rights, pedigreed cattle, etc. Kirk never again beheld the Huntly roisterers, so cordial to him, nor indeed the old town of Huntly, with its memories of George MacDonald and its warlike earls, the ruin of a castle brooding over it. Aye, what shadows we are, and what shadows we pursue!

Yet perhaps that Huntly revel, innocent enough, was one of the Timeless Moments known to T. S. Eliot — a moment never to be swallowed up by old Cronos, Time the Devourer. On that chance, Kirk recorded at some length the drinking bout, and *Queen's Quarterly*, in Canada, published his account. In those free and easy years, from 1948 to 1953, Russell Kirk would find himself caught up in more Timeless Moments than he deserved.

CHAPTER FIVE

Great Houses

An Unclassed American

Between 1949 and 1952, Kirk's existence seemed very like that of a character in one of George Gissing's novels — although not because of any deliberate emulation. Gissing remarked once that his characteristic contribution to fiction was the type of a young man "well-educated, fairly bred, *but without money.*" At an Atlanta bookshop, in 1944, Sergeant Kirk had picked up a copy of Gissing's novel of the London slums, *The Unclassed,* published in 1884. In his early thirties, Kirk himself was unclassed, it being impossible to fit this square peg into any round social hole.

His being an American, from the heart of Michigan, in itself sufficed to exempt him from stereotypes in English and Scottish society. More than that, he was not a professor, nor a man of business, nor a holder of office, nor a communicant of any church, nor an Oxbridge graduate, nor a journalist, nor an ideologue; nobody's servant, not an idler, not a worker.*

He was a quiet young man but able, if encouraged, to talk on a diversity of subjects and to spin yarns: that county families like. He was helpful at gardening and tree pruning, the avocations of country house families and indeed of the Queen. Thus the lords and lairds of Fife, and their consorts, came to like him.

As for the middle classes — nearly everyone in Britain, during

---

*An acquaintance at Rugby remarked to Kirk, during these years, that when the British workingman began to call himself a worker, he ceased to work.

those post-war years, putting forward a claim to be bourgeois — Kirk's grandfather, Frank Pierce, had been an archetype of such; and Kirk got on well with professional people and merchants.

And the working classes? Why, Kirk's boyhood had been spent in the railroad yards, and he knew well the rougher quarters of North Lansing and of Detroit. He could shift about readily enough from class to class, he understanding English and Scottish classes before ever he crossed the Atlantic, in consequence of much reading of Trollope, Hardy, and other novelists.

Most Americans do not well apprehend the nature and function of social classes. In America, class demarcations are less distinct than in Britain — and in turn, such British distinctions are, or at least used to be, less marked than in the Continent. Many Americans labor under the illusion that they exist in a classless society — and are startled if informed that the classless society was the goal of Karl Marx.

Americans often find it difficult to conceive that an upper class of birth and manners still exists; they fancy that aristocracy vanished with the waning of the Middle Ages — although they still approve somebody possessed of "good manners." When Americans think of *upper class,* they identify that status with the possession of much wealth; and indeed there has been, and remains, considerable connection between manners and wealth, although a more subtle relationship than is commonly recognized. Nevertheless, the rich man and the gentleman are not identical — especially not in Europe.

Once, Kirk happening to mention some old country houses of Fife to Jim Creighton, another American student at St. Andrews, Jim — who had been a naval officer in the Second World War — was astonished. "Why, do you mean there still are old families living in those places?" Jim, while at St. Andrews, was lodged only a few miles from some of the country houses described by Kirk.

Or on another occasion, when Kirk was conversing with members of the Committee on Social Thought at the University of Chicago, and had said something about the views and influence of the British landed classes, his companions seemed puzzled. "We don't know any such people," one professor told him.

Neither, for that matter, did Jim Creighton and the Chicago professors know any crofters, nor any railroad men who labored in the yards outside Detroit. It is quite possible to live wholly within one's own class. But that is not a very good way to understand the human condition nowadays. Kirk, being unclassed rather than immersed in one class, could get on very well with the people who lived in great old houses, the people who lived in Hebridean but-and-bens, and the people who lived on the skirts of the railroad yards. It has been written that a gentleman is a person who never calls himself one. One may add that to ascend in society, one must not be a climber. Even nowadays, wealth is no card of admission; indeed, wealth without manners will not ingratiate.

Russell Kirk came to know the lords and lairds of Fife and their ladies — not that he had planned or expected to call on them. In the beginning, he visited the big houses through notes of introduction from George Scott-Moncrieff, of the shabby clothes, the empty wallet, the cleft palate — aye, "Scomo" of the innocent charm, and perfect manners. In mind and morals and manners, Scomo was the archetype of the gentleman. Scomo sent a note about Kirk to Major Ralph Christie, laird of Durie, member of the Fife County Council; and another note to an eminent Scots sculptor, Hew Lorimer, R.S.A., of Kellie Castle, in Fife; and thus commenced Kirk's acquaintance with many county families.

During the days when Kirk lived there, Fifeshire still could be called, not altogether in jest, the Kingdom of Fife, almost an autonomous realm within Scotland. The road bridges across the Forth to Edinburgh and across the Tay to Dundee did not then exist; one travelled by train or ferry, not very speedily. This meant that one did one's shopping in St. Andrews or the county town of Cupar, and the merchants thereof prospered accordingly. This meant also that Fifers had to entertain themselves — which they did with pipe bands and country dancing, for instance. Also this meant that old customs of many sorts prevailed still and that the county families knew one another, rather than spending their time in Edinburgh or London. Even agriculture, highly successful then in Fife, was affected by Fife's peculiar situation: horses, rather than tractors, then did most of the ploughing, and a multitude of thatched stooks like African huts stood in the fields at harvest-time.

All along the Forth shore of the East Neuk of Fife ran what James VI had called the golden fringe to the beggar's mantle of the Kingdom of Fife: the venerable fishing ports of Crail, the Anstruthers, Pittenweem, St. Monans, Elie, Earlsferry, Largo — and other such havens along the southern shore of West Fife, but these latter fallen on evil days, in part. Kirk strolled the unspoilt coast of the East Neuk innumerable times, coming to know every wynd and close of those tarry fisher towns. In one of them, Pittenweem, once notorious for its retired pirates and active witches, later he would acquire and restore an ancient house with crowstepped gables, facing the market square.

Like the fisher towns, the castles and country houses of Fife had survived the vicissitudes of Britain between 1914 and 1948. Still, many a handsome country house stood empty; Kirk might have bought one for five thousand pounds — had he possessed any such sum. Those families and those houses he came to know so early as the summer of 1948, sometimes making his way to them afoot across the East Neuk. With three of those families he formed intimate friendships, and in those great houses, in following years, he would be a guest for weeks or months at a time; and he would entertain the children of those houses, or some of them, at Mecosta.

The families were the Lorimers of Kellie, the Christies of Durie, and the Lindsays of Balcarres. They were distinguished people in marvellous houses.

Kellie Castle

Kirk — about whom Scott-Moncrieff had sent a note to Kellie — soon came to know the Lorimers of Kellie Castle. With two or three St. Andrews students in tow, Kirk intruded upon Hew and Mary Lorimer and their three children when they were at tea in Kellie's walled garden. Hew was the best of the Scots sculptors of recent decades; several of his works are at Kirk's house of Piety Hill now, and his colossal allegorical figures adorn the façade of the National Library of Scotland, in Edinburgh. Mary Lorimer, who painted portraits of children, was the most convivial and cheerful of women. Theirs was a most Catholic house; it would have overjoyed G. K. Chesterton, had he ever been there.

And what a house! The lower portion of the oldest of its three towers had been built in the fourteenth century; the bulk of Kellie Castle was sixteenth-century work. Inside were splendid molded-plaster ceilings and other fine features. Over six centuries, only three families successively had dwelt here. Professor Lorimer, Hew's grandfather, had most carefully restored the castle in 1876, after it had been quasi-derelict for half a century. With its tall, tall windows looking down from Kellie Law upon the Firth of Forth and the Bass Rock, Kellie was not a fencible house, though there survived in its architecture some touches of a fiercer age; rather, it was one of the first great houses of a time of peace — in Fife and the Lothians, at least. Indeed Kellie was a dream of peace and beauty, remote even from the antique port of Pittenweem, where the old Earls of Kellie had maintained another lodging, Kellie Lodge, as winter residence. Kellie Castle was sufficiently chill in winter, but the Lorimers never noticed that: it was a place of splendor, not of comfort, with no electricity or other modern convenience during Kirk's years at St. Andrews; there had been even no fixed bathtub in the day of Sir Robert Lorimer, the great architect, Hew's father. The great families of yesterday, disdaining bourgeois comfort, built for grandeur. Until Hew Lorimer's time, Kellie was innocent even of stuffed easy chairs and sofas.

Kellie's traditionary ghost was consonant with the Castle's eerie beauty: a pair of red slippers, given to descending the turnpike stair within the thickness of the wall of the oldest tower. John Lorimer, the Edwardian painter, Hew's uncle, had used the uppermost floor of that tower as his studio. Afraid of encountering the empty red slippers as he descended to the Great Hall at nightfall, he habitually had shouted to the old gardener outside to ascend and escort his master to safety.

Kirk never happened upon the red slippers, even though for a whole month he was the solitary castellan of Kellie, while the Lorimers were in France. He did then enjoy one uncanny night when rooks and jackdaws whirred and cawed about Kellie's towers in the wee hours, perhaps giving an alarm: very possibly some two-footed predators, aspiring to Kellie's plenishings, were without that night — a band of gypsies having that day been encamped at a Devil's Acre a few miles distant. If indeed those gypsies or tinkers had waked the birds and the King Charles spaniel that barked furiously in the close, the marauders were frustrated by Kirk's kerosene lamp, flitting from window to window. At length, rifle in hand, Kirk sat triumphant in silence upon a window ledge in the entrance tower, with a full moon illuminating the Bass Rock. Such was the last siege of Kellie, a fortalice troubled enough during the two centuries when the wild Oliphants had held it.

Kirk's friendship with the Lorimers has endured warmly for three generations. Kellie is National Trust property now; kindly Hew died in a Fife nursing home; but the two Lorimer sons and the daughter remain intimate with the Kirks, in whose library building at Mecosta are fixed the originals of three of Lorimer's allegorical figures for the National Library of Scotland — that is, the models in Hopetounwood limestone from which the colossal reliefs in Edinburgh were carved in situ, Kirk on the scaffolding with the sculptor one fair day. Kirk's three stone reliefs are Theology, with the sword of faith; on Theology's right, Law, bewigged and grasping a book; on Theology's left, History, with a long scroll and a quill pen. These carvings, with their Celtic dignity, may outlast the Common Reader.

People are meant to live forever, Kirk came to reflect with the passing of the years. Why do they perish? Plato and Saint Paul tell us that they do not perish — and Saint Augustine of Hippo, too; they merely depart from us. Mary Lorimer is in her grave now, but is fixed in Kirk's memory by her blithe spirit, her humor, and her coffee — the best ever brewed for guests; and Hew Lorimer, solitary, later entered eternity. What timeless moments Kirk spent with them!

Durie House

Another grand house with which Kirk became well acquainted was Durie, near Leven, a big old estate of many farms, in effect a kind of agricultural frontier post marching with the mining and manufacturing of West Fife. The Lorimers were friends of the Christies of Durie, who also were connections of George Scott-Moncrieff. On one wet autumnal day, accompanied by Miss Anne Thompson of Dundee (later a pretty doctor of medicine), Kirk made his way up from the ugly bustling town of Leven, on the Forth, through Scoonie Den, to Durie House: a perfect eighteenth-century mansion, Adam style, with suggestions of an earlier Scots tower house in the ashlar of its walls, which turned a delicious purple in hue when wet. A noble specimen of a Scots doocot, or dove-cote, or pigeon house, stood upon a knoll nearby, overlooking the massive granary and other structures of the home farm. Durie was one of the best-built houses Kirk ever had the good fortune to inspect — seemingly strong almost as Brunelleschi's Strozzi-Guicciardini palace in the Via

Romana of Florence, which withstood German mines near the end of the Second World War.

In those years, Durie's hereditary proprietor was Major Ralph Christie, the surviving archetype of the eccentric Scots laird of the old school — generous, hospitable, humorous, an omnivorous reader, a seeker after occult knowledge. Once upon a time, in the First World War, he had been a major of infantry, once a Theosophist, latterly a county councillor, and always an accomplished raconteur. Margaret, Mrs. Christie, a Swedish lady of good family, stately, capable, charitable, was loved by everyone. Durie sometimes was bursting at the pointing with young Swedes and other Continental connections, entertained and teased by the three rambunctious jolly Christie children. Ralph Christie, a generation older than his wife, had departed from the Theosophists because he preferred beef and beer to their vegetal fare; but he remained familiar with all manner of things occult. What ghost-story-telling sessions he and Kirk were to have, a bottle of gin between them, in Ralph's business room!

Handsome Durie was the haunted house *par excellence* — though also the most livable of all great houses, activity occurring in all of its many rooms, and its every meal a feast prepared by Margaret, often with great bowls of sour cream and raspberries for dessert. In the dining room, perpetually looking down upon such merriment, hung the posthumous portrait of Chillianwallah Christie, Old Captain Christie, Ralph Christie's grandfather, reputed Durie's principal spectre. He was said to have made himself known to visitors to the house, this old laird with one arm (the other having been lost at the battle of Chillianwallah, in India), for decades after his death; even Mrs. Annie Besant, that formidable reformer and occultist, had encountered him. The complex tale is too long to relate in this book. Although lodged for months at a time in the great bedchamber, with its molded-plaster ceiling, that had been Chillianwallah's, Kirk never even heard the revenant laird, let alone saw him.

Also Durie was endowed, perhaps for eternity, with Mr. Boofie with Cobwebs in His Eyes, an ancestor who had written nonsense in great ledgers in a garret room for most of his early existence and had declined to depart from that little chamber even after having been interred in the ruined kirk of Scoonie. Boofie, the dread of the Christie rising generation, two decades later would be quite as alarming, though unseen, to the imagination of Kirk's daughters when they enjoyed a summer at Durie.

The Christies had held Durie since 1776; the founder of their fortunes had been a Tory merchant expelled from Maryland, who had been appointed commissary general to the British forces in North America. Coal from the mines of the Durie estate had been exported to Holland during the eighteenth and nineteenth centuries; happily the seams had been exhausted before Ralph's time, for otherwise the British Coal Board would have created an open-cast-pit devastation round Durie House, effacing Durie's fertile farms. Even so, the industrial town of Leven, once mostly the property of the Christie family, steadily encroached upon the Durie lands with hideous rows of public housing, so that during Kirk's St. Andrews years and later those dreary lodgings abutted right upon the policies of Durie House. But the young laird, Peter, Ralph Christie's elder son, has taken the farms into his own hands, and holds the frontier against "development."

The young Christies grew up to be Kirk's close friends as their parents had been before them; and those children's children, too. Before long, quite conceivably, Ralph Christie's great-grandchildren may take a dreadful joy in games of creep-mouse played with them by the legendary Dr. Kirk, a figure of antique grandeur. Much more about Durie and its laird may be found in Kirk's fifth book, *Beyond the Dreams of Avarice*.

Balcarres House

Some miles to the west of Kellie and more miles to the east of Durie stands the enchanted palace of Balcarres, with its park, its craig, its Gothick folly, its den, its village of Colinsburgh. Since the Second World War it has been the residence of the Earls of Crawford and Balcarres, whose line runs back through nine centuries of Scottish history.

This, the third great house of Kirk's Fife years, is larger far than either Kellie or Durie but not so handsome in its exterior, which is chiefly nineteenth-century work. Within, however, are such treasures in paintings and books as staggered the imagination of the young American writer befriended by David and Mary Lindsay, Earl and Countess of Crawford. There is a hall of the late sixteenth century panelled with fantastic carvings from the Low Countries, and the nineteenth-century interiors are majestic. "It all seems like a museum!" exclaimed one visitor brought to Balcarres by Kirk. "We had hoped you wouldn't think so," replied the Earl of Crawford, with a smile.

At Balcaskie House — the creation of William Bruce, architect to Charles II — between Kellie and Pittenweem, Mrs. Margaret Anstruther had presented Kirk to David and Mary Crawford. For some reason they took a liking to the young man, who then had published no book; they invited him to Balcarres. He set out from Kellie to walk there but was trapped by a rainstorm in the village of Arncroach and had to be picked up by the premier earl on the Union roll and transported by Rolls Royce to that maze of a house amidst woods and pastures. "I am rescued by an earl from a deluge," Kirk remarked to his host. Such was the beginning of years of friendship.

David Lindsay, twenty-eighth Earl of Crawford, eleventh Earl of Balcarres, was chairman at one time or another, it seemed, of everything artistic or learned — the National Trust for England, the National Art Collections Fund, the National Gallery, much else — always unpaid, of course. Why, he had been chairman of coal rationing for the north of England during the Second World War, paying for office space and staff out of his own diminished pocket. Mary, a daughter of the ducal house of Devonshire, loved simplicity and seclusion and rather disliked having servants about; she always was delightful to converse with. She and Kirk spent many a day pruning the ancient yews about the roofless Gothic chapel behind Balcarres House — where now David Crawford is buried, under a stone designed by Hew Lorimer.

The Crawfords had given up Haigh, the gigantic seat of the family near Wigan, after the Second World War, withdrawing to the relative modesty of Balcarres. This inescapable retrenchment had required the dissolving of the Lindsay Library at Haigh, the most ambitious private collection of books in all the world, systematically formed by generations of Lindsay earls and intended to comprehend every branch of knowledge — although the decay of the Lindsays' fortunes, with the fortunes of all their class, had frustrated the completing of that high design. Some thousands of the rarer books had been carried up to Balcarres; but these magnificent remains David Crawford described as "the shadow of a shade."

A Norman knight had founded the Scottish house of Lindsay in the eleventh century: the "light Lindsays," debonair, ingenious, for many generations relishing poetry and the arts. An earl of the Balcarres branch had written the first book on early Italian painting — a work disliked by John Ruskin, though the book moved Ruskin to his own studies of that subject. David, twenty-eighth Earl of Crawford, was the perfection of all those generations of what Burke called "the unbought grace of life"; he resembled one of the Kuge nobles of old Japan, patrons of high culture. He had been a diplomat and a member of the House of Commons (from Lancashire) before inheriting his peerage, and he was said to be the most eloquent man in the House of Lords since Lord Rosebery. He was splendidly handsome, with a noble carriage of his head. Old Reginald Fairlie, the architect, told Kirk that Lord Crawford's father, an eminent Tory politician, had been "nearly perfect — perhaps a little haughty. The present Lord Crawford is perfect."

His days were spent in writing letters on behalf of all those societies and galleries of which he was chairman. Now and again he made speaking trips to America and elsewhere. He was a chief authority on the genuineness of paintings — detecting, incidentally, a number of false "masters" sold to American collectors and museums by Sir Roger Duveen.

Balcarres's pictures were even more overwhelming than the books — paintings and other works of art of many periods and schools, down to the nineteenth century (no "modern" art, or little thereof), filling salon after salon, corridor after corridor. Even an outbuilding was crammed with Della Robbia terra-cottas in packing crates. The Balcarres collection of Italian primitives was the finest in private possession. Kirk's fancy was taken especially by two very early Italian panoramas of the monks of the Thebaid, by an unknown hand; the third painting by that hand of that subject is in the Uffizi. It was appropriate enough to encounter in Fife these fantastic scenes of little Egyptian eremites and their cells, for the Thebaid hermits had modelled themselves upon what they had read about the Culdees, the Scottish Christian hermits of the most misty of centuries, the founders of learning at St. Andrews. Reynolds and Gainsborough, Romney and Opie loomed large on Balcarres's walls; but this book is no catalogue.

The most ghostly picture was hung on a wall opposite the door of the room where Kirk lodged at Balcarres: a Dutch portrait of a rather sinister young man who ticked. Lord and Lady Crawford and Kirk twice stood before the picture to make quite sure that it ticked, loudly and intermittently: it did. They never could account for that: it was no deathwatch beetle in the frame.

Balcarres too had its eerie phenomena; there was even a "coffin path" up the Craig, affrighting to dogs, beneath which a number of funerary stone cists had been unearthed. (Culdee burials, perhaps?) But Lord Crawford discouraged talk of the ghostly. His grandfather had been one of the principal patrons of Home the medium; seances had been held at Balcarres, and at the end of one of those sessions, a young woman had been found dead in her chair. Also the twenty-sixth earl's corpse had been stolen from its "braw coffin" in a crypt by Ceres Kirk — perhaps taken by a crazed hanger-on of that occult circle. Such memories were not heartwarming in the enchanted palace of Balcarres, where Lord and Lady Crawford slept quite alone, except for an occasional guest like Kirk, all the windows of the ground floor barred with steel shutters closed every evening.

Recollections of life at Balcarres might fill a book. Here it must suffice to say that Russell Kirk acquired in the company of Lord and Lady Crawford an understanding of what Pico della Mirandola meant by "the dignity of man." In character as in manners, David and Mary Crawford represented to perfection the gentler side of many centuries of breeding. T. S. Eliot (also a visitor to Balcarres) agreed with Kirk, in their correspondence, that the Crawfords were the best exemplars of their class — as Eliot describes class in his *Notes towards the Definition of Culture*. Or, in Burke's phrases, David and Mary Crawford stood conspicuous in what Burke called the natural aristocracy, as well as in the hereditary.

> To see nothing low and sordid from one's infancy; to be taught to respect one's self; to be habituated to the censorial inspection of the public eye; to look early to public opinion; to stand upon such elevated ground as to be enabled to take a large view of the widespread and infinitely diversified combinations of men and affairs in a large society; to have leisure to read, to reflect, to converse; to be enabled to draw the court and attention of the wise and learned wherever they are to be found; to be habituated in the pursuit of honour and duty; to be formed to the highest degree of vigilance, foresight, and circumspection, in a state of things in which no fault is committed with impunity, and the slightest mistakes draw on the most ruinous consequences.

Such was the unbought grace of life represented by the Craw-fords. The destruction of their class is now far advanced. "There is no expectation of continuity here, or next to none," Lord Crawford said once to Kirk. (In this particular prediction, although in few other judgments, David Crawford erred; for Balcarres stands undiminished still.) Within eyesight from Balcarres Craig, old houses and castles were demolished, caught fire, or, long derelict, succumbed to dry rot and roof leaks: Largo House, Kinnaird on its windy headland, Kil-conquhar Castle, lesser places. What would remain by the year two thousand?

"The future will be so uninteresting," the Earl of Crawford remarked to Kirk in the 1950s. Life on a humane scale, at all levels of society, was retreating before the mass age: the little houses and little shops of Fife were failing as were the great houses. The guardians of the arts and the amenities of seven centuries of civilization, like the Celts of the Twilight, still went forth to battle — but not often to victory. "We are growing old," the Earl said of himself and his allies in the struggle to preserve beauty and diversity, as he and Kirk passed the ruins of Largo House one day. "No, we *are* old." That was in the 1970s.

Kirk had some hand in Lord Crawford's being elected rector by the students of St. Andrews University, and dedicated to him his *St. Andrews* volume. Perhaps a hundred letters from David or Mary Crawford are in Kirk's files — the Earl's in his minute and almost illegible holograph, wit and wisdom to be redeciphered if ever there is leisure. A conscience had spoken to a conscience. Surely we are more than ships that pass in the night.

Those three great houses, and others such in Scotland and England that Kirk came to know, helped to emancipate him from the provincialities of place and class — much as his reading of great works of history and humane letters had emancipated him from the provinciality of time. His Fife years of peace and charm, spent among old books, in old houses, in discourse with urbane and kindly men and women a generation older than Kirk, gave him such an education as is not to be bought in the graduate schools of Harvard or of Yale, and such a detachment from the ephemeral as had become most difficult to attain in a sensate age.

Walking late one day along the flank of Largo Law from Bal-carres toward Largo, Kirk paused to survey the distant line of fisher towns of the Golden Fringe, their roofs of red pantiles splendid in the sun's dying glow. He seemed to find himself outside the confines of Time. Like C. S. Lewis, he was surprised by joy. In a contented solitude, he enjoyed a vision of perpetuity, and his lone self in harmony with all creation. (Spaniards do well to name girls Soledad.) It was as if his soul would possess always that Fife prospect, though the antagonist world would efface the great houses and the little towns.

"But time runs on, runs on . . ." Swinging his stick, he strode downward toward the coastal road and literary obligations. That still moment at the intersection of time and the timeless had passed, though never to be forgotten; one is fortunate to experience a few such moments, or any, in the course of a life. They are our best evidence of eternity.

Castle Borstal

The great houses were dwindling in number during Kirk's years in Scotland. He attended the muckle roup, the great sale, at Melville House, in the Howe of Fife, which Scott-Moncrieff had called "best of the Fife mansion-houses." And out of that sad day came another of his essays, "Hung with Spanish Leather," later included in his volume *Beyond the Dreams of Avarice*.

Yet country-house life survived death duties, the land tax, rates, and the loss of servants at a good many estates. To so many castles and country houses was Kirk invited, during his St. Andrews years! Among them was Earlshall, across St. Andrews Bay, a fine laird's house with symbolic figures painted on the panels of the ceiling. Sir Robert Lorimer had restored the house with high success, even the bakehouse, and had added a very Gallic gatehouse. There was Falkland Palace, much of it ruined by Cromwell's troopers, where lived the kindly Creighton-Stuarts. Kirk found his way to curious Myres Castle, property of the Fairlies, where housemaids could not find their way back to their own bedrooms, so labyrinthine was the place. He went several times to Balcaskie, between Kellie and the Forth, a seventeenth-century masterpiece, where Madge Anstruther, with her Anglo-Irish manners, welcomed him to her terraces above the Forth.

Later he came to know well houses beyond Fife, in Galloway and Perthshire and Angus and Aberdeenshire and the Lothians and Peeblesshire. At Whittinghame, in East Lothian, the Earl and Countess of Balfour, Gerald and Natasha, entertained him in the fifteenth-century tower they had restored, behind which still flourished the yew under whose screening branches the murder of Darnley had been plotted; they took him on more than one occasion to visit East Lothian's other castles and mansions, some ruined, some sound. And there was Houston (c. 1600), restored by the architect Ian Lindsay in the devastated regions of West Lothian; Mrs. Lindsay baked the best gingerbread on either side of the Atlantic . . . But the full list of delightful country places and of generous hosts and hostesses would grow too long.

What became of the castles and mansions that no lord, laird, or member of the professional aristocracy could or would maintain or restore? Some were pulled down, being impossible to let; some caught fire and burnt; some collapsed from dry rot and deathwatch beetle; some became schools for a time, among them Melville and the huge formal house built in 1817 at Whittinghame. Yet others were made places of confinement. One such seems worth describing here.

On the northern shore of the broad Firth of Tay, between Dundee and Perth, stands Castle Huntly. When Kirk called there, in 1950, it had become a Borstal. Britain had many Borstals: these were, and are, disciplinary quarters for juvenile delinquents and juveniles more than delinquent, taking their names from the first such reformatory for young boys, established at Borstal in Kent in 1902. With two friends, Kirk drove through the decrepit ancient gates of Castle Huntly, up to the castle itself, standing in handsome green lawns.

Built for the most part in the sixteenth century, Castle Huntly is a great, tall, strong building of reddish-brown rubble, with the square towers, crowstepped gables, and steep stone-slab roofs that give Scottish architecture, down to the eighteenth century, a distinctive character. Upon this castle's face, late in the eighteenth century, a builder influenced by the famous Adam brothers clapped a neoclassical porch and entrance hall, contrasting oddly with the medieval work frowning above it. Dark, austere, and nobly situated, Castle Huntly is said to have had a curse upon it. The last private proprietor drowned in the Tay with his immediate family, their boat capsizing;

and then the castle passed into the hands of the state, which converted the place into a Borstal.

The three unexpected visitors, two of them Americans, were shown about Castle Huntly Borstal by the chief warden, a tired, good-natured little man. Stripped of all its plenishings, the castle had become a barracks for boys, a number of whom stared dully as the visitors made their way from room to room, all rooms chilly. The policies, including some terraces looking on the Tay, were kept up decently by the boys, most of whom had thick Glasgow accents. Along one of the paths, Kirk noticed the remains of a sixteenth-century Scots sundial of stone, laid out dismembered to form a border to a walk.

"You have quite a fine and rare sundial here," Kirk said to the warden. The man raised his eyebrows: "Oh, is that what it is? I had the boys break it up to line the path." On the terraces stood several remarkable allegorical statues, Scottish Renaissance carving of which very few specimens remain in the whole country; Kirk hoped silently that these mossy representations of the Seasons would not go the way of the sundial.

This warden, Kirk found, had grown somewhat sensitive to criticism of his care of an ancient monument. A month before Kirk and his companions arrived, the warden had a low wing made of gray concrete tacked on at the back of the castle; it squatted hideously upon the living red rock of the castle's foundation, above the old dungeons. "Only last week," said the warden to Kirk, plaintively, "a fellow from the Arts Council came here to inspect. He saw this new wing — we need it very much — and he turned quite furious. He said to me, 'Did anyone give you permission to build that monstrosity? You have committed an atrocity!'" The warden's meek eyes appealed to Kirk for sympathy. "I simply do not understand that chap's way of thinking. Now if I had my way, I'd knock down the whole castle and build a modern camp here."

Castle Huntly being state property, it was and is improbable that the wardens or anyone else will be permitted to pull it down altogether, no matter how much the Borstal boys knock the place about. Certainly there was some utilitarian advantage in making country places like Castle Huntly into reformatories: here, if anywhere, Borstal boys would see that something more exists in life than the slums or the town-council housing projects from which they had come. In

Britain, as in America, managing a reformatory for the young is weary work; many of the boys are repeaters; and whatever the Borstal might do to give them some discipline, it cannot accomplish much to put a different light into those dull and sullen eyes which, now and again, met Kirk's furtively. Borstal work, for the most part, is a species of delayed baby-sitting.

The conversion of castles and country houses into places of confinement of one sort or another, and the ominous increase in rates of criminality about 1950, were developments that British social reformers about the beginning of the twentieth century little antici-pated. And before 1914, at least, country-house proprietors would have laughed at any such suggestions. About 1948, Ralph Christie of Durie had conferred with his man of law about his inherited house's future. "Do you know what such places as this will become?" inquired his Edinburgh lawyer, rhetorically. "Why, lunatic asylums!" Christie had smiled just a trifle uneasily. Durie, at this writing, continues to function as the center of a biggish agricultural estate; but it went otherwise, during Kirk's own time in Scotland, with many another house of Durie's sort.

Even at the end of the Second World War, or perhaps especially then, the characteristic British humanitarian reformer, socialist or liberal, believed that by means of positive law and economic levelling a new society could be established in old Britain: the country would become one smiling "garden city," and the welfare state would abolish the economic causes of crimes. But disillusion set in fairly promptly after 1950. The Quaker philanthropist and writer Seebohm Rowntree, who had planned the new society before the twentieth century began, in his old age grew aghast at the morals and manners of the rising generation; while Lord Beveridge, architect of the welfare state, be-came so dismayed at the irresponsibility of the English masses that he questioned whether universal suffrage might not have been a colossal mistake.*

In no aspect of society did this disillusion grow more thorough, during the Fifties, than in the matter of juvenile delinquency. Rates of crime and minor offenses more than doubled in Britain between

---

*See B. Seebohm Rowntree and G. R. Lavers, *English Life and Leisure: A Social Study* (London, 1951); and the same authors' *Poverty and the Welfare State* (London, 1951).

the beginning of the Second World War and the early Fifties. It became very difficult to recruit enough policemen to keep an intermittent watch upon gangs of young toughs and vandals. Offenses against both persons and property increased alarmingly from year to year, without cessation. For the humanitarian social planner, this phenomenon was difficult to explain. Crime, such reformers had thought, resulted from poverty and ignorance; so higher wages, more modern housing, and more compulsory schooling would put an end to that ancient affliction.

Yet by the Fifties wages were higher than ever they had been before, both relatively and in absolute purchasing power; full employment had very nearly been attained; millions of houses had been built by local authorities, with national subsidies, and rented at modest charges to the working classes; the school-leaving age had been raised everywhere to sixteen and immense sums spent upon the enlargement of school facilities. Actual poverty, according to Seebohm Rowntree's sociological surveys, had been virtually abolished in Britain. Yet, all this accomplished, the rate of lawbreaking, of both violence and fraud, continued to rise apace; and the habit of obedience to law, once stronger in Britain than anywhere else in the world, actually seemed to diminish in proportion as the works of the welfare state grew in volume: a paradox, to say the least.

The highest rates of offenses, for instance, were found not in what old-fashioned slums remained. On the contrary, the police of the Fifties had far more trouble in many of the new county-council or town-council housing schemes, with their front gardens and wide streets and improved plumbing. Nor was it in regions dominated by old-fashioned heavy industries such as mining and iron forging that the mischief was greatest: rather, the newer communities dependent upon newly established "light industry" experienced more crimes against persons and acts of vandalism. The raising of the school-leaving age in Scotland promptly was followed not by an increase of earnestness and civility among young people; no, there came a doubling or tripling, in many towns, of acts that warranted committal to a Borstal.

It seemed to Kirk, he strolling about the lawns of Castle Borstal, that the twentieth century's reformers in Britain tended to accept with a naïve and disastrous eagerness the facile theory that social order is merely an exercise in social-democratic economics. A sentimental utilitarianism argued that prosperity would abolish sin. It was a shallow argument, ignorant of history; for had it been true, all rich men's sons, these many centuries past, would have been perfectly virtuous.

To the student of history, as contrasted with the doctrinaire positivistic reformer, it seems that people are decent, when they are decent, chiefly out of habit. They fall into habits of decent conduct by religious instruction, by settled family life, by assuming private responsibilities, by the old incentives of private gain and advancement in rewards for decent conduct. When the individual seems to run no risks; when food, shelter, and even comforts are guaranteed by the state, no matter what one's conduct may be; when the state arrogates to itself a complex of responsibilities that formerly were undertaken by church, family, voluntary association, and the private person — why, then the old habits of decency are weakened, and the police constable and the Borstal are required to maintain precariously by compulsion what once was taken for granted in Britain and elsewhere.

Shortly before his visit to Castle Huntly, Kirk had walked at night along Niddry Road, on the outskirts of Edinburgh. The corporation of Edinburgh, some years earlier, had decided to solve the problem of slum crime by resettling the roughest Edinburgh households in neat new houses at Niddry Mains. The experiment failed. Niddry by 1950 had become a more dangerous place than any part of the old town, and the Saturday night when Kirk strolled somewhat timorously along Niddry Road, he observed that nearly every solitary pedestrian he passed had with him an immense and surly dog on a leash, apparently as insurance against rough gangs of "Teddy boys" and the like. Niddry Mains had become a good recruiting ground for Borstals. As others had pointed out, it is not slums that make the people, but people that make the slums. And at bottom the remedies for slums are not bigger wages, or bricks and mortar, or huge new schools, but instead those habits of decency and responsibility beyond the grasp of welfare-state measures.

As Kirk said good-bye to the warden of Castle Huntly Borstal, that worthy still fretted about unkind words addressed to him by the gentleman from the Arts Council. "No, I cannot understand a chap like that," he repeated, mildly enough. Then his tired eyes brightened a trifle, as there flitted to his mind, so devoid of imagination, a tag from a wardens' training school. "That man must be living in the

Past. As for me" — and here he endeavored to throw back his little shoulders, as if marching into a brave new dawn — "as for me, *I* live in the Future."

The Future? Those Borstal boys, gathered in a street-corner sort of knot at the castle door, stared soddenly at their custodian and at the American visitor. They thought little about the Future, Kirk suspected, whether in the Gallowgate of Glasgow or on the lawns of Castle Huntly; and the Present was sufficiently boring for them. Kirk hoped that his host the warden might cease to live in the Future; for one does not relish the notion of a Future in which all folk will be so many Borstal boys, washed and fed and watched by the state in model camps established amidst a few surviving "cultural monuments" of an age that knew how to build for posterity.

Ninfa

Some forty miles southeast of Rome, in the shadow of the Volscians, stands the most curious country house Kirk ever encountered. For most of this century the rural residence of the great Roman family of Caetani has been at Ninfa, "a medieval Pompeii," where they fitted up the medieval *Palazzo publico,* the town hall, standing amidst ruins, as their country place.

Kirk made several expeditions to Rome during his Fife years. When he was about to commence one of those Italian trips, Lord and Lady Crawford suggested that he call on their "cousins" — they were distant connections — at Ninfa. At Balcarres, earlier, Kirk had met a fellow guest, Mrs. Howard (married to a member of that great English family), the only child of the Duke of Sermoneta, Prince Caetani. So, having a few days in Rome that year, Kirk prevailed upon a girl at the Embassy of the United States, Miss Barbara White, to drive him down to Ninfa.

Before arriving at Ninfa, they went up to the hill town of Sermoneta, surmounted by the Castello Caetani, where *cento bambini,* little children from cities, then spent a happy summer in the castle, which still is habitable. This was a principal stronghold of the Caetani in medieval times; also they held a tomb fortress on the Appian Way, the tomb of Caecilia Metella, from the age of Augustus. Two medieval popes were of the house of Caetani, one of them Benedict Caetani,

Boniface the Eighth, "keen, learned, brave, unforgiving," who was captured and insulted in the Caetani hill town of Anagni by an agent of the king of France and by the leader of the hostile princely family of Colonna, in the year 1303 — and died not long thereafter.

Far below Sermoneta, in the marshy valley at the foot of the Volscians, lies Ninfa, which in classical times had its nymph; and one can imagine a nymph emerging from the pool or little lake that is found within the ruins. But the ruins themselves are medieval, not classical: once upon a time Ninfa was a considerable place, with a cathedral, the apse of which still stands. Feuds tormented the town, and in the seventeenth century, the malaria of the Pontine Marshes (not drained until Mussolini's time) drove out the remaining population. Today Ninfa has no inhabitants but its lords. For in the present century, the Caetani made a park or garden of the whole ruined little city within the broken medieval walls and settled themselves in the *Palazzo publico,* which consists principally of one vast vaulted chamber, so that it is a most picturesque residence but not a perfectly convenient one.

Kirk gave his calling card to one of the *contadini* at this strange country house and was directed to the gardens, where he and his companion encountered Mrs. Howard, who presented him to her parents. The Duke of Sermoneta, last of his line, was very old and infirm, but a cordial host. The Duchess of Sermoneta, Marguerite Caetani, a Bostonian by birth, had become wholly Italian in appearance and manner. She had founded, and edited, the international literary periodical *Botteghe Oscure* (named after the "Street of the Dark Shops" in Rome, on which the Palazzo Caetani faces); also she knew much about paintings, and had a valuable collection in her Paris apartment — which quarters she lent generously to people she did not know well, and suffered the theft of some paintings therefore. She and Kirk had much to talk about.

The walled park of Ninfa was a wonder of color: every flowering plant, shrub, or vine of southern Italy seemed to be there. It was lotusland, for one might have dozed in the vegetal labyrinths, happy in the warmth and the perfume of the flowers, day upon day — as, it seemed, the aged Duke was doing. Were they haunted, those magnificent gardens, planted amidst scraps of churches, palaces, and buildings of all sorts, all quite roofless, all abandoned three centuries gone? They did not seem so. Perhaps the perfect manners and generous ways of the Duke and the Duchess had laid to rest any unquiet spirits of the old fierce times. Ninfa seemed outside time; there entered Kirk's head the first three lines of Eliot's "Burnt Norton":

> Time present and time past
> Are both perhaps present in time future,
> And time future contained in time past.

No, not haunted by those who may have suffered here at the foot of the Volscians; yet there was a hint of presences:

> There they were, dignified, invisible
> Moving without pressure, over the dead leaves . . .

The Caetani had been a brave and graceful race; such presences welcomed the visitors from distant lands.

The courage of the Caetani was undiminished during the German occupation of Rome. As American troops advanced slowly from Anzio, to the south, the German military government in the city proceeded to arrest anyone suspect — including Jews, who had been little troubled so long as Mussolini's government stood. The Duke and Duchess of Sermoneta were then living in the Caetani palace in the Via delle Botteghe Oscure; the ground floor was let to the Spanish government, which had installed its embassy there. A good many fugitives from arrest by the Germans had sought refuge on the upper floors of the Caetani palace, where the Duke and the Duchess took them under their protection. German officers demanded their surrender; the Caetani refused. Then the Germans prepared to storm the Palazzo Caetani. But at the gate the German force was confronted by Spanish sentries, instructed by their ambassador to deny passage through the embassy to the palace's upper floors. Not being authorized to commence war with Spain, the German military governor of Rome fumed pusillanimous. So the Caetani and their sought-after guests remained within the palace, inaccessible above Spain's embassy, until the American forces entered Rome.

The Caetani seemed imperturbable. Communist emblems and exhortations appeared on signposts along the roads in the neighborhood of Ninfa when Kirk was there. But what of that? The Caetani, and ancient families like theirs, had survived the Nazi power; they would outlast the Communist power; over the centuries, many centuries, these Roman princes had been endowed with the high old Roman virtue of *firmitas*.

The Caetani, indeed, were the oldest noble family in all Europe. For centuries they had claimed to be descended from a Roman house of some eminence. But skeptical nineteenth- and twentieth-century historians had smiled: most of the great palaces along the Corso had been built by men of power who had come to Rome from elsewhere; and surely no extant Roman house could justly lay claim to trace its lineage to some time the other side of the Dark Ages — why, even before the reign of Gregory the Great.

Then, in 1939, excavations were commenced under the Duomo of San Pietro, in search of Saint Pietro's bones; such diggings were resumed in 1952. Far below Bernini's altar of the seventeenth century, archeologists discovered impressive tombs, built before the Age of Constantine, of powerful families of the Empire. Early in the excavations, two tombs of the Caeteanius (Caetani) family, one of them very grand, were discovered; the remains of the Caetani ancestors had been laid there from the middle of the second century A.D. to the middle of the fourth.

In 1983, Russell and Annette Kirk, speechifying in Rome, would clamber down to these chambers of the dead. No other family in Italy or elsewhere can demonstrate such continuity, surviving the collapse of classical civilization.

At Balcarres, in 1950, the Earl of Crawford had told Kirk that almost no prospect of continuity for Balcarres House was conceivable. Yet forty-three years later, his son Robin Lindsay, the twenty-ninth Earl, is at Balcarres still; nothing seems to have changed there; the son Robin seems almost identical with David the father; and Kirk sat again by the fire with Earl and Countess, talking of the permanent things, and of their son, taking his perilous chances in Afghanistan. At Balcarres, as at other great houses he had known, Kirk thought of a passage from a book by a lady who knew the country houses of Ireland and Italy: Iris Origo's *Images and Shadows*.

Do the walls of a house sometimes become imbued with the nature of its inhabitants? I think so — and indeed, why should it not be so? Many people would agree that there are certain places whose walls are impregnated by centuries of faith and prayer. . . . And so, too, I believe that, on a more modest scale, the walls of some private houses may also be colored either by good or evil: in short by the character of those who live there.

In such houses there often was conferred what Burke called "the unbought grace of life." If all those houses perish, the twenty-first century will be graceless. And if the cozy little cottages are swept away altogether, to clear the ground for "housing" of egalitarian hideousness — why, then the common man will have been converted into the proletarian, and the people into Marx's masses. These processes were well advanced during Kirk's Scottish years and have made much headway since. When both great and small are broken, mediocrity remains; but boring mediocrity cannot forever sustain a civilization.

CHAPTER SIX

The Conservative Persuasion

A Doctor of the Schools

During the years 1951, 1952, and 1953, there lapped at Kirk's feet that tide in the affairs of men "which, taken at the flood, leads on to fortune." Kirk refused to take that tide — and doubtless has been the happier for his negative choice, preferring to dwell far from the madding crowd.

In 1951 his first book was published, winning praise; in 1952 the oldest university in northern Britain conferred upon him its highest arts degree, then held by only one other living scholar; in 1953 *The Conservative Mind,* his major book, enjoyed a remarkable success. Thereupon, resigning his academic post, Kirk withdrew to his ancestral village. Disliking the prospect of becoming either professor or politician, he made himself a man of letters. He did not altogether abjure the world, the flesh, and the devil, but he cast off vanities. There follows some account, chronologically, of these swiftly successive events.

Any aspirant to the St. Andrews degree of doctor of letters was confronted by severe preliminary requirements. To be admitted to candidacy, a prospective research-student must have published already writings of some significance; a period of five years must have expired since he had received his last previous degree (which might be the Ph.D.), and he must have the agreement of a St. Andrews professor to supervise the candidate's studies in his discipline.*

*Or such were the requirements until very recent years. Today (1994) the degree is conferred only upon distinguished members of the University's staff,

Moreover, it was expected that the candidate's resulting dissertation must be deserving of publication; it was assumed, indeed, that publication would follow. The dissertation must be approved by a distinguished external examiner in addition to St. Andrews professors. These requirements previously had repulsed all candidates but one — and he the St. Andrews professor of German literature.

Kirk's army years provided the interval between candidacy for degrees. And before arriving in Scotland, he had published essays in serious periodicals: *College English, The South Atlantic Quarterly, Michigan History.* While he resided at St. Andrews, his essays would appear in more journals, British or American: *The English Review Magazine, Comment, The American Council of Learned Societies Newsletter, Queen's Quarterly, Prairie Schooner, Western Humanities Review, The Review of Politics, The Yale Review, The University of Kansas City Review, The Sewanee Review, The Western Political Quarterly, The Dublin Review, The Contemporary Review, World Review, History Today, The Fortnightly, The Month;* also in St. Andrews publications. For him to survive, it was necessary for him to obtain such literary prizes as were offered at the university: he won the first prizes for the essay and the short story, and even a prize for a poem, his only poem ever. Thus Kirk met the requirement for serious publication as a D.Litt. candidate and was enabled occasionally to consume not merely high tea but a real dinner.

What mattered more, in 1951, when Kirk was thirty-two years old, the University of Chicago Press published his first book, *Randolph of Roanoke: A Study in Conservative Thought.* (Later, in 1962, an enlarged edition would appear, with some of Randolph's speeches and letters appended; and in 1978, a third and still larger edition.) This book established an enduring friendship with W. T. Couch, a brilliant scholarly editor, then head of the Chicago press.

Randolph met with a cordial reception from the reviewers — indeed, there were no hostile reviews. Kirk's master's thesis at Duke University (though the critics did not know the book's origin) was much praised by Samuel Flagg Bemis in *The Yale Review;* by B. I. Bell in *The Commonweal;* by the scholarly historical quarterlies; by the *New York Herald Tribune* and some other big papers. A review by

---

or, as an honorary degree, may be awarded on rare occasions at graduation ceremonies.

W. C. McCann in the radical New York *Daily Compass* for some time shielded Kirk against assaults from the literary Left, those gentlemen taking it that, despite the word "conservative" in *Randolph's* subtitle, any author so heartily approved by the *Compass* must have his heart in the left place.

All this made Kirk a minor literary lion in Scotland — although at Michigan State he encountered more envy than approbation among most of his colleagues, with the conspicuous exception of Richard Dorson, the folklore authority (himself much published), later a friend in need. Christopher Hollis reviewed *Randolph* in the London *Tablet*, attracting to Kirk the attention of some influential Catholic thinkers in Britain. Professor Bemis hinted that a Yale appointment might be possible.

In the spring of 1952, three learned men read Kirk's fat dissertation on conservative thought in the line of Burke: T. M. Knox, the distinguished professor of philosophy, later vice chancellor of St. Andrews; W. L. Burn, the Durham University historian, author of *The Age of Equipoise*; and J. W. Williams, the professor of history at St. Andrews — he having consented to read it in typescript after all, once the dissertation was bound. They found it good.

Within a few months it would be published in America under the title *The Conservative Mind*; the London edition and a Spanish translation would appear not long thereafter, and a German translation in 1959. Some account of the book's reception will appear later in this chapter.

So, early in July 1952, Russell Kirk was granted the degree of *litterarum doctorem*, the highest arts degree of the senior Scottish university, taking precedence of all mere doctors of philosophy. (Only the M.D., at St. Andrews awarded for distinguished scientific research in medicine and not to ordinary graduates of medical schools, stands on a plane with the D.Litt. St. Andrews requirements for the Ph.D. have been less exacting than those for the literary doctorate.)

The formal gown of a St. Andrean doctor of letters is a vast awkward saffron affair, resembling the robe of a Buddhist monk; Kirk was the first American to acquire it, and may be the last. Long later, when he was to wear it on occasion at Mecosta, Kirk's little daughters would call him the Great Pumpkin. Indeed, presently he fell into the habit of wearing it at Hallowe'en, telling fortunes by the Tarot so impressively garbed, to the dreadful joy of Mecosta's rising generation, scores of whom besieged Piety Hill every October 31. With it went a rakish black velvet cap, modelled on that of John Knox in his St. Andrews years. Such an academic regalia having to be especially ordered, Kirk placed an order with a draper well in advance.

But when graduation day arrived, the draper confessed that he had quite forgotten about the unique gown. The ceremonies would commence in a quarter of an hour. Kirk sent an emissary scurrying to the university registrar, asking if he might be graduated *in absentia;* the officer sent back word that a gown must be procured somehow, for this doctorate was the university's highest gift. Kirk then ran to the Roundel, Professor Williams's medieval mansion, hoping to borrow his old friend's Oxford gown. He was confronted at the Roundel's carved doorway by a dwarfish serving woman, one of a peculiar St. Andrews breed that Kirk thought might be Picts.

Maid: "See the Professor? Why, he's not up and aboot yet: 'tis but noon."

Kirk: "All the same, I'll see him."

Maid: "What, in his bedroom?"

Kirk: "Just so."

Having dashed up the stair, Kirk found Jack Williams abed, his large nose quite red. "Ah, Russell," sleepily, "I had meant to attend your graduation today, but I felt a trifle indisposed . . ."

"That's quite all right, Jack; I've only come to borrow your gown."

"You're welcome. But where is it? Not in that cupboard? Look in the corridor. No? Try my robing room at the College."

Back across St. Andrews Kirk dashed to discover at the United College of St. Salvator and St. Leonard a tattered black Oxford master's gown, made for a man more than six feet three inches tall. Gathering this garment about him, he hastened to the graduation hall and stumbled over people's feet to his place.

At once his name was called. Still he had no hood to go with the gown; but as he made his awkward way to the platform, he snatched from an acquaintance named Dugald Blue the hood of a bachelor of education (from the sublime to the ridiculous) which had a yellow lining. Turning this hood inside out, he presented himself before the Duke of Hamilton, the University's chancellor, who capped him with the literal cap of John Knox. Such haste and confusion would beset Kirk all his life thereafter.*

Now a doctor of the schools, Kirk possessed the credentials entitling him to profess true doctrine at any university that might tolerate him, and that without suffering the dreary pedantic years of the typical American doctorate. In the orders of precedence in American academic processions, thereafter he would go before all except doctors of Oxford and Cambridge (and after all, those sluggish foundations conferred doctorates in philosophy merely) or of a few Continental medieval universities that might happen to turn up. Yet he was to employ saffron gown and black cap only occasionally, never setting foot upon the "tenure track" (a hideous phrase scarcely ever heard so late as 1952) up and down which his degreed contemporaries would stumble.

He would be visiting distinguished professor from time to time, over the decades, in New York, California, Michigan, Indiana, Alabama, Colorado, and Scotland; but he preferred unsalaried independence. Kirk had known some professors of lively imagination; yet he had known more who, in Burke's phrase, were limited by "drydocked minds." What he sought was not an academic specialist's sinecure but a field for his imagination to plow.

That summer, having crossed to Hook of Holland, he wandered in the Rhineland and along the Mosel with an American colleague, Stebleton Nulle, and later in Switzerland. The noble medieval cities of the Rhineland and the Mosel — Cologne, Mainz, Coblentz, Trier, at all of which Nulle and Kirk spent a few days — still lay partially in ruin. Paupers from eastern Europe, fugitives from the Russians, dug furiously for articles of value in the mountains of rubble and debris — once the municipal watchmen went off duty in the evenings. The deliberate bombing of towns long famous for their architectural beauty, the "Baedeker raids" had been initiated by the Royal Air Force, but the Luftwaffe had been swift to retaliate; in Britain,

---

*Just forty years later, the Kirks' second daughter, the thoughtful Cecilia, would be awarded the degree of master of philosophy in history in that same St. Andrews graduation hall. Her parents were present for the graduation, and in their company was Mr. Jeffrey Nelson (sometime assistant to Dr. Kirk), a young man of unusual talents of a literary and philosophical character, like Kirk, a native of Plymouth, Michigan. He and Cecilia would be married late in 1993, at the cathedral in Grand Rapids.

Coventry had been the cathedral town worst smashed. In the Rhineland, praise be, the incendiary bombs tested at Dugway Proving Ground had not been employed. Kirk never has visited Dresden — now prospering again, he is told — where the gel bomb did its worst execution.

At frontiers, he presented United States passport No. 57 — a document received at first with suspicion by officers, and then, found genuine, handed back with some awe and the tipping of caps: this must be the fifty-seventh most important citizen of the United States. (Actually, it was merely the fifty-seventh passport issued at Glasgow's consulate-general in that year.) He lodged in the oldest inns he could find, those being as cheap as picturesque. He was perfectly carefree: his large book completed, he wondered vaguely how he might spend the rest of his life. Yet neither then nor on any other occasion lifelong did he make any long-range plans or come to any positive decision: he was good at making firm negative decisions, a no-sayer, but otherwise left the future to providence.

In September he went aboard a Greek ship, accompanied by Pongo McClellan, who was to engage in American graduate studies, first at Michigan State, then at the University of Chicago. They rejoiced in the spectacle of a bo's'n who looked exactly like Anthony Quinn, and in the company of innumerable bare-legged American girls returning from their first European tour. On September 15 they landed at Quebec, where Kirk's kinfolk met their ship and drove them all the way to Michigan.

Kirk returned to his huge classes at Michigan State, and McClellan became a graduate assistant in the department of history. They found rooms in a decayed house on an alley behind the massive People's Church, in what Kirk called the Kasbah of East Lansing. The front door of their ground-floor apartment would not stay shut while they were absent; masses of dead leaves blew in, and presently a bobtailed wild cat took up residence with them. They very nearly poisoned themselves fatally with their own cookery; neither cared to wash dishes often, so that the most curious fungi or bacterial cultures began to arise from their kitchen sink. A representative of the Guggenheim Foundation later came to talk with Kirk about his fellowship; Kirk muttered some words of apology for the condition of their rooms, but the amiable functionary said, "That's typical." After publication of *The Conservative Mind,* now and again some man of importance would find his precarious way up their crazy broken front steps, he unannounced — and surprised more than they. They were careless of the possibility of marauders, college students not being thieves in those years, and they two possessing nothing worth carrying off.

Academic standards at Michigan State were sliding downward — by the deliberate policy of John Hannah, MSC's aggrandizing president, the equivalent of President Boomer in one of Stephen Leacock's burlesques.* Kirk would describe that lamentable process in the 1954 volume (for 1953) of *Collier's Yearbook* (by this time, along with *Collier's Encyclopedia,* edited by W. T. Couch), and later in his book *Decadence and Renewal in the Higher Learning* (1978). By March 1953, it became clear that the College was committed to the educational degradation of the democratic dogma, at least in the Basic College with which Kirk was affiliated. Growthmanship! Beat the University of Michigan (Ann Arbor) in numbers enrolled, if in naught else! Vast new dormitories were under construction. "Comprehensive" multiple-choice examinations, so stupidly prepared (or was it by design?) as to reward mediocrity and penalize the more thoughtful undergraduates, were administered *en masse* in the fieldhouse. The question for Kirk was whether he should continue, well enough paid, in this academic barbarism, or whether he should fold his tent like the Arab, and as silently steal away.

Liberalism and Conservatism in 1952

By the time Kirk returned to the United States in 1952, at the end of his St. Andrews years, it was clear that the American electorate was turning conservative — even if most people entertained only a vague notion of what the word "conservative" signified. The conquest of eastern Europe by the Soviet Union, the triumph of Mao

---

*Hannah did possess a doctorate — conferred upon him by MSC, *honoris causa,* at his installation as president. He had wedded the daughter of the previous president. His earned degree, also from MSC, was in poultry husbandry. Not long later, the Michigan legislature elevated Michigan State College of Agriculture and Applied Science to the dignity of University. "This used to be a cow college," Kirk's friend Warren Fleischauer of the English department said, "but now it's Michigan's udder university."

and the Chinese Communists, and the decline of British power had alarmed the American public; like it or not, America had become the principal conservator of order, justice, and freedom against Communist aspirations to universal dominion. In domestic polity, the New Deal had run its course: the Great Depression was long past, and quite different measures seemed to be required for a quite different era. The insolence of the big labor unions had resulted in a public reaction against them; taxation, the national debt, government's arbitrary way with business and industry, and an oppressive bureaucracy were loudly complained of; centralization of political authority was resented by many. At the end of twenty years in power, the liberal Democrats were about to give way to the conservative Republicans.

"Liberalism," a term popularized in the United States by Franklin Roosevelt and his adherents, had lost its vigor, even though liberal attitudes and prejudices remained strong in intellectual circles, most of the serious press and publishing trade, and a large part of the mass media of communication. The term had become almost synonymous with the increase of centralized political power, egalitarian economic designs, growing fiscal burdens upon the public, and an attitude of "no enemies to the Left." As Francis Wilson had written in 1951, "The perennial rebirth of conservatism becomes apparent as liberalism disintegrates through the falsification of its own revolution." Thus the American political pendulum swung swiftly, in 1952, toward a conservative resurgence.

But toward what manner of conservatism? For a decade, the most conspicuous and influential conservative public man had been Senator Robert Taft, who called himself a liberal conservative, accurately enough. Taft knew that there was more to conserve than material interests. "Before our system can claim success, it must not only create a people with a higher standard of living, but a people with a higher standard of character — character that must include religious faith, morality, educated intelligence, self-restraint, and an ingrained demand for justice and unselfishness," Taft had written in 1944. "In our striving for material things, we must not change those basic principles of government and of personal conduct which create and protect the character of a people. . . . We cannot hope to achieve salvation by worshipping the god of the standard of living."

Amen to that, Kirk had thought at the time. In practical politics, he had been an obscure Taft man.* It had seemed as if Taft, so hard-working, so patient, would win the Republican presidential nomination in 1952 and go on to an intelligently conservative presidency — founded in foreign policy upon a realistic understanding of the national interest, in domestic policy upon a humane apprehension of the needs of a society disrupted by the War and by tremendous technological and demographic changes.

But by a narrow margin Taft had been defeated at the Republican national convention during the summer of 1952. It was General Eisenhower who would go to the White House. From abroad, Kirk had watched the process by which one Republican faction had undermined the true leader of their party so that they might elect a popular general (though always of the chairborne command), a political neophyte. Had Taft been nominated, he would have defeated Adlai Stevenson, though presumably by not so large a margin as did Eisenhower. With Taft as president, the United States might have entered early upon far-reaching conservative measures — something more substantial than Eisenhower's chief accomplishment, which was the paving of America with gigantic highways, ruinous to the railways and beginning to collapse thirty years later. Eisenhower and his people did retard the advance of the welfare state in America but did little to give flesh to the conservative imagination.

It would have been difficult to discover a public man less imaginative than Dwight Eisenhower. His national presidency was foreshadowed by his presiding over Columbia University: one incident at Columbia must suffice as illustration. Carlton Hayes — who had been Roosevelt's ambassador to Spain and was a famous historian, one of Columbia's principal scholars — was approached by the Metropolitan Museum of Art. The Museum had been endeavoring to obtain Eisenhower's assent, as president of Columbia, to an intended major project of collaboration between University and Museum; but the Museum had been unable to obtain any response at all from the

---

*Taft and Kirk never happened to meet. Taft lay dying in a hospital at the time Kirk's *Conservative Mind* was much in the news. A journalist asked him if he had read that book. Taft chuckled: "You remind me of Thurber's *Let Your Mind Alone.*" He implied that he had been too busy in conservative action to read about conservative thought.

educator-general. Therefore the Museum asked Professor Hayes to intercede in person.

The elderly Hayes made his way to the outer academic defenses of Eisenhower's redoubt on Morningside Heights, and, after repeatedly explaining his mission and himself to administrative pickets and sentries, he was admitted to a secretary's office. That confidential clerk never had heard of Carlton Hayes, then perhaps the best-known scholar in the humane disciplines at Columbia. He was compelled to recount afresh his association with the University and why it was that he presumed to speak on behalf of the Metropolitan Museum — virtually to outline a *curriculum vitae*. At length, partially satisfied that Hayes was not an impostor or an assassin, the secretary consulted an appointment book and said, "I suppose, then, that we can arrange an appointment with President Eisenhower on . . ." She named a date three months distant.

"No, thank you," replied Carlton Hayes, and slowly walked away. He never did see Ike.

It was said by wags that Truman had demonstrated how anybody could be elected president and that Eisenhower had shown how no president was needed at all: America's overwhelming military strength during the early Eisenhower years, and the economic boom resulting from consumers' demand pent up during war years, saved Eisenhower from any necessity for much thought, let alone imagination. As for his rambling and almost incoherent discourses in the White House — why, one marvelled that the general government was carried on at all. A man with frequent access to the White House, in 1953, would tell Kirk that at first the staff had endeavored to persuade President Eisenhower to read certain important documents; he did not do so. Then they had prepared brief summaries of those documents; he did not read those either. They found that they could explain grave concerns to him only by large simplified graphs and diagrams, exhibited on a wall, with a pointer to indicate what they signified. Robert Taft could have guided him, and was very willing to; but Taft died when Eisenhower had been only a few months in office.*

*In 1955, at Marcia Davenport's house on the East River, Kirk would meet with several people who had been active in supporting Eisenhower's candidacy for the Republican nomination and against Stevenson. They had been quite cut

Such was the quality of imagination possessed by the amiable gentleman elected chief executive in November 1952. The liberals' political imagination was exhausted, but it seemed as if the conservatives' political imagination had not yet been born.

Except for an isolated public man here or there, in Congress or out of it, the popular conservative impulse seemed quite leaderless in 1952. It had no organization and no serious journals or other modes of intelligent expression. As Richard Brookhiser was to write in *National Review* in 1981,

> *The Conservative Mind* appeared at a time when the very title seemed a paradox. The American right wing was an intellectual rag-tag, about as coherent as the Iranian parliament: robber barons and free-enterprisers; Communists turned Americans; America Firsters turned McCarthyites; Midwestern Republicans and Confederates; with Peter Viereck on the sidelines whispering all the while that the True Prince was Franklin D. Roosevelt. Even the poets whom Russell Kirk admired had no practical effect, hardly any practical interest; to the extent they mucked in politics at all, they seemed content to follow an antique drum.

Conservatism is the negation of ideology — as H. Stuart Hughes would put it a few years later. But a conservative impulse, if denied intelligent leadership and moral imagination, may be diverted banefully into ideological fanaticism; there had been seen something of that sort in Germany, although the thinking German conservatives had held out against Hitler, often to their destruction. No clear and present danger existed in the United States, about 1952, that conservatives' frustration would take the form of a totalist movement. But it remained conceivable that people of conservative impulses might descend into mere silliness, adopting an ideology of absurdity; some folk waved the banner of "libertarianism," a genteel form of anarchism.

Among these ideologues of the alleged Right, the most conspicuous was Ayn Rand, the author of an ideological novel of extreme

---

off from Eisenhower since he had entered the White House and were puzzled as to the sources from which he obtained advice. Did it all come from that hard-bitten politician Sherman Adams, guarding Eisenhower's door — Governor Adams, who had been given a vicuña coat?

and ruthless individualism entitled *The Fountainhead;* later her novel *Atlas Shrugged* would have tremendous sales. Miss Rand, born in Russia, made a living in Hollywood. Communism has been called the inversion of Christianity; Ayn Rand, reacting against practical communism, negated the negation. But she did not turn back to Christianity or any other religion: she was a militant atheist and materialist. She devised a curious ideology called Objectivism, in the social form of which Communist commissars would be supplanted, in effect, by capitalist commissars: with them, as with their Marxist equivalents, getting and spending would be the whole aim of human existence — plus some rather brutal sexual activity. Objectivism would wax during the Fifties and wane during the Seventies. It won the allegiance of a number of *Playboy* bunnies, among others.

Hating collectivism and sentimentality, Ayn Rand was determined that the modern world must rid itself of what she called "altruism" — that is, the theological virtue of charity — and exalt self-interest. Literally she would have put the dollar sign in the place of the cross. At every opportunity she preached the doctrine of "the virtue of selfishness." It is a sign of metaphysical madness that the ideological zealot insists upon his followers' total acceptance of the most repugnant and improbable of his doctrines; so was it with Ayn Rand. If one will concede that selfishness is a virtue, one will concede anything: even a man perfectly selfish himself works against his own interest if he urges other folk to be equally selfish; it is as if a burglar, moved by principle, should urge his neighbors to rob his own house.

Other varieties of the illusion called libertarianism were somewhat less crazy than Objectivism, but all were fantastically impractical. Many libertarians thought Soviet Russia no real menace: free trade and cordial handshakes would work happy conciliation; they would sweep away the state almost wholly, or perhaps altogether, as Marx aspired to. Somehow enlightened self-interest would cure all the ills to which flesh was heir. These groups constituted merely what T. S. Eliot called "a chirping sect," petty political sectaries of the sort Burke pictured as "the insects of the hour," noisy as they were ineffectual, ideological cliques forever splitting into sects still smaller and odder, but rarely conjugating.

It was inconceivable that these libertarians, whose only conservative aspect was their attachment to private property, could transform the United States into a utopia of moral negation and no recognizable rule of law. Yet they appealed to the strong individualistic strain in the American character, with its virtues and its vices. So it was quite conceivable that under certain circumstances they might pervert the popular conservative impulse into theater of the absurd, at the very time when a responsible conservatism of right reason and imagination was required to maintain a tolerable civil social order and to renew a personal order. So far as elections went, the good old causes of Bimetallism, Single Tax, or Prohibition enjoyed a better prospect of success in 1952 than did Libertarianism. But libertarian nonsense might make inroads upon conservative common sense. Otherwise libertarians were not worth writing about, in the early Fifties or later.

Kirk had meant his book *The Conservative Mind* to be a guide to politics as the art of the possible, as far removed from the varieties of anarchism as from varieties of socialism and of liberalism. He had meditated on the subject for a long while, and had been four years in the preparation of the book. He had not anticipated that it would appear at precisely the right time.

For at the beginning of the Fifties, the West and much of the rest of the world stood in need of a conservative renewal. The pace of change had been too rapid — in politics, in morals, in technology, in shifts of population, in methods of production, in patterns of living — ever since 1914, say, or perhaps for two centuries past. Two world wars had ravaged half the globe, doing even more mischief through their destruction of customs, institutions, and settled patterns of life than through their physical devastation. A series of violent revolutions had established squalid oligarchies or dictatorships far more oppressive than the regimes that they had overthrown. The reign of law, the traditions of civility, the sense of community, and the very family were shaken even in those countries that had escaped war and revolution. Clearly this was a time for the restoration of public and personal order, for settling down and healing wounds.

Samuel Taylor Coleridge had written that Permanence and Progression exist in a healthy tension within a tolerable society. If, then, one might identify Permanence with the conservative impulse and interest, and Progression with the liberal impulse and interest, it was high time at the beginning of the Fifties to advance the claims of Permanence, of the conservative understanding of human nature and society. It might be otherwise in a different age: in some old Egyptian or Peruvian society, where the dead hand of routine lay heavy upon everyone and nothing seemed to alter but for the worse, it would have been well to advance the claims of Progression, of healthful innovation. But mankind in the twentieth century did not suffer from stagnation. On the contrary, the pace of change was centrifugal and vertiginous; the center could not hold; generation could not link with generation. The nineteenth-century doctrine of sure Progress stood refuted by events, and liberals' meliorism was undone. If humankind should continue to progress in the same direction, it would progress to a precipice, and over that precipice. There was needed most urgently, by the Fifties, a renewed preference for the old and tried, against the new and untried.

Such reflections had caused Kirk to write his large exercise in the history of ideas and of institutions. The need for a serious book of this character had seemed to him, even when he was an undergraduate, so obvious that he had assumed the existence of a number of writers at work upon conservative studies. Yet the years passed, and still no such book was published. Then he had undertaken the task himself, despite his limitations; and when his book at length was published, he found that no one else had been writing so ambitious an account of this important and timely subject.

The book was a work of intellectual history, with considerable reference to institutions and political parties, from the middle of the eighteenth century to the middle of the twentieth. With the exception of a section on Tocqueville, it was confined to British and American writers and public men: to have attempted to extend the work to the European continent, or even farther afield, would have required two more volumes at least. At first, knowing how conservatives had been beaten back during two centuries from one ditch to another, Kirk meant to give his book the title *The Conservatives' Rout;* but his publisher, somewhat more sanguine, persuaded him to alter that to *The Conservative Mind, from Burke to Santayana.* More than Kirk had anticipated, his book would do something to convert that rout into a rally.

Kirk had hoped that his book might open eyes to a central concept of politics, not born yesterday, by which the claims of freedom and the claims of order may be kept in a healthy tension, avoiding extremes. In other words, the book was a lesson in normative politics, historically considered, expounding and criticizing the literature of that subject. At the time of its publication, American liberalism was intellectually and morally desiccated; American radicalism was confined to little knots of eccentrics; American libertarianism, patently absurd. Thus *The Conservative Mind* rushed in, perhaps where angels fear to tread, to fill that vacuum of intellect and imagination which nature abhors.

While still at St. Andrews, Kirk had been reasonably confident that his book would attract attention and exert some enduring influence. He had written it carefully and with conviction — in what has been called evocative prose. He summoned up dead authors, dead statesmen, dead controversies; also he evoked readers' memories. Concepts and phrases had seemed to bombard his consciousness from outside, as they did the imagination of men so diverse as Albert Einstein and St. John Perse.* But he had not expected the huge splash, literary and political, that his book made when it was tossed into the American pond in April 1953. It was as if a thoughtful multitude had been awaiting a novel intellectual event.

There had already been built up a body of scholarship derived from the works of Edmund Burke, the greatest of British political writers. All profound political movements draw their strength from some earlier body of belief: twentieth-century socialism from the Marx of the middle of the nineteenth century; Russian revolutionary violence from French Jacobinism; radical liberalism from Rousseau, whom Burke had called "the insane Socrates of the National Assembly." Kirk's source of wisdom was Edmund Burke, and by 1952 a good many other thinking people had rediscovered Burke. Kirk came to know many of these scholars in 1951 and 1952, particularly Ross J. S. Hoffman of Fordham University, with whom he traveled in Ireland; Carl B. Cone, who wrote a two-volume life of Burke; Thomas Copeland, who produced the new grand edition of Burke's correspondence; and a dozen others. He formed a close friendship with Peter Stanlis, then at the University of Detroit, to whose new book *Edmund Burke and the Natural Law* Kirk wrote a foreword. Kirk found a powerful intellectual ally in Robert Nisbet, whose book

---

*For Einstein's and Perse's conversation about "original" concepts in physical science and in poetry, see Andre Maurois, "The Illusions of Science," in his book *Illusions* (The George B. Pegram Lectures), 1968.

The Quest for Community was published in the same year as *The Conservative Mind.**

Kirk's appeal to the high authority of Burke began as a trumpet blast in the summer of 1950 in an essay in *Queen's Quarterly* entitled "How Dead Is Edmund Burke?" This was the first of an outpouring of essays and books about Burke as the source of the renewal of order. From the typewriters of Kirk and a score of other writers an intellectual counter-revolution had commenced. "History begins with Burke," Lord Acton wrote. Also there begins with Burke the modern understanding that the great problem of politics is the maintenance of a tolerable tension between the claims of order and the claims of freedom.

Soon talk of Burke was heard on every campus. Presently, at a gathering of intelligent undergraduates who had just listened to a Kirk lecture, a wag was heard murmuring,

"From Burke to Kirk and back again,
We move from age to age."

The Conservative Mind Breaches the Walls

Henry Regnery Company brought out the book. (Alfred Knopf would have published it, had Kirk agreed to reduce it in length by half; for years Knopf would resent bitterly Kirk's having taken back the typescript from him.) Henry Regnery, whose book-publishing venture was only a few years old, already had published books by Max Picard, Robert Hutchins, Victor Gollancz, Ernst Jünger, Mortimer Smith, Montgomery Belgion, Romano Guardini, Gabriel Marcel, and other writers of distinction; also a good many books dealing with the Second World War and current affairs. Regnery was then, and is now, the principal publisher of writings of a conservative cast — though not books of that inclination exclusively.**

*An account of these intellectual developments and of the friendship between Stanlis and Kirk can be found in the anthology *The Unbought Grace of Life: Essays in Honor of Russell Kirk,* ed. James Person (Peru, Illinois: Sherwood Sugden, 1994), pp. 31-50.

**Henry Regnery, man of literary and musical talents, was to publish nine more books by Kirk, plus a whole series of Regnery paperback classics edited by Kirk. Kirk often visited Henry and Eleanor (who came of an old Philadelphia

"I got my job through the *New York Times*," Kirk might say, for the marked approbation of that paper's *Book Review* could make any book a best-seller, while its disapprobation or its ignoring of a new book could be an author's disaster. Promptly upon publication of *The Conservative Mind,* the *Times Book Review* printed a lengthy review, with pictures, by Gordon Chalmers, president of Kenyon College, most heartily commending Kirk's study. "The author of *The Conservative Mind* is as relentless as his enemies, Karl Marx and Harold Laski, considerably more temperate and scholarly, and in passages of this very readable book, brilliant and even eloquent," Chalmers wrote. "It is history as well as argument. Familiar decades and political theories and controversies which usually, in our lifetime, have been illuminated by a searchlight from the left, are here revealed in unfamiliar highlights and shadows by Mr. Kirk's dexter beam." For some weeks, the *Times* continued to list the book in its column of recommendations.

It was taken up lengthily in other major papers as well — for one, by August Heckscher in the *Herald-Tribune;* even the Kirkus Book Review Service, usually acerbic, had kind things to say. Harrison Smith for the Saturday Review Syndicate, John Chamberlain in the *Chicago Tribune,* William Henry Chamberlin in the *Wall Street Journal,* a conspicuous review in *Fortune,* and other reviewers and review media praised this innovating book.

After some hesitation, *Time* magazine, on July 6 — with George Washington's picture on its cover — devoted its entire book section for that issue to *The Conservative Mind,* with several pictures and much praise. To write that review, *Time* had borrowed from its sister magazine *Fortune* an editor looked upon as *Fortune's* liberal, Max Ways. Someone told Kirk that the book converted Ways to conservative ways; certainly his review converted a great many *Time* readers. This conspicuous attention sold out the book's first printing immediately.

Quaker family) at their happy, antiquated house in Hinsdale, Illinois, and entertained the four Regnery children. Henry was the most intelligent and courageous publisher in the country, rowing against the intellectual tide. They became close friends and allies. They traveled together in northern Italy and Switzerland, and also met from time to time in London. Regnery introduced Kirk to Wyndham Lewis, Roy Campbell, Max Picard, and other European and American authors published by the firm of Regnery.

After some delay — Regnery having much underestimated the probable sales of Kirk's book — a larger second printing was made available. Over the next three decades, *The Conservative Mind* would go through six revised editions (including the London edition by Faber and Faber, which T. S. Eliot brought out), many printings, various paperback printings by two different houses, a Spanish translation, and a German one. Few politico-historical books in the twentieth century have enjoyed such a record — or so much influence, direct and indirect.

The weeklies and quarterlies took it up — though, curiously, not the leading monthlies. John Crowe Ransom reviewed it at length for the *Kenyon Review*, Brainard Cheney for the *Sewanee Review*; it was approved by Clinton Rossiter in the *American Political Science Review*, by John Hallowell in another political-science journal. In a third political-science quarterly, the socialistic reviewer wrote that "aphorisms burst from Kirk's pen like bombs." *Partisan Review* published *two* long reviews in different numbers — not converted, but impressed; that magazine's editors even attended a party for Kirk. The *Yale Review*'s piece by L. P. Curtis reinforced the book's reputation. Norman Thomas and Francis Biddle (who had been Roosevelt's attorney general) reviewed it in unconservative publications; they were opposed, but after their fashion respectful.

Among the reviewers in German publications were two famous men, Golo Mann and Wilhelm Röpke; they endorsed the book unreservedly. In Britain, after the appearance of the London edition, it was reviewed by other scholars and writers of importance, among them Michael Oakeshott, Colin Clark (in a four-part series in successive numbers of the *Tablet*), George Catlin, Marcus Cunliffe, and Christopher Hollis. Some time was required for doctrinaires of Left and Right to recover from this breaching of their walls by *The Conservative Mind*. Two years later, Frank Meyer denounced the book, in the pages of the *Freeman,* as "collectivism rebaptized": an extreme individualist, Meyer (formerly a Communist) suspected Kirk of being a Trojan horse within the conservative camp. He was not alone: some persons who thought of themselves as conservatives took approbation of a book by the *New York Times* as *prima facie* evidence of iniquity.

All this attention to Kirk's second book would assure, during the next few years, reviews of his later books in influential quarters:

Harper's, for instance, would defend his *Academic Freedom* against Kirk's adversaries. *Time* and *Newsweek* both would publish articles in which Kirk was described as one of a highly select band of "America's leading intellectuals" (he being the only conservative so denominated) — a description not wholly to Kirk's relish. W. T. Couch warned Kirk that an initial grand success of this sort might be followed by defamation; thirty years later, Couch would write to him that he was astonished at Kirk's continuing reputation and influence.

R. A. Nisbet, whose important and enduring book *The Quest for Community* was published soon after *The Conservative Mind,* told Kirk that *Mind* was the first book to have broken the barriers erected by America's liberal dominations and powers. Indeed it would open the way for a spate of other books about conservatism or by conservatives not ashamed of swimming against the tide — nay, even, in August Heckscher's words about *The Conservative Mind,* welcoming "Mr. Kirk's proud justification" of the term "conservative."

Kirk's book made clear for many the signification of the word "conservative," so often confounded with nineteenth-century liberalism or with mere stodginess.* Some people who had assumed that they were liberals now discovered their own conservatism. *Mind* seemed to attract lawyers, doctors, and other professional people especially — perhaps because *Time* lay on their waiting-room tables. It was well received by Catholics, in part because of its emphasis upon Newman and Brownson. Thousands of Americans who never opened the book nevertheless were influenced by its tenets: for it was quoted over the decades, with or without acknowledgment, in many newspaper editorials and columns, on the electronic media of communication, in sermons and campaign speeches. Practical politicians were somewhat slow to become acquainted with the book, for men in public office tend to read little once they have left college and entered upon the hurly-burly of political candidacy: they are kept too busy speechifying and answering constituents' complaints. Yet as time passed, more and more public men came to know Kirk's name

---

*Kirk's favorite definition of the term is contained in a work of reference frequently consulted by him: Ambrose Bierce's *Devil's Dictionary.* "Conservative, n. A statesman who is enamored of existing evils, as distinguished from the Liberal, who wishes to replace them with others."

and something of his writings; judges, too. *Mind*'s ideas moved outward in circles of increasing circumference in the American pond.

One consequence for which Kirk had hoped, and which Anthony Harrigan of the Charleston *News & Courier* had told him to be of the first importance, was republication of many of the conservative writers discussed in *Mind*. Through Regnery's Gateway paperbacks, Kirk himself soon brought out, with his own prefaces, new printings of selected essays by Orestes Brownson, of Burke's *Reflections on the Revolution in France*, of J. Q. Adams's translation of Gentz's *American and French Revolutions Compared*, of Babbitt's *Literature and the American College*, of Bell's *Crowd Culture*, of Marcus Aurelius and Epictetus; later, a handsome new edition of Babbitt's *Democracy and Leadership*, published by Liberty Classics.

Kirk's examination of John Adams and John Quincy Adams helped to revive interest in their writings; Coleridge, too, and Calhoun. Kirk was allied with Arthur Schlesinger, Jr., in renewing attention to Orestes Brownson, and with John Lukacs in pointing out Tocqueville's enduring significance. His summaries of the work of James Fitzjames Stephen, Henry Maine, and W. E. H. Lecky had something to do, years later, with new editions of their books; also, perhaps, with the printing of paperback editions of some of Brooks Adams's books, and a second edition — after an elapse of a century and three quarters — of the works of Fisher Ames. Kirk had a hand (along with the larger hand of George Orwell) in bringing about fresh attention to George Gissing, who had been forgotten except for his *Private Papers of Henry Ryecroft* and *New Grub Street;* but now biographical and critical studies of Gissing appeared, and many of his novels would be reprinted during the Seventies. When, in 1950, Kirk had published an essay on Gissing and had talked of writing a life of Gissing, a man in London publishing had scoffed: who would be interested in Gissing? The same person, in the *Times Literary Supplement*, sneered at *The Conservative Mind. Sed vincit* Gissing, apostate from socialism.

So it was that *The Conservative Mind* — working through a kind of intellectual osmosis and popularized through newspapers and mass-audience magazines, radio and even television commentators, and other media of opinion — gradually helped to alter the climate of political and moral opinion. A generation later, Kirk's works would be cited and quoted by the president and the vice president of the United States.

War with Behemoth University

Kirk had become the most widely published member of the staff of the Basic College, MSC; indeed, his periodical publications were more numerous than all those of other members of the large staff combined. Under the policy of publish or perish, Kirk might survive until the Greek calends. Yet when the members of the staff of the department of the history of civilization — poor serfs burdened by heavy teaching loads — were circularized as to their opinions on how large a part publication should count for in advancement and salary, Kirk replied, "No part": the function of the Basic College, he said, was teaching, not research.* The notion that all teachers should write and all writers should teach was a fallacy. As a college teacher, Kirk was tolerably successful, even with huge classes and the roar of construction machinery outside on the ever-expanding campus: he had the knack of dramatizing in his lectures historical episodes and figures. (In the Basic College, however, professors weren't supposed to lecture: they were told to carry on a Socratic dialogue with perhaps fifty students — sometimes more — simultaneously. And the educational theory of Professor Hopkins on one end of the log and a student on the other end requires that student to be eager for knowledge; at MSC in 1953, few students were.)

From its beginning, the Basic College was a blunder and a boondoggle. It was designed to provide "general education" for freshmen and sophomores; its program certainly was generalized, but it was not education. Initially, six departments — natural science, physical science, written and spoken English, literature and fine arts, history of civilization, and effective living — offered to teach all things to all men and all women. While Kirk was abroad in 1952, a reorganization had occurred. The departments of natural science and of physical science had been consolidated, imposing a hopeless task upon teachers of the sciences, for only an abstract and

---

*During 1953, Kirk published thirteen essays or articles and five lengthy book reviews in serious periodicals: *Southwest Review, Journal of the History of Ideas, The Month, The South Atlantic Quarterly, The Sewanee Review, The Pacific Spectator, University of Toronto Quarterly, The Church Quarterly Review, History Today, Queen's Quarterly, The Review of Politics, The Western Political Quarterly, The Yale Review*. Also one short story of his appeared: "What Shadows We Pursue," based upon an eerie experience of his as bookseller.

ignorant educationist (of such was the College's board of examiners composed) could have supposed that all these sciences (including mathematics) have much in common except that word "science." The departments of effective living and of literature and fine arts were abolished, some of their functions being transferred to surviving departments. History of civilization became "humanities," and upon this department were inflicted most of the former functions of the two effaced departments.

Even before having dumped upon it the functions of literature and fine arts and of effective living, the poor department of the history of civilization had labored under insuperable difficulties. Professor and students raced through a fat, dull textbook, all the way from primitive man to President Truman, a blur of Good Guys and Bad Guys: the best possible vindication of Alexander Pope's admonition that a little learning is a dangerous thing. There was no leisure to drink deep from the Pierian spring. As the department's chairman confessed, only a thin veneer of culture could be bestowed upon the students: "But it's surprising how many of them are successful later in life." What were nine-tenths of the students looking for, anyway? Why, certification and subsequent money — not wisdom and virtue. And now the members of this department were required also to veneer the students thinly with literature, fine arts, and a compound of philosophy, sociology, and erotic knowledge. Bring on more students! The dean had proposed to entitle the new consolidated department The Department of Man; in this, though in naught else, he found himself restrained by the staff.

Kirk went to Scotland in the summer of 1953, while all this compost was steaming. There he lived in the eighteenth-century cottage at Kellie, the grieve's cottage where Archibald Constable, the Napoleon of booksellers, had been born; he wrote essays and short stories in solitude, and enjoyed leisure enough to think of what he ought to do about Michigan State. Meanwhile *The Conservative Mind* was fascinating reviewers and scandalizing liberals and radicals. It would be sin and shame to linger longer in the Basic College's Garden of Attalus, injecting into sham students pseudo-intellectual nostrums that would do them more harm than good. He was all in favor of liberal learning — aye, in favor of genuine general education; no academic specialist, he did not desire to teach graduate courses; but why live a lie?

From Kellie, he sent to the head of his department his letter of resignation. If he were needed, he would return to teach for the fall term, he said; but after that he must depart, for conscience' sake. The chairman replied, very tardily, that Kirk's views considered, it was honorable for him to resign; but he would be needed for the fall. Kirk went back.

Having arrived at MSC, he was informed that he would not be needed after all. Although he had no money and no immediate prospects, Kirk was not discomposed; he would go north to Mecosta. The College's public-relations people gave it out that Kirk had resigned "to pursue a literary career" — which at the time he had not even thought of doing. When a reporter from the student newspaper came round to him, Kirk told him his true reasons; and the interview was published. At that, the College's office of public relations heaped vituperation upon him; his department head and a colleague even went on radio to defame him. This treatment vexed his friend Richard Dorson, the folklore man, who asked a meeting of the local chapter of the American Association of University Professors to protest such intemperate assaults on a scholar of international reputation. But one member said, "Let's get back to discussing the dangers of McCarthyism": that was the end of that. At this juncture, there appeared on the campus a journalist from *Time,* intending to write a piece about the bubbling intellectual activity at Big Ten schools. He asked to see Kirk. "I don't know where you could find him," said his cicerone. "Let's go talk with Duffy Daugherty" — the head football coach.

Kirk, whose wants were simple, was somewhat amused at all this. He had no cash on hand, as usual, but he had reputation. Once his resignation became widely known, he received invitations or approaches from better institutions than MSC: the University of Chicago, the University of Michigan, the University of California at Riverside, Yale, two Catholic universities, Kenyon College, Wabash College, others. Even John Hannah, president of MSC, sent him a polite letter, inviting him to confer; it was whispered to Kirk by others that Hannah, alarmed at all this publicity, intended to offer this annoying dissident some exalted post by way of conciliation — temporarily, anyway. Kirk declined to see him. "He seems to have burned his bridges behind him," said one officer of the College. That martial analogy pleased Kirk: indeed he had meant to do just that. Next year he published in *Collier's Yearbook* a detailed account of this fracas at

MSC. In their discomfiture at Kirk's resignation, the MSC oligarchs had forgotten Kirk's ready access to journals of opinion and even to works of reference.

That battle won, Kirk went up by bus to Mecosta. It would not have done to serve for hire at an institution so deprived or depraved of imagination as was MSC by 1953. Nor was he tempted by the kind approaches of superior institutions: he really did not desire academic community, although it would have been better than MSC's academic collectivism. Now and again, in later years, he would be visiting distinguished professor, for short periods, on one campus or another. As for a "literary career," he never had thought that possible at any stage in his young life. Still, perhaps he could earn a competence by writing articles and reviews, it costing little enough to live at Mecosta; he was being asked to lecture (with fees), too. The example of Scott-Moncrieff scarcely would encourage anybody to look for riches through writing; nor the example of George Gissing, whose *New Grub Street* was among Kirk's favorite novels. Nor are the royalties from such sober books as *The Conservative Mind,* critical successes though they may attain, sufficient ordinarily to sustain their authors; for that matter, Kirk had been paid no advance whatsoever for *Mind.* Yet as things turned out, Kirk would become a professional man of letters, one of a tiny tribe, for the rest of his life.

Russell Kirk, J.P. of Morton Township

At Mecosta, among its lakes, where the blue heron flapped over the swamps and the beaver still splashed in his pond, there lived in the Old House Kirk's widowed and blind grandmother, Eva Pierce, and his two great-aunts, Norma and Frances Johnson, among their souvenirs. Their existence was simple and unchanging; they seemed content enough. They could be humorous; they were kind to Russell, that stormy petrel of the family. From the great-aunts Kirk garnered many tales of Mecosta life, especially its grimmer side, and those went into his vignettes and stories.

Next door, in a cedar-post cabin, lived his little Aunt Fay, with her husband, Glenn Jewell. Kirk took many of his meals with them, Glenn looked after some of his affairs, the Jewells became as parents. Title to the Old House and its grounds, and to the Johnson forty acres, now was in Glenn Jewell's name; Kirk soon bought the property from him for six thousand dollars. On the upper floor of the Old House, he fitted up for himself two rooms and a bathroom: the Spanish room became his study and library, the Red Room his bed-chamber. He paid a monthly stipend to great-aunts and grandmother; life was tranquil.

Up here his great-uncle Raymond had kept his books, which Kirk had inherited. Not everybody quite liked coming up those tall stairs to these high-ceilinged silent rooms: Kirk himself, now and again, would pause at the foot of the staircase, fancying the presence of something; but nothing showed itself. Years later, one young woman insisted that she had perceived near the stair-foot a large uncanny cat — which, rather like Alice's Cheshire Cat, inexplicably vanished. Be that as it may, the Spanish room was conducive to the writing of ghostly tales, and Kirk, seated at his grandfather's library table and employing his great-uncle's archaic L. C. Smith Model No. 1 typewriter, wrote several such — soon published on either side of the Atlantic.

A neighbor owned a large brick building or complex of build-ings, most of it in the form of a gambrel-roofed or "Dutch" barn, which during the Second World War had been a little factory for children's oaken stools and adults' cigarette-rollers; Kirk bought that building and converted it into his library, when the weight of the books shelved upstairs in the Old House had begun to warp the house's beams. An old man five feet high did the carpentry for a wage of a dollar an hour, and Kirk's uncle Potter Jewell installed plumbing.

Potter was a hearty and hardy outdoorsman, admired by every-body, infinitely gentle and thoughtful with little Fay. They had no children. He was cheerful always, even after emphysema began to take hold upon him. As township supervisor and member of the county board of supervisors, he kept a kindly eye upon the township's poor, forlorn, and aged — of whom there were a good many. His good manners were natural to him. What an admirable companion! Kirk would take this aunt and uncle with him on two extended trips to Britain and the Continent.

Still farther north, at Baldwin, Kirk's father and stepmother settled in the Fifties, moving up from Detroit; his stepmother, Billie, had been born at Baldwin. The younger Russell Kirk bought for them a large and handsome old house, always coveted by Billie, and restored it; somehow he always contrived to find the money for such restorations, which became a passion with him. The Baldwin house, too, had its spectre, "Herman," a previous occupant and a very convincing ghost, who was in the habit of tramping about heavily upstairs, and seemingly shifting the heavy furniture there, when only one person was downstairs.

The elder Russell Kirk continued to drive an engine on the Chesapeake and Ohio, which ran through Baldwin to the lake port of Ludington, so long as his health would permit him to work. He was plagued with heart disease, severe diabetes, blindness presently, Lord knew what else; yet he lived patiently on to a ripe old age with no vices, not even bad temper. He never read anything his son wrote, but the younger Russell dedicated to him his *Enemies of the Permanent Things*. Later, after marrying Annette, Kirk would acquire a smaller house for his parents, next door to Piety Hill, and shift them down there, at their request. So Kirk had about him a congeries of elderly people, some of them very elderly; looking after them in one way or another would have bound him to Mecosta, even had he wished to go elsewhere for any great length of time — which he did not wish. One by one, the elder generation would drop away; Aunt Fay, by 1985, would be the last of them.

Obedient to the precept of Archilochus, Kirk had beaten a strategic retreat to Mecosta, that he might fight another day. From the Spanish Room, where he pounded away, usually at least twelve hours of the day, upon his inherited typewriter, he fired salvos at dull or cranky educationists, those of MSC in particular; these pieces were published in *National Review*, chiefly. He wrote for encyclopedias; he wrote prefaces for great books; he wrote for various weekly journals of opinion; he turned out several more books on that venerable L. C. Smith machine.

He had no regular income, no diversions except outdoor ones (chiefly exploring lakes, swamps, and Dead Stream in his boat), no wife, and no car — until he acquired a 1937 Chevrolet, high off the ground, useful on sand trails and in pastures where the stumps from the lumbering days remained. Mecosta had good walking country still, along deer-hunters' tracks, and an inveterate walker Kirk was. He was happy. He planted pines and spruces, thousands of them. Such was his life during the year after he had departed from Michigan State.

But it should not be thought that Kirk became such a recluse as did his contemporary Salinger, the author of *Catcher in the Rye*. The demand for his lectures quickened, on college campuses particularly, coast to coast; in one year of the Fifties, he would speak to nearly a hundred audiences. He lectured on everything under the sun, though on conservative thought most frequently. All this began for him with the Daly Lectures, at the University of Detroit, a series of six or eight evening talks to a general audience commenced very soon after his leaving MSC. The Detroit Jesuits at the University were infinitely civil to him; one of them coached him in public speaking. Lecturing, for years, was a more lucrative source of income than writing.

He was active in practical politics only in Michigan, and there principally as a campaigner against the abolition of rural schools: a fight that was lost. Not long after nearly all the rural schools had been wiped out of existence, it was discovered that in many ways they had been more effective than the consolidated monstrosities that had supplanted them; but the fell deed was done, thanks to the fallacious arguments of James B. Conant and his kind. Kirk had in common with Arthur Schlesinger, Jr. — with whom he debated once before a big crowd at Harvard, and whom he was to meet on other occasions — a detestation of Harvard's President Conant.

Of course he was active enough, on a national scale, in political and educational controversy. On request, he contributed several pieces (including an exchange with Schlesinger) to the *New York Times Magazine*. On the first occasion of these, an editor of that magazine interviewed him at the Century Club, in Manhattan. "How was it that you became the intellectual spokesman of the Republican party, Dr. Kirk?" the editor inquired.

At that moment — it was one of those incredible coincidences in one's life that tempt a man to fancy, with the Hindus, that all existence is *maya* — there passed by a gentleman who overheard this inquiry and stared with marked disfavor at Kirk; he could have played Envy in Marlowe's *Dr. Faustus*. "Hello, Emmett," said the *Times* man. "Dr. Kirk, have you met Emmett Hughes?"

Kirk hadn't until then, and never did again. Hughes was Nelson Rockefeller's man, a publicist for Liberal Republicanism who had yearned to be styled "the intellectual spokesman of the Republican party." And here, by some concitation of the backward devils, Hughes was compelled to witness this accolade bestowed upon that confounded conservative Kirk — and by the *New York Times!*

In plain fact, Kirk distinctly was not the intellectual spokesman of the Republican party. No hot partisan, he had not the least connection with the Eisenhower White House. But the Eisenhower administration possessing no true intellectual spokesman at all — doubtless it seemed to Eisenhower's people a superfluity or an impertinence, this notion of having to turn to intellect — the *Times* must dub someone or other such a Republican spokesman, to set against Professor Schlesinger, intellectual spokesman of the Democratic party. So knighted, Kirk drew his sword of imagination and hewed away at his friendly adversary Schlesinger, and other Democratic champions.

Thus elapsed Kirk's first year of emancipation from Michigan State, in Mecosta or Manhattan, Detroit or Los Angeles. He was awarded a Guggenheim Fellowship for a study of British society, to commence in the autumn of 1954; on November 6, he landed at Liverpool; out of some months of rambling in Scotland and England would emerge most of his collection *Beyond the Dreams of Avarice.* He would be back at Mecosta by April 1955, after becoming better acquainted with western Europe, as well as with Scotland. No, he was no recluse — even though his Aunt Fay accused him of being that.

The prophet was not without honor in his own land. At the behest of Supervisor Jewell, the citizenry of Morton Township, almost as one man, elected Dr. Kirk to the high office of justice of the peace, to fill a vacancy on the Republican slate. (He never would be elected to any other office, except that of delegate to various county and state Republican conventions.) A few years later, justices of the peace would be abolished by a new Michigan constitution; the office was far sunk in decay, statewide, during Kirk's several years of tenure. He never tried a speeding motorist; he would have been quite willing to marry young couples, especially if the brides were pretty, but none asked him to join her in wedlock. Nor did he collect any emoluments, save on one thrilling occasion that he was to record fictionally, later, in his short story "Fate's Purse."

This was a search for treasure trove. There dwelt a short distance east of Mecosta, on a farm held for a century by the same family that came from the Mosel to homestead it, a miser generally referred to as Jingo Cracky — that being his favorite ejaculation. He was long and lank as a Dürer figure of Famine incarnate, and as dirty a being as one could hope to behold. He had cattle, fruit, many hives of bees, crops; he spent next to nothing, ingeniously, outdoing even Scots of the old sort in frugality; he would buy week-old bread and store it in his deep-freeze — his only indulgence, that contraption, but paying for itself — and not consume it until satisfied that he must yield to the demands of the flesh.

While Kirk gloried in his judicial office, Jingo Cracky came to a timely end, at an advanced age. His drowned corpse was discovered in a stream in his woods, his old tractor sitting upon it: apparently he had gone down there to cut more firewood — though scores of cords of it were piled, rotting, by his desolate house — had climbed off to adjust the machine somehow, and had been trapped when the tractor started up of its own accord.

Supervisor Potter Jewell was appointed administrator of Jingo Cracky's estate. Jingo had laid away treasure on earth, if not in heaven, everybody knew; and it was suspected that a portion of his riches lay buried within his domicile. Recently there had been an unsuccessful attempt to break into Mecosta's bank nocturnally; some boys had robbed drawers and candy machines at the school; an old man, perhaps mistaken for Jingo Cracky, had been attacked by two-footed predators. Burglary was a rare offense then in Mecosta County, nearly all households having deer rifles and other weapons ready to hand. Still, an attempt might be made on the house of the late Jingo; it would be well to search for Jingo's hoard before others should.

Potter telephoned the undersheriff. "Today we're going down to Jingo's place, Ed. Russell's buckling on his six-shooter as justice of the peace, and you buckle on yours, in case anybody makes trouble for us, and we'll see what we will see."

They took with them the brother of Jingo, his heir apparent, a Lansing accountant, quite so parsimonious as Jingo. The two had fought whenever they met, but one could understand Jingo's motive in bequeathing his presumptive fortune to the accountant. One could fancy Jingo declaring, "There's one thing you've got to say for him: he'd save my money."

Kirk carried a long spade: as the youngest of the party, he would do the digging. He charged the estate, later, for his manual labor, and was paid: his sole recompense for years of judicial service to his fellow citizens.

Jingo Cracky's forlorn little house would have been pathetic evidence — to anyone ignorant of the dead man's habits — of an extreme poverty worse than that of any welfare client. In the bedroom, a single worn blanket lay upon the cot. The man's wardrobe had consisted of two pairs of overalls, in one of which he had been buried; the other, stiff with dirt, was hung on a wire hanger suspended from the ceiling, looking as if some invisible being were occupying the garment.

The four treasure-seekers descended to the stone-walled deep cellar, where hundreds of jars of preserves, the unconsumed accumulation of years of Jingo's obsessive home canning, lay as if in a catacomb. Executor, undersheriff, and justice of the peace were led by the heir apparent to an inner room with a floor of sand. "Now of course I don't know where my brother kept his money," said Jingo's brother, "but if I were you, *I'd dig right over there!*"

Kirk dug, and unearthed several glass jars. Opened, they were found to contain little cylindrical rods of something, every roll sewn about with newspaper. Kirk cut them open: every roll, in the first five jars, was composed of greenbacks of various denominations. But within the sixth jar, the newspaper wrappings contained merely corncobs. "Why corncobs?" asked Potter, astonished. "Could anybody have substituted corncobs for twenty-dollar bills?" At this, the heir apparent, previously garrulous, fell silent.

They took the contents of the jars upstairs to the kitchen table to count the money. Kirk, as teller, had recorded several thousand dollars — when a hulking shape loomed in the doorway.

That robber gang, at this juncture? Kirk's imagination was suffused with visions of glory. In the mind's eye appeared the newspaper heading, "Mecosta J.P. Wipes Out Bandits." Quicker than Bat Masterson, he was drawing his revolver and thumbing back the hammer; but Ed the undersheriff cried, "That's a federal man!"

So the hulking shape was: an agent of the Internal Revenue Service. For years Jingo Cracky had written on his income-tax forms "No Income." The mills of IRS grind slow, but they grind exceeding fine.

Potter, as executor, eventually discovered assets far exceeding the value of the cellar hoard: mortgages on many farms, stocks, bonds. Jingo Cracky had been one of the richer men of the county. "Thy money perish with thee, because thou hast thought that the gift of God may be purchased with money." Jingo had lived lifelong in misery, only that a brother-miser might inherit all he had saved. "Never save any money!" Kirk had learned from Bernard Iddings Bell. How wise an admonition, easily obeyed by a man of letters who never had money to spare!

On settlement day, Kirk presented his bill for ten dollars for manual labor and personal attendance, and Potter Jewell his substantial bill as executor of the estate. There were present the heir apparent and his grown son. Tight-lipped, they raised no objection to these charges; doubtless their lawyer had informed them that the executor and the justice of the peace were charging merely the minimum under Michigan statutes.

Then Mecosta's garage proprietor presented a bill for twenty-nine dollars and seventy cents, his charge for removing from the creek bed the tractor that had drowned Jingo Cracky, repairing it, and returning it to the farm. At this, the heir apparent's son, chip off the old block, gasped in indignation, and cried loudly, "That just shows what people won't do for money!" Aye, as reading of Longinus had taught Kirk in college, "Love of money is the disease which makes men most grovelling and pitiful."

Such was Mecosta, Kirk's stamping ground in the *corrida* of the twentieth century. Whatever its deprivations, Mecosta served well enough as a base for forays against the antagonist world: Kirk never had understood how a man could get work done if he sat all day in an office at New York or Washington, at the mercy of all comers. From Mecosta he would sally forth frequently, meeting people of like mind.

Various people urged Kirk to stand for public office: the Michigan Board of Education, for a beginning, or election as delegate to Michigan's approaching constitutional convention; grander posts later, perhaps. But he possessed neither the money nor the leisure requisite for such campaigns; he was a workingman. Besides, the serious writer on politics, if he is skillful, in the long run exercises far more influence upon public opinion — and, indirectly, upon public policy — than most public men can hope to obtain. Later Kirk would be offered various posts of a cultural sort in the Nixon and the Reagan administrations; for the same reasons, he declined with thanks.

At various universities and colleges, chairs would have been provided for him: an "academic career." But Kirk was puzzled that anyone should think he would desire such an appointment. The meager, backbiting life of a university town did not attract him; nor did the crowd of half-literate "students" enticed to the campuses at the end of the Second World War, who objected vehemently to any tolerable intellectual discipline. The books and essays Kirk wrote would do far more to improve minds than could his sitting in some ugly little office, correcting test papers. Lecturing for a few weeks a year, as visiting distinguished professor, to selected students of some ability, or at least curious about the life of the mind, was all he could manage.

Of Jeremy Bentham, Leslie Stephen writes, "He had not the strong passions which prompt commonplace ambition, and cared little for the prizes for which most men will sacrifice their lives." That was true enough of Kirk, too, although Bentham and he had naught else in common. Kirk's refusal, about 1953, to take that tide in the affairs of men which leads on to fortune was not unwise. His renunciation gave him a life of independence (of the sort praised by classical philosophers), a congenial literary occupation, and a Mecostan existence unpolluted by carbon monoxide and other progressive poisons. Also it gave him opportunity to defend the Permanent Things against their numerous adversaries in many quarters, he not tied to any interest.

Kirk's decision meant that at Mecosta he would enjoy little social intercourse, unless outsiders came to him. This isolation made him the more productive of books, essays, and stories. When William F. Buckley, Jr., then engaged in founding *National Review*, visited Kirk to enlist him as a contributor to that new weekly, the convivial young gentleman from New York inquired what Kirk did for friends in this remote village. For answer, smiling, Kirk swept his hand to indicate the shelves of books on all four sides of the big room: there reposed his friends, men and women of letters. In 1955, Kirk remained very much a lone wolf, expecting or fearing he would be thus lupine lifelong. Seven years later, how his life would be transformed!

CHAPTER SEVEN

The Literature of Order

Among Illiberal Men of Letters

By the 1950s, liberalism was in the sere and yellow leaf imaginatively, although still dominant in the universities, in serious periodicals, and in the book trade. Lionel Trilling lamented this in *The Liberal Imagination,* published in 1950. He put it bluntly: "Our liberal ideology has produced a large literature of social and political protest, but not, for several decades, a single writer who commands our real literary imagination. We all respond to the flattery of agreement; but perhaps even the simplest reader among us knows in his heart the difference between that emotion and the real emotions of literature."

To the monumental literary figures of the twentieth century, Trilling went on, "the liberal ideology has been at best a matter of indifference." Proust, Joyce, Lawrence, Eliot, Yeats, and other writers had "no love of the ideas and emotions which liberal democracy, as known by our educated class, has declared respectable. So that we can say that no connection exists between our liberal educated class and the best of the literary minds of our time. And this is to say that there is no connection between the political ideas of our educated class and the deep places of the imagination."

Very true that was. Yet Trilling, in 1950, perceived no conservative imagination to challenge liberal dullness: "For it is the plain fact that nowadays there are no conservative or reactionary ideas in general circulation. . . . The conservative impulse and the reactionary impulse do not, with some isolated and some ecclesiastical exceptions, express themselves in ideas but only in action or in irritable mental gestures which seek to resemble ideas."*

Three years after Trilling wrote those sentences, *The Conservative Mind*, a rock tossed into the stagnant pond of American intellectualism, made waves not to Trilling's liking. In *The Liberal Imagination*, he had suggested that a renewal of the conservative imagination might healthily stimulate the decayed liberal imagination: "It is not conducive to the real strength of liberalism that it should occupy the intellectual field alone." But after the publication of *The Conservative Mind* and its friendly reception, Trilling no longer professed to welcome a conservative challenge; he even deleted a commendatory reference to Burke that had appeared in the first printing of his book. The liberal trumpet had been blown; the challenger had appeared, surprisingly; the liberal sword stuck in its scabbard.

The New York Times Book Review, accurately, had categorized *The Conservative Mind* as *belles lettres* — and for several weeks had listed that exercise in imagination among recommended new books. Although scholars in political science paid considerable attention to Kirk, he was not of their number, declaring that politics was an art, not science. *The Conservative Mind* admitted him to such quarterlies of humane letters as *Sewanee Review, Kenyon Review,* and various British magazines; also to such magazines with strong literary emphasis as *Yale Review* and *The Month.* It was as historian of ideas and as literary critic that Kirk would write, even though from time to time he would be elevated to the dignity of distinguished visiting professor of political science. He meant to wake the moral imagination through the evocative power of humane letters.

Also the publication of Kirk's first two books attracted to him the attention of those illiberal writers — some of them already, or soon to be, among Trilling's "monumental figures" — to whom "the liberal ideology has been at best a matter of indifference." It would be erroneous to call them "writers of the Right," for some scarcely thought at all in political terms, and others knew that loose employment of the words "Left" and "Right" (borrowed from the nineteenth-century Chamber of Deputies in France) leads one into the trap of

---

*In the middle Fifties, Daniel Bell could discern only two genuinely conservative men of letters, lonely figures "without influence": Allen Tate and Russell Kirk.

ideological infatuation. Kirk's literary friends, some of them eminent, who rejected or ignored the liberal ideology may better be described as the literary party of order. It was order in the soul, chiefly, that interested them; but they knew, most of them, that the commonwealth too requires principles of order. Some of them were willing to be called conservatives, others not; labels are of no great consequence; they were no ideologues, no politicizers of humane letters. With George Gissing, they had come to understand that politics is the preoccupation of the quarter-educated — but that it cannot be abandoned wholly to the quarter-educated.

When Kirk rode into the lists of the literary tournament, at the beginning of the Fifties, the literary party of order stood in a forlorn minority; so it stands today. The literary party of disorder — an ill-sorted crew of nihilists, fanatic ideologues, and purveyors of violent sensation — were masters of the field; they are still, but now their hegemony is shaken somewhat.

Nature imitates art: so Oscar Wilde instructs us. Whether or not natural sunsets imitate Turner's painted sunsets, surely human nature is developed by human arts. "Art is man's nature," in Burke's phrase: modelling ourselves upon the creations of the great writer and the great painter, we become fully human by emulation of the artist's vision.

Or such is the upward way. But also there exists the path to Avernus, the way of degradation. The art of decadence and nihilism, the literature of meaningless violence and fraud, present us with the image of man unregenerate and triumphant in his depravity. This is the domain of the literary party of disorder.

In our time, the disciplines of humane letters and of scholarship are disputed in a Debatable Land by the partisans of order and the partisans of disorder. In this clash, often the enemies of the permanent things gain the advantage. Yet their victory is Pyrrhic; for in undoing order, they undo themselves. Preferring to reign in hell rather than to serve in heaven, they make a Waste Land, and are condemned to dwell therein. In Burke's words, "the law is broken, nature is disobeyed, and the rebellious are outlawed, cast forth, and exiled, from this world of reason, and order, and peace, and virtue, and fruitful penitence, into the antagonist world of madness, discord, vice, confusion, and unavailing sorrow."

The frontiers of that antagonist world of the rebels against nature and art have been extended, figuratively and literally, in our day; and many innocents have fallen trophy to the enemy. Through fanatic politics, the champions of disorder lay waste justice and freedom: a Pol Pot, having spent sufficient years in Parisian cafes imbibing Marxist dogmata, returns to Cambodia to slaughter a third of his nation. Somewhere in the pages of Sainte-Beuve one encounters the revolutionary playwright who gestures from his window toward the ferocious mob pouring down the boulevard: "See my pageant passing!"

Ideological servility in letters earns its ounce of gold at the devil's booth. T. S. Eliot touched upon this urbanely in his *Criterion* review of books by Leon Trotsky and V. S. Calverton, in 1933: "There are obvious inducements, besides that — never wholly absent — of simple conversion, to entice the man of letters into political and social theory which he then employs to revive his sinking fires and rehabilitate his profession."

In 1933, when Eliot wrote that telling rejection of Marxist criticism, Kirk was in high school, reading Trotsky's *History of the Russian Revolution* with a certain grudging admiration for the author but an abhorrence of the phenomenon. Trotsky rose in the antagonist world, and the antagonist world devoured him.

Without quite knowing it, Kirk joined the literary party of order upon having read Trotsky — and Rostovtzeff, too, in the same year. Kirk's first essay in a national magazine was published three years later; it had to do with the permanent things. Twenty years later, he found himself in the company of talented men and women of letters who had not surrendered to the antagonist world.

In this chapter there are set down observations about several American writers of the Fifties, friends and allies of Kirk; British and European vignettes of such people will be found in the following chapter. It is significant that none of the writers described here lived in New York City, the center of publishing, book reviewing, and literary cocktail parties: as T. S. Eliot put it, residence in New York City was the worst form of expatriation for American writers.

Bernard Iddings Bell, Polemical Canon

In an earlier chapter there was mentioned Kirk's correspondence, while a sergeant, with Albert Jay Nock. Kirk had just then begun to publish essays in quarterly reviews. Nock was very good about replying to Kirk's letters, possibly because Kirk was a soldier who approved Nock's opposition to Franklin Roosevelt's foreign policies. (Nock had written that the Principality of Monaco, or the Grand Duchy of Luxembourg, would have resorted to war with the United States if sent such an ultimatum as Cordell Hull, Secretary of State, had delivered to Japan.)

As was mentioned earlier, Nock and Kirk discussed Marcus Aurelius in their letters. The Emperor meditates upon the lovely ripeness of figs, just before they fall into deliquescence; and Kirk raised the question of whether this thought is an image of Roman society at its Antonine argentine perfection, on the eve of decadence. There is a certain fascination with decadence, of the sort remarked in the first century by Livy: "We Romans are in love with death." But Nock would not grant that any whiff of decadence hung about Marcus Aurelius himself.

Nock's individualism was so thoroughgoing that he could not endure those tender personal ties most men and women long for. He strode on solitary toward his latter end. "One has few companions [on the path to the river], latterly almost none, and one is content with that. One or two are willing to go the whole way with me, which troubles me a little, and I hope they will not insist. They are young, and taking this journey just for company would break the continuity of their lives, and be but a tedious business, besides."

This deliberate isolation was that of Marcus Aurelius, who enjoined himself, "Live as upon a mountain." Through letters, Kirk walked beside Nock, down the path to the river, to Nock's end.

Old Mr. Nock of Canaan, Connecticut, introduced Kirk through correspondence to "a gentleman of some intellectual distinction" (Nock's description), Dr. Bernard Iddings Bell — probably Nock's most intimate friend, so far as Nock admitted people to any degree of intimacy. Later, Bell and Kirk would spend many days together: at Chicago, in the Bells' apartment at the top of a baby skyscraper; in London, together with their common friend T. S. Eliot; at Scottish country houses, Balcarres in particular. But by that time, Nock had tramped all the way down to the river.

Canon Bell was the author of many small good books, nearly all of them now out of print: *In the City of Confusion, Beyond Agnosticism, The Church in Disrepute,* and others deserve restoration to booksellers' shelves. Late in his life, his *Crowd Culture* attracted considerable attention; his articles appeared in the pages of the *New York Times Magazine*. In the pages of *Commonweal* and elsewhere, Bell commended Kirk's first book and other writings. Friendship with this little bulldog of a canon was Kirk's direct opening to literary circles.

It is one of the marks of human decency, Eliseo Vivas remarks somewhere, to be ashamed of having been born into the twentieth century. With reason, Canon Bell excoriated our century. For broad influence, he was the most distinguished Episcopalian clergyman in the United States; he had an English reputation, too, and a large audience among many Catholics and many Protestant bodies. Famous as a preacher, he was also a powerful and clever writer, his books being sold in the tens of thousands. His sermons were read and discussed by a public few Christian apologists have reached since Victorian times. A High Churchman, he made no concessions to social gospellers, liberals, latitudinarians, modernists, humanitarians, or public-relations experts.

He was so hot against entrenched selfishness and stupidity that he was denounced as a communist; he was so hot against malign collectivism that he was denounced as an apologist for reaction. Such abuse delighted B. I., who rejoiced in a good fight. No one ever had the better of him in a battle of wits. Easily incensed, he was ready to forgive; and he was a man of honor scrupulous in distinguishing persons from opinions.

His life was one long fight. Only from a condition of voluntary poverty, Thoreau tells us, can a man justly criticize society; and Canon Bell did not hesitate to pay that forfeit. Although well rewarded as lecturer and author, he spent his income in good works and donated much of his own stipend when he was counselor to Episcopalian students at the University of Chicago. In educating his only son (who died at the threshold of manhood), in extensive travel, and in devotion to his ordained duties as priest, he spent his money as it came — and that on principle.

For when Bell was a little boy, he learned something from his grandmother. Straited in their means, his grandparents had been frugal, saving all their lives to build and furnish a house to their liking. In old age they achieved their aim, and their house was built and well plenished; and just then old Mrs. Bell discovered that she was suffering from an incurable cancer. Put to bed, she had her grandson called in, and said this to him: "Bernard, your grandfather tells me that they are going to have to put me under drugs soon, and then I will not be able to talk with you. So I wish to tell you now what I have learnt from life. I have had a long life, and rather a hard one, and I have learnt this: *Never save any money.*"

The anecdote and the tone were characteristic of B. I. Bell. He set himself to saving souls, instead, after studying history at the University of Chicago, and after working for a time as a paddy wagon–chasing newspaper reporter. In 1910 he was ordained a priest in the Episcopal Church; and his influence in that church became perceptible, even though often he stood in a forlorn minority at church convocations.

At the age of twenty-eight, he was dean of a cathedral (at Fond du Lac, Wisconsin); at thirty-two, he was ministering to the spiritual needs of fifty thousand sailors at Great Lakes Naval Training Station; at thirty-four, he became president of St. Stephen's College (now Bard College), where he served with distinction for fourteen years but resigned when the trustees would not support him in his code of manners and other matters. (He had insisted that students rise when a professor entered the classroom — a violation of democratic dogmata.)

To Bell, when he was president of St. Stephen's, came young Robert Hutchins, son of the president of Berea College, seeking a post as an instructor in English literature. Bell, who knew the elder Hutchins, inquired of the young man why he wished to teach: "Do you love English literature, Mr. Hutchins, or do you feel a vocation to teach, or what is your motive?"

"I want to earn enough money to put myself through law school," Hutchins answered, his arrogant head held high.

"Why should you earn the money?" Bell asked. "That's an awkward way to go about it. I know that college presidents do not get large salaries, but your father has many wealthy friends, any one of whom would be happy to lend you the money for law school; once successful as a lawyer, you could pay back the sum. Why not do that?"

"Because," said Hutchins, sustained by much self-assurance, "I don't mean to be obligated to anyone." Clearly he anticipated approval of such fine Emersonian self-reliance.

"Then, Mr. Hutchins, we don't want you at St. Stephen's."

Young Hutchins was angry: "Why not?"

"Because, Mr. Hutchins, we don't want anyone in this college who is too proud to be obligated to anybody."

Long later, when Bell spent years counselling Episcopalian students at the University of Chicago, Chancellor Hutchins studiously refrained from speaking to him. Christian humility was not among Hutchins's virtues, and soft answers were not among Bell's vices.

Bell stood against the degradation of the democratic dogma in American education, and he rallied round him many spirits, though there were times when he stood almost alone. His book *Crisis in Education* was one of the first to undertake demolition of vulgarized Deweyism. Bell was no respecter of the secular dogma that "one man is as good as another, or maybe a little better." Had we now a dozen more like him, we might cleanse the intellectual sty in the closing years of the twentieth century.

B. I. died poor, being blind and unable to lecture or write during his final year; it was saddening to sit with him then, as Kirk did from time to time. He laid up his treasure in heaven.

Once Kirk listened to Bell's preaching at St. Martin's-in-the-Fields, then still being restored from the bombing; and Bell spoke, amidst the rubble and hideousness of London, for that great continuity and essence the Church, in the tone of the Fathers of the early centuries and the divines of the seventeenth century from whom his inspiration came. And once Kirk gave away a bride — being married to Pongo McClellan, who had come over to America and entered into friendship with Canon Bell — at a wedding that Bell performed. If there be any contagion in holiness, Kirk may have some chance for redemption, with B. I. Bell for his intercessor.

Richard Weaver, High Realist

While Kirk was a partner in the Red Cedar Bookshop, East Lansing, the University of Chicago Press published the first book by Richard Weaver, *Ideas Have Consequences*. (Weaver detested that title, conferred by the publisher.) Kirk saw that the little book was important; featured it in his bookshop; invited Weaver to East Lansing to address the George Ade Society (a creation of Kirk and his partner, Adrian Smith). That was in 1948. Before he died at the age of fifty-three, Weaver published another good book, *The Ethics of Rhetoric;* four more volumes appeared after his death, *Visions of Order, Life Without Prejudice and Other Essays, The Southern Tradition at Bay,* and *Language Is Sermonic.*

Fellow conservatives, rare birds in the academic grove of 1948, Weaver and Kirk became close allies. It was not that they agreed in everything: Weaver understood Burke ill (interpreting him as Buckle had) and was given to positions unnecessarily dogmatic — for instance, his assertion of an *absolute* right to private property, a notion that cannot be sustained in any society. But both were defenders of immemorial ways, old morals, old customs, old loves, the wisdom of the species, the life of rural regions and little communities. In 1984, Kirk would receive an Ingersoll Prize — the Richard M. Weaver Award for scholarship in humane letters.

Ambrose of Milan taught that it has not pleased God to save men through logic. Richard Weaver assented to this, knowing as he did the nature of the average sensual man and the limits of pure rationality. Yet with a high logical power, Weaver undertook an intellectual defense of inherited culture, and of order and justice and freedom.

Weaver lived seriously and austerely all his days. A shy little bulldog of a man from the mountains of North Carolina — born at the town of Weaverville, founded by his ancestors — he taught for nearly two decades in the College of the University of Chicago. He saved his money in the hope of buying a little house at Weaverville, for a day when college teaching should end — something that never came to pass. Solitary by nature, he did not marry, and inhabited a single room in an obscure Chicago hotel; he never travelled. At International House, that cheerless structure, he breakfasted frugally, sometimes joined by Pongo McClellan or by Thomas Copeland, the Burke scholar. Stoically he endured the ferocious Chicago winters, wearing two overcoats often, so that he seemed wider than tall. Some of his Chicago friends did not encounter him during the course of a whole year, so seldom did he leave office or hotel room.

A Southern Agrarian, Weaver was offered at Vanderbilt University the professorial chair being vacated by Donald Davidson, at least for a year. He expressed his doubt that he would care to stay permanently at Nashville: for a great city like Chicago — so he said — offered amenities not to be found in state capitals. Precisely what advantages Weaver discovered for himself in Chicago, it was difficult to surmise. He lived chaste and withdrawn; his work left him no time to indulge in theater or concert; he attended an Episcopalian service once a year only, the solemn liturgy stirring him so deeply that he would abstain for another twelve months.

Among his handful of Chicago friends was Bernard Iddings Bell, who said to Kirk once, "Richard Weaver distresses me: every day he grows more like a little gnome." Truly it was no friendly climate of opinion in which Weaver found himself enveloped, so that he withdrew to the fastness of his books. Yet he never lost himself in pedantry or antiquarianism. Meant to expose and to restrain the illusions of the twentieth century, his books and his teaching (once he being chosen best teacher of the year in the College) were instruments for action.

Among philosophers, Plato was Weaver's mentor; and among American statesmen, Lincoln. Although a declared Southerner, in politics Weaver was a conservative Republican, an heir to the old Mountain Whigs. Such convictions did not find favor for him in the Academy, but he remained an intelligent defender of the Academy's rights and duties. "The more democratic society is, the more it tends to be jealous of exemptions and exclusions of any kind," he wrote in a pamphlet about academic freedom, "and therefore it is well to emphasize the purpose of academic freedom. . . . Generally speaking, Western man has believed that there is a truth which is knowable, that only a portion of the truth has been discovered, and that therefore the work of study and teaching should go on."

Weaver's books brought a consciousness of such truth to a good many who never saw him — and few of whom ever wrote to him, for a certain awe of that author existed. As a public speaker, Weaver had no talent; logical and resolute although his printed pages are, his is not generally the high rhetorical style, and so his chapters are not wholly persuasive when read aloud. But high consistency and honesty often win over some readers of his books who have begun in hostility.

Once Weaver came to visit Kirk at his old house in back-country Michigan. Mecosta, smaller and more remote than Weaverville, also was less tamed than was Weaver's birthplace. Professor Weaver was startled by Kirk's narratives of rural hardihood and decadence, of a kind he had encountered only in William Faulkner's novels. Although occasionally humorous, Weaver took life for a very serious business. His bulldog jaw seemed to resent Kirk's fondness for pretty girls, frivolous creatures indifferent to ideas; his forehead furrowed in puzzlement when Kirk told ghost stories. "I think I know what you mean, Russell," Weaver murmured when Kirk concluded his yarns: for Richard Weaver, allegory or parable lurked behind every flimsy appearance. If he knew what Kirk had intended, it was more than Kirk knew. Other friends occasionally committed the blunder of supposing Kirk to be a deep metaphysician, much read in Hegel and the like, when actually Russell Kirk cherished Edmund Burke's observation that nothing is more consummately wicked than the heart of an abstract metaphysician in politics.

No man was less romantic than Weaver — but none more strongly attached to failing causes. In the cause of peace and humility, he struck manly blows. Vanity he knew not. In his *Visions of Order,* he assaulted the "presentism," scientism, and democratism that are subverting the old order of civilization. He did not despair. Thus he concluded his autobiographical essay "Up from Liberalism":

> Somehow our education will have to recover the lost vision of the person as a creature of both intellect and will. It will have to bring together into one through its training the thinker and the doer, the dialectician and the rhetorician. Cognition, including the scientific, alone is powerless, and will without cognition is blind and destructive. The work of the future, then, is to overcome the shallow rationalism and scientificism of the past two centuries and to work toward the reunion of man into a being who will both know and desire what he knows.

This Platonic view gave purpose and direction to Richard Weaver's life and work. Weaver was surprised at the attention paid to *Ideas Have Consequences.* That book, reprinted several times, continues to win some of the rising generation away from twentieth-century nominalism.

Weaver's will did not fail him, but his heart did. In the spring of 1963, he was found dead in his rented room near the University. Yet Weaver had sowed deep his intellectual seed, and although he left no heirs of his body, the heirs of his mind may be many and stalwart.

Donald Davidson, Unreconstructed

On his annual expeditions from Nashville to the Bread Loaf School of English at Middlebury College in Vermont, Donald Davidson took pains to avoid passing through New York City. The most southern of Southerners, Davidson had been a leading member of both the Fugitives and the Agrarians, who stood high in American letters and thought during the Thirties and the Forties, and are no negligible influence even now. Some of those southern writers and scholars fell away or fell silent, but Davidson labored undiminished to the end of his life.

Christian humanism, stern criticism of the industrialized mass society, detestation of communism and other forms of collectivism, attachment to the ways of the Old South — such were the principles uniting the Southern Agrarians (overlapping with the Fugitives, who had begun publishing their magazine in the Twenties), so much discussed in the Thirties. The twelve essays of their anthology *I'll Take My Stand* were approved by T. S. Eliot and other reflective people; yet also the Agrarians met with much hostility and ridicule. Today many read their work with greater understanding and sympathy.

The Agrarians were genuine conservatives during the era of Franklin Roosevelt; so, despite the attention those writers obtained nationally, it was not easy for them to get their writings published — or, once published, to be kept in print. Nevertheless, their high talents gave them a degree of ascendancy over humane letters in America, even in Manhattan, until recent years — when the literary oligarchs of *The New York Review of Books* overthrew the remnant of the Agrarians' influence.

They illustrated wondrously well Lionel Trilling's observation that the twentieth-century writers possessed of imagination distinctly were not liberal. Allen Tate was so bold as to publish his *Reactionary Essays;* all the Agrarians reacted against modernist materialism. Of the original Agrarians, Kirk met and corresponded with Davidson and Andrew Lytle.

Kirk first discovered Davidson in 1938, when Davidson's polemical book *The Attack on Leviathan* was published: a copy appeared on the new-book shelves of Michigan State's library. It was an eloquent denunciation of political and cultural centralizing: strongly impressed, Kirk took it that Davidson's readers must be numbered in the hundreds of thousands. Actually, Kirk was one of the very few readers of the first edition; in the Fifties, he would name it in the pages of *The American Scholar* as the most deserving neglected book of recent decades; a reprint house would bring out a second printing in 1962, and then Kirk's review would result in substantial sales. When Davidson and Kirk first met in the Fifties, Davidson would marvel that Kirk had come upon *The Attack on Leviathan* at all; in a letter to Kirk dated June 10, 1955, he would explain why few copies of his book existed:

> I now own the copyright; it was assigned to me by the University of North Carolina Press, just a few years ago, after Lambert Davis came in as editor of the Press — and after I had a terrific row with him. I was assured by my lawyer that I had grounds for a suit against the Press, but I did not have the money to carry the suit through. When Bill Couch [editor of that Press in 1938] printed the book, he left some hundreds of copies in sheets, to be bound up as demand might occur. During the interim, after Couch left and before Davis came in, a man named Wilson filled in as editor. He undertook to "clear the stock room," and since the *Leviathan* had not been selling in quantity, he "pulped" the stock of my book that was in sheets, and so, in effect, put the book out of print, since only a few bound copies remained. But he did not notify me before taking this action and give me the opportunity to buy the stock, as the contract required the publisher to do. Furthermore, I discovered that the Press was withholding from me fees for reprint permission — quite an accumulation of them, it happened — and I had to come down hard on them to get the money that was due me. It was obvious to me that the book was being in effect "suppressed," and though Lambert Davis, Wilson's successor, protested that it was not so, I knew very well that if the book had been "liberal" or "radical," rather than "conservative," it would have been kept in print, or would have been reprinted, for it was continually being cited and was in some demand. Davis, by the way, in an interview he had with me in Nashville, had the gall to explain to me that he was a "Christian Socialist."

Kirk had similar experiences with certain publishers — although none of his books had been pulped, and some were substantial financial successes. His book on Randolph of Roanoke made him known to the Southern Agrarians; he was, indeed, a Northern Agrarian. With Davidson, who introduced Kirk when he lectured on academic freedom at Vanderbilt University, he felt a strong sympathy, both literary and political.

To Reginald Cook, director of the Bread Loaf School of English, Davidson wrote on October 22, 1955, "Earlier this week, we had Russell Kirk for a lecture at Vanderbilt. He performed very brilliantly and solidly, before a large and responsive audience in the University chapel on the topic 'What Is an American Intellectual?' He dealt, pretty much, with the 'alienation of the Intellectual' (who, at an earlier stage, would be Emerson's 'scholar') from the society of which he should be a part. Most of my Monday and Tuesday went into various meetings (and some social parties) with Russell Kirk."

It was good of Davidson to spend so much time with the visitor to Vanderbilt, for at that very hour Professor Davidson was much involved in measures to deal with the consequences of the Supreme Court's decision requiring racial desegregation of public schools. "I would hesitate to predict how long we shall be in this strained condition or how it will all turn out," Davidson wrote to Cook in the same letter. "How peaceful and remote Vermont seems, in contrast. I hope your peacefulness, which you cherish, will enable you to keep charity in your hearts for us."

The violence that Davidson had feared would be averted, in some degree through his efforts and those of his friends, but public-school standards in Tennessee and elsewhere suffered badly as a result of compulsory integration and "busing," and so continue to suffer to the hour of this writing.

Interference by federal judges — and federal troops — with the functioning of schools was another conquest of the fell spirit of nationalism that Davidson had described in *The Attack on Leviathan*. His devotion to the Old South, and to Tennessee especially, moves much of his poetry.

In 1927, Davidson had published *The Tall Men,* some of the best verse in a decade of many good poets. The Tall Men are the heroes of old Tennessee. This book's prologue was entitled "The Long Street" — which is the symbol of modern industrial existence, sterile and stifling, in opposition to the agrarian freedom of which Davidson was the most consistent and persistent defender. The Long Street is the desolation of an iron age of "dead men under a pall, nameless and choked."

Thirty-five years later, in his *Poems, 1922-1961,* Davidson returned to the charge, speaking undismayed, though beaten in many a fight, for the good old cause,

> For us, deliberate exiles, whose dry sod
> Blossoms athwart the Long Street's servile rage . . .

Even in rural Vermont, Donald Davidson felt the sneering hostility of the liberal intellectual, detesting a South known chiefly through the New York press and the New York stage:

> But Vassar bugled, Amherst bayed, and Yale
> Picked up the scent. They gave tongue on my trail:
> 'Admit! Confess! Nostalgic! No, he fights
> Historical process . . . Absurd Monuments. . . .
> Remember what? Gastonia? That makes sense!'

In his poem "Old Sailor's Choice" he describes a twentieth-century Ulysses of the Long Street on his voyage to Hell and beyond. Contrary to the counsels of a modern Circe, he chooses Charybdis over Scylla, though modern men lust for Scylla's deadly embrace, "the monstrous lips, the darting neck of their love-death."

> And I saw the stretching neck and the grinning teeth
> In the soundproof room where artificial daylight
> Blacks out the scudding clouds and the churning storm-wrack,
> And the secretary with half-naked breasts
> Extends the telephone on a crimson claw
> And murmurs Washington is calling!

Washington did not call Donald Davidson. More than one old friend sank into a rather dull liberalism; Davidson fought on against Leviathan and Scylla.

Davidson had an erect military carriage. His students and disciples, even posthumously, invariably referred to him as Mr. Davidson. Andrew Lytle was uneasy with his friend Davidson's Puritanism; once Lytle was shown a photograph of the extended family of the Davidsons, and none of them was smiling. And yet Donald Davidson was a lovable man, warmhearted. In Burke's aphorism, "They will never love where they ought to love who do not hate where they ought to hate."

The South's pace of change has been more rapid and more overwhelming than even the gloomier of the twelve original Agrarians predicted. Old Nashville has been thoroughly demolished and uglified, Strickland's Capitol on its hill besieged by the arrogant office towers of state and federal bureaucracies. Davidson lamented to Kirk in 1955 that the Vanderbilt campus had been converted into metered parking lots. Since Kirk knew the South during his year at Duke and his army years, the face of things has been altered; never again, presumably, will there be distinctively Southern architectural styles. Much else has gone by the board.

With the dwindling of Dixieland has come relative economic prosperity. Even so oldfangled a place as Farmville, in Southside Virginia, one of the two most Southern regions of the South (the other, according to Richard Weaver, being Middle Tennessee), is bustling and almost affluent compared with what it was a quarter of a century ago. The rural pattern of existence, defended by the Agrarians, still endures here or there south of Mason's and Dixon's line, but it has been brutally buffeted during the past fifty years.

To wipe out Southerners of the type of Davidson and Lytle may be more difficult. Modernity is doing its best to complete such liquidation by sweeping away — in the South as elsewhere — the sort of schooling that men of their stamp profited by.

Tide what may betide, the Southern Agrarians will loom large in histories of American thought and letters. With liberalism in America fallen nearly mindless, some of the rising generation will discover in the Fugitives and the Agrarians a healthier imagination.

Flannery O'Connor: Notes by Humpty Dumpty

At the house then called Cold Chimneys, in Smyrna, Tennessee, where Brainard and Fanny Cheney lived, Flannery O'Connor and Kirk met — for the first time and the last, here below. This occurred in October 1955; in Kirk's fancy, the occasion does not seem so far distant in time. For a conscience spoke to a conscience then, and the soul of Flannery O'Connor endures.

She happened to greet Kirk in the broad entrance hall of the handsome old house, which had been built by a Carpetbagger. Kirk had not known that she too would be staying there, and he had read nothing of hers. As she says in her published letters, *The Habit of Being,* she and Kirk were shy with each other. Probably she had not expected the portentous author of *The Conservative Mind* (as Eliot puts it, "the mild-mannered man entrenched behind his typewriter") to look like "Humpty Dumpty (intact) with constant cigar and (outside) porkpie hat" (Flannery's description of Kirk). For Kirk's part, noticing her crutch and a bandaged leg, and knowing nothing of the disease that had fixed upon her, he inquired whether she had broken that leg; she said no, but did not explain.

Kirk's first acquaintance with her power of imagination came that evening or the next, when she read aloud "A Good Man Is Hard to Find." She mentioned that a young man in Los Angeles had asked for permission to adapt the story for a film, he being a doctoral candidate in theater arts; he had chosen "A Good Man" because "it would be cheap" to produce.

"Cheap and nasty," Kirk offered. She smiled. Flannery went on to tell how she had named The Misfit in her story after a real escaped criminal by that appellation who had popped up in the Georgia papers. Kirk drew parallels from Michigan experiences. As Flannery mentions in a letter, she and Kirk were better at talking in the company of the Cheneys and of fellow guests than when left alone in a parlor. Kirk regretted that he had not told tales of his Scottish wanderings afoot, which might have amused and interested her.

Probably she was interested in Kirk because, as an informed Catholic, she had read his essays in *Commonweal, America, The Month, The Dublin Review,* and other Catholic periodicals — though Kirk still was unbaptized in any church. Then, too, "Lon" Cheney, their host, had reviewed *The Conservative Mind* sympathetically in *Sewanee Review.* She herself was to review Kirk's *Beyond the Dreams of Avarice,* published in 1956. Long after Flannery's death, Kirk would be shown her library books, desk, chair, and all plenishings — preserved in the library of Georgia College at her town of Milledgeville; and there he would find her copy of *The Conservative Mind,* with her marginalia.

There was much they should have talked about during that weekend with the Cheneys. They seemed to agree on everything —

she from the Milledgeville farm, he from the old judge's house at Mecosta. Although Kirk's junior in years, she was in advance of him: when Flannery died in 1964, Kirk — then forty-five years old — had begun to apprehend truths that Miss O'Connor had discerned at the age of thirty. It turned out that she had read Kirk's *Program for Conservatives* and his *Academic Freedom*. Of Kirk's Works, she wrote later that "Dr. Johnson would almost certainly admire them, both for their thought and the vigor with which it is expressed." That approbation was heartening in a bent world.

In her letters she refers to the title of a magazine Kirk then was intending to found, *The Conservative Review;* she begins to doubt whether the review will take on flesh. It did, eventually, but under another title, *Modern Age* — a quarterly still published. As matters worked out, the first number of the review appeared too late for the publication of an essay by Donald Davidson and an article about Flannery O'Connor by Ashley Brown, which Kirk had meant to print. He never had occasion to write anything about Flannery but two or three syndicated newspaper columns, an unsatisfactory mode for discussing so complex and subtle a writer.

The impression that she made upon Kirk by her presence was as strong as that created by her stories, which Kirk began to read on his way back from Tennessee to Michigan. Having acquainted himself with nearly everything that she had written, he wrote to T. S. Eliot — then his London publisher — that he really ought to read her, if he hadn't already. (There was little among new fiction that Kirk commended to Eliot.) He replied, in February 1957, that he had seen a book of her stories when he had been in New York, "and was quite horrified by those I read. She has certainly an uncanny talent of high order but my nerves are just not strong enough to take much of a disturbance."

He would have admired Flannery O'Connor as he admired Simone Weil, and for much the same reasons, had he penetrated below the surface of Flannery's stories to the power of her moral imagination, growing from a faith like Eliot's. But that did not come to pass. "Similarly with another book shown me in New York," Eliot went on in the same letter to Kirk, "a novel by Nelson Algren; that is terrifying too and I do not like being terrified. Apart from the general aversion to prose fiction which I share with Paul Valéry, I like pleasant, sunny comedies such as I write myself."

Eliot was unaware that a gulf was fixed between Nelson Algren (whose name he garbled in the letter) and Flannery O'Connor: the gulf between the diabolic imagination and the moral imagination, a subject discussed by Eliot himself in *After Strange Gods*. As for Eliot, so for Flannery, "the reverence and the gaiety" were not "forgotten in later experience"; no, not in "bored habituation," or fatigue, or tedium, or "the awareness of death, the consciousness of failure . . ."

Had TSE summoned up courage sufficient to read Flannery through, he would have discovered her similarities to Nathaniel Hawthorne, one of the few major American authors Eliot admired. For what fascinated Flannery was sin — and redemption. As Pope John Paul II wrote very recently, without an understanding of the nature of sin it is not possible to form a conscience — or to become fully human. That is the teaching of *The Marble Faun, The Blithedale Romance, The Scarlet Letter;* it is the teaching of Flannery O'Connor through "Southern Gothic." Kirk well understood her fantastic and her depraved characters, their twisted faith and all, because precisely such people lived about him in Mecosta County; they emerged repeatedly in his own stories, many of those written long before he met Miss O'Connor, and which presumably she never saw. His "Off the Sand Road" might have come from Flannery's typewriter; so too, except for their revenants, his "Behind the Stumps" and his later "There's a Long, Long Trail a-Winding" and "Fate's Purse."

So far as Flannery professed politics, she stood with the Agrarians — adding a Catholic element. "It is . . . a rethinking in the obedience to divine truth which must be the mainspring of any enlightened social thought," she wrote in her review of *Beyond the Dreams of Avarice,* "whether it tends to be liberal or conservative. Since the Enlightenment, liberalism in its extreme forms has not accepted divine truth, and the conservatism which has enjoyed any popularity has shown no tendency to rethink human truth or to reexamine human society." But Kirk had done both those things, she added, making "the voice of an intelligent and vigorous conservative thought respected in this country." That review was not called to Kirk's attention until Flannery had been dead for twenty years.

Kirk felt so swiftly drawn to only one other writer that he met — George Scott-Moncrieff, so like Flannery in character and conviction. In sorrow, Flannery told Kirk how the bishop of Savannah had demolished, next to the cathedral, one of Savannah's finest old houses, to clear the ground for a thoroughly hideous school (now disused but unhappily still standing). George Scott-Moncrieff, quite as Catholic as Flannery and as much a cherisher of the historic past and its monuments, would have expressed himself on such a melancholy subject in similar wry comic phrases. Neither of those two ever read the other, more's the pity.

It might please and amuse Flannery O'Connor to read these paragraphs, so tardily written. Yet she must have surmised, with her quick charitable insights, that the taciturn Humpty Dumpty esteemed her. Beyond time, we two, who met but once, may be enfolded in the community of souls.

A Decade of Intellectual Battle

During the Fifties, a renewal of the mode of thought somewhat vaguely called "conservative" occurred in the United States; it is described in detail by George Nash in his large and careful book *The Conservative Intellectual Movement in America since 1945*. Despite being a Michigan backwoodsman, Kirk knew many of the scholars and writers who contributed to this renewal. He could not cry, like Shakespeare's Coriolanus, "Alone I did it!"

But there existed no concerted "conservative movement" in the sense of an organized and systematic effort. Sidney Lens, the Chicago radical with whom Kirk debated from time to time, once asked if he might be invited to a large gathering of conservative intellectuals, to study them and argue with them. Kirk replied that Lens would have been welcome — had any such conferences ever been held. Endeavoring to bring together a few eminent men of business with men of ideas, Kirk did hold in his own library a few little meetings extending over two or three days. Among those who participated were W. C. Mullendore, chairman of Southern California Edison; Colin Clark, the economist, then at Oxford; B. E. Hutchinson, retired treasurer of Chrysler Corporation; Benjamin Casanas Toledano, later a courageous Republican politician in Louisiana; Louis Dehmlow, a young Illinois industrialist; James McCauley, the Australian man of letters; two or three Mecosta County men. (Kirk did the cooking for them.) Such was the scale of the infamous conservative plot so dreaded by publicists of the Left.

There was no money at all behind the conservative intellectual renewal, either from individuals or from foundations. The total sum that Kirk personally was able to raise from friends to found a conservative review was less than a thousand dollars.

Yet the climate of serious opinion was beginning to alter, even in the Academy. In either Britain or America, it takes some thirty years for a body of ideas to be advanced, promulgated, discussed, and at length accepted or rejected by the thinking portion of the public. It was so with the Fabians in Britain; it has been so with the conservative intellectual impulse in the United States.

Differences of opinion and character were obvious among the scholars of a cast of mind more or less conservative; but during the Fifties it became possible to speak of a body (if an ill-defined body) of serious writing and teaching, concerned for the permanent things and friendly toward constitution, convention, and custom. This general school of thought could be distinguished from the oldfangled surviving nineteenth-century liberalism that the press generally confounded with conservative thought. Here it is possible to mention some of the intellectual leaders in this development with whom Kirk was fairly well acquainted; there were others — William Yandell Eliot, at Yale, for instance — whom he never encountered personally.

R. A. Nisbet, the historical sociologist, whose book *The Quest for Community* was published not long after Kirk's *Conservative Mind,* impressed even doctrinaire liberals. Daniel Boorstin, among American historians, loomed large; later he would become head of the Smithsonian Institution, and then Librarian of Congress. Among the political-science people there were Francis Wilson, at the University of Illinois, the author of a little book too little known, *The Case for Conservatism;* John Hallowell, at Duke University; René de Visme Williamson, at Louisiana State; William McGovern, at Northwestern University, a towering man who in earlier years had made his way to Lhasa disguised as a Chinese porter.

Kirk had a close ally in Frederick Wilhelmsen, then in California, a professor of philosophy and a disciple of Belloc and Chesterton. He was closer still to certain professors learned in Burke — Peter Stanlis, at the University of Detroit, and Ross J. S. Hoffman and Father Francis Canavan, at Fordham. Two Englishmen resident in the United States exerted a conservative influence: Raymond English at Kenyon College, and Thomas I. Cook at Johns Hopkins. Harvard University still tolerated some scholars unashamed of being rather conservative, but not many: probably Crane Brinton was the best known of them. At Cornell, Clinton Rossiter wrote a much-quoted book about American conservatives, but later, in a letter to *Time,* declared that he was not and never had been a conservative himself.

Emigrés from Europe contributed much toward the restoration of political sound sense in America. Two historical scholars (not that they agreed about everything, or that either wished to be tagged as "a conservative") gained a wide hearing: Eric Voegelin, from Austria, and John Lukacs, from Hungary. Robert Strausz-Hupé, an urbane diplomat from the wreck of the Austro-Hungarian system, helped to improve American understanding of international policy. At Notre Dame University, Gerhart Niemeyer, a German, was a strong pillar; and at Johns Hopkins, Gottfried Dietze, another German, who continues to call himself a liberal — Continental or "proper" type. Kirk got along especially well with Ludwig Freund, at Roosevelt University, one of the two survivors of the first plot against Hitler. Freund, who spoke English perfectly (having been a German soldier in the First World War and an American soldier in the Second), did not write it equally well: Kirk had to render into genuine English Freund's articles for *Modern Age,* but Freund never guessed that the compliments he received for his essays' style were in consequence of Kirk's editorial revisions.*

Pass we now to the Fourth Estate. Among editors of large newspapers, James K. Kilpatrick of the Richmond *News Leader* and Jameson Campaigne of the Indianapolis *Star* were conservative voices; presently Stanton Evans, also in Indianapolis; all three wrote books. Kilpatrick would become the most influential of all nationally syndicated columnists. The *Los Angeles Times* then was the most powerful of conservative daily papers.

Among journals of opinion early in the Fifties, the Catholic weeklies *The Commonweal* and *America* occasionally published arti-

---

*Freund encountered Hitler face to face only once — in a men's washroom at Munich, when Hitler was making his way toward power. Walking toward the single washbasin, Freund saw a man hurrying toward that object — and recognized Adolf Hitler, detested by him. Resolved that the malign demagogue should not wash his hands first, Freund ran to the basin. "But Hitler defeated me. Seeing that I would get there first anyway, he stopped, bowed with Viennese courtesy, and said 'After you, sir.' He had converted me into a boor."

cles by conservatives. There was *Fortune,* with its conservative editors Duncan Norton-Taylor and John Davenport. Later Kirk would write for that monthly two of his more influential articles; but of course *Fortune* primarily was a business magazine. There existed precariously the monthly *Freeman,* edited at one time or another by Max Eastman or John Chamberlain; yet the *Freeman* (founded originally by Albert Jay Nock), with its small circulation, was more the voice of liberalism old-style than of conservatism. Such quarterlies as *The Yale Review, The Sewanee Review, The Virginia Quarterly Review, The South Atlantic Quarterly, The Southern Review,* and *The Georgia Review* were not unfriendly to conservative views — especially if such contributions were not directly political. As for popular magazines, *Reader's Digest* and *The Saturday Evening Post* and some others were politically conservative enough, but they did not influence the Academy.

It was a curious phenomenon that in the United States of the Eisenhower era, with conservatives victorious in practical politics, no thoughtful weekly or monthly magazine was much concerned with conservative ideas and policies, and the quarterlies of the Left had no conservative counterparts. Ross Hoffman, Geoffrey Stone, and Kirk had it in mind, from 1952 to 1954, to bring out a weekly magazine of conservative opinion to stand against the eight weeklies of a liberal or a radical complexion: the London *Spectator* and *Time and Tide* would have provided good models. But the three hopefuls possessed no real money, and presently Stone (who had written a book about Herman Melville), the intended editor, went off to settle in the Tyrol.

Then strode forward young William F. Buckley, Jr., to undertake such a publishing venture. Kirk had met him but once, finding him cordial and able. Months before *National Review* brought out its first issue (in November 1955), Buckley had invited Kirk to become an editor of the new magazine. But Kirk did not consent — although five years later he would assume the editorship of *The University Bookman,* a small quarterly allied with *National Review.* It would have been awkward to help edit a weekly at eight hundred miles' remove; and, contributing as he did to so many periodicals, Kirk preferred not to be identified as a chief member of the innermost editorial circle of one weekly periodical in particular. But he did agree to write a regular page, "From the Academy," for the new magazine; and he was to keep it up for a quarter of a century. Most of the time, Kirk lived quite outside the Academy; yet the *National Review* people seemed to think of him as a donnish type, which he never had been. He wrote about education at its several levels; the page became highly popular; also, he being then without assistance of any kind in his Mecosta fastness, it overwhelmed him with correspondence from parents distraught at the wretched schooling inflicted upon their offspring. In his page's early years, while Frank Meyer was *NR*'s book-review editor, Kirk often was asked to contribute to the magazine's literary pages, and all his own books were reviewed therein; it would be otherwise with *NR*'s later book-review editors.

Kirk had little in common with some of the people on *National Review*'s lengthy masthead — on which he declined to have his name appear. He was ill at ease with Willmoore Kendall, a Rousseauistic populist; and with Frank Meyer, a former Communist who had transferred his zeal to something called Fusionism. Two writers and scholars with whom Kirk associated closely soon began to contribute to that magazine: the urbane Ernest van den Haag, who in his youth had escaped from an Italian prison for anti-Fascists, and the cosmopolitan Thomas Molnar, who had survived years in Nazi concentration camps. Van den Haag was sociologist, psychologist, economist, literary critic; Molnar wrote books without number, among them *The Decline of the Intellectual*. Then there arrived Jeffrey Hart, at first calling himself a "Kennedy conservative," influenced by Kirk's books. Erik von Kuehnelt-Leddihn, *National Review*'s chief European contributor, was an old friend of Kirk: twice or thrice Kirk had visited him at Lans, high in the Tyrol. Not much united *National Review*'s editors and regular contributors except their detestation of collectivism.

In the course of twenty-five years' association, Kirk visited the shabby offices of *National Review* not more than six or seven times — and then usually on business with the publisher, William Rusher. When necessity took Kirk to Manhattan, he did not consort much with the *literati*, except for occasional lunches or dinners with Molnar or van den Haag. His Manhattan hosts were Charles Teetor, an adventurous manufacturer of bedspreads and pillows, once a Marine sergeant, and his charming wife, Mickie. In the writing trade, doubtless Kirk would have much improved his opportunities had he consorted with publishers, writers, editors, Madison Avenue, and the principal reviewers of books. Nevertheless, Kirk's constitutional aversion to running happily with the hounds, which had made him a conservative and later would make him a Christian of sorts, impelled him away from the self-proclaimed intellectuals and, in Hawthorne's phrases, toward holding "a little talk with the conservatives, the writers of the *North American Review,* the merchants, the politicians, the Cambridge men, and all those respectable old blockheads who still, in this intangibility and mistiness of affairs, kept a death-grip on one or two ideas which had not come into vogue since yesterday morning."

The *North American Review* was long dead, but presently Kirk would devise his own successor to it. Although Kirk tended to shy away from literary circles, in the middle Fifties he was a most prolific man of letters.

His book *St. Andrews,* a history and description of university and town, was published in London by B. T. Batsford, during 1954. Some of the photographs therein had been taken by Kirk. The book made Kirk a celebrity in the old gray town for decades to come; it never was published in the United States.

Also in 1954, his polemical work *A Program for Conservatives* appeared, published by Regnery in Chicago. Very widely reviewed, it obtained a book-club adoption, and over the years would appear in three later editions, two of which would bear the revised title *Prospects for Conservatives.*

In 1955, Regnery published his *Academic Freedom: An Essay in Definition,* in which Kirk argued that of the many difficulties in the Academy after the Second World War, the worst was the deliberate lowering of academic standards to create the mass campus — with unpleasant consequences for professors. The book roused the wrath of university presidents — or tyrants — so different as Minard Stout, of the University of Nevada, and Robert Hutchins, formerly of the University of Chicago.

His *Beyond the Dreams of Avarice: Essays of a Social Critic* was published by Regnery in 1956. This volume was a collection of his more important periodical essays, about half of them concerned with British society and letters; that portion of the book had been made possible by a Guggenheim Fellowship awarded to Kirk.

The American Cause, a slim volume about American moral, political, and economic institutions and principles, was written because of the ignorance of such matters that had afflicted many American soldiers during the Korean War. It was published by Regnery in 1957; later there appeared a paperback edition, with an introduction by John Dos Passos. For some time the Air Force Academy used *The American Cause* as a textbook.

Originally written as a series of pamphlets for use by Republican Women's clubs, Kirk's slender book *The Intelligent Woman's Guide to Conservatism* was published by the New York firm of Devin Adair in 1957. A paperback edition was brought out several years later.

Kirk would publish no books from 1958 to 1960: editing the infant *Modern Age* and serving as research professor of politics at C. W. Post College — and presently university professor of Long Island University — kept him too busy. Yet he did turn out, during the period from 1957 to 1962, a great many periodical essays and articles, several pieces for encyclopedias and yearbooks, fourteen prefaces or forewords for books by new or old authors, and a congeries of pamphlets and printed addresses. Also there were published during the Fifties some nine of his short stories, chiefly uncanny or mystical tales.

In the quondam factory on Franklin Street, Village of Mecosta, Kirk enjoyed the mighty advantage of being able to write and read in solitude all night, when he chose, undisturbed. Celibate and childless then, Kirk was able to entertain thoughts of yet more elaborate undertakings. Why had the old *North American Review* given up the ghost? Why might not it be raised from the dead? Or a simulacrum thereof created?

It should not be fancied that Kirk then dwelt disconsolate in a rural solitude. He was kept company by the cheerful Marian, that very pretty charmer with waist-long red hair, a bachelor of arts in literature, who from time to time came to Mecosta, fetching along her cat, to drink in the words of wisdom of the Sage of Piety Hill. Presently Kirk took this blithe young person to St. Andrews, where she enrolled in graduate studies. Theirs was an innocent comradeship.

Back at Mecosta, Kirk resumed his meditations about a conservative journal of ideas. About the middle Fifties, *National Review,* moving manfully and hopefully toward a conceivable circulation of one hundred thousand copies, provided tolerably well for weekly journalism of a conservative inclination. But still there existed no monthly or quarterly magazine in which views not conceived just yesterday might obtain a friendly hearing. Journals of that character, among them *The Bookman* and *The American Review,* had gone down to Avernus during the Thirties. With a few associates, Kirk proposed to remedy that sore lack.

Right Reason Does Not Pay

In 1955, endeavoring to found a conservative quarterly in collaboration with Henry Regnery and a few others, Kirk discovered how difficult it was to raise money for any cause genuinely conservative. It had been so with Eliot's *Criterion* in England, a generation earlier. They attracted writers for the journal, among them some distinguished men and women. It was otherwise with funds.

Approval for their undertaking was widespread and cordial, extending to liberal quarters. "Even inveterate liberals ought to look with favor on the revival of sound conservative journalism," Kirk wrote then in *Commonweal.* "For a conservatism of ignorance, like a liberalism of ignorance, is a curse to society; while a conservatism of reflection is a proper counterbalance to a liberalism of reflection." He pointed out that although the majority of Americans were conservative in their preferences and prejudices, they lacked intellectual leadership in the serious journals.

This Kirk plea was commended promptly by the editors of the *New York Times.* "We wish him well," they wrote in response to his *Commonweal* declaration, "not because we are so wildly conservative but because we think Mr. Kirk is a thoughtful man with scruples."

It was not without irony that Kirk clapped the name *Modern Age* upon a new quarterly of ideas. At first it had been his intention to entitle the magazine *The Conservative Review,* but friends had dissuaded him, fancying that the Tower of Siloam might tumble upon editor and publisher should they be so temerarious as to proclaim openly their attachment to the permanent things. Next he had inclined toward *The Federal Review,* but Henry Regnery suggested that people would think of the Federal Reserve Board. *Modern Age* the periodical became, in sardonic defiance of the fads and foibles of the twentieth century.

At the beginning of this century, dictionaries of the English language had defined *modernity* as "the quality or state of being modern; modernism in time or spirit" — appending to this definition, in brackets, "Rare." *Modernism* then was a literary term chiefly, signifying some novel word, idiom, or expression. Nine decades later, *modernity* and *modernism* have been erected into terms political and sociological, implying neoterism on principle; preference for change over permanence; exaltation of the present era over all previous epochs; hearty approval of material aggrandizement and relative indifference toward a moral order; positive hostility, often, toward theism. About the time when the first number of *Modern Age* appeared, *modernity* and *modernism* were terms of approbation in most quarters. The Modernists of the twentieth century have been the intellectual heirs of the Utilitarians of the first half of the nineteenth century and of the Positivists of the latter half of that century — even although few Modernists read Bentham or Comte attentively now.

Certain Modernist excesses incited Kirk to try to found a periodical comparable to the vanished *Bookman* and the *American Review* that might publish reflections on the permanent things and offer some intellectual resistance to a reckless neoterism. Eliot's *Criterion* and, more recently, the short-lived Chicago quarterly *Measure* had been such journals; they had expired several years before Henry Regnery and Kirk set their faces against the Modernists.

Modernism is not confined to any especial party, faction, or class; rather, it is a cast of mind and character. The Modernist mentality, aspiring to universal dominion, ranges from cosmology to sexuality; and everywhere it is overweeningly arrogant.

Three books, published during the decade before the first number of *Modern Age,* particularly helped Kirk to apprehend the significance of the cult of modernity and impelled him to take up the cause of the wisdom of yesteryear.

The first of these to appear was *What Ails Mankind? An Essay on Social Psychology,* published in English translation in 1947 by the French peasant-philosopher Gustave Thibon. Thibon looks upon the Modernists with pity and loathing. "My quarrel with all 'progress' of the scientific or the revolutionary type (they are fundamentally the same thing) is that it carries the infection into the interior of the social body under the pretence of curing a sore on the skin," Thibon writes. Kirk reads Thibon still.

The second book in this anti-modernity list is a slim volume by a psychologist, Charles Baudouin, published in English translation in 1950, *The Myth of Modernity.* The wars of 1914 and 1939, Baudouin writes, undid in men's minds the myth of Progress — which then was supplanted by the myth of Modernity. A point emphasized in Baudouin's little book is that the Modernists delight in the "clean sweep" — the obliteration of memorials of the past — notably in the uglification of once-beautiful cities. It remained for Lyndon Johnson's urban renewal, in full swing a decade after the first number of *Modern Age* appeared, to apply the Modernist doctrine of the clean sweep to American towns great and small.

A year after the English translation of Baudouin appeared, Regnery published in the United States a translation of Max Picard's moving book *The Flight from God,* first published in Switzerland in 1934. The Modernist, repudiating the divine as he repudiates the past, is the man of the Flight. Picard sketches the Modernist's falseness:

> Man is proud of being a manufacturer, and proud that he must engage in a specific kind of manufacture for each situation. Love, kindness, fidelity, his manufactured products, seem to him novel, as if they had no previous existence. And love, fidelity, kindness, all these, do not seem really to be there; rather, it is as though they were making a first or a final appearance, as in a theater. . . . In reality, love, kindness, fidelity, do not show themselves, not even for the brief moment when the Flight has need of them! They show themselves only in discussion and idle chatter, and are swallowed up in them. Only this endures in the Flight: discussion.

Amen to that, Kirk thought on reading this passage from Picard. Endless discussions, endowed by governmental bodies and tax-exempt foundations, are the festivals of Modernity: valueless discussions about "values," for instance, ending in a consensus that values cannot be defined. It was not this sort of Modernist fatigued and pointless discussion that *Modern Age* was meant to advance.

The obdurate adversaries of Modernity, in short, were raising their voices half a century ago in Switzerland, France, and other lands. *Modern Age* was intended to become, in considerable part, an American protest against the illusions of Modernity; and so it has remained.

"One of the rules of the psychological-literary game of our time is to oppose 'life' to 'morality,'" Thibon writes. "I say again that this dichotomy will make our descendants laugh." Those descendants conceivably may laugh harder still at the notion of twentieth-century folk that their era was the culmination of human striving, when in truth the notions of Modernity brought upon the whole world a ruin worse than that which fell upon Roman civilization in the fifth century. That hard truth, along with the search for means of redemption from Modernity, became the preoccupation of *Modern Age*.

The editors and backers of sober reviews of limited circulation are animated by their attachment to what they conceive to be right reason. Such a temperate magazine *Modern Age* was intended to become; and not an ideological publication seeking to indoctrinate in secular dogmata. The founders of *Modern Age* aspired to inform and to persuade.

But who subsidizes right reason? Most serious quarterlies modestly thriving from 1955 to 1957 were sheltered within the grove of Academe, and even there annually had to plead for some few crumbs from the university's table. Those reviews that enjoyed no direct academic sponsorship were journals of the Left, that Left having more reverence for "intellectuals" than did American conservatives. The founding fathers of *Modern Age* backed and filled for two years, hoping vainly for conservative passengers with well-filled purses to come aboard their frail vessel. But no such voyager picked his way down the desolate quay.

The quarterly's founders found next to no money. In a bank account at Mecosta, Kirk had deposited a few hundred dollars, small-ish donations from well-wishers. All of this sum was used up paying contributors to the magazine's first two numbers, and presently Kirk was paying such out of his privy purse, although he received no salary, ever, as editor. (In this, he learned later, he was like Eliot in the early years of *The Criterion*.) One poet-contributor, unconservative, complained that Kirk hadn't paid him so much as he expected and deserved; Kirk replied humbly that he was sorry, but couldn't pay out more money than he could earn through his own literary endeavors. The poet, who may have fancied that *Modern Age* obtained subventions from evildoers of great wealth, then relented. So far as income goes, editors of journals like *Modern Age* and *The Criterion* would be better off frying chicken for Colonel Sanders's heritors.

The first number of *Modern Age* appeared, notwithstanding, in 1957; among its contributors were Richard Weaver, Felix Morley,

Frederick Wilhelmsen, Geoffrey Wagner, Julián Marías, Anthony Kerrigan (translations from Ortega y Gasset), and Francis Russell. In later numbers, during Kirk's editorship, were such distinguished scholars and writers as Wilhelm Röpke, John Courtney Murray, Lynn Harold Hough, Leo R. Ward, Thomas Molnar, Will Herberg, Gerhart Niemeyer, Harry Elmer Barnes, Otto von Habsburg, José Maria Gironella, Margaret Coit, Donald Davidson, Austin Warren, Peter Stanlis, Marion Montgomery, William Henry Chamberlin, Louis Bredvold, Raymond English, and Mortimer Smith. Among contributors during the years after Kirk ceased to be editor were Martin Buber, Bertrand de Jouvenel, Karl Jaspers, Max Picard, Sir Herbert Read, F. R. Leavis, Karl Lowith, Eric Voegelin, F. A. Hayek, Eliseo Vivas, and Milton Friedman. Despite vicissitudes, the quarterly endures to the present under the able guidance of George Panichas.

Kirk resigned the editorship at the end of 1959. He and Collier (the managing editor, in Chicago) had disagreements in policy; that being so, it would have been next to impossible to direct the magazine from Mecosta, two hundred miles to the north. Besides, as an impecunious but travel-fond bachelor, Kirk would have been unwilling to settle down to full-time editorial labors. "When anybody wants to get hold of Russell he is always in Scotland," Flannery O'Connor complained to a friend.

Modern Age's early numbers obtained a surprisingly friendly reception from unconservative quarters — even from Norman Cousins of the *Saturday Review.* From Antioch College, Louis Filler, the historian of the Progressive Era, sent this to the editor: "Although I must confess to being what a fellow-traveler once called (he was not being complimentary) 'really a liberal,' and committed to something somewhere between the different things I think Thoreau and Lincoln had in mind, there is no question but that conservatism is the dynamic intellectual movement today on our national scene, such as it is, and merits thought and consideration."

Surviving vicissitudes, *Modern Age* remained a principal medium for the discussion of large questions down through the Eighties — when Kirk returned to that journal as a contributor, and indeed its most frequent contributor.

During the Fifties, Kirk took ship across the Atlantic and back at least once each year; in some years he crossed both ways three times. Yet he remained rooted at Mecosta. At a convention of the

American Political Science Association, an intelligent young radical who wrote for *Partisan Review* accused Kirk of being a rootless cosmopolitan. Rather a *rooted* cosmopolitan, Kirk replied: that spring he had planted thousands of saplings upon his barren acres, many of them with his own hands.

In Britain and in the Continent, he knew as many *literati* of order as he did in America; some of those will figure in the next chapter. One of the purposes of *Modern Age,* as of Eliot's *Criterion,* had been to establish some communion among the better minds of Europe and America. And not knowing how long, between the colossi of East and West, the old civilization of Europe might endure — why, Kirk had best see the things and see the men while still they stood.

CHAPTER EIGHT

Poets, Statists, and Ruins

The Perplexities of Europe

Materially, by the late Fifties western Europe had recovered from the devastation of the Second World War. But politically, Europe was unstable; and morally, all was adrift. In the autumn of 1957, *Modern Age* having been launched upon a sea of troubles, Kirk participated in two European conferences of some significance.

At that hour when Communists and other ideologues were busy ripping to shreds the wardrobe of a moral imagination in eastern Europe, Asia, and Africa, people of a different cast of mind had turned tailors in the West, doing what they might to stitch together once more that serviceable old suit variously called "Christian civilization," "Western civilization," "North Atlantic community," or "the free world." Not by force of arms are civilizations held together, but by the threads of moral and intellectual belief. In the hands of the Fates are no thunderbolts: only threads and scissors.

One of those two large conferences was held at St. Moritz, Switzerland: the tenth-anniversary meeting of the Mont Pélerin Society, composed mainly of political economists. The other met at Bruges, Belgium: the Conference on North Atlantic Community, an assembly of political theorists, serious journalists, political leaders, and men of business. Both groups talked for a week, stitching away at their work of restoration.

The common bond among the members of the Mont Pélerin Society was belief in the enduring relevance of the "classical" political economy: classical not in the sense of Greek and Roman learning, of course, but the doctrines and substance of a competitive industrial economy, developed principally in the closing three decades of the eighteenth century and the first three decades of the nineteenth. A chief founder of the Society, and its president in 1957, was F. A. Hayek, then at the University of Chicago, famous for his book *The Road to Serfdom* — although his later volume *The Constitution of Liberty* (in which he was assisted by Kirk's friend Edwin McClellan) is more important.

As the word "conservative" was and is used in the popular press, the Mont Pélerin Society — which, issuing no manifestoes or publications, existed for discussions "to contribute to the preservation and improvement of the free society" — was conservative. So far as social first principles were concerned, however, most of its members had their intellectual roots in eighteenth- and nineteenth-century liberalism. But a considerable diversity of opinion could be discerned, nevertheless: Wilhelm Röpke of Geneva, for instance, was what Walter Bagehot would have called a "liberal conservative," a believing Christian, an opponent of "the cult of the colossal"; while Ludwig von Mises, survivor of the Austrian school of economists (but living in the United States), was the disciple of Jeremy Bentham, dedicated to pure efficiency — what he called himself at the St. Moritz meeting (though with a degree of irony), an "entrepreneurial Marxist."

This body took up questions of the day: aid to "underdeveloped" countries (which most members opposed), the European Common Market (which they favored). All in all, a fair number of members seemed in 1957 to be moving away from the more extreme doctrines of nineteenth-century Benthamism, yet remaining strongly attached to liberal concepts of the free market and political liberty — although, in later meetings, they would not move very far. Bentham's "greatest happiness principle" and pleasure-and-pain calculus were rejected by several speakers, notably French. (Americans and Englishmen were most numerous among the participants; then French, German, Swiss, Italian, and Dutch nationals, with a sprinkling from other countries.)

Near the end of the week's proceedings, for all that, the presidential address by Hayek went counter to the trend of much of the conference. Reading a paper entitled "Why I Am Not a Conservative," Hayek rejected the recrudescence of conservative ideas. Kirk was called upon, abruptly, to reply to Hayek, and did so impromptu; the exchange is described by Henry Regnery in his *Memoirs of a Dissident Publisher*.

Conservatives, Hayek declared, are timid, authoritarian, paternalistic, anti-democratic, anti-intellectual, illogical, mystical, and many other distressing things. (Those epithets amusingly resembled the abuse heaped upon Hayek himself by professors of the Left after the publication of *The Road to Serfdom*.) Yet he confessed that most liberals, old-style or new-style, were no more to his taste, and approved of merely two political thinkers, Tocqueville and Acton. The choice of these mentors — both of whom were Catholics, while Hayek was distinctly anti-Catholic — seemed odd in the light of his nineteenth-century rationalism. For his part, Hayek declared, he was not a liberal in the popular twentieth-century sense, nor yet a "libertarian," but an Old Whig. Now the original Old Whig was Edmund Burke, the original conservative: Burke's *Appeal from the New Whigs to the Old,* even more than his *Reflections on the Revolution in France,* is the touchstone for conservatives. That fact left Hayek's stand not wholly clear.

When Benthamite liberalism stood at the height of its influence, Sir Walter Scott observed, "The Whigs will live and die in the belief that the world is governed by little tracts and pamphlets." Scott meant, among other things, that the New Whigs (and their Liberal successors) tended to leave out of their reckoning some of the deeper longings and instincts of the human heart, relying wholly upon private rationality and appeals to self-interest. But really the world is governed, in any age, not by rationality but by faith: by love, loyalty, and imagination. One of the reasons for the decline of the liberals in the twentieth century has been the doctrinaire narrow view of human nature and society taken by leading lights of liberalism. An intense preoccupation with economic questions — productivity is all! — has afflicted the liberals from the closing years of the eighteenth century to those of the twentieth century. Hayek himself suggested that he was not unaware of such shortcomings; yet he brushed aside the religious origins of social order.

Behind Hayek's chain of reasoning — and, to an extent still greater, behind the arguments of such other members of the Society as Mises and Alexander Rustow of Heidelberg — seemed to lie the assumption that if only a perfectly free market economy could be established universally, all social difficulties would dissolve. But this was very like saying that if only the Sermon on the Mount were universally obeyed to the letter, sin would vanish from among men.

The trouble is that the Sermon on the Mount will not triumph until the end of all things earthly. There exist reasons for believing that the ideal universal free market is nearly so difficult of attainment.

The world, in short, never is governed merely by little tracts and pamphlets; nor can an economic order long endure apart from a moral order. The Society's meeting was held high among the Alps, in the Romansch-speaking district of Switzerland, where an ancient tongue and ancient ways have persisted little altered. The Grisons are governed not by little tracts and pamphlets but by living traditions. If the better features of oldfangled liberalism — or Old Whiggery — are to be joined to an intelligent defense of continuity and stability in society, much may be done to resist the fell spirit of totalist collectivism, which detests equally the conservative and the liberal understanding of social order.

Among the medieval canals and towers of Bruges, the Conference on North Atlantic Community sought for means to resist the totalist assault upon civilization. The College of Europe (situated at Bruges) and the University of Pennsylvania were this conference's sponsors; and the meeting was meant to provide some moral and intellectual equivalent for the North Atlantic Treaty Organization. Representatives attended from all NATO countries except Portugal, Turkey, and Greece.

The Conference was divided into several working groups: religion and spiritual values; education and language; scientific and technological advance and economic problems of Western civilization; causes of tensions; the North Atlantic and causes of totalitarianism; the North Atlantic and the underdeveloped world; institutional framework. At the week's end, these several groups presented reports, and general recommendations were adopted. An Irish participant, the writer Monk Gibbon, remarked in a plenary session that the conclusions of the working groups were platitudes; but platitudes are true; that is why they are platitudes. By and large, the Conference did examine seriously the foundations of a common civilization and was remarkably free from extreme views. The stand taken by the Conference against the Communist powers was forthright and well expressed.

Among the participants were conservatives, liberals, socialists, and Christian communitarians (these last led by Adriano Olivetti, the Italian industrialist); there were no Communists or fellow travellers, though some of the social democrats present called themselves Marxist. Within the ranks of participants who called themselves socialists, indeed, there seemed to be more marked animosities than were visible among the conservatives, liberals, socialists, and communitarians taken generally.

For instance, Kirk got on amicably with the English trade-union M.P. George Brown, then talked of as a possible future Labour prime minister. (Later he was created Lord George-Brown, a life peer.) Some years earlier, after visiting Poland, Brown had declared that the Polish Communist regime had realized the totalism of Orwell's *1984*. After Brown had left the room, there came up to Kirk a young parliamentary deputy from Denmark, a Social Democrat.

"That Brown and his British welfare state! Disgusting! Boring!" said the Dane.

"What sort of socialist are you?" Kirk asked.

"Why, I am a Social Democrat, and speak for the people, but I don't believe in the welfare state — monstrous!" The outburst of ideological passion in western Europe after the Second World War was diminishing, and party leaders were beginning to settle for politics as the art of the possible.

At the Conference, naturally some subjects were slipped over uneasily, for the sake of general agreement upon resolutions; upon other subjects uneasy compromises occurred. In the group concerned with economic problems, John Davenport, an editor of *Fortune* then, endeavored vainly to insert a recommendation favoring the institution of private property; the phrase itself was anathema to the socialists. Yet when that group's recommendations were presented in plenary session by their *rapporteur* (the English socialist Arthur Gaitskell, brother of Hugh Gaitskell, leader of the Labour party), the original stand of the socialist members had been much modified by discussions, so that Gaitskell spoke of capital as a scarce thing, not to be lavished recklessly upon every "underdeveloped" country, and of "trade, not aid."*

---

*Kirk had been told that in 1954 a New York publisher had been present in a London office when Hugh Gaitskell had entered, bearing a copy of the London edition of *The Conservative Mind*. "This book will set back socialism a generation!" Gaitskell had said, disapprovingly. But actually that book made less of a stir in Britain than in America.

In the group concerned with totalitarianism, some of the socialist participants were bent upon including a reproof of the Spanish and Portuguese regimes; but no one doubted that the real menace to the North Atlantic countries came from the Communist East, and "national" communism had no sympathizers. The group's condemnation of "national" and "decentralized" communism (with Yugoslavia in mind) was drawn up by a Belgian socialist, Arthur Wauters, once ambassador to Moscow. In the group's final report, there occurred no reference to Portugal, and the censure of Spain was moderate.

With so much concurrence upon first principles, the North Atlantic community seemed to have come a good way toward intellectual harmony. The Conference did not attempt to define precisely the common patrimony of Europe and America: there would have been too much squabbling at the outset had such an attempt been made; it was assumed that some common heritage of moral principle, of culture, and of social institutions did exist. Prudently the Conference refrained from drawing up any such abstract document as the United Nations' Universal Declaration of Human Rights. This lack of precision, however, had the disadvantage of leaving unuttered the beliefs that had commanded the loyalty of most people either side of the Atlantic. In his closing address to the Conference, Paul-Henri Spaak, the militant Belgian politician, got briefly to the heart of the matter when he declared that the unifying element in the North Atlantic community was Christianity. But he hastily qualified this doctrine by adding "as enriched by humanism and the French Revolution." Now humanism in one form — that of Erasmus and More — did enrich Christianity. The French Revolution did nothing to Christianity but kick it downstairs. Equivocation from a politician usually unequivocal was a concession to the rationalists and egalitarians present, but it suggested an ambiguity that necessarily afflicted a preliminary attempt among anti-collectivists to find common ground in the Age of Ideology.

If on a few occasions the proceedings at these two international conferences resembled those of the Bellorius Tercentenary Celebration in Neutralia, as depicted in Evelyn Waugh's post-war satire *Scott-King's Modern Europe,* still the conferences gave one some reason to think that Oswald Spengler's *Decline of the West* was not to be justified promptly by the event. Yet it is not conferences that determine for good or ill the course of civilizations. The minds of seminal thinkers — Voltaire or Newman, Burke or Marx — are more powerful movers; and the minds, too, of men and women less eminent, in every age, who produce works of humane letters and of scholarship that speak to the imagination and the reason of the rising generation. In Europe and in Britain, Kirk came to know some such, most of them a generation older than himself, during 1957.

The Humane Economics of Wilhelm Röpke

Mindful of Burke's detestation of "sophisters, economists, and calculators," Kirk regarded with some suspicion the practitioners of the Dismal Science as a body — even though, in later years, he would write a textbook in economics for high-school students. In general, they were a blinkered breed, worshipping the false god Efficiency.* Kirk exempted from this indictment W. A. Orton, David McCord Wright, and a few other political economists of the Fifties.

Especially he exempted Professor Wilhelm Röpke, of Geneva. It was Röpke's advice, carried out by his disciple Ludwig Erhardt, that had produced Germany's economic recovery after the War. More than a technical economist — though he was that, too, in high degree — Röpke was a social thinker of unusual penetration.

He was no apologist for an abstract "capitalism." His influence extended, indeed, to some curious quarters. He discovered, for instance, an interesting Italian disciple. Professor Röpke was invited to Florence to have a medal or some other distinction conferred upon him. Upon arriving at the railway station, he found an escort of mounted carabinieri awaiting him. Escorted soon to the Palazzo Vecchio, he was received there by a throng of all the rank and fashion and officialdom and Firenze's intelligentsia, greeting him with high

---

*The more imaginative economists were aware of this failing among men of their discipline. Take Orton, in *The Economic Role of the State*: "Let us therefore praise the great god Efficiency. All he demands is that we make straight his path through the desert and purge the opposition. . . . We arrive at 'justice' without mercy, 'liberation' without liberty, 'victory' without peace, 'efficiency' without effort, 'power' without potency — because the means we collectively employ lie on a plane so different from that of the ends we humanly desire that, the more they succeed, the more they fail."

ceremony. This crowd parted abruptly to make way for some personage of importance, who hurried straight up to Röpke. The man approaching him was seemingly effeminate, fantastically dressed in unusual colors, fat, gesticulating. This person seized Röpke's hands to kiss them ardently. "Maestro! Maestro!" he ejaculated; then, bowing low, he retired backward into the assemblage.

Röpke had been astonished at the splendor and cordiality of this gathering in his honor; he was yet more surprised at the adulation of this conspicuous person. "Who is that gentleman?" he inquired of an official host.

"Why, don't you know him, Professor Röpke? He is your disciple, the man who invited you here and arranged this ceremony. He is the chief of the Communist party of Florence."

Italian Communists notoriously differ from their comrades elsewhere in Europe: already, at the time of Röpke's visit, they were endeavoring to appear respectable — even bourgeois. (Their gangs had been conventionally ferocious enough, however, at the time of the final fall of Mussolini, murdering hundreds in Milan, Turin, and other cities.) Their Firenze chairman seems to have perceived in Röpke an economist fruitful in means, however much he might differ with him in ends.

Röpke and Kirk met at two gatherings of the Mont Pélerin Society, and once at Geneva, and elsewhere; they corresponded fairly frequently during the Fifties, and Kirk suggested the title for one of Röpke's books published in America, *A Humane Economy*.

Röpke had been a fearless opponent of the Nazi regime, and he assailed the Communists with equal vigor. He was all energy. When skiing, he disdained chairlifts and funiculars: having whizzed down, he would clamber up a peak on shank's mare. Man is made for action, not for ease. Röpke's intellectual action, expressed in his several books, was a resolute endeavor to humanize the industrial order and to undo the mischief worked by Nazis and Communists.

That scholar's humane imagination may be suggested by an incident Röpke related to Kirk while he was Röpke's guest in Geneva, about 1957. During the Second World War the city of Geneva had allocated garden plots along the line of the vanished city walls to citizens wishing to grow their own vegetables in a time of food shortages. This use of public land turned out to be popular; the city continued the allocation of plots after the war.

Röpke heartily approved of this undertaking, which both enabled people to obtain independently part of their own sustenance and provided the satisfaction of healthy achievement outside factory walls. When Ludwig von Mises came to visit Röpke at Geneva, Röpke took his guest to inspect those garden plots.

Mises sadly shook his head: "A very inefficient way of producing foodstuffs!"

"But perhaps a very efficient way of producing human happiness," Röpke told him.*

A stern opponent of socialism, Röpke was no enthusiast for an abstract capitalism. In *The Social Crisis of Our Time* — of which book Kirk brought out a new American edition in 1991 — Röpke wrote of a "Third Way" that was not gas-and-water socialism nor consumer cooperatives nor a managed economy. Instead it was economic activity humanized by being related to moral and intellectual ends, humanized by being reduced to a humane scale. Röpke proposed to abolish the proletariat, not by reducing everyone to proletarian status — the method of doctrinaire socialism — but by restoring property, function, and dignity to the mass of folk.

Humanizing of economic structure — *à la taille de l'homme* in the phrase of Ramuz — was the kernel of Röpke's proposals. These were not detailed; they were not buttressed by statistical tables; but they were cheering. Röpke reminded his auditors and readers that the art of political economy has an ethical foundation, and that the purpose of industry is personal security.

He believed in government from local institutions upward, not in government by a centralized bureaucratic elite; he believed, too, in economic organization from the bottom up. He hoped for a society with reverence, manners, stability, and secure personal rights; he saw that if we do not restore such a society, presently we will have no

---

*In the chapter entitled "Avenues of Approach and Examples" of Röpke's *The Social Crisis of Our Time* (first published in 1942), he mentions that "a friend of mine in Rotterdam" was showing "a dogmatic old-time liberal" workers' allotments. The liberal "on seeing these happy people spending their free evenings in their gardens could think of nothing better than the cool remark that this was an irrational form of vegetable production." May Röpke, to spare Mises' sensibilities, have identified the distinguished economist merely as "a dogmatic old-time liberal" in the pages of *The Social Crisis* and have shifted the scene from the garden plots of Geneva to the garden plots of Rotterdam?

civilized society at all. The work of the French Revolution must be undone, not to reinstate a rule of force but instead to venerate again just order, coherence, authority, and hierarchy, established by prescription and consent. Society cannot be organized "in accordance with rational postulates while disregarding the need for genuine communities, for a vertical structure."

The same infatuation with rationalism that terribly damages communal existence also produces an unquestioning confidence in the competitive market economy and a heartless individualism "which in the end has proved to be a menace to society and has so discredited a fundamentally sound idea as to further the rise of the far more dangerous collectivism." In such a world, where old landmarks have been swept away, old loyalties ridiculed, and human beings reduced to economic atoms, "men finally grasp at everything that is offered to them, and here they may easily and understandably suffer the same fate as the frogs in the fable who asked for a king and got a crane."

Kirk's wanderings in Switzerland — usually in winter — confirmed Röpke's argument that modern society need not accept ugliness and boredom with a shrug of resignation. Two or three times Kirk visited the town of Thun, at the foot of Thuner See, high peaks about it and the beautiful long lake stretching southward from its miniature harbor; he perceived how ingeniously the Swiss had reconciled the old world with the new.

From the station one crossed the river, made his way through twisting streets lined with ancient but well-preserved houses, and presently reached the hill on which stand the square-towered schloss and the old church. From the battlements of the schloss one looked down upon the remains of the city walls, the rathaus, and the immaculate prosperity of the place.

And then one discovered that Thun also was an industrial town of some importance, for across the railroad tracks were factories and warehouses looking as busy as the old town was sedate. Here was an industrialism that had not blighted a society's traditional life. Zurich, Basel, Bern, Fribourg, and other places far larger than Thun had been nearly as successful in keeping industrial existence decent. What a contrast with the industrial blight that was sweeping over a great part of the world!

Often the Swiss have been accused of lacking imagination. Then what should be said of social imagination in Russia, or in Britain, or in the United States? Röpke spoke of the human condition; but Moscow, London, and Washington were obsessed by the gross national product.

Otto von Habsburg, Justiciar

To Kirk's mind, the best political essay that he published during his editorship of *Modern Age* was "The Divine Right of Minorities," by Otto von Habsburg. The Archduke Otto, head of the greatest of European houses, was better informed about events of the time than was any other man Kirk ever met. Also, possessed of a philosophical habit of mind and a good education, he manifested a power of political imagination exceeding that of any American or British public man with whom Kirk was acquainted.

His convictions were expressed in small compass in his little book *The Social Order of Tomorrow: State and Society in the Atomic Age* (published in America in 1959); they resembled closely, in many particulars, the convictions of Wilhelm Röpke. He wrote many books, among them a very interesting life of his great ancestor Charles V. It was not as a pretender to the imperial throne that he wrote and spoke: he labored under no illusion that he might rule as the Emperor Franz Josef had ruled so long, or even as his father the Emperor Karl had ruled so briefly. At one time the Archduke Otto told Kirk that he did aspire to become, conceivably, justiciar in Austria — that is, to revive the medieval office of justiciar, above party, with the high duty of safeguarding the laws — a kind of "repository of laws," to borrow Montesquieu's phrase. But that did not happen; indeed, the Archduke and all the house of Habsburg were forbidden by law, until very recent years, to enter Austria at all. Even when that law was changed, Otto did not return to Vienna, which he had left at the age of seven: the socialist labor unions threatened a general strike if he should. (He would make brief trips into Austria, but did not take up residence.) The Austrian socialists were proscribing one of the most able and intelligent men in Europe, and one of the most tolerant and far-sighted.

No, what Otto von Habsburg sought was not personal power or family restoration, but the restoration of the genius of Christianity to the politics of the twentieth century, so ravaged by ideological fanaticism. He did not mean that Christianity should be the province of a party; rather, he said that Christian faith upheld the dignity of man, set bounds to arbitrary power, and was "the great bulwark against totalitarianism's promise of immediate success." This teaching, and his analyses of present discontents, dangers, and hopes, he uttered round the world, decade upon decade.

His path and Kirk's crossed often in the Fifties: on the speakers' platform at Turin; at the University of Detroit and in a Grosse Pointe mansion; in Upper Bavaria, where the Archduke and his large immediate family lived in a nineteenth-century house built by an actor, in the village of Pöcking.

About the time when Kirk called upon the Archduke at Pöcking, a first son had been born to him and his consort Regina, née the Princess Regina von Sachsen-Meiningen. This visit had been arranged by Kirk's Salzburg friend Thomas Chaimowicz, a classical scholar and a Jew, founder of the Edmund Burke Society of Austria; the Archduke had no warmer admirer and supporter than Dr. Chaimowicz, son of a Viennese textile manufacturer. The Habsburgs in power had been the protectors of minorities, Jews among them. When Theodore Roosevelt inquired of Franz Josef how he saw his imperial place in modern times, the Emperor answered, "To protect my people from their government."

What Kirk found at Pöcking was a vigorous and cheerful household, intellectually lively, gracious in manners. The Archduke, forever writing, forever speaking, had no touch of melancholy about him: he was too busy for that. In his mind's eye, at the moment, Kirk contrasted this imperial family with Chateaubriand's gloomy descriptions of his waiting upon the exiled Bourbons at Prague and at Edinburgh. The Habsburg abilities, so conspicuously successful over many centuries, seemed to be undiminished in the latter half of the twentieth century.

The Archduke, something of a futurist, knew that those who ignore history are condemned to repeat it. As he wrote in his *Modern Age* article, "It is characteristic of a generation that has lost its sense of historical perspective and become so self-centered that it no longer sees the continuity of which it is a part. In rejecting its past, it has renounced its future, and sometimes its erratic and futile measures in the present convince one that these are the desperate activities of those who truly anticipate annihilation. The perspective of history has been lost because history gives up its meaning only in the perspective of eternity."

A powerful sense of duty animated him. The Emperor Franz Josef is said to have declared, "Only three things matter: work, duty, honor." The Archduke Otto so acted, exiled, a statesman without a state. Ever since his youth, he has travelled very widely, observing, speaking, advising, sometimes in peril of violent death. He was imprisoned for a time by Hitler. Contriving to reach the United States during the Second World War, he found President Roosevelt very friendly, and was welcome at the White House whenever he might call. Late in September 1940, he found Franklin Roosevelt in high spirits. "Otto," the President said, "I have good news for you. It has been a secret business, but the event will have occurred before you have opportunity to discuss it with anybody. Tomorrow we land at Dakar!"

This business was the descent upon Dakar, on the coast of Senegal, by Free French troops with British transports and naval support. It was the intention of the Allies to secure a base in French West Africa, then held by the forces of Vichy; and thence, eventually, to link up with Allied forces in North Africa.

Roosevelt went on to predict to the Archduke swift victory in Senegal. "But that will be only the beginning, Otto." Africa would become an American sphere of influence, American democracy spreading throughout the Dark Continent. (Such had been Colonel House's plan, in Woodrow Wilson's administration.) Of all African ports, Dakar, on the fifteenth parallel of latitude, was closest to the United States — or, more precisely, to America's Caribbean possessions. Free French troops and British ships might take Dakar from Vichy, but it was Roosevelt's intention to make that an American military base. "We will push the French and British colonialists out of Africa."

General Charles de Gaulle in person commanded the Allied force meant to land at Dakar; the whole design was his.

"General De Gaulle may disapprove of your plans, Mr. President," the Archduke commented.

Roosevelt laughed angrily. "Who is De Gaulle? What is France? If the French object, we'll wipe them off the face of the earth."

On September 22, 1940, the artillery of the Vichy French garrison at Dakar beat back the Allied fleet. Although before long the

Free French obtained access to other ports, and a good deal of territory, in French West Africa, it was not until December 1941 that the United States entered the war, and Operation Torch, the Allied invasion of North Africa, did not come to pass (at Roosevelt's insistence on this strategy) until November 1942. The notion of an American base at Dakar never took on flesh, although of course it became American policy, after the War, to encourage nationalism and self-determination in "emergent Africa."*

Franklin Roosevelt was not an evil man, Otto von Habsburg remarked to Kirk, after describing that White House exchange about Dakar. But power intoxicates, the Archduke said; and even granted good will, a man possessed of unchecked power almost certainly will do mischief. Ruinous miscalculations like the 1940 descent on Dakar sometimes are unhappy consequences of the arrogance of power. The restraining of centralized political power, Otto knew, is more difficult by far in the twentieth century than it had been in medieval times.

The tireless Archduke might turn up anywhere in the world. Once, in the Sixties, Kirk encountered him on an escalator at the Dallas airport, he going up, Kirk going down. Before Kirk could speak, the courageous, solitary little figure of the head of the House of Habsburg had vanished in the crowd. But what could one have said, at a moment's passing, to an emperor *de jure* on an escalator?

In the Seventies, Russell and Annette Kirk would attend a lecture given by the Archduke at a chicken restaurant in Frankenmuth, Michigan, the Knife and Fork Club of Saginaw having invited him. Although he lectured brilliantly, with a wealth of detail, about the international tensions of the time, the Knife and Fork gentry stared at him with dull eyes; not one intelligent question was put to him. What fortitude on the lecture circuit! Afterward he conversed for hours with the Kirks and the Saginaw couple who were his hosts that night. There must have run through his mind, often, the admonition, "Say not the struggle naught availeth."

---

*President Roosevelt's interest in securing Dakar as a base of operations long before the Pearl Harbor disaster brought the United States into the war is touched upon in Eric Larrabee's *Commander in Chief: Franklin Delano Roosevelt, His Lieutenants, and Their War* (1987). Larrabee mentions Roosevelt's assessment of Winston Churchill as a "British colonialist" in African affairs.

Sometimes the lives of two men, remote from each other in distance and in station, are plaited curiously. It was so with the Archduke Otto and Russell Kirk — though the kindly hand of Dr. Thomas Chaimowicz may be detected in this connection of the two. For there would arrive at Piety Hill, in 1982, the first Archduchess ever to set foot on Mecostan soil: Her Imperial Highness Walburga, a tall daughter of the Archduke Otto. ("Will she be wearing her crown?" asked Andrea Kirk, aged seven years.) The Archduchess was to spend some months in the United States, acquiring the craft of serious journalism, and she sought the Kirks' advice. In no time at all she was flying about collecting information for her *Reader's Digest* articles. Her father's political inclinations and talents were inherited by Walburga, alone among his daughters; Walburga became her father's aide in the European Parliament.

For by the Seventies, a federation of western Europe was in progress, and Otto von Habsburg was in the forefront of the movement. First Baden elected him its representative to the European Parliament, and then Bavaria elected him. At Strasbourg, his energies and eloquence were poured into the Parliament; personally he was popular even among the radical members. It was all rather like the ascendancy gained by the personable king in G. B. Shaw's play *The Apple Cart*. At last, as he grew old, the Habsburg's voice counted for something in the affairs of Europe. Ability will tell, even in a democratic age.

And in 1984, the Archduke Karl von Habsburg, elder son of Otto, would make his way to Piety Hill; he would spend most of the summer there, reading Burke, participating in the seminars in Kirk's library, being introduced to American practical politics through the Reagan presidential campaign. Adventurous, humorous, interested in everything under the sun, a hunter and a soldier and a navigator, easy in manner — why, Karl fascinated everybody of all ages. Undoubtedly he would follow his father into politics. Already he had seen much of the world, and already he possessed the intelligence of the heart. At length he would fly back to Austria (where he was studying law) to debate on television with Bruno Kreisky, the former chancellor.

Although Kirk had been abashed at being expected to play Aristotle to Karl's Alexander, he found the young Archduke quick of apprehension, if fonder of action than of theory. Even with the handicap of the grandest of European names, he would go far. What's in a name? Why, sometimes a high patrimony, both genetic and cultural — Burke's unbought grace of life.

The Imagination of T. S. Eliot

In 1948, when Kirk kept a good bookshop, not a few young people still fancied that Eliot expressed their own romantic nihilism. Many books about him having been published since then, that illusion no longer prevails. Eliot's descent into the numinous depths of the soul is not the path to Avernus; and "Difficulties of a Statesman" no longer is mistaken for an ideological poem.

Eliot and Kirk first met face to face in a little private hotel in Edinburgh, during the Edinburgh Festival of 1953, at which Eliot's play *The Confidential Clerk* first was performed. Kirk was to review for *The Month* that comedy; and Eliot, of the firm of Faber and Faber, was planning to publish the London edition of *The Conservative Mind*.

At that first encounter, Kirk was moved by Eliot's kindness — an impression confirmed by their meetings and correspondence for several years thereafter. The poet had passed through great sorrow to resignation and hope.

Recent psychobiographers have endeavored to discover vast dark secrets in Eliot's life. But the truth about his sorrow is quite simple and not at all extraordinary: he married young, imprudently; he loved not wisely but too well; his first wife, Vivienne, was neurotic from the first, became unbearable, and presently went mad. She vanished into an asylum; not until after her death did Eliot marry a second time, and wisely. Millions of men in the twentieth century have suffered from broken marriages, and Kirk never found the details of other folks' marital troubles a fascinating topic — even though it delights many psychobiographers. But great poets, who perceive much more clearly than does the average sensual man, also may feel more deeply. Eliot's friend Conrad Aiken might shed wives and mistresses casually enough, but with Eliot it was far otherwise. Out of that sorrow and his search for consolation through faith arose Eliot's major poems.

Until, long later, Kirk prepared to write his big book about his friend Eliot, he knew next to nothing about the disastrous first marriage. This ignorance produced a *faux pas*. One day in 1954, Kirk had spent some hours with Wyndham Lewis and his wife in their Notting Hill studio flat. The next day, Kirk lunched at the Garrick with Eliot and someone else (Herbert Agar?). As the three were putting on their coats to leave, Kirk remarked to his companions that Froanna Lewis was an admirable woman; he had fancied from reading Lewis's novel *Self Condemned* that Mrs. Lewis was another sort of person. Upon the utterance of this judgment, Eliot and Agar fell totally and distressingly silent. What had Kirk done? Wasn't it cricket to mention ladies at the Garrick Club? This blunder occurred four years before Eliot married Valerie Fletcher, who brought to him peace. To refer to Lewis's wife was to rouse memories of Eliot's first marriage, a subject never to be discussed; no man guarded his privacy more jealously than did Eliot.

On a wide variety of other subjects, Eliot talked with Kirk and wrote to him at length. What a voluminous correspondence he must have kept up, painstakingly and interestingly, busy though he was! The two met at the Garrick, at the Authors' Club, at Eliot's little office in Russell Square; they had friends in common — B. I. Bell, George Scott-Moncrieff, Lord Crawford, Henry Regnery, Wyndham Lewis, Roy Campbell, others. Kirk had subtitled the first edition of *The Conservative Mind* "From Burke to Santayana." Eliot remarked privately to Regnery that perhaps Santayana was not important enough to justify such an association — though he had been on very friendly terms with that philosopher (a complete materialist), and at one time Eliot, Santayana, and Ezra Pound had thought of collaborating in a book about education. In later editions Kirk enlarged his section on Eliot, and set down the new subtitle "From Burke to Eliot" — for indeed those two better consisted.

In 1952, while in Fife for a season before publication of *The Conservative Mind,* Kirk endeavored to entice Eliot into an expedition to Cyprus, that once-enchanted island. The Egyptians were then demanding the withdrawal of British troops from the country: at Cairo, on January 26, 1952, "Black Saturday," a mob had massacred the British occupants of Shepheard's Hotel, roasting some alive and dismembering others in the streets; the hotel and much more of central Cairo had been burnt. Cyprus, at that same season, was about to explode in revolution against British rule.

Eliot suffered from arthritis and other complaints; his doctor, who must never have read newspapers, had suggested that his distinguished patient ought to spend the winter in a warm, dry land — "Egypt, perhaps, or Cyprus." About that archaic recommendation clung the odor of nineteenth-century British confidence.

So, fancying archaic things, Kirk took up that proposal. Eliot and he ought to travel to warm and dry Cyprus, bomb-ravaged, garroting Cyprus, land of the prickly pear, so that they might fulfill the ghostly lines of "The Hollow Men":

Here we go round the Prickly pear
At five o'clock in the morning.

They might be so fortunate as to terminate, Kirk went on, not with a whimper, but a bang! — refuting the final line of that poem. But Eliot stuck to London, and Kirk never did adventure to Cyprus.

Eliot had published his *Notes towards the Definition of Culture* in November 1948, a month after Kirk had settled at St. Andrews; Kirk had read the slim book immediately, and has re-read it several times since. *Notes* relates the poetic imagination to the political imagination.

From the beginning, it had been Eliot's purpose to defend "lost" causes, because he knew that no cause worth upholding is lost altogether. He had sworn fealty to the permanent things, understanding that these permanent things are not the creations of men merely. As the inheritor of the purpose of Vergil and Dante, Eliot endeavored to "redeem the time, redeem the dream."

The things for which Eliot stood are not difficult to make out. First, he was moved by what Unamuno called "the tragic sense of life." Were it not for the hope that man is made for eternity, we should be wretched. Accepting dogmata, Eliot renewed in this century the apprehension of the theological virtues.

Second, Eliot abided by ancestral wisdom: the Hebraic and Christian and classical patrimony of culture. As Eliot expressed this in his essay "Tradition and the Individual Talent" (1917), "Some one said: 'The dead writers are remote from us because we know so much more than they did.' Precisely, and they are that which we know."

Third, Eliot sought to recover the idea of a community of souls, joining the dead, the living, and those yet unborn. The disorder of modern politics is produced by the decay of that community in spirit.

Replying to Karl Mannheim, Eliot wrote of modern political theory: "Being occupied only with humanity in the mass, it tends to separate itself from ethics; being occupied only with that recent period of history during which humanity can most easily be shown to have been ruled by impersonal forces, it reduces the proper study of mankind to the last two or three hundred years of man. It too often inculcates a belief in a future inflexibly determined and at the same time a future which we are wholly free to shape as we like."

What Eliot's revolution in literature gave to his age was a renewal of moral imagination — with social consequences, potentially. Eliot's orthodoxy, expressed in new forms, offered something more attractive to mind and heart than could either liberalist aridity or the ominous People's Hall of Culture. Literature and society both depend upon belief in a transcendent order, Eliot reminded the twentieth century. "If you will not have God (and he is a jealous God) you should pay your respects to Hitler or Stalin," Eliot wrote in *The Idea of a Christian Society*. Eliot scandalized many because he went all the way to "the awful daring of a moment's surrender" — that is, surrender to the divine.

"It is a tendency of creative literature, when it rises above a certain level," Rebecca West concludes in *The Court and the Castle*, "to involve itself with statecraft and religion: to exist and to belong to Him." Eliot involved himself with both, boldly submitting his strong private rationality to the authority of dogmas. But to the popular statecraft of his own time, Eliot did not surrender: against totalism, he set the idea of a Christian society.

"There seems to be no hope in contemporary politics at all," he had written in *The Criterion*, in 1933. As he wrote to Kirk, "A decline in private morality is certain to be followed in the long run by a decline in public and political morality also." Before humankind stretches a dark age: "We are destroying our ancient edifices to make ready the ground upon which the barbarian nomads of the future will encamp in their mechanized caravans," he put it in *Notes towards the Definition of Culture*.

Eliot's was a lonely voice in the Forties and Fifties; today he is echoed by many thinking people — among them not a few who derided him formerly. There are no lost causes because there are no gained causes, Eliot argued in his essay on Francis Herbert Bradley. "We fight for lost causes because we know that our defeat and dismay

may be the preface to our successors' victory, though that victory itself will be temporary; we fight rather to keep something alive than in the expectation it will triumph." That passage, Kirk found heartening often.

Eliot's adversary H. G. Wells, so influential between the Wars, died despairing for humanity. Eliot will endure because he was a man of imagination, while Wells was a man of fancy. Eliot knew that men may redeem the time only if they apprehend the timeless; that the dream may be redeemed only if one distinguishes between those false dreams that issue from between the gates of ivory, and those true dreams that issue from between the gates of horn.

"After such knowledge, what forgiveness?" Gerontion soliloquizes. The shallow presumption of doctrinaire rationalism, Eliot argued, has stranded us in cactus-land. "Where is the wisdom we have lost in knowledge?/Where is the knowledge we have lost in information?" Those lines from *The Rock* now speak to many of the rising generation — even if some of that generation turn to strange gods.

Eliot wrote to Kirk in August 1964, hoping to see him in London soon. But Eliot died in January 1965, on the day when Russell and Annette Kirk were in the air on the way to South Africa. Four years later, in the old church at East Coker, Kirk would pray for the soul of that wise and good friend. On the oval memorial tablet was graven the line borrowed from Mary Stuart: "In my end is my beginning." There came into Kirk's consciousness lines from Young:

> Still seems it strange, that thou shouldst live forever?
> Is it less strange, that thou shouldst live at all?
> This is a miracle; and that no more.

The Truth about Roy Campbell

Another of Kirk's friends of the Fifties, the lyric poet Roy Campbell, by accident went over an Iberian cliff, though he had survived wounds and injuries in several countries. To die in an automobile was an ironical end for Roy, who had loved horses and bulls but detested all machines. Kirk called him "the last of the scalds," for, like the Viking scalds, Campbell was fearless, outrageous, and reckless, at once a doer of deeds and a singer of them.

Loving freedom and tradition, he was beaten by Communists in Toledo and beat literary ideologues in Bloomsbury. He commanded four hundred of the King's African Rifles — many of them cannibals — in East Africa; he was storm-tossed in the Hebrides, anathematized in Durban, torn by wild beasts in Africa, buffeted by the critics of the Left. At one time or another he was sailor, shepherd, soldier, war correspondent, secret agent (an ineffectual one), hunter, horse trader, bull breeder. And always he was a poet of high imagination and skill. Spain he loved above all other lands. Despite the violence of his career, he was the gentlest of companions. Kirk spent days with him in Chicago and in London.

No man ever found more pleasure in life than did Roy Campbell — interested passionately in sea creatures, in insects, in children, in Christian faith, in the world of letters, in Mithraic symbols, in gypsies, Africans, ancient towns, ancient ballads. Once he told Kirk that he could have sat happily for a thousand years under Spanish oaks, watching the pigs feeding on acorns.

Much of the whimsical variety of the man may be gleaned from his autobiography, *Light on a Dark Horse* (which deals with his life only to the outbreak of the Spanish Civil War, he never finishing his projected second volume). But one does not learn from that diverting book how humane was this fighting wanderer and scoffer at modernity.

Campbell was an undismayed champion in arms against the gloomy powers that unnerve modern man. He never feared to brandish the sword of imagination. As he wrote in his Civil War poem "To the Survivors,"

> For none save those are worthy birth
> Who neither life nor death will shun:
> And we plow deepest in the Earth
> Who ride the nearest to the Sun.

Some people embroider the truth; and yet they may be more modest, and in essence more truthful, than certain men and women who pride themselves upon their literal veracity. Roy Campbell interwove his fact and his fiction. In reading his autobiography, one cannot be quite sure that, in many particulars, it is a factual narrative. Did Roy really wage that desperate fight against gypsies on a bridge near Toledo? Who can say? Were Roy alive, one might obtain only a poetic answer from him.

Much of Campbell's account of his adventures in the Civil War is grisly reality, and some of it is fanciful. Camilo Cela, the Spanish man of letters (whom Kirk met in Palma de Mallorca) was asked whether Roy's soldiering against the Reds was to be accepted soberly. "What does that matter?" Cela objected, in very Spanish fashion. "Campbell wandered along the front, sometimes as a journalist, sometimes with a gun. Put it down that everything he wrote was perfectly true. The real Campbell is the Campbell of his books."

Roy's was the true poet's awareness that high truth is symbolic, rather than matter of fact. The poet's interpretation of reality is elastic, but it is not false because of that latitude. Truth is a coy mistress who lets no mortal possess her utterly. Yet the poet is more favored by her than are the dull, prosy souls who confound petty detail with wisdom.

One evening Kirk was with the poet, his wife, their beautiful daughter, and Campbell's close friend Rob Lyle. "This fellow," Campbell said, nodding toward Lyle, "is writing a book about me, and he's caught me in seven great whopping lies already."

Roy was unabashed. Mary Campbell mentioned that Roy had lied when he declared that he had been a shepherd during his vagabond years in Provence. "You never were a shepherd, Roy. You lived among shepherds, but you never were one yourself."

"You don't know that," Roy retorted in his amicable way. "There are years of my life you can't account for. I might have been a shepherd."

On another occasion, when Kirk happened to mention his month-long residence in the Hebridean Isle of Eigg, Roy remarked that he had been torpedoed twice in troopships off the Small Isles, and had swum to shore, using as his landmark in those wild waters the volcanic peak called the Sgurr of Eigg. Having visited in Eigg the graves of nameless soldiers and sailors drowned off that island during the War, Kirk accepted as fact this heroic feat. In reality, it turns out, the transport *Antenor,* with Sergeant Campbell trying to control the terrified troops aboard, did very nearly founder in the seas between Scotland and Ireland; and out of those five dreadful days came Campbell's powerful poem "One Transport Lost." But the *Antenor,* after such peril, limped back to Glasgow.

If one would understand Campbell, the first thing to do is to read G. K. Chesterton's romance *Manalive,* published in 1921, about the time when Campbell (in the words of Peter Alexander, his biographer) "tramped about southern France, a bearded long-haired figure in shabby clothes who was several times mistaken for an escaped convict." It is doubtful whether Chesterton and Campbell ever met. Nevertheless, Roy Campbell was Innocent Smith of *Manalive* — wanderer, enthusiast, commonsense philosopher, pistol-packing servant of God. Even Innocent's eccentric endless romance with his own wife was paralleled by Roy's tempestuous (but finally idyllic) relations with Mary Campbell.

A passage from *Light on a Dark Horse* suggests the identity with Innocent Smith: "I hate 'Humanity' and all such abstracts; but I love *people*. Lovers of 'Humanity' generally hate *people and children,* and keep parrots or puppy-dogs." The real life of Roy Campbell, exaggerate and fabricate though Campbell did, was more fantastic than the fictitious life of Innocent Smith.

Aye, Roy was Innocent; also he was the original of Victor Stamp in Wyndham Lewis's novel *The Revenge for Love*. Stamp, duped by Communists, had gone to his death over a Spanish cliff, as Campbell one day would in Portugal. Wyndham Lewis once told Campbell, "I never loved anyone, Roy — except possibly you, a little." Indeed, Campbell was easy to love. "Wyndham Lewis is always trying to kill me off in his novels," Campbell told Kirk.

Perhaps Campbell's most enduring work is his rendering of the poems of Saint John of the Cross, published in 1951, with a preface by Martin D'Arcy. "Roy Campbell carries us with him to Spain and into the presence of a Saint singing of the love of God," Father D'Arcy wrote. Edith Sitwell, in her foreword to the third volume of Campbell's *Collected Poems* (1960), declared that "Roy Campbell was one of the very few great poets of our time." Stephen Spender, once Campbell's bitter enemy, did not rank Roy so high; but he was very ready to concede, recently, that Campbell was "the author of a number of resplendent poems unique in modern English verse."

Campbell wrote with passion, out of ardent and sometimes horrible experience of the twentieth-century world. The Primate of Spain confirmed Roy and Mary just before the Red militia seized power in Toledo (except for the besieged Alcazar) and murdered the Campbells' Carmelite confessors, together with all the other Carmelite monks. Out of this Toledo terror rose Campbell's poem "Toledo, July 1936":

> . . . high above the roaring shells
> I heard the silence of your bells
> Who've left these broken stones behind
> Above the years to make your home,
> And burn, with Athens and with Rome,
> A sacred city of the mind.

Writing often of death, Campbell glowed with his love of life: Innocent Smith, again.

"At certain strange epochs," says Innocent Smith in Chesterton's *Manalive,* "it is necessary to have another kind of priests, called poets, actually to remind men that they are not dead yet. The intellectuals among whom I moved were not even alive enough to fear death. They hadn't blood enough in them to be cowards. Until a pistol barrel was poked under their very noses they never even knew they had been born. For ages looking up to an eternal perspective it might be true that life is a learning to die. But for these little white rats it was just as true that death was their only chance of learning to live."

That passage might have been Campbell's retort to his literary adversaries; certainly it is in Roy's tone. But there was no malice in Campbell. To quote again from *Manalive,* "His eccentricities sprang from a static fact of faith, in itself mystical, and even childlike and Christian."

Kirk had taken his chances in clouds of poison gas, on peaks of the Rockies, and in alleys of New Orleans; he had walked the streets of Detroit with a sheath knife at his belt. But to Roy Campbell he most humbly took off his Borsalino hat. Dead? Not that incandescent soul.

The Solitary Fortitude of Wyndham Lewis

People have called Percy Wyndham Lewis the most uncivil man of the century. Yet to Kirk he was courteous and generous. Lewis spent his life trying to escape from the prison-house of self; and if the arrogant ego looms so large in his books, that is because he knew the ego for his enemy.

When Kirk knew this innovator in painting and in the novel, he was old and blind and sick, living at the top of an old house in

Notting Hill — which, with his mordant humor, he called Rotting Hill. Since the days when Kirk visited Lewis in his studio, that quarter of London has sunk from bad to worse; there Jamaicans and Cockneys fought in the streets; the building where Lewis lived fell to the house-breakers of the London County Council, along with much else near Notting Hill Gate.

Henry Regnery suggested that Kirk call upon Lewis, whose books Regnery published in America. Long interested in political theory, Lewis had made his secretary read aloud to him *The Conservative Mind*. Distrusting Regnery as he distrusted all publishers, Lewis preferred to meet Kirk alone. Earlier, when Regnery had asked Lewis out to dinner, Lewis had insisted that they dine at the Hyde Park Grill: "It's very expensive; you understand that you're paying." Kirk invited Lewis to join him there, that restaurant indeed being very good; but on the appointed evening, Lewis fell sicker; and so their meetings occurred at the Lewises' studio flat.

Although their personalities were radically dissimilar, Lewis and Kirk got along well. The old tiger encouraged Kirk to tell him anecdotes of Michigan life and asked him to name and describe "a conservative city": Kirk obliged with a description of Grand Rapids. (Kirk undertook a defense of Lewis's *America and Cosmic Man* against Lewis's hostile American critics.)

They sat in that gloomy studio, with Lewis's admirable wife by his side, he drinking little bottles of champagne — his doctor denying him most other strong drink — that Eliot had brought to him from France. Before Kirk he had set a bottle of brandy — the drink of heroes, according to Samuel Johnson — and Kirk drank it to the lees, at Lewis's urging. Conceivably Lewis might not have been so hospitable, had he been able to see the inroads his guest was making upon his stock. For Kirk's friends Geoffrey and Dora Stone had visited Lewis in 1949; earlier, he had been their guest in America. They dined with him and Froanna. Lewis had grown increasingly uneasy as the food was consumed, complained about inflation, was about to offer them brandy — and then said, "But of course you must be going" — and virtually pushed them out of the door. Lewis's most recent and most thorough biographer, Jeffrey Meyers, conjectures that Lewis feared the Stones might convert Froanna to the Catholic faith — awkward for Lewis, because then their marriage would have had to be validated by a Catholic ceremony. However that may be, certainly

[221]

Lewis was poor, and certainly he often was rude; yet he was cordial to Kirk.

The editor of *The Yale Review*, in 1955, asked Kirk to write a long article about Lewis's work, and the result much pleased Lewis, who was more accustomed to denunciation. He objected, in a letter to Kirk, only to Kirk's assertion that Lewis was loveless. If Lewis did not know how to love, at least he knew how to hate well; and his candor made him the most detested literary man of his time.

All the charlatans detested Wyndham Lewis. They abhorred him because he, an original, would not tolerate shams. From first to last, he struck out for himself: in painting, in criticism, in politics, in fiction. He created his own styles, and he mocked the people who aped him. A real bohemian, he flayed the pseudo-bohemians of the beards and the toreador pants who made unconventionality conventional. Because the Communist was a sham radical, Lewis loathed him; because the modern leader of society was a sham gentleman, Lewis caricatured him. For good or ill, Lewis was genuine all through.

Being an unconventional champion of the upper-middle-class culture of the nineteenth century, Lewis despised the "progress" of the welfare state in Britain. He found the level of medical practice decayed under the National Health Service — a sore spot with an old man ailing and often in want of money — and his stories and vignettes of hospitals and doctors, in his closing years, are among his most biting productions.

Lewis put no trust in man. He saw society sinking into an abyss, and because he dared to say so, Bloomsbury called him a Fascist. In point of fact, his politics were those of nineteenth-century liberalism: distrusting all power, he protested against restraints upon individuality. But where the liberals substituted Progress for Providence, Lewis would let no utopian sham fill the void: one of the few men with the courage of his convictions, he laughed, Democritus-like, amidst the crash of worlds.

Jeffrey Meyers applies to Lewis the judgment of Samuel Johnson on Savage: "The insolence and resentment of which he is accused were not easily to be avoided by a great mind, irritated by perpetual hardships, and constrained hourly to return the spurns of contempt, and repress the insolence of prosperity; and vanity may surely be readily pardoned in him, to whom life afforded no other comforts than barren praises, and the consciousness of deserving them."

Despite Lewis's literary celebrity and his eminence as a painter, his writings reached only an astonishingly small body of readers during his whole lifetime, and his pictures sometimes were sold for pittances. Reviewers often were brutal with him, chiefly because he was a man of the Right and never ran with the hounds. He aspired to be the detached observer; certainly he was detached from everything popular. As Kirk wrote of him in 1955, drawing a parallel with old Thomas Carlyle, "God, Freedom, and Immortality are not his; yet there in Notting Hill still sits (in this time of buckram masks and literary phantasms) a man."

Jeffrey Meyers observes that Lewis's "political judgment was seriously defective" and that if he had not written political tracts, "his reputation would have been much greater." The latter judgment is incontestable; as for the former, surely Lewis was erratic and inconsistent in his political polemics; yet some very shrewd observations may be found in his political writings; and the political judgments of those numerous writers who fancied that Stalin had opened the way to the terrestrial paradise were conspicuously more defective than Lewis's. Although he denied being a reactionary, Lewis reacted most healthily against the Communist party, in London or in Spain, "sham underdogs athirst for power; whose doctrine was a universal Sicilian Vespers, and which yet treated the real poor, when they were encountered, with such overweening contempt, and even derision." As Roy Campbell pointed out, a human body that cannot react is a corpse; and so it is with a body social.

Lewis was an unflinching rationalist — or so he seemed, most of his life. Meyers touches on Lewis's "antipathy to religion." But the matter is more intricate than that. A little essay might be written about Lewis's general friendliness toward Catholic priests in his fiction, and his commendation of Catholic hospitals as the only surviving institution in which a patient might feel safe. His kindest reception during his dreary years of exile in Canada was at Catholic colleges. Anglican priests, true, more than once were the butt of his mordant wit. But of Lewis's *Time and Western Man*, Father Martin D'Arcy wrote that it was "one of the most significant books of our age." And then there is Lewis's trilogy *The Human Age*, of which the first volume, *The Childermass*, was published in 1928: is that antipathy to religion, or a fantastic exercise of the religious imagination?

Lewis never wrote an intended final fourth volume of *The* *Human Age*. That series of sardonic fables or fantastic novels shows us existence beyond the jaws of death: the divine and the diabolical are in contest. Hugh Kenner, in his essay "The Trial of Man," appended to *Malign Fiesta* (the third volume of the existing trilogy, the Inferno of Lewis's twentieth-century Divine Comedy), describes Lewis's intention at the end of his days.

According to Kenner, Lewis had concluded, "after so many years' involvement in the death agonies of the Europe he had known as a boy, that its tragedy lay in the loss of a common religion. He spoke of his mother, a Catholic who had ceased to practice her faith without, apparently, repudiating it, and of his own growing interest in the Old Religion. He spoke of being converted, if he could find the right instructor. . . . Had Lewis been ten years younger *The Trial of Man* [the intended concluding volume of *The Human Age*] might have inaugurated yet another, and utterly radical, new beginning."

The philosophical novelist had come a great way from *Tarr,* his first novel, to his aspiration at the end. For *The Trial of Man,* barely commenced by the dying blind genius, was to have been Wyndham Lewis's vision of salvation.

Wreckers pulled down Lewis's studio flat the day after he died; they had been eager to demolish it earlier; they flung his drawings on the floor, mutilating some. This treatment would not have startled Lewis, who so early as 1914 had written ironically, "When you hear a famous man has died penniless and diseased, you say, 'Well served.' Part of life's arrangement is that the few best become these cheap scarecrows." Lewis had paid a bitter price for setting himself against the spirit of the age.

Among Ruins

Eliot, Campbell, and Lewis were three twentieth-century literary men of order whom Kirk read closely and about whom he would write something substantial. But he met others.

There was Robert Graves, at his remote house near Deyá, in Mallorca; they talked of magic and shared a detestation of Logicalism, the ideology outlined in Graves's romance *Seven Days in New Crete:*

Logicalism, the death of spirit, the illusion that man is made for production and consumption merely.

There were Anthony and Elaine Kerrigan, of Palma de Mallorca and Dublin, accomplished translators of Unamuno, Ortega y Gasset, Borges, and other authors in Spanish. When first Kirk came to them in Palma, the place was nearly perfect; as he returned over the years, philistine builders and tourists devastated the lovely city.

There was Erik von Kuehnelt-Leddihn, in his Tyrolean village: Erik the compulsive traveller, master of many languages, critic of democratism, knight-errant of political freedom.

There were literary allies in Milan and Rome, Madrid and Avila; they entertained Kirk in grand style during the Fifties and the Sixties.

There was Max Picard, on his mountainside overlooking Lugano, the author of *The World of Silence,* of *The Flight from God,* of *Man and Language,* of *The Human Face:* Picard, who would have been welcomed by the Seven Sages of old. Kirk would give Picard a chapter in his *Enemies of the Permanent Things*.

There was Sir Compton Mackenzie, in his book-crammed Georgian house at Edinburgh; at three in the morning (Sir Compton, like Kirk, being a creature widest awake in the wee hours), they talked of good books and better cigars.

There was Robert Speaight, actor and biographer, who long played Thomas à Becket in *Murder in the Cathedral* and wrote one of the more memorable autobiographies of the twentieth century, *The Property Basket*.

And there were yet others whose names and talents are touched upon elsewhere in this book. These all were members of the invisible Party of Order that withstood decadence: in their diverse ways, they contended against the antagonist world. Most of them did not despair: with Eliot, they demanded, "Do you need to be told that whatever has been, still can be?" Some of them, again with Eliot, hoped to rebuild the Temple, "Remembering the words of Nehemiah the Prophet: 'The trowel in hand, and the gun rather loose in the holster.'"

They labored among forgotten or ruined temples, from the empty medieval churches of York to the Greek columns of Akragas. The Hebraic, the classical, the Christian patrimony were theirs. Kirk would find his way to many of the ruins of fallen orders — from the brochs of Orkney to the Roman remains near Rabat, from the broken priory at Sligo to the ghostly fortress city of Stari Bar.

A sense of the fragility of human institutions came upon him strongly at the place now called Agrigento, where he spent some days in the course of a Sicilian expedition, accompanied there by his friend Jay Gordon Hall, a chief political agent of General Motors. (This may seem curious company for Kirk, who had called the automobile "a mechanical Jacobin"; but Dr. Hall was a disciple of Cicero and something of a Latin scholar, and a friend to the permanent things.)

Upon great barren ridges in the south of Sicily, looking across the African Sea toward Carthage, stands Agrigento — which city the Greeks called Akragas, and the Romans called Agrigentum, and in medieval times was Girgenti. The town itself, a place of fifty thousand people, is medieval still, crowned by the sirocco-worn cathedral of golden stone on the site of a great Greek temple.

The ghosts of the fifth-century Greeks hover over the place, and tourists come to see the splendid line of Greek temples that stand upon the southern ridge, right against the ancient walls. Akragas was better than Athens, better than Delphi; Pindar called it the loveliest of mortal cities.

Agrigento has its eerie charm and beauty still, though modernity has endeavored to uglify it. According to varying estimates, there were two hundred thousand to eight hundred thousand souls in the Akragan commonwealth in ancient times; the medieval and modern town occupies little more than a corner of the site.

Also Agrigento today is a sullen and sinister place. Not long after Kirk explored it, robbers took the collection of classical coins from the museum, and the Mafia shot down the chief of police upon his doorstep. The principal bookshops, when Kirk was there, were in the hands of Communists; a conspiratorial knot of young men with fast cars dominated the declining Hotel des Temples; everywhere Communist placards were plastered to the crumbling golden walls of the medieval hive. In the sour faces of Agrigento one did not see the boasted merriment of Sicily; but then, the Girgentines were sour before the Communists came. Edward Hutton, early in this century, wrote of the coming of industrialism — principally because of the great sulphur mines — to this marvellous place: "Yes, that world of misery and sulphur swirls round the high acropolis of Girgenti and trickles down to the sea at Porto Empedocle. It does not spoil the southern landscape . . . but it certainly sours the Agrigentines and marks them with the stigmata of industrialism."

The living rock beneath the whole of the medieval town is honeycombed by strange passages, entered from a grim gateway in the Piazza del Purgatorio, out of which incessantly stream vapors from this underworld, vanishing in the dry air of the streets; and these infernal regions are older than the glory that was Greece. As in Hadrian's Villa, as in every civilization, Hell lies just below the surface. The oldest temple is dedicated to the infernal water-deities, a labyrinth, utterly dark: this is Sican, although the conquering Greeks made it a temple of Demeter and Proserpine. The first famous ruler of Akragas, the terrible Phalaris, roasted his enemies in a brazen bull. Beauty is very old at Agrigento, but so are evil and terror.

Empedocles, the greatest native of Akragas, said that his fellow citizens lived as luxuriously as if they expected to die on the morrow but built as if they would live forever. Luxury, indeed, was an immediate cause of their ruin. In the conflict with Carthage, the masters of Akragas forbade their soldiers, while on field duty, to carry about more than three blankets each, with two pillows.

In the end, the merciless Carthaginians came over the high walls at night. The richest man in Akragas and his friends barricaded themselves in a temple, set fire to it, and so perished. By morning, most Akragans were dead or enslaved; the remnant fled eastward. The Carthaginians burnt the city, temples and all.

Modern folk do not build as if they expected to live forever: little erected today will stand a century from now. We live, nevertheless, as luxuriously as if we expected to die tomorrow. The common assumption is that the culture of the United States and of the West generally will endure to the end of time. So the men of Akragas may have thought of their fairest of mortal cities. Yet a sterner race, equally but more exclusively bent upon material acquisition, snatched all from them.

At least the ruins of Akragas stand. But if the modern "free world" comes to catastrophe, nothing will survive the destruction of the political order. There will be no majestic columns of American temples two thousand years from now; there will not be even monumental tombs or the mosaic floors of vanished splendid houses in the shade of almond trees. A broken America, a broken West, would leave no ghosts. With modern folk, it is survival as a living society, or else oblivion.

Kirk thought on such things at Agrigento. The survival of any culture, or of the material fabric of a civilization, requires vigorous imagination and readiness to sacrifice. By dullness and complacency are intellectual and social orders undone. Arnold Toynbee speculated that the "internal proletariat" and the "external proletariat" might put an end to the civilization of the West: the bored and demanding masses of industrialism, the belligerent totalist powers. Might the moral imagination be waked in time in America, western Europe, and the "developed" (but morally and intellectually enfeebled) world? Things seemed to be in the saddle, riding mankind, to borrow a phrase from that unreliable optimist Emerson. The event might be in the hand of God; yet God helps those who help themselves.

At the end of his Sicilian wanderings, Kirk boarded an Italian liner at Palermo, then still scarred by the American naval bombardment during the War. It might be by American imagination and energy that the time would be redeemed; or by American complacency and materialism that mere anarchy would be loosed upon the world. For his little part, Kirk could do no more than return to his antiquated ancestral typewriter in the memory-haunted old house at Mecosta.

"Never attack a man armed with a typewriter," someone in Long Island had told him. Yet the pen (or the typewriter) was not so keen a weapon as it had been when John Taylor, the Water Poet, had declared that it "cut more keen than whips or rods": Demon TV was riding mankind already. Nevertheless, Kirk meant to cut and thrust.

CHAPTER NINE

Belief Will Follow Action

A Flying Buttress of the Church

Russell Kirk's parents had not troubled themselves to have their child baptized. To what church, indeed, would they have taken him, not themselves having been baptized? No more had his grandparents been. Those elders, when he had been a small boy, had encouraged him, mildly, to attend a Sunday school; but when he had ceased to go, they had not admonished him. His family's attitude, so far as small Russell had been able to make it out, had been that belief in divine omniscience did not require one to pray in church, or even at home; and that many churchgoers were whited sepulchres. The Kirks and Pierces and Johnsons seemed unaffected by Darwinian doctrines, either in scientific or in vulgarized form; they kept Sunday decorously enough, with a collective family feast; but church — at least after the Spiritualist Church at Mecosta burnt — simply did not interest them, or seem pertinent to their temperate and diligent lives.

Marjorie Pierce Kirk taught her son little bedside prayers and read to him from a children's Bible, as did his aunts. But from the age of ten to that of thirty or more, he entered churches only very rarely, and then from mere curiosity. Although much read in the writers of antiquity, at thirty-five he knew next to nothing of the great Christian authors, except for Dante and for Samuel Johnson.

Yet by 1948, about the time when Alfred Kinsey's influential and silly book *Sexual Behavior in the Human Male* was published, Kirk, an instructor then at Michigan State, had become aware of the melancholy consequences of the widespread decay of religious con-

[229]

victions. The prurient public interest in Kinsey's alleged findings was evidence of such decadence. Kirk published in *The South Atlantic Quarterly* (April 1949) his mordant reflections on Kinsey, an essay entitled "Statistics and Sinai," his first recognition in print of the origin of morals in an acceptance of the transcendent.

"I am a partner in a bookshop," he wrote; "it is grimly amusing to survey the people who come asking for the Kinsey Report. There are some, of course — and this being a college town, they are more numerous than at most shops — who really think it a scientific document and buy it accordingly. But the bulk of Kinsey-buyers are the sort that, with a slight alteration of environment, would be gathered round the witch-doctor's blaze or rolling in the pious ecstasies of the extreme dissidence of dissent. They want any god but God; and Statistics now serves. Dr. Kinsey may think he is emancipating people; but most of them he is merely unbuttoning." (This essay was reprinted in Kirk's book *Beyond the Dreams of Avarice*, in 1956.)

His studies in Burke, beginning systematically about 1948, gradually introduced Kirk to Richard Hooker and other great Anglican divines; and he acquired a handsome set of the works of Sir Thomas Browne, so that he came to know *Religio Medici* and *Christian Morals*. He began, too, the study of John Henry Newman, reading his works through, so that Kirk might discuss Newman intelligently in his intended doctoral dissertation. He was won over altogether by the wisdom and the style of Cardinal Newman, and from Newman he learned the meaning of Authority, and how general convictions are formed.

Therefore it was on no road to Damascus that Russell Kirk, in erring reason's spite, came to believe in the Apostles' Creed. His was an intellectual conversion, if conversion it may be called. After Kirk had read for years about ultimate questions, and reflected upon them, late in 1953 he obtained formal instruction in Catholic doctrine from a wise and towering Jesuit professor of classics, Father Hugh O'Neill. That learned priest was somewhat surprised to learn that Kirk's reason for seeking him out was merely the yearning of intellectual curiosity: Kirk desired to have the principal dogmata explained to him, that he might truly understand.

"Don't many people come to you to learn the meaning of the creeds?" Kirk inquired. The priest replied that such were few indeed: it was out of some tormenting sorrow or psychological disturbance or ghastly miscarriage in life that men and women typically sought the consolations of religion.

What Kirk had been seeking was not so much consolation as understanding: knowledge of the source of authority in faith and morals. By what principles are we to live here below? And how are we to know that those principles, or norms, or doctrines, or dogmas, are true, and were true, and will be true?

Newman it was who introduced Kirk to the complexities and assurances of Authority. "Conscience is an authority," Newman had written in his essay on John Keble; "the Bible is an authority; such is the Church; such is Antiquity; such are the words of the wise, such are hereditary lessons; such are ethical truths; such are historical memories, such are legal saws and state maxims; such are proverbs; such are sentiments, presages, and prepossessions."

This is a long way from the error that Coleridge had called bibliolatry. Through what Newman named the Illative Sense, truths are borne in upon the mind, falling into place most intricately. It was the intellectual love of God that worked upon Russell Kirk; he never became an enthusiast, but the doctors of the schools persuaded him.

This book not being a work of apologetics, it is unnecessary to trace in detail the ways in which Kirk came to Christian belief: a rather slow and complex process it was. Reading the fathers of the Church, Augustine and Gregory and Ambrose especially, Kirk gave up his previous spiritual individualism. *Securus judicat orbis terrarum, bonos non esse qui se dividunt ab orbe terrarum in quacunque parte terrarum:* this he learned from Augustine of Hippo. "The calm judgment of the world is that those men cannot be good who, in any part of the world, cut themselves off from the rest of the world." Therefore the Church had been raised up.

The Stoicism of Kirk's military years was not effaced, but it was transmuted very gradually. Stoic insights had blended with Christian revelation in the early years of the Church, in the West especially; so it came to pass in Kirk's meditations also. Forty years later, Kirk's wife, bred up in high orthodoxy, would call her husband a Stoic still. Quite as there subsists Christian humanism, there endures Christian Stoicism.

In 1952, an incident in East Lansing pushed Kirk very nearly into the office of *defensor fidei*. He belonged to a little club of professors associated for the discussion of aesthetics. One evening the question was raised, "What first principles should modern men affirm?" — or some such inquiry. The answers offered were characteristically and innocently liberal. Provoked by banality, and somewhat irritated that religious belief apparently was to be omitted entirely from the discussion, Kirk put in, "We must begin with the principle that the fear of God is the beginning of wisdom."

This startled Kirk's colleagues, and none of them was wholly pleased; perhaps most took Kirk's declaration as a witticism. "You mean the love of God, don't you, Russell?" said one well-wisher. But Kirk replied that it was not so denominated in Holy Writ. (This exchange is more fully reported in Kirk's book *The Intemperate Professor,* published in 1965.) Thinking that he might as well have the game as the name, thereafter Kirk occasionally brought Christian doctrine and parable into his discourses, unbaptized heathen though he still remained. Slowly orthodoxy became his doxy, and heterodoxy another man's doxy.

Long years later, *Who's Who* asked certain persons whose succinct biographies appeared in those formidable red volumes to contribute statements describing their goals in life. Kirk was one of two Michiganians so invited. Most of the responses throughout the United States consisted of the affirmation of ambitions to make a great deal of money, succeed conspicuously in industry or the professions, or the like — all this justifying Tocqueville's reflections on American materialism. Kirk's reply, however, was sufficiently succinct: "To know God and enjoy him forever."

This very curious goal, openly professed, attracted some attention in the press. How very original of Kirk, and yet how puzzling! Who'll buy that? The catechetical affirmation, once familiar to every Christian communicant (at least of the more conventional denominations), had become by the 1970s an exotic and eccentric quip.

As Kirk's interests in church history and theology grew, his essays on such subjects began to appear in the serious quarterlies and monthlies: *The Sewanee Review, America, Christianity Today, The Contemporary Review, Commonweal, The Dublin Review* (since vanished, to our loss), *The Church Quarterly Review* (a survivor from the Oxford Movement, no longer published), *The Fortnightly, The Month, Fortune, The Newman Review,* and others. Some readers assumed that Kirk must be a Catholic, although his work occasionally was published in Protestant journals.

So it would come to pass that few were much startled when, in 1964, Kirk would be received into the Catholic Church. What Hoxie Neale Fairchild wrote of T. S. Eliot's "conversion" was quite as true of Kirk's: "One might say that he became a Christian on discovering that he already *was* one — a very common type of conversion."

This slothful and irregular Pilgrim's Progress was encouraged or accelerated somewhat, from time to time, by certain eminent men of the cloth. When, in 1964, little Father McDuffie (who kept a pistol hanging at his bedhead), of the Newman Center, Central Michigan University, gave Kirk formal instruction on the eve of his baptism, that witty priest — a Newman disciple — found the candidate already acquainted with much Christian doctrine. Some of that knowledge Kirk had acquired from parsons and priests; also some of it from observation during his wanderings.

The Canon of the Ghostly Tales

Throughout the twentieth century, the idea of Providence has been out of fashion. Yet sometimes the friends one happens to meet, or the enemies, seem to have been introduced to one by a providential intervention in the ordinary course of life. Is it mere chance that brings about such meetings? Arthur Koestler argues that coincidence is an illusion; that everything which occurs is an incident in some tremendous scheme as yet impenetrable by human intelligence. May it be, after all, that a beneficent providence may respond to the earnest call of a human heart? And that a retributory providence may give unto the wicked "their hearts' desire, and send the iron into their souls withal"?

In the ancient city of York, Roman before it was English, stands the little medieval church of St. Martin-cum-Gregory. On an autumnal day in 1949, toward evening, Russell Kirk viewed the old stained glass in the windows of that church; on departing, inadvertently he left his walking stick in the church porch. The next day he wrote to the rector of the grander church of Holy Trinity, Micklegate, in whose charge St. Martin-cum-Gregory lay, to inquire if the stick had been found and whether it might be kept for Kirk until he should pass through York again.

The stick having been found in the church porch, some weeks later Kirk called at Holy Trinity rectory, set in the middle of the medieval graveyard of a priory church, where monks' bones had a way of poking up through the lawns. There he met the Reverend Basil Smith, a vigorous northcountryman, whose friendship Kirk was to enjoy for two decades.

Had there been another thousand parsons of the Church of England like B. A. Smith, there could have been no talk in that land, about the middle of the twentieth century, concerning a "post-Christian era." Along Micklegate, between the medieval arch of Micklegate Bar and the River Ouse, he had resuscitated a parish long neglected. Of the seventeen medieval churches then standing within the walls of York, his was the most thriving. Also he was a scholar, and would write a good book about Dean Church. He found time, too, to take a large part in preserving York's rich architectural heritage. Without his intervention and success in finding help, little St. Martin-cum-Gregory, for instance, would have been demolished.

His rectory was a peaceful, dignified place, handsomely furnished with pieces that the Smiths had picked up prudently at sales. Kirk particularly appreciated their doxological clock, chiming "Praise God from whom all blessings flow" every quarter of the hour. Mrs. Smith, Phillis, served the most sumptuous afternoon teas anywhere in Britain. This old-fashioned charmed setting was embellished by the Smiths' Siamese cats, with their secretive ways.

As the years passed, Kirk stopped often to talk with the rector and stay a night or two or three. Later, when Basil had been made a canon of the cathedral chapter and treasurer of York Minster, Kirk lodged with them in a strange, large, evocative ancient house within the cathedral precincts, where there was plenty of room for all the Canon's fine books and the old china and figurines his wife collected.

Basil Smith and Russell Kirk both relished ghostly narrations, in which York was rich. In his large library was a collection of the books of Sheridan Le Fanu; during stays with the Smiths, Kirk would read leisurely in the three-volume original edition of Le Fanu's *The House by the Churchyard*. No book could have been more appropriate to the place. Holy Trinity Church, with its twelfth-century nave and its Roman fragments, had been notoriously haunted, some years before, by apparitions passing in silhouette against the stained glass of the great east window. And there were those monks' bones forever surfacing in the garden; the janitor burnt them in the rectory's furnace.

Basil Smith himself had written, though never published, five longish uncanny tales, very convincing, rather in the manner of M. R. James. In 1980, eleven years after the Canon's death, Kirk arranged their publication, with an introduction by himself, under the title *The Scallion Stone*. Into these stories Smith had woven fragments of local legends and of personal experience. Canon Smith knew that the whole of human existence is suffused with mysteries, and that pitfalls have been dug for the vagrant erring soul. A man of the light, he was aware of the brooding unregenerate darkness that has menaced mankind from the beginning of human existence. After a fashion, these tales are parables of that fascinating perilous darkness, which suddenly may envelop the unwary or the fallen. Kirk first read them in typescript, he sunken into a vast soft bed of yesteryear in the old, old house — once the gatehouse to a vanished palace — that was called Precentors' Close, hard by the Minster.

Ever since 1948, York had been a haunted town to Kirk; he had first beheld its streets at night, with rain falling, the Guildhall a roofless wreck — for the bomb damage of the War was then still unrepaired. One of Kirk's own eerie tales, not published until 1976, "Saviourgate," set in York, had some connection with Basil Smith.

For on one of Kirk's early visits to the city, the hours had passed too swiftly; and he found himself under the necessity of trotting to the railway station to catch a London-bound train. Not knowing well the complex pattern of the medieval streets, he stood in danger of missing that train. As he hurried through the darkening lanes, he glimpsed a short street of handsome neat houses, Queen Anne or Georgian, admirably preserved; he longed to inspect that street, but lacked the time, and so hurried on to catch the train. Try though he would on later expeditions, he could not find that charming unblemished antique street with its whitewashed doorsteps and its dim lighting.

When Kirk told his antiquarian host about this, Basil Smith suggested that Kirk's description would be most nearly matched by Saviourgate, a street that by the time of their conversation stood uninhabited and desolate. Upon reflection, Kirk concurred. (This was in 1955.) How long before had Saviourgate fallen to its ruined condition? "About 1914," said Basil. No rational explanation ever has been found for that momentary glimpse of yesteryear's street Russell Kirk experienced in 1949.

Once, when Basil Smith said his evensong office "in the draughty church at smokefall," Kirk sat in a dark pew before him, the Canon's whole congregation that evening. This was a moment out of time, Canon Smith and Dr. Kirk seemingly lodged at what Eliot calls "the still point of the turning world," enfolded in the eternal community of souls. That timeless moment has heartened Kirk ever since. He never told the Canon so; yet perhaps Basil Smith knows now, if he did not know before.

Smith's parish of Micklegate, exclusively fashionable in the nineteenth century, over the decades had turned into a working-class neighborhood, some of it slum. Basil Smith had renewed Christian belief in that venerable parish, through kindness and sensible sermons. Later, when he was Treasurer of the Minster, he preserved for posterity ancient properties possessed by the cathedral chapter since the high Middle Ages; also he took a principal part in the restoration of the Minster. Basil Smith knew that "the contract of eternal society," joining dead and living and those yet unborn, finds its expression, in part, through the visible fabrics of a culture, brick and stone.

"You and I are living at the end of an age," he told Kirk, as they sat by the fire in his parlor. "The old civilization dissolves swiftly about us." Like C. S. Lewis, whom he much admired, Canon Smith did what he could to redeem the time, in the order of the soul and in the order of the commonwealth — although he suspected, with Eliot, that probably no more could be done than to keep glowing through dark centuries a spark that some future generation might employ to rekindle the warming fires of a culture moved by love and beauty.

More than from books, one learns from exemplars. Kirk learned more from Basil Smith than ever Smith guessed. In the fullness of time, Kirk would become a Christian communicant, though not of the Church of England. In no small part, it was B. A. Smith who converted Kirk by example.

What induced Kirk to enter the forgotten little church of St. Martin-cum-Gregory, and why had he been so absent-minded as to leave his stick in the porch? What impulse prompted Basil Smith, a few weeks later, to ask Kirk in for tea? How was it that Kirk many times, over the years, dined and slept at Micklegate Rectory or Precentors' Close, though his home was four thousand miles distant from York? Why one falls in with vessels for honor, or with vessels for dishonor, remains a mystery. What we seek subconsciously, somehow we succeed in finding. "And if thy light be darkness, how great shall be that darkness!" Once a man has chosen, even though unconsciously, a power begins to work upon him. Things are put in one's way; doors are opened; and whether one walks in, or turns round upon the threshold, must depend upon his will. Kirk willed to be worthy of Basil Smith's friendship.

Smith's book *Dean Church: The Anglican Response to Newman* led Kirk deeper into the study of the Anglican tradition. In later years, after publication of his book *Eliot and His Age,* Clifton Fadiman and many others would ask Kirk why T. S. Eliot did not go all the way to Rome, once he had declared himself a Catholic in religion. That would have been almost unnatural in Eliot, Kirk would reply: the splendor of the old English churches, the grandeur (surpassing the Roman) of the Anglican liturgy, and the wisdom of the English divines of the sixteenth and seventeenth and eighteenth centuries encompassed Eliot. Upon Kirk, living in the backlands of Michigan, no such dim Anglican light shone. Yet very nearly Basil Smith made an Anglican of him — not at all by evangelism, but by strength of example.

Over the years, Kirk came to know every lane within the white stone walls of York, and a good deal of York *extra muros.* Among towns, only St. Andrews stimulated his imagination more strongly. He was present, incidentally, when the oldest-known rosary in England was discovered under a little soil just below a window of the Treasurer's House. For archeologists, York afforded many opportunities; and for sociologists, too, in the early Fifties. A very great event there, Kirk in attendance, was the revival of the York cycle of Mystery Plays in 1951.

Those religious dramas had not been presented in York since 1580, in which year Shakespeare had been sixteen years old: the Reformers had forbidden their celebration, finding the Mystery Plays superstitious. So they vanished from the streets between 1580 and 1951, the corporation of York reviving them in the latter year, in conjunction with the Festival of Britain (their medieval inspiration contrasting radically with the secular modernism of the South Bank Exhibition at London). Kirk became well acquainted with Canon Purvis, whose version of the Mysteries was presented that summer with the ruined arches of St. Mary's Abbey as backdrop.

About the York Mysteries of 1951, Kirk wrote one of his more substantial essays, "York and Social Boredom," soon published in *Sewanee Review* and later included in his book *Beyond the Dreams of Avarice* (1956 and 1991). As Kirk wrote on that occasion, it would not do to judge the condition of faith and taste in York by the revived Mystery Plays. Their audience was select and generally upper-middle class, the performances had the charm of artistic novelty, and the state of mind and conscience those plays embodied really ran counter to the vast social tendencies that ever since Newcomen and Watt, Paine and Bentham, had been sweeping Britain away from her immemorial ways toward a grimy secular world of uniformity, suspicious of beauty, contemptuous of belief. Nine-tenths of the population of York had become indifferent to religion; to the Mysteries, in 1951, they preferred the carnalities of the cinema and the cheap press; more and more, the people of England drew upon the moral and intellectual capital of England's yesteryear.

The dismal faces Kirk saw in the sickly mercury-vapor glare of nocturnal queues at fish-and-chips saloons, those slack mouths or vicious eyes of men and women who had forgotten that there exists an end in life, might dominate the Welfare State. The materialism of twentieth-century social reformers, Kirk reflected, often was the inverted image of humanitarian social theories of the nineteenth century.

This boredom of the laboring classes was paralleled, in Britain and elsewhere, by the boredom of the intellectuals and the artists, with honorable exceptions here and there. In the course of criticizing Ezra Pound, in 1933, T. S. Eliot had suggested that "with the disappearance of the idea of Original Sin, with the disappearance of the idea of intense moral struggle, the human beings presented to us both in poetry and in prose fiction today, and more patently among the serious writers than in the underworld of letters, tend to become less and less real. . . . If you do away with this struggle, and maintain that by tolerance, benevolence, inoffensiveness, and a redistribution or increase of purchasing power, combined with a devotion, on the part of an élite, to Art, the world will be as good as anyone could require, then you must expect human beings to become more and more vacuous."

Having forgotten Original Sin, the world had grown vicious and violent, as well as vaporous. What the culture of the twentieth century was experiencing, religious convictions having so diminished, amounted to evidence of the truth of Christian teaching. "Belief will follow action," John Henry Newman had written. About the middle of the twentieth century, Russell Kirk began to act as if the Christian understanding of the human condition were true; and right enough, belief began to follow. "I believe; help Thou my unbelief." Yet another thirteen years would elapse, after his talks with B. A. Smith and his Yorkshire walks, before Kirk would profess his faith in the world beyond the world. Meanwhile, although no pillar of the Church, he served tolerably well as one of its flying buttresses.

From the Night Club of the Holy Ghost to the Shroud of Turin

Strolling the byways — sometimes wintry — of several lands from 1948 to 1963, Russell Kirk thought often of ultimate things. Sleeping usually at the oldest inns, contriving to subsist pleasantly on a few dollars daily in Scotland, England, Ireland, Wales, France, Germany, Switzerland, Austria, Italy, Sicily, Spain, Mallorca, Tunisia, and Morocco, sometimes he did thirty miles a day in rough country, pack on his back, and two or three times some forty miles. He had become one of that dying breed, the peregrine seekers after knowledge, although time had been when folk walked all the way from Edinburgh to London, and back again, without anyone taking that for an extraordinary feat.

Once, while he wandered over the North York moors, a jet fighter broke the sound barrier thousands of feet above him. The fighter and he were the only moving things within his range of vision — the oldest and the latest means of transportation. But he was seeing every detail of a charming landscape, and the jet's pilot saw only, like flashes of nightmare, the infinity and the terror of the sky and a vague earth reduced to abstractions.

Man afoot encounters stimulants to his imagination; not so, usually, man aloft. Dr. Kirk and his friend Philip Barney (once an American intelligence officer) were strolling along the Appian Way, to the south of Rome, where that ancient tomb-lined road runs close to Ciampino airport. As they stumbled among fallen masonry, a big military plane roared overhead, about to land; and Barney studied it, planes being in his line of work.

But Kirk's eye was caught by something very different. A few yards ahead, two women were seated upon the fragments of a Roman tomb. One was bending her head deferentially before the dominant figure — a gaunt intense woman in gaudy but shapeless clothing, gesticulating with an ominous finger. Clearly the second woman was telling her companion's fortune. Kirk knew her for the modern version of a Roman witch, the spiritual inheritor of the horrid witches of the Esquiline comminated by Horace two thousand years before.

Interested extremely, Kirk moved gently nearer. Then the witch rose menacingly, pointed at him her fatal forefinger, and cursed him at some length in the dialect of the Campagna. He prudently beat a retreat.

A minute later, Barney and Kirk turned back toward the Immortal City. "Had you seen one of those jets before?" Barney inquired.

"Jet?" Kirk said. "Why, I was fascinated by that witch. She cursed me. What jet?"

"Witch? Right here at noon? You sure have an imagination, Russ."

Where other people saw an ordinary sunset, William Blake saw a host of angels crying "Glory, glory, glory!" Perceptions depend upon imagination and previous experience. Ordinary human senses measure only a small range of the phenomena that are in heaven and earth. Dogs, for instance, hear sounds imperceptible to humans even at close range, and can be summoned by whistles silent to the human eardrum. In a mechanized world, the average man — aye, even the average educated man, or perhaps especially such a one — tends to fancy that everything somehow is an exercise in technology. Kirk suspected that a people whose imagination has been atrophied by the machine may lose the faculty for ruling themselves.

Kirk's knapsack travels were concerned more with saints than with witches — though he was favored with some eerie little adventures in the course of his pilgrimages. He read every evening as he made his way from town to town, castle to castle, church to church. A good many young men of some education seem to think it their duty to read German metaphysicians while travelling; but not so Kirk. His favorite philosophers were those Catholic skeptics Unamuno and Santayana; but he was more strongly influenced by two great literary critics, Americans both, the humanists Irving Babbitt (also a walker in Europe) and Paul Elmer More. *The Skeptical Approach to Religion,*

More's slimmest book, joined for Kirk Platonic insights and Christian hope.

His expeditions afoot took almost a theological and an ecclesiastical turn, as if some power outside himself were at work. He was invited to address the Clergy School of the Province of York (a kind of annual convocation of the clergy, sponsored by the Archbishop), meeting at Scarborough, on the subject of the Anglicanism of Edmund Burke — a lecture soon thereafter published in the *Church Quarterly Review*. Kirk walked all the way from Edinburgh, crossing the empty Lammermuirs, lodging overnight at douce Duns, and pressing on through Berwick and Bamborough to Scarborough. That was in 1951; even in the middle of the twentieth century, Lammermuir was no unco' canny, and Kirk perceived a strange little silent figure in the gloaming, hard by the roadway; and himself much frightened a cottager by calling to him out of the blackness, "Can you give me the time?" — Kirk then seated on a mound that indubitably would have been taken, in an earlier age, for a fairy knowe, "with laughter under the hill"; perhaps the terrified cottager still took it for such, and Kirk for a bogle. Such chance encounters are among the larger rewards of nurturing one's imagination.

Such perils notwithstanding, Kirk strode eventually into Scarborough, above the North Sea, sound in wind and limb; and at dinner was seated on the right hand of Dr. Cyril Garbett, Archbishop of York, the author of *In An Age of Revolution,* who had his misgivings about King Mammon and King Demos — as did Kirk. "Nehemiah describes how the walls of Jerusalem were rebuilt in the face of the enemy; all took part in the work either in the actual building, or in the bearing of burdens; 'everyone with one of his hands wrought in his work, and with the other hand held his weapon,'" Cyril Garbett wrote at the end of his book. "The Church must continue day by day to build up and enlarge the city of God; but in its hands it must hold its weapons ready for any emergency which may suddenly arise."

During the next four decades, the most formidable adversary of the Church of England, and of all Christian churches, would not be the nuclear-bomb war that Archbishop Garbett thought all too possible; instead, the menace to the Church's fabric would be the miners and sappers of contemptuous disbelief, called by Christopher Dawson the "secular humanists."

Despite its afflictions, the Church of England seemed healthy enough by the side of the Protestant churches of northern Europe; at least the Anglicans kept most of their churches open to the pious and the curious, most of the day. In the Netherlands one found great medieval churches permanently locked.

The year after his lecturing in Scarborough, Kirk for the first time set foot on a Rhine steamer — at once recognizing that vessel and its crew for the ungainly craft and grotesque personnel of the "Katzenjammer Kids" comic strip of his tender years. In company with Stebleton Nulle, a colleague from Michigan State, Kirk voyaged upstream to the bomb-ravaged Rhineland cities, of which Mainz was the slowest to recover from its agony.

They landed and lodged at Mainz. Kirk found the Romanesque cathedral, restored by order of Napoleon but later battered by order of the Allied air command, one of the more interesting of the great churches he had come upon. After dinner Kirk went out walking — unaccompanied by Nulle, who fancied that two-footed predators would lurk in the ruins.

Strolling solitary in the dark, Kirk presently saw on the other bank of the Rhine, amidst ruins, a bright blue neon sign, *Zum Heiligen Geist,* from which a blue burning arrow pointed round a corner. What an invitation to the third person of the Trinity! Kirk contrived to find a bridge, cross the river, and poke about dark rubble-strewn streets; then, turning a corner, he reached his hoped-for rendezvous. The Holy Spirit descends where it lists, not disdaining ruins.

What Kirk found, however, was not the Dove of Christian symbol, but a venerable building converted to twentieth-century tastes and uses. This was the Hospital of the Holy Ghost, erected late in the Middle Ages as a hospice for pilgrims to the shrines of Mainz, Cologne, and other cities of the Rhineland. But when Kirk arrived at its door, the hospitality was of another sort, for in the hospital now was lodged the Holy Ghost Night Club, given over to things profane.

From without, the Holy Ghost Night Club seemed rather a decent, though not busy, secular establishment. Had Kirk at the moment enjoyed the company of a pretty and bold American girl, as was his wont in travelling, he might have entered, his companion serving as protection against those young women of the demimonde who run their fingers through one's hair. But knowing also that one ought not to venture into night clubs unless one's pockets jingle, Kirk lurked outside in the Rhine mists. In Nuremberg at that time, a successful night club called itself, with sufficient candor, "Erotica." But the Night Club of the Holy Ghost, perhaps weighed down by its centuries of charitable proprietorship, did not seem given to strip-tease, and the proprietor or manager paced the walk outside his door, still modestly hopeful of custom.

Our era knows few Christian pilgrimages, except those to the modern shrines of Lourdes, Fatima, or Medjugorje. In medieval times, pilgrimages were undertaken for the washing away of sins or in the hope of miraculous relief from the ills of the flesh. No one today rides with Chaucer's pilgrims to the tomb of Saint Thomas à Becket at Canterbury, or to the shrine of Saint Andrew the Apostle at St. Andrews, or to the tomb of Archbishop Boniface at Mainz. So it is that the medieval hospices for penitents and suppliants, if they survive at all, become night clubs or (as at Nuremberg) restaurants; and the Holy Spirit to which they were dedicated must be sought elsewhere.

Yet even in a post-Christian era, Kirk reflected, given up to the boring fleshly idols of the night club, the Dove descends still, touching in solitude the hearts of a Remnant. And Kirk recollected that Christianity, even in the Age of Faith, always had been a scandal.

He came to know the great churches of Spain better than those of Germany, and those of Avila especially. Cold, dry, austere, and in part derelict, the ancient and noble city of Avila stands upon a high spur of the sierra, looking in winter upon snow-drowned mountains. In Avila is the stony convent, not at all altered, where Saint Teresa experienced her visions. In the austere vestibule of that convent, the skeptical Kirk felt a presence — so strong a presence that women he knew, later, would run sobbing from the place. At Avila had been born George Santayana, that skeptical champion of convention and tradition, much read and re-read by Kirk.

An impression equally strong, but of a character somewhat different, was made upon Kirk by the modern monument and church of Los Caidos, high in Castile, on the southern slope of the Guadar-ramas, where tens of thousands of Spaniards perished gallantly in their Civil War. This is Santa Cruz of the Valley of the Fallen, hollowed out from a wild mountain.

Viva la muerte! Spanish soldiers had cried throughout those terrible years, hurling themselves upon destruction. Long live death!

Fascinated by the phenomenon of death, the Spaniard — from the philosopher Unamuno to the shepherd above some such forgotten town as Chinchon or Colmenar de Oreja — knows that man is made for eternity. And so the Spaniard builds noble shrines to those who have passed beyond the bourne on that mysterious journey transcending time.

Within the mountain, a tremendous church, with sculptures and tapestries, overwhelms the visitor to its sombre Spanish grandeur. Atop the peak, an immense stone cross, thrice the height of the Statue of Liberty, stands as the symbol of sacrifice and suffering. Thousands of the dead lie in catacombs, deep within the living rock. And at the back of the mountain, a stone monastery lodges the guardians of Los Caidos. Besieged by the bitter mountain wind in winter, burnt by the Iberian sun in summer, Los Caidos looks down upon barren Castile, contemptuous of the kingdoms of the earth.

From Castile's heights, Kirk's ecclesiastical memories glide to the embanked Tiber. It was his custom, on his many Roman expeditions, to lodge at the Albergo Minerva, Rome's oldest hotel (not counting medieval inns), at the heart of Rome of the Middle Ages, but with the splendid bulk of the Pantheon looming high above the next piazza. It was not Michelangelo's San Pietro that Kirk frequented, but Santa Maria sopra Minerva next door, the Dominicans' church, Rome's only Gothic church, that has for its footing the remains of a temple of Minerva. And he made his way often to Santa Maria in Aracoeli, where there projects above the pavement the remains of an altar said to have been erected by Augustus in veneration of the Unknown God who would be born in his reign. Even in the sixth century, men knew this church to be ancient.

But it will not do to catalogue here Rome's three hundred and sixty-five churches and major chapels. The church with the greatest significance for the twenty-first century, Kirk would come to believe, is situated far to the north, in Torino: the cathedral of San Giovanni Battista, rebuilt in its present form near the close of the fifteenth century. For within its walls, behind the apse, is the Chapel of the Most Holy Shroud. There, on the altar, is the silver casket holding the urn that contains the burial garment of the crucified Jesus of Nazareth.

Kirk entered the cathedral casually, on an afternoon in the summer of 1957, while he was in Turin for a conference of

Kirk's great-grandfather Amos
Johnson laid out the village of
Mecosta, built Piety Hill, and served
as a judge in Mecosta County.

Estella Russell Johnson, wife of
Amos, is said to have been a
medium of considerable talents in
the years before Kirk was born.

Frank J. Pierce, Kirk's maternal
grandfather. Self-educated — but
well educated for all of that —
Pierce exerted a powerful formative
influence in the life of Kirk.

Glenn "Potter" Jewell and his wife,
Kirk's Aunt Fay. Late in life, the
Jewells became as parents to Kirk,
sharing the grounds of Piety Hill
with him during the Fifties.

Kirk's father, Russell Andrew Kirk,
a railroad engineman

Kirk's mother, Marjorie Rachel Kirk,
second daughter of Frank Pierce

Kirk's birthplace in Plymouth, Michigan — one of the earliest prefabricated
dwellings, which had been purchased by Russell's grandfather from Sears,
Roebuck, and Company. It was located hard by the railway station, and
steam locomotives puffed and hooted a few rods distant, day and night.

Kirk in the arms of Frank Pierce, the grandfather with the tear-gas fountain pen, outside the Sears Roebuck house in Plymouth

Frank Pierce *(right)* with an associate on the steps of Plymouth United Savings Bank. While serving as manager of the bank, Pierce faced robbers several times, only once yielding any money from the vault, and then while staring down the muzzle of a submachine gun.

Russell Andrew Kirk with his children, Carolyn and Russell

Kirk at the age of seventeen,
in 1935

Sergeant Kirk while stationed at
the Dugway Proving Grounds,
Utah, in 1942

Kirk at about the age of thirty-four, when he completed his doctorate at St. Andrews University in Scotland in 1952. His dissertation, on British and American thinkers in the line of British statesman Edmund Burke, was published soon afterward as *The Conservative Mind.*

THE

CONSERVATIVE

MIND

from Burke to Santayana

RUSSELL KIRK

Chicago · HENRY REGNERY COMPANY · *1953*

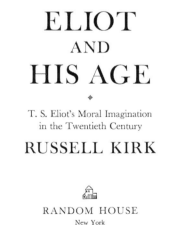

ELIOT

AND

HIS AGE

T. S. Eliot's Moral Imagination
in the Twentieth Century

RUSSELL KIRK

RANDOM HOUSE
New York

Above are the title pages of two of the most important of Kirk's books, *The Conservative Mind* (first published by Henry Regnery in 1953), which established his reputation on both sides of the Atlantic, and *Eliot and His Age* (1971), a fine example of his later work as a man of letters.

Durie House, Fife, Scotland, the estate of Major Ralph Christie, "one of the best-built houses Kirk ever had the good fortune to inspect"

Kellie Castle, Fife, Scotland, the home of sculptor Hew Lorimer and his family. Portions of the structure date back to the fourteenth century, but most of the construction was completed in the sixteenth century.

Kirk with his good friend
George Scott-Moncrieff
Photo courtesy of the *Big Rapids Pioneer*

Annette with friend Mickie Teetor,
who encouraged the relationship
between Courtemanche and Kirk

The Kirk-Courtemanche wedding party. On the left are Annette's brother
Regis Armand Pierre and father Regis Henri; on the right are her mother
Mary (née Cullen) and sister Marie Ellen.

Russell and Annette Kirk on their wedding day, September 19, 1964

Above, Killarney, Ireland, July 20, 1966. Annette rode through the Gap of Dunloe; Kirk walked the nine miles.

Right, the Kirks with their first child, Monica (1967)
Photo courtesy of the *Big Rapids Pioneer*

Above, Kirk and Annette reading to their three small daughters (1970)

Right, Kirk's burglar-butler Clinton Wallace and Felicia at Piety Hill (1972). The fierceness of Clinton's appearance in this photograph is the result, at least in part, of difficulties associated with getting used to a new set of teeth.

Kirk with his four daughters (*above*, 1976; *below*, 1978)

Kirk in Scotland (shown here in 1961) often made his way afoot, sometimes walking as much as thirty miles a day. It was at this time that his gothic novel *Old House of Fear,* set in Scotland, was published and became a best-seller.

The Kirks in the library at Piety Hill (1968)

Dressed for their parts in Mecosta's 1973 Fourth of July parade are
(*from left to right*) John Mulcahy, Jerry Schiffer (holding Felicia),
Clinton Wallace, and Regis Courtemanche.

The Kirks canoeing on the Little Muskegon River (1977)

Kirk outside his Piety Hill home prior to the Great Fire.
Photo by Bill Rabe

The Great Fire, Ash Wednesday 1975. It leveled the Old House and
consumed many mementos but spared body and spirit of all inhabitants.
Photo courtesy of the *Big Rapids Pioneer*

The Old House was replaced with a new structure designed by Kirk's friend, architect James Nachtegall.   Photo by John Lyon

This dining room was added at the back of the New House after the fire.
Photo by Sam Knecht

Annette and Russell celebrating their twentieth wedding anniversary (1984)
Photo by Jay McNally

The Kirks at the White House with President Richard Nixon (1972)
Photo courtesy of the White House

The Kirks at Piety Hill with Malcolm and Kitty Muggeridge
(Christmas 1978)

Kirk with Kenneth Cribb and President Ronald Reagan at a Christmas party in the Indian Treaty Room of the Old Executive Office Building (1982)
Photo courtesy of the White House

A presentation by Annette on the report *A Nation at Risk* at the U.S. Capitol in 1983. The event was sponsored by the Heritage Foundation.
Photo by Chas Gaer Photography

From left to right, Karl von Habsburg, Rosemarie Chaimowiczs, Walburga von Habsburg, and the Kirks in St. Mark's Square, Venice. Thomas Chaimowiczs took the photo.

The Kirks with Pope John Paul II at the Vatican (1983)
Photo courtesy of the Vatican

The Kirks with Michigan's governor, John Engler (1993)
Photo courtesy of the Mackinac Center

At this dinner in late December of 1991, Kirk received the Salvatori Prize for writings on the American Founding. Seated at the front of the table (*from center to right*) are Kenneth Cribb (president of the Intercollegiate Studies Institute), Holly Coors (who gave the invocation), and Richard DeVos (who delivered the benediction); to DeVos's right is Edwin Feulner, who presented the award. Photo by Creative Arts Photography

Cleanth Brooks and Andrew Lytle with the Kirks and the Wilbur Fellows
in residence at Piety Hill during the summer of 1989
Photo by Robert Barclay

Participants in a 1992 seminar at Piety Hill pose with constitutional lawyer
William Bentley Ball *(far left)* and Judge Brevard Hand *(far right)*.
Photo by Robert Barclay

Above, a seminar in the Kirk library. Leading the seminar with Kirk is Burke scholar and ethicist Vigen Guroian. Note the figures above the fireplace, shown below in greater detail: these are the original studies for the huge carvings that Hew Lorimer sculpted for the National Library of Scotland. The models, carved in Hopetounwood limestone, represent *(from left to right)* Law, Theology, and History.

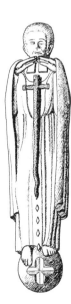

Above, the four Kirk daughters in 1990 *(from left to right):*
Andrea, Felicia, Cecilia, and Monica
Photo by Robert Barclay

Below, Cecilia Kirk on her graduation day at St. Andrews University in 1992.
She received the M.Phil. in history forty years after Kirk received his D.Litt.

Kirk outside his library in 1993
Photo by Robert Barclay

economists, sophisters, and calculators. Of the Shroud he had little more than heard. With astonishment he perceived photographs of the Shroud that displayed the face and the form of the crucified Christ: this was the source for the representation of the dead Jesus copied for many centuries by the artists of the brush and the artists of mosaic. The face was wondrously distinct, almost accurate as a plaster death mask: a strong face, composed in death, with long straight hair, and bearded. Only from this shadow portrait have succeeding generations of men known the countenance of God in the flesh of man. Upon that linen are the evidences of the Passion: the spear-wound between the ribs, the marks of the nails through the wrists, the coagulated streams of blood.

There is every reason to believe this relic to be genuine, and nearly all of it two millennia old, and that it enshrouded the body of Jesus, and not another. Kirk was astonished, in 1957, to learn that the Shroud had survived the fall of successive dominations and powers, the crash of empires, the disintegration of civilizations. Here at Turin it still was preserved!

At the time of Kirk's first visit to the Chapel of the Shroud, some ventured to surmise that the sweat of the dying man, mingling with unguents applied to the body before entombment, somehow had left upon the winding sheet this mold, as it were, of the dead man that once lay within. In recent years that implausible theory has been exploded. So have all other theories about some natural phenomenon that might have produced the image upon the Shroud. It is not, and could not have been, a painting; nor is it a scorch; nor is it a chemical reaction. No other such shroud image has been discovered anywhere, ever, by any archeologist. Teams of scientists and technicians have been unable to come to any scientific conclusion about the origin of the image.

Some talk now about nuclear fission, hinting that the particles of energy, negative and positive, which made up the fleshly envelope of Jesus of Nazareth — why, that those atoms disintegrated in a fraction of an instant, leaving upon the Shroud's linen something very like a photographic positive. Thereafter was the energy, the "virtue," that had made up the body of Jesus of Nazareth as abruptly reconstituted and reassembled, in the Garden? It is known in this century that energy, according to the laws of thermodynamics, can neither be destroyed nor created. Was what occurred in Tomb and Garden and elsewhere indeed the greatest of all miracles: the Resurrection in the flesh? Did there repose at Torino the long-preserved evidence of the central dogma of the Church, the Resurrection of the flesh and the life everlasting?

In 1957, however, it did not enter Kirk's mind that the Shroud was something much more than an amazing relic that somehow had survived translation, over twenty centuries, from Jerusalem, to Edessa, to Constantinople, to Cyprus perhaps, to the south of France, to Torino. It did not occur to him that the vindication of the Shroud, at the close of the twentieth century, might be a theophanic event, or else the forerunner to a theophanic event that might turn the world upside down much more sweepingly than had the political revolutions of the eighteenth century.

That the Gospel account of the Resurrection might be found literally true at the end of two thousand years — why, any such surmise was horrid to many twentieth-century folk. If the Resurrection should be conceivable, might not a Last Judgment be conceivable? And who could put up with that? It is not possible in these pages to enter into the controversies of recent years concerning the Shroud's origin and significance. More scientific investigations are in progress; and the Shroud will be next exhibited in 1999, for it is taken from the urn every thirty-three years. If by the end of the twentieth century the modern age's priests, who are called scientists, should certify that the Shroud indeed appears to have been Jesus' winding sheet and that the image upon it is inexplicable in physical science's laws of matter — why, then an Age of Faith might return.

Such reflections would enter Kirk's mind as decades passed. Some thirty-two years later, he would find himself, his wife at his side, back in that Chapel of the Most Holy Shroud. Round about the cathedral of San Giovanni Battista, in Torino, Italy's city of automobiles, there whirled the triviality and the concupiscence of the twentieth century. And against the Resurrection and the Redemption there fiercely contended, in Torino as elsewhere, the allures of the world, the flesh, and the devil.

A silent barefoot monk, in cowl and gown, undistracted, paced perpetually round and round that silver casket within its shrine of black marble, keeping vigil. Presently he said mass in that sanctuary, with only Russell and Annette and an Italian friend, Mario Marcolla, for congregation. Beyond the cathedral's bronze doors, the world went its busy and unheeding way.

> Remember therefore how thou hast received and heard, and hold fast, and repent. If therefore thou shalt not watch, I will come on thee as a thief, and thou shalt not know what hour I shall come upon thee.

For Russell and Annette, side by side in the great church at Torino, those sentences leaped up electric in their memories, and they held fast, and still keep watch.*

*In February, 1986, there was held at Elizabethtown College, in Pennsylvania, an interdisciplinary symposium entitled "The Mystery of the Shroud of Turin," organized by Dr. Wesley McDonald, friend and disciple of Kirk. (McDonald was professor of political science at Elizabethtown.) The Marguerite Eyer Wilbur Foundation, of which Kirk was president, helped to finance the symposium. There participated six of the American scientists and technologists who, in 1978, had been members of the Shroud of Turin Research Team, investigating the nature of the famous relic. Kirk presided over the roundtable discussion of these and other speakers. All but one of these experts concluded that there exists no scientific explanation for the image on the Shroud: it is a unique phenomenon.

Yet in October 1988, the Archbishop of Turin announced that carbon-14 dating of certain threads in the Shroud had revealed the relic to be of medieval, not ancient, origin. Immediately fresh controversies arose. Were the threads or fragments of the Shroud used in carbon-14 dating taken from the original fabric, or were they part of a sixteenth-century mending that occurred after fire-damage? How far is carbon-14 dating reliable? Other aspects of the 1988 announcement have been challenged formidably. The Vatican since has been investigating the case. Doubtless much more will be heard about the Shroud when next the silver casket is opened again and the most mysterious of relics once more exhibited.

CHAPTER TEN

The Art of Politics
and the Art of Love

Kirk's Works

By the early Sixties, Russell Kirk could be regarded as a thoroughly
established author, even though his writings went against the grain for
the intellectuals of the day. He had become literally a practicing doctor
of letters, an emulator of Dr. Samuel Johnson, but did not live on New
Grub Street. To the surprise of professors, he made money by his books
and essays, and presently by his fiction: not enough money to oblige
him to employ a broker, but sufficient to permit a frugal Scoto-Ameri-
can to travel, to invite people to lunch or dinner, and even to sustain
dependent or partially dependent kin — his grandmother Pierce, his
two great-aunts, his father and stepmother. In the later Sixties and the
Seventies, many more dependents would make their way to Piety Hill.

A second source of income was lecturing, chiefly on college
campuses, although occasionally to civic groups and business organi-
zations. As extemporaneous speaker, formal lecturer, or debater, Kirk
found himself in demand. Lecture bureaus in Chicago, San Francisco,
New York, Boston, and Virginia Beach, found engagements for him.
During the Fifties he spoke on some two hundred campuses, sometimes debating such well-known liberals or well-known radicals as
Arthur M. Schlesinger, Jr.; Carey McWilliams, Sr.; Carey McWilliams,
Jr.; Sidney Lens; Hubert Humphrey; Clifford Case; Eugene McCarthy;
Norman Thomas; John Roche; Michael Harrington. There would be
more debates, and fiercer, in the Sixties.

He talked about everything under the sun: Edmund Burke, nuclear weapons, American blunders in foreign policy, socialism, conservatism, the decay of liberalism, economics, historical determinism, first principles of morals, the idea of the hero, Cardinal Newman, Henry Adams, John Randolph, textbooks, decadence in education, philosophical historians, the ghostly tale, much else. His audiences generally were friendly, if surprised — having expected, perhaps, that they were to hear a ferocious ideologue.

All this writing and talking, it turned out, could not suffice to make ends meet, even for a frugal Scot, what with rising expenses. Therefore he returned in some degree to the Academy, having been invited by R. Gordon Hoxie, president of Post College, in Long Island, to offer one course, one term of the academic year, as research professor of politics. For several years, in the late Fifties, he conducted small classes of this sort, discussing Tocqueville chiefly; some of the classes met at the neighboring air base of Mitchell Field. He made some enduring friends on Long Island's Gold Coast.

He lodged at the grand old Garden City Hotel, standing in its own gardens; he was able to afford a room there, but not a room with bath. Later he lived in a seventeenth-century house close to Post College — that is, a house built at the end of the seventeenth century by Dutch settlers, not far from the frontier of New Amsterdam with New England.

His solitary evenings in the Garden City Hotel gave him opportunity to write, mostly for his own entertainment, a Gothick romance, conforming to the canons of Ann Radcliffe as described by Walter Scott: an antique genre, forgotten. The tone of the narrative, which Kirk entitled *Old House of Fear,* was more nearly that of Stevenson than of Radcliffe or Scott. The story was set (under other island names) in the Small Isles of the Hebrides, which Kirk knew well. The new firm of Fleet published it in New York in 1961.

The romance's popular success astonished the publisher. *Time* reviewed it lengthily, with a photograph of a rather sinister Kirk emerging from the doocot at Durie House (Kirk being in Scotland when the book was published). Many other cordial reviews appeared, so that the first printing was sold out in no time; there came to pass a second edition, and various large paperback printings by Avon paperbacks. More copies of *Old House of Fear* were sold than of all Kirk's other books combined.

This triumph of a literary form of yesteryear opened the way for a vast flood of allegedly Gothic romances, written by women or at least with the names of females as authoresses on the cover. Kirk shared the sentiments of Nathaniel Hawthorne, who had found himself emulated and imitated, if not plagiarized, by "a damned mob of scribbling women." *Old House of Fear*'s phenomenal reception is examined by Oscar Collier in his book *Write and Sell Your First Novel* (1986).

Some readers began to fancy that there were two scribbling Russell Kirks: one who wrote grave historical and political works and essays for the literary and scholarly journals, and another who wrote *Old House of Fear* and published uncanny tales in *London Mystery Magazine* and in *Fantasy and Science Fiction*. The latter group, as represented by the Count Dracula Society (a Los Angeles club interested in the Gothic novel and horror movies), appointed him a knight commander of the order of Count Dracula. Victor Gollancz brought out a London edition of *Old House of Fear*. Had Kirk been bent upon acquiring riches, he could have followed up this first-novel success with other fantastic tales and have grown rich as Midas or Croesus, perhaps, long before the name of Stephen King resounded among publishers. But Kirk had written the romance for his own amusement; and he wrote to improve, rather than to entertain; years would pass before he would turn out another novel.

His writing for the serious monthlies and quarterlies continued during the late Fifties and the early Sixties. His best work appeared in *The Sewanee Review* and *The Yale Review,* where he could write at considerable length for intelligent readers. He was the most frequent North American contributor to *The Month,* published by the Farm Street Jesuits, with Father Philip Caraman as editor then. *The New York Times Magazine* solicited several pieces on divers topics. *Fortune* published two long special articles from his typewriter. Of American church-related publications, he wrote chiefly for *The Catholic World, The Critic, Commonweal, America,* and *The Lamp.*

In 1960, Kirk assumed the presidency of The Educational Reviewer, Inc., a non-profit educational corporation; he began editing its quarterly, *The University Bookman*. A contract was arranged with *National Review* for that magazine to distribute the *Bookman* to all its subscribers. This small quarterly, consisting chiefly of serious reviews of serious books and of essays on education, was financed by dona-

tions from individuals and foundations interested in educational reform. In the beginning the *Bookman* had twenty-four pages per issue,
but eventually rose to the grandeur of forty pages. To the magazine's
pages there were attracted a number of able essayists and reviewers.
For the first thirty years of *The University Bookman,* Kirk was paid
merely a token honorarium as editor, and correspondence with readers and contributors took up more of his time than he had expected.
The little publication exerted influence: when a book was favorably
reviewed in its pages, a good many copies of that book were sold;
and in later years, when the *Bookman* commended a new children's
magazine, the subscription list of *St. Paul's Family Magazine* doubled
within a month.

Kirk's success as a romancer brought about the curious consequence of turning him into a newspaper columnist, nationally
syndicated. For the new book-publishing firm of Fleet was owned
by old George Little, the proprietor also of General Features Corporation, one of the principal distributors of columns and other
features to daily and weekly newspapers, with offices on Park Avenue,
New York. Not long after *Old House of Fear* was published, General
Features suffered the loss of Sydney Harris, the Chicago columnist,
who had transferred his talents to the publishing empire of Marshall
Field. Little bethought him of that skillful writer Russell Kirk to fill
the gap left by Harris's departure. Would Dr. Kirk consent to write a
lively column, five days a week, for national syndication, half the
proceeds to go to Kirk, half to General Features?

Many feel called to newspaper syndication, but few are chosen.
Wisdom is not required for column-writing, but cleverness helps.
There is not nearly so much profit in that occupation as most people
fancy: men who have been writing for big papers for half a century,
as did David Lawrence and Walter Lippmann, build up reputation,
influence, and emoluments; but it is otherwise with most syndicated
scribblers. John O'Hara, the novelist, quitting the occupation in disgust after a single year as a syndicated columnist, remarked that local
editors who happen to disagree with something or other a columnist
has written may summarily "fire" him — even though such editors
never would have been privileged to enjoy fifteen minutes' conversation with the syndicated columnist in question. The sum most
papers pay weekly, even for the work of famous columnists, is astoundingly small.

Yet Kirk accepted George Little's invitation; so in April 1962, a good many daily papers began publishing "To the Point" by Russell Kirk. It was understood between Little and Kirk that this was to be a "general" column, much resembling Sidney Harris's — about subjects of widespread interest, rather than concerning politics merely (although partisan politics are meat and drink to most newspaper editors).

Kirk's first five columns were entitled "Student Poverty"; "Two Senators" (Eugene McCarthy and Barry Goldwater); "Beaver Traps"; "Are You Sure You Want a State Doctor?"; and "Who's an Intellectual?" Soon he found that readers were most interested in columns about children, schooling, the family, the outdoors, good books, curious corners of the world, and personal reminiscences — distinctly not in politics, practical or abstract. But most newspaper editors, be it said to their shame, live and die in the delusion that what the public desires is chiefly political gossip, exhortation, and execration, such being the taste of the editors themselves.

Be that as it may, "To the Point" achieved an immediate popularity; with every day that passed, some more daily papers subscribed. In part this was because public opinion, in 1962, shifted swiftly in a conservative direction; few columnists of a conservative persuasion then existed; a leading one, George Sokolsky, had just died. William Buckley had commenced a newspaper column very shortly before Kirk did, without Kirk knowing that the editor of *National Review* so intended; thus two conservative writers seemed to have popped up to satisfy public demand, like two jacks-in-the-box. In the beginning, even many newspaper editors found Buckley and Kirk to be fresh voices, fairly interesting.

This column-writing was ephemeral work, of course. Kirk received an enormous volume of letters from readers across the country; responding to the mail became a task much more formidable than writing the columns. Many of those letters were intelligent and kindly; not a few readers kept scrapbooks of Kirk's columns. Kirk was made aware from time to time that he had comforted a young girl in the bloom of her youth, or an old man on a winter's night. Also, somewhat to Kirk's surprise, public men read his columns and occasionally wrote to him about political concerns; and still more surprising, this or that Kirk column did actually affect voting in some legislative body.

[253]

So matters went for "To the Point" during 1962 and about the beginning of 1963: a steady increase of influence. It became in circulation a column of the second rank, with prospects of achieving the first rank. But then occurred, successively, the murder of President Kennedy, the succession of Lyndon Johnson, the American intervention in Vietnam, and the presidential candidacy of Barry Goldwater. Those events altered radically the current of public opinion in the United States, incidentally giving a nasty knock to the circulation of Kirk's column.

The Ascent of Barry Goldwater

Any reflective person who has moved within the circles of power becomes aware that the full story of many major events never is made public. After all, nothing is deader than dead politics; the public soon loses interest in yesteryear's doings, even though that public, or part of it, may have been passionately attached to some political cause; and, out of prudence or out of weariness, the actors in yesterday's political drama often let the dead bury the dead. It may be said that behind every textbook history lies a secret history, that arcane account known to but a few. And in the twentieth century, when the telephone has nearly supplanted letter-writing for most folk, historians frequently are unable to find documents that might make fairly clear what actually happened in some struggle or controversy of a generation or a decade gone.

So it is with the endeavor to make Barry Goldwater president of the United States. Perhaps a dozen books about that campaign were published within a few years of Lyndon Johnson's defeat of Senator Goldwater, but none of them contains the entire truth. Nothing sinister has been concealed; it is merely that Goldwater's enemies were content with defamation, ignoring what Goldwater and his people actually said and what principles they really held, while Goldwater's admirers, passionately devoted to their candidate, did not trouble themselves to examine closely the causes of his rejection at the polls. Also some persons who did the most to advance Senator Goldwater were sedulous to cover their tracks — even though their motives had been blameless and their conduct honest.

[254]

Chief among these latter was an influential friend of Russell Kirk: a certain Dr. Jay Gordon Hall, by occupation a political agent of General Motors Corporation, by conviction a champion of the Permanent Things. Suave, humorous, and very gentlemanly, Hall had taught history and was a considerable Latin scholar; his exemplar was Marcus Tullius Cicero. Later Kirk travelled with him to the Greek cities of Sicily; a whole chapter might be written about their wanderings there and in Britain, but just now the Goldwater connection needs to be related.

Dr. Hall had read Kirk's first book, *John Randolph of Roanoke,* so soon as it was published, and had called upon Kirk at the rookery where Kirk then dwelt, behind the People's Church in East Lansing. Their tastes in politics and in letters turned out to be identical. Thus began a friendship and an alliance that endured until Hall's death — he debonair to the very end — at his house in Bloomfield Hills, in 1988. What was a Ciceronian doing as a political operative — something grander than a lobbyist — for General Motors? Why, no sooner had Hall been awarded his doctorate by the University of Chicago than he began to think of the power for good that might be exercised, in politics especially, by the manipulating of the influence of great industrial and commercial corporations. He had in mind, possibly, James Burnham's book *The Managerial Revolution.* To understand the industrial discipline of Detroit, styled during the Second World War "the arsenal of democracy," he worked his way up in the factories — first Ford, then General Motors. His education and his shrewdness raised him eventually to the post of second-in-command of General Motors' political office, which labelled itself "business research."

Hall labored very hard indeed, at two demanding tasks. The visible task was dealing with state legislatures, and sometimes with the federal executive and legislative branches, for the protection and advancement of General Motors' interests — labor legislation, taxation, pricing by automobile dealers, and the like. The invisible task that Hall took upon his shoulders was the defense of the American republic and the social order that Americans had inherited. On Ciceronian principles, he endeavored to bring forward candidates for high office who might be counted upon to stand for what had not been born yesterday; for such public men he would find financial backing; he would introduce them to people of like mind; he would write their speeches; he would plan their campaigns.

Now the mighty at General Motors knew next to nothing of Dr. Hall's invisible political operation. Great corporations are nonpartisan, really, out of fear of what might be done to them in retaliation by some faction that the corporation had offended. Their executives may contribute funds to the treasuries of the political parties — favoring whichever seems most likely to win the next election — but such great industrial corporations are not conservative, except in the sense that they are moved to conserve and augment their stockholders' investment.

Had the serried ranks of General Motors vice presidents known what their agent Dr. Hall was doing out of his concern for the American republic, they would have fired him, Hall told Kirk. Barry Goldwater was not General Motors' candidate for the presidency, but he became Jay Gordon Hall's candidate, and Hall recruited others, among them Dr. Kirk.

A good many conservative Republicans had wished to nominate Senator Goldwater at the Republican national convention of 1960. After Richard Nixon's defeat by John F. Kennedy, the conservative wing of the Republican party steadily grew until it amounted to the party's majority; and Barry Goldwater, the bold and outspoken Westerner, became personally more popular than his liberal Republican rival, Nelson Rockefeller.

This book not being a political history of the United States in the latter half of the twentieth century, only a very succinct description of Senator Goldwater and his convictions follows. In 1961, Goldwater was fifty-two years old and had been in the Senate since 1952; there he had set his face against liberalism, including Republican liberalism. No politician ever was more likeable, or more candid.

"I believe with Burke," Goldwater would write years later, "that each present generation has a contract with the generations which preceded it and the generations which will come after it, and by that contract we are required to preserve what we perceive to be good for society and to attempt to improve what we perceive to be evil. I understand that liberty and property are indivisible. . . . I think most conservatives commence with an understanding that human beings are not perfectible on this earth, nor can they erect and maintain perfect institutions — political, economic, or educational."

Jay Hall had introduced Goldwater to Kirk's writings, and presumably the preceding paragraph reflects the influence of Kirk. Also

Goldwater had put together a book himself, with the help of Clarence Manion and Brent Bozell: *The Conscience of a Conservative,* of which some three and a half million copies were sold. That little volume at first directed a great deal of attention to the conservative senator, but in the long run it did mischief to his presidential candidacy, it being attacked as harshly doctrinaire. He began writing a newspaper column, syndicated by the *Los Angeles Times;* a hundred and forty papers subscribed at the height of Goldwater's popularity.

By January 1962, Goldwater was on his way to the Republican presidential nomination, although his candidacy had not been announced. Kirk found himself at that splendid hotel named The Breakers, Palm Beach — popularly known as God's Waiting Room, what with the many valetudinarians to be seen in lobbies and dining-rooms. He was there to meet with Barry Goldwater, William Buckley, William Baroody (founder of the American Enterprise Institute), Stephen Shadegg (Goldwater's campaign manager in Arizona), and J. G. Hall. This gathering had been arranged by Dr. Hall as an intellectual council of war, convened in February.

The meeting cannot be said to have accomplished much. Baroody already was maneuvering to obtain thorough control over Goldwater's campaign, he perceiving the Senator's charisma, of which much could be made. Presently he would succeed in that ambition to corral Goldwater, and once the campaign was really under way, he would exclude Hall, Buckley, and Kirk from any part in it. Baroody's management destroyed whatever chance Goldwater retained of defeating Lyndon Johnson, but out of the fracas Baroody gained a handsome new suite of Washington offices and access to many well-heeled backers of Goldwater.

At The Breakers, one request had been made of Kirk: that he publicize Goldwater's rebuke of Robert Welch and the John Birch Society. It was felt by all present that the exaggerated denunciations of Eisenhower and others by the impetuous candy manufacturer Welch, and the general temper of the Society he presided over, would injure Goldwater's candidacy, should Goldwater's opponents be able to link him with extreme views. On January 29, aboard an airplane, Goldwater had been interviewed by a reporter from the *New York Times* and had made it very clear to the journalist that he repudiated the support of Robert Welch and his sort. But to Goldwater's surprise, this firm statement had not been mentioned by the *Times* during the days that followed. Would Kirk see that this repudiation was brought to public attention? Would Kirk, Mecosta mouse, please bell the cat?

Kirk did that by writing for *America,* the Jesuit weekly, an article entitled "Conservatives and Fantastics." It appeared as the first article in the magazine on February 17, 1962.

"Responsible conservative leaders in this country are beginning to be annoyed by fantastic political behavior that masquerades under the word 'conservative'," Kirk wrote, in part.

> America, more than ever before in her history, stands in a situation necessarily conservative: our nation is the guardian of a just social and civil order against the menace of the total society. This hour requires what Paul Elmer More called the positive factor of conservatism: "its trust in the controlling power of imagination." And I think we are about to see the rescue of the American conservative interest from freaks, charlatans, profiteers, and foolish enthusiasts. American conservatism, I think, will emerge from noisy confusion into purposeful and consistent action.
>
> On January 29, Senator Barry Goldwater made public a formal statement to the effect that the John Birch Society ought to remove Robert Welch from its presidency, or else dissolve. Several weeks earlier, Senator Goldwater had described Mr. Welch — on the television program "Meet the Press" — as an extremist. Though never connected with the Birch Society, and reluctant to condemn an organization that has attracted a good many well-meaning and able people, Mr. Goldwater has felt it necessary to make it clear that responsible conservatives cannot condone political silliness. This is the beginning, probably, of a general effort by enlightened American conservatives to reform, or else cast off, the political fantastics who have been clinging to their coattails. . . .
>
> To set one's face resolutely against the Communist domination is one thing; to cry havoc at every breath of liberal or radical opinion is quite another. Tolerant by nature, Barry Goldwater has spoken out with firmness against hysteria. And I think he will prevail among American conservatives, and even persuade some American liberals.

Once Kirk's piece was published in *America,* the *New York Times* publicized Goldwater's remarks on Welch — quoting Kirk as the authority. No mention was made of the fact that Goldwater's declaration had been made earlier to the *Times'* own reporter. Much more omission of Goldwater's words, or misrepresentation of them, would occur before and after his presidential nomination.

John Birch Society zealots began assailing Kirk, at his lectures or in print, so soon as his *America* article was published. They wrote vehement letters of protest to *National Review,* where Kirk's page on education appeared regularly. At this late hour, Bill Buckley, who had urged Kirk to write the anti-Welch article, now wrote to him inquiring whether he were not too severe upon John Birch. "You set me in the forefront of your host," Kirk replied, "so I go raging about the land on my black charger, a Bircher's head at my saddlebow."

Kirk's more direct service to Goldwater, in the early stages of the campaign, was the writing of speeches that Goldwater delivered at Notre Dame and at Yale; they were well received, even by some Irish Catholic Democrats at Notre Dame. These were the only speeches Kirk ever consented to write for a candidate for office, despite the illustrious examples of Jonathan Swift and Samuel Johnson, not to mention "Duke" Coombe, as ghostwriters. These lecture fees Goldwater turned over to Kirk, who in turn contributed the money toward some of the expenses of publishing *The University Bookman*.

On March 7, a new organization of youthful conservatives, Young Americans for Freedom, held a grand rally in Manhattan, with Senator Goldwater as chief speaker. There on the platform with Goldwater was the burly little form of Russell Kirk — blinking under the merciless kleig lights, perspiring in his antique evening-dress — along with George Sokolsky, William Buckley, Admiral Lewis Strauss, and other conservative worthies of that era, they being recipients of honors that evening.

Forceful and good-natured though Senator Goldwater's address was, Kirk recalls little more about it. For Kirk's eye and mind were upon the co-chief of the ushers, Miss Annette Yvonne Cecile Courtemanche, with whom he was not yet so well acquainted as he would wish to become. (That fair-faced and statuesque young lady had been secretary of the first organizational meeting of Young Americans for Freedom, at Sharon, Connecticut.) When speechifying was over, nearly all the platform guests and organizers, the breathtaking Annette among them, went off to a late cocktail party. But Kirk, so averse to cocktail parties as was T. S. Eliot, strolled solitary through the dark to the Manhattan apartment where he was to sleep that night. Later he learned that Annette had thought Russell Kirk's departure sad. But back to Senator Goldwater.

On May Day, Kirk's syndicated column for General Features — his second syndicated column published — compared, favorably to both, Eugene McCarthy and Barry Goldwater. Kirk pointed out that Goldwater was even more vexed at the antics of "radical right" groups than was McCarthy at silly "liberal" outbursts. "His book *The Conscience of a Conservative*," Kirk wrote, "together with his admirable performance at the Republican Convention of 1960, endeared him to the rank and file of American conservatives; he is quite the opposite of the old fogey that some commentators pretend he is. Zooming about in his jet plane, Barry Goldwater is far better adjusted to the twentieth century than are certain professors and journalists who write as if the issues of the 'Sixties were the problems — now substantially solved — of the 'Twenties and 'Thirties."

Goldwater's fair prospects of May 1962 grew fairer still as the months passed. Kirk kept up with Goldwater's progress in his syndicated column. The Senator's attack on the Kennedy administration's policies concerning Cuba and Katanga gained ground for him. By October 22, Kirk pointed out that Goldwater, despite the growth of his popularity, was not eager to assume the presidency:

> For one thing, the thought of Himalayas of paper-work appalls a man of action like Barry Goldwater. Also, as Walter Bagehot remarked a century ago, conservatism is enjoyment; and a conservative like Mr. Goldwater does not view the man-devouring job of the twentieth-century presidency as fun. More and more, it is to be feared, only those will seek the presidency who love power for its own sake, whatever its price in work; and such men are not ideal presidents for a free country.

So affairs political went swimmingly, in the autumn of 1962. *Time* magazine had estimated that were a presidential election to be held in 1962, Goldwater would defeat Kennedy in the Electoral College. As Goldwater's repute rose, Kennedy's declined. Kirk was cheerful — and not merely for reasons political.

The Conservative Beauty of Springfield Gardens

In February 1960, Kirk had been invited by AWARE, an organization opposing Communism in the theater arts, to speak at the Hotel Wellington (then elegant) near Columbus Circle, in Manhattan. This was a meeting of young people, undergraduates chiefly, of a conservative bent, or at least opposed to Communist ideology.

In the hotel lobby, Kirk was greeted cordially by a Mrs. Courtemanche and her younger daughter, Marie; they were fashionably dressed, well-mannered: Kirk supposed they might well come from Long Island's Gold Coast, they looking rather like Oyster Bay or Locust Valley ladies, possibly neighbors of his friends Franz and Betty Schneider. At the moment he did not surmise that these two new acquaintances, their rather aristocratic name of Courtemanche having only historical associations for him (for the Sieur de Courtemanche had built Fort St. Joseph, in the southwest of Michigan, when all that region was swamp and savagery), would come to figure very largely indeed in his life.

Entering the ballroom, Kirk glanced at the program, finding to his surprise that someone was to speak on his recent book *The American Cause* before he was to speak on educational standards, and that the person talking about his book was Miss Annette Courtemanche, elder daughter of the lady he had met a moment before. Kirk seated himself in the audience; soon Miss Courtemanche appeared at the rostrum. The impression made by that young lady is best conveyed by a Scots ejaculation, Wow!

Miss Courtemanche was nineteen years of age, a junior at Molloy Catholic College for Women, in Long Island, trained in public speaking by the nuns of Mary Louis Academy and of Molloy Catholic College. Her carriage was perfect, and she spoke clearly, with a high seriousness, her eyes demure.

Hers was an exquisite beauty, a unique one, difficult to describe. One was hard put to say from what race she came. She possessed a blooming Irish complexion, high cheekbones, a noble nose (perhaps French), and unblemished symmetry of countenance. That splendid and somewhat haughty face (relieved by a sweetness and innocence of expression) was crowned by long, long black hair, admirably groomed. Her figure would have been approved by the sculptors of antiquity. Such a face, such a shape, as drift through dreams!

This delightful creature praising his book! Kirk watched her, awed. Presently he was at the rostrum himself, speaking coherently enough on educational standards, but scarcely cognizant of what he said, for Annette's eyes were upon him now. To his high satisfaction, but also somewhat to his alarm, at lunch he found himself seated directly opposite this talented and resplendent young person.

Annette conversed intelligently and winsomely. Kirk thought, "Whomever can this girl marry?" So elegant, so self-possessed, so vivacious, so guileless, so fond of books, so obviously of good family! (Here Kirk recollected how at the beginning of the eighteenth century the Sieur de Courtemanche, with many tomahawks and scalping knives at his back, had descended from Quebec upon Kirk's New England ancestors.) What young man could aspire to Miss Courtemanche's person?

Had Kirk but known, at that moment she was mulling over that question herself: she had consented to speak at this conference because her mother had told her, "You'll be the only girl on the program." At that Annette had reflected, "I might meet somebody there." Indeed, she did meet somebody — but not quite the sort of somebody toward whom the matrimonial fancies of a nineteen-year-old belle usually incline.

It did not enter Kirk's head, there in the Hotel Wellington, that one day Miss Courtemanche might choose to marry *him*. In 1960 Kirk was forty-two years old, not handsome, totally unaccomplished in the arts of dancing and swimming, proficiency in which usually is expected of men by pretty girls. Yet Miss Courtemanche seemed to like him. They parted that afternoon, but not for many months. In his *National Review* page, Kirk soon described the seminar at the Hotel Wellington, mentioning Miss Courtemanche as "surely the most beautiful champion conservative doctrines ever found."

That summer, the Intercollegiate Studies Institute held at Grove City College a week-long conference for undergraduates. Kirk was to speak on theories of history. Upon arriving at the handsome campus, Kirk was even more pleased than surprised to find Annette Courtemanche as one of the students. He was a little embarrassed at encountering so soon the Athena whom, presumptuously, he had so praised in *National Review;* but Miss Courtemanche, who by this time had attained the great age of twenty, did not appear to be displeased. He had no opportunity to talk with her alone, various boys obtaining her attention after lectures. But she took copious notes of his learned talks, and from time to time smiled upon him.

In the autumn, Annette arranged for Kirk to lecture at Molloy College, she being president of the student body there. Presently she scheduled lectures for him at other colleges about New York City.

Visits to her house in Springfield Gardens commenced. The marvellous girl came of French, Indian, and Irish stock; as a child, when tanned and with her black hair in a single braid, she had been nicknamed Pocahontas. Her father, hard hit by the Great Depression in Pennsylvania, had shifted to New York City, where briefly (about the time Annette was born) he was a doorman at an apartment house on Riverside Drive — an employment contrived for him by one of his sisters, Lola Courtemanche, a showgirl in the Ziegfeld Follies. Later, at various times, this Regis Henri Courtemanche had been a designer of jewelry in Greenwich Village, a decorator, and a tool-and-die maker; still later he would become bursar of a private school. He was a handsome, energetic man with some liking for good books.

Mary Cullen Courtemanche, wife and mother, a most earnest Catholic who reared good children, was something of a power in Long Island, organizing civic committees for better schools, for better buses, for summer camps for young people, for the diminishing of air pollution. Active in conservative causes, Mrs. Courtemanche had organized the only bloc of delegates pledged to the presidential candidacy of General MacArthur, at the Republican Convention, 1952. She was secretary to a judge, part time.

Annette's parents, her brother Regis Armand Pierre Courtemanche, her sister Marie, and Annette lived in a little house that had stood solitary amidst marshes until what is now Kennedy International Airport was much enlarged and households displaced by that expansion were moved — yes, their very houses were transported — to become the Courtemanches' numerous neighbors.* The elegant Annette slept in an unheated garret. Kirk was somewhat pleased to find that the young lady's family, like his own, would have been sociologically classified in Britain as "working class," in America as "blue collar." To Courtemanches and Kirks, class distinctions

---

*An older brother of Annette, Gerard Courtemanche, already had left home and married. Annette's sister, Marie, later became an able teacher of the deaf.

scarcely existed: they dressed well, dined well, and schooled well the rising generation. Annette was closely acquainted with the Roosevelts of Oyster Bay and their cadet branches; Mrs. Courtemanche moved influentially in Republican political circles and in church concerns of Long Island. On Sunday evenings they kept a good table, with many interesting guests taking part in conversations. Kirk was mightily taken with this close-knit family, whose elder daughter played the accordion and the piano, and with naïve pleasure displayed to Dr. Kirk many handsome books in the household library.

The Courtemanches were familiar with Kirk's articles in *National Review* and with most of his books. Annette's witty brother, the younger Regis Courtemanche (then a teacher of history, later a professor of that discipline), approved this visitor. Now and again, as the Goldwater campaign took form, Kirk encountered Annette at political gatherings, notably the Young Americans for Freedom rally in Manhattan on March 7, 1962, where she and her friend Doris Sukup (another Long Island beauty) directed the ushers. Occasionally Annette put on a golden sash identifying her as a Goldwater Girl; all eyes followed her.

A Kirk-Courtemanche correspondence had commenced. Even when lecturing at Post College, in Long Island, Kirk had no way of seeing Annette, public transportation to Springfield Gardens being most difficult, and he possessing no automobile. Most of the time he was back at Mecosta, seven hundred miles distant; he was long accustomed to the art of writing interesting letters; his epistles were welcome at Springfield Gardens. Thus 1962 and much of 1963 passed away, the exchange of letters steadily becoming more frequent. Annette was graduated from Molloy Catholic College for Women; became a teacher of English and drama at Floral Park Memorial High School; presently shifted from her parents' house at Springfield Gardens — a community already sinking in the social scale, and growing dangerous — to a little apartment at Valley Stream; settled her affections on nobody. "There's nobody to marry in Long Island!" she and her girlfriends were given to lamenting, half seriously.

In the summer of 1962, Annette and her petite friend Peggy Travers (who sang at Goldwater gatherings) took ship to Europe, two innocents abroad, flirtatious teachers, bound for such towns, presumably romantic, as Heidelberg, Berlin, Rome, and Paris. Russell Kirk somewhat timidly had offered to accompany them, as *cicerone* and *cavaliere servente,* but his offices were rejected, the young ladies preferring to be footloose and fancy-free. That summer Kirk made his solitary way back to Scotland, staying most of the time at Durie, Kellie, and Balcarres.

As the end of summer approached, the peregrine Annette — somewhat resembling Daisy Miller in Henry James's novelette — wrote to Russell that she was on her way to Britain to visit him, leaving Peggy in Germany. Very nearly down and out in Paris, Annette on arrival in London contrived to borrow enough money for a rail ticket to York, where the obedient Russell met her on the station platform. So far there was little in their association to suggest courtship; and yet Annette must have begun to feel rather like the fictional Daisy Miller, interested in Winterbourne — that character who resembles his creator, Henry James. Russell Kirk had his similarities to Henry James — his relatively formal manners, his reserve, his moving in country-house circles and literary circles, his life as a middle-aged American bachelor much at home in Britain. It may have been so early as 1962 that there passed through Annette's mind the momentary reflection, "Wouldn't it be a pity if Dr. Kirk didn't have children!"

They stayed with Canon and Mrs. Smith in the cathedral precincts; that first evening Kirk took the Smiths and Annette out to dinner, causing Miss Courtemanche, a zealous Papist, to miss Sunday mass for the first time in her young life. This she confessed to a priest upon returning to Springfield Gardens, offering as excuse the necessity of having to dine out during the hour of the last mass; but her confessor would reprove her: "Pleasures of the flesh!"

After showing the Conservative Beauty some of the antiquities of York, her respectful admirer took her north by train to East Lothian, where Gerald Balfour, Lord Traprain (later the Earl of Balfour), picked them up by car and bore them off to the well-wooded great estate of Whittinghame, where Natasha, Lady Traprain, and the Balfours' little girl were much taken with Annette; the daughter besought her autograph. The vivacious and easy-mannered Annette carried herself very well indeed at this her first encounter with a peer and a peeress.

The next day they two took train to Fife, and Kirk showed his resplendent guest the amenities of old St. Andrews and took her the round of country houses. At Durie, the old laird and Kirk gathered mushrooms on the lawns for their dinner and nursed Annette through convalescence from a severe cold, easily acquired in Scotland.

Those Fife days passed too swiftly; it was nearly time for Kirk to get back to writing and Goldwater campaigning in America. Kirk took Annette down to Edinburgh for the Festival of 1962. She was introduced to George and Eileen Scott-Moncrieff, at James's Court. After many years as a widower, Scomo had married an American art student, Eileen, a girl about Annette's age, a friend of George's daughter Lesley. From the beginning, Eileen and Annette got on well. The gulf of years between Scomo and Eileen was far greater than that between Russell and Annette: a vague suspicion passed through Annette's consciousness that just possibly Russell had some personal motive in thus showing her that October and May might be cozily compatible.

Lesley Scott-Moncrieff went with them to a performance of *King Lear,* one of the lesser but better events of the Edinburgh Festival. This was the last night of the Kirk-Courtemanche Tour of the British Isles. About midnight, Kirk knocked at the door of Annette's chamber. "Yes?" she called, somewhat sternly, possibly fancying that Dr. Kirk had turned suddenly amorous.

"I just brought you some postage stamps, Annette," replied Kirk, humbly — and pushed the stamps under the door. Next day he was off to New York, and she to Ireland, where she would visit friends of friends.

Yet they were not parted long. In September, Kirk participated in an ISI summer school held at Post College. Annette, very busy with her high-school teaching and directing of plays, came over from Floral Park to greet him. He took her to meet Dr. Gordon Hoxie, the president of Post College. After her departure, Hoxie inquired of Kirk whether he was thinking of marriage. Kirk replied that it was quite out of the question.

"That girl would marry you," said Hoxie, referring to Miss Courtemanche. Smiling, Kirk shook his head. But the judgment of Hoxie would be vindicated, two years later, by the event.

For the following twelve months, Kirk and Annette met only on his occasional trips to New York, she or her brother sometimes meeting his plane at the airport. Late in the summer of 1963, they two having corresponded a great deal meanwhile, Annette decided to visit Russell at Mecosta. Thither she drove in her little Corvair, accompanied by her pretty friend Peggy Travers. Arriving late at night, the girls drove through the village of Mecosta without realizing it was their intended destination; never before had Annette been farther west than Scranton, Pennsylvania. Kirk lodged them in the Red Room of the old house. Next morning, Annette inquired of Russell, "Where's the Italian restaurant? Where's the Chinese restaurant? Where's the Chinese laundry? Where do all the people live? How near is the nearest town — about two miles?" For the first time she came to know that America is not all one vast Long Island.

Kirk's uncle, aunt, and two great-aunts received Annette cordially, but with some trepidation: like Gordon Hoxie, they perceived the shadow of events to come. Annette was so magnificent, larger than life! They entertained the notion that her kinsmen must be very high-born indeed, and that she must be accustomed to a most sumptuous manner of living. "There are many beautiful girls, Russell," said Aunt Fay. "I've always thought you ought to marry a woman a little older than yourself."

"Then I'd be marrying a grandmother, Faydie," said Kirk. Uncle Potter, saying nothing, clearly admired his nephew's friend Annette Yvonne Cecile, Catholic though she was, and he a Mason. No one at Piety Hill guessed that Annette and Russell never had spoken of marriage, nor that Daisy Miller never had been kissed by Winterbourne.

Kirk showed Annette and Peggy the rustic delights of Mecosta County, among them Lost Lake and the sand trails of the back country. On the final evening of their stay, in his library, he told them their fortunes by the Tarot — an art he had been taught by Ralph Christie of Durie. Kirk wearing a devil's mask of rubber, and robed in his saffron gown of a doctor of letters, and capped with the black cap of John Knox, the girls were suitably impressed and distressed. Before them on the round oaken table of his library, Kirk spread out the strange symbolic cards of the Tarot; he laid beside the cards a case of crocodile hide, containing two Sumatran throwing knives.

Kirk does not know how to account for the eerie verdicts of the Tarot cards, and has ceased to tell Tarot fortunes. In part, the reading is simply the conventional significations of the many cards, as recorded in a Tarot manual. Yet also the unusual intuitions of an accomplished Tarot-reader play a large part; and (or so it long seemed to Kirk) some form of thought transference from the mind of the subject to the mind of the cartomancer commonly is involved. Beyond such possible insights lies a mystery yet more arcane: a power of prediction of events very difficult indeed to explain on any ground. Are we bound by fixed fate? Is there foreknowledge absolute? In Kirk's experience, the fortunes foretold by the Tarot very often are predictions of disgrace or of death, and just such catastrophes often come to pass, after no great interval. Are the Tarot cards devilish? No, Kirk no longer amuses his guests by cartomancy.

On a hot night, a tall candle burning on either side of his face, Russell Kirk, D.Litt., told the fortunes of the two frightened Long Island belles. Of Peggy, the cards said that soon she would have to make a decision that would determine the whole course of her life, to its end. Annette's fortune was more complex and more alarming.

By Kirk's reading of the cards, Death stood at Annette's right hand — imminent peril of death, rather. Annette being but twenty-two years of age, and lovely, and much beloved of Russell Kirk, this prospect could not be put bluntly. Instead, Kirk told his subject that someone near and dear to her might be in peril of death, but that a trusty friend would be at hand on the occasion.

The next morning the three of them, in Annette's Corvair (unsafe at any speed, thundered the omniscient Ralph Nader), drove north to Mackinac Island, where they lodged in the Grand Hotel and saw the historical sights. That evening Kirk took Annette, without Peggy, to the Casino or Grandstand at the head of the golf course beside the huge quaint summer hotel. (Annette had invited Peggy, too, but that perceptive dear had declined: "Dr. Kirk wants to talk with *you*.") They devoured coconut snowballs, a trifle shy either with the other, despite the intimacies of their Scottish journey. To Annette — although nothing occurred, not even the patting of a hand — this encounter was "their first real date." As he said good night to her at the door of her room, she wondered whether he might try to kiss her, and what she ought to do should he try; but, whether to her relief or to her chagrin, Dr. Kirk remained Winterbourne to her Daisy. Was ever there a courtship more respectful and more good-natured? For Annette had begun to recognize this happy association as a species of courtship with which previously she had been unacquainted.

Departing from the antique enchantment of Mackinac Island and its Grand Hotel, Annette and Peggy and Russell drove for two days across Ontario, on their way to New York City and Long Island. From Ottawa they would have one more day's journey, southward to

New York; the girls would resume their teaching, and Kirk, bound for Europe, expected later to travel in northern Africa, writing newspaper columns along his route.

On Sunday of the Labor Day weekend, 1963, they three were whizzing along the great highway, a few miles north of Kingston, New York. Annette, a skillful and a speedy driver, honked a slow car out of the passing lane and increased her speed. Then a rear tire of the Corvair blew out.

Annette took the shaking car off the concrete into the green strip between the north and south lanes of traffic, braking so that the Corvair would not plunge headlong into the opposing thick stream of northbound vehicles. She braked a little too hard; the rear of the car rose up, for the Corvair was turning heels over head. Kirk's immediate thought was for the charming faces of the two girls in the front seat, should the windshield burst in upon them. In the back seat, with the young women's dresses and jackets hanging next to a window, Kirk was turned topsy-turvy.

He found himself in total darkness, as if that of a coffin, swathed in fabrics, atop him some long metal lid. It took Kirk two or three seconds to understand that the girls' clothing, flung down in the crash, was wrapped about him; and that the back seat had turned over, pinning him between the roof of the car and that seat-frame. He heard Annette calling, "Peggy! Russell! Are you all right?"

Kirk does not remember how he contrived to fling the back seat off himself and scramble out the small window; but he did it in an instant. Little Peggy had popped out her window without difficulty, and Annette out the door on the driver's side. The Corvair was fit only to be towed away for junk.

The car's trunk had burst open, and their luggage was scattered on the grass. Several cars pulled over to view the disaster. Annette's Catholic missal lay disconsolate among the luggage, and was snatched up by a preacher who took it for a Bible. Exhibiting it to the little congregation that had gathered behind the wreck, he cried, "See, she had the Good Book with her!" commencing a succinct sermon for the occasion.

Hailing a passing car full of young men, the intrepid Annette sped away to the nearest police post to report the disaster. There she was confronted by a grim-faced highway policeman who told her how lucky she was to be alive. "I know!" Annette replied. "No, you don't," the policeman said. He went on to tell her that a few hours earlier, a dark-haired girl of Annette's age, a teacher, driving a small car, had been killed on that very stretch of highway, and he had moved the corpse.

Annette, Peggy, and Russell contrived to lug their baggage aboard a bus at Kingston, and presently arrived at the Port Authority bus terminal, in Manhattan; there Annette telephoned one of her admirers, a stalwart young radio announcer, to collect and transport them in his car.

When Peggy reached her parents' home, she found a message waiting from her friend Donald, announcing his firm intention to accept a post at Hong Kong: either she must marry him and accompany him to the Orient, or else they two forever would be parted. It was the great decision determining her whole future, predicted by Kirk's Tarot cards three nights before. She accepted Donald's proposal, and not long after off to Hong Kong they went, and lived happily ever after. This chapter of this book is no work of fiction.

As for Annette's Tarot fortune, indeed Death had stood at her right hand, but a trusty friend, who in his life had escaped all manner of perils, had been near her at the crisis. Another girl, whose mother Annette arranged to lunch with some weeks later, had perished violently on that strip of highway: a teacher much like herself. Annette, Peggy, and Russell were unscratched. One thinks again of Arthur Koestler's argument that everything happening in this world is part of some tremendous intricate design into which human intelligence never has penetrated far.

At a lunch counter in the Kingston bus station, shortly after the ruin of Annette's Corvair, Annette told Kirk how sorry she was that he had been endangered; it was her fault. "Yes," said Kirk, "you've shaken me up, and now you'll have to spend the rest of your life taking care of me."

Miss Courtemanche glanced away, with a slight smile on those perfect lips of hers. "I don't know I'd go *that* far."

He was tempted to reply, "Think about it, Annette" — but did not quite dare. A day or two later he was off to Scotland, and would go thence to call on his friends the Kerrigans in Palma de Mallorca, and then to Rome, and after that to Roman Africa. From Fife, Edinburgh, London, Palma, Rome, Tunis, Kairouan, Fex, Rabat, Salé, Casablanca, Marrakesh, Tangier, Gibraltar, Granada, and Malaga, letters and postcards would be dispatched daily to the Maiden of Springfield Gardens; also, from Morocco, a rug, a Berber bracelet, a brass tray. At her apartment, Annette would exhibit to her friends these gifts and would sing to them the praises of Dr. Kirk, the writer. "I have always had," Daisy Miller remarks to Winterbourne in Henry James's story, "a great deal of gentlemen's society." Similarly, Miss Courtemanche always had a great deal of such society; but to her gentlemen callers, in 1963, almost compulsively she would discourse of her friend Russell Kirk, his adventures, his learning, his wit, his books.

"Why don't you marry the guy?" asked one disgruntled admirer, with irony.

Of course she couldn't. But wouldn't it be a pity if Russell Kirk were to father no children! And he was her best friend; she told him everything. She entertained waking visions of a future in which she, married (the face of the future husband being a blank always) and surrounded by her little children, would receive the avuncular visitor Dr. Russell Kirk, her best friend, he bearing gifts for her offspring. Somewhat confusing, this vision; but then, she was too busy directing her school's performances of *The Music Man* and *Oklahoma!* to fret overmuch about her future state. Anyway, she and Peggy had agreed that early marriage was the pits. Where would Russell be tonight — the Pillars of Hercules?

CHAPTER ELEVEN

Private Victory and Public Defeat

Roman Ruminations

From Mallorca, late in September, that busy year of 1963, Kirk flew to Rome. The Ecumenical Council of the Vatican was at its lively deliberations again, and simultaneously there was held in the Immortal City a grand conference of the Centro di Vita Italiana, a new organization of conservative inclinations intended to clear some common ground, intellectually speaking, upon which members of Italian political factions and men of intellect from other countries might meet amicably enough.

Next to Kirk, on the plane that was bearing them to the great new airport near Ostia, sat the youngest of the bishops attending the Ecumenical Council — Bishop Mendoza, from Ecuador, aged thirty-four years. Kirk and his companion (Anthony Kerrigan, the translator and poet) asked this bishop how it had come to pass that he had been elevated to a see (where most of his flock were Quechua-speaking Indians) at so tender an age. "In Ecuador we have a proverb," he replied, "which runs thus: 'Guile compensates for youth.'" Aye, in 1963 the Catholic Church, in Ecuador as elsewhere, seemed to require a certain craftiness, as well as sanctity, to survive in an age of ideology.

In Rome, the terrible adversary of Christianity, Communism, lay hard by the gates of the Vatican, in the picturesque slum of Trastevere. In 1963 the big Communist party grew stronger with every month that passed. And Pope Paul VI, still an uncertain quality in the eyes of many Catholics, sat in the seat of Saint Peter, with the heavy duty of defending orthodoxy against the heresy, or inverted religion, of Marxism.

Old Pope John XXIII, powerfully influenced by his secretary, had entertained hopes of gaining concessions from the masters of the Kremlin by some measures of conciliation. Also he had entertained Nikita Khrushchev's son-in-law at the Vatican, to the dismay of many members of the Curia, and of most Italian anti-Communists. *L'apertura a sinistra!* The peril had been worse in 1948, when every bank in Milano had been guarded at its doors by squads with automatic weapons at the ready; but not a few Italian conservatives, in 1963, were declaring that John XXIII unwittingly had given the Communist Party of Italy a million votes at the previous national election, by receiving Adzhubei as the legitimate representative of the Soviet empire. For the Communist and near-Communist press and party workers had claimed that this papal gesture proved clearly how no real barrier lay between Catholicism and Communism. Why not vote the Communist ticket, then? It appeared that a good many Italian working-class women, previously obdurate against Marxism, had taken such advice — or, at any rate, were not so strong as they had been previously in dissuading their husbands from hearkening to those Communists.

A different course might be expected from Paul VI, formerly Monsignor Montini, papal secretary of state under John, and recently enthroned: so Kirk was told by knowing Romans, among them his host in Rome, Prince Rospigliosi, who took Kirk round to clubs and restaurants. The new pope was by nature and instinct a man of order, Rospigliosi stated; knowing this, the Conclave had accepted his candidacy with little dissent.

While Kirk spent that week in Rome (lodged, as usual for him, at the Albergo Minerva, which then swarmed with ecclesiastics, its rates being low for a hotel nominally first class), the Pope addressed journalists from all over the world. He pointed to the empty chairs where the bishops from eastern Europe should have been sitting — but were not sitting, because the governments of the lands beyond the Iron Curtain would not permit them to attend the Ecumenical Council. Paul VI told the newspapermen from Soviet "people's democracies" that those vacant chairs signified the hostility to religious freedom that still prevailed evilly in their countries.

Although he had commenced an administrative reform of the Curia, Paul did not intend any sweeping alterations in the structure of the Catholic Church. When, later, the Catholic monthly *The Critic* asked Kirk to defend the doctrine of papal infallibility, as represented in the person of Pope Paul VI, Kirk endeavored to excuse himself, telling the editors that surely there must be church historians and theologians, better informed than was Kirk, who would willingly undertake such a chore. "No, there aren't such people," *The Critic* informed Kirk. Therefore Kirk did support the Pope on the question of infallibility, pointing out that this doctrine, so much assailed by modernists, was a necessary fiction, like the English legal doctrine that the king can do no wrong, or like the American assumption that decisions of the Supreme Court of the United States are final, without possibility of appeal to any other authority. An ultimate power of decision on questions of faith and morals must repose somewhere; church councils cannot be meeting perpetually; so it is simply in the nature of things that papal infallibility must be sustained by the Church.

Paul VI had a high respect for long-established patterns of order. Prince Rospigliosi made this sufficiently clear by telling Kirk of an incident in the reign of John XXIII which probably has been published nowhere until now. Mrs. Clare Booth Luce, while American ambassador to Italy, had drawn up a fairly elaborate plan for the reform and reconstruction of the Universal Church. The Luce magazine empire had enthusiastically applauded the elevation of John XXIII to the papal throne, especially in the pages of *Time*, and generally had approved John's policies and pronouncements. Mrs. Luce may have expected, therefore, that if out of gratitude only, the Pope would proceed promptly to alter the structure of the Church on the lines supplied to him by so eminent an American Catholic, diplomat, playwright, and novelist as Clare Booth Luce.

Yet whole months passed, and the Church worldwide remained unreformed. Mrs. Luce summoned her spouse as reinforcement. Highly vexed that the Vatican had not yet acted, Henry Luce flew to Rome to demand the reason why.

Prince Rospigliosi, that model of urbanity, previously had been Henry Luce's agent in Africa. Luce demanded of him that he arrange an audience with the Pope. Even for the head of a Roman princely house that had itself supplied a pope (Clement IX), to arrange such a confrontation was neither possible nor desirable. Rospigliosi did take Henry Luce to see the papal secretary of state, the soft-spoken and courteous Monsignor Montini.

"How may I be of service to you, Mr. Luce?" Montini inquired.

Luce made it very clear indeed that he wanted to know what had been done to implement his wife's plan, so kindly supplied to the Vatican, for modernizing and thoroughly revising the Church. Weeks had passed, and then months, and still the Church went its ancient ways!

Monsignor Montini explained most civilly that the Vatican was very grateful for Mrs. Luce's detailed recommendations, and he doubted not that great good would come of them. "But you must remember, Mr. Luce, that the Church moves deliberately and with caution — slowly, if you will. From time to time, this caution has declined into tardiness; on the other hand, much mischief may come of imprudent haste. It is well to achieve a consensus of the learned and virtuous." Committees of the Curia must be appointed to discuss the plan of Mrs. Luce; indeed, such bodies already had begun preliminary conversations and researches. The Secretary of State very much regretted that it had not been found possible to proceed in a fashion somewhat more gratifying to Madame the Ambassadress, who had honored the Church by . . .

Here Luce broke in angrily, demanding evidence of what, if anything, had been accomplished already, and a definite date by which his wife's reforms would be implemented.

"Mr. Luce," Prince Rospigliosi interposed, somewhat sharply, "you must remember that you are addressing a high dignitary of the Church. At the least, you must lower your voice."

Yet Henry Luce departed in dudgeon, or at least in low dudgeon, from the audience chamber. As he went out, he said to Rospigliosi, indicating Monsignor Montini, "Mark my words, that fellow will never be pope!" But Providence does not much regard the vexation of the lords of the press.

The Roman conference of the Center for Italian Life was concerned with matters other than the structure and liturgy of the Church. What is called "Western civilization" (more accurately, "Christian civilization"), with its roots in classical and Hebraic culture as well as Christian culture, seemed less secure in 1963 than it had been since the Middle Ages, perhaps. Modern ideologies, mass counter-culture, and the triumph of technology all had undermined, in their several ways, the venerable traditions of humane learning and of the inherited social order.

Scholars and writers from nine countries were present at this conference, to discuss their common cultural tradition and how it might be reconciled with national differences. Everybody present had a conservative mind, in the sense of opposing collectivism and cultural mediocrity or decadence. Several Americans spoke — William Buckley, Thomas Molnar, John Dos Passos, Kirk.

Dos Passos, born in Madeira, presided over the conference's first session, speaking with shrewdness and force on how the writer has the duty of serving his time by defending the common heritage of order, justice, and freedom. Not many years earlier, Dos Passos — in 1963, the most eminent living American novelist — had been fancied by many to be a man of the Left. Paul Elmer More, a generation gone, had described one of Dos Passos's early novels as "an explosion in a cesspool."

But by 1963 the American political tradition, and traditions of civility in general, had no more sincere champion than John Dos Passos; he had published a whole series of books on the American political experience, in a spirit of approbation. The youngish Italians who had organized this conference venerated him.

Italian Liberals, Spanish Carlists, Austrian monarchists, and twenty other groups of various political shadings were represented at the gathering in Rome; and Catholic, Greek Orthodox, Protestant, and Jewish writers and scholars attended. Meeting near the column of Marcus Aurelius, at the heart of medieval Rome, the men attending endeavored to renew the cement that had held together, despite passionate differences of opinion, the tessellated pavement of European and American civilization. Until late in the eighteenth century, when the utopianism of the alleged Enlightenment (renounced by the participants in this Roman conference of 1963) led many into perilous paths, men of letters rarely had been radical advocates of change. The growth of Marxism, after the middle of the nineteenth century, turned other writers and scholars toward the Left — and sometimes to their own destruction.

Yet by 1963 the fearful spectacle of what Communist ideologues had done with the works of the mind had shaken some writers of the Left. This Roman conference was meant to hearten "intellectuals of the Right." Men of that inclination have gained some ground since 1963 — though the more eminent of their number have been writers of Russian or Polish origin, rather than of the Mediterranean culture.

About 1963, thinking Italians began to turn away from *l'apertura a sinistra,* and the deliberations of the Center for Italian Life were a manifestation, if not a major cause, of that change of heart.

Twentieth-Century Barbary

From Rome, at the beginning of October 1963, Kirk flew to join Thomas Molnar in what had been the Roman Province of Africa and two thousand years later was a re-emergent Moslem despotism. It was Kirk's first expedition to that continent out of which, the old Romans knew, "come all things strange." His friend Molnar, the author of *The Decline of the Intellectual* and many other books and a most lively survivor of Nazi concentration camps, would write about their expedition in his book *Africa: A Political Travelogue* (1965). Therein Kirk appears as something of a figure of fun. In the passage that follows, Molnar writes of their being pleasantly accosted by a Tunisian charmer clad all in leather:

> "Are you tourists?" she asked in French. In fact, it was not hard to ascertain that we were. I wore only a shirt and trousers, but my companion, famous not only for his writings but also for his passion for covering numberless miles on foot, was unmistakably a tourist, though a strange one. He wore, under the sun of North Africa, a suit, necktie, a felt hat, heavy shoes, and a heavy, knotty walking stick. All the children of Tunis, and later those of mysterious Morocco, looked at us with open mouths as we passed.

Kirk protested to Molnar, however, that in Africa and India only mad dogs and Englishmen go hatless in the noonday sun, and that not even Englishmen go stickless in such lands, so abounding in sturdy beggars and masterless men.

Nowhere are Roman ruins thicker than in Tunisia. For this, from the days when Scipio took Punic Carthage until the Vandals broke into the city, was the Province of Africa, wondrously rich and prosperous. Saint Augustine was born in Carthage, to a patrician family, and died in neighboring Hippo, when the Vandals were at the gates.

Kirk and Molnar spent some days in Tunis and the country round about. In Carthaginian and Roman times, the town on the site of Tunis, across the bay from Carthage, was a slum; now it is the capital of a secular state. But the greatness of this land is gone, one coming here chiefly to view the ruins.

Going up to the Moslem town of Zaghouan, thirty miles inland from Tunis, one finds the springs from which the Romans took their water to supply the great Antonine baths at Carthage, and from which Tunis's water comes today. Here stands at the fountainhead the Temple of the Nymphs, built in the Emperor Hadrian's day. A colossal Roman aqueduct runs in ruin, across arid hillside and plain, all the way down to the coast.

The ruined Roman cities of Tunisia are many, sacked by Vandal and Arab. Of them, Carthage is the most evocative of the grandeur that was Rome. Although the Romans, having destroyed forever the Punic power, sowed with salt the site of the Carthaginian capital, later they built their own city there beside the sea. The hill called the Birsa, where the Carthaginians made their last ghastly stand in citadel and temples against the conquering Romans, is surmounted nowadays by the nineteenth-century Catholic cathedral, built by the French. (Ten months after Kirk's visit to Carthage, the Tunisian state arbitrarily converted the cathedral into a museum.) One sees elsewhere the Tophet, the pit in which those Carthaginians sacrificed children, and many Carthaginian tombstones.

Water made this land fruitful. But its forests were hewn down by Vandal and Byzantine and Arab, erosion followed, and the splendid works of irrigation crumbled to dust. On this blasted African shore, blackmail, freebooting, and kidnapping became the principal industries, until Decatur, Eaton, and other Americans taught the Barbary pirates some lessons.

No strong political power endures forever. In those times, when Roman emperors were bred up in the Province of Africa, no man expected that all this splendor would become the abomination of desolation. Only after Alaric's barbarian Goths had taken Rome did Saint Augustine see that Roman might, too, was a vanity that must pass; and he wrote *The City of God*, about the community of souls that endures when the cities of this world have been given up to fire and sword.

In the amphitheater of Carthage, still to be seen, Saint Perpetua and Saint Felicia (after whom Kirk's third daughter would be named) and many other Christians gave up the ghost. One finds, too, a little subterranean church dedicated to Saint Monica, Augustine's mother (after whom Kirk's first daughter would be named). Yet early Christian site though Carthage was, Islam triumphed long ago; virtually the only Christians there now are resident Europeans. Their villas and those of rich Tunisians stand on the sites of big Roman houses, looking across the magnificent bay. Habib Bourguiba, president of the new Tunisian Republic and powerful as any Bey of Tunis in the old days, in 1963 was building himself a palace on those heights.

Quite as Christian belief was shrinking in Europe during the 1960s, Moslem faith was attenuated in Tunisia. Molnar and Kirk made their way to the oasis and town of Kairouan, founded by the conquering Arabs in the year 670. It is one of the sacred cities of Islam. Here stands the famous mosque built in the ninth century, with a slender primitive minaret, which Molnar and Kirk ascended by its narrow winding stair, to obtain the fine view over the medieval town. They found no one at the summit, nor met any one on the stair; yet when they had returned to the ground, there sounded from the top of the minaret a voice calling the faithful to prayer. "Where is the man?" they asked their guide. "How did he get up there?" "There is no man," they were informed. "It is a recording."

They entered the great mosque, having first removed their shoes. The magnificent stone columns within had been plundered from Roman public buildings in Carthage and elsewhere. Nobody at all was praying there: the only other visitors were a gaggle of German tourists in lederhosen. From the grand mosque at Kairouan, the spirit of Islam had departed so utterly as had the spirit of Christianity from the cathedrals, or former cathedrals, of the Netherlands.

One intelligent citizen of Meknes, in Morocco, told the two travellers that along with faith in Allah and the Koran, sexual morality, and personal responsibility generally, were fast declining among Moslems. Increasingly, he said, children were disobeying their parents; many girls became pregnant, no one knowing the fathers; the idea of duty was weakening in its power. This state of affairs he attributed to a vague progressivism. For one thing, he lamented, Moslem mothers increasingly arrogated the whole rearing of the children to themselves, pushing out the fathers — and discipline. Although formerly the father had quoted passages from the Koran to his children, in 1963 the custom was neglected. Public morality was no more heartening. The more loudly a North African government proclaimed itself to be popular, progressive, and socialist, the more corruption was evident.

In previous centuries, the power of even sultans and beys had been checked by the religious authority of the *cadi,* the Koranic judge. But such new masters as Ahmed Ben Bella, in Algeria, had only contempt for the claims of religion. In North Africa, and in Libya and Algeria particularly, the modern state might become more cruel and less efficient than any European domination.

From Tunisia, Molnar and Kirk flew to Morocco. Although Moroccan troops just then were fighting against Algerian forces along the desert frontier in the extreme southwest, in Morocco's cities no sign of war was to be perceived — except for *lab-el-barod,* the powder war, the mock battle, at the oasis city of Marrakesh.

Outside Marrakesh's crumbling ancient walls, Berber tribesmen had a temporary encampment, a multitude of round, neat white tents. They had been summoned to do honor to two foreign guests, the Emperor Haile Selassie and Mrs. Jacqueline Kennedy. The city folk of Marrakesh were somewhat discomposed by the Berber presence: "Very fierce fighters," said the Americans' guide.

Amidst the drifting dust (the rains not having fallen yet upon Morocco that October), the Berbers' robes were clean and colorful. Of an evening, Molnar and Kirk hurried down toward their camp, for the chief men had sent word to the city that foreign visitors would be welcome at their cooking fires and their dances this appointed evening.

Doubtless the invitation was meant chiefly for Mrs. Kennedy and her party. As Molnar and Kirk made their way toward the Berber fires, out of one gate of Marrakesh rolled several black closed carriages, drawn by handsome Arab horses: the Kennedy party, shepherded by some of the courtiers of King Hassan, thus made a gesture of response to the Berbers' invitation. But those carriages merely glided along parallel to the wall, a half-mile distant from the Berber encampment, and then vanished through the next gate of the city, not to be seen again — no face having been visible within any of the several carriages.

Not caring whether or not anyone watched them, the Berbers took a formidable joy in their own militant *razzia.* Many wore daggers in long silver sheaths; their horsemen carried long antiquated guns bound with silver, which they fired manfully into the air (the guns being charged with powder only) as they dashed about on their horses in simulated warfare. All during the day, this irregular cavalry had galloped up and down outside the walls for the entertainment of the townsfolk, now and again a band firing simultaneously at the command of a chief; tossing up their guns and catching them; standing up in their saddles. They were playful, but not to be trifled with. A gang of city toughs, depraved-looking young men with heavy criminal faces, came down on motorbikes to the Bedouin camp, perhaps seeking what they might purloin; some man of mark among the Berbers spoke a few stern words to them, at which the gang gaped — and departed most hastily, back to their alleys behind the city walls.

The dancers were better still. As dark came on, scores, perhaps hundreds, of knots of desert men formed on foot among the tents, and presently each little cluster of tribesmen commenced to stamp and chant — some with the accompaniment of simple native instruments, others with only a little drum for beating time. Their desert rhythms were ancient, and to the stranger scarcely distinguishable one from another. All the dancers were male, and men chiefly in the prime of life. They were quite tireless. The little cooking fires cast shadows upon them in the twilight. Their audience, from the neighboring old town, the Medina, watched respectfully.

Presently Molnar and Kirk noticed that they two were the only non-Africans in this whole great crowd. Both the Berbers and the Marrakesh townsfolk seemed pleased to have them present; perhaps they took these two foreigners for members of the Kennedy entourage. A young and courtly Berber, presenting them with lamb on skewers, invited the visitors to join his circle; he said in French that he hoped they would not take offense at the ludicrous rubber masks some of the dancers wore — "all in fun." (Among those masks were ones of Jack Kennedy and Dick Nixon; also grinning paper-white rubber countenances of an admiral, a coquette, a drunkard, a salesman.) Capering and cavorting, this particular circle of comic dancers played their respective roles, always keeping time, mowing and goggling and laughing cordially in the visitors' faces, yet maintaining a certain courtesy. Under the masks, the lean and dignified bedouin lost their solemnity, so that a set of Italian clowns could not have been less inhibited. The crowd of watchers stared at Molnar and Kirk hopefully and sympathetically, to see if they enjoyed the fun — which they did.

[282]

After an hour or two of this, Molnar and Kirk strolled homeward in the dusty night, through neglected arcades and groves of palms. Not a great many human beings still live a life more austere and comfortless than that of the Berbers. Yet they retain pleasures more genuine, often, than those of coddled modern man, who cannot ride an Arab barb, or really dance with abandon, or laugh at his own aches, pains, and privations.

In search of the Moslem culture of yesteryear, Molnar and Kirk penetrated to the old pirate lair of Salé, within its great grim circuit of walls, between the Atlantic and the estuary of the Bou Regreg — by which Salé is parted from Rabat, the capital. More than a hundred and fifty thousand people dwelt within those walls in 1963 — though how anyone could count them within that rabbit warren, Kirk couldn't guess. Moroccan tourist agencies made scant mention of Salé, for the place was desperately poor and crowded, and the populace said to be still somewhat militant children of Islam. But also Salé was the true old Morocco.

The two American men of letters crossed the estuary in a rowboat, paying a ragged ferryman three or four pennies; then they plodded along the shore to a monumental gateway. Once through that gate, they found themselves in a labyrinthine market, the *suk*, where — as at the Devil's Booth of Vanity Fair — all things were sold. There was no proper market square, for within the inhabited regions of Salé are next to no open spaces. The Christian captives of the seventeenth century, enslaved by the ferocious Salé Rovers of that corsair republic, must have felt that the jaws of Hell had closed upon them once they were prodded into the hot and stinking maze of Salé.

Yet also Salé was curiously like the towns of the Holy Land at the time Jesus of Nazareth was born. Within three minutes, Molnar and Kirk passed the gateway of a caravanserai, still full of horses, mules, donkeys, and camels, architecturally descended from the inn where the infant Jesus lay in a manger. Next they brushed past a young woman on a donkey, a baby in her arms, like Mary on the flight into Egypt; then they encountered a blind and scabrous beggar, a Lazarus. Just outside the sea wall — built handsomely and almost indestructibly of ashlar by the last Moriscos driven out of Spain — miserable hovels leaned against that fortified barrier, and between wall and ocean were great dunghills, very like that on which Job languished, to be comforted by his peculiar comforters, *sidi bu zibbula.* Atop one of those dunghills, when Molnar and Kirk passed through the sea gate and came out upon that barren shore, was seated a public reader; about the foot of the dunghill stood his audience of the poorest of the poor, and he was crying aloud to them from the Koran. On the neighboring dunghill, another reader had established himself, and to his audience he was crying aloud from *Das Kapital,* in translation. In this fashion did Jesus address his disciples.

In modern Salé, as in ancient Israel and Judah, grinding poverty is accepted as part of the nature of things. In a moment, the visitor is transported from the age of affluence to the age of pressing want — which, after all, has been the ordinary condition of most folk in all ages. Ever since freebooting and slavery were suppressed, old Salé has been a "depressed area" — although hardly an underdeveloped area, the population density exceeding that of Manhattan, and Salé's people very industriously turning out, in their little workshops open to the street, large quantities of rugs, brass trays, jewelry, and other Moroccan handicrafts, nearly all of which are sold retail in Moroccan towns more popular with the tourist: free enterprise and perfect competition.

Great poverty does not necessarily bring with it great misery. Accepted by most people as their ineluctable lot, poverty loses its terrors. The folk of Salé, in 1963, listened to the street musicians playing their primitive instruments, and occasionally would drop a small coin into the musicians' cup; they drank fragrant tea at the tiny cafes; they tended their dark little shops in the lanes. The rest was the will of Allah. Unlike Tunis, unlike Casablanca, Salé was crowded with mosques and the faithful.

No inconsiderable part of the population was engaged in beggary — a phenomenon increasingly observed in American cities. For the pious Moslem is commanded by the Prophet to bestow charitably a tenth of his income. One may see in Salé people bestowing alms who are themselves poorer than the poorest folk in America. Blinded by diseases of the eye, crippled by diseases of the foot, mutilated from birth by horrid afflictions, the Salé beggars in their rags nevertheless scrape up the means of survival. In the Moroccan climate, if they have not even a lean-to against the seawall, they can sleep in the open air.

Some day, conceivably, the fanatic on the dunghill, crying aloud the words of Karl Marx or of some other sanguinary ideologue, may succeed in waking internecine hatreds in Salé. But never can the ideologue put an end to Salé's poverty, without sweeping away the city: there are too many people, and nature's bounty is too scanty. "The poor we have always with us," Jesus of Nazareth prophesied. Both Christianity and Islam preach reduction of wants, and resignation. A very different gospel was preached by the advertising agencies of Kirk's native land.

The makers of policy in Washington, Kirk reflected, and the majority of members of the Congress of the United States, understood ill Tunisia's version of modernism and Morocco's version of traditionalism. They fancied that Islam no longer mattered; that the modernist Shah was secure on his peacock throne; that the hideous murder of the king of Iraq and his prime minister would usher in Mesopotamian democracy. Such misapprehensions, Kirk thought, would have grave consequences for America before many years elapsed.

But nothing could be done about that, at least by Kirk, in 1963. It was time for Kirk to return home, that something might be done about love and politics.

Goldwater vs. Rockefeller

Back at Mecosta before the middle of November, Kirk took up the Goldwater cause in his syndicated column. His three columns of Monday, Tuesday, and Wednesday, November 18, 19, 20, amounted to a prolonged commentary on Senator Goldwater's ascendancy. Wrote Kirk,

> Some admirers of Senator Goldwater tell me, gloomily, "Mr. Goldwater can't be nominated — he's too honest, so the Big Boys will stop him before the Convention." On the other hand, some detractors of the Arizona senator inform me, "Goldwater's too extreme for the Republicans to think of following him."
>
> Writing a few days ago in the *New York Times Magazine*, Mr. Tom Wicker endeavored to play a variation on this theme. He argued that the odds against Mr. Goldwater, for either nomination or election, are very great, because — well, because history is against him, mostly. Besides, Senator Goldwater leads only a faction

of the Republican party, said Mr. Wicker; therefore his feat of attaining the nomination would be astounding, equalled heretofore only by William Jennings Bryan.

The trouble with these analysts, I think, is that they look upon Mr. Goldwater as somehow the leader of a little splinter group, like the men who went out to David in the Cave of Adullam. Only very gradually is it dawning upon both the pro-Goldwater enthusiasts and the anti-Goldwater zealots that the Goldwater "faction" substantially is the Republican party.

In his concluding Goldwater column, Kirk ridiculed the suggestion that some "dark horse" candidate — Henry Cabot Lodge, Robert S. McNamara, Margaret Chase Smith, George Romney, or Richard Nixon — might sweep triumphantly through the Republican primaries and capture the National Convention.

Despite the events of the twelve months that followed these predictions, Kirk demonstrated that he was a far better prophet than Tom Wicker. On November 20, 1963, it appeared certain that Goldwater would win the Republican nomination, and probable that he would defeat President Kennedy on election day, 1964.

Yet then, on November 22, 1963, just two days after Kirk's column entitled "Nomination Follies" was published, John F. Kennedy was assassinated in Dallas. The popularity of President Kennedy's "New Frontier" policies had been decreasing steadily. But now no Republican could campaign against the New Frontier; that would have been like campaigning against the good works of a martyr.

On the afternoon of the murder of President Kennedy, Kirk was lecturing to a good-sized and civil audience at Macalester College, in St. Paul. Word of the shooting leaked into the auditorium during the middle of Kirk's talk. It was a mark of the good manners prevalent at Macalester College that perhaps half of Kirk's audience remained in their seats until he had finished his formal remarks.

All was changed in American practical politics by that assassination. The fickle sympathy of the public promptly shifted to Kennedy's successor, Lyndon Johnson; in the months after the murder, there occurred silly mass-media muttering about the murder having been planned by "right-wing extremists," when actually the killer, Lee Harvey Oswald, was a radical fanatic who may have been an accomplice of Fidel Castro.* This backlash against conservatives would not be the decisive issue in the presidential election nearly a year later; nevertheless, it heavily impeded the Goldwater movement.

Barry Goldwater knew how dreadful a blow had been struck against his prospects. Fifteen years later, he would write, "At the beginning of December 1963 it was my considered opinion that no Republican could prevail against Lyndon Johnson. President as a result of a great national tragedy, he could not be held accountable for the errors of his predecessor. Fate had muted all the issues I might have used in a confrontation with Jack Kennedy."

All the same, Goldwater was persuaded by his more eminent supporters, Senator Norris Cotton in particular, to make a stand for conservative principles. "My critics have remarked, and in retrospect I must agree with them, that my inner circle of advisers had very little experience in the politics of campaigning. Baroody, an intellectual, had devoted his career to dealing in abstracts, pursuing 'ideal public policies.' Jay Hall had a greater understanding of the practical ways to reach the voters than the others, but he had never been in charge of a campaign."

Baroody made sure that Jay Gordon Hall ("Gordon" to his family and such intimates as Kirk) would not be in charge of this desperate campaign. Kirk would be active as a Goldwater speaker during both the primary contests with Rockefeller and the presidential contest with Johnson. He would address public meetings and campus audiences in Michigan, Georgia, California, Indiana, and Illinois. But his invitations would come from local Republican organizations and Goldwater backers in this or that state, not from the Goldwater campaign organization dominated by Baroody. Nor was Kirk ever consulted on policy, or asked to help in any other fashion, by the national campaign people. Their treatment of William Buckley was similar.

---

*Chief Justice Earl Warren, chairman of the commission appointed to investigate the assassination, presently stated that the whole truth about the murder might not be made known for a century. Kirk took up this peculiar declaration in one of his newspaper columns. In a letter to Kirk dated May 5, 1964, Congressman Gerald Ford, a member of that commission of investigation, wrote, "Personally I regret as much as anyone the statement that some of the story 'may not be made public for decades.' I believe and trust that our report will give 'the whole story.'" That did not come to pass.

Kirk's syndicated column, notwithstanding, was useful to the Goldwater campaign, as was Buckley's column, carried in more newspapers than Kirk's. Kirk's "To the Point" appeared several times a week in the *Los Angeles Times,* the biggest paper west of the Mississippi, in the most populous of states, so the Goldwater enthusiasts of California were eager to have him speak there. Even so, the public-relations firm handling the Goldwater account in California did next to nothing to publicize or enlarge Kirk's speaking schedule, either before the California primary or before the election. Reeling from unfair assaults by Republican rivals and managed by the inexperienced, the Goldwater campaign seemed in peril of collapsing before the autumn.

First the Rockefeller people, the Scranton people, and other liberal Republicans heaped abuse quite shamelessly upon the senator from Arizona; later President Johnson's people cudgelled him still harder. Newspaper editors, most of them, swiftly joined the pack; and of really big newspapers, by November 1964, only the *Chicago Tribune* and the *Los Angeles Times* still supported Goldwater's candidacy — the *Times* lukewarmly. On television and radio, strident voices cried that to support the extremist Goldwater would be sin and shame. So various editors ceased to print Kirk's "To the Point," adherence to Goldwater being the Mark of the Beast.

This book not being a history of political parties, detailed description of the vicissitudes of the Goldwater presidential campaign is left to other political analysts. Senator Carl Curtis's *Forty Years against the Tide* (1986), with an introduction by Kirk, contains a straightforward account of the misrepresenting of Goldwater by both Republican and Democratic adversaries.

Later in 1964, Kirk would campaign for Goldwater in the primaries, and then in the weeks shortly before the election, chiefly in California. But meanwhile he was busy with his own campaign to win Annette.

Clamp Your Padlock on Her Mind

When Annette greeted him in Long Island on his return from foreign parts, he kissed her hand, after the Austrian fashion. She was mildly embarrassed: "What is this ritual?" Not long later, Kirk sent her a copy of Jessie Weston's book *From Ritual to Romance,* which augmented her suspicions about Russell's attentions and intentions — as if there could have been any reasonable doubt.

Daily Russell sent her letters or postcards, some typed on airplanes, others written from hotels or colleges, as he speechified from coast to coast. He sent her closet dramas, farces, written for her eyes only: "Annette in Hades"; "Who Is the Fairest of Us All?"; "Diary of a Maiden Voyage"; and others, in all of which the heroine was a certain maiden named Annette, and the hero a short, infatuated admirer of many guises. These plays, some written more or less in the style of Christopher Marlowe, were many typed pages long, and became Annette's dearest possession, trophies of her charm.

Whenever Kirk flew to New York, a member of the Courtemanche household would pick him up at Kennedy Airport, so close to Springfield Gardens. Annette's brother Regis teased her: "Russell's coming to see you tomorrow; you can collect him at the airport." She insisted that "He's coming to see all of us, not me." Indeed, Kirk did take out the whole family to dinners, in Long Island and New York, which increased his popularity with the parents; no other suitor of their elder daughter had done anything of that sort.

As for Kirk, he remained uncertain of just how he stood with the Conservative Beauty — and dared not press his addresses very far, lest he be rejected, and so everything lost. His literary successes and his political undertakings would be dust and ashes without Annette. He was now forty-four years of age — twice as many years as Pocahontas Courtemanche had lived. She had been born about the time he had been graduated from Michigan State; she had been dancing on her front porch to Elvis Presley records when he published *The Conservative Mind.* She esteemed him. Could she love him? The odds were that he had been foolish to pursue this lovely girl, so sought after by everybody. He recollected a passage in Gissing's novel *The Crown of Life:*

> For the men capable of passionate love (and they are few) to miss love is to miss everything. Life has but the mockery of consolation for that one gift denied. The heart may be dulled by time; it is not comforted. Illusion if it be, it is that which crowns all other illusions whereof life is made. The man must prove it, or he is born in vain.

Annette was taken out from time to time by several young men, among them three Germans, each named Wolfgang, whom she had encountered during her European wanderings in company with Peggy. What advantage had Kirk over them? Only that he appealed to her mind. Prior's lines in "A Lover's Padlock" were pertinent:

Let all her joys be unconfined,
And clamp your Padlock — on her mind.

Whether or not great beauties require minds to achieve their ends, Annette Courtemanche was endowed intellectually as well as physically. She was much commended as a teacher of English in high school. In humane letters her taste was sober: the only novels she was given to quoting were Dickens's *Great Expectations* and Kingsley's *Hypatia*. (One of her nicknames was Hypatia; also someone conferred on her the nickname Esmeralda, after the innocent gypsy beauty in Hugo's *Notre Dame*.) Of short stories, Hawthorne's "Feathertop" was her favorite. Her knowledge of history and of political theory was scanty. But in philosophy and theology she was schooled already far beyond what is expected of the graduates of liberal-arts colleges, and the lovely Thomist continued to read and to meditate in those disciplines. She having a vast curiosity, one of Russell's attractions for her was that he seemed a walking encyclopedia. She could chatter like a magpie; but when earnest in her discourse, she could become deeply moving.

"What do you see in me, a child of the modern age?" she asked Russell once. He saw in her a beautiful and desirable woman; and, more, a soul possessed of goodness and wisdom.

Now and again she frightened him by her hauteur. When it had begun to seem as if they two were joined in affection, abruptly Annette might bring Russell the suitor up short by a reprimand. Dining with her family one evening, Kirk made some reference in his talk that vexed Annette. "When I tell you not to do a thing, I want you not to do it!" she cried, as if reproving a child. Her parents were astonished, and Kirk dismayed, at her tone. Had he fallen from favor? He did not then understand how affianced girls, in a final teasing gesture of defiance, may cry, "Mind your manners, or you may not catch me even yet!" Annette's air of cold command — Kirk called her Ozymandia sometimes — really was the last crumbling barrier before giving herself to him.

[290]

With Chuck and Mickie Teetor as chaperones, Russell and Annette went up to a New Hampshire ski resort. The resort's proprietor had read Kirk's conservative works. "What's this with Courtemanche?" he inquired of the Teetors, he being surprised at the learned conservative's close association with the glowing girl young enough to be his daughter and striking enough to have followed her Aunt Lola into the Follies. In private, Mickie Teetor said to Kirk, "Russell, if you win Annette, you will be delightfully happy; if you lose her, you will still enjoy the even tenor of your ways."

Apparently not troubled by their disparity in years, Annette had begun introducing Russell to her Long Island friends of her own age. She had found Dr. Kirk usually amusing, sometimes wise, and respectful of her intelligence.

They saw each other only intermittently, Kirk usually being at his typewriter in Mecosta, or lecturing at some university, or wandering about on political business. His long, long letters continued to arrive daily; there were telephone calls, although Kirk detested the impersonality of telephone conversations; and they commenced to exchange tape recordings, telling one another of the day's experiences and reflections. Annette's voice was marvellously sweet on those tapes.

Reading those letters and listening to those tapes, Annette would cry, thinking "But I can never marry Russell!" And then, one night, she bethought herself, "Why can't I marry Russell?" True, he never had formally proposed; yet he had written to her that every male bird first marks out his territorial domain before sending out his call for a female bird to mate with him — an observation borrowed from Robert Ardrey's book *The Territorial Imperative* — and had implied clearly enough that his territory of Mecosta was ready for a spouse. Besides, what man wouldn't wish to marry her?

So Annette, on March 19, 1964 — thereafter known to them as the Letter Day — sent to Russell Amos Kirk a letter which declared to dear Russell, "I have decided that our marriage is inevitable."

"Like death and taxes?" Russell would reply, in his letter of gratitude written that same night. Before his letter could reach his darling, Annette telephoned him. "Did you get my letter, Russell? Did you like what it said?" Indeed he did.

Formally engaged on May 20, Annette's twenty-fourth birthday, they began making plans. He was to be baptized in the Catholic

Church before their wedding: only indolence, the press of business, and lack of guidance had impeded his arranging to be received earlier into the Church. No wedding day was set, for Annette had intended to undertake graduate studies. In a little conference of Annette, Russell, and the younger Regis at the Garden City Hotel,* it was agreed among the three of them that Annette should spend some months at the School for Scottish Studies, Edinburgh; that her brother should work for a doctorate at the London School of Economics; and that Russell meanwhile should stick to his scribbling. (Regis was to be Kirk's best man at the wedding, before flying to London.)

This compact did not endure. Once kissing commences, the best-laid schemes o' mice an' men gang aft a'gley. By August, at Mecosta, Annette and Russell would be of one mind: only after the wedding would Annette go abroad, and then of course with Russell. The sacrament of marriage was to join them at Our Lady of the Skies, Idlewild (Kennedy) Airport's Catholic Chapel — since demolished, not even one brick being obtained as a memento — on the nineteenth of September, 1964. That sacred building was chosen not because Kirk and Miss Courtemanche were jet-setters, but because it was a chapel-of-ease for Annette's Springfield Gardens parish.

"Don't give me a diamond for my wedding ring," Annette told her betrothed. "Just give me my birthstone." Here, as in various other matters, Annette was ingenuous; she had no notion that the emerald is costlier far than the diamond. Eager to please this gem of a fiancée, Kirk procured that emerald ring, long before the ceremony.

This merry, passionate, pious, loquacious, lucious, contemplative young beauty, this long stalk of loveliness, was giving herself to him that she might cheer his life and bear their children! Indeed, this would be the crown of life, and he all undeserving.

---

*They would not look upon the delightful old Garden City Hotel again: a few years later it was demolished and its park devastated. (Still later, a new hotel, somewhat garish, would rise on its site.) The Victorian Hotel, where Russell and Annette would first stay in St. Andrews, also would be swept away, a few years later.

A fatality seemed to attend their lodgings. The New Hampshire ski lodge of their courtship was consumed by fire some six years after their marriage; the Old House at Mecosta would vanish in smoke and flame in 1975.

To the California Primary

On May 25, five days after his engagement to Annette, Kirk resumed a series of syndicated columns about the contest within the Republican party. To everyone it was clear that Governor Rockefeller must win the primary in California on June 2 if he were to have the least chance to win the Republican party's presidential nomination at the Republican National Convention in San Francisco, in the middle of July. Rockefeller had allocated more than four million dollars of his campaign chest to the last days of the Californian fight; Goldwater, about half a million.

At last all the columnists and news magazines were saying what Kirk had been predicting for many months: that Senator Goldwater would stride into the national convention with many more delegates behind him than the total for all his rivals combined. And yet Goldwater had his troubles. At Madison Square Garden, in Manhattan, on May 12, twenty-two thousand people cheered him; but some of his supporters were disappointed by his speech. His performance on national television the following day had been dull and almost feeble. Many signs existed that the Goldwater staff required much improvement. His speeches of recent months had been noticeably inferior to his addresses a year earlier. The performance of the Washington "Goldwater for President" headquarters often was cumbersome, and sometimes seriously offended the sensibilities of the state and local volunteers who were the heavy infantrymen of the Goldwater phalanx.

At the invitation — the pressing invitation — of some of those state volunteers in California, Kirk flew to Los Angeles, where he established himself in the Beverly Wilshire Hotel and spoke in Goldwater's favor at various colleges and to Republican groups. He talked privately with Stephen Shadegg, Henry Salvatori, Patrick Frawley, and other Goldwater leaders. It appeared certain that the vote in the primary would be very close; indeed, all the polls showed Rockefeller ahead. Should Goldwater be beaten badly on June 2, just conceivably he might still have a hard battle to win at San Francisco, despite the large total of delegates pledged to him already from many states.

Mrs. Vernon Luck and other Goldwater people besought Kirk to employ what eloquence he had on Goldwater's behalf, at this late hour; Kirk said he would do his best. Money was found on short notice, quite apart from the Goldwater campaign chest, to pay for one-minute radio broadcasts, every hour or half-hour, on some ten Los Angeles radio stations. (Then and later, Kirk found political advertising on radio, as distinguished from television, surprisingly efficacious — and inexpensive; this was true especially in Los Angeles, where a considerable portion of the citizenry listened to radio as their cars struggled along the jammed freeways.)

Dr. William Teague, vice president of Pepperdine College, was enlisted in this project. In 1964, Kirk still was nominally research professor of political science at Post College and university professor of Long Island University, although that year he was not lecturing at all at Post. The radio interview went much as follows.

> DR. TEAGUE: Dr. Kirk, you are research professor of political science at C. W. Post College, in New York. Do people in New York believe that Governor Nelson Rockefeller would be an able president of the United States?

> DR. KIRK: No, sir. A great many people in the state of New York regard Mr. Rockefeller as an advocate of high taxation, think him feeble in the field of foreign policy, and fear that he stands for centralized power. Even in New York City, the giant Goldwater rally on May 12 demonstrated that Rockefeller lacks enthusiastic support in his own state.

Versions of this interview, with some alterations in the text, were "saturation broadcast" every hour or half-hour during the concluding three days of the primary contest. The ladies and gentlemen who paid the bills to the Los Angeles radio stations told Kirk, after the vote totals were announced on June 3, that Kirk's comminations of Rockefeller had supplied Goldwater with his slim margin of victory. Indeed, saturation political dialogues on radio stations are effective vote-getting; Kirk found that later in Michigan campaigning for which he paid from his own pocket.

On Thursday, May 28, Kirk's friends arranged a press conference for him at the Beverly Wilshire. Reporters and columnists for both the *Los Angeles Times* and the *Los Angeles Herald-Examiner* attended, and reporters from the big suburban papers; also newsmen and cameramen from three or four of the Los Angeles television stations and people from radio stations. Kirk addressed them on the theme of what Senator Goldwater really stood for, and why Kirk supported him. Then the media asked the expected urgent question: "Which man is going to win the primary?"

"Goldwater."

"How can you say that, Dr. Kirk, when every poll shows that Rockefeller will be the winner?"

"One has to know how to analyze polls, ladies and gentlemen. Also I have been talking here in California to a good many knowledgeable people."

"By how much will Goldwater win, then?"

"One per cent of the popular vote."

And so it came to pass, or very nearly so. For some years thereafter, Kirk would enjoy a good reputation among journalists for arcane knowledge of the drift of public opinion. When all the ballots had been counted and the results were announced on the morning of June 3 — hey presto! Barry Goldwater had been approved by a margin of some 58,000 votes, out of a total of approximately 2,100,000 ballots cast in the Republican primary. In his column of June 8, Kirk crowed on his own dunghill, the *Los Angeles Times*. Who would be so naïve thereafter as to repose faith in public-opinion polls? he inquired rhetorically.

Louis Harris's poll had predicted a result of fifty-five per cent for Rockefeller, forty-five for Goldwater. Mervin Field's poll had given Rockefeller forty-six per cent, Goldwater thirty-seven, with seventeen per cent undecided. Samuel Lubell's poll, though somewhat more canny, had indicated a victory by Rockefeller. George Gallup's poll, although earlier showing Rockefeller well ahead, evaded prediction in the closing days of the contest — by instead asking folk the burning question of whether they preferred, among eminent Democrats, Robert Kennedy to Adlai Stevenson.

"Were Messrs. Harris, Field, and Lubell led astray by their prejudices and preferences?" Kirk asked in his column. "It is disagreeable to eat crow, but these gentlemen cooked their own dinner."

Kirk did not attend the Republican National Convention at the Cow Palace, San Francisco, beginning July 13: the result was foregone. As Kirk had told his "To the Point" readers in 1963, Goldwater would enter the convention with more pledged delegates than would have all the other presidential candidates combined. He was nominated on the first ballot: 883 delegates voting for Goldwater, 214 for Scranton, 211 for other candidates.

In Holy Matrimony

Matters went ill with the central direction of the Goldwater campaign from the victory at the Cow Palace onward, but Kirk had no hand in that general management. Speeches prepared for Goldwater's delivery by Karl Hess and Harry Jaffa did the candidate sad mischief. Greater harm was worked by Rockefeller, Keating, and Romney, who deserted the national presidential campaign; and the fatal blow was struck by the mass media, who gleefully publicized the charge that Goldwater was "trigger-happy."

Kirk was not invited back to the fray until the hurly-burly was nigh done. Thus he had two months before marriage to spend in harmony with the happy Annette, whose hauteur had changed — for the time being — to a sweet deference. Much of that interval they were at Mecosta, where Annette even condescended to walk the woods trails with her betrothed (although he never would succeed in converting her into an outdoorswoman) and to cruise with him about Lake Mecosta in a new and especially built rowboat he had named "Annette" — this despite her dread of bodies of water.

In September, their wedding was pleasantly simple, Annette's high loveliness and air of exaltation being grander than any cere-monial ostentation. Three priest-friends said mass and administered the sacrament of matrimony. Russell Kirk was half dazed at his good fortune. He recalls in the congregation of friends the mustachioed countenance of old Hoffman Nickerson, the author of *The Armed Horde,* with his wife, Bea, traveller and writer, who once fought off a scoundrel atop the walls of Salé — both gathered to eternity now. "Do you take this woman . . . until death do you part?" Aye, and beyond those jaws of death.

A reception, with a huge cake and a single bottle of champagne, was held at the Courtemanches' little house. Bill Buckley was con-versing in the Courtemanche kitchen; Thomas Molnar, too, was there; and Scomo's son, Michael Scott-Moncrieff. And now Annette, who had ardently kissed everybody as they filed out of the chapel, took her husband by the elbow: it was high time to fly to Michigan.

Tony May, M.A., Sancti Andreae, with whom, a few years before, Kirk had explored Caithness and Orkney, would drive them to the airport. He had brought over from Britain a Rolls Royce Phantom Second hearse, hoping to sell it to some American collector of automobiles. In this vehicle of antique grandeur, with a large Goldwater sign astern, they very nearly tipped over when ascending an airport ramp, the left-side wheels of the hearse spinning in air; but Tony did get them to the baggage counter undamaged, and wished them lifelong happiness. Things went otherwise with kind Tony, an Elgin laird's son; next year they would visit him as he lay dying of some tropical affliction by the Thames in a long, long ward of a hospital seemingly built for the Crimean War. For a few years Tony had served the British West Africa Company, with consequences to his health:

> Beware, beware the Bight of Benin.
> Few come out, though many go in.

Tony was the first of Russell's and Annette's wedding guests to cross the bar and put out to the sea of eternity.

Joined here and hereafter, off to Michigan bride and groom flew. First they lodged at Russell's cabin on Lake Mecosta; they would stay there until snow should fall heavily, and then shift to the Old House in the village. Morton Township farmers and farmers' wives came to shivaree the newlyweds; one celebrant flung a stick of dynamite into the ravine across the trail, to startle Annette; when the fuse failed, he clambered down the gully and lit the fuse again, this time successfully. Long Island had no such goings-on.

From Lake Mecosta, presently they went to Beaver Island, in upper Lake Michigan; the tourist season being past, they were nearly alone in the inn. Russell had fancied that Annette might feel at home, for that forested island was populated with Irish, French, and Indians; but distinctly she did not feel at all at home; no great wild forest passion burned in her bosom.

Russell could not complain of this, for if Annette did not embrace the wilderness, with passionate affection she embraced him. "Beauty passes," Kirk meditated privately during the early days of this marriage. He thought of how, with the elapse of time, Annette's perfect face might grow wrinkled, and her supple figure fat. Why cannot beauties remain forever young?

Yet three decades later, marvellous to relate, Annette would be slimmer than before and altogether unwrinkled: beautiful when she attained her half-century, and still admired by everybody, heads turning when she made her way along the corridor of an airplane. At the age of three she had been a Conover model, but under the photographers' cruel lights she had squalled too loudly to continue long in that infant profession. Now she commenced a fresh career as beautiful wife — and, God willing, beautiful mother.

Campaigning for a Lost Cause

While Russell and Annette had dallied by the shores of Lake Mecosta during the summer, the Goldwater campaign had faltered badly. What had done Senator Goldwater the most damage was the controversy about tactical nuclear weapons.

Quite early in his campaign, Goldwater had declared that under certain circumstances, North Atlantic Treaty Organization field commanders should be permitted to use "tactical" atomic weapons against an enemy, if suddenly attacked. President Johnson and other Democrats wrought mischief to Goldwater's candidacy by misrepresenting this observation so as to make it appear that the senator from Arizona was "trigger-happy."

Tactical weapons are those used in more or less conventional battle, against military personnel, and are relatively short-range instruments: atomic cannon and low-yield atomic bombs for employment in the field of battle are such "tactical" devices. By contrast, "strategic" nuclear weapons are big missiles with atomic warheads, designed to destroy enemy bases and cities.

Senator Goldwater, a major general in the Air Force Reserve, had no intention of authorizing field commanders to use *strategic* nuclear weapons. But he said that if, during war, the president should be incapacitated, or if communications should be interrupted, then American generals in the field should have authorization to employ *tactical* armament in defense.

If Goldwater was "trigger-happy" in this grave matter, then so had been Presidents Eisenhower and Kennedy, for both those presidents, apprehending the "tactical weapons" problem, had given field commanders to understand that they might use their limited nuclear weapons if, during war, they could get no instructions from the White House.

During 1964, the governments of western Europe, very uneasy with President Johnson's policy of centralizing total control of atomic missiles in Washington, talked of dissolving the North Atlantic Treaty Organization; President de Gaulle had begun to create France's own independent atomic armament. The Goldwater policy of authorizing field commanders to use tactical nuclear weapons in emergencies and of permitting the European states to defend themselves if attacked was in fact calculated to reduce "atomic" tensions and the proliferation of nuclear weapons. The Johnson scheme of a single nuclear push-button, dependent on a single executive's presence and judgment, seemed by far the more risky concept.

But Goldwater's adversaries, Democratic or Republican, perceiving in the "trigger-happy" charge a very promising means of reducing Goldwater's popularity, continued to build up a massive propaganda against him as a reckless advocate of nuclear bombing. On the eve of the Republican National Convention, Goldwater had been asked during discussion on the "Meet the Press" television program what he would do to end the war in Vietnam. He replied that there was talk in Washington about possibly employing low-yield atomic bombs to defoliate the Ho Chi Minh Trail, so that troops from North Vietnam would be exposed to air observation and harassment as they moved south — but he added, "I don't think we'll do that."

Despite this Goldwater demurrer, the mass media immediately announced that Goldwater would use nuclear weapons in Vietnam. In the major newspapers appeared such banner headings as "Goldwater Says Use Atomic Bomb" and "Defoliate Vietnam, Goldwater Demands." The American democracy, always very reluctant to engage in foreign wars, was being induced to ask itself this question: which candidate would involve the United States in war — Johnson or Goldwater? A good many Americans seemed unaware, there having been no formal declaration of war against North Vietnam, that the United States had already been very deeply involved by Presidents Kennedy and Johnson in the ruinous conflicts of Indo-China.

Who would pull the trigger? That stupid inquiry became the central issue in the presidential contest of 1964, when so many more realistic questions required discussion. In October, the Greater Chicago Adult Education Council arranged a debate between Kirk (representing the Republicans) and Hans Morgenthau, the theorist on foreign policy (representing the Democrats). Professor Morgenthau, though thinking Barry Goldwater quite unfitted for the presidency, conceded that the gentleman from Arizona was "most engaging, warm-hearted, an honest and decent human being." On the other hand, though Dr. Morgenthau preferred Johnson's policies, he confessed that in character Johnson was "less engaging than Goldwater, complex, difficult, highly intelligent, very vain," oppressed by a conviction that he had an historic mission, and marred by "an enormous ego."

Kirk asked, of these two men, which seemed better qualified by personality to keep a prudent watch on that atomic trigger? People with White House "inside dope" were saying that not long before, in a fit of anger, Mr. Johnson had flung a telephone straight through a window. Certainly that President often was short-tempered. At the beginning of the Tonkin Gulf encounter, unauthorized by Congress, he had ordered air raids (allegedly retaliatory) all along the coast of North Vietnam. Was Johnson's then the most restrained finger to rest upon a trigger?

Louis Cheskin, of Cheskin Associates, scientific pollsters, was present on the platform at the Morgenthau-Kirk debate. In a private conversation, Cheskin told Kirk of a brand-new poll concerning the Johnson-Goldwater contest that his firm had taken. It was the Cheskin policy to conduct their polls only in selected representative areas or among selected groups, rather than endeavoring to poll nationally and superficially, and not to ask directly "for whom will you vote?" but instead to ascertain voters' underlying prejudices of a political sort — and so to deduce from underlying opinions how those questioned actually would cast their ballots on election day.

Cheskin had just then conducted such select polls-in-depth in the key swing states of California and Indiana. In this subtle Johnson-Goldwater poll, Cheskin had presented to his select representative sample of voters a questionnaire with some one hundred items, each of which had three possible responses. No question asked directly what candidate for the presidency the respondent would support at the voting booth. On several important questions, the respondents clearly preferred Goldwater's principles to Johnson's — centralization of power, for one. But on the really decisive question, Johnson scored far better than did Goldwater. It was this: "Suppose that Lyndon Johnson and Barry Goldwater were out hunting deer. Do you think that either of these candidates would fire at the first movement in the brush?" A substantial number of Cheskin's respondents thought that Johnson would fire recklessly. Approximately twice as many respondents, however, believed that Goldwater would fire at the first movement in the brush.

On this opinion or prejudice, Cheskin told Kirk, would the presidential contest be decided a few weeks later. The popular prejudice against Goldwater on the trigger-happy issue was so powerful as to outweigh prejudices in his favor on some other issues. Cheskin predicted the margin by which Goldwater would lose; as matters turned out, Goldwater on November 7 would do a little better, although not much, than Cheskin had estimated. Once elected, Lyndon Johnson would become far more trigger-happy in Vietnam than ever Goldwater would have thought of being.

In the last fortnight of the presidential struggle, Russell and Annette — for she, too, was a political activist — were asked to help the Goldwater candidacy in California. With their base in Los Angeles, up and down the coast they scurried, sometimes in company with Hollywood actors and actresses of the Goldwater persuasion. (Annette, in orange dress and grand-brimmed orange hat, would be asked in airports and department stores, "Are you a famous star?") Kirk flew in little planes to towns in the high desert and the mountains, speaking on every conceivable political issue. Also he was the principal Goldwater representative at the political meetings of southern Californian universities and colleges, at that late hour.

Only once, during the whole course of the Goldwater primary and presidential campaigns, did Kirk come face to face with the Senator, and that was during the final fortnight. Goldwater was passing into the Beverly Wilshire Hotel, Kirk passing out the same doorway; and Henry Salvatori, Goldwater's chief booster and backer in California, was holding open the door for the two of them.* Kirk was on his way to speak on Goldwater's behalf at Claremont Men's College; Goldwater on his way to Chavez Ravine, where a very big rally of Mexican-Americans had been organized by another friend of Kirk, old Walter Knott of Knott's Berry Farm and Ghost Town.

---

*Only a few of the men of large means whom Kirk happened to meet between 1950 and the present writing were given to reading serious books and to taking long views in politics or any other works of the mind. Of those few, Salvatori was probably the most intelligent, and certainly made the most prudent use of his money in support of scholarship.

What occurred at Chavez Ravine that evening sufficiently illustrated the insufficiencies of the Goldwater staff. The Spanish-
speaking crowd there ordinarily had voted the Democratic ticket,
when they had voted at all. But on two issues they were seriously
discontented with policies of the Johnson administration; they might
be persuaded to vote against Johnson. The first of these issues was
the massive baneful program of so-called urban renewal, "war against
the poor," aimed chiefly at black and Hispanic urban districts, which
was destroying their *barrios* in southern California. The second of
these issues was the bracero program, under the terms of which
Mexican laborers had been permitted to reside temporarily in the
United States for seasonal work, especially harvesting; this program
was popular with Mexican-American citizens because it provided
lucrative employment for Tio Paulo or some other kith and kin from
south of the border, but the Johnson administration had terminated
that bracero program.

All that Senator Goldwater needed to do at Chavez Ravine, then,
was to express his wholehearted opposition to the excesses of urban
"renewal" and to tell the crowd of his approbation of the bracero
program. His stand on these concerns was clearly expressed in his
record in the Senate. He might have prefaced such remarks by a few
words of homely horse-trader Spanish.

But what Senator Goldwater actually did was to read a speech
supplied to him by his staff, in which he advocated kindly toleration
of minorities. In their *barrios,* then at any rate, Mexican-Americans
clearly constituted the majority, not a minority, and to them the word
"minority" tended to carry the connotation "black." Mr. Goldwater
said nothing about the bracero program or about urban renewal. No
shifting of Mexican-American sentiment to Barry Goldwater occurred
in southern California at the last hour.

On election night, Russell and Annette and a good many other
people had crowded into the Goldwater Victory Celebration at
Anaheim, in Orange County, a region where Goldwater was held in
higher respect than anywhere else in the country, with the possible
exception of certain districts in Arizona. The results appeared on
television soon enough: Senator Goldwater carried six states and 38.5
per cent of the popular vote, being undone by the accusation of
trigger-happiness. This seemed a catastrophic defeat, but in comparison with the defeats of Democratic presidential candidates McGovern,

Mondale, and Dukakis in years to come, Goldwater did fairly well against great odds. Ronald Reagan, whose lively speeches on behalf of Goldwater had been perhaps the most effective strokes of the campaign, would inherit Goldwater's national following, his principles, and his charisma — but only after the elapse of sixteen years.

Meanwhile, Lyndon Johnson was an American Caesar: abroad and at home, disaster would follow close upon his decisions. His opportunity it was to order a great many triggers to be pulled almost daily in Vietnam.

CHAPTER TWELVE

Imagination and
Practical Politicians

Infusing Political Imagination

Paul Roche, translator of the old Greeks and a considerable poet in his own right, once told Kirk that he had thought of a means for reforming the political administration of Britain. He would require that there be appointed to advise each cabinet minister some competent poet. The minister would be expected to listen to his poet, whether or not, upon serious reflection, the minister finally should accept the poet's counsels. And thereby the minister's folly would be diminished somewhat.

For what poet, Roche inquired rhetorically, would have been deluded for an instant by grandiose designs for paving Britain with tarmac, building American-style superhighways running practically everywhere, doing mighty mischief to the ecology, destroying much of Britain's best agricultural land, smashing through historic towns and lovely rural regions, undoing British Railways? Yet just such a policy had been followed in the United Kingdom by both Labour and Tory governments — until at length Experience, that hard master of fools, had shown everyone the costly silliness of the undertakings of the Ministry of Transport. A competent poet might have dissuaded a minister of transport from such Lagado projects; for the poet possesses imagination, which includes a certain power of foreseeing the consequences of actions. Paul Roche went on to suggest to Kirk other instances of the potential utility of poets.

This suggestion seemed to Kirk equally applicable to the American Republic. Ever since Kirk's birth, the Republic had confronted grave difficulties, in domestic concerns and in foreign. The Republic had muddled through — yet not because of any high degree of imagination among its chief executives, nor among the leaders of the Congress.

The word "poetic" is employed here in its larger sense: to borrow from the old *Century Dictionary,* "poetry" signifies the art of exciting "intellectual pleasure by means of vivid, imaginative, passionate, and inspiring language." And by "poetic imagination" is meant those powerful insights of the armed vision that transcend Benthamite calculations of utility.

This present chapter of memoirs, departing from chronological continuity, touches upon the imagination possessed by Herbert Hoover, Norman Thomas, Eugene McCarthy, Lyndon Johnson, and Richard Nixon, with all of whom Kirk enjoyed some acquaintance, having encountered them during his occasional forays into politics as the art of the possible. Some of those encounters may be found comical; one may as well laugh as cry.

When one writes of American presidents and of gentlemen who yearned to be chief executives of the United States, there comes to mind the harsh judgment of James Bryce upon most American presidents since "the heroes of the Revolution died out with Jefferson and Adams and Madison": down to the end of the nineteenth century, "The only thing remarkable about them is that being so commonplace they should have climbed so high."

American politics fared somewhat better, perhaps, after Bryce wrote those lines: Theodore Roosevelt, Woodrow Wilson, Herbert Hoover, and some other party leaders were gentlemen of considerable intellectual attainments. Yet intellect is not identical with imagination. Very rarely did truly imaginative candidates win office in twentieth-century America.

Roman men of rhetoric and philosophy, of the stamp of Cicero or Seneca, found it their duty, without question, to enter ardently into the politics of the commonwealth. By and large, it has been otherwise in twentieth-century democracies, with the exception of France chiefly; and one may doubt whether the part of French men of letters in such public concerns often has been salutary. Although Kirk knew a good many politicians at various levels, he never felt impelled to stand for election (except for being twice elected justice of the peace of Morton Township) or to seek appointment to office (except for serving on Michigan's Bicentennial Commission). Know thyself! Kirk possessed neither talent for what H. L. Mencken called boob-bumping nor administrative abilities. He was offered one post under the Nixon administration and several under the Reagan administration; he shook his head, though the invitations were kindly intended. Knowing himself more poet than professor, he kept in mind Nietzsche's barb that in politics the professor always plays the comic role. Then, too, his lack of means and his reluctance to compromise would have been obstacles.

In this era, the man of letters or the scholar of a philosophical habit of mind may accomplish something to refurbish political imagination, to infuse into it some element of poetry — but by publishing books and delivering lectures, rather than by appearing at the hustings or converting himself into a public administrator. What men of literary talents may contribute was suggested by T. S. Eliot in his *Notes towards the Definition of Culture* and his address to the Conservative Union in 1955. As Eliot put it, "The question of questions, which no political philosophy can escape, and by the right answer to which all political thinking must in the end be judged, is simply this: What is Man? What are his limitations? What is his misery and what his greatness? and what, finally, his destiny?" William Butler Yeats, who from time to time expressed political wisdom in his writings, became absurd when he adventured into political action; Robert Frost, who made no such practical essay, exercised a subtle influence for political sound sense that will endure.

In his smaller way, Kirk believed that his political function it was to work upon the body politic by endeavoring to rouse the political and the moral imagination among the shapers of public opinion — that large category including political leaders; opinion makers of serious journals, the mass media, the academy, and the church; and that unknowable crowd of individuals who, as Dicey points out, influence their neighbors by the strength of their convictions. By talent, he was a writer, a speaker, an editor. In the long run, conceivably he might demolish some molehills, if not move mountains. The only weapon with which he was skilled was the sword of imagination. His prose had been called "evocative" — rousing old memories and old hopes, visions that pass between the gates of horn.

What Kirk might do to some effect was to point the way toward a more imaginative politics.

He wrote and spoke, Isaiah-like, to a Remnant; yet Remnants may swell to majorities. Editors, broadcasters, professors, clergymen, lawyers, and physicians paid more attention to him than did holders of public office; nevertheless, some public men were influenced. Certain senators and members of the House, in Washington, read and commented upon *The Roots of American Order* or *The Conservative Mind;* Richard Nixon twice read *A Program for Conservatives;* Ronald Reagan followed Kirk's "From the Academy" page and his syndicated column; Supreme Court justices commended this or that book of his; he spoke fairly often in Washington to audiences of civil administrators. At the end of three decades, his views began to take on a certain venerability in official quarters — even among ladies and gentlemen who never had opened one of Kirk's books. One day, being escorted through the White House by Kenneth Cribb, chief advisor to President Reagan on domestic policies, they encountered David Gergen, who danced attendance upon a series of presidents — a White House Vicar of Bray. Mr. Gergen expressed his sorrow that President Reagan was not present that day to see Dr. Kirk; how delighted the President would have been! When Gergen had passed by, the waggish Cribb said, grinning, "He's not one of us" — conservatives, he meant — "but he bows to the Icon."

This was mildly heartening, as well as amusing, to Kirk the Icon of the Reagan administration. But the infusing process was painfully slow. "Winning is the name of the game" for most public men — a slogan popularized by publicists for George Romney, who rose superior to it. Kirk frequently marvelled that the Republic somehow continued to blunder on prosperously enough, despite the deficiency of imagination — and of right reason — among these votaries of ephemeral success by candidate and party. For the real aims of the game of politics are order and justice and freedom, not the winning of polls and primaries.

The shallowness of practical politicians, as a species, struck Kirk forcefully when he watched the television debate, in 1976, between Gerald Ford and Jimmy Carter. They stood like dolts under the scrutiny of television cameras, neither of them prepared to debate without intensive coaching, and both unable to think of anything to say while waiting for technicians' blunders to be mended. What a contrast with Lincoln and Douglas!

It was said that Ford and Carter were "political animals." Doubtless so. What chiefly distinguishes the human kingdom from the animal kingdom is the power of imagination possessed by the human race. Carter and Ford were innocent of poetic fancies. Mr. Ford was proficient as a committee strategist in the House, and later master of the veto while President; Mr. Carter's skill as a Georgia courthouse politician elevated him to the headship of his party. But they were political animals merely.

When a poet named Solzhenitsyn offered to call on President Ford, he was repelled at the outer defenses of the White House, rather as the historian Carleton Hayes had been repelled by the White House staff in the first Eisenhower administration. Of Solzhenitsyn, Ford said privately that the exile must be seeking an interview merely to obtain publicity and so sell more of his books. Through tribulations, Solzhenitsyn had developed that sort of political imagination urgently required in America near the end of the twentieth century — and that sort of moral imagination, too. Ford was not interested. Dante was fortunate not to have encountered in Can Grande della Scala a forerunner of Gerald Ford.

The Stolid Integrity of Herbert Hoover

In the second chapter of these memoirs it is mentioned that in junior high school the precocious politician Russell Kirk had flung into a wastebasket a large bulletin-board photograph of President Herbert Hoover. Three decades later, Kirk had come to think otherwise of that gentleman.

W. C. Mullendore, president of Southern California Edison when first he and Kirk met, had been very closely associated with Hoover for many years; he called him The Chief. Mullendore visited Kirk at Mecosta several times, and spent days with him elsewhere; Kirk several times stayed with Mr. and Mrs. Mullendore in their big and handsome, but crumbling, mansion off Wilshire Boulevard, Los Angeles. They exchanged letters from time to time. Mullendore was a kindly man, quite well read, concerned for the common good.

The time came when, in 1960, Mr. Hoover was looking about

for a new director for his Hoover Institution of War, Peace, and Revolution, at Stanford; he asked Bill Mullendore to ask Russell Kirk for the names of possible candidates for the post.

Kirk offered suggestions, but the idea entered Mr. Hoover's head that Kirk himself might be the best director. Kirk told Mullendore that though he might be qualified in point of knowledge, he possessed no administrative talents that he knew of — his only experience of that sort having been as an army sergeant. Nevertheless, Mr. Hoover asked Kirk to call upon him at the Waldorf Towers, in the middle of Manhattan, and gave him breakfast. Kirk noted that the Waldorf hot breakfast was cold by the time it reached the Hoover table; kings in former ages notoriously had suffered from that very deprivation, it taking so long for hot dishes to reach the king's chamber.

Mr. Hoover looked his years. Having injured his spine while on a South American mission for President Truman, he was in some pain constantly; also his eyes gave him trouble, and his hearing was imperfect. But intellectually he remained very alert, and he was hard at work on a volume of his memoirs.

Kirk did not mention the Hoover Institution post during their conversation; and perceiving his guest's disinclination, the experienced diplomat Hoover did not touch upon the possibility. (Eventually Glenn Campbell was appointed.) But Kirk's talk with the old gentleman was memorable.

Kirk inquired of him — this conversation preceding the Republican National Convention of 1960 — whether he thought Senator Barry Goldwater would make a good President. Hoover replied with a prompt and unequivocal "Yes." Dissatisfied with Republican conventions and many Republican programs ever since 1932, Hoover saw in Goldwater a man of principle, unafraid to make hard decisions. "They never have taken my advice before," Hoover said apropos the Republican Conventions, "and so I sha'n't attend this time." Declining health kept him from the 1964 convention, too.

Hoover was one of the more learned of American presidents and — with the two Adams presidents — one of the hardest working. He published in *The Saturday Review* a very good essay, written in his later years, presenting evidence and argument that the mysterious Fourth Horseman of the Apocalypse must symbolize Revolution. Fighting hard all his life against war, hunger, and pestilence, Hoover perceived in the terrible revolutions of the twentieth century not a liberating force, but instead the debasing — perhaps the destruction — of civilization. He established that well-conceived Hoover Institution, devoted to the study of war, revolution, and peace, with its unique library of materials related to those themes — even copies of the most obscure ephemeral pamphlets — and its scholarly publications.

As for administrative abilities and long successful experience of public affairs, Herbert Hoover had been better qualified for the presidency than any other man of his time — nay, perhaps the best-qualified man in the whole history of the Republic. It was even being said, by 1960, that Hoover could have led America out of the Depression — the coming of which he had expected — had not his austere personality been overwhelmed by Franklin Roosevelt's charisma. Patient, tireless, and a model of dignity, Hoover had in him no touch of the demagogue.

While the close friend and adviser of President Woodrow Wilson, Hoover had foreseen the towering part that America was to take in the international affairs of the twentieth century. His management of international relief of famine and devastation foreshadowed the "foreign aid" undertakings of the late Forties, the Fifties, and later — although Mr. Hoover achieved far more satisfactory results from far smaller means.

He was a great mining engineer and an entrepreneur of genius; his talents were diverse. What other public man, and what public man's wife, would have been capable of the labor of translating Giorgius Agricola's *De Re Metallica*, which Mr. and Mrs. Hoover published in 1913?

Yet his was an engineer's mind, going for hard fact, with the usual limitations of such a cast of mind as well as with its practical merits. Until late years he had called himself a liberal, and rightly so: lack of the higher imagination was a deficiency of the better liberals in their nineteenth-century heyday and their twentieth-century decline. One may be highly intelligent, as Mr. Hoover eminently was, without being at all imaginative. In 1932, Mr. Hoover had seemed stodgy, while Governor Roosevelt had seemed imaginative — although Roosevelt read only detective stories. Mr. Roosevelt trounced the great administrator. *Sic transit gloria mundi.*

Shabbily treated by his successor in the White House, Hoover the oldfangled liberal never gave up his struggle for the improvement of American politics or for the restoration of peace, order, and tolerable conditions to the torn twentieth-century world. The reports of the Hoover Commission, instituted in part during the Fifties, did something to make American government more efficient and honest. Such labors were very much in the spirit of nineteenth-century liberal reforms in Britain and elsewhere.

Yet the complexity of world affairs and of America's domestic concerns, in the years that followed the First World War, required statesmen with imagination of the sort with which Disraeli had been endowed — or, to a somewhat lesser degree, Theodore Roosevelt's imagination. In particular, the historical imagination was needed. That sort of imagination was not Herbert Hoover's.

That imagination lacking, Hoover's humanitarianism led him into generous but baneful blunders in Europe, just after the First World War. Joseph Alsop and others have reproached him for his program of famine relief in Russia, which in practical effect secured the Bolsheviki in power when otherwise their regime might have collapsed. (Maxim Gorki had sent Hoover a letter of praise for that grand-scale act of humanitarianism.) Of course Hoover had not intended to shore up the dictatorship of the proletariat; with Wilson, he had seen from the start that the Russian Revolution was devastation. The sanguine but unimaginative liberal cast of mind, often dominant in both Wilson and Hoover, is curiously ineffectual in foreseeing long-run consequences of today's major decisions.

Another miscalculation of this sort is recorded in Hoover's exhaustive memoirs — although Hoover does not set it down as a miscalculation. The incident reveals at once the strength of Hoover's prejudices and the naïveté of his notion of the future of Europe.

In 1919, after the Communist dictator Bela Kun had fled from Hungary to Russia, Hungary was left without a government; a body of trades-union leaders meeting in the parliament house at Budapest claimed to be a legislative authority, and appointed ministers. At this juncture, in August, the Archduke Josef von Habsburg travelled by train from Vienna to Budapest; very promptly declaring himself the representative of the imperial and kingly house, he had obtained the obedience of the municipality, and, with ten policemen under his command, arrested the social-democratic ministers. His action was countenanced by the only body of troops then in the Hungarian capital, a battalion of Rumanians under orders from Queen Marie.

He proclaimed the restoration of Habsburg authority, the Kingdom of Hungary still existing *de jure.*

Hoover then was a power both in Woodrow Wilson's administration and in the Big Four (the Allies' Associated Governments, each with an administration at Paris, and representatives of the Big Four at Budapest.) Overriding men in the Wilson administration who wished to proceed cautiously with the Archduke's assumption of power, and opposing too the inclination of various British and French soldiers and administrators to support the Archduke Joseph, Hoover insisted that the Habsburg be compelled to resign and withdraw. Hoover informed President Wilson that he must act at once, or "the tyranny of the Habsburgs will be restored throughout Europe." Hoover argued that if the government of the Archduke were left in power for merely ten days, it might acquire legitimacy and support.

He told the Council of Five, at Paris, "I consider that the American Army fought in vain if the Habsburgs are permitted to retain power." In an interview with the United Press, he declared that he would resign, ceasing to labor in the American Peace Conference, unless the Habsburgs were expelled from Hungary. And, with permission of the Big Four, he sent to Budapest a telegram that compelled the Archduke Joseph to withdraw.

Now the Dual Monarchy of Austria and Hungary had been no tyranny, but a constitutional system, highly tolerant of minorities; the Emperors Franz Josef and Karl had been humane rulers devoted to duties. This final defeat, arranged by Hoover, of the Habsburg authority produced a successor regime in Hungary scarcely to Wilson's and Hoover's liking; and later this exclusion of the Habsburgs left Central Europe exposed to conquest first by the Nazis and then by the Soviet Union. The Wilson-Hoover policy did not result in that idealized "national self-determination" or "open covenants openly arrived at" or a Central Europe "safe for democracy." Ultimately, Hoover's undoing of the Habsburg power — Hoover's policy so liberal, so democratic, so naïve — destroyed any possibility of redressing the balance of power in Europe, and reduced to a hideous servitude Hungary and the other succession states. Wilson was an able writer of histories; Hoover, too, had some knowledge of recent history; yet they were not sufficiently imaginative to apply historical lessons to the crises of their time.

In the course of their Waldorf Towers conversation, Kirk raised this subject with Mr. Hoover, inquiring of him whether he had repented of his decision of 1919. But Mr. Hoover had become hard of hearing; when he chose, he could be *very* hard of hearing. So he became at this juncture, not replying to Kirk's question; a pause occurred; then they passed on to other subjects.

Certainly Hoover was no revolutionary and no economic leveller. But he was an ideologue of sorts — holding the ideology of Liberalism, "a great philosophy of society" (so described in his little book published in 1934, *The Challenge to Liberty*) and also an ideologue of democratism. Whatever political structure or theory did not conform to the American pattern of liberalism and democracy was suspect to Mr. Hoover; and the Dual Monarchy, presided over by the house of Habsburg, did not so conform; therefore it was crushed; and totalist powers presently occupied its ruins. In the long run, even the statecraft of good intentions goes to rack and ruin — supposing it founded upon ideological prejudices, including the prejudices of democratism. For ideological dogmata impede political imagination.

Had Hoover been able to rouse Americans' imagination in 1932, the course of American domestic policy and probably of foreign policy would have been quite different for the following decade. Mr. Hoover knew how to restore stability and was eager to maintain the peace. As Samuel Johnson put it, it is no more true that "he who leads free men must himself be free" than it is that "he who drives fat oxen must himself be fat." Nevertheless, the public man who needs to wake popular imagination must himself possess some visionary power, or he will fail. That power was required in 1932; more practical talents could not suffice in that year of unrest; and Mr. Hoover was found wanting. Yet no more honest or able man (for practical talents) ever occupied the White House. Saying good-bye to that old gentleman in 1960, Kirk respected Herbert Hoover more than he had abhorred him in 1932.*

*For Herbert Hoover on the regime of Bela Kun, the brief regime of the Archduke Joseph, and related matters, see Hoover, *The Memoirs of Herbert Hoover: Years of Adventure, 1874-1920* (1952), pp. 397-405; Hoover, *The Ordeal of Woodrow Wilson* (1958), pp. 134-41; Hoover, *An American Epic*, vol. 3 (1961), pp. 358-78; T. T. C. Gregory, "Overthrowing a Red Regime," *The World's Work*, June 1921, p. 164; *Papers Relating to the Foreign Relations of the United States: The Paris Peace Conference, 1919*, House Document no. 93, 78th Congress, 1st

Fellow-Travelling with Norman Thomas

Twice Kirk found himself on the platform with Norman Thomas, candidate for the presidency so often, beginning in 1928. Astoundingly tall and even more gaunt, Thomas was invincible in debate. By the time Kirk argued with him, the quick intelligence and sardonic wit of the formidable Socialist had been reinforced by age and responsibility: Thomas had become an institution, the old man eloquent.

Kirk first heard Thomas speak in the People's Church, East Lansing, when Kirk was a freshman, in 1937. Michigan State College's authorities had forbidden use of any campus lecture hall by that dangerous radical Thomas; therefore, unperturbed and not reproaching MSC's concept of academic freedom, Thomas addressed a very large crowd in the big church. This was natural enough: he had been a minister at one time, and had a talent for comminatory sermons. His socialism was Fabian, distinctly not proletarian. Young Kirk's impression of Thomas as a man was favorable, though he disagreed with some of the speaker's first principles.

Near the end of the Fifties, Kirk took part in a symposium at Bowdoin College; the other speakers were Senator Clifford Case and Mr. Norman Thomas, the three presumably representing conservatism, liberalism, and socialism. Case, having said nothing memorable, departed early after basking in the adulation of students who actually could converse with a live Senator.

Thomas was interesting, as always. He had much to say in praise of Eleanor Roosevelt, and, by implication, not a great deal to say in praise of her husband, although he did not object in the least to FDR's having stolen socialists' clothes while they were bathing. (Socialists of Thomas's breed were a well-scrubbed lot.) No one could doubt the honesty of this levelling gentleman.

Bowdoin then retained the old custom of compulsory chapel once a week for undergraduates. But Bowdoin's dogmata were as

---

Session, vol. 7, 1946, pp. 768-77; "Hoover Says Oust Archduke at Once," *New York Times,* August 22, 1919, p. 6; and "Hoover's Plan to Oust Joseph from Hungary," *New York Times,* August 24, 1919, p. 3. See also Murray N. Rothbard, "Hoover's 1919 Food Diplomacy in Retrospect," in Gelfand, *Herbert Hoover: the Great War and Its Aftermath, 1914-23* (Herbert Hoover Presidential Library Association, 1975), pp. 87-110.

attenuated as those of Kirk's Pierce ancestors. It was hoped that one of the three guest speakers would lecture at chapel. Case seemed not to have been invited to occupy the pulpit; Kirk, as yet unbaptized, was invited — to the relief of Thomas, who told Kirk that he had ceased long ago to believe in the transcendent. So Kirk addressed the undergraduates on ethical norms in literature. The students were very civil, and some seemed genuinely interested, if surprised: they informed Kirk that this was the first chapel talk in their experience at all related to religion or morals.

It was to Thomas's credit that he did not profess "Christian socialism"; there was no humbug about him. He knew that Jesus meant to save sinners, not to give commands to the dominations and powers of this earth; Thomas understood that religion is a means for ordering the soul, not for ordering politics and economics. In his morals, nevertheless, he was an example of Christian rectitude, and in private discourse charitable toward his adversaries. He had reviewed Kirk's *Conservative Mind* at some length, on its first publication, and though opposed to its postulates, Thomas had not misrepresented the book. Rather oddly, he had objected to Kirk's referring to the "emotional storm" of Wesleyism; not sneering at honest fervor, Kirk had not intended that phrase to be derogatory. But Thomas was a thoroughgoing rationalist, capable indeed of rousing strong emotions by his speeches, yet seeking to persuade chiefly by his reasonableness. George Orwell, so contemptuous of most fellow socialists, probably would have approved of Thomas.

This rational presidential candidate never labored under any illusion that he might be elected, or that any other socialist candidate might attain the presidency. His hope it was that by standing for the highest office he might help to tug the major parties — the Democrats, anyway — somewhat in his direction, and obtain a hearing for his humanitarianism. In that he enjoyed success; late in life, after he had ceased to run every four years, he pointed out a trifle smugly that many of his objectives had been attained by the New Deal — though Roosevelt was no socialist. He found no following among the labor unions; and, at the height of public discontent, in 1932, he had obtained fewer than nine hundred thousand votes, to Roosevelt's twenty-three million and Hoover's sixteen million. His mission was not to the American masses.

In 1961, a few years after the Bowdoin encounter, Thomas and

Kirk engaged in amiable controversy at Bucknell University. At an evening question session, they were seated on the platform along with Michael Harrington and the *chargé d'affaires* from the embassy of Ghana. (The Ghanian ambassador abruptly had been summoned back to Africa by the dictator Kwame Nkrumah, presumably to be chastised for something or other.) What followed was sufficiently illustrative of Thomas's candor.

The Ghanian diplomat, a short man in a robe, proceeded to deliver a brief address castigating the white race in general and Americans in particular. Very likely he had found this approach well received by liberal white audiences; he may have obtained standing ovations elsewhere. Passionately he shook his finger; he fulminated. Whites in America were wicked oppressors of the black man . . .

His address was brief because at this point Norman Thomas, who had been staring at the *chargé d'affaires* with increasing disfavor, rose up spectrally and interrupted him. "Stop right there," the old socialist commanded. "That's nonsense you're talking. What right have you to criticize the United States? There's a great deal going on in your country that I don't like: jails full of political prisoners . . . You attack us because we once had slaves in this country. That was a century ago. We'd have had no slaves here if your chiefs hadn't sold them overseas."

"That is not so," the alarmed Ghanian gasped. "We have sent our scholars to Oxford to prove it is not so."

"Then your scholars will be perpetuating lies," Thomas told him. "Besides, why do you denounce America, and not the Arab states? There are no slaves in America today, but there are slaves in Arabia, black slaves."

The Ghanian was staggered. "Well, there are not as many blacks in Arabia as here, so the Arabs cannot be so bad."

"That's because they were so badly treated by the Arabs," Thomas retorted. "They died. Generally blacks have been treated well here, so they have multiplied."

Overwhelmed, the Ghanian sank back into his chair; the audience gave Thomas the enthusiastic applause that the *chargé d'af- faires* had coveted for himself. Nobody but Norman Thomas could have carried off this refutation so magnificently.

Never a fellow traveller with the Communists, Thomas had no kind words for the squalid oligarchs of Asia and Africa. He was keenly aware of the menace of the Soviet Union and the threat of Communist infiltration into certain American circles. No man was a more consistent champion of civil liberties everywhere — in this, he was a great way removed from the editors of the British *New Statesman and Nation* and the editors of the *Manchester Guardian* in Malcolm Muggeridge's years with that paper. When Kirk wished to learn whether this or that intellectual or publicist actually was a Communist, he would ask Thomas, who invariably was accurate and candid in such identifications.

The morning after this Bucknell exchange, students transported Thomas and Kirk to a little airport and abandoned them there. (On the way, a girl inquired innocently of the two of them as to who Whittaker Chambers had been; Thomas agreed with Kirk that Hiss had been a Soviet agent.) Rain coming down heavily, their flight to New York was cancelled. A stranded television salesman, knowing nothing of either lecturer, had rented a car; he offered to transport them so far as Newark. Off they went wetly across Pennsylvania and New Jersey, chatting politely — rather like the intellectual anarchist Peter Ivanovich and the conservative Councillor Mikulin, met in a railway carriage in Conrad's novel *Under Western Eyes* — though dropping no hints about double agents.

At Newark airport, the two caught a bus to Manhattan, both being bound for Long Island. Thomas was surmounted by a lambskin cap from Pakistan, and Kirk wore a Tirolean hat with badges affixed to it. Thomas seemed twice Kirk's height. As well they might, a middle-aged couple near the back of the bus stared intently at this ill-sorted pair of men.

As they left the bus on Manhattan's west side, the woman hissed to her husband, "I *know* I've seen that man somewhere before" — nodding toward Thomas.

"Of course," her husband answered omnisciently. "That gentleman is Mr. Bernard Baruch."

Thomas missed this dialogue, but Kirk recounted it to him. He did not mind having been taken for the eminent financier. Three belligerent little boys tried to snatch the travellers' bags and thrust them into a taxi, but Thomas and Kirk resisted and flagged their own cab; the scalawags howled obscenities after them. "I like to carry my own bags," said Thomas, benignly.

At Pennsylvania Station, two admirers recognized Thomas and expressed their devotion. This seldom occurred, Thomas told Kirk:

"The quiz people are always putting my face above one of those questions, 'Can you identify these men?' I'm included as the puzzler." Yet nobody looked in the least like him.

Thomas was a genuine social democrat; in that, though in nothing else, he resembled Aneurin Bevan, the firebrand or bully of British socialism. Both of them put their attachment to democracy above their socialist ideology.

Under thoroughgoing socialism, even in Britain, generous natures like Norman Thomas's are chucked into the dustbin once their party is established in power. In his failure to apprehend what triumphant socialism must become, Thomas lacked imagination. Perhaps a graver fault was what Paul Elmer More called another deficiency of radicals — their naïve trust in the goodness of human nature. For all his detestation of the Marxist tyrants of three continents, Thomas (like Ralph Waldo Emerson) could not accept the reality of original sin. Perhaps he was invincibly ignorant of the Fall. Yet by the intention are we judged, so that like enough Thomas is gathered in with the sheep, notably unsheepish though he was here below.

Lyndon Johnson, American Caesar

At the Bruges conference on Atlantic community, in 1957, Kirk had met Amaury de Riencourt, the author of *The Coming Caesars,* published that year. Unless measures of restraint should be undertaken promptly, Riencourt wrote, the United States would fall under the domination of twentieth-century Caesars:

> Caesarism is not dictatorship, not the result of one man's overriding ambition, not a brutal seizure of power through revolution. It is not based on a specific doctrine or philosophy. It is essentially pragmatic and untheoretical. It is a slow, often century-old, unconscious development that ends in a voluntary surrender of a free people escaping from freedom to one autocratic master. . . .
>
> Political power in the Western world has become increasingly concentrated in the United States, and in the office of the President within America. The power and prestige of the President have grown with the growth of America and of democracy within Amer-

ica, with the multiplication of economic, political, and military emergencies, with the necessity of ruling what is virtually becoming an American empire — the universal state of a Western civilization at bay. . . .

Caesarism can come to America constitutionally, without having to alter or break down any existing institution. The White House is already the seat of the most powerful tribunician authority ever known to history. All it needs is amplification and extension. Caesarism in America does not have to challenge the Constitution as in Rome or engage in civil warfare and cross any fateful Rubicon. It can slip in quite naturally, discreetly, through constitutional channels.

Just so. Caesarism slipped into the White House constitutionally, if not naturally, with the murder of President Kennedy in 1963 and the succession to executive power of Lyndon Johnson, a hard man of no discernible principles, long a rather unsavory power in the Senate. The plebiscitary democracy would elect Johnson Caesar in 1964; but Johnson's military failure would undo him, despite his *panem et circenses,* and a rebellious senator would strip him of the purple. If Caesars do not win their battles, they fall. In this, though not in much else, perhaps it was well that the war in Vietnam was lost.

In an address entitled "Credulity and Incredulity among the Intellectuals," delivered at the University of Southern California in 1970, Kirk would hint that President Johnson deliberately contrived the naval engagement in the Tonkin Gulf which promptly brought American troops into the war; very recent evidence tends to confirm that suspicion.

On the wall of Kirk's library hangs a photograph of Kirk with President Johnson; both are smiling; it is well to be civil to Caesar. It might be thought that Kirk would not have been eager to visit Caesar in the Oval Office of the Executive Mansion; he was not. But Mrs. Preston Davie, imperious patroness of the Robert A. Taft Institute of Government, dragged him thither. Kirk, with James McClellan, had just published a book about Senator Taft, and in 1953 Senator Lyndon Johnson had delivered a funeral eulogy of his colleague. Mrs. Preston Davie had determined that a copy of the Taft book must be presented formally to President Johnson therefore, and photographs taken. Her will was done. The occasion, in 1967, had its comic relief.

Annette would not be denied participation in this White House presentation. With her husband she flew to Washington, carrying with her in a basket their tiny baby, Monica. They lunched at the old Occidental, now demolished, members of Congress stumbling over Monica in her basket beneath their table; they lodged at the old Willard, then not long for this world — though destined to resurrection in 1985. Telephoning the White House with her accustomed audacity, Annette insisted that she be included in the ceremony; the young Southern staffer at the end of the line gave way.

Leaving Monica to a sitter, the Kirks gained entrance to the White House and proceeded so far as a desk at which sat a Marine sergeant in dress uniform, the President's Cerberus. "Identification, please!" Nearby, in dudgeon, stood Howard Samuels, the undersecretary of commerce, with two young aides hovering nervously behind him; he had neglected to put into his briefcase any acceptable document of identification.

"But I've got to get in: I have an urgent appointment with the president," Samuels was pleading. "I'm the Undersecretary of Commerce!"

"No identification, no admittance," said the Marine. Those were assassin-haunted times. Nodding to Kirk, "You, sir?" Having displayed his passport, Kirk was permitted to pass the desk.

Annette endeavored to follow him; the Marine barred her way. "Identification, miss?" She protested that she was the venerable doctor's spouse — which did seem somewhat improbable. "Every person has to have his own identification, miss."

Mrs. Kirk opened her purse. Alas, she had brought the wrong one; this purse contained no driver's license, no passport, no scrap of . . . But wait, there was something. It was a playing card, the knave of hearts.

At the Magic Castle club in Hollywood, one enchanted evening, Blackstone the Magician had told Annette to write her name on any card. She had chosen the jack of hearts, and the great Blackstone had thrust it back into his pack; and later, inexplicably, Annette had discovered that card in her purse. There it still lay.

Producing the jack triumphantly, the audacious Annette cried to the sergeant, "Here it is!" and thrust it into his hand.

Cerberus stared at the card bemused. "You're Annette?"

"Yes, it says so right there."

"And this is your identification?" Cerberus may have taken her for Annette Funicello, the comic actress, though Annette Kirk had grander charms.

"Of course."

"Well, then, I suppose I'll have to accept it. Pass on."

Up the elevator the Kirks went, and as they rose they could hear Howard Samuels loudly complaining, "You let her in with a jack of hearts, and I'm the Undersecretary of Commerce!" (He still waited there, frustrated, when the Kirks returned; an assistant still had not brought back the required card of identity. But years later, even after the wounding of President Reagan, it would remain possible to penetrate the White House with the flimsiest of identification, and to encounter the President in a corridor; Kirk would do it himself. Such are the manners of democracies, sometimes with perilous consequences.)

In the Oval Office with President Johnson were Mrs. Preston Davie, complacent, and two Democratic senators who had been on good terms with Robert Taft — Byrd of Virginia, Tydings of Maryland. Lyndon Johnson towered tall and masterful, clearly a bad man to have for an adversary. The Taft book was presented, and the president exchanged some brief remarks with Kirk; photographs were taken while Annette strolled behind the presidential desk, examining photographs of Lady Bird, Linda Bird, and other people at the ranch.

True to his reputation if to naught else, President Johnson wheeled and dealt with Senator Byrd and Senator Tydings the while. He knew Kirk for a syndicated columnist, but surely never had opened any of his books. "Stay in school! Stay in school!" Johnson had shouted, over television, to the rising generation. Yet this Caesar had no need of books: he had been the vainglorious disciple of Experience, that famous master of fools.

Every inch a Caesar LBJ looked; he might have sat to Michelangelo for the carving of a statue of a barracks emperor. Experience, nevertheless, had not taught this imperator how to fight a war. To fancy that hundreds of thousands of fanatic guerrillas and North Vietnamese regulars, supplied by Russia and China, might be defeated by military operations merely defensive — plus a great deal of bombing from the air, destroying civilians chiefly, that bombing pinpointed by Johnson himself in the White House! The American troops in Vietnam fought admirably well — how well, Kirk's friend General S. L. A. Marshall described unforgettably in his books — but their situation was untenable. "Imagination rules mankind," Bonaparte had said — Napoleon, master of the big battalions. Had Johnson possessed any imagination, he would have sealed Haiphong, as Nixon did later: only so might the war have been won.

Afflicted by *hubris,* Johnson Caesar piled the tremendous cost of the war — a small item was the immense quantity of milk flown daily from San Francisco to Vietnam, American troops not campaigning on handfuls of rice — upon the staggering cost of his enlargement of the welfare state at home. One might have thought he could not do sums. He ruined the dollar and bequeathed to the nation an incomprehensible national debt. Both guns and butter! It had been swords and liturgies with earlier emperors.

No, Johnson did not open books: with Septimius Severus, he might have said, "Pay the soldiers; the rest do not matter." Had he not Robert McNamara, creator of the Edsel, to counsel him? Power was all, and surely the power of the United States, under Johnson's hand, was infinite. All the way with LBJ! There came into Kirk's head, in the Oval Office, a passage from Amaury de Riencourt:

> With Caesarism and Civilization, the great struggles between political parties are no longer concerned with principles, programs and ideologies but with *men.* Marius, Sulla, Cato, Brutus still fought for principles. But now, everything became personalized. Under Augustus, parties still existed, but there were no more *Optimates* or *Populares,* no more conservatives or democrats. Men campaigned for or against Tiberius or Drusus or Caius Caesar. No one believed any more in the efficacy of ideas, political panaceas, doctrines, or systems, just as the Greeks had given up building great philosophic systems generations before. Abstractions, ideas, and philosophies were rejected to the periphery of their lives and of the empire, to the East where Jews, Gnostics, Christians, and Mithraists attempted to conquer the world of souls and minds while the Caesars ruled their material existence.

All the way with LBJ!

It is with variations that history repeats itself. Ignoring history, LBJ was condemned to repeat it.

Morally, he was the worst man ever to make himself master of the White House. The corrupt antics of Bobby Baker and Billie Sol

Estes did not bring him down, although he had been intimately connected with both.

In June 1961, an agent of the Department of Agriculture, Henry Marshall, had been found shot to death in Texas. Marshall had been about to expose the criminal wheeling and dealing of Billie Sol Estes, and in that wheeling and dealing Lyndon Johnson, then vice president, had participated. A justice of the peace declared the murder of Marshall to have been suicide.

But in March 1984, a grand jury in Robertson County would look into the mystery. A federal marshal and Billie Sol Estes would testify before that jury. Estes, under immunity, swore that the killing had been decided upon at a meeting at Vice President Johnson's Washington residence; Johnson had given the order and directed a hanger-on of his, Malcolm Wallace, to execute it. The grand jury believed Estes, it appears, and concluded that Marshall's death had been a homicide; no one was indicted, for the grand jury presumed that the murderers already were dead.

Such frequently is the way of Caesars. Like some other Caesars, Johnson, from small beginnings, accumulated while in public office a large fortune. No one ever accused him of the vice of scrupulosity. An ill man to deal with, Lyndon Baines Johnson.

Yet Eugene the Poet, Eugene the Giant-Killer, would fetch Caesar down.

Eugene McCarthy: Poet as Politician

Few chief executives of the United States have preferred poetry to pushpin. Yet a few politicians, usually members of the permanent opposition, have confessed to such eccentric tastes. Among them was Randolph of Roanoke, about whom Kirk wrote his first book. The chief recent example of the breed is Eugene McCarthy, for whose presidential candidacy Kirk cast his vote — after beholding Ford and Carter on television — in the Bicentennial year of 1976.

The most interestingly complex of all recent aspirants to the presidency, McCarthy obdurately called himself a liberal during years when that appellation was sinking in popular favor — although he abjured all forms of liberalism earlier than Franklin Roosevelt's. This contrariness was characteristic of his Irish nature. In theory, actually

McCarthy was a conservative: he declared that Edmund Burke was his political mentor, and no one more warmly praised Tocqueville. He read seriously and wrote intelligently. In the White House — *per impossibile* — he might have turned the most imaginatively conservative of presidents.

McCarthy never ran with the hounds. He was at once candid and comical. He and Kirk first met at a debate, with a large audience, in Boston. After the exchange, sponsored by the Paulist Fathers, a reception was held for the two debaters. Up to Senator McCarthy came a zealous young Paulist, inquiring, "Senator McCarthy, don't you think that Jack Kennedy is the finest president this nation ever has had?" (This occurred during the first year of the Kennedy administration.)

"No," said McCarthy, unsmiling.

The Paulist, though taken aback, returned to the charge: "But surely you agree, Senator, that President Kennedy has given this country a new hope, a new vigor, a sense of moving forward toward great things?"

"No," said Eugene McCarthy.

The Paulist persisted: "But of course you'll agree with me when I say, Senator, that the Kennedy family have brought to our life a culture, a refinement, a meaningfulness, that we have not known before."

"No," said Eugene McCarthy.

"But — but Senator McCarthy, surely Jack Kennedy is a very nice man personally?"

Eugene McCarthy turned his back upon the Paulist and slowly walked away. He knew how to say no, he was not ensnared by cliché and slogan, and he had a poet's attachment to truth.

Later McCarthy and Kirk debated at the University of Minnesota. During the question period, a man in the audience asked the two if they didn't think that the greatest menace to the United States was the John Birch Society. Kirk said no, observing that the Birch Society had neither power nor money. Senator McCarthy seconded him, remarking that the resources of the Birch Society were tiny, by the side of the wealth and influence of the Kennedys and the Rockefellers.

Another person in that Minnesota audience inquired of McCarthy how he could explain his membership in so sinister an organization as Americans for Democratic Action. McCarthy answered,

"The ADA have taken so many foolish stands that often I have thought of resigning from that organization. But nowadays it has become worse to be called 'a former member of the ADA' than to be called merely a member; so I have remained within."

McCarthy mentioned privately to Kirk on this occasion that he had been able to support Hubert Humphrey for the Democratic presidential nomination in 1960, for "Hubert often says foolish things; but when compelled to act, usually he is sensible enough." He mentioned that J. F. Kennedy's part in his West Virginia primary contest against Humphrey, what with the buying up of black preachers and other costly tricks, was the most corrupt episode in the history of American elections. Incidentally — this not from McCarthy — that primary cost Humphrey also a vast deal of money. To pay his debts, he became involved in a shady deal about a disused steel mill sold to the Turkish government and shipped to Turkey — where it was discovered to be junk.

Once Kirk had as assistant William Odell, trained as a graphoanalyst. Having examined a specimen of Senator McCarthy's handwriting, Odell pronounced him rebellious, a hard master, and desirous of power. Yet McCarthy's only considerable assertion of power was his unseating of President Johnson by running a good second in the New Hampshire primary of 1968. It is said that his chief bill introduced in the Senate, during his years there, was a measure designed to protect that curious bird the loon, endangered in northern lakes — a conservative proposal heartily endorsed by Kirk. Senator McCarthy generally was a no-sayer on Capitol Hill. The function of the no-sayer is highly valuable, and essentially conservative.

It was McCarthy's proclivity for no-saying, and his refusal to be any lobby's servant, that persuaded him to leave his Senate seat after his first unsuccessful seeking of the Democratic presidential nomination. Probably he despised many of the radical young folk who rioted at Chicago in support of him. But also he had the support, then and later, of some of the better minds and consciences among the rising generation.

Eugene McCarthy's finest act was his undoing of Lyndon Johnson, who had succeeded in displeasing both Left and Right, in New Hampshire's Democratic primary that year. McCarthy assailed Johnson's ruinous conduct of the war in Vietnam. It is said that a good many New Hampshire Democrats thought erroneously that McCarthy had opposed Johnson for not having prosecuted the war with sufficient vigor; at any rate, after McCarthy had run him a close second in the popular vote, Johnson knew that he could not be re-elected.

In turn, McCarthy soon was undone by Robert Kennedy, who had not ventured to bell the cat before McCarthy boldly denounced Johnson. Had that Kennedy taken office, a good many people might have wished Johnson back again. Vindictive, ruthless, lustful, efficient, Attorney General Kennedy of the shrill voice and the three-finger handshake was such a one as never should be chief magistrate. In the spring of 1968, Robert Kennedy and Kirk were among the participants in a symposium at the University of Alabama.

The student chairman introduced Kennedy — who had arrived hours late, keeping everybody waiting, and would fly away immediately after his brief speech — as "the next president of the United States." Succeeding the Attorney General on the platform, Kirk remarked that Kennedy never would become president. A murderer's bullet, on June 5, brought that prediction to pass: Kirk, sitting in a Fifth Avenue apartment just below the apartment of one of the Kennedy clan, saw on television that slaying.

In later contests for the presidency, McCarthy was not a serious contender — and yet, as Norman Thomas had done, he elevated the tone of electoral politics somewhat. In 1976, during the course of a Texas debate with Frank Mankiewicz (then working, *sub rosa*, for Jimmy Carter), Kirk found himself publicly announcing his endorsement of McCarthy's independent candidacy. He did not know that Mr. McCarthy was quite the sort of person needed in the White House; on the other hand, Kirk did not know that McCarthy wasn't. In some degree, public men with poetic insights possess that armed vision to which the razor's edge becomes a saw.

A president who would be no man's servant — surely no prisoner of the big labor unions — might have acted with decisive courage; instead, the country was given the quasi-populist Carter, infirm of purpose. In McCarthy there was nothing of the demagogue; in his little book *Frontiers in American Democracy* he had mentioned that the Senate had suffered much from the constitutional amendment establishing popular election of senators. In *The Ultimate Tyranny* (1980) he would scourge bureaucracy and the cult of political efficiency; in that year he would endorse Ronald Reagan's presidential candidacy. Although no hot partisan, McCarthy had been hot for imaginative politics.

It is entertaining, although profitless, to wonder what manner of president the witty gentleman from Minnesota might have become — he seeming by nature a mordant critic of central authority, rather than an Ozymandias. But enough! As T. S. Eliot reminds us, all time is unredeemable. McCarthy might have saved the Democratic party from its increasing perversity. It remains surprising that at one time he came fairly close to accomplishing just that.

The Fortitude and the Failings of Richard Nixon

Kirk's graphoanalyst assistant examined specimens of the handwriting of Mr. Richard Nixon, at a time when President Nixon's reputation was at its summit.* Nixon, his handwriting suggested, was far from being the ruthless practical politician of frequent caricature; instead, he was somewhat dreamy and idealistic. His principal ambition, as revealed in a holograph analysis, was to possess an enviable reputation with future generations. Although conservative by conviction, he was extremely fond of ingenious innovations; yet, lacking imaginative power of his own, he sought to gather round him men of creative talents, fertile in suggestions.

Late in the autumn of 1967, when Nixon was planning to have another go at the presidency but had not publicly announced his intention, he invited Kirk to meet with him privately in his New York law office. Doubtless he was collecting advice from various well-inclined persons; perhaps also he had in mind possible kind words in Kirk's syndicated newspaper column. (The two had exchanged notes from time to time, and had spoken from the same platform in Washington, but had not previously conversed.) It was Mr. Nixon's custom, then and later, to consult with persons presumed to have some political imagination.

*The art of graphoanalysis, dubious though it may appear to many, frequently is employed as evidence of character by personnel offices and also in trials at law. William Odell, just out of the army, became the second young man to serve as Kirk's literary assistant; he happened to be an accomplished graphoanalyst.

Their talk concerned foreign affairs — Vietnam in particular. Kirk protested that his host knew far more about the subject than did he, but Nixon encouraged him to expatiate. He mentioned that he had obtained Dr. Henry Kissinger as his advisor on foreign policy; Kirk approved. (He had corresponded with Kissinger as a contributor to Kissinger's Harvard magazine *Confluence*.) Then Nixon asked what, if elected president, he should do about the Vietnamese war.

"We must do what the admirals call 'going to Haiphong,'" Kirk replied. Were that port sealed, the chief source of supplies to the Communists of Hanoi would be blocked. The Chinese would not interfere, Kirk said, what with the enormous losses they had sustained in Korea in Truman's time. The Russians might be given sufficient warning not to send ships into Haiphong after a formal declaration of blockade: their stake in Vietnam was not big enough for them to risk confrontation with American seapower. Mr. Nixon agreed; that was just what he meant to do; and later that was what he did, successfully, when in office.

Their conversation proceeded to more general themes of foreign policy. Mr. Nixon declared that he always had believed this to be the American Century and that President Wilson was his exemplar in such great concerns. (Kirk had his misgivings about this discipleship to Wilson, but did not voice them.)

Having said good-bye to Mr. Nixon, Kirk paused at the door to show photographs of his old house and his young wife to Patrick Buchanan, then and later, in the White House, Nixon's honest and intelligent assistant. Mr. Nixon stood some feet distant, smiling his thanks; Kirk did not think he could see the photographs.

Some ten or twelve days later, Kirk and the beautiful Annette were strolling upper Fifth Avenue; they noticed a considerable crowd assembled before Tiffany's (where Annette's brother once had been a repairer of jewelry). Was a mob trashing Tiffany's? Looting on a larger scale had become almost commonplace during the Johnson administration. But as they drew nearer, they found that it was a crowd of giggling and screeching shop girls, mostly, gathered about a tall man.

"It's Richard Nixon!" Annette exclaimed. "Introduce me!" "Some other time," her husband murmured. But the strong-willed Annette thrust her husband forward through the shop girls, much as Mary of Guise pushed the reluctant Earl of Arran to the assault on St. Andrews Castle.

"Good morning, Mr. Nixon," said Kirk. Hesitating only for a fraction of a second in the midst of the mob of autograph seekers, Nixon replied, "How good to see you again, Dr. Kirk — only twelve days after our conference!" Nixon was excelled only by Jim Farley in powers of total recall of names and faces and related details — the most precious of all gifts for a democratic politician. He addressed the shop girls: "I want you all to meet a famous writer that you've heard of, Dr. Russell Kirk." The young women gazed uncomprehending upon that mysterious grandee; none sought Kirk's autograph.

Mr. Nixon engaged Annette, who was most fashionably dressed, in conversation amidst this chaos. "Can it be," he inquired, paying a graceful compliment, "that you live in that old farmhouse at Mecosta, Michigan?" He had seen Kirk's photographs, after all, some days earlier, though standing some distance from them; he had remembered Kirk's village. By such talents, as through political courage, persistence, and quick grasp of affairs, the trolleyman's son ascended to the presidency.

The youthful Annette came off happy from that first encounter with Mr. Nixon; not so happy from the second one.

On April 1, 1972, the President's press secretary telephoned Mecosta to inquire whether Kirk could be in Washington on April 4 to confer with President Nixon. Answering the telephone, Annette asked whether the occasion was to be a general press conference, for her husband never attended those. Ron Ziegler replied that this was to be a private conversation with the President, "on general questions." Kirk flew to Washington, Annette insisting on going along, as was her imperious wont.

That day great crowds of young people, and radicals not so young, were pouring into Washington. North Vietnam's troops, on March 30, had crossed the demilitarized zone in great force; the South Vietnamese divisions had fallen back in confusion, and the Nixon administration was moving to shore up Saigon's resistance to the Communists. Protest, protest!

Patrick Buchanan and his wife greeted the Kirks at the west wing of the White House; they shook hands with Henry Kissinger in a corridor. Annette having been deposited for the time with Mrs. Buchanan, Kirk was ushered into a private conversation of forty minutes with the President.

Unperturbed by the demonstrators in the streets, Mr. Nixon was leisurely in manner, assured, cordial. (Five weeks later, he would order the mining of the harbor of Haiphong, which by summer would compel Hanoi to suspend military operations against Saigon.) The President seated himself on a sofa by Kirk's chair. Indeed, the questions he raised were of a general and fundamental character. Something was said about assistance to independent schools, but nothing about Vietnam or about domestic politics of the hour. Their talk turned soon to perennial questions.

Some weeks earlier, at Kansas City, President Nixon — in the course of being interviewed by mass-media people — had raised the question of whether America might be decadent. He was the first president ever to suggest that disturbing possibility. This subject became the principal theme of his conversation with Kirk.

It became clear that Mr. Nixon felt lonely, despite his high rating in public-opinion polls — a popularity that would lead to his overwhelming defeat of George McGovern in November. "Where do presidents obtain their support when unpopular decisions have to be made, Dr. Kirk?" He did not mean himself only. "I know that people think I have the support of big business, but I find that when I'm in trouble, big business is absent. On some questions I can count on George Meany and the AFL. I don't have many friends in the press; there are some in the Academy. I still have Main Street . . ."

"As I needn't tell you," Kirk commented, "poor Main Street counts for less with every day that passes." Nixon nodded. Kirk felt rather like Chateaubriand, consulted by Louis XVIII: he could offer only the coldest of comfort.

At the end of February, Kirk had written in his column for the Los Angeles Times Syndicate, "Mr. Nixon is the least liable of public men to set himself up as a kind of secular supreme pontiff, advised by a college of self-righteous intellectuals. Moralistic attitudinizing is more in Senator George McGovern's line."

Nevertheless, the possibility of American decadence was much on Mr. Nixon's mind that April afternoon: the rotting of great cities and the violence within them, the widespread addiction to narcotics, the fierce protests of militant pacifists against action in Vietnam, a general mood of discouragement. "I can speak to some effect against drug abuse and such questions," the President told Kirk, "but I don't think that people wish me to turn preacher."

[331]

What might be done — not just today, but in the long run — to revive America's spirits and old national character? The President put the question earnestly: "Dr. Kirk, have we any hope?" He repeated it: "Have we any hope?"

"That depends upon public belief, Mr. President," Kirk suggested. "Despair feeds upon despair, hope upon hope. If most people believe the prophets of despair, they will seek out private hidie-holes and cease to cooperate for the common good. But if most people say, 'We are in a bad way, but we still have the resources and the intelligence and the will to work a renewal' — why, they will be roused by the exigency to common action and reform. It is all a matter of belief."

Kirk went on to offer the example of the Byzantine Empire, which — despite beginnings not altogether healthy — endured for a thousand years, experiencing alternately eras of decline and eras of reinvigoration. "No human institution lasts forever, Mr. President; but the United States is young, as great powers go; and presumably three-quarters of our existence, at least, lies before us. Our present troubles may be succeeded by an age of greatness." Such was the substance of Kirk's reply.

The President's spirits revived; he said that so he always had believed; and indeed generally he had been a sanguine politician — perhaps too sanguine. (In Washington's streets, at that hour, young persons in jeans or stranger attire were denouncing him as sanguinary, for letting Hanoi and Haiphong be bombed.)

As their conversation drew to a close, the President asked Kirk, "What one book should I read?" Kirk raised his eyebrows. Mr. Nixon added that he never watched television, knowing that for a waste of time; therefore, despite his duties, now and again he had the opportunity to read a serious book. "Yet I don't have time for many books. I am always asking Moynihan or Kissinger for the title of one book, and they give me a list of a dozen books on some subject; but I haven't time for a dozen books. What one book should I read?"

Kirk did not hesitate. "T. S. Eliot's *Notes towards the Definition of Culture.*" Mr. Nixon wished to know why. His bookish advisor mentioned that Eliot discusses the relationship which should exist between men of action and men of ideas, and touches upon many of the fundamental difficulties of culture in the twentieth century; he examines those norms upon which civilization rests, and matters raised by the President himself.

Kirk had just published his big book about Eliot. "I can read that in your book, can't I?" Nixon asked.

"Yes, Mr. President; but it would be better to read Eliot's book; I'll send you a copy." Whether Nixon made time to read Eliot, Kirk never learned; but at the President's second inauguration, a rabbi speaking at the White House quoted from Eliot's choruses in *The Rock;* so some Eliot influence is to be suspected.

The President rose. "I understand that your wife is here with you; I must see her again."

Annette was ushered in. Kindly questioning her, Mr. Nixon found that she had attended a Catholic college. He asked her if she were a Catholic; she was.

Turning to Kirk, "But you're not a Catholic?" Kirk declared that he was.

"But in *A Program for Conservatives,* you say you're a Puritan." Mr. Nixon's wondrous memory had dredged up an obscure aside in that book at the time it had been written in 1954.*

"Watch out for the Jesuits," the President added, with a smile. The brothers Berrigan, S.J., had been after him and Secretary Kissinger; one of the pair even had contemplated kidnapping Henry Kissinger. But Mr. Nixon's admonition was playful, he having a Jesuit of a different stamp among his advisors.

Next Mr. Nixon bent over his desk to open hidden drawers and extract souvenirs for the Kirks: trinkets for the daughters, cuff links and a presidential ashtray for Russell Kirk; he dispatched a page to fetch from a safe a golden compact for Annette — "not that she needs it."

More than once, Kirk had called his vivacious spouse the Mistress of the Faux Pas. Now she fully justified that sobriquet. It seemed to her undignified for the President to extract trinkets from drawers; besides, she and her husband were not tourists. She was embarrassed, therefore, and unsure of what to say by way of thanks.

There came into her head a line from "The Vision of Sir Launfal" that her husband was given to murmuring facetiously as

---

*Kirk had been told that *A Program for Conservatives,* at the time of its first publication, had been thrust upon Richard Nixon by Congressman Hiram Bingham, the patriarchal Republican from Massachusetts; but the President had acquired another copy not long before the conversation with Kirk, and copies had been distributed among some members of the White House staff.

he tagged after her in shopping malls. There being a lull in the conversation while Mr. Nixon opened more drawers, she uttered that line of James Russell Lowell's poem with her accustomed distinctness, rather loudly:

"At the devil's booth, all things are sold!"

Mr. Nixon was not much read in the poets. He paused over his desk drawers, saying nothing; the silence was chilly. Then he straightened up and faced the Kirks, looking upon them from his full height, unsmiling. Annette sensed that she had used the Lowell line in not quite the right context. The amused smile she had expected to receive from the president did not appear on his face; instead she received a cool if puzzled stare.

That moment's silence seemed to endure for an hour. "We campaigned for you in California, Mr. President," Kirk offered. The door opened; there appeared a page, grinning from ear to ear — as if, Annette later remarked, he were thinking, "Wait till I tell this to the boys downstairs!" The Kirks retreated.

When Annette had entered the presidential office, there had been outside only a page, on a stool. Now there stood without three capable men, somewhat grim, their hands thrust into their pockets. Annette smiled placatingly at those Secret Service agents.

As Russell and Annette made their way down the corridor, Kirk murmured to his wife, "It's fortunate that your husband is not an ambitious man."

This time she was apt at quotation: "Ambition should be made of sterner stuff."

That night, Mr. Nixon, with his accustomed intrepidity, went down to Lincoln's monument to converse with demonstrating boys and girls. Unlike President Johnson, he did not confine his speechifying chiefly to military bases.

At the height of the Watergate fracas, Kirk would write in a newspaper column, "Mr. Nixon is not a crook." And Nixon, borrowing, would tell the public on television, "I am not a crook." That was true, and Annette had intended no such imputation. Again unlike Johnson, he had not accumulated mysteriously, during years in public office, a huge private fortune; he never had made much money until he turned to the practice of the law after his defeat by Kennedy. But after the staff report of a Senate committee that investigated the Nixon income-tax returns — a report outrageously partisan and unjust —

most of the American public concluded that the president of the United States had endeavored to swindle the Internal Revenue Service. That final blow made his impeachment certain, his conviction probable, and his resignation inevitable.

Nixon was brought down by his closest associates in the administration, "pragmatic" men with no scruples when "winning is the name of the game." It was John Mitchell, Nixon's friend and former law partner, who gave assent to the mad scheme of invading the Democrats' headquarters in the Watergate, so eventually ruining President Nixon; and Haldeman and Erlichman, counsellors to the president, were false to their patron. Nixon's endeavors to save such shoddy associates from the consequences of their folly blighted his aspiration to be esteemed by future generations. And among other disastrous consequences, the Watergate scandal brought about the Communist conquest of South Vietnam.

So what is one to say about imagination in the Nixon administration? In the lowest, prudential sense of the word, one is astounded at the stupidity of "pragmatists" who could fancy that burglarizing the Watergate would be a game worth the candle. Were they so thoroughly unimaginative that they could not foresee possible failure and what that failure would bring upon their heads? As for the higher moral imagination, how could they conceive, lawyers as they were, that fancied partisan expediency could justify breaking of the law by the guardians of the law?

So it was that despite Nixon's endeavor, in part successful, to attract to his administration men of imagination, he chose as certain close subordinates men who could not see beyond their noses, intoxicated by power, terrified of losing that power — and faithless into the bargain. It was from lack of imagination that the Nixon administration fell.

An intimacy with great poetry might not have saved Richard Nixon from his fall; yet it might have made him shrewder, paradoxical though that may seem, in concerns of state and judgments of character. Like Eliot's Coriolan, Nixon wanted that peace and confidence "at the still point of the turning world." Like Coriolan, he was engulfed by committees and commissions; and presently the voice of the crowd was heard: RESIGN RESIGN RESIGN!

During Nixon's first administration, Kirk had been invited by Patrick Buchanan, the ablest of the President's inner circle, to take a

Washington post in which one actually would have been paid well for concerning himself with the works of the imagination. But Kirk recommended another writer for that appointment; he did not mean to be converted into a cultural bureaucrat; and besides, to paraphrase General Sherman (substituting Washington, D.C., for Texas), had he owned both Hell and Washington, he would have rented out Washington and lived in Hell. Through his books and essays and, indeed, through his fiction too, Kirk would continue to try to infuse some imagination into America's politics. Kirk's refusal, during the Watergate frenzy, to join the journalistic hounds in pulling down the President led many newspaper editors to cease to publish Kirk's column "To the Point"; so before Mr. Nixon's resignation, Kirk gave up his syndicated column altogether, emancipating himself from what Arthur Machen had called "that damnable vile business, journalism."

CHAPTER THIRTEEN

The Last Homely House

Beyond Politics

If the American democracy could choose to be ruled by such a one as Lyndon Johnson, what point was there in taking any direct hand in practical politics for the next four years? Kirk's syndicated column grew less political: in the November election, 1964, Johnson had obtained such a majority in both Senate and House that resistance to his "Great Society" follies was almost vain.

So Russell and Annette, the political battle lost, took passage on the Bremen for Southampton — Annette being seasick, first class, for the whole of the voyage, so that she would scarcely set foot on a deck thereafter. They sped by railway to the Kingdom of Fife, very cold that winter, to make the rounds of country houses and ancient burghs, where Annette was greeted with wonder and enthusiasm.

At Pittenweem, the most picturesque of the medieval fishing ports of Fife, Kirk had begun the restoration of a delightful white-harled old house with crowstepped gables that stood on the market square — a dwelling, derelict, that he first had noticed in 1948. Lady Crawford had suggested to him that he acquire the house, to save it from demolition, which house-breaking would have spoilt the appearance of Pittenweem's High Street. He had bought the house for a hundred pounds, and the land behind it for another hundred; but the cost of restoration, when all the bills came in, would be twice what he had estimated. This house, Number 40 High Street, had been built at the beginning of the eighteenth century, but it incorporated the walls, running at right angles to the later house, of a dwelling perhaps three centuries older. Number 40 High Street even had its peculiar ghost, the revenant of Palmer the gypsy painter, who had been hanged by the neck until dead.

Restoration had not sufficiently progressed, in the winter of 1964, for the Kirks to lodge in their own tenement; in 1966 they would spend the summer there on the market square of Pittenweem; but later they would have to sell, at a loss, that beloved little ancient house, to meet their growing expenses at Mecosta. Kirk's short story of witchcraft, "The Reflex-Man in Whinnymuir Close" (first published in 1984) would have the tarry wynds of Pittenweem for its setting.

So the Kirks lodged in castles and in country houses. They were with the Lorimers at Kellie Castle for a grand Christmas party, 1964, fires blazing in all fireplaces and fifty or sixty guests talking animatedly (and a Lorimer gift for every guest). Those log fires were very necessary, what with the north wind coming down over Kellie Law upon the tall castle with its tall windows. Indeed, the cold grew so severe that Annette could not endure it, and even Russell shivered in his heavy Scottish suits. Therefore they fled from Fife to South Africa, on January 3.

While they were in the air half way to Johannesburg, T. S. Eliot died in London; they did not come to know that until long later, for their month in South Africa was a period intensely busy. Annette was terrified nocturnally by a hyena in Kruger National Park, and by a wild tropical storm on the lip of a cliff at Majubaskloof. They called upon Chief Matanzima, prime minister of the Transkei, and his brother the Transkei's minister of education; they attended the season's first session of Parliament, at Pretoria; Kirk went down a diamond mine.

By February 1965, the Kirks were back at Mecosta — at least Annette was, for Russell found himself speechifying all over the country. They had moved from their cottage on Lake Mecosta to the Old House of Piety Hill, sharing it with Russell's surviving great-aunt, Norma Johnson, whom Annette persuaded to tell her tales of the old Spiritualist seances of the Johnsons. Aunt Normie herself sometimes seemed a revenant, gentle though she was, and a reader of good books.

Kirk's bibliography was growing, although after his marriage he found himself less able to write for the literary and scholarly quarterlies: they paid little, and married men require money. In 1963, Fleet had published a collection of his *National Review* essays and syndicated newspaper columns, *Confessions of a Bohemian Tory: Episodes and Reflections of a Vagrant Career.* Fleet it was that brought out, too, the first collection of his occult and mystical stories, in 1965 — *The Surly Sullen Bell: Ten Stories or Sketches, Uncanny or Uncomfortable, with a Note on the Ghostly Tale.* This was very well received by the review media; presently a London paperback edition appeared; also an American paperback edition, under the title *Lost Lake* — which was the title of one of the Mecosta vignettes within the volume. This collection and his earlier *Old House of Fear* induced the Count Dracula Society, a Los Angeles league of *afficionados* of uncanny tales and horror movies, to bestow upon Kirk the high distinction of Knight Commander of the Order of Count Dracula.

In 1965 there appeared also his book *The Intemperate Professor, and Other Cultural Splenetics,* published by Louisiana State University Press, a collection of his essays on colleges and culture; religion, morals, and culture; wealth and culture; and beauty, community, and culture. (A revised edition would be brought out by Sherwood Sugden in 1988.) It may be worth noting that from 1958 through 1966 he published no book dealing with political theory or practice. Despite his activity in the Goldwater campaign, there had echoed in his mind Gissing's aphorism: politics is the preoccupation of the quarter-educated.

The summer of 1965 was spent by Russell and Annette chiefly at Pepperdine University, where he had been induced, as distinguished visiting professor of politics, to offer a course in Modern Political Movements. His students were somewhat surprised to learn that to Professor Kirk, Modern Political Movements meant the French Revolution.

Los Angeles smog notwithstanding, those Pepperdine weeks were pleasant. In 1962, for some weeks, Kirk had been visiting distinguished professor at Los Angeles State College, an interesting time. He liked Los Angeles, where his syndicated column in the *Times* made him many friends. Their apartment was near a race course. After mass, a priest inquired, "Are you race-track people?" His suspicion may have been justifiable, for he beheld the shapely Annette in one of her flamboyant outfits, and Dr. Kirk in his gambler's Palm Beach suit of black, with a gold stickpin in his tie.

"Now we're going to live like real people!" Annette had exclaimed when, at Mecosta, they had received the invitation from Pepperdine. Her husband promptly had composed a jingle suitable for radio or television, on this theme:

Living like real people, living as people should,
In our little apartment, ten miles from Hollywood;
Taking it free and easy, watching the go-go girl,
Living life with abandon, living it in a whirl . . .

The ghosts from Mecosta, temporarily pretending to be real people living as people should, learned during their stay in Los Angeles an arcane doctrine that has comforted them ever since. This came from the lips of Father Martin D'Arcy., S.J., whom Kirk had met in New York some years before. The wisest of Jesuits, Father D'Arcy was visiting Loyola University, Los Angeles; and a vice president of that institution, Father Lucy, S.J., acquainted with the Kirks, arranged for Russell and Annette to dine at a good restaurant with Father D'Arcy and himself. Annette, on the appointed evening, was somewhat tardy, as usual, in arraying herself even as a lily of the field; the two Jesuits waited, and Kirk watched Father D'Arcy, old, lean, handsome, and intense, dramatic with his grand-brimmed, shallow-crowned clerical hat, pacing up and down before their door.

Kirk prized Father D'Arcy's several books, especially *The Sense of History, Secular and Sacred*. The most important of those books was *The Mind and Heart of Love: Lion and Unicorn, a Study in Eros and Agape*. That volume Russell had sent to Annette during their courtship, and it had been a major influence upon the Conservative Beauty in her decision to let her best friend become her husband.

Father D'Arcy was astonished and delighted when Kirk told him that for months, before their marriage eleven months past, he would quote to Annette passages from *The Mind and Heart of Love*, adding his own comments on the theme. Martin D'Arcy said that such unexpected acknowledgment of influence makes a man feel that he has not lived in vain.

He and Kirk had various friends in common, T. S. Eliot among them; they fell to talking at the dinner table, that August night, about country houses they both knew — and then about the ghosts of those country houses. Loyola's vice president stared in amazement, first at

D'Arcy, then at Kirk. "Why — why, you fellows really *believe* in ghosts!"

"Of course," said his fellow Jesuit; "the evidence is indubitable" — and resumed his spectral narrations.

He was a perfect raconteur. One of his most interesting adventures had been his discovery, in a Dublin junk shop, of the portable altar of John of Gaunt, later possessed by Mary Stuart; he had tracked down the precious thing's rightful owner, a beautiful Brazilian widow, who had given him the altar in return for his trouble, she being rich beyond the dreams of avarice. But George Gordon, S.J., then head of the Farm Street Jesuits, had forbidden D'Arcy to display it, lest the Jesuits be thought a wealthy order.

All this fascinated Annette, but she was eager to question Father D'Arcy on a theological point of burning interest to her, and question him she did. She knew that the sacrament of marriage is said to work an eternal union; yet how may that be if, as the Gospel according to Luke has it, in heaven is no marriage or giving in marriage?

Father D'Arcy had written a penetrating little book, *Death and Life,* published during the Second World War, and difficult to obtain. In its pages he remarks that the Christian understanding of the life eternal is an arcane doctrine. But his reply to Annette was less shadowy than the treatment of the subject in his book.

"Heaven is a state," D'Arcy told Annette, "in which all the good things of your life are present to you whenever you desire them" — not in memory merely, not somehow re-enacted, but present, beyond the barriers of time, in all their fullness. Thus husband and wife would experience in eternity, when they should will it, what they had experienced within mundane time, linear time; and human creatures, resurrected, will have perfected bodies.

But Hell, Father D'Arcy continued, is a state of being in which all the evil one has done is eternally present — and there is no escape from it. So it is that human creatures make their own destiny, their own Heaven and their own Hell. "Why, this is Hell, nor am I out of it," says Mephistopheles, in *Doctor Faustus.* If people firmly believed this doctrine — that our every decision for good or for evil, here below, is eternal, and determines our eternal state — why, how differently most folk would live! (This aside is Kirk's, not D'Arcy's.) We are in eternity now. This teaching of D'Arcy's, Kirk thinks, directly influenced T. S. Eliot; one can perceive its substance, and that of May

[341]

Sinclair's short story "Where Their Fire Is Not Quenched," in Eliot's last play, *The Elder Statesman*. The whole arcane doctrine is bound up with what we call Time, and with whether one thinks of time as Cronos, Time the Devourer, or of time as did the Hebrew prophets, psychic time, a relationship with the divine.

After that evening of good talk, Kirk never saw Father D'Arcy again here below, although years later he and Annette visited the noble Martin D'Arcy collection of religious art at Loyola University, Chicago. D'Arcy and he would correspond during the year Kirk was finishing his book *Eliot and His Age* — that is, in 1970. There occur timeless moments, Eliot tells us; surely that dinner with Father D'Arcy and Father Lucy was one such. So, indeed, Martin D'Arcy assures his readers near the end of that small book *Death and Life*.

In the heavenly state, D'Arcy writes, when "the phase of corruption has passed into the permanent state of incorruption, thanks to the life-giving power of the spirit which lives in Christ, the identity of this new self with its past will be clearer than that of any Cinderella who had been changed into a queen." God will not withhold "the experiences which made us what we are and bound friends to us by affection and vow. Nor will those experiences be just memories, for memories mean that something has been lost and that we are spiritual orphans. 'I will not leave you orphans: I will come to you.' . . . In the day of the reward we will not have to ask for anything, for all things, all joys and all loves will be ours. Memories will give up their dead and the past will live again in this fullness of life."

"O Death, where is thy sting? O Grave, where is thy victory?" That promise it was which caused Christian faith to rise upon the ashes of the classical culture; that promise, renewed and believed afresh, may yet breathe vitality into a dissolving moral order. Certainly Father D'Arcy's words and presence gave to Russell and Annette Kirk a glimpse of eternity that has not faded with the passing of the years.

Denizens of the Safe House of Piety Hill

Once the spirited Annette had become chatelaine of Piety Hill, the constitution of things there was altered marvellously. Openhanded, glowing with life, and discerningly compassionate, Annette Courtemanche Kirk turned the shadowy old house, without altering its character, into a center of charitable and intellectual undertakings, so that often it was crowded with people of all sorts and conditions. She was beloved by people of all ages and both sexes, which caused the telephone — Mecosta 8, Mecosta Telephone Company — to ring at all hours; and the mail-box — P.O. Box 4, Mecosta — to overflow.

The blithe spirit from Long Island busied herself immensely and effectively. Far more than her reserved husband, soon she was accepted as a Mecostan. She poured her energies into Saint Michael's Church; she became chairman, presently, of the county board of social services. Later she founded the Mecosta County Council for the Arts and restored a one-room schoolhouse. She commenced to fill Piety Hill with a congeries of long-term guests, from earnest disciples of Russell Kirk to outcasts of Poker Flat.

The gates of Piety Hill, like those of the palace of Dis, stood open night and day; visitors from Megalopolis or from foreign parts marvelled that the house's doors never were locked against the antagonist world. Kirk assured them that as Sparta's walls had been the breasts of her men, so it was at Piety Hill: the place always had potential defenders in the form of Kirk's assistants and students, often redoubtable young men. Before his marriage, Kirk had told timorous guests and kin, "Who'd invade this house? It's notorious that the place is haunted; downstairs live two witches, and upstairs lives a mad doctor, a justice of the peace who collects weapons of war" — his references being to his pair of aged and somewhat uncanny great-aunts, and to himself.

"Your house is wonderful but spooky," a visitor from Crakow remarked. In a time of violent crimes, Piety Hill stood inviolate, a safe house in more ways than one, a place of refuge for some that had escaped from tyranny and others whom society had cast out; also for numerous handsome cats and a stray dog or two.

Even before she met Russell Kirk, Annette had hoped to bear four children. Four daughters did appear successively; more about them presently: Monica Rachel, born in 1967, would justify her name by soon growing very much attached to matters of the hearth and the heart; Cecilia Abigail, born in 1968, would become intelligent, independent, often piquant; Felicia Annette, born in 1970, would develop into a gentle and shy beauty, in the fullness of time embracing the books of Laurens van der Post; Andrea Seton, born in 1975 soon after the Kirks' Great Fire of Piety Hill, the self-styled

[343]

Fire Baby, would be of good cheer, dancing and drawing, affectionate, imaginative. These girls would appear frequently in Kirk's newspaper columns.

Piety Hill's increase of population made necessary the house's enlargement. In 1970 there was added a huge wing of brick, a tail wagging its dog, four stories high, connected with the original house by a passage: the New House in the Italianate style of the Old House, with a grand drawing room and thirteen other chambers. A prudent steel sliding door parted New House from Old. Now Piety Hill was ready for inmates. How many and various those would be!

Near the end of the Seventies, there arrived from California young Jas Scott-Moncrieff, eldest son of George Scott-Moncrieff by Scomo's second marriage. His stay at Piety Hill was a blessing to him after his long journey. "This is the Last Homely House!" the boy exclaimed.

His reference was to Tolkien's volumes *The Lord of the Rings,* the sacred trilogy of the more imaginative among the rising generation of the Sixties and the Seventies — among boys, that is, the girls generally preferring C. S. Lewis's *Chronicles of Narnia,* or later the romances of Madeleine L'Engle. Tolkien's Last Homely House, a refuge secured both by warriors and by enchantment, was Rivendell, where the master was the ageless Elrond Halfelven, keeper of the greatest of the formidable Rings of Power. His ring, Vilya, Elrond wielded for the purposes of "understanding, making, and healing, to preserve all things unstained." At need, Elrond would draw his sword. "But the House of Rivendell was not a fortress, nor a camp of war," according to J. E. A. Tyler's learned commentary upon Tolkien. "It was a place of learning, of merriment and of quiet, beside a running stream, deep in a forest-clad northern valley. There, with his children, his loremasters, and many of the Chief Eldar of Middle-earth as his counsellors, Elrond dwelt until the end of the Age."

No more overwhelming compliment could have been paid to Kirk than this. Indeed, Loremasters and Chief Eldar were to be encountered from time to time at the Last Homely House of Piety Hill, come to converse with young people from the Intercollegiate Studies Institute or merely to forgather with Kirk-Elrond's household: Cleanth Brooks, Andrew Lytle, George Nash, William Ball, Peter Stanlis, Edward Ericson, M. E. Bradford, Frederick Wilhelmsen, Count Nicolai Tolstoy, William Kirk Kilpatrick, Paul Vitz, Michael

Aeschliman, Thomas Howard, Marion Montgomery, Bela Menczer, John Lukacs, Stephen Tonsor, Gerhard Niemeyer, William Campbell, Charles Moser, Antony Sullivan, Roger Scruton, others. Younger scholars, too: Russell Hittenger, Vigen Guroian, Mark Henrie, Gleaves Whitney, Marco Respinti, Greg Wolfe. Politicians, too, were entertained there frequently, and local societies of antiquaries. Annette, in crimson gown or in white, made everybody jolly, sometimes flamenco dancing for them; Elrond-Russell was induced to lecture on everything under the sun or to tell ghostly tales.

Of all such occasions, Annette's most cherished was the coming of Malcolm and Kitty Muggeridge, Malcolm — along with Russell — to talk about "Pilgrims in the Dark Wood of Our Time" to college students ready to commence that pilgrimage. The Muggeridges were lodged in what ordinarily was the bedroom of Russell and Annette, a chamber embellished by a large fireplace; Annette assigned them that room because English people rejoice in open fires.

The second Kirk daughter, Cecilia, then aged ten years, sat in the front row to hear all of Malcolm Muggeridge's lively if lugubrious lectures, closely attentive. After the Muggeridges had departed, Annette asked her daughter, "Cecilia, did you understand everything that Mr. Muggeridge said?"

"Not all of it," Cecilia replied, "but more than I had expected." She was their philosophical child.

An even closer relationship came to pass between the Muggeridges and the youngest Kirk daughter, Andrea, then a three-year-old. It had been infant Andrea's habit to creep into bed between her parents, coming in the wee hours from her room to theirs. One night she forgot that her parents had shifted temporarily to another chamber.

"We had a visitor in our room last night," Kitty Muggeridge remarked at breakfast next morning. "About three o'clock, one of the doors opened quietly. We thought of your ghostly tales of this house. A little white figure entered and climbed into bed between us: very frightening!

"The little shape lay there for some time. Then she looked at Malcolm and me. She said, 'I think I must be going now,' and she left the bed and the room."

"How long did she stay?" the embarrassed Annette wished to know.

"Long enough not to give offense," Kitty Muggeridge smiled.

As for the lectures on the Dark Wood, the select audience found the communication of the doom-speller Russell Kirk virtually sanguine by contrast with the Muggeridge vaticinations.

In the Seventies, the first wave of refugees received at Piety Hill came in consequence of the triumph of the public policy of abortion on demand. Kirk had been the chief speaker at the initial rally (on the riverfront at Detroit) of Michigan citizens opposed to a state initiative to make abortion lawful; the pro-life people, at the polls, had defeated the proposal nearly two to one, but the Supreme Court of the United States, in its infinite wisdom, had undone them. The compassionate Annette, active in Alternatives to Abortion, then had Piety Hill certified as a temporary home for unwed mothers. They came, from all classes and conditions, and Annette saw them through pregnancy and childbirth — even supervising, white-masked, in the operating room of a hospital; she arranged adoptions while private adoptions still were permitted by Michigan's regulations.

Some girls came from good families, others from the depths. One unwed mother fetched in her sister, not then pregnant, yet liable to find herself in that condition soon. The sister's consummate ambition was to become a go-go dancer, but she had not risen so high.

As he ascended the stair of the New House upon having returned from a speaking tour, Kirk met a strange young woman, one of whose eyes was of glass; she was barefoot and garishly attired. "Good morning," said Kirk.

"Hi," said this visitor, with a sidelong glance, and proceeded down to the kitchen.

Seeking out his wife in their bedroom, where early Medici prints of Da Vinci's Jesus and Mary were hung above the fireplace, Kirk inquired, "Who is that person I met on the stair?"

Annette explained, a trifle uneasily, that the young woman, sister to the house's current unwed mother, had plied the world's oldest profession in Grand Rapids. Her apartment had been invaded by a narcotics pusher who had assumed permanent possession of the quarters and the girl. A notorious desperado, under indictment for murder, the pusher habitually went belted about with guns and knives. As her condition of servitude had worsened, the would-be go-go girl had determined to go.

But she had left in the city cherished possessions, especially her television set. The indomitable Annette resolved to obtain these for her guest. She proposed to quondam Sergeant Kirk that they and allies should raid her Grand Rapids apartment. This dashing act considerably appealed to Kirk, but he suggested that the police be invited to participate, too, arriving in armored cars. Eventually the goods and chattels were obtained by stealth.

Yet their one-eyed guest did not linger for more than a fortnight. "It's too richy here," she pronounced, longing for the less genteel fleshpots of the city. They gathered from the one-eyed girl's sister that august architecture was a protection against marauders from Grand Rapids. Annette had inquired whether acquaintances of the sisters — their mother having been a zealous member of the Outlaws motorcycle gang — might come to Piety Hill uninvited.

"Naw," said the unwed mother, "they'd be scared."

Piety Hill, with its antique furniture, its statuary, paintings, and old engravings, doubtless looked richy to girls from desperate slums. Yet appearances deceive: money always was wanting, much as it was wanting in Scottish and English country houses, or in Italian *palazzi*, Kirk's income being irregular. He never had owned a share of stock, a bond, or other such intangibles. Like the grasshoppers that perish, the Kirks took small thought of the morrow. From kith and kin they had inherited obligations and good example merely. What matter? Sometimes people would ask the laird of Piety Hill, taking him to be prudent and prosperous, how might they best invest their money during a decade of inflation. "Spend it," Kirk would say. "Spend it on schooling your children, on your house, on hospitality, on good causes." He knew well enough that should nobody lay away capital, the national economy would decline; but there was no danger of such profligacy; one could rely upon most people's frugality or avarice.

The wave of the unwed presently was succeeded by a wave of Asiatic guests. After the fall of Saigon came the Vietnamese. Captain An and his ten dependents were lodged for three years in a house next to Kirk's library before settling in southern California. Little energetic Captain An had commanded a strong force of Vietnamese soldiery cooperating with the American Special Forces, a risky undertaking; he had been surrounded nightly by a considerable bodyguard.

"You commanded so many, and yet were a captain?" Kirk inquired. "Where were your superior officers?"

"In Saigon," said An, without comment.

The bright and pleasing Vietnamese children performed admirably in the local schools, and as they grew older were graduated from colleges. They were succeeded by a Chinese-Vietnamese family, boat people who had found their way to Mecosta.

Then there came the wave of Abyssinian guests, fugitive from Marxist tyranny. Some young ones, residing at Piety Hill for years, were put to school by the Kirks. These were the children of a leading writer in Addis Ababa, once a cabinet minister then imprisoned, later heroically remaining in his country because of his leadership in the Ethiopian Church. One Ethiopian, or Tigrean, with the fuzziest hair imaginable, had been sent under compulsion to Moscow, there to be trained as a Communist indoctrinator. Rescued by Amnesty International at Nicosia on his return flight, this Johannes Gebrehiwot presently had found himself installed without occupation, a stateless person, in the house of an old lady at Tucson. Friends gave him the Kirk name and address; he was transported to Piety Hill for residence and counsel; eventually employment was found for him, and then he enrolled in college. Later he shifted to California, and, being industrious and clever, soon acquired two houses there.

Who didn't turn up at Piety Hill, scholars and waifs, flotsam and jetsam of the twentieth century's disorders, for short stays or long? There were Scots, American Indians, Italians, Swiss, poets, wayward young folk, professors deprived of academic posts, students of International College tutored by Kirk, musicians, painters (one of them an Indonesian who had come by way of the West Indies and Texas), folk of three or four colors. The place seemed rather like Samuel Johnson's house in Gough Square, where the garret had been inhabited by Scots laboring away at the Dictionary, as well as pensioners who otherwise might have begged on the street.

Annette spent endless hours counselling and consoling the unfortunate and the perplexed. An ancient Indian, Frank Chickum, who had travelled with Barnum and Bailey, turned up now and again, drawing pictures of animals for the Kirk daughters; he seemed to have climbed out of the property basket of *The Fantasticks*. The Kirks called him the Death Angel, for Annette's mother had died promptly after his first call at Piety Hill, and her father after his second; they grew uneasy about feeding him. He claimed to be a hundred years old, which was false; he claimed to have been a soldier during the

First World War, which was true. He had been surprised to find that Belgians "spoke our Indian language" — that is, a French patois. At one time the undersheriff was about to arrest him or to expel him from the village, but he declared that he was a guest of the Kirks (having slept in the woodshed, without Kirk's knowledge), and that connection secured him against molestation by the undersheriff. Indeed, Piety Hill had become a "safe house." Incidentally, Chickum, or the sinister side of him, became a character later in Kirk's short story "The Princess of All Lands."

The Kirks' stolid housekeeper, Mae Cole, one of Mecosta's Old Settler community, with her Indian carriage and backwoods lore, maintained some physical order in that lively house. More than one person remarked that Piety Hill seemed like the house of the Addams Family, in Charles Addams's *New Yorker* cartoons.

Kirk bought a little house immediately adjacent to Piety Hill for his parents and moved them down from their own haunted house at Baldwin. Annette's father, a widower, came from Long Island to Mecosta, lent Kirk a hand, and settled down, remarried, near Kirk's library. Old Aunt Fay lived on into her nineties in her cabin beside the big house.

It was not surprising that some of the villagers of Mecosta looked with awe or trepidation upon the cosmopolitan or outlandish crew at the Kirks' place. Russell's and Annette's grand-scale Hallowe'en celebrations, with Gregorian chant played at slow speed from on high, and tapes or records of howling wolves and shrieking cats, and costumed capers on the leaf-strewn lawn to trick two hundred trick-or-treaters, understandably became the talk of the town, and a dreadful joy to little people.

Rumors of the uncanny doings at Piety Hill seemed to have worked upon the mind of a pretty young matron, new to Mecosta, who came to Annette for advice about educational films. This caller was a born-again Fundamentalist, active in a recently founded Accelerated Christian Education school erected in the most desolate township of Mecosta County. As she and Annette conversed, the young woman noticed some object in the drawing room — a carved copy of a Catalonian retablo, perhaps, or a Jerusalem Bible. "Oh, you're Catholics!" she exclaimed. "I'm so glad!"

"Why are you glad of that?" Annette asked, thinking of her visitor's evangelical zeal.

[349]

"Because they told me downtown that you're all pagans in this house, and sacrifice living cats."

If the Kirks sacrificed, it was to no Dark God. There were victims aplenty at Piety Hill, true — the victims of Marxist regimes in Europe, Asia, and Africa, to whom the Kirks had given shelter.

Kirk contrived stealthily to extricate from Poland, after the declaration of martial law in 1981, Professor Rett Ludwikowski, author of several learned books, together with his beautiful wife and their children. (In this they were much helped by Robert Reilly, of USIA, and an American consul of Filipino stock.) The Ludwikowskis were lodged for two years next door to the Kirk library; then Dr. Ludwikowski obtained a good post at Catholic University.

Later there came to the Kirks, from Zagreb, a high official of the People's Republic of Croatia, with wife and son, the man to study with Kirk, to write a book about the failure of the Yugoslav economy and political structure, and to achieve political sanctuary in the United States. Ivan Pongracic became a professor of economics at a Wesleyan university.

At one time or another there appeared at Piety Hill a Bolivian senator; Hindu gentlefolk from India; a divorced young woman, complete with string bikini, from Brazil; a pair of female dwarfs, professional ghostwriters, who cooked messes of spaghetti in the Old House's kitchen and prevailed upon Kirk to inscribe to them a copy of one of his books that they had purloined from a public library; Lord knows who else. Rather like Walter Scott at Abbotsford — although Kirk's works were not so readily sold as the Waverley Novels had been — Kirk sometimes stood in peril of being eaten out of house and land. To restore Piety Hill, it had been found necessary to sell property he had acquired in his celibate years: their little ancient house in Pittenweem, his Plymouth birthplace, their Lake Mecosta cottage, other holdings. But the Vergilian motto on the Kirk armorial bearings above the arched entrance to Piety Hill runs *adjuvante Deo* — completed, "God helping, work prospers."

Clinton Wallace, Hobo in Residence

Of all the denizens of Piety Hill, the most pathetic, gigantic, irritating, and (after his fashion) lovable was a man who had spent most of his life in prisons or tramping the roads. Unwitting, he was to stand as a model for the reluctant hero in Kirk's best-known tale, "There's a Long, Long Trail a-Winding." He lived with the Kirks for six years and then was buried in their family plot; he deserves a section of this chapter to himself.

On a Sunday morning in 1966, Annette, coming out of the rural church of Saint Michael, saw a tall and massive man at the door of the rectory. "Can you spare a dollar for a bum?" he was asking the priest. The beggar did not look indigent: he was handsome in a Viking way, with thick white hair well brushed, and better dressed than most of the parishioners. Having obtained his dollar, the man began to trudge along the road to Mecosta. The neighbor with whom Annette had ridden that morning took this pedestrian for somebody temporarily lacking a car; he gave him a ride.

Except for a wild blue eye and the lack of some teeth, the man was most presentable. He spoke with a down-East accent. Having informed Annette and the driver that he was a bum, he asked to be let off in Mecosta to beg a meal at a cafe. As they drove on, they saw him emerging from the restaurant, rejected.

A few minutes later, Annette burst upon Russell, who lay abed — being too frequently given to indolence on the Sabbath, the charge brought against his Pilgrim ancestor Abraham Pierce — and shouted, "Russell, do you want to meet a bum? Can I ask him in for lunch?"

While her husband arose, Annette dashed down the stair and out the front door. Already the huge figure of the tramp was a distance down the road, plodding through the snow. "Sir, sir!" she called. "Do you want to have lunch with us?" He accepted the invitation; later he would tell the Kirks that this had been the first such invitation he had received in all his life. His benefactress had worn a coat of many colors and an Auersperg hat; he told her that she looked like something from the film *Dr. Zhivago*.

Kirk arrived downstairs to find Clinton Wallace already seated at the kitchen table with Annette and great-aunt Norma. He was reciting poetry: Gray's "Elegy in a Country Churchyard," quatrains from the *Rubaiyat,* and the lines by "A Person of No Quality":

Seven wealthy towns contend for Homer dead
Through which the living Homer begged his bread.

For decades he had read in public libraries and Christian Science reading rooms, and the one quality upon which he prided himself was his memory: he was at once blessed and cursed by the power of total recall. Born in an island off the coast of Maine, he had run away from a brutal father when he was fifteen or sixteen, and ever since had been a homeless wanderer. Now, in the dead of winter, he was tramping toward the Pacific coast, for no reason in particular; he kept to the country roads, dreading the violence of the cities. The man was immaculately clean, dressed in very decent wash-and-wear clothing, and innocent of luggage. (He carried his toilet articles in a coat pocket.) Having fed him, they drove him some miles on his way and gave him two dollars and a paperback copy of Kirk's *Old House of Fear*.

He was back a fortnight later, snow having blocked the passes of the Rockies. This time Annette told him that when next he should come, he could be lodged in their lake cabin and given employment. "We'll never see Clinton again," Kirk murmured to her as Clinton departed the second time, "what with your having menaced him with work." Some four years elapsed; then both the Kirks and Aunt Norma received handsome Christmas cards from Clinton. He was lodged in Graterford prison, in Pennsylvania; he thanked his hosts for their kindness and inquired after their well-being. Kirk entered into correspondence. It was ascertained that Wallace might be released on parole, had he a sponsor. Through the local parole officer, the Kirks learned what they needed to know about this unusual being. He had been sentenced first for robbing a church poor box, and later for attempting to escape from prison. Although his prison record was long, he never had been charged with any serious felony: no violence, no armed robbery, no offenses against women or children. The Kirks got him out, brought him to Piety Hill, commenced to pay him a salary — which he spent chiefly upon presents for the Kirk children and lottery tickets.

Although incredibly strong, Clinton endeavored to avoid physical labor. He did enjoy setting the table and pouring the wine; Kirk dubbed him his burglar-butler. He was useful in minding the little daughters, but spoilt them, to the best of his ability, by indulgence and servility. He was an innocent, a child himself, despite all his hard experience of the world: he laughed immoderately at movie cartoons, was ecstatically happy at birthday parties, and had the temperament of a boy of fourteen. A prison psychiatrist had classified Clinton as "dull normal," but he was neither. He read and memorized not only good poetry but some serious prose. There had been some utilitarian advantage in this talent: it had made him a successful panhandler, a second-hand Vachel Lindsay or W. H. Davies.

Despite his size, strength, Viking head, and roving life, he was timid — though he had fought professional pugilists at county fairs (invariably being beaten) for the sake of five or ten dollars. His stentorian power of lung, employed in necessity, had aided him in the prison hells. The worst thing about prison life, he observed, was the foul language: "every other word a curse." He detested the jail-house lawyers, with their never-ending discourses on the Miranda and Escobedo cases: "There's no good talk in prisons any longer." Capital punishment he vigorously approved. "They're beasts who ought to be put out of their misery," he said of the more evil prisoners; they endangered the non-violent inmates and the guards. Prison cells had been made too luxurious, with television sets and carpets; being sentenced to a term had become small deterrent to many habitual criminals.

For truancy from school, he had been first flung into jail about the age of fourteen — into a cell with old offenders. He could quote a wealth of prisoners' doggerel besides Shakespeare, Eliot, and Frost. Haunted by memories, he slept badly. Once he had shared a cell with a murderer who had cut off his wife's head; Clinton had lain awake o'nights, feeling his neck to make sure his own head still was on. Pilfering church poor boxes, in hard necessity, was the offense for which he had usually been sentenced; he knew those acts to have been sacrilege. Clinton was a Catholic, though not in communion, for he could not bring himself to enter the confession box.

Unschooled and unmachined, Clinton was unemployable by anyone except the Kirks. A hobo's life was degrading, he observed: "You have to humble yourself." He was awkward as a good-natured bear, breaking everything, and even burning down the house — an event described below. "Clinton is a baby," tiny Felicia Kirk said of him, judiciously: "You have to tell him to mind."

He was conservative in his social views. "Nobody ever was reformed by prison," the convict instructed the Kirks. "You have to begin by saying, 'I know I did wrong,' and take responsibility." He derided the idea that criminals are victims of social circumstance.

[353]

There remained to him a sense of humor and a child's endowment of wonder. Kirk asked him what he would do, were he to win a million dollars in the state lottery. "Why, Russell, I'd just sit back and take it easy." He was doing that already at Piety Hill.

Clinton was highly willing to entertain at table by his recitations and anecdotes. At the last dinner-party of the Kirks in which he participated, he burst into one quatrain of Omar that he never before had quoted:

> Why, if the Soul can fling the Dust aside,
> And naked on the Air of Heaven ride,
>   Were't not a Shame — were't not a Shame for him
> In this clay carcass crippled to abide?

Those lines Kirk had quoted at the end of "A Long, Long Trail a-Winding," in which Frank Sarsfield (really Clinton Wallace) had died in a snowdrift. Just one year after that story was written, and a week after Clinton had recited that quatrain at the party, the Kirks' telephone rang in the wee hours: Clinton Wallace had fallen dead in a snowdrift. He had been walking home after seeing the film *Across the Great Divide*.

A monsignor gave him a funeral, and Clinton was interred beside Annette's parents in Saint Michael's cemetery. Gracia Virgo, the Kirks' young friend, long resident at Piety Hill, dreamed that she saw Clinton turning over in his open grave. And to Kirk, not long later, came a dream still stranger. The doorbell rang: Kirk answered it. There stood Clinton, his eyes closed. Although always he had been scrupulously clean, now he was all bespattered with earth. The giant collapsed into Kirk's arms, and Kirk woke. In spirit, was that wanderer, that huge child, drawn back to the only permanence he had known, the Last Homely House?

Clinton had been a ghost-seer, or ghost-hearer, at Piety Hill. Several times he had heard the Crying Baby; more than once a voice in his bedroom, at dawn, had moaned "Agnes" or (he thought later) "Amos"; after the Old House burned, he still had heard the Crying Baby, a voice outside his second-story new bedroom, coming from the ground where formerly the old lying-in room (for pregnant women) had been. (An American-German baroness and a Polish cook had encountered such alarming phenomena in the Old House room where Clinton had slept, so his reports enjoyed substantiation.) With such precedent, what wonder if an impulse moved the poor soul to return?

Ash Wednesday: The Death of the Old House

As history runs in Mecosta County, the bracketed house built by Amos Johnson was venerably ancient, as if it had been Traquair or Cawdor in Scotland. No house endures forever. "Old houses have stood long enough if they stand until they fall with honor," says Bradwardine, in *Waverley*.

In February 1975, Kirk was visiting professor at Olivet College. On Ash Wednesday, he attended a Congregational service early in the morning at the college chapel, and in the afternoon he read Eliot's *Ash Wednesday*, in part, to his students, and played a record of Eliot reading that mysterious poem himself. That night he was roused from bed by the news that his house, a hundred miles to the north, was burning; and the Old House already was beyond saving.

There had been forewarnings. About Christmas, in 1973, a smouldering fire had occurred at the base of the Old House's chimney; it had been put out and the chimney's footing repaired. At Christmastide 1974, a woodcutter, Archie Meyers, had told the Kirks sadly how his own stone house had been burnt the previous day by the collapse of the sand-brick chimney: and he had enjoined the Kirks to take inventory of their furnishings.

In the dining room of the Old House was a handsome mantelpiece, obtained by Kirk from Bridgend House, in Perth, where John Ruskin had spent summers in his boyhood. This was a chimneypiece in the style of Robert Adam, the architectural genius from Kirkcaldy, ornamented with Grecian figurines. (Bridgend House had been demolished some years earlier; Kirk had stored the chimneypiece at Kellie Castle until the Kirks embellished the interiors of the Old House.) A fire was kept blazing there every winter day, so hot that the brick back of the fireplace warmed the kitchen too, and Annette had her misgivings, pooh-poohed by her husband, about safety.

On leaving for Olivet College, Kirk had instructed Clinton Wallace to keep the fire going overnight — meaning that the embers should be banked so that a blaze might be rekindled easily in the morning. But Clinton resented laborious instructions of that sort. On Ash Wednesday evening, he left a great fire blazing in the dining room; Annette objected. "Russell told me to keep the fire going," Clinton growled — and marched off to bed.

About midnight, Clinton heard a great crash in the old House, and went into the dining room, which was filling with smoke. He opened windows to clear the room, so creating a fatal draught.

The upper portion of the old sand-brick chimney had fallen into the attic. Flames soon burst out. Annette, upstairs in the New House, mysteriously sensed that something or other was wrong. She flung open the door at the head of the stair — and saw Clinton entering the New House by the sliding door. "Fire, fire!" Clinton was shouting.

"Close that door, Clinton!" Annette commanded — an action that saved the New House from destruction. Gracia Virgo, Annette's confidante, hurried the three little daughters next door to Aunt Fay's cabin; the bewildered Clinton was left there too. Annette, barefoot, dashed through the snow to rouse one of Kirk's assistants, Dennis Flynn, who slept upstairs in the Old House. He was a deep sleeper: only by throwing snowballs repeatedly at his window could Annette rouse him. Choking in the thick smoke, Dennis tumbled down the stair and burst out the front door, in the nick of time.

There was trouble getting through a call to the volunteer fire company, but eventually three or four crews from Mecosta and neighboring villages responded, and fought to save Piety Hill. One fireman, in an asbestos suit, plunged like a salamander into the heart of the house, but could make no headway against the flames. The white-pine house was a tinderbox, and it was a bitter night, with a high wind blowing against the house.

Within a few hours everything had vanished; not one stick of furniture was rescued; the keepsakes of five generations perished. The poke of gold dust that Isaac Pierce had brought from California was melted, as were several antique gold watches in the same chest; the fierce wind deposited in the school yard, down the hill, little golden nuggets from that wild smelting. The organ was consumed, and a framed Piranese. The Sunderland wall plaque, with its great staring eye and the legend "Thou God seest me" entered into eternity, and much else besides. Masses of ancestral papers were consumed, and all the silver and china were lost, and an ivory triptych, and rare prints, and cases of family books. Kirk was grieved especially by the loss of Amos

Johnson's majestic walnut bed, on the high head of which ghostly knocks had been heard over the generations. No scrap of anything survived, except for a tiny saucer with a design of roses upon it.

Although its tall brick face was grimed with smoke, the New House stood almost intact; but deprived of its parent Old House, that huge wing was a grotesque cube. Two trees were consumed, and some shrubbery, but the splendid old maples facing the streets endured only scorching that could be remedied with a pruning saw. Kirk looked upon this ruin when he arrived home in the morning. It was well for him that he had read the Stoics over and over.

Next day a schoolmate said to little Cecilia Kirk, condolingly, "I'm sorry to hear that your house burned down." Cecilia, too, was stoical: "That's all right: we have another one."

The local Jehovah's Witnesses declared that the house had been burnt by the demons (invisible ones, that is) who inhabited it. In photographs of the burning taken by neighbors, there appeared to be figures at some of the windows, amidst billowing smoke — even faces. The face most distinguishable seemed to be that of Russell Kirk, in the bay window of the Spanish Room, where he had written most of his books — but Kirk had been a hundred miles distant on the night of the fire. What was this shade? In spirit, Kirk was bound up with the Old House beyond time.

Innocent Smith, in Chesterton's romance *Manalive,* says that he would not be very surprised to find in Heaven the lamp post and the green gate of his own dear house. Heaven is a state, Father Martin D'Arcy had told the Kirks, in which all the good things of one's temporal life are eternally present, whenever one desires them. If that be so, Annette and Russell and their daughters shall have the Old House always.

In the New House, a good many old pieces and things acquired by Kirk on his travels were untouched by the fire. The huge family portraits providentially lay in a wing of Kirk's library, down Franklin Street, awaiting repair of their frames. Some articles of antique furniture, resembling those lost or even identical with them, might be bought in second-hand shops and restored. Other old prints in Kirk's collection might be framed — though the complete series of Rowlandson's caricatures for *Dr. Syntax,* which had hung on a wall of the front parlor of the Old House, seemed irreplaceable. In short, it was just possible to turn the clock back.

Gradually a new-old Piety Hill took form. Their friend James Nachtegall, a Grand Rapids architect, drew up designs for an Italianate house more striking than the old one had been. Once Michigan had been rich in Italianate houses; doubtless the restored Piety Hill would be the last ever constructed in that archaic but very practical style.

At the back of the New House, a long dining room was added, with a half-gambrel ceiling made of white-ash seats and backs of pews, obtained from the demolished old church of St. Michael. The huge door-frame for this new room was taken from the demolished old courthouse at Big Rapids: it had been the doorway to Judge Amos Johnson's courtroom there.

As for the front, there was created a fine entrance hall panelled to the ceiling with carved French walnut that once had adorned the interiors of the elevators of the Conrad Hilton Hotel in Chicago, before elevator boys were abolished. This hall and much else were created by John Mulcahy, once a building inspector in Harlem, who with his wife and children had been enticed by Annette, years before, to shift to more tranquil Mecosta.

Many other architectural features, snatched from the jaws of the urban renewers of western Michigan, were incorporated in the fabric, interior or exterior. There was the gigantic mirror with carved and gilded frame, extending from floor to ceiling, installed in the drawing room: it had been affixed to a wall, originally, in a Grand Rapids grand hotel of bygone years, the Cody House, but Annette had chanced upon it in a Chinese restaurant. Lions and griffins, stone or iron, these too from demolished buildings, were pressed into service to adorn the exterior. There was constructed a new grand bedroom, the Gothick Room, wainscoted and otherwise embellished with handsome carved materials from vanished churches.

Above the limestone arch of the new main entrance was set a red sandstone inscription taken from some vanished Grand Rapids mansion of a hundred years gone. *Adjuvante deo labor proficit,* Vergil still instructs us. True at the Old House, and to be true at the New. And, astounding coincidence — if indeed what people call coincidence is merely happenstance — this square inscribed stone, found in a Mecosta County junkyard, bore above its legend the coat of arms of one sept of the Scottish Kirks.

A ninety-foot crane carried up to the summit of the restored house a massive cupola or bell-cote from the demolished hospice of the Little Sisters of the Poor, in Grand Rapids — this too discovered in a wreckers' yard. Children were let out of the Mecosta school to behold the elevation of the cupola, a man aboard it, to the roof platform.

More rooms were contrived on the top floor, previously unfinished, and on the basement floor. After interruption by the Great Fire, the bustling life of Piety Hill returned; more guests poured in. Visitors new to the place would say to Kirk, "This is a very old house, isn't it?" He would reply, "That depends upon your standards; of course there are many newer houses. The oldest block of this house goes back to 1970." The Kirks' restoration was more successful than those of the Stuarts or of the Bourbons had been. Burke had written that an enduring society must be a blending of the old with the new; the Kirks had accomplished just that with their house.

When the restoration was virtually complete, Kirk found himself fifty-nine years old, and the work had left him deeply in debt. But Piety Hill was more than an ornament to the county: it was a house of many functions, like Rivendell "a place of learning, of merriment and quiet." There, emulating Elrond, Kirk would employ his ring of power, such as it was, for "understanding, making, and healing, to preserve all things unstained." What Elrond lacked at Rivendell, Kirk had at Piety Hill: a wife with her own magic, a lovely doctor of souls. Without that magic, she might have perished some months after the Great Fire.

The Kidnapping of Annette

During Clinton's six years at Piety Hill, occasionally he still ventured forth from that safe house — to the Upper Peninsula, Wisconsin, and Minnesota, chiefly, keeping to the country roads and the villages — but he reported that a hobo's life had become precarious. He had found himself riding with narcotics peddlers, bank robbers, madmen. He was some sixty years old, but his size and formidable face must have afforded considerable protection. There was no telling what one might encounter in these times, this Good Thief declared: "People's morals have gone to pieces." Now and again it passed through Clinton's mind that he might end not in St. Michael's cemetery but in some unmarked swamp grave. The aura of Kirk's ring of power did not extend far beyond the grounds of Piety Hill, when personal safety was in question. And so Annette discovered.

The Conservative Beauty was driving alone, hurrying north from Lansing, where she had participated in a meeting of Michigan's Bicentennial Commission. Kirk was away at Hillsdale College, and she disliked leaving the four daughters for long, even though there were Piety Hill inmates to watch over them. It was a cold October day, and she was on a highway not much travelled.

At a stoplight in a village along that road, Annette noticed a young girl hitchhiking. She wore, this seeming sixteen-year-old, a faded sweatshirt and jeans; she had no coat and no suitcase. Probably this was an artless runaway, Annette thought. Should she pick her up and help her? She had taken in several runaway girls. One more opportunity, one more burden. Annette decided to leave her decision to providence. Turning the corner, she drove round the block. If the girl should still be there when she came full cycle to the stoplight, she would take her in.

There she was still, looking confused. Annette opened the door and beckoned her in. They sped northward.

At close range, Annette could see that the girl was two or three years older than she had fancied: chunky, not ugly, her face swarthy and rather hard.

"Mind my smokin'?" the girl asked. She spoke with something of a Southern poor-white intonation and accent.

"Have you had anything to eat?" Annette inquired. The girl nodded, drawing on her cigarette. "You ought to have a coat in this weather," Annette continued.

"I travel light. I'm comin' north from Florida; I'm going to Pompey Eye, where my daddy lives. My brother beat up my daddy, an' I'm goin' to settle it."

"I don't know where Pompey Eye is," Annette told her, "but I'll take you as far as I can. I've got to get home to my babies." Already Annette suspected that she shouldn't take this girl home with her.

The girl's face softened a trifle. "I never had no babies. I got married when I was thirteen, but they put seven slugs in my husband's head the next day, so I never had no chance to have no babies. You got a husband? What's he do?"

Annette thought it well to be vague. "He teaches." That occupation being outside her world, the girl made no comment. She had not given her name, and Annette did not offer her own.

Tossing away her cigarette butt, the girl drew a big bottle of glue from a pocket, removed the cap, and sniffed it deeply. "My daddy, he tol' me not to use more'n one o' these a week." Annette, a very speedy driver, kept her eyes on the road.

"You're pretty," the girl observed dispassionately. "You look like Loretta Lynn."

"Do you like Loretta Lynn?" — this asked cautiously.

"She's O.K." The girl took another deep whiff of glue.

"You're pretty too," Annette offered. She must establish some sort of rapport with this stray. "Why, you could fix your hair like mine." She offered detailed suggestions. It wouldn't be long, she trusted, before the junction for Pompey Eye — wherever or whatever that might be — should come up.

And a few minutes later, there appeared a highway sign pointing west: "Pompeii." "Here we are," Annette announced, her spirits reviving. "You can get another ride here: I must get home to those babies of mine."

"Yeah," the girl drawled, emphatically, "but I'm goin' to Pompey Eye."

She pulled up her sweat-shirt, ostentatiously. Thrust into her jeans, settled in her groin, was an efficient-looking pistol. She looked hard at Annette.

"I suppose I can take you to Pompey Eye." Having taught dramatics, Annette could control her voice and her face. She swung the station wagon left, into the Pompeii road.

"What are you doing with the gun?" Annette asked, so quietly as she could.

"I'm takin' it to my daddy," the girl told her, in her slurring drawl. The glue-sniffing seemed to be affecting her. "It's my birthday present to him. My daddy's an Indian. He likes to shoot up things."

"Why, I'm part Indian too." Annette knew that she must not lose what frail camaraderie she had established with this passenger. "My great-grandmother was an Indian."

A truck with two men in it whizzed past them. "Men!" the girl snarled. "I hate men. If you hadn't of picked me up, I might of got in that there truck with them two. You know what they'd of done to me then?" She proceeded to describe in detail what she would have experienced, sparing no obscenity.

Annette thought it prudent not to dissent from this discourse on the iniquities of the opposite sex. She even added some strictures of her own. The girl seemed to warm toward her a little.

"I shot a man day before yesterday," the girl remarked, casually enough. "Got a ride in his truck, an' he started pawin' me, an' he wouldn't stop, so I pulled this here gun an' shot him in the leg."

Annette raised her eyebrows in sympathetic interest.

"'You shot me!' he says.

"'Yeah,' I says. 'Git out!' I make him git out o' the cab — it's dark — an' then I drive round the block. When I come back, he's still sittin' there.

"'Git back in an' drive!' I tell him.

"'But I'm bleedin',' he says to me.

"'You kin still drive.' So I make him drive me to the edge o' the next big town, an' then I jump out an' run for it. Men!"

Annette thought it prudent to change the subject. The girl's eyes were glazed now from her glue-sniffing. "Does your mother live in Pompey Eye, too?"

"Naw, she's livin' in Lansing with ten niggers an' a wetback. I stopped by to see her, but she called me bad names. So I shot her in the backside, las' night."

Annette wondered to herself whether the mother remained in the land of the living. "What did your mother say to that?"

"She says, 'Daughter, I'm sorry!' She was sorry, all right."

How much of this mad narration was invention, how much truth? Annette could not tell. It was fortunate for her in this plight that an unending flow of talk came to her naturally. She groped for some bond of sympathy with this girl. "You poor kid!" She put her right arm round the girl's shoulder. "You've had a hard time."

The road to Pompeii, so little travelled, seemed interminable. Probing in her talk, Annette discovered that both she and her passenger had been born under the sign of Taurus: she made much of that link. Also she found that the girl approved of babies, and so she talked much of her little daughters. The girl continued to sniff her glue bottle. Neither of them mentioned the gun; there was no need to.

At last they reached Pompeii, a half-derelict hamlet with a grocery store and a gas station that was closed. Soon this trial would be over! "Where can I let you off? Does your daddy live on the main street?"

"Naw, he lives a piece out in the woods." The girl stared at her, and gestured. "Keep goin'."

They took a dirt road through desolate country, turning twice. This is how I'm going to end, Annette thought. For the first time in her life, she despaired. This girl will take the car, and never let me return. Would they kill her or keep her for ransom?

On either side of the narrow road lay bleak scrub, trees and bushes leafless. Rain hadn't fallen here for a long while: everything was parched and dusty. Presently the scrub gave way to swamp on either side of the track. Big birds flapped in front of the car. Sullenly brooding, the girl sat silent beside her, nearly out of this world.

In the course of that last ghastly stretch, perhaps for fifteen minutes, Annette relived her life in her mind's eye, as she had read that dying folk do. She thought most acutely of how she was expected at home already, with her little girls. There came to her imagination flash upon flash of vivid memory: marrying Russell, happiness with the babies, books in their library unread, rambles in Scotland . . . "Life is wasted on the young," she thought. Where had she read that? How much more she could have done in three decades! In her terror, she found herself suffused with an intense awareness of the beauty of life. There came to her scenes from Thornton Wilder's *Our Town*. It occurred to her that the little false-fronted village of Mecosta was Our Town. Now she wouldn't even be buried at St. Michael's, in an Our Town graveyard.

"I wan' you to meet my daddy," the girl was saying.

Annette suppressed a shiver: this was like being invited to meet Grendel's mother. Was she to be daddy's birthday present, along with the gut-gun? Daddy liked to shoot up things.

"Yes, that would be nice — someday," Annette forced herself to reply. It came to her that this girl, murderous and sentimental, had her being in a fanciful world of television soap operas and thrillers, evanescent shadows, flickering and maudlin and bloody, to be snapped off upon impulse.

"You and I have a lot in common," Annette went on, intensely. "We're both Indians. We're both born under Taurus. You love babies and I love babies."

The girl nodded dreamily. Achingly aware of the gut-gun, Annette sensed that her companion had not forgotten it either. An apt mimic, Annette fell half-unconsciously into the girl's own poor-white speech, eliding and slurred, patched with shallow TV clichés. "My daddy's gonna like you."

And then they arrived at the back of beyond, the end of this sinister ride. A kind of lean-to hovel, more like hogan than house, stood in an old clearing. It was unpainted and covered with tarpaper. "There it is!" the girl cried excitedly, waking from her torpor. No smoke rose from the hut.

The driveway, if it could be called that, was overgrown. No car was to be seen. The road was so narrow that the station wagon could not be swung easily round in it. Between hovel and road stood a cover of thin young leafless poplars. Nowhere was animate life discernible.

There came no sound, no movement, when Annette stopped the car. This place was dead, dead, dead. "Oh, fine: you're home now," Annette contrived to say.

"You gotta come in an' meet my daddy," the girl commanded her.

"They'll be so glad to see you," Annette babbled, "on your daddy's birthday. I'd love to come in — but you know, my babies. Why, they'll be cryin' an' cryin' for me!" She was pleading in the very richest soap-opera tones: one couldn't possibly overdo the act with this psychotic girl, this prisoner in Plato's cave where insubstantial shadows were taken for reality. "Now you love babies an' I love babies — you know that!"

The girl had slid halfway out of the car. "My daddy's gonna like you," she said.

"I gotta git home to them babies," Annette implored, wide-eyed. "I'll see you an' your daddy next time, I promise."

Out of the car now, the girl stared, shook her head, glanced toward the shack. Annette, reaching over, slammed shut the right-hand door of the car. The girl swayed where she stood. Annette gunned the motor. Would the girl draw her gut-gun and fire? She was one of Tolkien's trolls, masters of the desolation that hemmed in Rivendell.

Everything blurred. Sure of nothing, Annette had no time for the rearview mirror. Was the girl stumbling toward the tarpaper shack? Go, go, go!

Backing and cramping the wheel, Annette frantically turned the station wagon around, stepped on the accelerator, and bounced down the empty dirt road, through swamp, through scrub, making for Pompeii. No shot came.

Behind Annette lay emptiness, the horror of the void. That lean-to cabin may have been abandoned altogether — no daddy, no brother. In her stumbling ferocious glue dream, that girl might have confounded present with past. She had herself been little more than a walking and talking phantom, a deadly negation that could pull a trigger.

Speeding northward toward Mecosta, Annette felt energy and reality flow back into her. Against odds, she had been given renewed opportunity to know the wonder of life. With every day that passes, other women perish in some such fashion. Kirk formed his short story "The Princess of All Lands" out of Annette's misadventure and escape.

It was well to be lodged in the safe house of Piety Hill; yet even to such a sanctuary came visions of terror. Sharon Wright, the daughters' baby-sitter, dreamed such a dream. She heard something at one of Piety Hill's doors; she opened that door a crack, in her dream. Two ghastly men began to force their way in. At Sharon's cry, Clinton Wallace, so huge, hurried to the door from his bedroom. On seeing the intruders, he scuttled back and locked himself in. Such was the dream.

Annette having been told of this nightmare, next day she and Sharon recounted it to Clinton. "If anything like that should really happen, Clinton," Annette said, "you'd help us, wouldn't you?"

"I don't know what I could do, Annette," responded the titular burglar-butler. "There are so many violent people on the roads today."

"But Clinton, you're so big and strong!"

"They might be armed, Annette."

"At least you could shout at them, Clinton, with your great big voice. Really, wouldn't you help us?"

"Well, I suppose I could try. But I don't know what I could do about it."

Nevertheless, this Cowardly Lion turned out once to be good at need. There came to a door of Piety Hill, Clinton responding to a knock, an impossibly tall young man. Later it was learned that this person at one time had been president of the student body at a Michigan college; latterly he had been making opium pipes, in company with other youthful dropouts, at an isolated house down the creek. Few would have cared to tangle with him. Doubtless Piety Hill looked richy to him; the great thing was to gain admittance.

Summoned by this brigand's sharp knock, massive Clinton flung open the door. Being little more than six feet six inches tall, Clinton was overshadowed by the intruder; but Wallace's tremendous depth of chest and burliness of frame were impressive. His splendid head, Viking nose, strong chin, and furtive light-blue eyes gave him the look of a sea rover.

"Yes?" Clinton bellowed, looking the caller up and down. No one could recognize criminal types more swiftly and accurately than could Clinton Wallace.

"I . . . I heard you rent rooms here," the pipe-maker stammered, intimidated.

"No!" the Viking guardian thundered. He slammed the door in this intruder's face.

Much taken aback, the brigand abandoned this unpromising attempt upon Piety Hill, went downtown, and stuck up the branch bank instead.

In Kirk's story "A Long, Long Trail a-Winding," the sober, amusing, and pathetic hobo giant turns out to be still better at need. Clinton Wallace declared himself to be "non-violent" — but Kirk suspected that he had made himself so only through a prudent prolonged repression of impulses; he never had resisted arrest, even though sometimes arrested without just cause. The meek shall inherit the earth, we have been told. Clinton Wallace inherited merely seven feet of it.

Clinton's closing years had been sufficiently happy. He had poured the wine for Justice Mary Coleman of Michigan's Supreme Court, and for many another distinguished guest at Piety Hill, too; and, sitting at table with them, had regaled the company with anecdotes and recitations of verse. Some folk are invincibly ignorant lifelong; others, fortunate, remain invincibly innocent, as did Clinton.

The Wolf Is Everywhere

Well at the back of the New House, Kirk planted three oak saplings from Sherwood Forest, kindly supplied by the Sheriff of Nottingham — not Robin Hood's adversary, but the current Sheriff, who sent also several Sherwood Forest acorns. The three saplings, intended to grow tall above the old croquet-ground, were named Monica, Cecilia, and Felicia. Later, one of the acorns germinated and arose from the soil by the woodshed; Kirk transplanted it to grow in a line with the saplings, naming it Andrea — who was born after that catastrophic event in the history of Piety Hill, the Great Fire of 1975. At this writing, the four young oaks, like the four young daughters, are strong and graceful.

For two generations, before Kirk bought Piety Hill, the house and grounds had been childless. As the Last Homely House, Piety Hill became the most cheerful of safe houses for small children, with Annette as the most sedulous of young mothers, and the most lovely.

At Mecosta, snowdrifts persist well into April; when the drifts vanish, the lilacs bloom. Like other animals, little children are intoxicated by the coming of spring. On the first warm and bright morning of April 1971, there burst out of the pantry door of the Old House Monica, aged three; Cecilia, aged two; and Felicia, aged eleven months — the latter two in their pyjamas. They commenced to caper and sing.

Monica, emulated enthusiastically by Cecilia, began piling stones on the back steps. "Stones for breakfast!" she shouted. "We're going to have stones for breakfast tonight!" Not to be outdone in fantasy, Cecilia tried to feed pebbles, exclaiming "'Tones for b'ekfas'!," to Felicia — who writhed in an endeavor to escape from her father's clutch and crawl down to the wan grass.

"Hush!" said Monica, "I hear a bird!" Cecilia spied a picturesque insect. Only Kirk's prompt exertions prevented Felicia from devouring pebbles in earnest.

Returning from the post office, Annette reproved Russell for surrendering feebly to the desires of their strong-willed daughters, who might catch cold outside; he protested that their gamboling could not be restrained. Before their marriage, in her famous Letter of Inevitability Annette had declared that any husband of hers ought to be ready to romp with the children. In 1971 she found her Russell, gray hairs (just then coming in) notwithstanding, all too liberally fulfilling her commandment.

In the spring of life, Kirk reflected, nearly everything is wondrous. The fortunate are those who have not lost their sense of wonder: who subsist upon the bread of spirit, laughing at the stones of dullness and hard materialism. It was a good omen that very little girls should be fanciful enough to set out stones for breakfast; that quality might serve them well, long later, in times and circumstances when many folk mistake stones for bread.

The life eternal is determined by what one says and does here and now: so Martin D'Arcy had said. With these three playful daughters, that spring morning, Kirk enjoyed one of those moments in which time and the timeless intersect: a glimpse of immortality. Heaven may be perpetual spring.

Those men and women who fail to perceive timeless moments are the prisoners of time and circumstance. Only by transcending the ravenous ego, and sharing their joy with others, do mortals come to know their true enduring selves, and to put on immortality. What Hell symbolizes is imprisonment within the ego, in the winter of discontent, Kirk had come to suspect.

Someday Monica, Cecilia, and Felicia must put away childish things, coming to know the ills to which flesh is heir. In Adam's fall, we sinned all: presumably Abraham Pierce, at Plymouth, had taught his offspring that line from *The New England Primer.* Yet the resurrection of spirit and flesh, of which Easter is the symbol, is promised to those who become as little children.

Evil, too, is childish, Kirk ruminated — in the sense that the evil man is trapped in the selfishness, the fierce appetites, and the wrath that are childish vices; the evildoer is one who never has learnt to order his soul. Yet in learning to restrain and discipline themselves, wee daughters need not lose that love of proliferating life which breaks out in spring. To the end, wonder can be found by those whose senses perceive the difference between stones and bread. To such, after travail, spring returns.

In a time when the mass media were proclaiming, almost daily, some new "national crisis" or "total revolution," it seemed well to grow up inured to terrors. Little Monica was making sure, in 1970 and 1971, that her younger sister Cecilia should become acquainted early with the dreadful.

Monica's favorite recording was "Peter and the Wolf." She enlarged on that adventure with much relish. Over the intercom, one evening, Annette and Russell heard Monica instructing Cecilia (both abed in their chamber) in the perils of this world. She spoke in the dark.

In quaking silence (she being unable to pronounce many words then) Cecilia listened to Monica's somewhat complex narration of the troubles that Peter, Sasha, and Sonia had with the Wolf — this talk embellished with episodes borrowed from "Little Red Riding Hood," "The Wolf and the Kids," and "Goldilocks and the Three Bears." At length Monica concluded, in deliberate and awesome tones, "And Cecilia, the Wolf is *everywhere*."

The consequent eldritch shriek of poor Cecilia could have been heard without employment of the intercom.

Too true, Monica: there was a lesson learnt vicariously at the age of four and a half years. All the children of Vietnam and Cambodia and Laos then were learning such truths the hard way, many of the boy children in those lands dying, gun in hand, at an age when American children had not yet escaped from the dull domination of Dick, Jane, and run, Spot, run.

In a violent time, Kirk thought, it is prudent to rear children on tales of peril — and of heroism. If enough of the rising generation take the heroes of fantasy for their exemplars, the wolf will find sustenance less readily. "What sharp teeth you have!" "The better to eat you with, my dear." Give us more woodcutters, in the nick of time.

Small children often are endowed with remarkable insights. If only their early eagerness to learn and their acuteness of perception could be prolonged through their school years!

Early in June 1974, Miss Monica Rachel Kirk, aged six years, and then ambitious to become a ballerina, startled her parents by her talent for abstraction. She was conversing with her sister Cecilia.

"Do you know what 'meditation' means, Cecilia?" she inquired omnisciently.

Cecilia replied that she did not know. For their part, Monica's parents had not been aware that Monica was acquainted with the word "meditation," let alone the concept.

"Meditation means thinking about God," Monica proceeded to instruct her sibling. "It isn't praying; it's sitting and thinking about God. I do it often in the parlor."

Although Cecilia had not recognized that word, actually she was quite so meditative as Monica. Only a few days earlier, she had surprised her mother by entering into metaphysical discourse.

Cecilia had been clowning in Annette's study, making a nuisance of herself, and her mother had reproached her. "All right," said Cecilia, cheerfully, "would you like me to ask you questions instead, Mama?" Annette assented.

"Well, then," Cecilia went on, "I've been wondering about this, Mama. I can imagine a thing that has no end. But I can't imagine something that has no beginning. Now how is it that God has no beginning?"

Despite Annette's Thomist metaphysics, little Cecilia had stumped her mother, at least for the moment. By way of demonstration, rather than of dialectic, their father set Cecilia, Monica, and their three-year-old sister, Felicia, in a row between opposed old mirrors, to show them the apparent infinity of their own images, reflected back and forth from mirror to mirror, the image growing smaller with each reflection, until at length imperceptible to the human eye. Perhaps the analogy was apt enough: for God, one mirror is what human beings call "future," and the other mirror what is called "past."

Not content with having perplexed her mother thus, Cecilia proceeded to the discipline of natural philosophy. She pointed out of the study window to a maple tree that Cecilia's great-great-grandfather had planted. "God made that," Cecilia declared. "But how did He do it? Mama, *how did He do it?*"

Cecilia had raised not merely the subtle theories of botany and silviculture but also the vast mystery of what is called "life" and how it comes into being. No one living could have given her a complete answer; but it is important not to shrug children aside with dusty and nearly incoherent answers.

The little daughters were able occasionally to stump Dr. Kirk, too. Early in March, Monica, pointing to a cirrus cloud, had asked her father how that cloud had taken form.

"I don't know, Monica," Kirk said; "I did once, but I've forgotten." Indeed it had quite passed out of Kirk's memory that a cirrus cloud normally consists of tiny ice particles.

"That's all right, Daddy," replied Monica, amicably. "I'll ask Clinton: he knows everything."

Walking the roads most of his life, Clinton Wallace had picked up in public libraries or in the lonely rooms of old hotels a tremendous fund of miscellaneous knowledge. Once he startled Kirk, in connection with some mention of change of regimes, by remarking "Arnold Toynbee writes of the susurrus of silken slippers descending the stairs, and the tramp of hobnailed boots coming up."

For facts, the burglar-butler's memory served well enough the daughters of Piety Hill. He was a gigantic battered child, and the little girls lovingly enslaved him and comforted him. The giant was happy in the hour of his death in the snow, as he returned over a bridge from seeing the motion picture *Across the Great Divide,* for he knew himself beloved. Of such is the Kingdom of Heaven.

By humane knowledge, by thoughtful work, by imagination and right reason and contemplation is the universal Wolf kept from the door. In 1970, Russell Kirk remained capable of repelling the Wolf. From the age of three to that of sixty, he never was lodged in a hospital. In recent decades he had smoked more cigars and consumed more chocolate than he should have; still, these vices aside, he remained hale and hearty in the 1970s, still capable of canoeing twenty miles a day on Little Muskegon or Chippewa, of walking thirty or forty miles a day on Scottish hills. And walking he did go, in foreign parts.

CHAPTER FOURTEEN

Wanderings in Precarious Places

Literary Blows in Defense of the Permanent Things

Marriage did not diminish Kirk's literary productivity. Lingering with him nocturnally in his library, Annette would read and then nap in the wee hours. Her husband was enormously busy endeavoring to defend the Permanent Things against the hosts of rash innovators; he had his work cut out for him, in the late Sixties and the early Seventies, for the radicals were out in force, in the Academy and in the street. They were mastering the quarterly journals of the learned societies; they were marching on Washington.

His essays appeared in more periodicals than ever, in those turbulent years: *Kenyon Review, Sewanee Review, Center Magazine, The New York Times Magazine, Book Week, Triumph,* and others — even in *Cosmopolitan,* the contribution to this last entitled "You Can't Trust Perpetual Adolescents." His *National Review* pages — mostly concerned with education at various levels, but occasionally touching on his travels and general reflections — attracted a great deal of attention and thrust upon him a burden of correspondence. Twenty years later, Kirk would wonder how he had contrived to complete all this writing, especially when their first baby, Monica, turned out to be nocturnal like himself, so that almost nightly he walked the floor with her.

Yet the books continued to appear. In 1967 Arlington House published his *Edmund Burke: A Genius Reconsidered,* which for some years was the only biography of Burke in print; Sherwood Sugden would publish a paperback edition, revised, in 1988. In collaboration with his friend James McClellan, in 1967, Kirk brought out *The*

Political Principles of Robert A. Taft, published by Fleet; as was mentioned earlier in these memoirs, with some reluctance Kirk entered the White House to present a copy to President Johnson, who held other principles. In 1969 there appeared a collection of Kirk's essays, *Enemies of the Permanent Things: Observations of Abnormity in Literature and Politics,* published by Arlington House; this volume had to do with the norms of literature and the norms of politics; Kirk thought it in some ways his most nearly original and imaginative book. A paperback edition, first released by Sherwood Sugden in 1984, soon went through two printings.

A really major book, *Eliot and His Age: Eliot's Moral Imagination in the Twentieth Century,* was published by Random House in 1971. Allen Tate, in his *Britannica* article on Eliot, named Kirk's lengthy study as one of the two books about Eliot recommended for a general survey of Eliot's life and writings. Interestingly, the most cordial reviews of *Eliot and His Age* appeared in weeklies of the Left, the *Nation* and the *Progressive;* Malcolm Muggeridge reviewed it approvingly in *Esquire.* Although a spate of books about Eliot followed hard on Kirk's book, *Eliot and His Age* continued to be discussed and recommended; Sherwood Sugden brought out a revised paperback edition in 1984, and another printing in 1988. Kirk was given a Christopher Award for the book.

A still fatter book, *The Roots of American Order,* was published by Open Court in 1974. This had been written at the request of Pepperdine University; the moving spirit there was Romuald Gantkowski, who had been a film director in Poland before the Communist triumph in that unhappy country. Pepperdine hoped to make a series of television films based on Kirk's book, and something of the sort may come to pass. This historical, political, and moral study continues to be used in university and college classes. The Open Court edition was succeeded by a Pepperdine University edition, in both cloth and paperback; in 1991, a third edition would be brought out, in the face of radicals' outcry against "Western civ" college courses. Huntington Cairns, C. Northcote Parkinson, Malcolm Muggeridge, Harry Gideonse, Elliot Richardson, and Robert Speaight, among others, praised *The Roots of American Order.*

More of Kirk's uncanny tales were published. "Balgrummo's Hell," set in a decayed great house in Scotland (suggested in part by Melville House), was published in 1967; some thought it the most alarming of Kirk's tales of the supernatural. "Saviourgate," set in York, was published in 1967, too. "There's a Long, Long Trail a-Winding," in which Frank Sarsfield is drawn from Clinton Wallace, became the most widely anthologized of all Kirk's tales, and for it he received the award for short fiction from the Third World Fantasy Convention; it was published in 1976. ("Third World Fantasy" may suggest an assembly of Libyan, Korean, and Peruvian terrorists entertaining political fantasies, but actually the phrase signified merely the third annual meeting of readers, from several countries, interested in quite recent literature of fantasy.)

During this period of the late Sixties and early Seventies, Kirk produced one novel or romance, *A Creature of the Twilight: His Memorials,* published by Fleet in 1966: a black comedy about an African civil war. Just as the book appeared in the bookshops, the Nigerian civil war erupted; it was as if Kirk had been given fore-knowledge of that sanguinary clash of racial, religious, and ideological rivalries. The novel's chief character, Manfred Arcane, haunted Kirk's imagination thereafter, demanding to reappear in print; yielding, Kirk introduced him into later short stories.

Despite this outpouring of books, essays, and articles, Kirk could not have supported his household, growing so rapidly, without his income — not very great — from the syndicated column; and, more importantly, from all the lecturing that resulted from his column being read in many cities. Travel to foreign parts helped to provide Kirk with subjects to write columns about; anyway, so Kirk told himself to justify his taste for rambling. Annette was left home with the babies, but that could not have been otherwise.

Reflections Near the Brandenburger Tor

"Precarious" was the word to describe the situation of most people in most of the world during the three decades when Kirk, usually afoot, went about inquiring into the human condition. The Second World War and the destructive revolutions that had followed it, breaking the cake of custom, left a great part of humankind in the state that psychologists call "anxiety," extremely doubtful of their future, living as dogs do, from day to day. The earthly paradise promised by ideologues had been transmuted into a tremendous Tophet.

Kirk was often in Austria, especially in Salzburg, where lived his friend Thomas Chaimowicz, who had introduced Burke's works to Austrians. Also he came to know much of Spain, and more of Italy, north and south. The wounds of war in Austria and Italy, and of civil war in Spain, were healing fast during those years; and one perceived that the Communists would not gain the mastery in those three countries, unless through the Red Army.

But in the Fifties, Sixties, and Seventies, the Red Army and the Soviet nuclear armament had to be reckoned with. Kirk had spent a week in West Berlin during 1957, years before the Wall was erected. The city's prosperity had been glowing, many people on the streets radiating confidence, having overcome adversity through strength of will. Also one came upon the living wrack of the war — skeletal folk, vacantly staring, deranged in the bombardment of Berlin or escaped, damaged, from East Germany.

Kirk had walked the length of the Kurfürstendamm, on past the wreck of the Kaiser Wilhelm Memorial Church, and along the avenue through the blasted Tiergarten, where nothing was to be seen except rubble. Presently, quite solitary, he had approached the Brandenburger Tor.

A short distance west of the Brandenburg Gate is the War Memorial of the Soviet Union, a simple structure (by contrast with the Russians' vast memorial in East Berlin). It stands upon a platform of blocks of marble taken from Hitler's Reich Chancellery. There, when Kirk had arrived, a Russian sentry bearing an automatic weapon was pacing. They two were quite alone.

From that platform, Kirk had stared across empty devastation to the immense massive ruin of the Reichstag, mysteriously burned in February 1933 — which destruction became Hitler's justification for seizing absolute power in the cause of order.

"What do you think of *me?*" that ghastly stone wreck seemed to demand of Kirk. Nobody at all could be seen anywhere in the vicinity of the Reichstag, which lay on the border of Russian-occupied East Berlin. No wall or wire marked any demarcation of the blasted-out terrain between the War Memorial and the Reichstag; nor were any people walking in that sinister area.

Why shouldn't Kirk stroll across that rubble-strewn intervening space — it could scarcely be more than two hundred yards to the Reichstag, and probably less, although somehow that treeless and grassless burnt-out expanse tended to puzzle the eye — and tour the empty colossal ruin? It would be something to remember; he might ruminate for a while, seated on some fallen block of stone. Nobody was to be seen over there, true; but neither was there any sign or billboard inscribed *Verboten*.

Kirk put his right foot off the marble platform. His left foot did not follow. For at that moment he heard distinctly a sound familiar from his days as a sergeant: an automatic rifle had been cocked.

The solitary American turned and looked at the Russian sentry, who averted his face. Nobody else was anywhere in the vicinity of the War Memorial at that moment; perhaps people were aware of some reason for not frequenting that spot. Had Kirk's left foot followed his right foot off that marble platform, very possibly the sentry would have fired. There had been no witnesses who might have contradicted the sentry's account of the incident. An unidentified stranger would have menaced the Russian zone of occupation in Berlin, if only by strolling unauthorized across scorched earth in the direction of the Reichstag; and orders were orders. Later, when the Berlin Wall was built, many men were shot down for trying to cross near the Brandenburger Tor.

Turning his back on the sentry, Kirk walked back to the avenue: there could be no standing orders to shoot visitors in the back, so long as they remained within the Allies' zone and did not make their way through no-man's-land.

This small incident signified for Kirk the precarious state not merely of everybody behind that famous invisible Iron Curtain, but of many other lands where everybody lived on the sufferance of squalid oligarchs or ideological fanatics. It is recorded on the ancient tomb of an Egyptian man of mark that he had enjoyed the distinction of never having been beaten with rods. Kirk, too, despite wanderings, somehow had been exempted from serious damage, perhaps chiefly because he was a citizen of the United States. He had lived for nearly forty years inviolate. He had been shot at, but never hit; he had needed to draw his sheath knife two or three times, but never had been stabbed; nay, he never had been brought before the bar of justice accused of a felony, a tort, or a fraud; for that matter, he never had been a party to a civil suit. These people of Berlin — how more roughly life had treated them! Kirk had lived what is called a charmed life. Doubtless a Scots canniness, inherited from Edinburgh and Galloway, had done something to preserve him from harm. But was there more to this seeming invulnerability? Was he preserved for some purpose? He thought of Lucy Ashton's song:

Look thou not on beauty's charming, —
Stand thou still when kings are arming, —
Taste not when the wine-cup glistens, —
Speak not when the people listens, —
Stop thine ear against the singer, —
From the red gold keep thy finger, —
Vacant heart, and hand, and eye, —
Easy live and quiet die.

For those obsessed with personal security, doubtless that was sound advice. Yet Kirk had rejected it all, save for the injunction against fingering red gold; and for that vice he had enjoyed precious little opportunity.

Disorder always had been the natural condition of man; order, the produce of elaborate artifice. The Second Reich had endured less than half a century, and Hitler's Third Reich merely twelve years of agony. Kirk was walking upon their pulverized monuments. "Change and decay in all around I see . . ." Kirk did not fancy himself born to set right the disjointed world; yet conceivably he had been spared much so that he might attempt to remind his contemporaries — or such people as still read sober books and attended sober lectures — that only the inner check upon will and appetite keeps the human race from self-destruction.

Will Ye Be a Protestant or a Catholic?

By 1968, the human impulse toward destruction of the species was raging in Indo-China, Nigeria, and other lands. Intellectually, that frantic impulse dominated university students on either side of the Atlantic; collegians busied themselves in undoing the works of the mind and shrieking the slogans of ideologies of which they possessed next to no knowledge. In Ireland, peaceful during the previous forty-five years, the old murderous feuds bubbling up afresh in 1968, exploded the next year, and have ever since ravaged the land. Kirk wandered in Ireland, in company with his Michigan friend Tom Galloway, just before the recrudescence of the Troubles.

During his St. Andrews years, Kirk had visited Ireland frequently. In 1949 he had published his essay "A House in Mountjoy Square," describing Dublin, where for a week he had lodged in the elegant slum of Mountjoy Square. At that time no country had seemed more peaceful and tradition-governed than Ireland, south or north. The following extracts from Kirk's essay suggest the striking difference between that Ireland of 1948-49 and the Ireland of twenty years later, when terrorists would begin to spring up so thick as if someone had sown dragons' teeth.

"Dublin is poor," Kirk had written in 1949, "and drinks her Guinness, and thinks now of New York, now of Rome — enamored of them both.

In the argot of the Black-and-Tans, the quarter of the old city round about St. Patrick's Cathedral (Swift is dust there, and Stella) was "the passage of the Dardanelles": every other high house held a sniper, in those days when men and boys in tattered overcoats swarmed out of the Coombe and out of the streets by St. Michan's, out of Ringsend, out of Mountjoy Square, urged on by their women, to burn the Custom House and blow up the Four Courts and die in the flames of the Post Office.

Where are those terrible fellows now? Why, at your elbow, crossing themselves as they pass the Augustinian church, asking you for a match, keeping an eye on the babies who roll marbles into the sidewalk-traps. They remain poor as they were then, as pious, as fond of poteen and oratory. But no longer are they Jacobins, and one suspects that even the half-plaintive fuss about ending partition heats few of them. . . . I do not think the Garda have an intolerably difficult job.

"Saints preserve us!" cried a middle-class Dublin woman to a friend of mine, upon learning that I had lodged in Mountjoy Square. "However does the poor boy get in there at night? Why, he'll find himself with his throat cut." The bourgeoisie of Dublin have trickled away to the southern suburbs, for the most part abandoning the old squares to other orders of society; and the illusions entertained by such Dublin folk concerning the mysterious proletariat differ little from those of middle-class people in

Manchester or New Orleans. For all that, in a week of poking about the dark streets I was accosted only by one woman with a whisky cough and by one boy, aged six, who wanted "the time, please, sir."

Aye, four decades and more of peace; but late in the summer of 1968, those "terrible boys" were plotting mischief again, although much more in Londonderry and Belfast than in Dublin. Galloway and Kirk commenced their Irish walking tour at Londonderry, called by all its residents simply Derry. Within the stout Protestant walls of Derry and for some miles outside those archaic fortifications, religion still is a power so explosive as it was four centuries gone. The Protestant establishment — which is Presbyterian, actually, more than Anglican, in Ulster — in 1968 was governing Derry much as it had ever since the defeat of James II at the Battle of the Boyne, in the seventeenth century. But by 1968, the rebels against that social establishment were mixing Marxist ideology and tactics of terror with their professed Catholicism.

Galloway and Kirk arrived at Derry shortly before Orangemen's Day, on which annual occasion the more militant Protestants of Ulster celebrate the landing at Carrickfergus, in the north of Ireland, in 1689, of that eminent Protestant champion King William III. In 1968, the Orangemen remained as zealous for William III, William of Orange, as if he had landed the previous day. Kirk found that the Orangemen's headquarters at Derry were in the palace of the Church of Ireland (that is, Anglican) bishops of Derry.

On the gable-ends of various old houses in Derry, the Orangemen annually had renewed frescos of martial scenes: William landing at Carrickfergus, William triumphing at the Boyne, and others. These copies of seventeenth-century paintings were twentieth-century political exhortations to fidelity to the Protestant creed and Protestant supremacy. In no other country, perhaps, was the distant political past so vibrant and passionate, sustained by religious fervor and embattled class distinctions.

A few minutes' walk from those gable-end paintings, Kirk and Galloway came to the church of Saint Columba, who had founded Derry in the fifth century. This long had been sacred ground to the Catholics of Derry. In the churchyard, masses had been said in defiance of secular authority until the Penal Laws had been repealed late in the eighteenth century. The Catholics of Northern Ireland, in 1968, often were speaking of their sufferings under King William's Penal Laws as if it still were perilous to celebrate mass. Catholics continued to drink water from the open-air holy-water stoup under the hawthorne trees near Saint Columba's Church, in 1968, as if it gave them strength against Protestants. A sign hard by pointed to the place of martyrdom of a Derry priest — at the hands of Protestants.

With some reason, Derry Catholics were complaining in 1968 that although they now had come to form the majority of Derry's population, they had been gerrymandered out of seats in the Parliament of Northern Ireland. To them, the political authorities of Derry seemed alien conquerors, even though it was impossible to distinguish Protestant from Catholic by physical appearance or by speech. To this ancient religious animosity there were being added, in 1968, Marxist teachings of class revolution.

Just outside Bishopgate, Kirk paused to survey old Derry Gaol, a vast prison in nineteenth-century Gothic style, by 1968 disused and scheduled for demolition, to make way for a supermarket. In Derry Gaol had been confined, down to the end of World War II, the Sinn Feiners and other rebels against British and Protestant authority. During that war had occurred here a famous jailbreak, the escaping Nationalists hoisting their banner over the walls.

At Bishopgate came up to Kirk a lanky Catholic, volunteering various tales of the Gaol. Cursing Derry, he declared it to be the most miserable of all towns. Having successfully begged a shilling from the American visitor, the lanky man bestowed his blessing and departed. Doubtless not very long afterward he was one of the handful of IRA Provisionals, the Provos, who commenced fierce rioting, and then shooting and bombing, in old Derry. The type was readily recognizable even by a stranger, and unquestionably the Northern Ireland Constabulary possessed detailed lists of the dozen or so IRA terrorists resident in Derry, and the score of "back-up men," older fellows, who supplied and concealed the front-line violent zealots. In an authoritarian land, martial law might have been declared late in 1968 or later, all the terrorists and back-up men arrested at their houses, and dealt with by court martial. But Northern Ireland is under the Crown in Parliament still, with all the protections of civil liberties that have grown up in Britain over centuries, so Kirk's shabby raconteur of tales of Derry Gaol, and his IRA comrades, have been enabled to torment Derry for the past quarter-century.

[381]

Having seen the sights of Derry, the most interesting town in the north of Ireland, the two travellers from Michigan took a bus six miles west, to the foot of the cashel, or hill fort, called the Grianan of Aileach, in Donegal — which is to say, within the Irish Republic. Kirk was somewhat surprised that a fairly thorough inspection of their local bus was made when they crossed into the Irish Republic: nothing of that sort had happened on Kirk's many crossings of the border of the two Irelands in earlier years. The hill surmounted by the Grianan stands on that border, its eastern slopes in Northern Ireland, its western in the Irish Republic.

Kirk and Galloway rather painfully ascended the steep hill by a path apparently little used, a barbed-wire fence running parallel with it; presently it entered Kirk's mind that the fence was the demarcation between the two Irelands. Twice, as they climbed, men emerged from farmhouses on the eastern slope, shotguns in their hands, and stared keenly at the American climbers — who found it prudent to crouch and take whatever vegetal cover they might encounter, as they climbed higher. These glimpses of armed farmers also somewhat surprised Kirk.

On reaching the Grianan, a concentric stone fortress of the Dark Ages, the walkers found to their chagrin that an easy paved road ran up the hill from the western side, so that their travail had been needless. This cashel and its outworks had been the stronghold of the O'Neills, Ulster's kings; it had been slighted by Murtogh O'Brien, king of Munster, in the year 1101. One could imagine its ruined ramparts shielding twentieth-century Irish factions in some border clash; what with those farmers' shotguns on the far side of that barbed-wire border fence, one could picture quite readily such an encounter.

After this, returning eastward, Kirk and his friend put up that night at the Causeway Hotel, architecturally ingenious and charming, surely one of the earliest tourist hotels; and in the morning they inspected the Giant's Causeway, often called one of the natural wonders of the world. Then, packs on their backs, they took the cliff-face path, "dangerous in parts" but somewhat improved by the Irish National Trust, some six delightfully alarming miles long (plus elfin caves beyond the end of the cliffs). It would not have done to clown on that track. The cliffs of Antrim stand some four hundred feet high, columnar basalt, perfectly precipitous; at almost any point it would have been difficult in some degree for one person, going in the opposite direction, to pass Kirk and Galloway; at some points on that scary path, which had no railing, either the traveller from the west or the traveller from the east would have had to retrace his steps, that a wider space might be found.

There arose in Kirk's imagination a grimly amusing scenario. In his mind's eye he found himself confronted, at the very narrowest stretch of the path, by a stalwart Irishman, a shotgun in the crook of his arm, who had come from the east, perhaps from Dunseverick. Necessarily this stranger and Kirk were at a stay; one or the other must retreat.

With a grin somewhat sardonic, this imaginary Irishman of Kirk's fancy said, "Now, sir, will ye be a Protestant or a Catholic?"

To which Kirk, in this imaginary encounter, would reply prudently, "I'm an atheist."

And then the sardonic Irishman, master of this situation, would inquire, "Yes, sir; and now, will ye be a Protestant atheist or a Catholic atheist?"

Kirk and Galloway followed the whole length of that cliff path, their right shoulders brushing basalt, and then took to the windy cliff lip for a mile or two, and at length passed through the magical coastal caves, to a chill and damp inn that night — without any sinister incident. A year later, or even a month later, lonely walks in Antrim on a broad highway, let alone a crumbly cliff track, might have been precarious. When nationalism, religious fanaticism, and Marxist ideology are compounded, some chance word or gesture may serve as catalyst to ignite a fatal explosion.

Down Glen Tilt with a Nationalist Zealot

Yet it was not in Ireland, but in the Highlands of Scotland, that Kirk and Galloway fell in with a nationalist ideologue, during the summer of 1968. They were making their rough way from the neighborhood of Braemar, near the springs of the Dee, over the uninhabited and almost pathless uplands to the head of wild Glen Tilt, and thence downward to Blair Atholl, near the very heart of Scotland. Many deer perish among the snows of Glen Tilt in winter; so do those few men and women, Southrons, who foolishly venture out of hunting lodges

into that wintry desolation. Tilt's scenic beauty almost makes roman-
tically perishing there worthwhile. From Braemar Castle to Blair
Castle is a taxing hill walk of some thirty-three miles, with no dwelling its whole length.

A mile or two up from the Linn of Dee, they were overtaken by
a hardy man, previously unknown to them, who had slept the pre-
vious night out of doors in the Lairig Ghru, the wildest pass in
Scotland. (For that matter, no door is to be found in the Lairig Ghru.)
Perhaps he still lives; probably so; therefore let him be called here
Colin, which is not his name.

Galloway and Kirk bore surnames indubitably Scots, and that
was well; for Colin detested the English virulently. In 1968, the
Scottish Nationalist party entertained high hopes of Scottish independence through the dissolution of the United Kingdom; the
government of Harold Wilson was seriously alarmed. In that year
Kirk talked with many members or well-wishers of the Scottish
Nationalist movement — journalists, poets, professors, engineers,
miners, farmers, town councilors. At least a large measure of devo-
lution of power to Edinburgh from Westminster seemed probable —
though the Nationalists desired more than that. No Scots parliament
had met since the Act of Union in 1707. There arose plans to make
that fine classical structure the old Edinburgh High School into a
parliament house.

The Scots Nationalists, in 1968, seemed to be filling a vacuum
left by long decline of the Liberal party, and more recently by the
unpopularity of the Labour party.

Now Colin, the Americans' chance companion in their arduous
crossing of the high moors and their descent of the canyon-like Glen
Tilt, was a Scots Nationalist of the most doctrinaire persuasion. He
called himself a miner; later Kirk learned from a reliable source among
the Nationalists that indeed Colin once had been a miner, but latterly
was a newspaperman. He spoke well, was affable toward the American
hill walkers, and appeared to be indefatigable.

Radical only in his nationalism, he was wrathy against Communism. As a British soldier in Malaya after the Second World War,
he had served in the "Iron Broom" that had swept out of the jungles
the Communist partisans (ethnic Chinese, not Malays). He would
have been an ill man to make an enemy of. Colin hated criminals as
fiercely as he detested Communists. Not long before, he had been

camping, with his wife, near a derelict hunting lodge in the very desolation through which the three hill walkers were tramping as he told his story. Along had come a large party of Borstal boys, taken on a Highland jaunt by a custodial officer, on the theory that a walk in the open air improves morals. Fearing his charges, this officer exercised next to no effective control over the young roughs. They encamped near Colin and his wife. Those Borstal boys proceeded to chop down for firewood the saplings in their vicinity — to the great vexation of Colin, lover of the wild — and to curse foully. In vain Colin appealed to the custodial officer.

Thereupon Colin, a man of average stature merely, transformed himself into an Iron Broom to set upon the Borstal boys, knocking heads together, disabling them with karate blows, belaboring them with his walking stick as he pursued the whole band over the high moor. He broke up their camp while the custodial officer stood aghast. "And wow! but he was rough," as the old Scots ballad had it.

Regaling Galloway and Kirk with such narrations as they made their painful way down Glen Tilt, the flints of the cart track through the marvellous Atholl forests tormenting their soles, Colin made it clear that he would stop at nothing to liberate Scotland from the United Kingdom. (Later a Nationalist friend hinted to Kirk that Colin may have had in mind some signal act of defiance.) With Colin's vehement rejection of Communism in mind, Kirk ventured to inquire what an emancipated Scotland would do, should the Soviet Union think of aggression against the revived nation-state. "The English would have to defend us, out of their own interest," Colin replied. He saw no obstacles to a conspicuous place for Scotland among the comity of nations.

Like some nationalist ideologues of other lands whom Kirk met from time to time, this Colin was a cheerful and friendly companion, so long as one did not venture to deny the possibility that his political aspirations might be given flesh. Nationalism often is a virulent force, an intolerant substitute for religious faith. Yet also it is possible for a reviving national awareness to restore to a people unity, purpose, and energy. No such fair prospect, however, has yet appeared in the bloody chaos of Serbia, Croatia, and Bosnia-Herzegovina, nor in the warring succession states of the overthrown tyranny of the Soviet Union.

[385]

Colin's hopes, nevertheless, were vain. During the two decades after 1968, at first events would favor Scottish and Welsh nationalism, and then the political tide would ebb.

In 1975, Parliament would enact a local-government statute that would deprive most Scottish counties even of their old names, and strip their old authority from ancient boroughs. St. Andrews, for one, would be deprived of nearly all its established powers of self-government and planning; the town, the oldest in Scotland, would be subjected to a bureaucracy situated at Perth, across the Tay. In 1979, the Labour government would be persuaded to permit a referendum in Scotland on the question of whether the Scots should establish an Assembly to deal with Scottish concerns; that body would be authorized, should forty per cent of the whole Scottish electorate approve the plan. But although the Nationalists and their allies won a majority of the votes cast in the referendum, that majority did not amount to forty per cent of the whole electorate — that is, a good many Scots did not vote at all on the question. No later attempt was made at establishing some sort of Scots parliament.

After that defeat, the Nationalists would fade into insignificance, losing their few seats in the House of Commons. Many English people would shift northward into Scotland, the Scots birthrate would decline relatively, and quite swiftly Scotland would slip toward the status of "North Britain" — the name bestowed upon the country by various public men of England during the nineteenth century. If Russell Kirk could not approve Colin's hinted strategy of protest and separation, or share his expectations, nevertheless Kirk would understand very well Colin's sorrow and his wrath.

And yet was Colin's cause, in the long run, quite forlorn? The Irish, from the eleventh century onward, somehow had absorbed and won over to the Irish nation successive waves of conquerors from Great Britain; grandsons of invaders became the defenders of Irishness. And the movement of societies through the world, as the twentieth century drew toward a close, was that of centrifugal force — the Russians' U.S.S.R. dissolving, the far-flung empires built by western European peoples already dissolved. Political nationalism was rising up on every hand, in defiance of the unifying influences of technology and world trade. If the powers at Westminster should falter someday — why, Colin and his like were waiting for crisis. From the middle of the eighteenth century to the early years of the

twentieth, Scots intellect and Scots courage had been mightily powerful in creating and administering the British Empire. Those Scots
talents just possibly might re-emerge in the twenty-first century to
work a restoration — much to the satisfaction of the ghost of Walter
Scott — at once cultural and political.

Colin and Tom Galloway conversed on such themes, and Kirk
(a few yards to the rear) meditated upon them, as the three strode
downward in the dark through the splendid forests planted by the
dukes of Atholl — even towering sequoias, transplanted long ago
from California, growing in the Atholl estates. In 1968, the Scottish
plantations of the British Forestry Commission consisted mainly of
dull clusters of small conifers, fit for nothing better than pit-props.

The night was black as the Pit when Colin, Galloway, and Kirk
groped through the wooded policies surrounding the great bulk of
Blair Castle. Midnight was past when the two Americans were admitted to the Atholl Arms, that handsome hotel built (along with
much grander works) by Sir Robert Lorimer, father of Kirk's sculp-
tor-friend Hew Lorimer. Colin declined their invitation to lodge with
them at the Atholl Arms; probably he had little or no money. Instead
he stretched himself on a bench in the little railway station, and they
never saw him after. God bring him to a better place than even
Edinburgh town.

That trek from Braemar to Blair Atholl was the most exhausting
walk Kirk ever had undertaken — worse than divers explorations in
Utah deserts. He was fifty years old now, and weighed more than he
should have, and foolishly he had not put on his feet the right sort of
boots. Galloway was a quarter of a century younger, and Colin the
Zealot at least a decade younger. "I admire the way you keep up," Colin
had told him near the foot of Glen Tilt, "I really do." Because nobody
ever before had suggested that Kirk would have difficulty keeping up
on a long walk in the wilds, Kirk was not altogether pleased by that
commendation. Annette had told him he seemed still a boy.

Scottish nationalism began to decline not long after Kirk returned to America; but the radical movement in northern Ireland, a
compound of nationalism with yesteryear's Catholicism and with
Marxist ideology, burst into violence not long later. Massive rioting
commenced in Derry during the annual Protestant march commemorating the thirteen Apprentice Boys who, in 1688, had closed
the city's gates to keep out the Earl of Antrim's Catholic regiment.

Much of the fighting of 1969 occurred well outside the walls, at the head of William Street, near the Catholic cathedral, St. Eugene's. The pretext for the beginning of bloodshed was that one Bernadette Devlin, heroine of the IRA, had been passed over, allegedly, for tenancy of a flat in a municipal council house; that apartment had been assigned, instead, to a family of several persons who happened to be Protestants, while Bernadette Devlin, unmarried, happened to be Catholic. Therefore murder and arson ever since have tormented Ireland, north and south.

Order and the reign of law lacking — so Kirk reflected at Derry and Carrickfergus — no civil society truly exists, and therefore no civil rights of any sort may be secured. The worst enemy of genuine civil rights is the fanatic who demands exclusive and unlawful privileges for his faction, who asks the impossible, and so receives nothing worth possessing.

In Northern Ireland, just a year after Kirk had strolled there, anarchists pretending to represent the Catholic minority were burning houses, shops, and pubs — mostly in the very Catholic districts they professed to be defending. By 1969, the rebellion in Ulster clearly was directed by fantastics of the New Left, of a type already familiar in the United States, France, Germany, and Italy. Those wild radicals no more represented the bulk of the Catholics of Northern Ireland than H. Rap Brown and Robert Williams, black militant extremists given to arson and kidnapping, could rightfully claim to represent the black population of the United States.

On the very day in August 1969 when the insurrection was fiercest in Derry and Belfast, a little riot was contrived at Dayton, Ohio, by white and black fanatics and charlatans who appeared to be paranoiacs. At the Professional Golfers' Association in Dayton, a gang of freaks, claiming to represent various "civil rights" groups, assaulted participants on the greens, endeavoring to break up the tournament. This action was designed to demonstrate its organizers' hostility toward the Dayton Chamber of Commerce.

The extremists' coalition demanded that the Chamber of Commerce, or anyway somebody in Dayton, must end the war in Vietnam, guarantee free access of everyone to all private clubs, hand out three thousand free tickets to the golf tournament, pay the coalition a sum in dollars ("for the poor") equal to the cost of the tournament, etc., etc. Who would have surmised that the Dayton Chamber of Commerce possessed such arbitrary authority over international, national, civic, and private affairs?

Taking frantic advantage of genuine grievances, in Derry as in Dayton, the New Left fantastics brought about violent disorders with the aim of demolishing the whole structure of order, justice, and freedom. Men have a natural right, said Edmund Burke, to be restrained from passionate actions that would work their own destruction. In the late Sixties, the state of society in America and in Ireland seemed quite so precarious as that tortuous path midway up the cliffs of Antrim.

Meditations in the Palace of Diocletian

Wandering for a fortnight in Dalmatia and Montenegro, late in 1969, Kirk had for companions Chuck and Ben Teetor, from the United States, all three of them visiting for the first time a state nominally Communist. Kirk meditated on the persistence with which human nature and civilized institutions reassert themselves after being battered by ideologues.

Sipping Turkish coffee at a table of the Café Luxor, in the ancient heart of Split, Kirk and the Teetor brothers saw pullulating about them a life almost indistinguishable from that of western Europe. Sitting at that table, they confronted the cathedral of Split, once the mausoleum of the Emperor Diocletian: for this square was the peristyle of Diocletian's palace, converted into a teeming fortified town by the Roman fugitives from Salona, after the Avars and the Slavs had broken through the defenses of Illyria.

Within that tomb-cathedral, mass was being celebrated while the three Americans watched the tourists from West and East swarm like bees in the piazza. The city guide standing outside the cathedral's doors might sneer at "the opiate of the people," but faith, the adversary of ideology, persisted all the same. Like the old Illyrians, the modern Croats rendered unto Caesar what was Caesar's; yet Caesars pass, and even whole peoples cease to be, and still the continuity of church and culture endure. Conceivably Christian belief may be strong, Kirk speculated, when Tito has been buried so long as Diocletian, that masterful persecutor of Christians.

On the hillside above Split, in 1969, Tito's name glowed enormously in neon; Tito's photograph was on the wall of every shop and restaurant. But one found the emblem of hammer and sickle nowhere; even police were conspicuous by their absence; ideology lay forgotten as Diocletian's edicts. Like Diocletian long before him, Tito had become the Protector, the shield against the menace from the steppes. But he had grown old; and after his death, the socialist state he had created would sink deeper and deeper into difficulties. By the beginning of the twenty-first century, like enough, the Church would rise upon his grave even as the Church had made its own the mausoleum of its enemy Diocletian.

The Communist ideologue knows two grand adversaries, Kirk reflected, there at the Café Luxor: the "opiate" of the Church and the comforts and vices of the bourgeoisie. Yugoslavia's revolution had failed to crush either foe. At Dubrovnik, great monasteries still warded the city's two splendid gates, and choirs still sang, while Marxist ideology faded to a shadow. In Split and Dubrovnik and other cities, the revolution-created "New Class" entertained itself elsewhere than in workers' canteens.

Some members of the New Class had deposited gold in Swiss banks, or acquired villas in Egypt; meanwhile, proletarian virtues decayed, and the old phenomena of the short-changing waiter and the sly pornographer and the gratuity-soliciting functionary were experienced afresh. Kirk and his friends voyaged along the shores of Dalmatia aboard the *Proletarska,* the "Proletarian Woman" — first class. All proletarians are equal, but some are more equal than others.

They found museums of the People's Revolution in every city — yet very few visitors to those museums. Architectural restoration, historic preservation, and archeological museums, nevertheless, were flourishing in 1969: Dalmatia's past had not gone down the Memory Hole. Excavation of the vast vaulted cellars of Diocletian's palace, packed tight with sixteen centuries' rubbish, was in progress literally beneath Kirk's feet as he sat in the Café Luxor.

The tyrant Tito, luxuriating at his island villa then, would leave behind him no such colossal monument as Diocletian's palace; by 1969 it was clear enough that future historians would regard Tito's domination as a brief distasteful interregnum, even less productive of art and architecture than had been Cromwell's Protectorate in England.

Far to the East, the strange god enshrined at Moscow had failed. "That belongs to America," a Pula taxi driver had chuckled, pointing to the moon and referring to the recent landing of the American astronauts. The man was proprietor of his own cab, a good new car; he saved money; he had kinfolk in San Pedro. In the humming yards of Pula, that year, ships were built that would make their way through the St. Lawrence and the Great Lakes to Chicago, or by way of Panama to the Pacific. Yugoslav ships' officers, amiable efficient men, knew the West well, and did not genuflect in the direction of Moscow.

Diocletian's imperial structure had survived in Illyria for a century and a half, and had endured after a fashion in Constantinople a millennium and more. Deficient in the Roman practical genius, and not shored up by the transcendent faith of Christianity, Tito's revolutionary transformation and its Russian model counted their domination in decades, not in centuries.

Ere the end of the twentieth century, no Yugoslavia would exist. An outrageous conglomeration of nationalities and cultures, Yugoslavia had been created at the end of the First World War to reward Serbia for her feeble part as an ally of the Western powers. (Serbia, of course, had brought on the terrors of that war by arranging the murder of the Archduke Ferdinand.) The realm of King Peter I had been tripled in extent by the annexation of Croatia, Slovenia, Bosnia and Herzegovina, Macedonia, and Montenegro — all those lands inherited by Tito and his Communist party in 1945. But so early as 1969, Kirk could discern signs that this forcible union of territories inconsonant in religion, language, and historical background would be dissolved by the rebellion of its ethnic elements against any sort of central direction. Already the Croats had begun to resist Serb domination; later the Albanians of Kossovo would take up arms against Serbian administration. And the inability of the economic structure — half socialist, half syndicalist — to produce goods and services adequately had caused, well before 1969, a general bitter discontent. People in the towns of Dalmatia and Montenegro seemed never to smile.

It would be well for the suffering incongruity called Yugoslavia to separate into its constituent states, Kirk thought. Nationalism — so destructive in Northern Ireland, so rebuffed in Scotland — might be the redemption of the diverse cultures of the Balkans — or else their scourge. Twenty years later (a good deal sooner than Kirk had expected), resurgent nationalism in Poland, Hungary, and other states of central and eastern Europe would put an end to the Communist despotisms over those nations.

During the unimaginative decades of the Seventies and the Eighties, there would occur much vague writing and talking about "global democracy" and "the global village" — nay, even of "the end of history" in a universal triumph, presumably eternal, of "democratic capitalism." Yet in truth the strong tendency of most quarters of the world during that era would be toward splitting, rather than toward conjugation. Latter-day liberals and that curious breed of Manhattanites called neo-conservatives both mistook the ebb tide for the flood. Men learn to love the little platoon they belong to in society, Burke had said. Not toward the big battalion, but toward the little platoon, eastern Europe and much else of the world had begun to shift so early as 1969.

After that serfs' son Diocletian, administrative and military genius, had taken his own life here in his Dalmatian palace in the year 316, the Roman Empire began to disintegrate. Diocletian, by heroic endeavors and extreme measures, had kept the empire coherent from Hadrian's Wall to the Euphrates, from the Rhine to the Atlas. But centralization and bureaucracy and unendurable taxation had worked as cancers within the Roman frontiers; the center could not hold; things fell apart.

Outside the mausoleum-cathedral crouches a sphinx of black granite, fetched here from Egypt by Diocletian; it had been carved nearly nineteen centuries before the Emperor took it from the valley of the Nile. Many dominations and powers, whole civilizations, have gone down to dusty death since that sphinx emerged from its block of granite. Diocletian's sarcophagus was empty; the days of Josip Broz, called Tito, were numbered, as were the days of socialism. The sphinx-monster of antiquity — the word *sphinx* means "strangler" — demanded, on pain of death, answers to most difficult questions. "What will happen next, little man?" the sphinx of Diocletian's palace seemed to inquire of Russell Kirk. Her stare was most menacing.

Yet she still is waiting for Kirk's reply. Although now and again Kirk was invited to lecture or to write about the future of civilization, he knew that he was playing a game when engaging in that enterprise. For no man can know the future: the event is in the hand of God. We cannot predict safely even tomorrow. For all one could tell in 1969, civilization might have been terminated the next week or the next year, by the employment of nuclear fission.

Only the past is knowable, even though history is an art, not a science. Through a fuller understanding of vanished civilizations, modern men might do something to postpone or avert their own destruction. Knowledge of Roman achievements and Roman errors — as symbolized, for instance, in Diocletian's palace — is relevant to the human condition at the end of the twentieth century as no arrogant speculation about the future might be.

"We learn from history that we learn nothing from history," Hegel wrote. The lessons lie there in the history books, he meant, but we ignore them, dunces that we are.

Kirk would make some use of the lessons to be learnt from Diocletian's age in his short story — set in Split in the last quarter of the twentieth century — "The Last God's Dream," published in his collection *The Princess of All Lands,* in 1979. Upon the face of a coin, acquired by Kirk, minted at Antioch in Diocletian's reign, one admires the Emperor's indomitable profile, strong nose, strong jaw; and one admires still his baths at Rome, his palace at Split. He abdicated and planted cabbages. As Kirk's character Manfred Arcane remarks in "The Last God's Dream," Diocletian was centric, and so kept the peace for twenty years — an achievement unequalled by the principal statesmen of the year 1969.

> He left a name at which the world grew pale
> To point a moral or adorn a tale.

But the tenth epigram of Pentadius, presumably written with Diocletian in mind while the Emperor yet lived, is more moving:

> Pastor, arator, eques, pavi, colui, superavi
> Capras, rus, hostes, fronde, ligone, manu.

> (As shepherd, ploughman, knight, I've pastured, tilled, subdued
> Herds, farms, and enemies, with herbage, hoe, and arms.)

With an obeisance to the last imperator deified by the Roman Senate, Kirk and his friends left the Café Luxor, took ship to Dubrovnik, and later came near to being shot by Albanian frontier guards. They explored the walled ruins of Stari Bar (the background of Kirk's later uncanny tale "The Peculiar Demesne of Archvicar Gerontion"), where doubtless Turkish ghosts lurked; and lodged in the old sea citadel of Sveti Stefan, where a monk painted and sold icons, and where the beach was reported to have indulged nude bathers. (On Kirk's return to domesticity, Annette inquired keenly into that licence, of which she had been informed by Roger Grandmaison, Mecosta's dentist; her Russell replied that he and his companions had beheld only one nude bather, but she was perfectly formed, and almost three years old.)

Kirk travelled to spy out the nakedness of the land, sometimes, but not of its women; his interest lay chiefly in such old masters as Diocletian, not in young misses, nor young mistresses. To Michigan he returned, for much public debating with radicals, to build a vast wing of brick to his ancestral house, and presently to be presented by Annette with a third daughter, Felicia Annette, whose first name was that of a little saint and martyr of Roman Carthage. It was a good name; but perhaps Kirk should have named the pretty baby after Diocletian's only child, the innocent Valeria, whom the evil Licinius put to death while her father still lived.

Much of what is called history records the fruits of original sin. Even the daughters of emperors exist only precariously. Order, justice, and freedom are garden plants; the natural condition of humankind is that of the jungle. In the year 316, Diocletian, who had been master of the world, was compelled to starve himself to death in his palace. In the year 1969, President Nixon was triumphant; five years later, his enemies would pull him down. It was a wonder, Kirk thought, that a tolerable human society could subsist at all. Prescription, custom, and convention enable generation to link with generation; but the cake of custom was being trampled under foot near the end of the twentieth century, much as the cake of custom had been broken about the beginning of the fourth century. All Kirk could do was to remind some thinking people of such hard truths, and to brighten the corner where he found himself.

"What book are you reading?" So John Davenport, then an editor of *Fortune,* inquired of Kirk in 1969.

"Polybius's *History,* Hampton's translation," Kirk informed his friend.

Davenport was taken aback; doubtless he had expected comments on some recent polemic or well-publicized novel. "Why?"

"For political wisdom, and evidence of the constancy of human nature," said Kirk.

At Split, as at Carthage, as at Rome, some classical wisdom had seeped into Kirk by osmosis. The ruling of many lands and nations had been too much even for strong Diocletian: he had but twenty-four hours in his day. Of several lessons which may be learnt at Split, one is this, whispered to Kirk by the ghost of Diocletian: the more that power is collected at a central point, the less good can it accomplish. That hard permanent truth had been thoroughly forgotten by most Americans of Kirk's time.

Musings in Taiwan

His mother never had travelled beyond Michigan, except for a honeymoon trip by train to Niagara Falls — where rain had fallen the whole twenty-four hours of Kirk's parents' stay. (That expedition had been possible only because they had obtained free passes on the Pere Marquette Railroad.) Russell Amos Kirk travelled a great way to somewhere or other from 1936 onward, every year. Although not so compulsive a world traveller as was his Austrian friend Eric von Kuehnelt-Leddihn, Kirk came to know well all of the several United States, except Alaska; to feel at ease in the lands of western Europe, save Scandinavia; and to set foot in several African countries. From time to time he received invitations to speak in Argentina, in Australia, in New Zealand, in Sweden; even to lecture on jurisprudence, under the patronage of the American State Department, in Burundi! But his friendships in Scotland, England, Ireland, the Netherlands, Germany, Austria, Switzerland, Italy, and Spain dissuaded him from venturing farther afield, life being brief; and, as he had learned from John Henry Newman, if we are to know anything well, we must rest ignorant of much.

To the Orient Kirk flew only once, and then in company with Ralph de Toledano, columnist and poet, and a man from the Columbia Broadcasting Service. It was the spring of 1974 when they arrived in Taiwan; later his fellow travellers would proceed to Hong Kong, but Kirk would refrain from blurring his impressions of Free China by continuing travel. He found in Taiwan and its dependent islands persuasive evidence of the virtues of smallness of scale in society.

At its nearest point to the Chinese mainland (the islet of Tatan, off Amoy), Nationalist China, Free China, was within swimming distance of Communist China. This was as if a mongoose confronted an elephant. Taiwan and its dependencies had, and have, approximately the land area of New Hampshire and Vermont combined; Red China was nearly a hundred times bigger. In population, Free China was outnumbered by Red China nearly fifty souls to one. Beijing (then styled Peiping) had the atomic bomb, and Taipei had not. Yet Taiwan, the only remaining Chinese province controlled by the Nationalists, went on building and planning and behaving as if the island republic were no more menaced than Switzerland.

For in the international balance of forces then existing, Taiwan could not be seized by the Communist regime. Red China had a more formidable adversary to deal with, the Soviet Union. Also Beijing dared not risk intervention by America's Seventh Fleet; for that matter, as Chou En-lai had declared publicly, Communist China then desired America's Far Eastern fleet to remain in Oriental waters, as a restraint upon Russian ambitions; and Red China had only some submarines for a navy. Moreover, the Soviet power itself found its interest served by the survival of an independent Taiwan: the more troops that Beijing must leave in Fukien to keep watch upon the island fortress of Taiwan, the fewer Chinese troops could be sent to the Manchurian and Mongolian frontiers. And even unsupported by either the United States or the Soviet Union, Taiwan in 1974 would have been too hard a nut for Red China to crack, even had it been found possible to transport troops across the Formosa Strait.

Militarily, Taiwan had become self-supporting. By agreement between Washington and Beijing, in 1974 American forces stationed in Taiwan were being withdrawn; fewer than six thousand remained at the time of Kirk's visit. Free China's expulsion from the United Nations had not enfeebled the Kuomintang, or Nationalist, power in Taiwan.

And, diplomatic recognition or no, the world was trading famously with Taiwan in 1974, the price being right. Taiwan was competing successfully with Japan in quality and cost of goods produced; Taiwan had supplanted Hawaii as the world's principal producer of pineapples. The island's exports exceeded those of the whole vast expanse of Communist China.

In this balance of forces, clearly Taiwan, the nominal Republic of China, in 1974 expected to endure and to prosper. A striking illustration of this was encountered by Kirk in Kinmen (Quemoy), the island lying in range of Communist artillery. For in Kinmen, overseas Chinese of Hong Kong, Singapore, and more distant lands were building private houses with a view to retirement — which was as if American citizens should build cottages for their sunset years at the naval base of Guantanamo, in Cuba.* Knowing that the Communist regime in mainland China had triumphed out of peculiar combinations of circumstances, the overseas Chinese of 1974 surmised that Chinese Marxism might collapse out of another peculiar combination of different circumstances. Of the two Chinas, Taiwan was the more stable. President Chiang Kai-shek was old and sick, the inmate of a military hospital. Chairman Mao Tse-Tung, too, infirm and rarely seen, was near his latter end. When they two vanished, great changes might come to pass, although gradually.

Legitimacy of government, the cardinal point in the political theories of Confucius, in 1974 still influenced strongly the Chinese mentality. Marxism was a Western ideology, quite without Chinese roots. Marxist dogmata struck at the heart of Chinese social institutions — especially at the family, still enduring in China as a social bond more tenaciously than in twentieth-century Europe or America. Between Confucian teachings and Marxist ideology there existed not even that link of heresy by which Marxism and Christianity were joined in Europe and Latin America: Communism was an alien system, imposed by terror.

While Kirk was in Taiwan, Chiang Ching, Mao's wife, visited Swatow, on the mainland nearly opposite southern Taiwan, that she might preside over the burning of some hundreds of copies of the writings of Confucius and his disciples; the reading of those classics was forbidden by the Communist regime. In Taiwan, the ancient Chinese culture was not proscribed. Yet Western technology, education, and patterns of thought were inundating Taiwan: the traditional Confucian modes of thought and custom had retreated to the temples, to some oldfangled professors with white beards and black pyjamas, to peasant villages distant from the principal roads.

In Red China, the new pattern of life was Western — in its Russian aspect. For Communist China was a grim caricature of Soviet

---

*Also the Chinese of Hong Kong and Singapore were purchasing gravesites in Taiwan because of the old desire of Chinese dwelling overseas to be buried in Chinese soil.

society, monotonous and boring, with its omnipresent secret police, its adulation of the machine (commonly an ineffectual machine), its reduction of the intellectual life and of art to servitude under Marxist dogmas. How visiting American liberals could idealize this hideous new Chinese society, as many of them had done after Richard Nixon and Henry Kissinger had undertaken their mission to Beijing, puzzled Kirk in 1974. What those visiting simpletons praised in the Red China of that year was not Chinese at all, but merely a bad copy of the Soviet misery that Alexander Solzhenitsyn had sufficiently exposed.

Yet in Taiwan also the new pattern of life was Western — in its American aspect. Free China's technology, free enterprise, amusements, schooling, administrative practices, and costume all were of American inspiration, in 1974. On the streets of Taipei, Kirk almost never encountered a girl in anything resembling traditional Chinese costume: miniskirts and hot pants had triumphed utterly. Taiwan's three commercial television stations reproduced, with Chinese actors and singers and overwhelming dollops of advertisement, America's TV wasteland.

Was the old China dead everywhere? Or did it remain possible that behind this Western façade there still dwelt a mentality distinctively Chinese, a moral order older than Marxism or even older than Christianity, a submerged culture which might react against this Western domination, bursting up with ancient power?

Lafcadio Hearn had remarked the Japanese talent for seeming to accept wholly the ways of the foreigner — and yet, in the long run, of assimilating those alien ways and reasserting old Japan in new forms. Whether Chinese culture possesses a similar power of recrudescence is yet to be ascertained. For the sake of diversity in the world, Kirk hoped so in 1974.

The Americanization of Taiwan alarmed some writers and scholars whom Kirk encountered. Those were aware that every old culture resists with all its power the endeavor of some competing culture to overcome and supplant it — quite as every living organism resists desperately the voracious attempt of some other form of life to assimilate to its own mode and substance the first organism.

The contest between the regimes of Beijing and of Taipei was not military merely or political merely. It was a contest also for the half-instinctive cultural loyalties of the Chinese people. Suspicion of "foreign devils" was for many centuries among the strongest characteristics of the Chinese. If the "Free China" of Taiwan should come to seem a mere imitation of the United States, how might Taipei hope to win over the hundreds of millions of mainland Chinese in the long run? If Chinese communism eventually should adapt itself in some degree to the old patterns of Chinese life, might not those hundreds of millions of Chinese come to endure communism for the sake of its Chinese aspect — irrelevant though Marxist dogmas are to Chinese society?

It was easy to understand the attractions of the American cultural pattern for the Chinese of Taiwan. America had been the protector; their army had been trained and equipped by the United States; America was their biggest customer; most of their younger professors had been educated in American universities; English was taught in all the schools; American investment in Taiwan bulked far larger than all other foreign investments combined.

And yet if Taipei, in the fairly near future, were to assert its legitimacy as the government and the culture of all the Chinese people, it must be something more than American China, as set against Russian China. The industrial efficiency of Taiwan, founded upon American methods, could not of itself supply a principle of cultural loyalty. Eventually the most populous of all nations would demand a culture of its own, rooted in the nation's collective experience.

Beijing in 1974 had decayed to a drab and dreary metropolis, half demolished, almost all its former splendor and vitality crushed by Marxist egalitarianism and Mao's grinding despotism. Taipei was a bustling, smoggy city with a population about the size of Detroit's, its buildings (except for temples) very like Detroit's — and its pursuits, too. The people of Beijing wore uniforms; the people of Taipei wore American fashions.

The capital and the culture of a future China must differ from both of these, if China were to renew its civilization. Several times, in ages past, China had been tormented for a century or longer by alien masters from beyond the Wall. From those epochs, China had risen up in an altered form, reasserting much of its old culture but adding to it new things Chinese. By the beginning of the twenty-first century, China might have recovered from its Russian affliction and its American affectation, Kirk reflected.

In 1974, Taiwan suffered from complacency, not from despair. Its afflictions were those of the affluent countries, inflation and excessive expenditure conspicuous among those troubles. Only in Kinmen and Matsu, the fortified islands within sight of the mainland, did the Nationalist Chinese remain fully aware of the great, grim power that would try to devour them so soon as the international balance of forces might be altered.

Several years before Kirk's trip to Taiwan, David Nelson Rowe had written, "There is a great deal of unthinking acceptance of everything American, and much equally unthinking rejection of what is traditionally Chinese. This is almost certain to lead to insufficient utilization of the real political and psychological assets inherited from China's past. There is no doubt that American influence is to blame for much of this."

Those sentences about the Taiwanese were even more true in 1974. Emulation of the United States had led the Chinese of Taiwan into various costly miscalculations and boondoggles, among them the obsessive desire to own automobiles — this in an overcrowded island not much bigger than Maryland. Among the consequences were severe pollution, hideous traffic problems, waste of capital, and social antagonisms.

Suppose, for example, that one were a Taiwanese villager, well enough fed and housed perhaps, but unable even to dream of possessing any such contraption as an automobile. Suppose that as one walked along a road with one's umbrella extended (for very often rain falls torrentially in Taiwan) a new car should roar by — and drench the pedestrian from head to foot with muddy water. Those proud chariots were doing precisely that, day in and day out, in Taiwan. Such arrogance could create class division far more swiftly than could clumsy Communist propaganda.

But America being the land of the automobile triumphant, so must Taiwan be. To create a speedway, Taiwan's public authorities had begun to construct, in 1974, the North-South Freeway, extending almost the length of the island, closely parallel with the coast. By the time it was finished, the cost would be a billion American dollars. One section of this boondoggle would be eight lanes wide. There would be thirty-seven land-consuming interchanges, American style. This superhighway would lie parallel with Taiwan's chief railroad, which was well managed and ran admirable swift passenger trains; it would drain off business from that more efficient means of transportation. Worst of all, the new freeway, with its ten toll plazas, was being cut through Taiwan's only fertile region, and would cover precious soil with concrete. The chief beneficiaries of the freeway would be rich Taiwanese eager to speed in their new cars — and, of course, the big contractors. Such was one consequence of foolish adulation of American folkways.

Yet there was more to the Republic of China in Taiwan than this conspicuous consumption. To understand the fortitude and tenacity of Free China, Kirk spent two days in Kinmen.

That island, or rather archipelago, was a fragment of old China, lying just off the great mainland port of Amoy. In 1949 the Communists took Amoy, but Kinmen had held them in check ever since. The island was all garden above and all fortress below.

Every other night, the Communist guns on the mainland and the Nationalist guns on the islands exchanged salvos — although in 1974 most of the shells were loaded merely with propaganda leaflets. Those guns were echoing as Kirk strolled with his companions, nocturnally shopping, along the chief lane of old Kinmen City, a pleasantly unmodernized town. "Just listen to that thunder!" exclaimed Ralph de Toledano, who had downed two or three whiskies before the barrage had commenced. It was not thunder out o' China 'cross the bay, but artillery.

The old houses of Kinmen, the country places particularly, with their ochre-tinted thick walls and the delightful pitch and slant of their tiled roofs, were the most eye-pleasing dwellings anywhere, to Kirk's taste. They seemed to emerge from one of those long, long rolled paintings of eighteenth-century China. Kirk was surprised that so many of them still stood, after twenty-five years of siege.

The assault on Kinmen had begun late in October 1949, when two divisions of Communist troops had stormed ashore. The island had been unfortified then, but the defending Nationalists had captured seven thousand of the enemy and killed several thousand others; many had drowned in the bay. For years thereafter, Mao's artillery, on the mainland near Amoy, had bombarded Kinmen — daily or nightly for some periods, sporadically in other months. On the two days when President Eisenhower had visited Taiwan, during 1960, the Communists bombarded Kinmen with nearly 175,000 shells, the most intensive fire in military history.

Kirk's host in Kinmen was the humorous Major General Wang T-chun — who had charge, among other things, of the radio and loudspeaker broadcasts directed at the Amoy Communists. General Wang declared that Kinmen was delightfully peaceful, a refuge from the tumult and smog and booming modernity of Taipei.

Kinmen had become impregnable as Gibraltar. On the surface, the island of Big Kinmen was all tranquillity. The strong garrison had planted innumerable trees, created parks and lakes, restored shrines. From the living rock, far below, they had quarried the tremendous Hall of Atlas, a theater and an emergency hospital. Food was exported from the island, from the fields that supplied food for the whole civilian and military population as well. Also Big Kinmen had a thriving distillery and even a commercial pottery.

At the Kinmen pottery Kirk bought a china peach, delicately tinted, with a Ming design of animal figures upon it. In Chinese tradition, the peach is a symbol of longevity. To manufacture fragile china within range of Communist guns was an act of audacity — and of piety. Through joining audacity with piety, the Chinese might redeem their civilization.

Life in the Taiwan of 1974 was not altogether idyllic. Like Israel, Taiwan was a garrison state. On checking out of his palatial hotel, Kirk discovered that he had left a small trinket in his room. Key in hand, he hurried back. As he turned the key in the lock, he heard some faint sound within the room. On entering, he found a window wide open — a very tall window that he had closed three or four minutes earlier. A decorative ledge just outside the range of windows was broad enough for a practiced man to make his furtive way from bedroom to bedroom. In his bathroom, Kirk noticed that his toilet-paper rack had been dissected, and that in the recess behind the toilet-paper roll was a device for holding a little tape recorder; the tape had been carried off, but the spy had lacked the time to put back the rack or close the window by which he had fled. Taiwan's Federal Bureau of Investigation, on a tour of which Kirk had been taken, was an efficient agency. Later Kirk found that copies of some of his books, posted by him to friends in Taipei, never reached their destination, some being returned to him by the Taiwan post office, and others simply vanishing. Any foreign devil might be a subversive.

Sixteen years later, Taiwanese investors would be building factories in Fukien, and developing other enterprises on the mainland, with the approval of the Communist regime. For their own economic advantage, the capitalists of Taiwan would have begun to restore the mainland economy that the Communists had ruined. Kirk would wonder whether the Taiwanese, or the ROCs, would not have been more prudent to preserve their separation altogether from the huge inchoate bulk of China. It was said that Chiang Kai-shek had been successful and happy in ruling Taiwan, for the mass of all China had been too much for his abilities, as it had been too much for other rulers before him. For more than forty years, Taiwan had known peace and prosperity — and, in strong contrast with Communist China, had known some freedom. The closer economic advantage might draw Taiwan toward the immense Chinese magnet, still merciless at its Beijing core, the greater the political peril.

Flying back to the United States, Kirk reflected high above the Pacific that despite his Stoic principles he was leading an epicurean existence. A beautiful wife, three charming little daughters, a handsome ancestral house in the country, gardens and woodlots to cultivate, no end of books to read, friends of all ages, expeditions occasionally to distant lands, good health, influence upon the course of affairs — why, it was well to bear in mind the counsel of Solon to Croesus, "Let no man call himself happy until the hour of his death."

CHAPTER FIFTEEN

Down with the Revolution!

Platform Duels

Although Kirk never took a vacation, in the sense of ceasing to write and instead lying serpent-like upon some beach, his expeditions to Europe, Africa, and the Orient during the Sixties and Seventies were relief from the verbal slashing and stabbing of controversy in which he was engaged, almost incessantly, while in the United States. In his syndicated column he assailed, Tacitus-like, fallacies and appetites of his era; and on the lecture platform he debated the more noted or notorious radicals of the turbulent years between 1965 and 1972; also he crossed swords of imagination with various eminent liberals.

Such platform duels, indeed, had begun to attract large audiences so early as 1962, and would occur sometimes after 1972; but the hottest exchanges happened between Lyndon Johnson's election to the presidency and Richard Nixon's election to a second term. Among Kirk's platform opponents during the Sixties and Seventies were William Kunstler, Max Lerner, Michael Harrington, Leonard Weinglass, Karl Hess, Ayn Rand, Saul Alinsky, David Lilienthal, Harold Taylor, William MacGregor Burns, Clark Kerr, Staughton Lynd, Malcolm X, Dick Gregory, Tom Hayden, Louis Lomax . . . He met many adversaries at many campus and public assemblies, and there were ever so many questions of the hour to be debated hotly!

So far as any pattern may be discerned in all this speechifying, Kirk was concerned with four very large questions, arising successively: anarchic radicalism on the campus, abortion and public policy, the state of the Church, and educational reform. Also, during the

Seventies and Eighties, from time to time he testified in federal and state courts as an expert witness in church-state litigation. In the role of polymath, he lectured from coast to coast on a wide diversity of other topics, among them "Is America Decadent?"; "The Return of the Philosophical Historians"; "The Persistence of Political Corruption"; "What's Wrong with Textbooks in Literature"; "The Literature of Decadence"; "Criminal Character and Mercy"; "Prospects for Conservatives"; "Will Independent Colleges Survive?"; "The Menace of Giant Ideology"; "American Presidents"; "Schooling for Wisdom and Virtue"; "The Supernatural in Fiction"; "Prospects for the American Family"; "Rediscovering Mystery: Imagery and Moral Imagination"; "Can Modern Civilization Be Reinvigorated?"; "Ideology and Prudence in Foreign Policy"; "Decay and Renewal in American Education"; and "The Roots of American Order." Because most Americans mistakenly revere syndicated newspaper columnists — a shallow breed, with few exceptions — he had so many invitations, until in 1975 he ceased to write his "To the Point," that during some years he was able to spend little more than half his time at Mecosta. Often he was asked to talk about Edmund Burke or T. S. Eliot.

Certain vignettes of these platform duels remain vivid enough in Kirk's memory. For instance, in a big auditorium at the University of Michigan, Kirk debated Tom Hayden — who arrived late, as was his custom (he wishing to make a dramatic entrance well after a debate had commenced). Leaping to the platform, Hayden (long before he became Mr. Jane Fonda) proceeded to denounce Kirk as the champion of a merciless capitalism; Kirk was reminded of the caricatures of the bloated capitalist, in evening dress and top hat, puffing on a long cigar, that had appeared in the Railroad Brotherhood's weekly paper *Labor,* in the days of his youth. But the audience began to laugh at Hayden, not with him; for Hayden's straw man bore not the least resemblance to Kirk, who had been discussing the afflictions of twentieth-century society. Puzzled by the students' mirth, Hayden spoke less rapidly; at which juncture there arose from the audience a huge young black man who growled, "Hey, Hayden, you got this cat Kirk all wrong!" Not many weeks later, Hayden was off to Newark to incite riots there; but he fled away when shooting began.

Or there comes to Kirk's mind the wild night at Ohio State University, not long after the violent struggle at Kent State University and the seizure of Attica prison by its inmates, when he debated the radical lawyer William Kunstler, whom he had confronted before at Boston College. The crowd was tremendous, many of the students seated in ideological blocs, some groups dressed uniformly — as Fidelistas, for instance. The militant black women, clustered together, shrieked intermittently. Kunstler, writhing snakelike as he gripped the podium, praised the criminals who had taken hostage guards and other prisoners and had hideously tortured to death some of their captives.

At the conclusion of the debate, several serious undergraduates asked Kirk to talk with them. He agreeing, the group proceeded to the student union, but found the doors chained so as to avert violence and vandalism. They walked on to the long avenue in Columbus that parallels the campus and leads to the state capitol. That street was lined with bars and bistros, frenetic music blaring from every door; it would have been impossible to converse at any of those joints. "Is there any coffeehouse or restaurant that doesn't have this music?" Kirk asked. The students put their heads together, but could think of no such oldfangled establishment in the neighborhood of the campus of Ohio State University, with its forty thousand students — or alleged students. Kirk took the students to his room at the campus hotel, where the only refreshment was cola from a machine, but this tiny remnant was able to discuss the politics of prudence. Such was the state of learning and of free inquiry at the mass campus of the Sixties and early Seventies.

A third recollection sometimes comes to Kirk: a debate at Fort Wayne with Dick Gregory. That towering black man, comedian and champion of negroes and Indians, talked so rapidly and so garrulously that Kirk scarcely could get in a sentence or two. Gregory was a man of real courage and honesty, no radical really. In the Watts riot, he had been shot in the thigh by black extremists while trying to calm the crowd; at the Democratic National Convention of 1968, in Chicago, he had acted in the same fashion by persuading a part of the wild crowd to follow him toward the stockyards, away from Grant Park and the Hilton Hotel. At Fort Wayne, two white men — probably college instructors — in neat business suits, rising from the front row of the audience, requested of him, "Brother Gregory, tell Dr. Kirk how much we need Senator Edward Kennedy as president."

"Ted Kennedy!" Gregory exclaimed, incredulously. "Ted Kennedy? If that Kopechne girl had been driving, and Kennedy had been left to drown in the car — why, she'd have gone to the chair by now. We don't want that sort of man for our president!"

Someone else asked Gregory if the United States didn't need a new constitution. "I don't want any new constitution," Gregory replied vigorously. "We couldn't have a better Constitution than the one we've got already. All I want is a piece of it."

Among the self-seeking agitators of those years, eager for power and money, delighting in "burn, baby, burn," moved by hatred, stood up in marvellous contrast fearless Dick Gregory, concerned for the common good, and sufficiently humorous and good-natured to restrain crowds, through his power of persuasion, from turning into mobs.

Those three occasions on the platform, so very readily recollected, might be supplemented and substantiated by two score more such, were there but world enough and time. Not a great many other men of conservative inclinations, during those years of shouting, came forward to share with Kirk the unpopular, and perhaps dangerous, duty of endeavoring to refute on the platform the fallacies and frantic misrepresentations of the demagogues. His stoicism served him well. At one college, a professor dubbed him "the unflappable Dr. Kirk." He was not the sort of conservative the radicalized students had expected; on some campuses, chapters of Students for a Democratic Society applauded him heartily, after hearing him out. With few exceptions, Kirk's platform adversaries of those ten combative years have gone into the dark since Kirk faced them, or have sunk into obscurity. When the most bitter debating ended, Kirk would be fifty-four years old, gray-headed, his photographed profile rather haughty. The Republic had not been radicalized: after a fashion, Kirk and his friends had outtalked and outwritten the enemies of the permanent things.

Rebellion against Boredom

Why did university and college students in the United States, during the late Sixties and early Seventies, convert classes into "teach-in" sessions about current affairs? Why did they shout down speakers, menace professors, and burn libraries? Much has been published about campus radicalism; Kirk commends particularly Edward Ericson's *Radicals in the University* (1975) and Klaus Mehnert's *Twilight of the Young* (1977). Kirk's speechifying on many campuses at the height of collegiate disruptions taught him that the principal enemy to tolerable academic order was Giant Boredom.

The psychiatrist Bruno Bettelheim, on the platform at Rosary College along with Michael Novak, Staughton Lynd, and Kirk, described the composition of radical organizations of students. (Bettelheim's personal experiences at the hands of the Nazis and in concentration camps added weight to his words.) At the core of every radical student group, he said, could be found a handful of clever young people who knew what they were doing and were seekers after power. These were surrounded by a much larger body of neurotic young persons with proclivities toward violence who served as the striking force of the inner cadre: precise in his employment of terms, Dr. Bettelheim called these latter activists paranoiacs. Then there could be turned out by the radicals, on occasion, a mob of boys and girls with no real commitment to the ideological cause, but ready enough for a varsity rag — bored, other-directed, happy at escape from campus routine, eager to be where the action was. Of such elements were the "idealist" student groups made up, and ordinarily the activists did not exceed more than five per cent of any student body, even on the more systematically radicalized campuses. The paranoiacs among them were capable of destroying offices, damaging libraries, setting off bombs, and beating fellow students or recalcitrant professors. The presence on campus of a few shrewd and energetic young ideologues often sufficed to paralyze the normal functioning of a big university.

Several pretexts for student protest were advanced: the war in Vietnam, Black Power, "authoritarianism" in universities, detestation of the "military-industrial complex," opposition to the Reserve Officers' Training Corps, others. Yet Kirk found that for the most part these causes were pretext merely. Really, the chief reason for students' discontent was boredom: boredom among the better students because the American university offered too little for mind and conscience; boredom among the poorer students because they never should have been enrolled at all.

"I'm not surprised at all that many young people — those who are naïve and searching for identity, as well as those who are quite mature and clearly motivated — 'drop out' of their studies." So wrote to Kirk a well-known editor and critic, professor and formerly administrator at a large midwestern state university.

Professor Bruno Bettelheim's recent statement before a Congressional committee was entirely accurate. As you know from your own past experience, many of our faculty have good reason to be disaffected, and their common reason is similar to the reason the students are unhappy and unruly.

One can easily lose his identity even before he becomes aware of it. The facelessness and namelessness of the modern university are horrifying. I just heard today that the appropriate Presidential commission in Washington is prepared to recommend that no universities be established and allowed to grow over a student body of ten thousand.* But what about the present monstrosities?

Aye, student and professor were victims of what Ernest van den Haag had called "America's Pelagian heresy." Old Pelagius, so drubbed by Saint Augustine, declared that all men will be saved eventually, without the operation of divine grace. The average American in our century has come to believe that all men may be saved through educationism, without need for thought. Mere enrollment in a college, the American Pelagians had become convinced, would assure a lucrative salary upon graduation, acceptance at the country club, tolerable manners, participation in middle-brow culture, exemption from military service, and moral equanimity.

Ever since the end of the Second World War, therefore, American campuses had been flooded by ineducable young persons uninterested in abstractions, and consequently incapable of profiting from years in college, because the higher learning necessarily has to do with abstractions. What once was academic community had become academic collectivism.

In this mob, the better students were resentful and frustrated, for general standards had been lowered below their interest or capacity. In this mob, the learned professor was deprived of dignity and influence, although he might lecture little and be paid well. In this mob, the teaching assistant and the research assistant were worked to the bone, paid a pittance; they developed the mentality of proletarians. Such was Dr. Clark Kerr's "multiversity": on the platform with Kirk and others at Tulane University, Kerr argued that the students were happy at Behemoth University.

*No such recommendation was published, however.

In 1953 Kirk had turned academic dropout, in protest against the deliberate lowering of academic standards and the insensate swelling of campus enrollments. Once upon a time, it had been easy to love *alma mater*; then there existed a humane scale upon the campus, and genuine principles of learning might be discerned. But in the academic crowd of 1969, Kirk had written, little love was lost; and that lonely crowd easily was converted into an academic mob — difficult for police to restrain because of its immensity. The student sans-culotte and the instructor-ideologue readily found followers in such a collectivity. What wonder that the campus sank into anarchy? The wonder really was that violent protest against academic anonymity and academic fraud had not burst forth earlier.

Bruno Bettelheim had described perceptively the mentality of campus rebels. They were led, he said, by students intellectually precocious but emotionally immature — little knots of bright young people, permissively reared, imperfectly schooled, and altogether un-acquainted with the limitations of human action. Such students felt that the typical mass campus had lost ethical purpose, intellectual relevance, and personal relationships; it had been perverted from its ends. They asked the right questions, though they knew few answers.

Subscribing to the American Pelagian heresy, fond mothers and fathers had shipped off to the campus certain young persons, trouble-some at home, who might have been directed to a different sort of public institution, were they to be institutionalized at all. It was hoped that the young paranoiac might sink comfortably into the campus ethos of sociability. At Behemoth University, however, the student with serious psychological disturbances was given not bread, but a stone. Intellectually rootless, and depersonalized by the vastness of the campus crowd, such a student, perhaps suffering from a proclivity toward violence, could become a willing storm trooper in the service of the smart young theoretical revolutionaries. He met no distin-guished professor; the imperfectly schooled young instructors whose classes he attended were incapable of offering him normative guidance. He grew bored; he grew angry; and presently a latent impulse toward destruction found a vent.

Such disaffected students were unopposed, and often abetted, by that large proportion of the students who had known nothing outside college but the Permissive Society, in which most appetites were gratified without labor, and in which authority was resented — though

[411]

unconsciously yearned after by most people. Such indolent students did not find it unpleasant that administrators and professors were reviled publicly; they knew no strong loyalties, and had been taught to revere nothing. So long as their own campus pleasures were not seriously interrupted, they would not support any academic order.

Add to these the mass of "students" present on the campus only to avoid the rigors of Vietnam, or for certification as potential employees, most of whom never would be graduated anyway — and it ceases to surprise that campus after campus fell under the domination of immature ideologues. To this pass the campuses had been brought by the educationist empire builders, by those professors who preferred governmental and industrial research contracts to the pursuit or dissemination of wisdom, and by the American Pelagian heresy — which last had produced, also, the degradation of the democratic dogma in public primary and secondary schools, so that the average college freshman had been prepared wretchedly for higher studies.

Preoccupied with vocationalism and sociability, many universities and colleges had neglected both the development of right reason and of those ethical insights that are apprehended through the rousing of the moral imagination. After enormous bricks-and-mortar expenditure, after infinite bragging about democratic culture, after promising a pleasant and affluent white-collar career to every boy and girl who could be lured into the degree mill — why, somehow this sham "education" had angered both the enterprising talents and the mediocrity of the rising generation. Mankind can endure anything except boredom. For two decades and more, American higher education had bored undergraduates, graduate students, and many professors. By the late Sixties, the paranoiacs were smashing the computers, while the ideologues were busy abolishing the liberties of the mind.

Kirk was writing, in 1969, about Behemoth University, the typical overgrown and flatulent campus, where the boast was "service" — service to industry, to government, to popular fad or foible, service to anything except Veritas. Service to King Numbers had been especially sycophantic. Yet King Numbers was easily bored, and ungrateful for flattery.

There survived some colleges and even universities that had yielded relatively little ground before King Numbers and that had made comparatively few concessions to pressure for reduction of intellectual standards. And it is true that some of these better campuses had been beset by rebellion nonetheless. Yet at such institutions, the violence was imitative of graver troubles elsewhere and was short-lived, repudiated by the large majority of students and professors. (The University of Chicago put down the ideologue and the paranoiac with only minor difficulties.) Where the decay of principle and discipline had not proceeded inordinately, loyalty to genuine academic community withstood fantastic innovation.

But at most of the institutions of a learning nominally higher, the development of a defecated rationalism, unchastened or uninformed by the moral imagination, had produced ideological yearnings and had roused literally burning impatience with the old perfections of man and society. American affluence and a fatuous social permissivism had turned out a college-age population often intellectually flaccid and insulated against the harsher aspects of the human condition — though sentimentally lachrymose whenever the "underprivileged" or "culturally deprived" were mentioned. Roughly speaking, the higher the student's background of prosperity, the higher the rebelliousness. Those childish revolutionaries would demolish their own economic foundations. On the other hand, where most students were children of hard-working parents, the radicals were unpopular: consider the eviction of radical Mark Rudd from the campus of Brooklyn College by Brooklyn undergraduates no sooner than he had set foot there, and similar resistance to ideologues and fanatics at Queens College and City College.

As for proximate incitements to rebellion, in part the campus troubles grew out of conscious emulation of recent "activism" elsewhere: the "civil rights" movement, Black Power aggressiveness, protest against the war in Vietnam. When undergraduates are unutterably bored, any varsity rag will do; the ideological trappings are incidental. Nor is it possible to forget that young people between the ages of nineteen and twenty-two, during the Sixties, had been fed the pabulum of television all their days. The TV producer found it necessary to solve within half an hour, or an hour at most, every personal and social problem. So students were indignant when the difficulties of the college, or the nation, or the world, were not resolved with equal celerity by the possessors of political or economic power. How happy everyone would become if only some wretched university president or some crepuscular military-industrial cabal should be brought to heel!

By its nature, the college is a place for academic leisure and reflection, not for action; a place for preparation, not for domination. When Kirk addressed students at the University of California at La Jolla, some of the disciples of the radical Dr. Herbert Marcuse were present. They informed Kirk that Professor Marcuse and he were singing rather the same tune: for Marcuse repeatedly had told his students that they ought to refrain from "activism" in college: their task it was to study and talk now, if they were to act effectively later. Had Karl Marx spent his years parading round Trafalgar Square with a sandwich board on which he had inscribed the legend "Off the pigs!" rather than burrowing in the British Museum, he would have been altogether ineffectual — so Kirk told Marcuse's students. In the course of his collegiate speechifying, Kirk found that it was quite possible to convince students, at least the better ones, that college and university are places for the acquiring of intellectual disciplines, for sober meditation and inquiry and pleasant discourse. But this comes to pass only when courses of study offer something for the mind, and when professors are something better than dry sticks or frustrated soapbox orators. When the Academy ceases to be boring, the student will cease to wave the bloody shirt.

Such was the sermon that Russell Kirk, D.Litt., preached from Atlantic to Pacific, and the Canadian frontier to the Gulf of Mexico, year after year. Occasionally, in the course of his peregrinations, he was rewarded by glimpses of intellectual farce. At Fresno, as his hosts of the State College were driving him to the lecture hall, their car passed a vacant lot next to a movie theater. The lot was crowded with shouting students, bonfires were alight, and some of the students were flinging bricks and stones against the theater's side wall.

"What are those boys protesting?" Kirk inquired.

"Nothing, really," he was told. "One of the broadcasting networks has hired them to put on a model riot; the film will be shown nationally."

"As a genuine demonstration?'"

"That's right, Dr. Kirk. The students are paid ten dollars an hour."

This simulated zeal of the Fresno students vanished about the time their bonfires were extinguished; and the professed zeal of the rising generation for the attaining of a Brave New World somehow trickled away about the year 1972, for rebellion had become boring, as well as fruitless.

Down with the Revolution!

Fifteen years later, Kirk would participate in a symposium on "Education and the American Dream" at Indiana University of Pennsylvania. The first speaker was Abbie Hoffman, the craziest and most repellent radical of the Sixties, obscene in his discourse, wearing apparently the same greasy clothes with which he had adorned his person in the glorious riots of yore. He professed his continuing devotion to the revolutionary ideals of the Good Old Cause.

"Revolution now!" he shouted at his student audience. (Instructors in sociology and political science had directed their students to attend this important lecture, on which they might be examined.) "Revolution now!"

The bored students, their feet up on the chairs in front of them, most of them chewing gum, wrote lazily on their notepads, "Revolution now." Some of them dozed. It was a far cry to Danton's "audacity, and again audacity, and always audacity!" Hoffman expired three years later, of drugs.

At an eastern Catholic college, twenty years after the Fresno demonstration, Kirk's third daughter, Felicia, enrolled in a political science course entitled "The American Experience." This turned out to be a tribute to the vehement radicals of the Sixties, team-taught by a man and a woman; though both were surviving (and probably tenured) radicals of the last stage of the Movement of the late Sixties and early Seventies, the female obviously begrudged the male such time as he spent lecturing, she desiring a monopoly of the platform. One subject was assigned to all students for a term paper: a study of one of the people conspicuously active in the debates and demonstrations of the Sixties. Felicia Kirk chose Russell Kirk as her subject, which doubtless chagrined her instructors, and surprised them more; but after all he surely had been active and voluble, and of all the students in that class, only Miss Kirk had direct access to the papers and indeed the continuing conversation of a noted activist of the Sixties, still quick.

To have been made aware by riot that something is amiss with the higher learning in America is some gain. This tardy awareness, however, has not flowered in conspicuous reforms. Therefore, on one pretext or another, academic anarchy may occur another day. Yet the university is not the Bastille, to be taken by frantic storm and razed to the ground; nor ought students to massacre the Invalides, dull dogs though some professors may be. The university is not a prison or a fortress, but a community of scholars — and not a community of one generation only. Those who would reform it must understand its past greatness and its surviving promise.

In the later stages of the student uprisings, Miss Joan Baez remarked that if one desires to work a revolution, the campus is an unlikely place to commence, that she was disgusted with the antics of campus radicals, and that she would have no more to do with them. Even such professors as taught Kirk's daughter Felicia will learn that lesson in time: for revolutions devour their fathers, as well as their children. Those who sincerely desire the restoration of the higher learning need to heed the admonition of Miss Joan Baez, leading the turbulent first rising at Berkeley: "Do it with love."

Kirk conducted a good many college classes during the Sixties and Seventies and Eighties, as distinguished visiting professor of something or other at a diversity of institutions — Los Angeles State College, Pepperdine University, Central Michigan University, Hillsdale College, Olivet College, Albion College, Troy State University, Indiana University, the University of Colorado, Grand Valley State University. Also twelve honorary doctorates were conferred upon him, in addition to his earned doctorate of letters. Though much bedoctored, Kirk settled on no campus.

He never encountered difficulties with radical students, though all about him disorder was seething. In the summer of 1965, at the Vermont Avenue campus of Pepperdine University in Los Angeles, across a freeway from black Watts, he taught a course in modern political movements, and explored Watts near the grotesque Watts Towers: the quarter was calm and cheerful-seeming. At the conclusion of summer school, Annette and he flew back to Mecosta. A day or two later, he telephoned the administration building at Pepperdine to turn in some final grades.

"We can't talk now, Dr. Kirk," a woman's voice panted. "The mob is coming down the street, and we're all leaving!" It was the great Watts Riot, gunfire and all.

Indeed, the mob from Watts did come down Vermont Avenue, smashing and looting; the mob paused at the main entrance to the Pepperdine campus; its scouts peered into the quadrangle. The staff prudently had fled. In the middle of the quadrangle, leaning backward in a chair, was a veteran janitor of Pepperdine, a man of color, saying nothing: he had served the University for many years. "The boy stood on the burning deck, whence all but he had fled . . ." Across the old man's knees lay a shotgun. Perceiving that, the mob from Watts turned tail and proceeded down Vermont Avenue, leaving Pepperdine unsacked.

Hillsdale College, rather remote in southern Michigan, had no such unruly neighbors. Kirk met classes there, one semester a year, for some seven years. Staff and students, with few exceptions, rejected the radical movements of the Sixties. Later Kirk would sell his library to Hillsdale College. Had finances permitted, he would have preferred to leave it to his wife and daughters, who desired to keep alive the "little platoon" of writers and students who, over the years, had professed to find at Piety Hill an oasis in the cultural wasteland.

Kirk estimated that some thirty years must elapse before most universities and colleges should recover from the follies of the Sixties; meanwhile the Academy would be dominated by yesterday's militant ideologues, who had bullied their way into tenure on the large majority of campuses — famous universities included. It was well that he had turned his back, in 1953, on the professorial existence.

The Slaughter of the Innocents

Another revolutionary agitation promptly succeeded the conclusion of the campus riots: the bitter dispute over whether women had the right to destroy their impending offspring, which controversy has raged ever since, a grim political question, right down to this writing. "Abortion on demand" was bound up with a more general revolt against traditional morality and old institutions; many of the spirits that had marched against college administration buildings now found their joy in proclaiming that the human fetus is not human.

By 1970, liberals had forced the abortion question to the forefront of public discussion. In surveys of public opinion, the *New York Times* put the question thus: "Do you believe that the termination of a pregnancy should be a matter of consultation between a woman and her physician?" Of course the large majority of the public responded in the affirmative, assuming naturally that a pregnant mother would consult an obstetrician, and that her pregnancy would be happily terminated by the birth of a baby. But that was not at all what the abortion-rights folk intended by that ambiguous word "terminated"; for them, the word meant a phrase from *Macbeth* — "ripped untimely from the womb."

New York, Colorado, Hawaii, and other states adopted innovating statutes permitting abortion; within a few months after New York's legislature so acted, some seventy thousand unborn children were put to death. This horror made other state legislatures hesitate. In Michigan an abortion bill was bottled up in a legislative committee, early in 1971.

A dozen of Kirk's syndicated columns, during 1970 and 1971, dealt with the abortion dispute. Kirk argued that a people who demand the inalienable right to destroy their own young are far gone in decadence. Various newspapers simply did not publish those particular columns, for the sympathies of editors and radio and television people generally lay with the "pro-choice" or pro-abortion faction. The advocates of abortion on demand were enthusiastic, much heartened by their triumph in New York particularly; they organized powerful lobbies in state legislatures and raised very large sums of money for propaganda in the mass media.

The right-to-life camp, earlier sluggish, now began to stir. In Michigan the opponents of abortion formed PTAAA (People Taking Action Against Abortion). On Palm Sunday, 1972, they held on the Detroit riverfront a Congress for the Unborn.

Because of his newspaper columns, PTAAA had chosen Russell Kirk to be principal speaker. Russell and Annette took down with them to Detroit their youngest daughter, Felicia, aged eighteen months, whose beauty (she inheriting Annette's face) was much admired by the pro-life activists who gathered at Veterans' Hall, a big newish building beside the river.

That quarter of Detroit where Woodward Avenue meets the river had been sufficiently picturesque in Kirk's high-school and college years. Very close to this spot, the Sieur Antoine de la Mothe Cadillac had founded Detroit in 1701. Here, in his youth, Kirk had taken the steamers for Put-in-Bay Island, in Lake Erie; here, in Vernor's marble palace, he had drunk many a glass of ginger ale with cream added; here he had sniffed pleasantly the odors from a coffee-roasting plant nearby; starting from this point, he had walked pretty girls along Jefferson Avenue to the concerts on Belle Isle. All that had been swept away by civic improvers; even the historic city hall had been demolished; the old core of Detroit had been supplanted by what

Kirk later was to call "the architecture of servitude and boredom." The nearby streets were half derelict and altogether dangerous.

To Kirk's surprise, the meeting's chairman, a negro, was an educational ally of his — Bob Johnson, a public-school librarian who was also president of the Detroit Education Association, a small union of teachers, distinctly not associated with the Michigan Education Association, the leaders of which gladly endorsed the alleged right to abortion.

Although a big man, Mr. Bob Johnson was not nearly so tall and ponderous as the four or five ministers who sat on the platform behind Kirk, pillars of rectitude. A physician or two and a judge also sat on the platform, silent, endorsing Kirk's speech. Not one Catholic priest joined the platform party, although in the audience were two elderly Jesuits. As for leading public men — why, the only politician bold enough to be seen on the dais with Kirk and the black Baptist clergymen was Mr. William Ryan, Speaker of the Michigan House, a labor Democrat who subscribed to the Catholic social doctrine of subsidiarity, a healthy-principled, intelligent man.

Perhaps a thousand people, most of them white, were in the audience. To them, Kirk declared that many well-meaning folk did not understand how abortion is the killing of a true human being — still in the womb, but as human as the people sitting at that moment in Veterans' Hall. To kill a baby who had yet to emerge from the uterus would be quite as immoral as it would be to kill a baby who had been breathing for a week. Kirk quoted at some length the remarks of Dr. Paul E. Rockwell, director of anaesthesiology at Leonard Hospital in Troy, New York. "It is my opinion," Dr. Rockwell had concluded, "that if the lawmakers and people realized that very vigorous life is present, it is possible that abortion might be found much more objectionable than euthanasia."

"Besides," Kirk went on in his exhortation to the Congress for the Unborn,

> we do not really obtain happiness by destroying the life closest to us. . . . What we fancy would make us happy may make us wretched, before long, if we yield thoughtlessly to impulse, doubt, or pain. A subtle sense of guilt endures, with reason; and a society in which abortion should be general would be a guilt-ridden society, suffering from subtle neuroses.

I propose that we vote in legislators who know reverence for human life, and vote out legislators who take baby-killing for the newest form of social emancipation. I propose that we employ every reasonable means to turn out of office those public men — and public women — who would approve the slaughter of babies; just as we ought to turn out of office such persons as might assent to genocide against Negroes or Jews or any other category of people. If we Americans have become too decadent to defend even the right to life of the innocent and the helpless — why, a sentence will be passed upon us all. "And that house fell; and great was the fall of that house."

The big Detroit television stations had their cameras focused on Kirk, and would broadcast a rather generous portion of his remarks that night. The two big Detroit dailies had sent reporters, and Kirk had given a copy of his speech to one of them; but no word of what Kirk had said to the Congress was reported in the press, that evening or the next day, even though one of the papers subscribed to his syndicated column and the other printed feature articles about him. In 1971, newspaper editors generally frowned upon pro-life reactionaries.

After much handshaking, exchange of promises, and compliments to the tiny Felicia Kirk in her basket — which sociability left them almost the last to leave Veterans' Hall — Russell and Annette Kirk made their way to a rooftop where, that Sunday afternoon, they had parked their rather battered automobile. From that rooftop all other cars had departed; but there remained a knot of unpleasant-looking men, seemingly engaged in a narcotics transaction. Then the Kirks discovered that their gasoline tank was empty.

What to do? No personnel of the parking garage remained on duty; presumably no gasoline stations remained open in downtown Detroit on Sunday evening, and they had no gasoline can in which to fetch fuel in any case. It would not do to leave Annette and the baby in the company of the grimy abusers of substances; and Russell had neglected to bring with him from Piety Hill his registered pistol. What to do, in the failing heart of the half-ruined city of Detroit, still unrecuperated from the wild riots of 1967, all about them the sinister silence that pervades the downtown area after business hours? Talk of the right to life, here amidst Muggerdom!

At this juncture there appeared, *deus ex machina*, Mr. William Ryan, Speaker of the House, who had driven up to the garage roof by some mistake, and who most kindly drove away again to procure gasoline for them. There had occurred in the wanderings of the Kirks other remarkable incidents of rescue, most notably one on the streets of the quarter of the Cape Coloreds in Port Elizabeth, South Africa — Annette, enfeebled, sitting on the curbstone and imploring Russell not to leave her in search of help as night fell. A solicitous man of color, rising out of nowhere, had got them back to their hotel. Now Providence had produced the Speaker as if he were a jack-in-the-box. Were theirs charmed lives?

Now the Michigan political battle about abortion, extending over nineteen months, commenced in earnest. Unable to extract their abortion-on-demand bill from legislative committees — Speaker Ryan saw to that — the "Pro-choice" (choice of life or death) people contrived to put the issue on the statewide ballot as an initiative. On November 7, 1972, the public would decide the question.

Meanwhile the Kirks speechified a great deal on the subject, Kirk campaigning against abortion in Massachusetts and Illinois as well as Michigan. Together they appeared on television. Annette began to take in a series of unwed mothers. The young women who took sanctuary at Piety Hill came from highly diverse circumstances: once a physician deposited with the Kirks a newborn infant who had entered the world unexpectedly in the back seat of a moving automobile. The little Kirk girls named him Jason and desired to keep him, but the waif had to be given up to the state for adoption, worse luck for him.

During the summer of 1972, a war of words concerning abortion was fought in Michigan. The bigger newspapers and most of the television stations clearly favored Proposal B, as the initiative for abortion-on-demand was designated on the ballot. In full-page newspaper advertisements, the pro-abortionists claimed that their cause was endorsed by practically every professional association and practically every church — except, of course, the reactionary Papist hierarchy. (Actually, in 1972, bishops and priests were remarkably feeble, most of them, in their condemnation of induced abortion.) Polls even indicated that more than half the Catholics of Michigan favored the right to abortion.

On September 1, a *Detroit News* poll revealed — at least to such people as think polling infallible — that less than thirty-seven per cent of the citizenry opposed Proposal B. On September 21, according to a later *News* poll, the opponents of abortion on demand numbered merely thirty-six per cent of the voters. But the people whom Kirk had addressed on the riverfront, months earlier, had begun to move.

By a poll of October 11, it appeared that forty per cent of the voters rejected Proposal B. The final *News* poll, published October 31, showed, to the surprise of liberals, that fifty-four per cent of the voters opposed abortion rights, forty-two per cent approved Proposal B, and four per cent were undecided.

On election day, November 7, Proposal B was rejected by a statewide majority of nearly sixty-two per cent. A month before the election, Dr. Jack Stack, a vociferous advocate of abortion on demand — he held some power in the Republican party and lived in Kirk's own senatorial district — had declared that the proposal would win sixty-two per cent of the vote. (Stack performed abortions, and Kirk had called him a son of a bitch, to his face, at a public meeting of Republican officeholders in central Michigan.) Dr. Stack's prediction was turned upside down. All Michigan counties except two voted against abortion on demand; one of those two counties was dominated by white university students, the other by affluent white-flight people. One of the black precincts of Detroit voted sixteen to one against abortion rights; every precinct dominated by black voters heavily rejected Proposal B.

Even in the closing decades of the twentieth century, it was not radical innovators merely who might gain their way through rallies and speechifying; such strategy could serve on occasion the defenders of tradition, too, as the struggle over Proposition B demonstrated. Kirk had not wasted his time, a year and a half earlier, when he had harangued at Veterans' Hall.

But two months and a fortnight after the defeat of Proposal B in Michigan, in the case of *Roe v. Wade*, the Supreme Court of the United States, seven justices to two, found that somehow the framers of the Constitution, in 1789, had intended to extend the shield of the federal government to women desiring to have abortions performed upon themselves — at any rate, during the first three months of pregnancy. Kirk's speech on the riverfront was undone. Or was it? More than twenty years later, the abortion question still is being debated in Congress, legislatures, and courts.

Down with the Revolution!

A Call to Reaction

The causes of the demand for legalizing abortion were bound up with the causes for the decline or the virtual secularization of Christian churches: widespread decay of belief in Christian dogmata brought with it a revolt against Christian morals. The dogma of the resurrection of the flesh and the life everlasting having been cast aside by many, it seemed to follow that the human fetus signified no more than the fetus of a dog or a cat.

Or so the zealots for abortion on demand insisted; and they intimidated many people, bishops among them. Kirk had thought it very curious that no priest had joined the black and white Protestant ministers on the platform with him at Detroit; equally curious that the archbishop of Detroit and the people about him had done nothing to publicize or encourage that riverfront rally. Among Catholic laity generally, it was otherwise: approximately half of the Michigan men and women active in the pro-life cause were Roman Catholics. Clearly the visible Catholic Church, its hierarchy and priesthood — with some honorable exceptions — had grown reluctant to frown on any movement called liberating or progressive. And this was painfully true in Michigan especially. The Church's trumpet gave an uncertain sound.

Annette Kirk, the child of an ardent Catholic family, the graduate of a Catholic school and a Catholic college, was much saddened by the changes in the Church that had commenced not long before her marriage; later she would take some part in the national deliberations of the Church. Russell Kirk, not baptized until 1964, nevertheless had contributed to Catholic periodicals long before that, and had been acquainted with influential ecclesiastics; he continued to write for Catholic publications. They were agreed that the Church was falling into disrepute.

Ever since the Second Vatican Council, the Church in America had been supposed to be "renewing" itself; certainly it had been in ferment. Enthusiastic Catholic renewers had proclaimed that the Church in America would make itself relevant to present social concerns and accomplish a prodigious reawakening of faith.

Had that happened by 1972 and 1973? Not so: more people had turned away from the Catholic faith with every year that elapsed during the asserted "renewal." The worst year of all was the period from July 1972 to July 1973: during those twelve months, weekly attendance at Catholic mass nationally fell from sixty-one per cent of parishioners to forty-eight per cent. The decline in number of communicants in the Archdiocese of Detroit had been far more severe than that in any other diocese in the United States.

This phenomenon was analyzed by two sociologists of the National Opinion Center at the University of Chicago — Father Andrew Greeley and Dr. William C. McCready. Writing in the *National Catholic Reporter,* these two students of opinion were gloomily candid: "The changes of the past year may well constitute the most dramatic collapse of religious devotion in the entire history of Christianity," they commented.

During the same period, 1972-73, church attendance by Protestants decreased slightly, and attendance by Jews at synagogues increased slightly. The Catholic Church in America, by contrast, was falling apart during those twelve months.

It was not the rising generation that left the Catholic Church during 1972-73. During the Sixties, attendance at mass by people less than thirty years of age had decreased sharply. But that falling away of the young had much diminished in 1972-73: during those months, taking of communion by members of this age group decreased merely by one per cent.

Something still more alarming than desertion by young people was occurring within the Church during 1972-73: older Catholics, most of them lifelong communicants, began to drift away from Catholic churches. Among Catholic parishioners fifty years of age or older, mass attendance fell from seventy-six per cent in 1972 to fifty-five per cent in 1973. Among Catholics between thirty and forty-nine years of age, attendance fell from sixty-two per cent to forty-nine. In short, the highest rate of attrition occurred among those Catholics who had seemed most faithful to their Church's magisterium and who had participated in the mass most habitually.

"The phenomenon is dramatic," Greeley and McCready observed. "We know of no other time in the course of human history when so many people — particularly older people — so decisively removed themselves from canonically required ecclesiastical practices." Far from renewing itself, by 1973 the Catholic Church in the United States seemed to be dissolving itself. Religious vocations had fallen dismayingly: no longer were there enough priests and nuns to do the Church's work adequately. Seminaries stood empty or nearly empty; a good many seminaries had been sold or converted to other purposes. Some orders of nuns received next to no novices. Conversions to the Church had dropped steadily during the previous decade.

Catholic parochial schools had closed their doors in increasing numbers, with the passing of every year since the Second Vatican Council. Many parents had reacted vehemently against innovations of the alleged "renewal" and had concluded that their children might be more free from heresy in a public school, with no religious teaching at all. Also many parish priests had lost interest in schooling.

"When a Catholic falls away," Samuel Johnson had said two centuries earlier, "he falls into nothing." By 1973, the laity were falling away fast. One aspect of "renewal" was supposed to be an increased active participation in the Church by the laity; actually, the "renewing" changes of the Sixties and early Seventies had been imposed upon the laity arbitrarily and often arrogantly. The laity had reacted to such bullying by staying home.

The typical Catholic layman resented prolonged tampering with the traditional liturgy; he was alarmed by the intrusion of radical political doctrines into Catholic homilies; he disliked the awkward English of the new "priests' Bible," so inferior to translations previously employed. A few more years of "renewal," it seemed to the Kirks early in the Seventies, would leave American Catholicism shattered to its foundations. Tardily, many priests, nuns, and "church mice" of the Church bureaucracy from Atlantic to Pacific had adopted the phrases and the attitudes of the student radicals and Black Power radicals of a decade earlier: a case of culture lag. Between them and many of the laity, a gulf had opened.

The radical movement of priests, nuns, church mice, and their faction reached its height during 1976. Its seeming triumph, but its real defeat, was the hierarchy's conference entitled "A Call to Action," nominally in celebration of the Bicentenary of the United States. Annette Kirk asserted herself at that tumultuous conference, with her husband as coadjutor.

Call to Action, otherwise known as the United States Bishops Conference on Liberty and Justice for All, met in the devastated city of Detroit (more dismal even than the city had been in 1971) from October 20 through October 23, with some thirteen hundred delegates attending.

The bishop of Grand Rapids had appointed Annette a delegate, she being well qualified as a woman, young, of Indian ancestry, wedded to a male chauvinist: in short, a Multiple Minority, presumably oppressed. Her husband, wearing a press badge, went along to guard her against the sturdy beggars and masterless men of the Cass Corridor, which howling slum marches with the convention center on the Detroit River.

What happened at Cobo Hall during four days of talk was to bring about sound and fury within the Catholic Church of America for some years — although a commotion not so loud and furious as the conference's organizers had hoped for, nor yet of quite the character they had intended. How much the majority of delegates actually intended to commemorate the two hundredth anniversary of the Republic may be gathered from this passage in one of the resolution documents adopted by the Assembly:

> While we affirm with gratitude all the positive elements in our heritage, we are conscious of our complicity in the many injustices committed at home and abroad through our uncritical acceptance of the social, economic, and political system in which we participate. We hear the cries of our oppressed brothers and sisters.

Scarcely anything more was said about those vague "positive elements." As for the bishops whose conference this was supposed to be, some never turned up; others, cardinals among them, appeared briefly and then fled; those who endured to the end learned something salutary in this school of hard knocks, perhaps. "You came here to listen, not to talk!" said a militant priest to an unhappy bishop who had attempted to utter sense at one of the workshop sessions. Persevering nevertheless, the bishop inquired, "People, do you know that there's a real world out there?" Cardinal Krol of Philadelphia, whose tall dignified form was beheld now and again, declared that the conference had fallen into the clutch of rebels. Many of the bishops were bruised at Detroit; next to nothing was said about commemorating the Bicentenary; and the large questions of liberty and justice were eclipsed by resolutions demanding the ordination of women, marriage for the clergy, civil rights or privileges for homosexuals, abolition of right-to-work laws, and passage of the Equal Rights Amendment.

[426]

In brief, Call to Action converted itself into a one-person/one-vote National Assembly (yes, adopting that ill-omened name of 1789), all dignities and ranks commingled and confounded. The Assembly presumed to instruct the bishops how to work all manner of radical alterations within and without the Church.

At this juncture there strode up to Kirk Monsignor Geno Baroni, of the National Center for Urban Ethnic Affairs, in the District of Columbia. (Soon, in the Carter administration, he would become the first Catholic cleric to be appointed an undersecretary [of Housing and Urban Development] in a President's cabinet.)

Embracing him, Monsignor Baroni cried, "Russell Kirk! You here! This conference doesn't really represent American Catholicism! Where are the professional people, the businessmen, the labor people?"

"This is a convention of the Church Mice, Monsignor," Kirk replied. By Church Mice, he meant members, paid or volunteer, of the spreading bureaucracy of the Church in America — functionaries whose chief work had become the filtering of government funds through an ecclesiastical apparatus; malcontent new-breed nuns and activist new-breed priests of the sort who found lettuce boycotts far more lively than visitations to the sick; members of parish committees and auxiliary organizations, provincial or parochial (at best) in their outlook, folk who had small knowledge of the real world beyond the shadow of the parish church in some neat suburb.

At Kirk's back as he talked with the Monsignor, and seated on the benches above his head, a grim-faced collection of nuns were knitting while they voted "Aye!" to all resolutions proposed. They looked very like Kirk's image of Madame Defarge and her lieutenant The Vengeance, knitting and rejoicing at the foot of the guillotine; doubtless those nuns would have relished being appointed to a revolutionary tribunal invested with the high justice, the middle, and the low.

Call to Action was the monstrous baby of Cardinal Dearden, of Detroit, upon whom the Church had conferred responsibility for celebrating the Bicentenary. Every participating diocese had been entitled to send nine delegates to Detroit. The bishops were supposed to select the nine, but many of the delegates seemed to have thrust themselves militantly upon timorous bishops; others were named because their faces were familiar to bishops; yet others appeared to have been nominated at random. In many dioceses, little or no preparatory study of the "working papers" had been undertaken. In consequence, although among the delegates there were a number of learned, sober, experienced, and moderate people, the majority were either aggressive social-action types or functionaries easily persuaded or intimidated by the militants. The guiding spirit at work among the real organizers of this conference had been that of Liberation Theology, reckless of consequences; a good while before Call to Action convened, witty Andrew Greeley had published a mordant description of the scheme shaped by Call to Action's organizers; his predictions were fully realized.

Those Jacobin organizers kept a tight rein at the conference. In the preliminary workshops, nobody was permitted to speak more than ten minutes. On the floor of the National Assembly, only the briefest debate was allowed, and no discussion whatever occurred concerning a number of important radical resolutions. The "working papers," drawn up before the conference began, were converted with few changes into resolutions; and even more startling manifestos, not mentioned in those working papers, were passed by voice vote in the frantic closing hours.

During this forced-draft adoption of resolutions about everything under the sun, there was read aloud, hastily, a resolution to the effect that the conference condemn management in some obscure Florida labor dispute. Annette Kirk struggled to a microphone to ask the floor chairman, Monsignor John Egan, a Machiavelli of Church politics, why some brief account of this mysterious dispute could not have been read aloud before the voting occurred. "Does anybody know about this?"

"That's a good suggestion," Monsignor Egan blandly replied. But the resolution already had been adopted by voice vote, any dissenters being drowned out; and the spate of resolutions swept on.

The National Assembly declared its will on subjects that for centuries had perplexed the most sagacious heads among theologians, church historians, moralists, and statesmen: the Church, the family, ethnicity and race, humankind, nationhood, neighborhood, personhood — all in the spirit of Robin Hood. The majority, experiencing no misgivings, desired not to be troubled with the facts. Consider the following resolution on "Defense of Human Rights." It was resolved that American foreign policy should allow "the development of political and economic systems that differ from our own. We urge that no economic or military support be extended to any government which displays a pattern of gross violations of human rights, whether based on political or religious grounds. We call upon the people of the United States to restrict any further government or corporate investment in these nations, allowing exceptions only for specific humanitarian needs."

Curiouser and curiouser, Kirk reflected. America was to tolerate political and economic systems that differed from her own, and yet must deny any public or private assistance to nations lacking America's own civil-rights pattern. Perhaps only Switzerland would qualify for aid. Was the United States then to allow the peoples of Africa to starve until their governments satisfy the stern requirements of the American Civil Liberties Union?

Some of the more innocent and moderate delegates to the conference had begun to suspect, by this time, that this Bicentennial gathering was dominated by ideologues who desired to politicize the Church and indulge their appetites for power. A number of the ideologue-delegates obviously regarded the Catholic Church in America as a potentially useful auxiliary of the extreme tip of the left wing of the Democratic party, though good for little else; other delegates were yet more radical in their aspirations.

For the majority of delegates, it appeared, "liberty" would be achieved by increased direction from government and from church bureaucracies. They would welcome whole new layers of sacred and secular bureaucracy, with abundant committee work at every level. To them, "justice" seemed to mean total equality of condition. Few, if any, of this ideological majority could have read Aquinas on justice, or even that admirable slim book *Justice* by Josef Pieper.

Possibly Cardinal Dearden may have grown uneasy with the tendencies of this National Assembly, though after all it was his creation. While he was addressing the conference from the middle of the floor, something indecorous occurred. There staggered across the hall a Detroit eccentric bearing on his back an immense cross, he bowed down by its weight. "Traitor!" he howled in seeming agony, "Traitor!" His loud reference was to Cardinal Dearden, notorious sufferer from the lust for innovation, patron of Call to Action. The protester, cross and all, was ejected from Cobo Hall, but Cardinal

Dearden, somewhat shaken, withdrew out the main door, applauded by many of the delegates. Kirk, puffing a cigar near the main exit, did not applaud. This lack of enthusiasm for the prelate was noticed by a small zealot nearby, who pointed out Kirk to a policeman, with the muttered request that Kirk too be ejected. But having noticed Kirk's press badge, the officer declined to offend the Fourth Estate.

"Is this the beginning of the end of the Catholic Church in America?" Kirk was asked by a young writer and editor who stood beside him. "Not so," Kirk told him. "These delegates have shocked and alarmed the bishops, and even the dullest and most progressive bishop is jealous to guard one thing — his episcopal authority. The boasted 'Five Year Plan' for implementing these crazy demands will be ignored by the bishops. And those bishops will find their resistance sustained by the huge majority of American Catholics."

As the conference ended, delegates and others were invited to affix their signatures to a document in which all those resolutions were recorded; the Kirks declined that honor. Outside Cobo Hall, as they departed, three lesbians were prancing and chanting, very like Macbeth's witches on the blasted heath. "Women, love yourselves," their placards declared. "The bishops don't."

There came to Kirk's mind a passage from John Henry Newman. "At this very time there is a fierce struggle," Newman wrote in 1836, "the spirit of Antichrist attempting to rise, and the political power in those countries which are prophetically Roman, firm and vigorous in repressing it. . . . At least we know from prophecy that the present framework of society and government, so far as it is the representative of Roman powers, is that which withholdeth, and Antichrist is that which will rise when this restraint fails."

In Cobo Hall, the majority seemed happy at the prospect of sweeping away the present framework of society and government to clear the way for "the rebirth of utopias," and they wasted no love upon Roman powers. This would not have surprised Newman. Satan is accomplished in his promises, Newman continued:

> Do you think he is so unskillful in his craft, as to ask you openly and plainly to join him in his warfare against the Truth? No; he offers you baits to tempt you. He promises you civil liberty; he promises you equality; he promises you trade and wealth; he promises you a remission of taxes; he promises you reform. . . . He scoffs

at times gone by; he scoffs at every institution which reveres them. He prompts you what to say, and then listens to you, and praises you, and encourages you. He bids you mount aloft. He shows you how to become as gods.

Just so. Pope Paul VI, then reigning, was mentioned only perfunctorily at the beginning of Call to Action's agenda: a three-minute film was shown in which, speaking broken English, the Pope welcomed the delegates; it was as if Call to Action deliberately mocked him. But the organizers of the conference could have been no better pleased with his successor, John Paul I. And when a cardinal from Cracow, that astonishing priest who knew altogether too much about Five Year Plans, was chosen by the Conclave — why, the American politicizers of the Church would be undone. Years later, the Kirks, in the Vatican, would exchange a few sentences with John Paul II — and for the first time in her life, Annette would find herself at a loss for words. John Paul II was both a man of thought and a man of action, as well as a man of prayer; but his thoughts and his actions were far removed from the ideology of Call to Action. He made himself the skillful renewer of Roman powers, that authority so esteemed by Newman, so detested by the New Breed of 1976.

The pronunciamentos of the Call to Action zealots promptly sank like stones. Most American Catholics of 1976 dwelt in the real world, not in the fantastic realm of humanitarian ideology. Most knew that liberty, justice, and peace are preserved and extended only through patient and prudent striving, that Providence moves deliberately, while the devil always hurries.

A human body that cannot react is a corpse; and this is as true of a body social that cannot react: so Kirk had learned from his old friend Roy Campbell. Against the Call to Action, the American bishops reacted healthily, and so did the Catholic laity of the United States. A little less than a year after the fiasco of the Call to Action at Detroit, in Rome the Conclave of Cardinals reacted against what Greeley and McCready had called "the most dramatic collapse of religious devotion in the entire history of Christianity"; the Conclave reacted also against "the rebirth of utopias" promised at Detroit, knowing such promises to be inspired by the Evil Spirit, engaged in what Newman called "warfare against the Truth." With the election to the throne of Peter of Karol Wojtyla, in reaction against the Church's ideologues, there commenced a genuine renewal of authority, tradition, the sacred, and the Good News.

A Tranquil Interval

The concluding four years of the eighth decade of the twentieth century were peaceful enough at Piety Hill. Kirk had ceased to write his syndicated column a few months after the Great Fire of Ash Wednesday, 1975; even had he desired to linger as a newspaperman, he had become too busy rebuilding Piety Hill to bother with daily scribbling. His decision to give up the column, which had been published for thirteen years, turned out to be prudent, despite Annette's dismay at her husband's casting away their only regular source of income; for he turned his typewriter to work more enduring, more to his taste, and better paid. For the destruction of the ancestral house on Ash Wednesday, Russell and Annette Kirk were granted one high consolation: the Fire Baby, Andrea Seton Kirk, born on the ancient feast of Saint Crispin, the twenty-fifth day of October, 1975: all unknowing, Annette had been carrying this child in her womb when the Old House burned utterly. Learning she was pregnant, she dreaded that the baby might be born without fingers or toes, or perhaps mindless, what with Annette's distracted state during and after the Great Fire. But far from suffering from her mother's shock, Andrea turned out to be the merriest of the Kirk daughters, the most affectionate and creative.

The Great Fire, which had consumed the Old House while Andrea was swimming vigorously in amniotic fluid (she then perhaps one centimeter long), fascinated the youngest of the Kirk daughters. When she was three, her father presented her with a little doll that had survived the fire by being in a cellar of the wing. "Is this from the Old Time?" she inquired reverently. For her, modern history had commenced in 1975. For some years, Andrea insisted on taking her meals from her father's plate, she sitting on his lap. Once enrolled in kindergarten — she had to walk only one block to the school — she said gratefully to her father, one evening as he was about to read to her, "Daddy, because of all the things you've taught me, I can answer the questions other children ask in school."

The splendid old mahogany dining table, London-made, that the Kirks had acquired after their Great Fire, would accommodate sixteen diners comfortably; and often every place was filled, what with Kirk's assistants, students, and guests; also there often dined at Piety Hill the refugees and exiles — Vietnamese, Chinese-Vietnamese, Ethiopians, Eritreans — who, escaped from squalid oligarchs, the Kirks lodged in one or another of the smaller houses that they held. (Some such families stayed with the Kirks for several years; later would come Poles and Croats.) Kirk the paterfamilias, at the long table's head, in those four tranquil years forbade the asking at dinner of either of two questions: "Have you seen *Star Wars*?" and "How do you think Jimmy Carter is doing?"

Between 1975 and 1980, Kirk's platform duels were fewer. Innovators in State and Church had been beaten back; the Academy was fairly quiet once more; rebels in the Church were licking their wounds. Thus he found the time to complete *Decadence and Renewal in the Higher Learning: An Episodic History of American University and College since 1953,* the chapters of which each discussed, consecutively, one year of decay. Gateway Editions (the new name of Henry Regnery's publishing firm, then managed by the younger Henry Regnery, with Kirk's former student, the cheerful and rather martial Dennis Connell, as sales manager) published the book in 1978. Nearly all reviews were friendly, despite the mordant belligerence of Kirk's chapters, but it did not obtain nearly so much attention as Bloom's *The Closing of the American Mind,* published some years later, which took up a number of the same themes.

In 1977, Kirk's mystical fiction emerged again in two volumes: a collection of his uncanny tales, *The Princess of All Lands,* published by Arkham House; and *Lord of the Hollow Dark,* published by St. Martin's Press, in form a Gothick romance, by intent a symbolic representation of the corrupting cults that had come up from underground in the latter half of the twentieth century.

Princess received many cordial reviews; the first printing soon was sold out, and the second printing did not last long. Edmund Fuller's review in the *Wall Street Journal* called much attention to the collection. Of the tales therein, four were set in Michigan, two in Scotland, two in England, and one in Croatia; all purported to occur in the twentieth century. "Sorworth Place," the first story in the book, Rod Serling adapted for his television series of occult and uncanny films; it was shown on the networks many times.

[433]

Lord of the Hollow Dark received relatively little attention, although it was praised by Robert Aickman, the most accomplished of writers of uncanny tales. It was a subtle, scary, complex book, in which there reappeared Manfred Arcane, the picaresque hero of *A Creature of the Twilight;* Kirk left his readers to puzzle out for themselves his meanings. A new edition, with Kirk's earlier story "Balgrummo's Hell" as prolegomenon, would be published by Christendom Press in 1989.

Kirk had fancied his purgatorial or hellish characters and scenes sufficiently terrifying; but his agent, endeavoring to arrange paperback editions of Kirk's fiction, told him that perhaps some paperback publisher of fantasy might find Kirk's works suitable for "their gentler women readers." The American public, particularly the boys and girls, had supped so long on literary horrors that their taste had become depraved. For that market, Kirk would not write, no matter how well rewarded. He never had written anything he did not believe to be true, or of which he had been ashamed, or of which he ought to have been ashamed. That resolve had given him perfect independence and a tolerable conscience, though it had left him innocent of stocks, bonds, and savings accounts. Like his literary mentor Walter Scott, he might convivially consume, what with guests, refugees, charities, and daughters to be well schooled, such small resources as he possessed. Yet because there was in the beginning the Word, he would not abuse words.

During 1975 and 1976 he had been a fairly active member of Michigan's bicentennial commission, appointed by Governor Milliken; that body did well to spend its funds chiefly upon historic preservation. Otherwise he had accepted no public office of any sort during the Seventies.

Charles Brown, who had known Kirk for a good many years, compiled a bibliography of Kirk's writings, which the Clarke Historical Library was to publish in 1981. Through the year 1980, his bibliographer found, Kirk had published sixteen volumes of history, politics, literary and educational criticism, and biography; five volumes of fiction; seven hundred and thirteen periodical essays; fourteen articles in works of reference; twenty-two introductions or forewords to books; forty-three published addresses, pamphlets, and miscellanea; one hundred and fifty major book reviews; seventeen short stories; and nineteen articles or essays first published in, or reprinted in, anthologies. Brown's bibliography listed only two hundred and twenty-two of Kirk's newspaper columns — ones selected for their merit; but the total number of syndicated columns published between April 30, 1962, and June 29, 1975, was in excess of two thousand. So, as "publications" are reckoned by colleges and universities under the "publish or perish" tenure policies, Kirk had to his credit more than three thousand publications — which doubtless would have conferred upon him precedence over all other professors everywhere, had he chosen to be a professor. He had been writing for publication from the age of sixteen to the age of sixty-two; and during the Eighties he would add very considerably to his list of books, essays, and published speeches.

From time to time, one friend or another had offered to secure for him an endowed chair in some discipline. Different friends urged him to take a post in the Nixon administration or the Reagan administration. To the first he would say, "I could have had that sort of thing when I was in my thirties, had I desired it"; smiling, to the latter, "How you must hate me, to try to convert me into a bureaucrat!" Irving Babbitt wrote that we must be happy in our work, or not at all. Kirk was well content with his work as man of letters, much as surviving illuminators of manuscripts may have been well content with their work even after Gutenberg had invented movable type. "A man may write at any time if he set himself doggedly to it," said Samuel Johnson. There is more to the knack of writing than that; but at any rate Kirk had been sufficiently dogged.

What had he accomplished by all that scribbling? "Scribble, scribble, scribble — eh, Dr. Kirk?" Why, from time to time a good many people told him that chiefly he had set in motion a train of ideas, that he had reminded a generation of the existence of permanent things in morals and politics, that he had struck the errors of socialism a dolorous blow and had chastened liberalism's presumption. But Kirk was not inclined toward the theory that history is made by books — not by abstract books, anyway. What Napoleon had said, though, Kirk found true in considerable degree — that imagination rules mankind. If Kirk had exerted any real influence during sixty years of writing, it was because he had been endowed with the talent to write imaginatively. Still undismayed in the year 1980, he whetted the edge of his sword of imagination.

CHAPTER SIXTEEN

Causes Gained, Causes Disputed

The Conservative Tide

By the spring of 1980, it was clear enough that most American citizens had turned politically conservative; and it was clear enough to Kirk, if not to others, that Mr. Ronald Reagan would be the next president of the United States. The intellectual movement to which Kirk had contributed at the beginning of the Fifties had become a popular cause — nay, a high tide in the affairs of men. Somewhat to his surprise, he not having been sanguine thirty years earlier, Kirk found that he had not labored altogether in vain.

On the eve of Ronald Reagan's great national victory, being invited by the Heritage Foundation to lecture in Washington, Kirk discussed publicly the large subject of the renewal of conservative thought and action. He began by pointing out that in nineteenth- and twentieth-century America, as in Britain, ordinarily the passage of some three decades had been required for a body of convictions to be expressed, discussed, and then at length incorporated into public policy — or else to be rejected. Usually this leisurely pace in the movement of public opinion had been to America's or Britain's advantage — in strong contrast with the mercurial politics of France, say. Such a fruition of ideas was making possible a political harvest in the United States by the year 1980.

A thoughtful, renewed conservatism, Kirk continued, had begun to appear in print at the end of the 1940s and the beginning of the 1950s, with the publishing of books and periodical essays by men and women of a conservative bent. Ideas do have consequences, as

Richard Weaver had written about that time; and a generation later, these conservative concepts, popularized, were about to enter into public policies.

It did not signify that most "activist" conservatives had read only scantly, if at all, in the serious conservative books of thirty years past; that was to be expected; serious thought always is vulgarized and filtered and transmuted, through newspaper editorials and Sunday sermons and college lectures and paperback books and even television programs, until a crowd of people perhaps wholly unaware of the sources of their convictions come to embrace a particular view of religion or of morals or of politics. As Henry Adams had remarked in his *Education,* during his editorship *The North American Review* had only a few hundred subscribers, and yet he found his journal's views plagiarized, happily, in hundreds of newspapers. Thus the average American citizen had no notion that his vote, in 1980, would be very strongly influenced, although indirectly, by certain books three decades old that he never had opened; nevertheless, it would be so.

Kirk drew a parallel with the Fabian Society in Britain, which had gained success in public policy only after thirty years of pamphleteering. But unlike the tightly concerted Fabian Society, the American intellectual renewal of conservative ideas, beginning about 1950, had been undirected and uncoordinated, the work of isolated individual scholars and writers only slightly acquainted one with the others' work, let alone enjoying personal acquaintance. Consider the names of men whose books had obtained some attention, perhaps as novelties, shortly before or shortly after 1950: Richard Weaver, Peter Viereck, Daniel Boorstin, Francis Wilson, William Buckley, William McGovern, Russell Kirk. When Kirk had published his book *The Conservative Mind* in 1953, he never had met any of these gentlemen except Weaver; nor had these persons met one another, with few exceptions. Nevertheless, the gentry whom Sidney Hook called "ritualistic liberals" took for a wicked conspiracy this recrudescence of conservative opinions. A rumor went round among professors of history, about 1954, that Daniel Boorstin, Peter Viereck, and Russell Kirk were plotting industriously to dominate the teaching of history in the United States. Actually, those three never had conferred together, and had met very rarely and then by chance.

Until this surprising renewal of conservative thought, liberal dogmas in morals and politics had been everywhere triumphant in the United States since the Twenties — as Lionel Trilling still declared, with some misgivings, at the end of 1949. Irving Babbitt and Paul Elmer More had been dead for years; Donald Davidson and Allen Tate were read as poets and literary critics only. In practical politics, the leading men of both parties then employed merely the vocabulary of latter-day liberalism. Yet, as if Trilling's remark had conjured spirits from the vasty deep, no sooner was his *Liberal Imagination* published than the literary adversaries of liberal dogmata rose up in numbers.

The renewal of conservative thought at the beginning of the Fifties had been paralleled chronologically by the decline and fall of the New Deal and by the abrupt ascent of Dwight Eisenhower to the grandest place among the seats of the mighty. Yet there had existed next to no connection between these two political phenomena, except that they both may have been produced, in part, by a general American boredom with the clichés of the New Deal and by the obvious feebleness of what remained of the New Deal measures during the Truman administration.

Arthur M. Schlesinger, Jr., had endeavored to taunt the "New Conservatives" for their failure to be appointed to office by President Eisenhower. But the writing conservatives of the Fifties were not disheartened at not having been created Eisenhower placemen. Some of the New Conservatives were hereditary Democrats; of the Republicans among them, most had preferred Robert Taft to Dwight Eisenhower. So far as conservative writers had aught in common, it was this: they were social critics, innocent of any design for assuming personal power. For one thing, they had set their faces against political centralization, so that a cushy appointment in Washington might have been a repudiation of their own convictions.

They had been sufficiently ignored by both Republican and Democratic presidents, except that Richard Nixon occasionally had invited one or another of them to the White House for general conversation. Now and again a United States senator or a member of the House of Representatives — rare birds, rare as men of business who took long views in politics — had sent to one or another New Conservative a note of appreciation. They had fared no better among state politicians. They had possessed no central apparatus; few publishers had approved their books; in the Academy they had been a forlorn remnant.

[439]

Still, they had not been ignored by the movers and shakers of public opinion. When Kirk's *Conservative Mind* had been approved by the *New York Times Book Review* and *Time,* a breach had been made in the intellectual ramparts that liberals watched. Through this breach other scholars and writers had fought their way: Robert Nisbet, Thomas Molnar, James Jackson Kilpatrick, John Lukacs, Frederick Wilhelmsen; a trifle later, Ernest van den Haag and Jeffrey Hart; a score of others. They had become allied, too, with older men, some of whom had been very different in their politics at an earlier time: such writers as James Burnham, William Henry Chamberlin, John Davenport, and John Chamberlain; such eminent professors as Will Herberg, Ross J. S. Hoffman, Eliseo Vivas, and Leo Strauss. Such economists as W. A. Orton and presently Milton Friedman, contemptuous of the planned economy, had weight in the Fifties. The resurgent conservatives made themselves heard. Since then the breach in the liberals' literary ramparts had been filled up with rubble and rubbish, but the liberal reviewers had not yet succeeded in stamping out altogether the forlorn hope of conservative writers who, having penetrated within the citadel, continued to lay about themselves with their swords of imagination.

There had sprung up weekly and quarterly magazines of a conservative temper. Some few book publishers, besides the courageous Henry Regnery, began to indulge them occasionally — even some university presses. Now and again people of a conservative bent were invited to speak upon campuses. There arose a national campus discussion society, distinctly conservative, which today is called the Intercollegiate Studies Institute, with its widely circulated *Intercollegiate Review* and other journals, and its lecture programs; there appeared also national and local "activist" student groups, most notably Young Americans for Freedom, of which M. Stanton Evans was prime mover.

This haphazard intellectual revival of conservative thought at first had affected American elections only a trifle. A considerable time is required for new or revived political concepts to supplant in American citizens' conscious and subconscious minds accustomed political loyalties and prejudices. Nevertheless, the immediate influence of the conservative renewal would have been larger, had not certain political accidents occurred: the extravagances of Senator Joseph McCarthy, the absurdities of the John Birch Society, the murder of President

Kennedy, the fiasco of Barry Goldwater's presidential campaign, Lyndon Johnson's Vietnamese war. Despite conservatives' protestations, liberal and radical publicists had tarred them with these alien brushes. Even so, the public-opinion polls had shown a steady increase in the number of Americans who set themselves down as "conservatives" — indeed, from the first such poll onward, conservatives formed the largest single segment of political preference. Political circumstances and an altered climate of opinion were pushing public opinion toward conservative measures.

The circumstances that worked upon the American public were obvious enough during the Fifties, Sixties, and Seventies. Inflation of the currency, burdensome taxation, oppressive political centralization, sorry confusion in the public schools, disintegration of great cities by grim social change, violent crime, feebleness and failure in foreign affairs — these were only some of the afflictions with which American citizens became unpleasantly acquainted from the end of the Second World War onward, although especially during the Johnson administration.

Because political administrations professedly liberal were in power while these grim troubles came to pass, and because liberal dogmas dominated the serious press and the universities, the American public tended to look for some alternatives to liberal slogans and policies. Never had any very large proportion of the American electorate embraced a thoroughgoing radicalism; therefore conservative measures slowly were recognized by the public as the alternative to liberal measures.

Adverse circumstances alone do not bring on a reformation or a renewal: for a people to take arms against a sea of troubles, there must be provided the catalyst of ideas, for good or for ill. About 1950, the emerging conservative thinkers had discerned the causes of national adversity, long before the general public had become aware of the difficulties into which the United States was sliding. Thus a measure of conservative imagination and right reason already had existed as the public, somewhat slowly and confusedly, had begun to turn its back upon the politically dominant liberalism. The handful of conservative writers and scholars, and those public men capable of serious reflection, offered an alternative to the exploded dogmas and measures of liberalism. Those fresh or renewed conservative concepts worked upon the public's discontent with the circumstances into which liberalism had brought the country: this union of thought and circumstance had made possible a general conservative movement.

Any intellectual and political movement, if it is to achieve more than ephemeral popularity and influence, must possess a body of common belief. That is not to say it must, or should, profess an ideology. For ideology is political fanaticism and illusion: as John Adams defined it, ideology is the art of diving and sinking in politics. By "a body of common belief," then, is meant here those general convictions and healthy prejudices derived from long consensus and social experience.

Such a body of common belief still subsists in the United States — perhaps more than in any other major country — during the latter half of the twentieth century. Here are some of its elements: persuasion that there exists a moral order, of more than human contrivance, to which human laws and usages ought to conform; confidence in the American Constitution, both the written Constitution and the underlying unwritten constitution of custom; attachment to representative government; suspicion of central direction; preference for an economy in which work and thrift obtain their just rewards; love of country — a love extending beyond the present moment to the past and the future of the nation.

Such are conservative beliefs and impulses. Their roots were not altogether withered in the Fifties and Sixties and Seventies, even if few could express such sentiments coherently. It is not surprising that in a time of tribulation and discontent, the American public had begun to listen to conservative voices.

Yet the fact remained that these conservatives did not march in lockstep. In one respect, this lack of unanimity was a virtue: it meant that conservatives were no ideologues; they approved diversity and individuality. Utopianism, oddity, and extreme positions, all the same, are not conservative qualities. Such failings were discerned easily enough in various aspects of the growing drift of opinion that was somewhat clumsily labelled "conservative."

One of those defects was the continuing obsession, particularly among people well endowed in the goods of fortune, with economics. This is not to denigrate the Dismal Science. A good economic arrangement had produced America's prosperity; and, still more important, it had been closely connected with private liberty. But economic security is no more the whole of the civil social order than wealth is the sole source of happiness. Economic success is a by-product, not a major cause, of America's success as a society. This point may be sufficiently illustrated by one of the inimitable anecdotes of Kirk's friend Erik von Kuehnelt-Leddihn. On one occasion, that compulsive traveller was addressing a gathering of Catholic businessmen in Detroit. At the conclusion of his remarks, a gentleman in the audience inquired, "Doc, do you know what history is?"

"Why, no," Kuehnelt-Leddihn answered. "Can you instruct me?"

"Sure. History is just economics, that's all — just economics."

In the mind's eye, one may see the ironic Dr. Kuehnelt-Leddihn replying: "Indeed? Tell me, sir, are you a Catholic?"

"Sure. I just made a novena."

"What a pity, sir, what a pity!"

"Why is it a pity I'm a Catholic?" — this belligerently.

"Because, sir, if you were not a Catholic, you might be appointed a professor at the Marx-Lenin Institute."

To embrace Marxist materialism and determinism in the name of another abstraction called "capitalism" is to deliver one's self bound to the foe. Conservatives do defend a free economy; they defend it, however, as bound up with a complex social structure of order and justice and freedom, founded upon an understanding of man as a moral being.

Sometimes allied with this economic obsession, among folk who called themselves conservatives or were so called, was the mode of belief labelled "Libertarianism," a demand for absolute civil liberty from the controls of government. If one demands unlimited liberty, as in the French Revolution, one ends with unlimited despotism. "Men of intemperate minds never can be free," Burke wrote. "Their passions forge their fetters."

Any good society is endowed with order and justice and freedom. Of these, as Sir Richard Livingstone wrote, order has primacy; for without tolerable order existing, neither justice nor freedom can come into being. To try to exalt an abstract "liberty," as John Stuart Mill attempted, is to undermine order and justice — and so, in a short time, to undo freedom itself, the real prescriptive freedom of a settled social order.

If they were to lead the United States, Kirk said in 1980, conservatives must appear to be, and in fact really must be, imaginative but reasonable people who would not claim that they could turn the world upside down. The American people were not about to submit themselves to the utopianism of a tiny band of chirping sectaries, whose prophet (even though they might not have had direct acquaintance with his works) was Jean Jacques Rousseau.

Genuine conservatives knew that man and society are not perfectible; they were realistically aware that Utopia means literally Nowhere. It always has been one of the conservatives' principal functions to remind mankind that politics is the art of the possible.

Were the conservatives of 1980 what John Stuart Mill had called conservatives in the Victorian era, "the stupid party"? Certainly a good many Americans who thought themselves conservatives were dull or apathetic merely. Others seemed interested chiefly in conserving their own advantages. "With conservative populations," Brooks Adams had written, "slaughter is nature's remedy." He had meant that mere plodding adherence to old ways would not suffice for survival in an age of fierce and rapid change.

During thirty years of growth of the American conservative movement, immense mischief had been done to the politics and the economic structure and the culture of the United States by liberal and radical notions and policies. Soon — within a few months — it would be up to conservatives to repair the damage, supposing them to know how to go about it. Were the conservatives of 1980 well prepared to undertake such responsibilities? No, not altogether; but then, time runs on, runs on, and nobody ever is well prepared for great duties, and the longer the delay, the more formidable a nation's difficulties would become.

Those who had begun a conservative intellectual renewal about 1950 had grown gray in opposition to liberal dominations and powers and to radical zealots of overturn. Those conservatives of the mind did not expect ever to be able to doze secure in lotusland. Prudent change being the means of a state's preservation, the great statesman has been one who could combine with a disposition to preserve an ability to reform. That awareness, and that sort of public man, the conservative movement had been endeavoring to develop. The conservatives' efficacy soon would be put to the test. Although they were not going to march to Zion, they might succeed in planting some saplings in the Waste Land.

Defending the Family

Conservatives of the 1980s were hard worked: they found it necessary to defend at all points the beliefs, customs, and institutions that until recently had seemed (like Kirk's grandfather's bank) strong as the rock of Gibraltar. Even the human family was assailed by the ideologues of modernity and collectivism, although the whole of society, from the time of the first true men to the age of nuclear fission, had rested upon the footing of the family. Often, during the Eighties, Kirk was asked to speak on the plight of the American family, and to write about the subject.

In 1983 he was invited to give the keynote address to the international Congress on the Family, meeting that year in Rome, during November. Several hundred people attended, the larger delegations from the countries of western Europe and of Latin America. Accompanying her husband, Annette was interviewed on Italian television concerning the recent report of the federal Commission on Excellence in Education. Russell had some opportunity of showing her the grandeurs of the Eternal City; she was especially taken with the house and tomb of Saint Cecilia, the catacombs of Priscilla, and the restaurant in the vaults of the Theater of Pompey.

To the polyglot Congress on the Family (with simultaneous electronic translation into several languages) Kirk said that the family has been held together by the strongest of human bonds — by love, and by the demands of self-preservation. The family commences in *eros,* but grows into *agape.*

The alternative to the vigorous family is the universal orphanage, Kirk continued. If the family disintegrates, there remain only two modes of human existence. The first of these is an atomic individualism, every man or woman isolated and self-seeking, suffering each from too much ego in one's cosmos. Such loveless individualism, the delusion of the nineteenth-century rationalists, does not endure long; for, as Aristotle put it, man is a gregarious animal. We yearn to love and to be loved, to belong to something bigger than ourselves. Besides, total individualism is the negation of society. We are made for cooperation — like the hands, like the feet, Marcus Aurelius says. When we cease to cooperate, the average sensual man becomes Cain, with his hand against every man's. In such a condition, there exists freedom of a sort, but it is what John Adams called the freedom of the wolf, as distinguished from the moral freedom of the truly human person. License of that sort, if prolonged, would put an end to the human race. So it is that if the family structure dissolves into an irresponsible solitary individualism, such a phase is adventitious and transitory merely. It is succeeded, ordinarily, by a different alternative mode.

This latter condition is compulsory collectivism. The political state becomes all in all: only in its most rudimentary, deprived aspect is the family tolerated. Children become the wards of the state, reared for the state's purposes; marriage survives simply to reduce the enervating consequences of promiscuity. That servile condition is described in a number of fictional dystopias of our century — by Aldous Huxley, by George Orwell, by Jacquetta Hawkes. Married couples cohabitate in barracks cells; or, if children are permitted to dwell with their parents beyond infancy, that is because they might be employed as spies upon their parents, as in Orwell's *1984*. Mere production and consumption, under direction of the state apparatus, become the exclusive ends of human striving.

Such a prospective extinction of the family is not fanciful merely. It has been the deliberate policy of the Communist regimes in China and Cambodia — although already the masters of China have found it necessary to modify their scheme. It was the design of the Bolshevik ideologues of the Russian Revolution, although the vestiges of Christian belief and custom among the Russian people impeded the fulfillment of this aspiration. And we would be foolish to ignore a strong drift in what is called "the West" toward the supplanting of the family by the Universal Orphanage. Vast schemes of state "child care," in the name of liberating housewives, in truth are designs for thrusting women into gainful employment, at whatever cost to small children — so that the state gains revenues, through taxing women's incomes.

Kirk went on to remark that adversity, good for the soul, also may reinvigorate the family. Suggesting various measures that might be taken to restore the family's vigor, he let cheerfulness break in. Human nature, imperfect though it be, is a constant, he concluded. Out of this human nature arises a healthy reaction against the degradation of the family. For love, which is stronger than death, also is stronger than the enthusiasts for copulation without population, stronger than arid humanitarianism, stronger than the computer, stronger than Caesar. And the family is the child of the fertile union of love with necessity. God willing, the champions of the family will overcome the death urge, the enemies of Adam and Eve, and the foul fiend.

Fourteen members of the Congress on the Family, the Kirks among them, were admitted to an audience with Pope John Paul II. Surely the burdens that John Paul II bore were heavier even than those endured by Gregory the Great. Gregory's principal adversary was barbarism, but near the end of the twentieth century the papacy was assailed by a heavy intellectual mechanism and materialism, by the concerted hatred of totalist ideologues, and by demands for "liberation" that called to mind Milton's line: "License they mean, when they cry liberty."

In the Renaissance audience chamber, the strong winning Pope, the restorer of the Church's spiritual authority, listened patiently to long addresses, his slippered feet tapping softly on the pavement to relieve the pain left by the terrorist's bullet that had struck his spine. Then he spoke himself at some length, in French. Seeing this remarkable priest and hearing him sing — for he sang to the men and women of his audience — Kirk knew John Paul for one of those very rare persons whose actions, in Burke's phrases, "have changed the face of fortune, and almost of nature."

It was this pope himself — previously laborer, actor, poet, philosopher, now sufferer and holy man — who contended against the spirit of the age, and who for his courage had become venerated by millions who stood outside the Church. What he was doing was more efficacious than what he preached. If indeed it was Andropov, master of the Soviet Union, who sent the Turkish gunman to Piazza San Pietro — why, Andropov had recognized his most formidable adversary, the priest who had grown up under Communist servitude.

At the conclusion of the audience, the Pope warmly clasped the hands of Annette and then of Russell. Annette contrived to tell him that some years before, in Cracow, he had joined in marriage a couple, Rett and Marguerite Ludwikowski, friends of his and of the Kirks. The Pope smiled in recognition: "Si, si, Ludwikowski!" He passed on.

The tremendous task of John Paul II, to borrow a phrase from T. S. Eliot, was "to save the World from suicide."

Two millennia after certain theophanic events occurred, tradition had grown dim; people were left chiefly with a Book, excessive veneration of which could become bibliolatry; men and women, rejecting authority, had fallen back upon private judgment; doubters and scorners had been at work for some centuries, especially the most recent two centuries. These were the new barbarians described by G. K. Chesterton:

> What though they come with scroll and pen,
> And grave as a shaven clerk,
> By this sign you shall know them,
> That they ruin and make dark.

The barbarians of the pen and the barbarians of the gun did not dismay John Paul II. Of all defenders of the family, he was the most moving.

The Triumphs and the Jests of Ronald Reagan

From 1964 onward, the activities of Ronald Reagan and of Russell Kirk had run in parallel lines. It was not that Kirk ever had been in consultation with Mr. Reagan, or had written speeches for him, as had Jeffrey Hart (who, like Kirk, followed in the steps of Edmund Burke and Samuel Johnson); no, the relationship had been casual, intermittent, and usually at a considerable remove. Yet they two (both writing columns) had been of one mind for the most part, ever since they had campaigned for Barry Goldwater's presidential candidacy — had campaigned simultaneously in California and elsewhere, that is, although never as a team.

On Reagan's announcing his candidacy for the governorship of California, Kirk had ventured to think that although Mr. Reagan would win that office, he would cut no great figure as a governor; for what did Reagan, Hollywood actor, know of political administration? Soon Kirk discovered that he had mistaken his man; for Mr. Reagan turned out to be an efficient and popular governor. Audacious as a politician, he actually dared to charge tuition at the state's institutions of higher learning: students, the children of affluence, sped about in their Jaguars honking furiously in protest against this outrageous demand that they pay money for college degrees. Some people complained that the Governor was false to the conservative cause, for he did not drastically reduce public expenditures and taxation; but as a political realist, Reagan knew that he had done well to prevent expenditures and taxes from increasing more than they did during his tenure of office.

Kirk commended Reagan as governor in his syndicated column and in *National Review.* A member of Reagan's inner staff kept the Governor and Kirk in communication from time to time. Both of them contributed essays to an anthology, *Seeds of Anarchy: A Study of Campus Revolution,* edited by Frederick Wilhelmsen. One of their bonds was that both had newspaper columns published by the Los Angeles Times Syndicate. Mr. Reagan read Kirk's *National Review* page and his newspaper column fairly often; if he read Kirk's books, he did not comment upon them.

As the contest between Reagan and Gerald Ford for the Republican presidential nomination became war, Kirk took Reagan's part in Michigan. Again, in 1980, Kirk would be active in support of Reagan's candidacy; the leader of the Reagan faction offered Kirk a place in the Reagan wing of the Michigan delegation to the Republican National Convention, but Kirk declined, disliking crowds, and indeed never attending any national convention. (He did attend Michigan Republican conventions, as a delegate.) Kirk's political influence was not of the sort that shouts upon the floor of large public assemblies.

Had the Republicans nominated Reagan for the presidency in 1976, rather than Gerald Ford, conservative measures would have prevailed during those four fateful years when, instead, President Jimmy Carter blundered at home and abroad, alienating even such Democratic partisans as Henry Steele Commager and Arthur M. Schlesinger, Jr. Had he been a presidential candidate in 1976, Reagan would have overwhelmed Carter as he was to do in 1980: Carter could not have withstood the popular rhetoric and charismatic personality of Reagan. For that matter, had the Republicans nominated Reagan in 1968, presumably there would have occurred no Watergate disaster; or if something of that sort had occurred, Reagan would have surmounted the episode, quite as he came off scatheless, during his second administration, from the storm that arose in Congress over secret dealings in Iran and the Levant.

After leaving the governorship, Mr. Reagan was persuaded to chair the committee of prominent Californians interested in promoting the production of a series of television films based on Kirk's fat book *The Roots of American Order.* At a luncheon meeting of those people, Reagan sat next to Kirk; the famous actor and politician seemed somewhat shy with Kirk, perhaps fancying that his luncheon neighbor was sober-sided and formidably learned; actually, Kirk himself was shy on that occasion, as often. They did talk of politics in Michigan, from which state Kirk brought Reagan good news, and Mr. Reagan expressed his eagerness to be matched against President Carter.

In 1979, beginning his third endeavor to obtain the Republican presidential nomination, Reagan won the electorate by his humor and his candor, as well as through the vigor of his speeches. Occasionally, like Goldwater before him, Reagan uttered some political howler; yet Reagan was able to recover better from the reproaches or the mockery of television commentators and newspaper columnists than Goldwater had been. Just after the Russians had invaded Afghanistan, Reagan was asked on television what course of action he would have taken about that, had he been president at the time. Unhesitatingly, Reagan replied that he would have sent American troops to Pakistan. Hearing this hasty declaration, Laurence Beilenson, who had been Reagan's Hollywood lawyer and who was a friend of Kirk too, telephoned Mr. Reagan. Colonel Beilenson, the author of books on diplomacy and counter-insurgency, had been the principal American liaison officer operating with Chinese troops against Japanese divisions in the interior of China, during the later stages of the Second World War in the Orient.

"Ron," said Beilenson in their telephone conversation, "whatever did you mean when you said that you'd station American troops in Pakistan. What would they do there? Would you intend to go to war with the Soviet Union in the heart of Asia?"

"You're right, Larry," Reagan said. "I made a mistake. I'll tell the media about it right away." Of course his repudiation of his blunder was little reported by the press or the electronic media. It would have been well, a few years later, if President Reagan had consulted Beilenson before stationing a body of Marines at anarchic Beirut; certainly his friend would have advised him against such foolish strategy, which would bring about America's only military disaster and humiliation during Reagan's two terms in office.

About foreign affairs and military operations Reagan had known little before he took his oath of office in Washington. Yet his audacity compensated for his ignorance; and, except for the terrorist assault upon the Marines at Beirut, he was successful in diplomacy and in limited war. His obvious sincerity would serve him well in his conduct of affairs of state; he was as persuasive with Gorbachev as with Mrs. Thatcher.

Kirk took next to no part in Reagan's successful presidential campaign; there was no need for him to do so; but he did predict the size of Reagan's popular and electoral triumph, more accurately than did any of the pollsters. Once Mr. Reagan had settled into the White House, Kirk began to receive from various folk newly appointed to office offers of appointment for himself to a congeries of high administrative posts, councils, commissions, and committees; with thanks, Kirk declined them all, although the invitations kept coming, all the way down to 1987. He would be more useful to the President, he told his Washington friends, by speaking and writing independently. His bachelor friend Kenneth Cribb left the practice of law to take an eminent post in the Reagan administration, and presently rose yet higher, becoming the President's chief advisor on domestic policy, in Reagan's second administration. Should he join the Reagan administration? Cribb had asked Kirk in 1981. "It's your duty," Kirk had told him. But Cribb, with no wife or child, could afford to live in Washington. Kirk, with his several hostages to Fortune, his lack of the red gold, and his role as Lone Wolf (which part had become second nature to him), labored under insurmountable difficulties, where acceptance of office was concerned. Also Kirk bore in mind H. L. Mencken's witticism about committees. The human body, Mencken had written somewhere, is so perfectly contrived that obviously it is the work of a single divine mind; but when God came to the teeth, he appointed a committee.

Now and again Kirk saw the President somewhere in the White House — a cheerful President Reagan. Kirk and Annette would recall especially a Christmas party in the Indian Treaty Room of what had been the State Department building when Kirk first had visited Washington, in 1936, but by the 1980s was styled the Old Executive Office Building. There the eldest of all the presidents of the United States — who also was the most popular president ever with young voters — glowed with energy and cordiality that afternoon, witty and ready of repartee. Despite a few facial wrinkles, President Reagan never seemed old. At that party in the Indian Treaty Room, the principal people of his administration near him, there seemed to radiate throughout the huge chamber the political and physical courage, and the kindliness, of the fortieth president of the United States.

To the American people, Ronald Reagan had become the Western hero of romance — audacious, faithful, cheerful, honest, and skilled at shooting from the hip. William Butler Yeats suggests that it might be well for one to make himself a mask, and wear it, and become what the mask should represent. Decades earlier, Ronald Reagan had put on the mask of the Western hero, and had lived the part, and had become the Western hero truly. He had proved that when, shot down at the door of a hotel and injured also by the Secret Service agents who had flung themselves upon his body, he had joked irrepressibly with his wife and with the doctors who had worked nip and tuck to save his life.

What blunders in office the Western hero had made had been eclipsed by his large accomplishments. His administration had opened the way to educational reforms, had reduced taxation and almost abolished (temporarily) federal inheritance taxes, had greatly reduced inflation of the currency, had brought about virtually full employment. In foreign policy, Mr. Reagan's Lebanese and Iranian failures were counterbalanced by his dramatic successes in expelling the Russians from Grenada and intimidating the dictator of Libya, heir to the Barbary pirates. And near the end of his term of office, President Reagan would vastly diminish the perilous rivalry with the Soviet Union.

In Reagan was no touch of pomposity. He did not take himself more gravely, nor the world more grimly, than he must. After suffering some defeat in the Congress, he did not repine, but laughed, perhaps. He had jested with bullets in him, and at the gravest moments in his career, or careers. There ought to be graven upon his tombstone — if ever Mr. Reagan should die, which seemed improbable there at the Christmas party in the Indian Treaty Room — the epitaph that John Gay wrote for his own grave:

Life is a jest, and all things shew it;
I thought so once, but now I know it.

Occasionally Kirk would write to President Reagan, now and again touching upon politics, but more often recommending some appointment. Most of these letters were not formally replied to, although Kirk would learn from one or another of his White House friends that Mr. Reagan had read every letter and had thought about Kirk's remarks. But when Kirk happened to touch upon the health or personal concerns of some friend they had in common, Mr. Reagan would take the trouble to reply promptly and personally, and perhaps to telephone the friend in question. John Henry Newman observes that Toryism is loyalty to persons; if so, Ronald Reagan was a Tory in the best sense of that term.

Near the end of his second term, and two days after his triumphant return from his conference with Gorbachev at Moscow, Mr. Reagan and his people, learning that Kirk was in Washington for a few days, invited him to call on the president at the White House. Tall and ruddy-faced, smiling broadly, President Reagan told Kirk that he was eager to take the campaign trail in the cause of his chosen successor, Vice President Bush. As the White House photographer took pictures of the two of them, the President told jokes to his guest.

These particular jokes had a political significance. For what President Reagan might say to that conservative writer Kirk, humorously, might serve to reassure some conservatively minded folk who had grown uneasy at Mr. Reagan's Russian negotiations.

He did not tell these jokes to Gorbachev, Mr. Reagan informed Kirk — which was sufficiently obvious from the jokes' nature, their point being that Ronald Reagan still thought the Soviet empire to be evil.

In the first of his two Russian jokes, Reagan pretended that he had been riding in a limousine through the Russian countryside, with Gorbachev at his side, Gorbachev having with him a KGB agent, and Reagan a Secret Service agent. Suddenly Gorbachev commanded the chauffeur to stop the car near the lip of a tremendous cataract.

"Jump down that waterfall!" he ordered the Secret Service agent. The American declined to do so.

"Why do you disobey me?" Gorbachev demanded.

"Because I have a wife and three children, sir."

Then Gorbachev turned to the KGB agent: "Jump down that waterfall!" Immediately the agent obeyed.

Horrified, the Secret Service agent clambered down to the foot of the cliff. There he found the KGB agent, bruised but living, wringing out his clothes.

"Why did you obey his command?" the astonished American asked.

"Because I have a wife and three children."

For Reagan's second jest, Kirk was to imagine the President addressing a high Soviet official.

"Just how high does Communism stand with the Russian people?" So Reagan, with an affectation of earnest naïve inquiry, represented himself as asking this Soviet dignitary.

"One point six meters."

"One point six meters? How can you be so precise? And what does that signify, 'One point six meters'?"

"It signifies that I've had it up to here," said the Russian, drawing his right hand smartly across his throat, just below the chin.

This was Ronald Reagan's imaginative way of telling Kirk, and Kirk's friends, that he still apprehended the grisly Soviet power against which he must contend in his negotiations.

Kirk saw Mr. Reagan once more in the White House, during his last week in office, when the President presented to Kirk and some thirty-five others the Presidential Citizens Medal; Kirk was the only man of letters so recognized. Someone should have presented Mr. Reagan with a tremendous medal, studded with emeralds, for having restored the repute and the popularity of the American presidency. But who was greater than he, that might have made such a presentation? In 1993, when Kirk called on Mr. Reagan in Los Angeles, the gentleman who had been the oldest of all American Presidents was undiminished still — alert, cordial, humorous, abreast of public affairs. He deserves praise from future historians.*

---

*Mr. Reagan was endowed with a certain power of imagination; successful actors almost necessarily have a talent for image-making. His successor, President Bush, expressed his distaste for the "vision thing." At that time, Kirk hoped that Mr. Bush was disavowing political utopianism; but no, it turned out that Bush really repudiated political imagination, so that he was unable to foresee probable consequences of his own policies and utterances. The Kirks, in 1988, had done much to secure a unified Michigan delegation pledged to George Bush at the Republican National Convention that gave him his presidential nomination. But soon they found Bush in the White House worse than unimaginative — merely silly, often.

So in 1992 Kirk became general chairman of Patrick Buchanan's campaign in the Michigan primary. Kirk's friend and neighbor John Engler, the successfully conservative governor of Michigan, was titular chairman of the Bush primary campaign; but this episode did not disturb their close alliance.

Annette's Educational Crusade

The years of the Reagan presidency became a period of public activity for Annette Kirk: she was appointed in the autumn of 1981 to the new National Commission on Excellence in Education (an unsalaried distinction), and for the following eighteen months was very busy with the Commission's meetings and hearings, in Washington and other cities. After the Commission issued its much-publicized report, *A Nation at Risk: The Imperative for Educational Reform* (April, 1983), she was much in demand across the country, and on television and radio, to discuss educational concerns.

Then in 1984 she was appointed a member of the Committee on Education of the United States Catholic Conference, doubtless in recognition of her active part in drawing up *A Nation at Risk*. For three years she worked with USCC, flying to Washington for meetings. The culmination of this conferring came in 1989, when she and her husband delivered jointly the United States Catholic Conference's annual Seton-Neumann Lecture.

Russell Kirk had fancied he was escaping from the task of writing and speaking about pedagogy and associated subjects. For a quarter of a century, commencing in 1955, he had written for *National Review* his page "From the Academy." That feature, he had been told, became the most attentively read page in the magazine; certainly it had involved him in massive correspondence with readers. But if "From the Academy" resulted in any improvements at any level of American education, over the years, Kirk was unable to discern such reforms; he longed to spend his time — he attaining his sixty-second birthday in 1980 — at writing of a more enduring sort. So he gave up "From the Academy" (having already ceased to write his syndicated column "To the Point" in 1975) shortly after Mr. Reagan's election in 1980. For twenty-five years he had rowed in the educational galleys. Let someone else take the oars now!

To his surprise and almost to his chagrin, his replacement as educational galley slave turned out to be his wife. They had neither solicited nor expected any federal appointment for her. (Later, she would decline a second educational appointment of the Reagan administration.) But she was known to a good many conservative Republicans through her membership in the Philadelphia Society, the discussion club founded by the Kirks' friend Don Lipsett; once upon a time she had been a public-school teacher; on the platform, she was a winning speaker; and she had four daughters still enrolled in various schools. Most of her seventeen colleagues on the National Commission in effect represented some educational organization or interest, or else were famous as scientists. If Annette Kirk represented anybody — why, her constituents were America's parents.

Russell Kirk was conscripted as her coadjutor, as he had been at the Call to Action in Detroit. Several times they jointly addressed intelligent audiences on the National Commission's work — most notably, perhaps, in a well-attended session held in the Capitol at Washington and sponsored by the Heritage Foundation. At the National Commission's meetings and hearings — Annette chairing, at Atlanta, the session on teacher education — she was effectively lively; her husband, no committeeman, would have been dully silent.

A principal cause of the creation of the National Commission had been concern over the superior industrial efficiency of Japan and Germany — which presumably had something to do with efficient schooling in those lands, and inefficient schooling in the United States. Annette endeavored successfully, at the Commission's meetings, to go deeper into the difficulties of American schooling; her especial interests were moral education and humane studies. This enlarged scope was reflected in some sentences of the final report: "Our concern, however, goes well beyond matters such as industry and commerce. It also includes the intellectual, moral, and spiritual strengths of our people which knit together the very fabric of our society."

Annette's influence in affirming the importance of humane studies, as distinguished from technical skills, resulted in the report's commendation of "the arts and humanities that so enrich daily life, help maintain civility, and develop a sense of community. Knowledge of the humanities . . . must be harnessed to science and technology if the latter are to remain creative and humane."

Annette encountered some difficulty in persuading certain of her colleagues to criticize, even by implication, the methods of training teachers in the United States; or to suggest that teacher-training schools might be held accountable for the sort of teachers they turned out. Nevertheless, *A Nation at Risk* did print this recommendation: "Persons preparing to teach should be required to meet high educational standards, to demonstrate an aptitude for teaching, and to demonstrate competence in an academic discipline. Colleges and universities offering teacher-preparation programs should be judged by how well their graduates meet these criteria."

Much though Annette had insisted upon the necessity for moral imagination in schooling, at the last moment it was discovered that the report did not contain even the word "imagination." A clause about imagination and ethical understanding, the first portion of which was suggested by Annette, therefore was inserted: "The teaching of *English* in high school should equip graduates to . . . know our literary heritage and how it enhances imagination and ethical understanding, and how it relates to the customs, ideas, and values of today's life and culture."

At the Commission's meetings and hearings one could notice a tendency to assume that only state-supported schools, commonly called "public" schools, were the National Commission's concern; sometimes almost to act as if church-related schools and independent schools did not exist. Annette's reminders that President Reagan had intended a wider purpose for the Commission produced a declaration, among the recommendations of *A Nation at Risk,* accordingly: "We wish to note that we refer to public, private, and parochial schools and colleges alike. All are valuable national resources."

On October 9, 1981, President Reagan, at the National Commission's first meeting, had urged its members to consider four fundamental principles: the primacy of the family in the educational process; educational competition; diversity in schooling, with emphasis upon independent schools; and the teaching of morality. Annette had paid more attention to these four concerns than had most of her colleagues. One of them, with reference to the teaching of morality, had remarked after the President left the room, "Well, I suppose if we took a vote on the Ten Commandments, we might agree on at least five." The Commission did not find it easy to achieve consensus on various other themes. One of the more controversial topics, which the National Commission did not even discuss thoroughly — although President Reagan was much interested in it, and had said so — was the possibility of recommending tax credits or voucher plans in aid of independent and church-related schools.

Various conservative activists who strongly favored proposals for tax credits or voucher plans had expected Annette Kirk to obtain the National Commission's endorsement of such measures — or, failing that, to resign indignantly from the Commission or to file a minority report. But Annette had ascertained, early in her service on the Commission, that not more than four other members would have joined her in recommending tax credits or vouchers, and none would have resigned in protest along with her. Had she parted from the Commission on this point, the Commission's majority then would have found it necessary to issue a recommendation *against* tax credits and vouchers. Instead, then, Annette chose to remain and to emphasize the primary right and responsibility of parents in the educational endeavor. *A Nation at Risk,* influenced by Annette's argument, put it thus: "As surely as you are your child's first and most influential teacher, your child's ideas about education and its significance begin with you. . . . Moreover, you bear a responsibility to participate actively in your child's education." She emphasized the necessity of virtuous example. In the report's phrases, "excellence in education cannot be achieved without intellectual and moral integrity coupled with hard work and commitment. Children will look to their parents and teachers as models of such virtue." These sentences, in effect, established a precedent for recognition by the federal government and by American educational agencies generally, of the principle that parents, and not the state, are the primary educators of the rising generation.

Just those "words to parents" were read aloud at the press conference on the day that the Commission's chairman, Dr. David Gardner, presented the report *A Nation at Risk* to President Reagan. The President replied that his administration would continue to work for the implementing of tuition tax credits and vouchers. One member of the Commission, at the moment standing next to Annette, at this angrily muttered, "Those things were not in our recommendations at all!"

Some time would elapse before the premises advanced by Annette were grasped, before the concepts of parental rights and responsibilities were fully understood. But in Chicago, the current experiment in parental control of neighborhood schools, widely publicized, is one beginning at putting such ideas into practice.

Until recently, the view that prevailed even among parents — often intimidated by educationists — was that the state educational authorities knew best. Educational bureaucracies, teachers' unions, and courts of law decided what and how children would learn; also with whom and where they must learn. Lip service was paid to parental involvement, so long as the existing educational establishment was not seriously questioned. Statements in *A Nation at Risk,* and discussions that arose from the report, had much to do with a tardy recognition, widespread, of parents as educators.

Two months after *A Nation at Risk* had been published, Mr. Patrick McGuigan interviewed Annette Kirk for *Family Protection Report.* He asked her, among other questions, what changes were needed to achieve long-term educational improvement.

Mrs. Kirk listed four: to make it clear that the fundamental ends of education are the imparting of wisdom and of virtue, for the sake of the person and of the republic; to radically revise procedures for certification of teachers and for accreditation of schools; to introduce a career ladder for teachers; to adopt voucher and tax-credit plans that provide equitably for public schools, independent schools, and church-related schools alike.

She was asked for her "philosophy of education." What she answered should have been more widely circulated:

> I believe there is a close relationship between the soul of the person and the well-being of society. When the health of the soul decays, society declines, and general decadence results. If decadence is defined as the loss of an object, we ought to begin our educational reform with an examination of the true ends or objects of schooling, the purpose of learning. . . . Education should impart ethical understanding of those enduring norms that make life worth living. Also education should enlarge our imagination, that we may appreciate truth and beauty in literature, art, and music. Without any element of such an education, people's lives are fragmented. The more true learning one acquires, the more one experiences awe at the mystery and miracle of life.

If Annette did not find the recommendations of the National Commission on Excellence in Education so imaginative as she wished, still that body succeeded in rousing a great deal of interest in nearly every state (although less in Michigan than in most states) in serious educational reform. At the end of the Eighties, *A Nation at Risk* still was being cited with respect.

While discussion of the National Commission's report was at its height, Annette was invited to join, for a term of three years, the Committee on Education of the United States Catholic Conference; as an earnest Catholic, she accepted readily. During her term, that Committee on Education was concerned particularly with the subject of moral education in the public schools. Annette, at that time the only laywoman among the Committee's many members, soon found that many Catholic educators hesitated to affirm any Christian concepts of education: they had been heavily influenced by Instrumentalist or secular-humanist theories of pedagogy prevalent at teachers' colleges. In an earlier interview, Annette had said, "In his *Idea of a University*, John Henry Newman declares that the aim of higher education is the acquisition of a philosophical habit of mind, which should enable us to distinguish between the essential and the inessential; that habit should enable us to make the best use of our time and talents."

With the very honorable exception of two or three bishops, Annette did not encounter much support for such an understanding among her colleagues of the Committee on Education; she was disappointed in the brief report, "Value and Virtue," distributed in consequence of the Committee's deliberations. Perhaps for that very reason, she and her husband were asked to deliver the USCC's annual Seton-Neumann Lecture, in Washington in December 1989. Annette began their joint address, which they entitled "Purifying the Dialect of the Tribe":

What happens to language when words lose all significance, when they have no history or objectivity, when they are deconstructed or denied a reality? This is what has happened in recent years in the departments of literature and philosophy in leading universities. Is it any wonder that there is a crisis in the teaching of moral education, if words, which are the tools to convey truths, have no objective meaning?

Russell Kirk took up his cudgel. "Nowadays we hear a great deal about 'teaching values' in schools," he began.

Although sincerely held by many people who mean well, this notion is a mistaken concept. For what true education attempts to impart is *meaning,* not value. This sly misemployment of the word "value" as a substitute for such words as "norm," "standard," "principle," and "truth" is the deliberate contrivance of the doctrinaire positivists, who deny that any moral significance of a transcendent or enduring character exists. In America, the notion of educational "values" has been thrust forward by sociologists and educationists of the Instrumentalist school; it is intended as a substitute for the religious assumptions about human nature that formerly were taken for granted in schools. A "value," as educationists employ that unfortunate word, is a personal preference, gratifying perhaps to the person who holds it, but of no binding moral effect upon others. Choose what values you will, or ignore the lot of them: it's a matter of what gives you, the individual, the most pleasure or the least pain.

Near the conclusion of their joint address, Annette exhorted their listeners to undertake a work of restoration:

> Let it be understood that the transmitting of the tradition of intellectual virtue is a complex process, much more than a matter of uttering platitudes in classrooms. People who seek to restore the moral aspects of schooling frequently call for abrupt reform and speedy results. One well understands this demand; one sympathizes with the exasperation of many a parent. All the same, the process of restoring meaning and moral purpose in formal education necessarily is a difficult one, requiring time for its attainment. We do not mean that it is a hopeless task. What once has been, may be again.
>
> If there is no education for meaning, life will become meaningless for many. If there is no education for virtue, many will become vicious. . . . Your mission and ours, then, is to make old truths new, to teach reverence for the past, for we are but dwarfs standing on the shoulders of spiritual and intellectual giants. We recall the words of Cicero when he describes how the neglect of an inheritance may lead to its dissolution. Where Cicero uses the word "Republic" we might include the word "Church." Cicero writes, "Our age inherited the Republic like some beautiful painting of bygone days, its colors already fading through great age; and not only has our time neglected to freshen the colors of the picture, but we have failed to preserve its form and outline."

The two Kirks were of one mind. In the cause of restoration —
in education, in Church, in State — they strove against the dominations and powers of the hour.

In Manhattan, when Kirk was courting young Annette, Mickie
Teetor had described Miss Courtemanche to others, in Annette's
absence: "Annette is one of the most beautiful girls in New York."
During the years of Annette's educational crusade, Mickie told Russell, "Annette has become a really wonderful woman!" Her beauty
was undiminished by the growth of her wisdom and virtue.

Martin D'Arcy's analysis of *eros* and *agape,* in his book *The Mind
and Heart of Love,* had much moved Annette and Russell in their years
of friendship before their marriage; and their own love had grown from
eros to *agape.* In Spain today, the verb *amar* has fallen out of use,
supplanted by *querer* — to desire. But the chivalrous *amar,* of ancient
days, was the bond between Russell and Annette as they spoke from
the same rostrum, twenty-five years after their marriage: *amamos.*

The Coming of the Disciples

During the eight years of the Reagan presidency, Kirk stuck to his
last, on the sound Roman principle of *ne sutor ultra crepidam;* or, in
the rendering of Sir Roger L'Estrange, "The cobbler is not to go beyond
his last." This is an admonition to a man to mind his own business;
and Kirk's proper business was writing and speechifying. He spoke
often at Washington, invited by the Department of Education, the
Heritage Foundation, and other public and private sponsors; but he
steered clear of political appointments, not flattering himself that he
possessed the least aptitude for office.

The books continued to come from his old typewriter. *Reclaiming a Patrimony,* a collection of his formal lectures, sponsored by the
Heritage Foundation, appeared in 1982; among the subjects discussed
were "Church and State in Conflict"; "The Perversity of Recent Fiction"; "Criminal Character and Mercy"; "The Architecture of Servitude
and Boredom"; "Regaining Historical Consciousness"; and "Audacity,
Rhetoric, and Poetry in Politics."

The editors of the big publishing firm of Viking Penguin asked
him to draw up an anthology of conservative thought, which was
published in 1984 under the title *The Portable Conservative Reader.*

In this rather painful labor of seeking out accurate texts and securing permissions, he was mightily helped by his disciple Wesley McDonald. The book, almost a companion to *The Conservative Mind*, did something to clarify in people's minds, during years when the word "conservative" was on nearly everybody's lips, the significations of that disputed political term. A long introduction by Kirk traced the word historically.

Watchers at the Strait Gate, another collection of Kirk's mystical tales, also appeared in 1984, published by Arkham House. The geographical settings of the tales — some of them quite new, others published in periodicals at the beginning of the Fifties — were diverse: Los Angeles, St. Louis, Morocco, New England, Edinburgh, Lansing, Mecosta, Kirk's birthplace at Plymouth, and northern Michigan: slices of Kirk's life.

The Wise Men Know What Wicked Things Are Written on the Sky (a line borrowed from Chesterton's long poem *The Ballad of the White Horse*) was published by Regnery in 1987; it was fairly widely reviewed and read.* This was a second collection of Heritage Lectures: it included several formal lectures on aspects of education, and others on prospects for the United States.

His *Work and Prosperity,* a textbook in economics for high-school students, was published by the Christian textbook firm of Beka Books in 1988. This manual was the final production of the Educational Research Council of America, with offices in Cleveland. Kirk had accepted the post of director of ERCA's social-science program, to fill a gap left by the departure for Washington of Kirk's friend Raymond English, the previous director. For several years, fairly well paid, Kirk spent several days a week, part of each year, at his Cleveland office, dwelling in hotels and exploring the heart of that city in the evenings. He brought out a new edition of the Council's social-science series — the best textbooks of their sort then published in the United States. In the end, ERCA folded its tents for lack of funds; but Kirk's economics textbook, which made the Dismal Science seem almost cheerful and actually was written in lucid English, survived the catastrophe, to appear independently, and was received cordially; even some colleges adopted it for use by their freshmen.

---

*This little book was warmly commended by Mr. Charles Colson, of the Prison Ministries.

A fellowship from the National Endowment for the Humanities, in 1985, gave him time to commence the writing of a series of essays and lectures on the Constitution of the United States — published by Regnery as a book in 1990. He particularly emphasized in his study the neglected influence of Edmund Burke on the framers and the interpreters of the Constitution. *The Conservative Constitution* undid the claim of the disciples of Leo Strauss that somehow the Declaration of Independence and the Constitution had conformed slavishly to the doctrines of John Locke.

Editing of others' books occupied a good deal of Kirk's time during the Eighties. He was able to bring out, in 1986, through the National Humanities Institute, a handsome new edition of Irving Babbitt's *Literature and the American College,* with a learned introduction nearly so long as the book itself, from Kirk's typewriter. At the request of Irving Louis Horowitz, of Transaction Publishers, Russell Kirk began editing a series entitled The Library of Conservative Thought; nearly all volumes would have introductions or forewords by Kirk. Among the volumes published in 1988, 1989, and 1990 were *Collected Letters of John Randolph of Roanoke to Dr. John Brockenbrough,* Mallock's *A Critical Examination of Socialism,* Scott-Moncrieff's *Burke Street,* Wilson's *The Case for Conservatism, Selected Political Essays of Orestes Brownson,* Davidson's *The Attack on Leviathan,* a collection of Stanlis's essays on Burke, and a collection of critical essays on Burke edited by Daniel Ritchie.

Kirk's production of periodical essays and articles was undiminished. His work appeared frequently in two new magazines, *Policy Review* and *The World & I; Modern Age* published something or other by him in most issues of that quarterly during the Eighties.

Tocqueville observes that the American democracy, though it does not formally persecute men of unusual talents, places in their way various impediments that will delay their success until they are too old and fatigued to accomplish much. Kirk, in the year when Ronald Reagan took office, was nearly eligible for Social Security benefits, and therefore (though actually still undiminished in mind and vigorous enough in body) reckoned ready for the conferring of public recognition. In the Eighties he received the Richard Weaver Award (for scholarly writing) of the Ingersoll Prizes — no empty honor, for there went with it fifteen thousand tax-free dollars, at once flung into the chasm of Kirk's debts. At the Mayflower Hotel, in

Washington, a grand dinner was held in his honor, sponsored by the Philadelphia Society, the Intercollegiate Studies Institute, and *National Review.* In 1987 he was appointed Fulbright lecturer at St. Andrews University, and during the same season he lectured at the University of Trier, the University of Groningen, and elsewhere in the Continent; in 1989, at Austrian and Italian universities.

In Germany he acquired considerable reputation as a political wizard by having predicted accurately, in an article for the monthly *Epoche,* George Bush's election to the presidency and the grand scale of Bush's victory, confounding German forecasters. But during 1991 Kirk would come to detest Bush for his carpet-bombing of the Cradle of Civilization with its taking of a quarter of a million lives in Iraq. Early in 1992, Kirk, along with his old friend Harry Veryser, would chair the effort to secure Michigan's delegates for the presidential candidacy of another friend, Patrick Buchanan.

Chapters about Kirk appeared in Henry Regnery's *Memoirs of a Dissident Publisher* and in John East's *The American Conservative Movement.* Late in December 1991, at Gunston Hall — which George Mason, framer of the Bill of Rights, had built in 1755 — Kirk was awarded the first Salvatori Prize for writings on the American Founding. Kirk's speech of acceptance, "The Marriage of Rights and Duties," reminded his auditors of the healthy tension that should subsist between the claims of order and the claims of freedom.

"I attest the rising generation!" old Edmund Burke had cried at the end of the trial of Warren Hastings. During the Nineties, Kirk could have called to witness many of the better hearts among the rising generation in the United States; indeed, members of that generation nearly drowned him in correspondence. Often the big drawing room of Piety Hill, and Kirk's library building, were full of young men and women attached to the Permanent Things — on some occasions so many as forty-five guests. Some of the disciples obtained university credits for studies with Kirk; others were literary interns with fellowships from the Marguerite Eyer Wilbur Foundation, of which Kirk had become president.

Early in the Seventies there had commenced the Piety Hill seminars, sponsored by the Intercollegiate Studies Institute (ISI). In the Eighties the frequency of these gatherings increased to three, four, or even five a year — rather a strain on Annette. Between 1973 and 1993, more than two thousand students, from all over the land —

[465]

and some from abroad — would participate in ISI seminars. Participants were lodged at the main house of Piety Hill, or in three small houses nearby that had been acquired by the Wilbur Foundation for literary fellows; others were put up at the Blue Lake Lodge, an old-fangled Michigan summer hostelry with a fine beach.

These seminars extended to a wide diversity of subjects. Among them were "Historical Consciousness"; "Christopher Dawson and Culture"; "Criticisms of the United States Constitution"; "A Humane Economy"; "Questions of Church and State"; "True Humanism and False"; "Our Cultural Patrimony"; "The Moral Vision of Solzhenitsyn"; "The Mind and Heart of Edmund Burke"; "T. S. Eliot and the Defense of Culture"; "The Achievement of Eric Voegelin"; "Democracy East and West"; "Humane Letters in an Age of Disorder"; "Literature and Ideology"; "The Little Platoon We Belong to in Society"; "Liberal Education"; "Burke's *Reflections on the Revolution in France*"; "The Political Novel"; "The Thought of Orestes Brownson"; "Natural Law."

The seminar participants soon perceived why Kirk preferred this rural solitude to a professorship with tenure at the University of Chicago or at Yale, say: at Mecosta he had pure air, quiet, woodland paths to walk, friendly neighbors, extensive grounds, and a library-and-office building a block from his residence so large and convenient that its rent, had it been situated in any city, would have consumed his income. How might one write here in the backwoods a syndicated newspaper column for thirteen years? How to communicate with the great world from this remote decayed village? Why, Alexander Graham Bell had organized the Bell Telephone Company in 1877.

The main topic for a seminar, which lasted for a weekend, might be historical, literary, or political; in general, it was the intention of the ISI's officers and of Kirk to encourage discussion of fundamental questions, rather than to engage in debate about controversies of the hour.

Somewhat to their surprise, the Kirks came to learn that apparently there existed nowhere else in the United States such gatherings in a country house, with leisure for fellowship and animated conversation. At whatever season of the year, Kirk would take the hardier among the participants walking the woods trails in the neighborhood of Mecosta; or those who could stay a day or two longer, he might take canoeing on the boulder-strewn waters of the Little Muskegon or the Chippewa.

What the disciples seemed to find at Piety Hill was not ideology — for the Kirks detested that — but the sense of continuity and permanence. Some of these students fell into the habit of telephoning Annette frequently — she being more approachable than her husband — to report on what was occurring in their lives, and to seek counsel on matters religious, educational, occupational, political, and marital.

Those sessions at Piety Hill somewhat resembled country-house weekends in Britain, as described by Edwardian novelists. On a modest scale, such gatherings had survived at Balcarres, Kellie, and Durie during Kirk's Scottish years. It was a far cry from Lord Falkland's seventeenth-century house of Great Tew to twentieth-century Piety Hill, but Falkland's and Kirk's beliefs and approaches were not dissimilar. "When it is not necessary to change," Falkland had said, "it is necessary not to change." Sharing that sentiment, Kirk had imparted it to his young guests at Piety Hill. At one seminar, Edward Giles, a Wilbur Fellow at Mecosta in 1987, arose to utter a brief informal disquisition on the idea of a gentleman. He might have been describing Lucius Carey, Viscount Falkland, in the seventeenth century, or John Henry Newman, in the nineteenth. Giles had recognized at Piety Hill the lingering perfume of an antique time, or the echo of an old song.

By the Nineties, there were dispersed throughout the United States a great many people in their middle years or their early careers who had read *The Conservative Mind* — the seventh edition had been published in 1986, and a fourth edition of *A Program for Conservatives* in 1989 — and had been moved thereby. Of the disciples who at one time or another had beaten a pathway to Piety Hill, some had become lawyers, and some teachers, some journalists, some professors; some were in the book trade, others had been ordained, yet others had obtained posts in government. They might leaven the lump of American society.*

With the publication of his first book, in 1951, Russell Kirk had begun to address a Remnant: those folk, he not knowing their number, who did not confound Change with Reform; who did not worship Dinos, flouting Zeus; who did not prefer a young mistress to an old

---

*One, Jeffrey Nelson, publications director of ISI, marrying Miss Cecilia Abigail Kirk just before Christmas 1993, might carry on Russell Kirk's literary raids against the enemies of the Permanent Things.

master; who did not cheer for King Demos, guillotining King Constitution; who did not fancy that God was dead. Letting cheerfulness break in occasionally, Kirk had not been quite so solemn as Isaiah.

In January 1993, Kirk and his former assistant George Michos were strolling the cliff-head promenade at Santa Monica. George was tall and young; Kirk was short and nearly three quarters of a century old, yet sufficiently dapper in his black Palm Beach suit, his black boots, and his broad-brimmed, flat-topped black leather hat; he swung a brassbound walking stick. They approached a bench upon which were seated an amiable bourgeois trio: middle-aged husband and wife and their daughter, apparently.

"That's a handsome gentleman you have with you," said the husband to George.

"That's because he's from another century," George replied.

But the trio on the bench mistook George's word "century" for "country."

"Does he speak English?" the wife inquired.

He did and he does; he even writes English, if sometimes in the manner of another century.

A few months after this encounter, during October 1993, Kirk was overwhelmed by a whole series of celebrations in honor of the fortieth anniversary of publication of *The Conservative Mind* and the seventy-fifth anniversary of the birth of that book's author. Large gatherings and formal banquets and presentation of awards occurred at Chicago, at Washington, and especially at Dearborn, Michigan, at the still-charming Inn, across the road from Greenfield Village of Kirk's youth.* This last was a two-day gathering, organized principally by Kirk's old allies Don Lipsett of the Philadelphia Society, Ken Cribb of ISI, Edwin Feulner of the Heritage Foundation, and Ron Robinson of Young America's Foundation, with many speeches by distinguished men and women about Kirk and Kirk's Works. By all this rejoicing and by much speechifying, coast to coast, during October, Kirk found himself cheerfully worn out.

---

*There at Dearborn and elsewhere, John Engler, governor of Michigan — the most intelligently conservative governor in the Union — was quoting Kirk in generous speeches: imaginative and practical talents allied. Engler had accomplished political wonders — cutting the welfare rolls justly, greatly reducing taxes on real property, curtailing the power of the teachers' unions.

Fifty-seven years had elapsed since Kirk first had drawn his literary sword and blown his literary trumpet. That Remnant he addressed had grown in numbers and earnestness; now and again it had taken a castle or a town. At the age of seventy-five Kirk could not ascertain accurately how far his exhortations had brought about such gains. What he might do to rouse others' imagination and courage, that he had done, to the best of his limited talents. It remained to keep keen the edge of his sword of imagination for another decade or conceivably longer. As no great cause ever is wholly lost — to borrow a sentence from Eliot — so no great cause ever is wholly gained.

Is Life Worth Living?

In some ages, what Thoreau says is true: most men lead lives of quiet desperation. They endeavor to evade answering the question "What is the purpose of human existence?" As children, they entertain vague expectations of some future happy condition and achievement; but commonly those hopes are dashed or much diminished once they flap or tumble out of the parental nest. After that, they may live as birds do, from day to day, until they starve or are caught by a cat. Nevertheless, many men and women are haunted by such nagging questions as "What is this all about?" or "Is life worth living?" And a good many, if pressed for an answer, will reply interiorly much as does T. S. Eliot's Sweeney Agonistes: birth and copulation and death, that's all. As to whether such a life, seemingly limited to reproduction and repetition, has significant value — why, some people may shrug, and others shake their heads.

Personal and social decadence, the consequence of the loss of an end or object in existence, come to pass when the shapers of opinion, sophisticated, not philosophers but philodoxers, find nothing worth living for — except sensation. C. E. M. Joad mentions certain characteristics of a decadent society: luxury; skepticism; weariness; superstition; preoccupation with the self and its experiences; a society "promoted by and promoting the subjectivist analysis of moral, aesthetic, metaphysical and theological judgments."

Into such a society Russell Kirk was born — or rather, born in the salad days of such a society, its decay accelerating swiftly as Kirk grew older. His parents did not question whether life was worth living: they lived by tradition merely, growing up decently, marrying when they were about twenty years old, bringing two children into the world, then dying — Kirk's mother giving up the ghost while she still could be called youthful, his father dying blind, sick, and old. Their experiences in the world were unremarkable; they performed their duties patiently, harming no one; they were loving parents. Marjorie Rachel Kirk lived hopeful of great prospects for humankind, but her cheerful spirit was snuffed out by cancer; the elder Russell Kirk accepted his tribulations uncomplaining, though he never had read the Stoics, or for that matter the book of Job. Had their lives signified something? Does anyone's life signify anything?

Time was when nearly all men and women, believing in some transcendent religion, had taken it that their little lives were bound up with some divine design, which they could not hope to comprehend wholly, but which gave meaning to their existence as persons. Such, at any rate, had been the doctrine imparted to them, and most of them had tried to conform their lives to that eternal purpose.

Russell Kirk's parents had inherited that body of belief, if in a vestigial form. That teaching had led them into honest and kindly lives. But the attenuated tradition that had sustained them was perilously weakened by the middle of the twentieth century. Performance of duties was giving way to eagerness for sensations. And that way lay decadence.

Livy, at the time the Roman republic collapsed, wrote that the Romans of his era seemed to have fallen in love with death. Such a death-urge, interestingly similar to the Roman phenomenon, was at work in America during Kirk's lifetime. (It is grimly amusing to compare Livy's description of the Bacchanalian rites, Book XXXIX of his *History*, with certain cult orgies of the twentieth century; Kirk, in his mystical romance *Lord of the Hollow Dark*, had ventured to picture the diabolic imagination at work in such a cultic initiation of his own time.) From the Second World War onward, the civilization of Europe and the Americas had stumbled into decadence: the moral order seemed to be dissolving. Subconsciously or half consciously, a great many people came to assume that really life was not worth living; the death-urge enticed them, as in Livy's time.

There came to pass a growing general indifference concerning the past and the future of the human species: an echo of the ancient Greek cry of ruthless individuality, "When I am dead, let earth be mixed with fire!" In the name of freedom, modernism had opened the path that leads to dissolution. Indeed, there is terror in a handful of dust. "There is no death," Gregory the Great, in the catacombs, had told his Roman flock. *"Viva la muerte!"* the nihilists of the dying twentieth century seemed to shout.

It was otherwise with Russell Kirk, who in 1993, on the eve of his seventy-fifth birthday, published two more books: *America's British Culture* (Transaction), a counter-buffet to Demon Multiculturalism; and *The Politics of Prudence* (Intercollegiate Studies Institute), addressed to the rising generation in search of principles. He was pro-life, although he did not dread his latter end except as it might trouble Annette and the four daughters. To them he could leave little but a handsome house, five acres, a sense of honor, and many happy memories.

At an early age, Kirk had learned from the discourse and the examples of his mother and his grandfather that life is well worth living. He had learned also that life ought to be lived with honor, charity, and prudence. Those and other enduring principles he had accepted on authority: "Believe what all men, everywhere, always have believed." Somewhat to his surprise, his adherence to those precepts brought strength and happiness into his life.

At the age of seventy-five, Kirk had come to understand that he had sought, during his lifetime, three ends or objects.

One had been to defend the Permanent Things, in a world where "Dinos is king, having overthrown Zeus." He had sought to conserve a patrimony of order, justice, and freedom; a tolerable moral order; and an inheritance of culture. Although rowing against a strong tide, in this aspiration he had succeeded somewhat, certainly beyond his early expectation, in reminding people that truth was not born yesterday.

A second had been to lead a life of decent independence, living much as his ancestors had lived, on their land, in circumstances that would enable him to utter the truth and make his voice heard: a life uncluttered and unpolluted, not devoted to getting and spending. In his antique vocation of man of letters, he had achieved that aspiration at Piety Hill.

A third end had been to marry for love and to rear children who would come to know that the service of God is perfect freedom. In his middle years, the splendid Annette had given herself to him and then given him four children, presently endowed with the unbought grace of life. Annette and he helped to sustain the institution of the family by creating a vigorous example.

Thus his three wishes had been granted; he was grateful. Power over others, and much money, he never had desired; he had been spared those responsibilities.

Both on authority and through his own insights and experiences, Kirk had come to understand that there exists a realm of being beyond this temporal world and that a mysterious providence works in human affairs — that man is made for eternity. Such knowledge had been consolation and compensation for sorrow.

Kirk stood ready to affirm his belief in such knowledge, and to be derided for it, despite his being no Hot Gospeller. Like David Hume, he was more skeptical of Rationalism than of Tradition — a worldly *defensor fidei*. Strongly influenced by Christopher Dawson and Eric Voegelin, Martin D'Arcy and Mircea Eliade, Kirk had come to conclude that a civilization cannot long survive the dying of belief in a transcendent order that brought the culture into being. The ideology of modernism bestrode the intellectual world from 1860 to 1960; after that, its power waned. As Arthur Koestler observed, yesteryear's scientific doctrines of mechanism and materialism ought to be buried with a requiem of electronic music. Once more, in biology as in physics, the scientific disciplines had begun to enter upon the realm of mystery. Kirk had become in his convictions both pre-modern and post-modern.

This Russell Kirk was a canny Scot with a relish for the uncanny. The one high talent with which he had been endowed was imagination, the power of raising up images of truth and terror in the mind; through images, he had come to know something of the world beyond the world. The armed vision, Kirk had discovered, penetrates through the skin of appearances to energetic reality; the unimaginative human being is dully confined to the provinciality of time and to the provinciality of place. His had been a romantic life, conducted on classical lines. Apprehending reality through images, he had succeeded in exhibiting those images of the Permanent Things to a good many people; and after his body was dust, his books would carry on that work.

As his seventy-second birthday had approached, his daughter Cecilia (soon to follow in his steps at St. Andrews University) had told him in her affectionately acerbic way, "You look like a bulldog."

He recalled having noticed, at the age of sixteen, his mirrored face, suddenly encountered — innocent and somewhat wistful. Now, the years having swept by giddily, he found himself with a bulldog visage, the veteran of many controversies, mordant on occasion, given to growling, but a good guardian of the threshold and the hearth, kindly with children.

Blessed or cursed with near-total recall, Russell Kirk descried in his kaleidoscopic imagination every scene of every year, almost, in his life. They all had poured by so hastily and tumultuously, and what had been done could not be undone. How very like he had been to Mossy in George MacDonald's tiny book *The Golden Key,* or to John, the latter-day pilgrim in C. S. Lewis' *The Pilgrim's Regress!* Then, too, in his seventh decade Kirk had come to note wryly his resemblance to the Little Fir Tree of Hans Christian Andersen's fable — long eager for the coming of some wondrous event, not apprehending that the splendor of life is here and now.

On the shelves of Kirk's library rest a good many books he never had found time to read through. How many thousands of hours had he wasted in dreamy reverie, after the fashion of the Little Fir Tree? No doctrine is more comforting than the teaching of Purgatory, in part the gift of Gregory the Great to the Church. For purgatorily, one may be granted opportunity to atone for having let some precious life run out like water from a neglected tap into sterile sands. Improving the living moment, Kirk must reform his meandering ways even at this tardy hour. There is the book of children's tales, long in contemplation, that ought to be written; and three more volumes of his integrated essays on various themes, already requested by a publisher, must be compiled; and more volumes for the Library of Conservative Thought (some thirty volumes thereof already published, by late 1994) must be edited. Aristotle instructs us that life is for action; Irving Babbitt, that we must find our happiness in work or not at all. What sort of action, and work for what purpose? The answer is catechetical: to know God, and enjoy Him forever.

This present life here below, Kirk had perceived often in his mind's eye, is an ephemeral existence, precarious, as in an arena rather than upon a stage: some men are meant to be gladiators or knights-errant, not mere strolling players. Swords drawn, they stand on a darkling plain against all comers and all odds; how well they bear themselves in the mortal struggle will determine in what condition they shall put on incorruption. His sins of omission and commission notwithstanding, Kirk had blown his horn and drawn his sword of imagination, in the arena of the blighted twentieth century, that he might assail the follies of the time.

Above the chimneypiece in the drawing room of Piety Hill there hangs an eighteenth-century sword, in its worn leather scabbard, of the Mogul Empire. Kirk obtained it from Count Jas Tarnowski, the great Polish collector of art. This sword was forged in Persia and adorned with silver mountings in France. The head of a leopard, delicately carved in ivory, is its hilt; the creature retains its slender fangs and its ruby eyes. Is it a court sword? Perhaps; yet its edge is jagged and hacked badly, as if this elegant weapon, one grim day, had been passionately employed in desperate battle against a steely adversary. With this pretty, deadly thing, Elrond of Rivendell, master of the Last Homely House, might have hacked at orcs.

Humankind has it on authority that riches cannot well pass through the needle's eye into the world beyond the world. Being unencumbered with pelf, Kirk is not distressed by that difficulty; his worn old knapsack will suffice him for the tramp from corruption to incorruption. In imagination, at least, may he be permitted to carry with him, into another realm of being, beyond time, his Mogul sword? That blade might repel certain Watchers — the old Egyptians dreaded them — at the Strait Gate. Quite conceivably imagination of the right sort may be so redemptive hereafter as here. Forward!

> I am for the house with the narrow gate, which I take to be too little for pomp to enter: some that humble themselves may; but many will be too chill and tender, and they'll be for the flow'ry way that leads to the broad gate and the great fire.
>
> *All's Well that Ends Well*, IV, v, 46-51

Chronology of Selected Events in the Life of Russell Kirk

1918   Russell Amos Kirk is born in Plymouth, Michigan, the son of Russell Andrew and Marjorie Rachel (Pierce) Kirk.

1923-32   Attends Starkweather School in Plymouth. His sister Carolyn is born in 1925.

1936   Graduates from Plymouth High School, enters Michigan State College of Agriculture and Applied Science, East Lansing.

1940   Graduates from Michigan State with a B.A. in history; enters Duke University, Durham, North Carolina.

1941   Receives M.A. in history from Duke University in June. Enters the U.S. Army in December.

1941-45   Serves in the U.S. Army, attaining the rank of staff sergeant in the Chemical Warfare Service, stationed at Dugway Proving Ground, Utah. Marjorie Kirk dies in 1942.

1946   Appointed an assistant professor of the history of civilization at Michigan State, teaching there one semester per year until 1953. Admitted for doctoral studies at St. Andrews University, St. Andrews, Scotland. Is a guest at several country houses throughout Fife during his years of study.

1950   Becomes a senior fellow at the American Council of Learned Societies.

1951   Publishes his first book, *Randolph of Roanoke: A Study in Conservative Thought*.

1952 Doctor of Letters degree conferred by St. Andrews, the highest arts degree of the senior Scottish university.

1953 Publishes *The Conservative Mind: From Burke to Santayana.* (In the second through seventh editions, the subtitle is "From Burke to Eliot.") Meets T. S. Eliot. Leaves teaching post at Michigan State after dispute with college authorities over academic standards. Moves into ancestral home, Piety Hill, in Mecosta, Michigan. Delivers the Daly Lectures at the University of Detroit during 1953-54.

1954 Publishes *St. Andrews* and *A Program for Conservatives.* Studies and travels in Britain on a Guggenheim Fellowship through 1955.

1955 Publishes *Academic Freedom: An Essay in Definition.* Meets William F. Buckley, Jr. Agrees to contribute a regular column on education to *National Review;* Kirk's first installment of "From the Academy" appears in November, in the magazine's first issue.

1956 Publishes *Beyond the Dreams of Avarice: Essays of a Social Critic* and a revised edition of *A Program for Conservatives* entitled *Prospects for Conservatives.* Is awarded an honorary doctorate from Boston College.

1957 Founds the quarterly *Modern Age,* serving as its editor for the first two years. Publishes *The American Cause* and *The Intelligent Woman's Guide to Conservatism.* Appointed visiting lecturer at the New School for Social Research, Manhattan, 1957-58. Awarded honorary doctorate of humane letters by St. John's University.

1958 Serves as research professor of politics at C. W. Post College and a university professor at Long Island University 1958-60.

1960 Meets Annette Yvonne Cecile Courtemanche. Assumes presidency of The Educational Reviewer, Inc. Founds *The University Bookman,* serving as editor until his death. Awarded an honorary doctorate of humane letters by Park College.

1961 Publishes a Gothic novel, *Old House of Fear.* Begins term as Justice of the Peace for Morton Township, Mecosta County, serving until April 1965.

1962 Begins writing syndicated newspaper column, "To the

Point," in April. Publishes a ghost-story collection, *The Surly Sullen Bell: Ten Stories and Sketches, Uncanny or Uncomfortable*. Also publishes a revised edition of his first book, *John Randolph of Roanoke: A Study in American Politics*.

1963   Publishes an essay collection, *Confessions of a Bohemian Tory: Episodes and Reflections of a Vagrant Career*. Awarded honorary doctorate of humane letters by Le Moyne College.

1964   Received into the Roman Catholic Church. Marries Annette Courtemanche, September 19, at Our Lady of the Skies, Idlewild Airport's Catholic Chapel, New York. Works in support of Barry Goldwater's presidential election campaign.

1965   Publishes an essay collection, *The Intemperate Professor, and Other Cultural Splenetics*.

1966   Publishes a novel, *A Creature of the Twilight: His Memorials*, and a second edition of *The American Cause*, with an introduction by John Dos Passos. Receives the Ann Radcliffe Award for Gothic fiction for *Old House of Fear* and *The Surly Sullen Bell*.

1967   The Kirks' first daughter, Monica Rachel, is born in July. Kirk meets Clinton Wallace, a hobo who later resides at Piety Hill for nearly a decade. Publishes *The Political Principles of Robert A. Taft*, co-written with James McClellan, and *Edmund Burke: A Genius Reconsidered*.

1968   Second daughter, Cecilia Abigail, is born in September.

1969   Publishes *Enemies of the Permanent Things: Observations of Abnormity in Literature and Politics*.

1970   Third daughter, Felicia Annette, is born in May. Is named a Knight by the Count Dracula Society for accomplishments in literature of the uncanny. Awarded honorary doctorate of humane letters by Loyola College.

1971   Publishes *Eliot and His Age: T. S. Eliot's Moral Imagination in the Twentieth Century*.

1972   Receives the Christopher Award for *Eliot and His Age*.

1973   Awarded honorary doctorate of law by Gannon College.

1974   Publishes *The Roots of American Order*.

1975   Piety Hill destroyed by fire in February. Not lost in the fire, Piety Hill's brick annex becomes the main section of a new, Italianate house built on the site. Ceases writing his newspaper column "To the Point." Fourth daughter, Andrea Seton, is born in October. Awarded honorary doctorate of civil law by Niagara University.

1977   Receives a World Fantasy Award for short fiction for "There's a Long, Long Trail a-Winding." Awarded honorary doctorate of journalism by Olivet College.

1978   Publishes *Decadence and Renewal in the Higher Learning.* Named a Heritage Distinguished Scholar; over the next fifteen years he delivers four lectures annually for a total of 60 lectures at the Heritage Foundation.

1979   Becomes president of the Marguerite Eyer Wilbur Foundation. Becomes director of the Educational Research Council of America's social science program. Publishes a collection of ghost stories, *The Princess of All Lands.*

1980   Receives an honorary doctorate of letters from Central Michigan University. Appointed a visiting Patton Professor at Indiana University, serving in that role for one year. Publishes a novel of the uncanny, *Lord of the Hollow Dark.* Ceases writing "From the Academy" for *National Review* in December.

1981   Russell Andrew Kirk dies. Awarded an honorary doctorate of humane letters by Albion College.

1982   Publishes a collection of Heritage Foundation lectures, *Reclaiming a Patrimony.* Edits and publishes Viking Penguin's *Portable Conservative Reader.*

1983   Elected president of the Philadelphia Society. Awarded an honorary doctorate of letters by Grand Valley State College and an honorary doctorate of law by Pepperdine University.

1984   Awarded an Ingersoll Prize, the Richard M. Weaver Award, by the Rockford Institute, for scholarly writing. Publishes *Watchers at the Strait Gate,* a collection of ghostly tales.

1985   Awarded a constitutional fellowship from the National Endowment for the Humanities.

1987   Lectures as a Fulbright Scholar at St. Andrews University. Publishes an essay collection, *The Wise Men Know What Wicked Things Are Written on the Sky.*

1988   Publishes an economics textbook, *Work and Prosperity.* Delivers a lecture in Monza, Italy, to honor the centennial of

T. S. Eliot's birth. Begins editing the Library of Conservative Thought, a series published by Transaction. He would edit thirty volumes in the series by the time of his death.

1989   Awarded the Presidential Citizen's Medal for Distinguished Service to the United States, by President Ronald Reagan in January.

1990   Publishes a collection of essays entitled *The Conservative Constitution*.

1991   Gives daughter Monica in marriage to Brian Scott Carman in July at St. Anne's Church, Mackinac Island. Awarded the Salvatori Prize for historical writing, in December.

1992   Accepts honorary chairmanship of Patrick Buchanan's presidential primary campaign in Michigan to express his disapproval of the direction of the Bush administration; serves in this capacity until the Michigan primary, in March.

1993   Publishes *America's British Culture* and *The Politics of Prudence*. Travels to England and Wales to visit places connected with the life of Christopher Dawson in preparation for editing Dawson's complete works. Hillsdale College establishes an American Studies program and an endowed chair in honor of Kirk. In October, is feted at a conference in Dearborn, Michigan, commemorating the fortieth anniversary of *The Conservative Mind*'s appearance and his seventy-fifth birthday; here he is presented with a special tribute by Michigan governor John Engler. Gives daughter Cecilia in marriage to Jeffrey O. Nelson in a Christmas wedding at the Cathedral of St. Andrew, Grand Rapids, Michigan.

1994   Completes his memoirs, *The Sword of Imagination*. Receives a copy of a *Festschrift*, *The Unbought Grace of Life: Essays in Honor of Russell Kirk*. Dies at home on Friday, April 29. A requiem mass is held on May 3 at the Cathedral of St. Andrew. Memorial services are also held in Washington, D.C., at St. Joseph's Church and in New York at St. Patrick's Cathedral.

Index

NOTE: References to Kirk's publications have been gathered in an entry following his name.

Index